DOWN AND OUT IN LATE MEIJI JAPAN

Down and Out in Late Meiji Japan

JAMES L. HUFFMAN

 University of Hawai'i Press ◈ Honolulu

23 22 21 20 19 18   6 5 4 3 2 1

Library of Congress Cataloging-in-Publication Data

Names: Huffman, James L., author.
Title: Down and out in late Meiji Japan / James L. Huffman.
Description: Honolulu : University of Hawai'i Press, [2018] | Includes
    bibliographical references and index.
Identifiers: LCCN 2017055855 | ISBN 9780824872915 (cloth : alk. paper)
Subjects: LCSH: Urban poor—Japan—History. | Urban poor—Japan—Social
    conditions. | Japan—History—Meiji period, 1868-1912.
Classification: LCC HV4147.A5 H84 2018 | DDC 305.5/692095209034—dc23
LC record available at https://lccn.loc.gov/2017055855

To Judith,
Whose values and passions inspired this journey
And to her children and grandchildren:
May they live in the world she dreamed

CONTENTS

ACKNOWLEDGMENTS

Writing intimidates me. It confronts me with a hundred inadequacies as I try to do justice to materials and a story that are bigger than I am. Never is that more true than when I sit down to write acknowledgments, partly because I know that I will inadvertently omit people who should be thanked and partly because it is impossible to articulate how deeply dependent my work has been on great numbers of people, many of them friends, some of them relatives, and quite a few strangers who have helped me even though they did not know me. They have given me access to materials, suggested paths to follow, and, above all, provoked ideas and made helpful critiques. It goes without saying that these people bear no responsibility for the errors and failings of this work, but they deserve immense credit for keeping me going and making this study one of the richest experiences of my life. Thanks!

Let me begin with groups and organizations. Two groups have given me intellectual homes since my retirement from teaching: the Midwest Japan Seminar, headed by Elizabeth Dorn Lublin, and Northwestern University's East Asia Research Seminar, which Laura Hein leads. In both of these, the intellectual energy of friends who share their research and discuss ideas has been as important as the specific suggestions about my work. I also am indebted to institutions that have supported my research financially: the Northeast Asia Council of the Association for Asian Studies (supported by the Japan-U.S. Friendship Commission), Wittenberg University's Faculty Research Fund Board, and the Japan-U.S. Educational Commission, which administers the Fulbright grant program in Japan. JUSEC director David Satterwhite was unusually helpful at an early stage of this project, with astute observations that helped me narrow and frame my study. And the University of Tokyo's Jōhō Gakkan granted me office space and library privileges under the directorship of Yoshimi Shunya, while the Waseda University Library repeatedly provided a research home.

Across the many years that I have been doing this work, I have been helped by endless people who have done special things—usually with nothing to gain for themselves—to make the late Meiji *hinmin* come alive for me. I think of Nashilongo Shivute, who took me to the Namibian township of Mondesa, where I found the statement that begins this book's sixth chapter; of James McMahon, who helped me gain access to Northwestern University's library and shared his enthusiasm for Japan; of Nishiyama Takanobu, the Shintō priest who guided my interviews in Totsukawa; of Willa and George Tanabe, who showed me what life could be for descendants of sugar plantation workers; of Pat Crosby, who gave me wise direction in deciding what approach the book should take; of documentary filmmaker Brent Huffman, who provoked several of the ideas in this book; of Paul Snowden, who made it possible for me to work at the

Waseda Library; of two wonderful mentors, Roger Hackett at the University of Michigan and Kato Mikio of the International House of Japan; and of the brilliant economic historian Nakagawa Kyoshi, who shared his knowledge and enthusiasm so generously in Kyoto, then took me to an exceptional meal near the Imperial Palace. There also was Hoshino Kaoru, my student and aide, who did translations and gave me such encouragement. Others who helped with special needs of this sort included Djeld Duits, who made it possible to secure several of the work's photos, Dave Barry at Wittenberg, Yamamoto Nobuto at Keiō University, and Sagawa Osamu at Zenshōen in Tokyo.

Among the most important contributions to this book were the perspectives inspired by people with whom I discussed the world of the late Meiji poor across the past few years. Kenneth Cukier gave me fresh ways of looking at things; Patricia Sipple provided insight into Japan's contemporary poverty; Susan Burns shared her expertise on Hansen's Disease; Gotō Ken'ichi helped me understand emigrant Japanese; Kobayashi Sōmei and Changhyun Lee shared their office at the University of Tokyo and helped me see things with new eyes; and my student Suzuko Kantarō gave me insights I'd never have had into Tokyo's *shitamachi* areas, while another student-turned-colleague, Dennis Frost, introduced me to pertinent materials in the Ueno area and kept me alive mentally with his constant ideas. Others whose thoughts have helped to shape this study—and me—include Timothy Cheek, Warren and Clara Copeland, Mitani Hiroshi, Terumi Imai, Linda Lewis, Jennifer Oldstone-Moore, Kaneko Yukie, Murai Norihito, Nakashima Reiko, Tammy Proctor, Shikata Norio, Stephen Smith, David Spengler, Eugene Swanger, Thomas Taylor, Donna Techau, Tomonari Noboru, Timothy Weston, and Samuel Yamashita. And there are, of course, those others whose names I will regret not mentioning just after this manuscript goes to press.

Then there are the colleagues who opened specific doors for my research, often places I could not have entered on my own. Iwata Mizuho and Ito Miyuki provided exceptional guidance in the Tokyo Fulbright office; Lucas Clarkson arranged my unforgettable time in Totsukawa Village; Kita Etsuko spent three invigorating days with me in the northern Kyushu area around Haki; and both principal Ōno Yasushi and teacher Mukaihira Shinji brought special energy to my Totsukawa interviews. Though I have said it before, I must say again that many of my greatest heroes are librarians, people whose ingenuity and helpfulness amaze me. Hayashi Rie at Tokyo's International House was repeatedly helpful in locating materials, as were Koide Izumi at the Shibusawa Memorial Foundation and Joan Hori at the University of Hawai'i—Manoa. So too were Fujii Kaori and Shiraishi Megumi at the University of Tokyo's Meiji Shimbun Zasshi Bunkō. Others who helped me find materials included Keiko Yokota-Carter at the University of Michigan East Asia Library; Aoki Mutsumi (Kokubungaku Kenkyū Shiryōkan); Tokiko Bazell and Dore Minatodani (University of Hawai'i—Manoa); Leah Pualaha'ole Caldeira, Tia Reber, and Matthew Yim (Bishop Museum); Higuchi Keiko (International House); Hirano Takako (Kyoto Buraku Mondai Kenkyū Sentā); Kusumoto Wakako (Shibusawa

Foundation); Gerald Marsella and Midori Oka (Peabody Essex Museum); Naitō Seizō and Nishiura Naoko (Kokuritsu Hansenbyō Shiryōkan); Nakata Reiko (Buraku Kaihō Jinken Kenkyūjo); Suzanne Smailes and Regina Entorf (Wittenberg University); and Tanimukai Hajime (Totsukawa Rekishi Minzoku Shiryōkan).

I am indebted too to a number of people who read part or all of the manuscript at various stages and made comments that improved the content and saved me from making some embarrassing errors. They included Sally Hastings, Charles Hayford, Laura Hein, and M. William Steele, as well as an anonymous reader for the press. Stephanie Chun, the editor at the University of Hawai'i Press, was as gracious and astute an editor as I ever have known, and Grace Wen, Drew Bryan, and Emma Ching gave me unusually helpful guidance in the editing process.

It now should be clear that I am in serious debt. None have put me in greater debt than my family. My sister Judy, once more, asked astute questions and gave me superb strategic advice. My Chicago family—Kristen, Dave, Grace, and Simon—touched me constantly by the way they maintained an interest and kept making just the right suggestions as I bombarded them year after year with details about slum dwellers. My Tokyo family—James, Nao, Ryu, and Nana—did the same, and they helped often with translations, pronunciations, and interpretation, even as they gave me meals and a futon during my many stays in Japan. And though I have long been a widower, my wife Judith was the guiding force across the dozen years I worked on this study. Her passion for justice prodded me to launch this study, and her spirit kept me going when I might have stumbled. Yes, I am a debtor.

Until the lion has his historian, the hunter will always be a hero.

—Anonymous[1]

The journalist Yokoyama Gennosuke found it curious that "even though society invariably is propelled by nameless people, social commentators focus on people with names. They leave out those who have no names."[2] He made his observation in 1910 after years of studying the nameless people, first as one of them, a teenaged student sleeping in flophouses and temples, and then as a reporter eager to understand what he called the *kasō shakai*,[3] or underclass (literally: society of the lower classes). For nearly two decades after becoming a reporter for the paper *Mainichi Shinbun* in 1894 at age twenty-four, he roamed the slums of Osaka and Tokyo; he also journeyed to the mountains of Ashio, where miners sucked in ore dust and died young; he walked the aisles of Kiryū textile factories, where teenaged girls cowered before lecherous supervisors; and he crossed the sea to find out how emigrants to Korea lived. Some of the people he saw were dullards, he concluded, "staring silently at the skies and sitting dejectedly around empty *hibachi*"; many were "intelligent and clever."[4] But all of them evoked a new Japan, an explosion of "modern" energy during the 1890s and 1900s that led to the growth of both wealth and poverty. While his peers chronicled the successes of the wealthy, he gave his attention to the have-nots. It is my intention to do likewise: to tell the story of how the poor—particularly those in the cities—experienced life in the late Meiji years.

Between 1888 and 1903, Tokyo's population grew by more than a thousand people every week, skyrocketing from 1.4 million to 2.3 million, while Osaka increased at half that rate, from 1.2 million to 1.7 million.[5] And the changes in urban life were phenomenal. In the decade sandwiching the turn of the century, Japan won two major foreign wars and became an imperial power. School attendance rates nearly doubled, according to official statistics, to more than 95 percent. The old elitist newspapers turned into mass mediums, read by slum dwellers as well as by officials. Trade exports tripled to three hundred million yen in the decade before 1902; foreign imports quadrupled; and the number of factories quintupled, providing work for thousands on thousands of those new city dwellers. And new train lines tied far-flung regions to the cities.[6] Newspaper anecdotes compiled by historian Aoyagi Junrō suggest the energy of the decade: 1896 gave Japan its first luxury toilet, a lacquered contraption that played music; 1897 brought electric fans and the first moving picture exhibition;

1899 introduced beer halls and long-distance telephone. Railway sleeper cars came in 1900, artificial rain in 1901, the first automobile ride and first railroad dining car in 1902. Not everyone understood or embraced the changes. When an electrical short burned down the Diet Building in 1891, the kerosene indus- try launched an ad campaign about the dangers of electricity. And when tele- phone service began to spread, people bombarded officials with questions about whether cholera could spread over the phone lines. But the changes were massive, and their impact was revolutionary.[7]

This study starts from the premise that all city residents, poor or rich, saw and felt the changes, whether they enjoyed the benefits or not. The urban his- torian Yazaki Takeo said that people in the "lower stratum of society . . . experienced little change in their daily lives, despite the remarkable changes taking place at higher levels."[8] He was wrong. Even the poorest of the poor were profoundly affected by Japan's modernization. Industrialization brought hundreds of thousands into the cities, where they performed the tasks that made affluent life possible. They may not have been affected in the same way that their wealthier neighbors were. Indeed, as the social historian Sally Hast- ings observes, within their abodes "the furnishings, the clothing, and the food remained much as they had been for centuries,"[9] and many of them watched with longing or resentment when they could not afford the newfan- gled things they were making. But the changes all around influenced the poor every day: in the work they did, in the way they saw the world, and in the way they saw themselves.

The goal of this study is to determine how Yokoyama's urban *kasō shakai* responded to the changes, to understand how it felt to live the life of a *hinmin*, or poor person. Before addressing that subject, however, we must answer sev- eral background questions regarding the nature and usefulness of the sources available for such a study, the kinds of images that underlay and shaped early accounts of the *hinmin*, and the interpretive and methodological approaches that will undergird this examination. Only after finding answers to those ques- tions will it be possible to deal fully and fairly with the work's fundamental questions: how Japan's urban poor lived in the last half of the Meiji era (roughly the late 1880s to the mid-1910s) and how they understood the world that sur- rounded them.

Kasō Shakai: How We Know About Them

The first issue is sources. If the poor were "nameless," were they also voiceless, and thus incomprehensible? It is true that very few of the late Meiji poor wrote anything for others to see. Four major sources of information, however, taken together, make such a study more than merely feasible. First, several late Meiji newspaper reporters gave significant portions of their careers to studying and describing the people who lived in the *hinminkutsu*, or "caverns of the poor" (usually translated as slums), which began to grow in Osaka and Tokyo after the 1880s. Second, officials concerned about the connection between the state's modernizing policies and urban poverty began in the mid-Meiji years to conduct extensive surveys of slum dwellers, factory workers, and general urban populations that provided a balance to the anecdotal approach that many journalists took. Third, intellectuals and opinion leaders wrote voluminously about the "lower classes" and the *hinmin* in an outpouring of essays and literary works, some of which were empathetic and careful about facts, others of which repeated long-held prejudices about the poor. And fourth, a small number of post-Meiji social scientists and historians have used the late Meiji writings and surveys to construct analyses of the broad social systems and structures that framed the *kasō shakai* experience. Taken together, these materials provide a great deal more information than I expected when I began this study.

The reporters' accounts merit special consideration, since they formed the baseline for most of the other work and serve as the central focus of my own study. When legions of people began moving into the cities and settling together in slum-like areas in the late 1880s, Japan's opinion-making community took note, and newspaper journalists began to write about what they called the new "*shakai mondai*," or "social problem." Yokoyama is the best known of a group that I call the "poverty journalists,"[10] but he was neither the first nor the last. In the late 1880s, Suzuki Umeshirō reported extensively on the slums in Osaka's Nago-chō for the newspaper *Jiji Shinpō*, and *Chōya Shinbun* ran stories on poverty in Tokyo. Then in November 1892, Matsubara Iwagorō began a ten-month series of colorful and emotive articles in *Kokumin Shinbun* on the hard life in Tokyo's poorest areas, drawing on his own difficulties as an orphan; he later published the articles in the book *Saiankoku no Tokyo* (Darkest Tokyo). In 1893, Sakurada Taiga (aka Taiga Koji) of *Nihon Shinbun* published *Hintenchi kikankutsu tankenki* (Exploring the hungry and cold realms of the poor), based on time he spent in the slums disguised as an ordinary resident. And in the late 1890s, *Jiji* ran successive articles on *Tokyo's Poor (Tokyo no hinmin)*, while *Hōchi Shinbun* did a three-week series on the notorious Shin'ami-chō slum in Tokyo's Shiba ward.[11] In addition, most papers reported almost daily on the darker sides of *hinminkutsu* life in their Page Three stories (*sanmen kiji*), where human interest materials were featured: the crimes, the epidemics, the suicides, the sensational and salacious.

These works were hardly uniform. Many reporters stood aloof from their subjects, treating poor people as inferiors and oddities. The best of the poverty journalists, however, brought empathy and professionalism to their investigations. Matsubara and Yokoyama, in particular, put on the tight-fitting pants and jackets of workers and spent weeks on end in flophouses and back alleys, sometimes handing out candy to children to encourage them to talk.[12] Matsubara wrote primarily from the observations of his eyes and the feelings of his heart and produced what some have called an "antecedent of the fact-based novel," while Yokoyama—who had studied under the pioneer novelist Futabatei Shimei, an advocate of greater empathy in the treatment of all social groups—wrote in a more clinical fashion, backing up his observations with copious data, using government surveys and interviews to test his conclusions.[13] The economic historian

Nakagawa Kiyoshi argues that the poverty journalists' interpretations evolved quickly, from late-1880s images of the poor as wholly other people who led "unimaginable" lives worthy only of fear and pity, to later depictions of people who were fully human if still pitiable.[14] By Yokoyama's time in the middle and late 1890s, Nakagawa says, the view had changed even more: "He did not see *hinmin* society as a different, outside world but as a part of the broader society," albeit a part whose problems demanded rigorous analysis in order to make society more equal and fair.[15] The writings of these reporters were voluminous, detailed, and, in Yokoyama's case, data-driven—enough so to lend confidence to a twenty-first-century writer trying to understand *hinmin* life.

Late Meiji: The Popular View

Late Meiji images of the *hinmin* were propagated primarily by popular writers who applied their own perceptions and preconceptions to the reporters' findings and came up with a simplistic image that blamed poor people for their own plight and doubted that they had the capacity to surmount it. They gave us a portrait filled with despair and inferiority, a picture, in a prominent novelist's words, of "savages who were more machine than human, more animal than machine."[16] A slightly more nuanced, more sympathetic image was articulated by a few surveyors and reformers, but their works amounted to a whisper within the day's general discourse. One reason for this was that the stereotypes of the popular writers played into widely held presuppositions in a society where differences of class and status seemed natural and normal. The Tokugawa-era status groups had been abolished legally at the beginning of the Meiji era, but society remained divided officially into *heimin* (commoners), *shizoku* (former samurai), and *kazoku* (nobility), and the sense of fate-ordained divisions, of better and worse, higher and lower, persisted among adults who had grown up under the earlier system. The novelist Tanizaki Jun'ichirō talked about how his mother, despite being relatively poor, loved to be "able to sit in a comfortable seat on a train, . . . carefully dressed like any prosperous middle-class matron" and, less cheerfully, about the humiliation he felt when he had to enter the home of his samurai-descended boyhood friend by a "narrow service door used by the greengrocer and fishmonger." Friends or not, poverty meant inferiority and had to be kept hidden. That experience, he said, impressed on him "keenly how very disagreeable a thing it was to be poor."[17] Western academic approaches reinforced such attitudes with the emergence after the 1890s of what David Ambaras calls a new middle class that saw education and wealth as the marks of virtue and ability. Influenced by both the old Confucian morality and a new "Anglo-American, Protestant-inflected moral vision," the rising middle class used "Western social scientific categories" to make the *kasō shakai* into "objects of ethnographic inquiry, pacification, and enlightenment for assimilation."[18]

The result was what Nakagawa calls an "it's-a-pity" portrait of *hinmin* society filled with characteristics and categories still familiar to readers today.[19] Matsubara, a one-time social Darwinist who argued that reality belied theories of progress and "the well-being of people,"[20] set the tone for the popular writings by titling his classic work *Darkest Tokyo,* a phrase that evoked what the literary critic Maeda Ai calls a world of "dark energy" where "the boundary between life and death itself seems to dissolve."[21] The title drew on two Western works: Henry Morton Stanley's *In Darkest Africa* and Salvation Army founder William Booth's *Darkest England, and the Way Out,* which said that "without some kind of extraordinary help," the poor "must hunger and sin, and sin and hunger, until . . . the gaunt fingers of death will . . . terminate their wretchedness."[22] The features of Matsubara's night-black place included a litany of *hinmin* characteristics that were repeated endlessly in late Meiji accounts of the urban poverty pockets and that continue to be applied to poor families in popular accounts even today. Understanding them should help us to assess the stereotypes that informed most of the Meiji writers and to confront our own instinctive way of seeing the poor.

"POVERTY AND VULGARITY"

All observers agreed that the most important feature of *hinmin* life was economic deprivation. *Hinmin* were poor; desperately so. For the popular journalists, that meant more than a mere lack of means, however; it was a qualitative thing, captured in Shiga Naoya's sniffing comment about his grandfather's home: "Everything smelled of poverty and vulgarity."[23] Almost always, popular pictures of poverty highlighted squalor, dirtiness, or eyesores. Matsubara talked about "the lice, the fleas, the mosquitoes, the offensive odors, the drunkenness, the stifling heat," and about the old man in a lodging house, popping tiny bugs into his mouth, a sight that "made it hard for me to remain seated."[24] Tanizaki likened the Asakusa amusement region's slums to "an over-turned trash bin."[25] And the painter Kaburagi Kiyokata rued a storyteller's toilet outside the windows of a bean porridge shop, where the "offensive odors . . . drove patrons to insanity."[26]

Squalor was accompanied by crime. Because they were poor, most writers suggested, members of the *kasō shakai* stole and murdered. Ambaras argues that in an effort to "establish their own superiority," the middle class reformers "defined particular types of deviance" as coming from class deficiencies.[27] Dramatic support for this view showed up daily in the Page Three stories that became standard fare in most newspapers after the 1890s. On January 4, 1900, a typical news day, Tokyo's largest newspaper, the inexpensive *Yorozu Chōhō,* reported in great detail on a near-murder that had occurred two evenings earlier in a park in Asakusa's slum area after "a group of merrymakers began to quarrel." A drunken man in his mid-thirties got involved in a quarrel, went off to buy a knife at a nearby street stall, then came back and started a fight. Blood was spilled and the man ran, bleeding heavily, to a nursing center, which sent him to a hospital, where he was in a precarious condition. Stories on the same page included two head slashings, one murder, and sundry police reports. Another Page Three story, selected at random from April of the same year, included reports on the suffocation of a baby, a burglary, and gambling arrests.[28]

And a scan of the third page of Tokyo's other major commoner paper, *Niroku Shinpō,* during the first five months of 1900 shows the same pattern. Violence of middle-class students received some attention; so did immorality among the rich and famous. But articles on *hinmin* crimes dominated: a young woman stabbed to death in the neck; a blind man stealing beef, onions, and beer; a priest-turned-extortionist; the pickpocketing of someone in a rickshaw; a series on "the true state of affairs among low class prostitutes" (*katō baiin no jikkyō*); and a graphic report about a musician who set himself on fire out of financial desperation.[29] The message implied by these stories was consistent: if you don't have money, you run amok.[30]

"HE IS POOR BECAUSE HE WANTS TO BE POOR"

Another set of popular images grew from the widespread conviction that poverty resulted from bad behavior and unfortunate choices. Few generalizations had wider currency than the idea that there was a direct relationship between moral behavior and having money. As a result, the *shakai mondai* writings brimmed with comments about work ethic, sexual promiscuity, eating practices, and frugality. Laziness headed the list. The poor might slave into the night pulling rickshaws; they might serve tables with knuckles raw from washing dishes in cold water; construction workers might die of exhaustion while rich young men lived lives of ease. No matter. The truism persisted: those who prosper are hard workers; those who starve are loafers. As a mid-Meiji journalist said of rickshaw pullers: "They will work no more than they absolutely must, and . . . they spend all they earn, knowing no other than mere animal wants."[31] No one put it more baldly than the Meiji Restoration leader Iwakura Tomomi, who said the poor "do not work because they are lazy; they bring about their own impoverishment."[32] When another reporter said he had heard some carters say, "We will not do such a foolish thing as working regularly,"[33] readers nodded knowingly: that was how poor folks thought.

The *hinmin* of these accounts were dissolute and morally loose too: heavy drinkers, philanderers, gamblers, thieves, wife beaters. The pioneer social worker Adachi Kenchū clearly saw things that way. "A major cause of juvenile delinquency," he said, "was the ease with which members of the lower class married and separated"; he added that the urban poor "know only lust, and their marriages and divorces are quick, easy affairs." Another moralist said, without evidence, that a tendency to unbridled sex made the slum dwellers like "lower animals."[34] Even the sympathetic founders of Futaba Nursery School on the edge of Samegahashi slum west of the palace moaned that children failed to thrive because "their families are bad. . . . They are only here at the kindergarten for six hours. After that they are free to absorb bad influences [at home]."[35] And the press echoed them with repeated tales about the immoral poor: the "troublesome son" in a Honjo sweets shop who was supposed to take 150 yen to the bank but spent it all in an Asakusa liquor store, or three carpenters who murdered a fellow merely because he humiliated them.[36] Yokoyama's writings were particularly full of moral judgments. He quoted a poor woman in Samegahashi district: "My husband drinks saké daily, never works, and idles away his time. So, I tell him all the time that he is poor because he wants to be poor. Then he talks back and argues for argument's sake. . . . He idles away his time." Women who did side work, the journalist said, "secretly waste it on food and drink." The rickshaw pullers? "They squander their monthly income on food and drink and when they have spent all their money, they rely on their more resourceful fellow *yado* to support them." And textile workers? A factory manager in the Kiryū-Gifu region said:

Factory girls . . . are hopeless. After we have given a present to a girl who worked hard, others bear a grudge against her boss and are oblivious to their own uselessness. Even when it is obvious that hard work will benefit them in the future, the girls merely count the days before each holiday . . . and pay no attention to their work. If we are not vigilant, girls make unacceptable goods, yet are unconcerned about their inferior workmanship.[37]

Yokoyama occasionally praised the poor, but comments about irresponsibility and laxity dominated. As Hastings has noted, the 1874 act that governed relief policies in the Meiji era was based on the view "that poverty was largely the fault of the poor individual."[38] Most middle-class citizens took that view as obvious reality.

"SOCIETY OF THE LOWER STRATUM"

A third set of images was rooted in the belief that the naturalness of hierarchy meant that the poor were inferior. The very phrases usually used to describe urban poor articulated the equation: "*kasō shakai*" or "*kasō kaikyū*," both of which meant the "society of the lower stratum," the "underclass," the "bottom layer." Being in the middle class meant being superior: having a better education, greater economic stability, more "civilization," in contrast to the lowliness of the poor. The women's rights pioneer Oku Mumeo recalled that when she quipped as a child that it might be fun to work as a weaver, her mother, "who was usually very gentle," rebuked her: "Absolutely not! That is something poor people do. I never want to hear you say that you want to become a factory girl again! I have never even set eyes on a factory loom." The harshness of the response "always remained at the bottom of my heart," Oku said, even after she had grown up and become an advocate of equality.[39]

Sometimes this condescension took the form of pity. The Youth Club of the middlebrow journal *Seinen: The Rising Generation* included this comment in a report on a famine in the Tōhoku region, "We must think of these poor people whenever we sit at our meal and put on our warm clothing, and must do whatever in our power to give them relief."[40] Even the socialist champion of the working poor, *Shūkan Heimin Shinbun,* exuded pity when it demanded justice, with endless lists of parents who abandoned their children, paupers who tried to drown themselves, and ill-tempered rickshaw pullers who attacked passengers, usually because they were "pressed by poverty."[41] The compassion was genuine; so was the condescending pity. Often the pity took the form of an assumption that poor people were simple-minded. When a "poor widow" ran back and forth trying to get a glimpse of the Emperor Meiji during an imperial procession in the summer of 1906, she was a "helpless rustic."[42] When a child in Higuchi Ichiyō's novelette *Child's Play* (*Takekurabe*) acted like a "buffoon," he was nicknamed "Mannen-chō," after the nearby slum by that name. Was that not how poor people acted?[43] As Yokoyama summed it up: "Poor people lack economic resources and are exceedingly deficient in their intellectual faculties."[44] That was why educators often placed poor youths into classes for the "feeble-minded" when they misbehaved.[45] Attitudes such as this are not, of course, limited to Meiji Japan: The social worker and educator Paolo Freire argues that "from the point of view of the dominators in any epoch, correct thinking presupposes the non-thinking of the people." He could have added "any region" to "any epoch," because his principle squared as well with Meiji Japan as it did with late twentieth-century Brazilians.[46]

"ALMOST WITHOUT CONSCIOUSNESS"

A fourth set of images—which persisted to the end of the era despite Nakagawa's hopeful analysis of changing perceptions—placed important elements of the *kasō shakai* beyond the pale of normal society. It was a short step from "simple" to "barely human." The journalist Harada Tōfū wrote in a 1902 report on *hinmin* generally: "They do not know the joys (*kōfuku*) of the world. They do not know the world's sources of pleasure (*omoshiromi*). They live their days almost without consciousness (*muishiki*)."[47] Yokoyama put it even more baldly in a discussion of rag pickers, who, he claimed, "seem to be an almost subhuman species only slightly related to other human beings on this earth."[48] And the novelist Natsume Sōseki had the protagonist of his novel *Kōfu* (The miner) comment that "I knew full well that the miner ranked only above the ox and the horse among beasts of burden and that it was no honor for me to become one."[49] One of the most damning features of this otherness was the widespread assumption that poor people lacked agency and hope. They were automatons who went through life's daily motions with neither the ability nor the inclination to control their own destinies; they were Fukuzawa Yukichi's commoners who, "when told to stand, they stand; when told to dance, they dance," people who "truly are spiritless and wear faces of brass."[50] They were, in the words of the humor magazine *Tokyo Puck*, the victims of faith healers and fortune tellers who "trade on the gullibleness of brainless folks."[51]

All of this was when they were visible at all. For most people in the middle class, most of the time, the *hinmin* simply did not merit observation. "The poor," says the economic historian Koji Taira, "existed somewhere in silence and darkness" because "Meiji Japan was too busy with the tasks of modernization and industrialization to pay serious attention to them."[52] Shoppers closed their eyes to the rag pickers on the street beside them, while guests of the rich Iwasaki Yatarō strolled in his walled Kiyosumi gardens in Fukagawa, oblivious to the slum that spread on all sides. Tanizaki's memoir, *Childhood Years*, is filled with rickshaw rides in which he is "jounced about on my mother's lap," but it has almost no pullers; the rickshaw men are backdrops.[53] The influential *Yorozu Chōhō* editorialist Uchimura Kanzō commented once that Japanese intellectuals had much to say about the "sweet cry of the geisha playing," but "no professor has yet described the thin *bitter* cry of the Japanese poor pulling jinrikishas or spinning cotton in Osaka factories."[54] That was why Osaka officials could carry out a "removal of the poor" policy during the city's 1903 industrial exposition, pushing out the people who lived in the area, with neither comment nor concern about where they would go. The lack of public outcry about their removal sprang less from callousness than from the fact that the poor were not objects of interest.[55]

The popular writings did not, however, focus exclusively on negative stereotypes. Empathetic images may have been harder to find, but they were there if one looked for them. Sometimes the brighter view showed up in simple expressions of respect or empathy: in the novelist Shimazaki Tōson's descriptions of turn-of-the-century Komoro as a place "poor on the surface but rich underneath,"[56] or in an *enka* singer's soulful descriptions of the impoverished workers among whom he lived:

> Of course, his dreams are boldly ambitious
> When hungry he goes to a tavern
> Where instead of chairs there are soy sauce barrels . . .
> One cannot hear the tale without tears falling.[57]

Sometimes, the empathetic nuance came in discussions of poverty's causes. As early as 1880, the journalist and future political leader Hara Kei had written in the newspaper *Yūbin Hōchi* that "despite hard work and careful management," many people were forced into destitution by government policies and social forces.[58] Drawing heavily on Marxist thought, which provided explanations for both poverty and inequality, the Osaka reformer Seki Hajime argued that responsibility for the *hinmin* plight lay not in personal failures of the "guiltless poor" but in "the system of capitalist enterprise" and the "cold-blooded industrialists who use machines as weapons to control their pitiful workers."[59] And Matsubara, who also was influenced by Marxism, observed in a set of writings on homelessness that most workers were paid only a tenth of what their labor actually was worth to society, adding in a pitying yet empathetic tone: "Should we not think about that fact when we see them bent over beside the road, freezing in rags, starving on food scraps?"[60] Most often, the empathetic view appeared as an undermelody, sometimes a countermelody, in works that emphasized the standard stereotypes. Yokoyama talked with admiration about the way the poor helped each other, even when he blamed them for not providing their children with an education. Matsubara balanced his criticism of workers' "sloth" and heavy drinking with discussions of what he called the "college of the poor" (*hindaigaku*), which taught anyone who would listen how to make do on very little and how to "bear, in an almost comedic way, whatever difficulty comes their way."[61] Even *Tokyo Puck* ran occasional cartoons about *hinmin* cleverness in outwitting creditors or tormentors. All but the glibbest of the writers admitted to certain redeeming features when they wrote about the *kasō shakai.*

On the whole, however, the positive images got lost in the popular writing: thin threads in dark tapestries. Facts, after all, are rarely sufficient to revise popular narratives. Certainly they were not in this case. To the vast majority of late Meiji readers, the poor remained a static and undesirable segment of society, lacking not only the means to live comfortably but the intelligence and values that a satisfying life required. They were vulgar; they were lazy, depraved, or self-indulgent; they lived on society's shadowy margins, inhabiting an inferior social plain; the lowest of them were barely human. Most important, they were responsible for their own plight. When an industrialist said that his employees were "more like bears or wolves than anything else," he would have drawn little negative response from most late Meiji observers.[62]

Later Years: The Academic Portrait

The generations after the Emperor Meiji died in 1912 gradually produced another set of lenses for viewing the *kasō shakai,* as a number of academics began to look at the poor in a more systematic way, often as proponents for relief programs. The background for their work was laid by a few late Meiji intellectuals who made the rise of urban poverty, or *hinkon,* a subject of broader academic and official concern, regarding it as "an integral part of Japan's modernization process."[63] The early sociologist Tongo Takebe, for example, commented in 1904 on the increasing numbers of believers in "the distributive justice theory" who saw "the relief of extreme poverty as the most vital project to be accomplished."[64] The German-trained economist Kanai Noburu took up the question of how poverty could be relieved. And the young Gotō Shimpei, who would go on to become one of Japan's most powerful colonial administrators, argued (with limited impact at the time) that poverty undercut Japan's ability to be a strong nation and thus called for state-sponsored relief programs. These men were outliers, but they set the stage for scholars such as Kagawa Toyohiko, the Christian social activist who, despite strong ideological biases, began to apply social science approaches to broader questions of poverty in the Taishō years, and the ethnographer Yanagita Kunio, who gave us monumental, deeply empathetic studies of folk life, particularly in the villages. By the late twentieth century, impoverished groups and individuals had caught the attention of a number of scholars, both Japanese and Western. Patricia Tsurumi, for example, did pioneering work on factory girls; Mikiso Hane detailed the travails of those in the "the underside of modern Japan"; Nimura Kazuo applied the social scientist's skills to the 1907 miners' riots in Ashio; Sally Hastings showed us the interactions between bureaucrats and the urban poor in Tokyo's Honjo Ward, particularly in the decades right after the Meiji era; Michael Lewis' lively translation of the *enka* singer Azembō's memoirs shed light on life at the street level; and

Irokawa Daikichi's examination of political consciousness in Meiji villages challenged stereotypes about farmers as disconnected and unsophisticated.[65] It is perhaps ironic that the studies of the Meiji poor seldom were carried out by economists, whose work tended to focus on national wealth, industrial growth, and state policy.[66] But they made it clear that the denizens of poverty led lives that were as complex and nuanced as those of the middle and upper classes.

The scholar who focused most systematically and extensively on the *hinmin* is the economic historian Nakagawa Kiyoshi, who has spent decades analyzing everything from government data collections to journalistic accounts in an effort to understand the social and economic structures that defined life for the late Meiji *kasō shakai*.[67] In concert with several other scholars, he has developed broad analyses of the society-level frameworks within which *hinmin* life took place, based on meticulous study of the quantifiable features of the *kasō shakai* experience: wage structures, family sizes, patterns of crime, and health. The picture Nakagawa and his peers have constructed differs, often dramatically, from what we saw in the popular portraits. While it largely ignores the specifics of daily life, it lays out the broad conditions that underlay those specifics. If an understanding of the popular middle-class images will help us confront our own preconceptions, a grasp of the scholars' picture should provide a framework for interpreting more clearly just how the poor themselves experienced daily life. A summary of their major points is thus in order.

HOW MANY *HINMIN* WERE THERE AND WHERE DID THEY LIVE?

Precise figures are impossible to come by, in part because Meiji writers did not generally make the kinds of distinctions about levels of poverty that Europeans such as Booth and Karl Marx did.[68] It is thought, however, that the very poor, generally referred to as *hinmin* (paupers) or *kyūmin* (destitute people),[69] constituted between 275,000 and 400,000 Tokyoites in the early 1900s, or 12 to 20 percent of the population; in Osaka, they likely made up between 200,000 and 340,000. Some scholars suggest that when all the nation's poor are counted—the farmers, the petty merchants, poor schoolteachers and lower civil servants, the jobless, the rickshaw pullers, the carpenters, the outcastes, the boatmen, the miners, the fishermen—they made up between 50 and 60 percent of Japan's total population and a good half of its urban citizens.[70] One reason the *hinmin* in particular drew so much journalistic attention was that by the 1890s, they lived in increasingly concentrated areas, in the *hinminkutsu*, or "caverns of the poor," noted above. In Osaka, that meant the southern parts of the city, especially Nago-chō in the 1890s, then, after a slum-clearance project there, in Namba and Imamiya.[71] In Tokyo, where poverty had been dispersed across the metropolitan area during the early Meiji years, *hinmin* began congregating after the mid-1880s in once-empty lands east of the Sumida River, a region popularly known as the "low city," or *shitamachi*. The neighborhoods of Mannen-chō in Shitaya, Shin'ami-chō to its south, and Samegahashi just west of the palace had come by the 1890s to be known as the city's "three great slums."[72]

WHERE DID THEY COME FROM?

The urban poor were a people on the move, geographically and economically. Some of their families had been in the cities for decades, working as night-soil collectors, porters, and cleaning people, or doing the leather work reserved for the outcastes known as *eta* or *burakumin*. Kagawa claimed in 1915 that slum dwellers were "all of the *eta* race": either families who had long lived in the cities or immigrants from *burakumin* villages in the countryside.[73] The truth, however, was that while most slum residents were indeed from the countryside, they came from regular farming and fishing villages, not from outcaste enclaves. Drastic economic policies intended to help urbanites and elites by combating inflation and the spiraling national debt hit rural Japan like a tsunami in the early 1880s. Rising taxes and tight currency policies sent rice and tea prices plummeting, forcing farmers in all parts of the country to sell off their property to wealthy landlords and sending children to bed hungry. One result was the nation's first sizeable immigration abroad, particularly to Hawai'i, where tens of thousands of Japanese took jobs on sugar plantations. Another was an even larger migration, predominantly though not exclusively of males, to the cities, where the move to modernity was creating new jobs. In the last half of the Meiji era, city surveys showed as much as four times the growth in the *shitamachi* regions, where the poor domestic immigrants congregated, as in the rest of the city. Fueling that growth was hunger and desperation: masses of young men and women, typically single, whose families decided it was better for everyone for them to leave home and seek work in the city.

WHAT DID THEY DO?

The short answer is that the urban immigrants did just about everything necessary to support life in a modern city. Although their occupations were weighted toward the physical and the menial, the variety of what they did was too rich and nuanced to be captured by the standard job classification categories. A survey of the very poorest in Osaka at the end of the 1880s, for example, divided those who "live in extreme difficulty" into more than fifteen categories, from pulling carts to making matches, from entertaining to running pawn shops, with the largest percentages classified as rag pickers or jobless.[74] A quick look at one analytical scheme—the regularly employed, the irregularly employed, and the self-employed—demonstrates just how varied *hinmin* work was.

The preponderance of those with *regular* employment—nearly half by the last Meiji decade—worked in industry, with great numbers in construction, textile factories, and the metal industries. Commerce, large and small, also provided regular incomes for many, in jobs as diverse as typesetting, waiting tables, selling clams or scrap metals, working as shop clerks, and providing towels in public baths. A majority of the *irregularly* employed were the day laborers who gathered each morning in specified locations to seek low-paying jobs, of-

ten in building projects. Families who took consignment work—rolling cigarettes or making matchboxes, for example—also made up an important
segment of the irregulars, as did the cart pullers who were called *tachinbō*
(loafers) even though they did what was probably the heaviest work for the lowest pay. The most colorful individuals occupied the *self-employed* category.[75]
Street and temple entertainers, for example, filled the public spaces with magic,
dancing, samisen-playing, and acrobatic tricks, smiling in public but "staring
silently at the skies and sitting dejectedly around empty *hibachi*" when weather
kept them inside.[76] And Tokyo's fifty thousand rickshaw pullers, most of whom
worked independently, did more than any other group to give poverty a human
face. It bears noting, as an aside, that those with no work at all formed only a
small group in the late Meiji years, with their numbers rarely rising above the
1 or 2 percent level.[77]

WHY WERE THEY POOR?

The answers to this question are as diverse as the theoretical approaches of the
people who write about it, but two points come through consistently in academic analyses. First, poverty had many causes. Some studies found the origins in educational levels, illness, and happenstance; some found poverty's
sources in transience or in the desperate conditions that parents passed on;
and a late Meiji questionnaire given to the *hinmin* themselves placed blame on
more than twenty causes, with economic factors such as unemployment and
low wages topping the list, followed by everything from illness to poor money
management to acts of God such as floods and fire.[78] There was, in other words,
no single cause of poverty. A second point, which has received less attention
than it deserves, was the arithmetic explanation: low wages. It is true that some
people drank or gambled away their income, but they were the minority. The
simple fact was that neither the coins that commuters handed over for rickshaw rides nor the wages that factories paid provided enough money for the
average family to live on. In November 1901, the journal *Taiyō* detailed the
bare-bones monthly expenses of the four-member family of an unnamed but
typical shop worker (*kozukai*). They came to 19.19 yen. His salary, by contrast,
was less than half of that: a mere 8 yen. The family eked by because both children and the wife also worked. Even their combined income was "barely sufficient to keep body and soul together."[79] The refusal of a capitalist society to pay
workers enough to survive gets only brief mention in most late Meiji explanations for poverty,[80] but the truth is that unjust wages were the major cause of
hinmin poverty.

WHAT WAS DAILY LIFE LIKE?

Although the scholars have not paid much attention to the way the urban poor
experienced life day-in and day-out—to people's emotional ups and downs, to
their personal interactions, to family tragedies and joys—their studies nonetheless suggest some of the key features of daily life that will frame the chapters
that follow. Among them:

Family Size

The late Meiji cartoonists and essayists pictured poor families as large; even the poor themselves sometimes blamed large families for their fellows' plight.[81] The reality was that the majority of *hinmin* had relatively small families. Several surveys in the 1880s, particularly in Osaka's Nago-chō, found that average family size ranged between three and four, while an 1898 study of poor regions in Tokyo's Yotsuya and Shitaya found averages of 3.6 and 4.5 respectively. A late Meiji survey that excluded single-resident abodes showed the average family in poor Tokyo regions with 3.9 members, in contrast to 4.2 for the city overall.[82] One reason the poor families remained small was high mortality rates, with one scholar estimating that fewer than a third of poor children lived to adulthood.[83] Another reason likely lay in the fact that, as Fabian Drixler has shown, most *hinminkutsu* residents had come from rural regions where a "culture of low fertility"—an "heir and a spare" philosophy—had kept family sizes low well into the mid-Meiji years.[84] Whatever the reason, poor families remained small on average, across the entire period.

Housing

Hinmin abodes took many forms, but they always were cramped. To the end of the 1800s, large numbers lived in the flophouses (*kichin'yado*) and tenement row houses (*nagaya*) that crowded urban slums. At the beginning of the 1890s, Matsubara found three to five families living together in a single room in many flophouses, with only screens to divide them. He described a night in a flophouse as "disgusting." "Think about it," he said: "doing day labor with a will and a body like iron . . . not getting your three meals a day, unable to buy the clothes you want, then paying three *sen* each night for this lodging."[85] The *nagaya* were only slightly better: whole families living in one room of three or four mats, with no kitchen, toilet, or running water. Things improved as the years passed, and a very few families began to have homes of their own. But as late as 1912, nearly three-quarters of the *hinmin* in Tokyo's Sumida River wards still lived in single-room rentals of six or fewer mats (about 108 square feet); not a single family in the Shitaya and Asakusa slums owned a house. A quarter of those in the *kasō shakai* had begun to share bathrooms with other families by then, and most had secured cooking facilities.[86] If adequate personal space is a sign of modernity, Japan's urban poor still had a long way to go.

Food

Food consumed two-thirds of the average *hinmin* family budget at the end of the Meiji era, and even so, meals were meager and boring. Many of Matsubara's most vivid accounts dealt with filling the stomach. He describes rickshaw pullers gulping down cheap bowls of soba, rice balls, and the "horsemeat that is eaten especially by the lower classes." He notes that on the rare occasion when there was a bit of money to waste, poor workers might visit a tavern to "have one drink, take one puff, eat a bit of vegetable, and leave." And he devotes many pages to leftover food stores, where surplus rice, fish, and greens from military schools or rich families were sold cheaply to long lines of people whose "crowded scuffles presented a fantastic spectacle." The household staple was rice of the "lowest quality," with a third of the shop worker's monthly budget—at least twice what was paid for rent—going to that. Other foods included miso, pickled vegetables, and shaved bonito flakes, which were "sold by the piece in the slums." And there was alcohol, which Yokoyama said was an important part of the food consumption in three-quarters of the *kasō shakai* homes. "These people may have become poor because of drinking," he said, "or it may be that because they are poor, these slum dwellers seek solace in drink."[87] He failed to add that they may have drunk alcohol because that was what people did, regardless of class.

Work Patterns

Nearly everyone in the *hinmin* community worked for pay, and for very long hours. In 1886, *Chōya Shinbun* reported that when children in poor families reached age seven or eight "it was customary for boys to work for merchants in Tokyo and for girls to go to Gunma Prefecture to work at weaving. . . . It was rare for children above seven or eight to be at home."[88] Nor did the situation improve much over time. One study of Osaka's Nago-chō estimated that more than 80 percent of females over age fifteen worked for pay, meaning that the vast majority of wives engaged in at least part-time work, even when their children were infants. At the end of the era, six of every seven Tokyo boys between the ages of fifteen and twenty were working to supplement the family's expenses.[89] And they worked long hours. A survey in 1910 showed the average *hinmin* household head working twenty-five or twenty-six days a month. Only three groups—rag pickers, day laborers, and construction workers—worked fewer than twenty-three days each month.[90] And the days were long. Streetcar conductors had their workday *cut* to fifteen hours (from sixteen) late in 1903, prompting a commentator to complain that these key railway attendants were treated like "cows and horses."[91] *Taiyō*, hardly a bastion of social activism, likened shop employees to "birds in a cage" in its 1901 report that clerks typically worked sixteen-hour days, with time off forbidden for anything except calamities such as the death of a parent.[92]

HOW DID THE SITUATION CHANGE OVER TIME?

The *kasō shakai* class, taken as a whole, was surprisingly dynamic, across time. Certain things remained constant across the late Meiji years: poverty itself continued, as it still does; the *hinmin* continued to be concentrated in certain geographical areas; life was still grippingly hard at era's end for huge numbers of people; and jobs never stopped paying badly. But for many individuals and families, life was filled with change, usually slow and frequently for the better. While many people stayed in poverty, most saw life gradually (even if glacially) improve, as they used meager savings to secure better living quarters, then pushed their children into jobs at least minimally superior to their own. One of the stock themes of the day's journalism was the poor child who, through hard work and filial behavior, got an education and moved "upward." Sometimes that theme merely reflected middle-class fantasies and values, but it had a ring of truth for many. *Kokumin*'s Matsubara estimated that four of every five young men who came to the city saw life get better over time.[93] And Nakagawa has found evidence that by the last Meiji decade a "new middle class" (*shin chūkansō*) had emerged in the *hinminkutsu* regions, typified by cohesive families with high levels of ambition and an expanding ability to spend more on nonessentials. While large numbers continued to fuel a "poor class" (*kasō kaikyū*), he argues, personal drive and the rising industrial economy produced increasing differentiation within *hinmin* society. Even factory workers, whose apartments still were tiny, were now paying rents by the month (rather than daily or weekly), putting in their own toilets, and installing tatami flooring.[94] An unfortunate result of progress, he notes, was that by era's end, "the city's poorest classes (*toshi kasō*) no longer felt a sense of mutuality with industrial workers."[95]

These economic improvements were accompanied (and spurred) by educational changes, as school increasingly became available to poor children. The grimness of the mid-Meiji situation had been captured by the governor of Osaka in 1894 when he said of poor children: "If we were to force them to attend school, their families simply could not make ends meet." Even the inflated official statistics found more than half of Tokyo's children unschooled early in that decade, meaning that a minuscule portion of *hinmin* were attending classes.[96] In the early 1900s that changed significantly, however, thanks in part to the gradual elimination of school fees, in part to official efforts to get all children into the schools, and in part to the creation of some special schools for the poor.[97] Most historians are skeptical about official claims that 97 percent of all children in Tokyo were attending the six years of school that were required from 1907 on,[98] but none doubt that there was progress. Nakagawa, for example, argues that even among the poorest families, three-quarters of children were in school by the end of Meiji, and Richard Torrance's painstaking work on popular reading in Osaka convinces him that "by the end of the Meiji period, . . . tens of thousands of men and women of working class backgrounds were forming the core of a mass readership."[99]

Taken as a whole, the scholars' portrait of the urban *kasō shakai* reveals hundreds of thousands of *hinmin,* living in tiny apartments, shanties, and flophouses in the slums and poverty pockets of Tokyo and Osaka. Their work, though most often physical in nature, was as varied as life itself, and many led colorful lives while others subsisted in gray obscurity. Although their poverty sprang from multitudinous causes, two precipitants stood out: that so many had migrated, yen-less, to the city, where they had neither roots nor social networks, and that they received abysmally low wages. Life was framed for most poor families by desperately cramped living quarters (often shared with other families in the 1890s); subsistence-level diets heavy on low-grade rice and light on protein and vegetables; the impossibility of making do unless everyone, including the children, worked; and the weariness caused by twelve- to sixteen-hour workdays and twenty-five-day work months. The grimness of this picture continued until well after the end of the Meiji period. It was not, however, a static or unidimensional situation. Hope, as we shall see, was surprisingly tenacious even in the poorest *hinminkutsu,* sustained by enough real improvements to make life bearable, on some days even pleasurable.

ONE MORE PORTRAIT: OURS

We have seen the two major views of the *kasō shakai.* The Meiji era's popular writers fashioned a narrative that resonated with centuries-old stereotypes, conveying vivid, sometimes lurid descriptions of people mired in poverty caused either by fate or by their own personal failings. The later scholars described a more dynamic set of social and economic structures that held hundreds of thousands of urbanites in uninviting slum regions, providing an analysis that was less colorful but richer in nuance and less prone to judgments about character. This study will draw on the portraits of both groups, as well as on writings they largely ignored, to render still another view: one that, while grounded in the social science data, focuses on the nuances and the human side of daily life. It will address the question of how the *hinmin* experienced the everyday, not just where they lived or what they ate but how they felt and how they coped. It will look at the many kinds of work that consumed their waking hours, at the assiduous efforts they put into staying healthy, at the challenges and tragedies that sent some of them to despair and suicide, and at the many ways they celebrated life and asserted their own agency. There will be no lengthy or explicit discussions of theory, even though the works of several highly theoretical writers have informed the study,[100] because such discussions would run counter to the goal of understanding how the *hinmin* themselves experienced life. This study will attempt, in short, to see the world not as the officials and scholars understood it but as the *hinmin* felt and lived it.

A few words, then, about methods and approach.

The first thing that needs to be emphasized is that this is a study of the *urban* poor, particularly in Tokyo and to a lesser degree in Osaka and other cities, between the 1880s and the mid-1910s, a period when writers were deeply concerned about the soaring *shakai mondai.* After an initial examination of the neighborhoods in which they lived, two chapters will describe the kinds of jobs they did, with one chapter on those who *built,* working particularly in factories and in construction, and another on those who *served* more directly, in everything from street performances to bath houses, from pulling rickshaws to providing sex. Then the study will shift to the nonwork hours, with a chapter on how *hinmin* families and individuals shaped their experiences into life, followed by a chapter on the harsh or darker sides of life—the crime, the illness, the fight with despondency—and another on the things that softened the impact of poverty: the assertion of agency and engagement in activism, as well as the festivals, street fairs, and holidays that demonstrated *hinmin* exuberance and spontaneity.

The book will conclude with two chapters on the nonurban poor, designed to put the urban experience in comparative perspective.[101] One of these chapters will provide an overview of the villages from which the urban immigrants came, with a focus on how rural poverty differed qualitatively from urban poverty. Another will look at Japanese workers who emigrated abroad, particularly more than eighty thousand who left their villages to work in Hawai'i's sugar plantations. While both of those groups shared much with their Tokyo and Osaka counterparts, their experiences also differed in ways that should help us understand more clearly what made the urban *hinmin*'s life unique.

Certain themes will emerge repeatedly. The first, the grim nature of poverty, needs no further explication here. The second is resilience. Poverty was not the whole of the *hinmin* experience. When the British writer James Lasdun tried his hand at natural farming in the 1990s, he complained of humiliating bosses and back-breaking work, but then added, "The strange thing, though, was that later I felt only satisfaction with the way I had spent my day, mindless and monotonous as it had been." He said his pay seemed "more honest . . . than any other pay I had ever earned."[102] Sentimentality aside, he was onto something that shows up often in *hinmin* stories: a balancing of hardship with a determination to make life meaningful and satisfying, which made most days more complex, more varied, and more complete than the popular writers realized. Even in the depressing world of the flophouses, people formed communities where they cooked together, reared children together, and laughed, "helping each other in times of affliction and rejoicing together in times of joy."[103] Even the poorest of families strategized and dreamed of better times when external circumstances suggested only darkness. Hardship may have appeared dominant to the onlooker; it blighted the lives of *hinmin* much of the time. But for most slum dwellers, the world was more complex than that. Difficulty and determination balanced each other; resilience was a central ingredient in the *hinmin* life recipe.

Agency provides a third theme. Simon Partner, a historian of Japan's rural communities, has questioned the impact of elite efforts to impose new social norms on commoners early in the 1900s. "I am left with many doubts," he says. "Can desire in fact be manufactured? Are ordinary people really so lacking in agency and initiative?"[104] The *hinmin* materials suggest they were not. Scholars and activists too often have dismissed Japan's *hinmin* as a "*lumpenproletariat*," what even Karl Marx called "social scum" with little sense of agency and limited revolutionary potential. This study will argue that they were wrong in at least two respects. In the nonpolitical sphere, it will highlight endless expressions of conscious selfhood and agency: in the decision of young men to move to the city, in the widespread refusal of *hinmin* to accept what Irokawa Daikichi calls the establishment's new "conventional morality,"[105] in housewives who swallowed their embarrassment and did evening sex work when they saw no other way to avoid starvation. Even in the political arena, there will be accounts of activism and agency. Matsubara argued that rickshaw pullers never would engage in organized activism, but he was wrong about that too. By the early

1900s, the pullers and thousands of their *hinmin* peers were taking to the streets in a string of popular protests that kept streetcar fares affordable and toppled cabinets. The poor took charge of their own lives with as much initiative as their peers in the middle classes. They may have had fewer resources to help them get what they wanted, but that did not prevent their active engagement in every phase of life, both private and public.

The most unexpected theme probably is joy. Neither "joy" nor its synonyms appear much in standard portraits of the urban poor. Like the nineteenth-century British explorers who wrote about "bacchanalian orgies" by women "of the lowest class" when they saw hand-clapping Trinidadians dancing at a Christmas mass,[106] Japan's popular writers saw expressions of *hinmin* pleasure through the lens of class-driven condescension: slum dwellers might seek relief in alcohol or sex, but they were too poor, too burdened by misfortune to know real joy. A serious look at the records, however, suggests that a different set of lenses might have revealed something else. Matsubara's overriding narrative line is one of misery, but when he sees a group of *hinmin* outside a leftover food shop, holding "their bamboo baskets, or their little buckets, or their miso strainers, and squatting on the ground, . . . or sitting down, or standing for several hours" to chat, "to hold a salon (*danwakai*)," as it were, he cannot help but exclaim, "What rich conversation material they had!"[107] It is an energized scene that suggests anything but dull depression. Similarly, when the newspaper *Niroku Shinpō* said in the spring of 1901 that it would sponsor a workers' friendship rally (*konshinkai*) for "the poor," more than twenty thousand people showed up for a day of dancing, music, comedy, and labor speeches, despite a government edict limiting the crowd to five thousand.[108] This was not an isolated happening. Celebrations did not make poverty noble, nor did they remove its grimness. But they made it clear that joyous festivities were more than mere distractions. They were central to *hinmin* life.

The Influences Behind This Study

My efforts to understand slum life as the *hinmin* themselves experienced it often have been exhilarating; they also have pushed me beyond my comfort zone. Many days have left me feeling like Shimazaki after an evening of eating stew in a farmer's home in the early 1900s: "I still have the feeling that I really cannot see things their way."[109] Seeing things "their way" has remained my goal, nonetheless. When the effort has seemed daunting, four writers have been particularly important in providing models and approaches for my work. The first is Edward Fowler, whose study of Tokyo's late twentieth-century day laborers in *San'ya Blues* is a model when it comes to giving voice to a population that in an earlier era would have numbered among the *kasō shakai*. Fowler immersed himself in the day laborers' world, living with them, drinking and eating with them, working alongside them. As he wrote, "It should be remembered that there is far more to life in the San'ya *doyagai* [lodging-house district] than that seen on the streets." He said one had to go into the living quarters and the bars and shops, and to go there at all times of the day and night, if one were "to grasp its economic raison d'être and the vital and mutually dependent relationship between marginal and mainstream society."[110] Although his specific methodology is unavailable to me, it is that kind of immersion, at least in the sources, to which I have aspired. I also have been influenced by Yale University's James C. Scott, who has labored to see the rural populations of Southeast Asia through fresh eyes. In *Domination and the Arts of Resistance*, Scott argues that peasants consciously construct double discourses: a public transcript and a hidden transcript, with the former employed in interchanges with those in power and the latter used to keep the powerful from knowing what they think. He postulates that "the greater the disparity in power between dominant and subordinate and the more arbitrarily it is exercised, the more the public transcript of subordinates will take on a stereotyped, ritualistic cast. In other words, the more menacing the power, the thicker the mask." He adds that the public transcript tends to follow "in close conformity with how the dominant group would wish to have things appear." Thus, the Ethiopian axiom "When the great lord passes the wise peasant bows deeply and silently farts."[111] Scott's focus is more explicitly political than mine, but his insistence on reading against the grain, on ferreting out the more nuanced, often cunning, meanings of statements and actions, is crucial to my study.

A third guiding spirit is Freire, who, like Scott, wrote primarily from a political stance in his classic *Pedagogy of the Oppressed*, describing class as "an important factor in our understanding of multiple forms of oppression." Although his discussions of politics and class struggle are important, my greater interest lies in his emphasis on the humanity and subjectivity of the poor among whom he worked, the people he called "the oppressed." The members of that class, he insists, have been systematically subjected to a "culture of silence," in contradiction of "man's ontological vocation," which is "to be a Subject who acts up and transforms his world." If the poor refuse to be subjected, he says, the dominant culture labels them "'inferior,' because they are 'ingrates,' 'shiftless,' 'diseased,' or of 'mixed blood.'"[112] It is this silencing, this dehumanization, that Freire rejects most forcefully. Like Scott, he demands that the poor be seen as fully human, labeling "the problem of humanization . . . humankind's central problem" and calling for the poor to see themselves not as failures in a normative system, but as creators and masters of a new world that enshrines humanity and compassion as its chief values. Freire ends the preface to his work with the declaration: "From these pages, I hope at least the following will endure: my trust in the people, and my faith in men and women, and in the creation of a world in which it will be easier to love."[113] The important feature of this argument, for this study, is his assertion that the "oppressed"— by extension the *hinmin*—must be understood as fully bodied human beings, worthy of as much respect as Yokoyama's "people with names." I disagree with Freire when he describes the poor as "unauthentic" when they allow the system to curb and restrict them;[114] that label reflects too political an understanding of authenticity. As this work will show, the great majority of the Meiji *hinmin* found ways to experience wholeness and authenticity, whether they engaged in politics or not. They found ways to live as full human beings within an unsympathetic system. They were—using Freire's words—"not 'marginal'" and "not people living 'outside' society,"[115] but full-bodied humans, as diverse and vibrant as any others.

My fourth inspiration is one of the nameless people: someone whose insight arose, for me, when I visited the Elmina slave "castle" in Ghana in 2011. The place is a fortress, a whitewashed structure on the shores of the Atlantic Ocean, which served for two centuries as a depot for holding and shipping off Africans to slavery in Europe and the Americas. On the second floor, the officials—first Portuguese, then Dutch—occupied breezy quarters with a sweeping view of the ocean beyond and a grim view of sweating, imprisoned Africans in the courtyard below. Often, the downward look was to choose, by whim, a woman or girl with whom to sleep that night or someone else, still by whim, to send to the dungeon. Nearly everyone in the courtyard eventually would pass through the "Door of No Return" to begin the Atlantic Passage. Nearing the end of my visit, my own view was upward, onto the walls of a room where artifacts were displayed. The epigram that heads this introduction, written by an anonymous inmate, caught my eye: *"Until the lion has his historian, the hunter will always be a hero."* Its relevance to this study needs no discussion.

One final issue has dogged me throughout this study: What right do I have, as a middle-class white American more than a century removed from the late Meiji world, to try to explain how the *kasō shakai* experienced daily life? What right, in other words, do I have to do this study? By many standards, I have little. At the same time, it could be argued that no one has more right than I do. So I have pushed ahead, and I need to explain why.

One explanation lies in the simple fact that the topic compels me. Having spent most of my career studying the Meiji press, I have found myself pulled increasingly to the commoners who are, in my view, the soul of Japanese genius. In every generation, Japan's governments have been criticized for being ineffective and inefficient,[116] but the country's energy rarely has lagged. Why? I suspect that one source of that energy lies in the way ordinary Japanese approach life. Studying the *kasō shakai* seemed one way to test that suspicion. A second reason lies in the paucity of historical work on the *hinmin*, particularly on the way they experienced life. The situation has improved only marginally in the last two generations. Even in an era when social history encourages studies of excluded groups, when the quotidian has become a mainstream topic, studies of "ordinary" people still focus heavily on middle-class and elite issues and writings: how people related to social and political systems, what the intellectuals and officials had to say about the commoners, what impact those commoners had on mainstream society. Understanding the lives of commoners as important in and of themselves, for their *inherent* worth, continues to be slighted, and thus draws me.

Finally, while I have spent my adult life as a middle-class journalist (briefly) and academic, I began it as a peasant, a fact that has both pulled me toward this study and influenced my interpretations. There is no question that the way I view society springs in profound ways from the rural, American, *kasō shakai* milieu in which I was reared. Born seven weeks before Pearl Harbor on a northern Indiana farm at the edge of a village of 206 people, with parents who spent sixteen-hour days teaching and farming in order to clothe us and put food on the table, I admit to a lifelong sympathy for poor outsiders and a chip on my shoulder toward what we called "rich snobbishness." We owned our farm, but when I began elementary school, we had no indoor bathroom. Nor did we have central heating until I was nearly finished with high school. If we left a glass of water out on winter nights, it froze. We never were destitute; indeed, we were no poorer than our peers. Education was central in our family, and we had solid social networks, of the kind that characterized rural Japan. Nonetheless, we were poor farmers.

That fact has had an important impact on my understanding of the *kasō shakai,* particularly on my view of the "salient characteristics" listed above. When I hear the word poverty, for example, I remember carrying eight hundred chickens out of our chicken house on a one-hundred-degree Sunday afternoon, all of them dead from heat suffocation because we could not afford a cooling system. I remember resentments toward certain "rich city cousins" whose visits left me feeling patronized. And I remember cringing when Dad told us at supper one night that he had cried in front of the elevator owner who had come to demand payment for bills that we did not have the money to pay. Dad was as gentle and strong a man as I ever knew; the idea of his crying shook me. That the "elevator man" might have been having trouble paying his own bills never entered my mind. Our "poverty" was never bad enough to make us go hungry; it did not make me feel less human nor did it take away my pride. But it acquainted me with anxiety over where life's basics would come from, and it left me touchy about the pretentiousness of people who had more means than we did.

Even more than that, those early years showed me that being poor should not be equated with an absence of those other three summary characteristics: resiliency, agency, and joy. Forced to be resilient, I must admit to finding a sometimes perverse satisfaction in knowing that we could make do without many resources. Having no bathroom, we would bring a chicken cleaning tub into the living room every Saturday night, which made the weekly bath both more communal and more fun. When I had to go to a band contest with my hands emitting the inerasable odors of a morning spent castrating pigs, I was embarrassed, but I also remember the faintly conspiratorial, even smug, satisfaction of knowing that smelly residues made me no less proficient a trombonist than "those city kids" who might patronize me. When the poultry house burned to the ground with its thirteen thousand chickens on a windy winter night, I never doubted that Dad would find new ways, no matter how hard, to put food on the table. Resilience was a fact, not a choice. Knowing that has affected the way I understand the Meiji *hinmin.*

Agency? We would have chuckled at the "highfalutin word," then laughed at any suggestion that we lacked it. We never had any question about being in control of our destinies, even when we complained that a lack of money would make it harder for us to get ahead. Had outsiders called me a victim, I would have been puzzled. Partly, this was because, like my peers, I was steeped in American shibboleths about equality and freedom; mostly it was because of the behaviors I saw around me each day. When Ira stood on a desk and challenged the second grade teacher, he may have been disruptive, but he was asserting agency. When several of us fourth graders produced our own rough-hewn plays for the second and third graders, we were taking initiative. When Dad decided to quit teaching one year and gambled everything on spending life solely as a farmer, that spoke to me of being in charge of one's own destiny, and when he went back to teaching after a year of farm disasters, that seemed like an agent making the best of what life meted out. If agency meant making "free" choices within the limits of the structures that enfolded us, those who peopled my world were agents. Knowing that would make me forever skeptical of people who question the selfhood and agency of poor people anywhere.

So too with joy, which was only slightly affected by being poor. I may have hated the hard work and economic challenges: the spooky midnight walks to the outhouse, putting groceries "on the bill" because there was no cash to pay, having no kitchen table in my early years, going to bed in my freezing room. But those things had nothing to do with life's pleasures. Church life provided one source of joy, a joy not all that different qualitatively from the temple festivals in Meiji Japan. There were potlucks; there were youth parties; there were teenage trysts after Wednesday night prayer meetings; there was Bible quiz competition. School provided a similar range of sociable gatherings: basketball games, vegetable-judging trips, junior and senior plays. So did family times, everything from listening to the state basketball tournament on a radio in the barnyard (no reception in the house) to swimming at a nearby lake. An outsider might have looked at us freezing in winter and sweating in summer, at our tears over bills we could not pay, at the failed crops and dying animals, and pronounced our lives harsh. And they would have been right. But I knew as a child, and I know now, that that judgment would have been simplistic. Life's hardships were simply the dark shadows in a life that, taken as a whole, was joyful. It is this knowledge that forces itself into my consciousness whenever I start to take difficulties as the whole of the *hinmin* picture.

This is not meant to equate life in mid-twentieth-century rural Indiana with that of the *kasō shakai* in late Meiji Osaka and Tokyo. It is meant, rather, to explain that growing up poor has influenced the way I read and interpret materials. It has given me, perhaps, an access to certain features of the *kasō shakai* experience that otherwise might be unavailable to me. The farm years have made me skeptical of observers who see the poor only through economic, political, or class lenses. Above all, they have left me convinced that every part of *hinmin* life is important and worthy of study, in all of its variety and complexity.

A final comment is in order about the way in which this work handles Japanese names. The body of the text employs the standard academic pattern of using surnames first, as is the custom in Japan. The bibliography and notes follow the style used in the work being cited, which sometimes entails using an author's given name first (most often without a macron over long vowels). Thus, the writer of *Childhood Years* (*Yoshio jidai*) is referred to as Tanizaki Jun'ichirō in the body of the work, just as he is in Japanese, but the citations list him as Jun'ichiro Tanizaki, following the usage of the published memoir, with the given name coming first and the final "o" devoid of a macron. In line with standard practice, long vowels use a macron, except for words and places that are used commonly in English without the macron.

CHAPTER 1

The Slum Setting
Moving In and Settling Down

> In Asakusa, everything is flung out in the raw. . . . Asakusa is a young
> punk. And bad or not, youth has charm, energy, and a progressive spirit.
> —Kawabata Yasunari, *The Scarlet Gang of Asakusa*[1]

Tension and stress surely filled the Ueki household on this late November morning in 1901, for Hidetoshi and his small family were typical (if there was such a thing) members of Tokyo's mushrooming poor population.[2] He worked as a general errand man, or *kozukai,* at a firm in the city's commercial district, spent a dozen hours a day running letters and packages to the post office, sweeping floors, cleaning windows and countertops, and dashing off to buy cigarettes for his superiors. Bringing home seven and a half yen a month for this work—less than half of what it cost the family to scrape by in a one-room apartment—he was poor even by the standards of what journalists called the "underclasses" (*kasō kaikyū*). He was not, however, at the bottom.

Why the tension? Hidetoshi would have been amused by the question. How could a household like his be anything *but* tense? For one thing, there was the exhaustion that consumed him every hour of every day, a weariness that made it hard to face life's insecurities serenely. Like the other three members of his family, he had long workdays, some of them sixteen suffocating hours. At least three nights a week, he finished his tasks so late that he had to stay on at the firm, getting what sleep he could on the office floor. Most weeks, he got a single day off; some weeks, none.[3] Tiredness and irritability were unavoidable. And the work situation affected relationships within the family. Ueki's two children should have been going to school, but the family could not put food on the table unless everyone worked. So school was an unfulfilled dream, and that worried Hidetoshi. Fifteen-year-old Tōru, the only son, worked full-time at a printing office and his thirteen-year-old sister Eiko put in twelve-hour shifts at a factory. Even Noriko, Hidetoshi's wife, had to do extra piecework when she was not cooking, or cleaning, or doing the wash, or mending holey socks for the third time, or buying rice at a leftovers shop. The living space produced tensions too, because there was so little of it. They all lived in a single rented room of about a hundred square feet, with neither bath nor kitchen. Life, in short, gave them neither space for privacy nor time to be together as a family. How could they nourish the filial relationships described in the ancient tales?

Most anxiety-producing of all was the lack of money. Even a bare-bones existence cost more than all four of the Uekis took in together. They bought the lowest quality rice and ate slivers of fish each day, with a tiny chunk of meat added on celebration days; mostly, they subsisted on miso soup and rice gruel. The journalist who wrote about them noted, "The enjoyment of three square meals, to use a common expression, is of course out of the question." Even with scrimping, it cost 19.19 yen a month to live, which was half a yen more than their combined incomes (see table 1). So how did they get by? They cut every corner possible; they worried; they sniffed out night work and an occasional extra job; small semiannual bonuses helped; they worried still more (God forbid that a crisis or accident should occur). When things got really bad, they took something to a pawn shop to get a small loan from that "universal friend of the needy" who made a living through what the *Taiyō* reporter called his "insatiable thirst for gain wrung from people in misfortune."[4] And some days Hidetoshi stole a few pieces of charcoal from work to keep the hibachi burning at home. If he and Noriko "tended to fly off the handle easily because they were always hungry,"[5] one should not have been surprised.

Table 1. "Ueki" family finances, in yen, 1901

Available monthly income		
Father	*kozukai,* commercial firm	7.5
Mother	supplemental work	2
Son, 15	printing office	5
Daughter, 13	factory	3
Miscellaneous (bonuses, tips, gifts, etc.)		1.2
Total		*18.7*

Monthly expenses				
rent	2	kerosene	0.3
rice	6.4	provisions	5
soy	0.3	bath	0.8
miso	0.36	hair cut	0.36
salt	0.05	hair dressing (woman)	0.12
fuel	1.5	incidentals	2
Total				*19.19*

Source: Taiyō 7, no. 14 (December 5, 1901), 5. The article says that, with overtime, Hidetoshi made up to 9.5 yen a month but that he could only turn over 7.5 yen to the family coffer because of "a few incidentals."

Fortunately, tension was not the whole story for the Uekis. The middle-class journalist who described their situation may have focused on how difficult it was for "such a class of people . . . to keep body and soul together," but a careful reading suggests that life also had another side. Like most of their peers in the late Meiji urban slums, the Uekis experienced life in all its rich complexity. Along with the anxieties and difficulties came humanizing activities that gave most days color and hope. Like their more affluent fellow citizens, they knew life as a multifaceted thing, filled with accomplishment as well as trouble, joy along with sorrow. And the indications of agency—that these people took hold of circumstances actively and intentionally—were numerous.

The grim budget, for example, showed a family determined to do more than merely subsist. Some eighty sen a month—a pittance, certainly, yet 4 percent of the total—was set aside for visits to the public bath, while forty-eight sen went to haircuts and "hair dressing."[6] Even saké was included explicitly in the "provisions" category, which accounted for more than a quarter of the budget. And the reporter noted that when Hideyuki turned over his monthly income to his wife Noriko, in keeping with Japanese custom, he kept a yen or two for himself for "buying tobacco" or "occasionally indulging in a drink or in some cheap delicacy." The assertion of agency also was clear in the way Hideyuki and his family undercut the system when circumstances demanded it or when chance provided the opportunity. The most telling piece of evidence lay in Hideyuki's practice of stealing petty things from his employer: a few coals from the bags of charcoal that the firm burned each day, a sen or two from the payments that customers made when he delivered goods, a couple of empty straw bags that could be exchanged for a free soaking at the local bath house. He never took enough to raise suspicion, but the gleanings were enough to make his family "a little better off than some employees with slightly higher salaries."

The Uekis were not, in other words, passive recipients of life's blows. Their options may have been limited but they made conscious decisions about the budget, cutting corners or stretching the unstretchable to make means meet needs and finding ways to enjoy a few of the guilty pleasures that are an essential part of the fully lived life. The *Taiyō* reporter does not talk about it, but there is no question that they also participated in the bustling festival life and street markets of their *shitamachi*, or "low city" area, because all people with their profiles did. And it is likely that they would have managed to save a sen or two a month since that was the experience of typical late Meiji *hinmin* families.[7] Life, in other words, was complex and varied for the Uekis. Poverty set them apart from their peers in the middle class; everyone knew that. But aspiration, agency, and pleasure were important features of life too, features that poor and rich shared, whether those in the more affluent classes knew it or not.

The first issue that confronted the great majority of Japan's urban poor in the late Meiji years was where to live. If daily life was driven by work and the need for food, it was framed by the physical spaces they called home. For that reason, it seems appropriate to begin this study with an examination of place: a glance at where the immigrant *hinmin* came from, then a fuller look at what their urban habitations, the *hinminkutsu* (slums) and other poverty pockets of Tokyo and Osaka, looked and felt like. These caverns of the poor may have been scorned by the middle classes; they certainly were overlooked in contemporary travel guides and in studies of modernity. But they were among the most interesting and dynamic areas in the cities of the 1890s and early 1900s. When the Nobel laureate Kawabata Yasunari called Asakusa a "young punk" that exuded charm and energy whether it was "bad or not," he was describing the alleyways and streets—a "turbulent vortex of people"—that the *hinmin* populated.[8] To know those alleyways and streets is the first requirement for knowing the *hinmin* themselves.

What Brought Them?

A small portion of the *hinmin* were longtime residents, particularly those in the *burakumin,* or outcaste enclaves that stretched back into the pre-Meiji generations. Even though outcaste status had been abolished officially in 1871, the *burakumin* communities continued in reality until well beyond the end of the Meiji era, with tens of thousands living in the poorest regions of Osaka, Kyoto, and Kobe and smaller numbers in Tokyo.[9] But the great majority of those who made up *kasō shakai* society were transient and rootless, immigrants from elsewhere in Japan. As the introduction pointed out, villagers and rural townspeople flooded Japan's cities in the 1890s and early 1900s, pushing the population of Tokyo from 1.3 million in 1897 to 3.4 million in 1920; that of Osaka from 750,000 to 1.8 million; that of Kyoto from 330,000 to 700,000, and, even more remarkably, that of Kobe from 190,000 to 640,000.[10] This great migration raises many questions, the most obvious being: Why? Japan never had had population shifts on this scale before. Why now? One reason lay in the new ease of movement, as trains and improved roads made travel easier than it ever had been. Another lay in communication: the spread of print media and education provided people in the remotest villages with an awareness of national trends and possibilities in far-off places. Modernity, in other words, facilitated migration.

The primary cause, however, was economic. Life always was hard for most rural people. As the farmer Nagatsuka Takashi wrote in his novel *Tsuchi* (Soil), which was serialized in *Tokyo Asahi Shinbun* in 1910, even in normal times "poor farmers were caught up in a vicious circle." If they could not afford fertilizer, their crops were skimpy, which forced them to supplement their income with side jobs, which left little time for "weeding and cultivating their own fields," which meant that "inevitably a time would come when they had nothing left to eat."[11] If that cycle described normal times on the farm, it barely hinted at the dire situation in the 1880s, when government austerity policies aimed at cutting national debt and curbing inflation resulted in a major depression that hit farmers hardest of all. Economic misery swept Japan's rural regions like a plague as taxes rose and rice prices fell, leaving household heads unable to pay their rents and mothers without enough grains to feed their children. Rice that sold for one hundred yen in 1881 brought just fifty-one yen three years later, and as many as a fifth of the country's farmers lost their land in the economic tidal wave. Bank-ruptcies more than tripled in the mid-1880s, and more than 367,000 farmers lost their fields because they could not pay land taxes in the eight years between 1883 and 1890. One newspaper reported that two-thirds of the residents of a village in northern Kyushu "had disposed of their belongings by public auction and were waiting for death."[12] Other stories circulated about families eating roadside grasses because there were no vegetables, making mushy cakes of arrowroot starch, and turning the despised leaves of ginger into salads.[13]

The most obvious answer to the difficulties, for many families, was to reduce the size of the household by sending at least one child to the city, where mo-dernity was creating new jobs. Sometimes parents would respond to the sales pitch of a recruiter from a factory or a brothel and hire out their younger chil-dren in return for a fee and a promise that extra income would be sent back home. Occasionally they would make connections with relatives or other vil-lagers who already had settled in the city. Not infrequently, ambitious or rest-less young men (occasionally young women) would decide on their own to leave. More often, the family would decide as a unit that it was time for the son to leave. During a series of village visits in the 1890s, the *Mainichi Shinbun* reporter Yokoyama Gennosuke heard many parents admonishing sons, "with all the wisdom and experience they can muster," to "leave their native villages, migrate to other places in order to find work, and establish their own families." They would talk about how hard village life was and play up the great possi-bilities offered by urban employment, he said, pulling out all the stops to strengthen the son's resolve as he pondered the heavy decision.[14] When a fam-ine hit northeastern Japan in 1905, the youth magazine *Seinen Kurabu* re-ported that more than thirty young women in Miyagi Prefecture decided that the only way they could save their "starving families" was to move out and take work in urban brothels.[15]

What the journalists saw with their eyes, government researchers confirmed in repeated studies during the late Meiji years. Tokyo population surveys, for example, showed that recent migrants to the city, labeled *kiryūjin,* or "tempo-rary residents," made up at least half of the total population in any given year. In 1907, some 62 percent of the city's residents were *kiryūjin;* in 1912, they consti-tuted roughly half of the population.[16] And most often the migrants settled in the *shitamachi* wards in the north and east where poverty was concentrated. In the last decade of the Meiji era, while the city as a whole saw an increase of 114 people for every thousand who had been there in 1903, the poor wards experi-enced increases of triple that rate, or 338 per thousand, with Fukagawa growing by a phenomenal 532 people per thousand.[17] Moreover, as one might have expected in a migration of this sort, males far outnumbered females in the *hin-minkutsu* areas, with 120 males for every hundred females in 1900 and 114 for every hundred in 1910. Surveys also showed that until the beginning of the 1900s, the poor regions of both Osaka and Tokyo had more deaths each year than births, evidence, says the economic historian Nakagawa Kiyoshi, that these neighborhoods were home to single young men who might have had sex but were not ready to marry and have children. An increase in the proportion of births in the last Meiji years suggests that many of those young men began to settle down and create families as their years in the city passed.[18]

The impersonal statistics may numb the brain, but the challenges that the new arrivals brought with them from their rural homes were anything but cool and academic. There was, for example, the frightening task of confronting a wholly unknown world. The novelist Inoue Yasushi describes the paralysis induced by strange foods and exotic clothing fashions in one early-century village boy when he visited the city for the first time. He "found it totally foreign territory," says Inoue; he felt "utterly outclassed" and holed himself up in his inn room for the length of the stay.[19] And that was on a mere visit. Rural immigrants had to live permanently with the unfamiliar things, with no place in which to hole up. They also had to live with the debilitating burden of having their "new hopes for good salaries" dashed in the brutal world of urban employment.[20] Most difficult of all, for many, was the challenge of scarcity. Farmers who emigrated abroad in these years usually had at least a minimal amount of savings for the voyage and the settling-in period. Not so the urban immigrants, who typically came "destitute and with nothing but the clothes on their backs."[21] Even finding a few sen for the first night's lodging and first day's food often was a challenge.

There also was the challenge of being alone, with the village's human networks a mere memory now. Dire conditions sent most of the young men and women to the city; a desire to escape rural insularity sent others. Few, however, realized when they left how bereft the cities would be of those things that had for generations made rural life liveable: the unpolluted skies, soaring mountains, camaraderie in the communal bath. Here they had neither natural settings nor human connections. Nor were there government programs to assist them. They usually arrived yearning for companionship but rarely found it, said the folklorist Yanagita Kunio.[22] The new, crowded sleeping quarters seemed like "bleak, sunless cages," added Yokoyama,[23] cages with no family members or village friends nearby to confide in. At first, most newcomers still thought of themselves a part of the old village family from which they had come, says the historian Kumazawa Makoto, but they quickly had to face a bleaker reality: "These people had, in fact, lost their homes."[24] New networks would take shape over time and new hopes would gradually grow, but at the beginning, when they arrived in the city, the entire package of challenges—the newness, the unrealistic dreams, the impoverishment, the lack of human networks or support systems—simply made city life grim. And the neighborhoods where they settled were as challenge-ridden as the young men themselves.

Where They Lived

The populist newspaper *Yorozu Chōhō* filled its New Year's Day columns in 1900 with comments about society's state at century's end. The last decades, said editor Yamagata Isō, had produced "such a great progress as has never been seen in the preceding centuries. . . . It almost appears as if the world has already reached the highest point of material civilization." Individual freedoms had multiplied and wars had decreased, he said in a burst of optimism, giving the world a realistic hope "of universal peace, the ideal of mankind." But unfortunately, all was not well: "So full, in fact, is the world of miseries, that we, weak as we are, almost stagger before them."[25] Near the top of his list of miseries was the growing scourge of urban poverty, particularly the unceasing spread of *hinminkutsu* and smaller pockets of poverty where those newcomers from the countryside were settling.

Yamagata did not make the connection, but the modern currents that filled him with such rapture, the "wonderful inventions . . . at work both on land and sea," had played a crucial role in creating the slums. With inventions had come factories, new professions, a rush of construction, demands for new products like sugar and cigarettes, and all those jobs that beckoned the rural poor. The editor's enthusiasm was understandable; the cities were exciting places in these years, bombarded daily with the unknown, the scary, and the inviting: gas streetlights, horse-drawn streetcars, ugly factory buildings, wider streets (some of them even paved), rickshaws, stores selling watches and Western-style suits, electric lights, waterworks, sellers of modern furniture, barbershops, beer halls, a discombobulating wave of modernity. And the immigrants had ridden that wave. Unfortunately, the onrush often felt more like a tsunami, inundating both the newcomers and the government workers responsible for managing urban spaces. Bureaucrats in Osaka and Tokyo had begun paying increasing attention to city planning by the late 1880s, but the swelling numbers made the task daunting. While officials put massive efforts into developing new parks, safer sanitation facilities, and better transportation routes, much of their energy, especially in Osaka, went into a less salutary effort simply to control "undesirable" elements such as factories, red-light districts, and the ever-increasing poor populations to keep them from spilling into or contaminating the cities' respectable areas.[26]

As a result, one of the important features of the last half of the Meiji era was the increasing concentration of the poor in the *hinminkutsu* and other, smaller poverty pockets near the factories and cheap entertainment areas. Although the "service classes" had been separated officially from the governing elites in earlier centuries, status—not wealth and income—had been the main criterion for separation. For that reason, the early Meiji years had seen the poor widely dispersed, particularly in Tokyo, with the very poorest, for example, staying in some five hundred flophouses scattered throughout the city and others residing in nearly all regions.[27] There were exceptions, particularly the concentrations of outcastes in Tokyo's Asakusa region and in areas such as Nishihama in Osaka, but poverty generally was spread out. Once job seekers began moving to the cities in great numbers, however, income-based separation became increasingly common, in part because immigrants looked for cheap housing near their work and in part because urban planning after the 1880s focused on segregating rich and poor and getting rid of slums in the central business areas. In Osaka, the poor were concentrated in the southern districts, particularly in Namba and Tennōji, as well as in the well-known region of tenements and rentals called Nago-chō, where, according to the journalist Suzuki Umeshirō, if "one ventures off the beaten path, one encounters people . . . crying aloud from hunger and cold."[28] After the turn of the century, the city government's slum-clearance project moved *hinmin* to Osaka's southern periphery where the Nipponbashi and Kamagasaki slums sprang up. In Tokyo, which had had more than a hundred *hinminkutsu* in fifteen wards as late as 1891,[29] the new immigrants settled overwhelmingly in the northeast, along the Sumida River in what was popularly called *shitamachi*.[30] While big slums such as Samegahashi in Yotsuya and Shin'ami-chō in Shiba near Tokyo Bay continued to house thousands of people, all but seven of the fifty-three new slums that appeared after 1890 were in the four "low city" wards of Asakusa, Shitaya, Fukagawa, and Honjo, a region that in 1911 housed 40 percent of the city's total population; five-sixths of its "very poor," including the long-standing *burakumin* enclaves; the largest concentration of rickshaw pullers, and just 5.6 percent of its cars.[31] These were the neighborhoods, in the words of novelist Natsume Sōseki, with "that cheap, dirty look peculiar to newly developed areas."[32]

With newness and concentration came a plethora of journalistic reports on these places where people had "customs, popular sentiments, and characteristics distinct from those of the general populace in Tokyo."[33] In the popular accounts, the poor areas all sounded alike: they reeked, they shocked the senses, they evoked some combination of pity and disgust. The pioneer journalist Matsubara Iwagorō set the descriptive model in the 1890s when he described the Shin'ami-chō slum as a region with "a degree of dirt and ruin that almost defies description." Here, he said:

> The alleys are a swamp of dirty water, dead rats are festering in the sun, . . . heaps of old clogs, spoiled rice and fish are lying about, the roofs are repaired with pieces of broken mats, and the place looks a fort in a wilderness that has been riddled by shot and shell. . . . It is the last refuge on the face of the earth, so crowded, oh so crowded with all its woe and misery, and so barren of all that makes life enjoyable or even bearable, and those who enter it have . . . abandoned hope.[34]

Other observers echoed him. A British sociologist visiting Osaka in 1911 talked about "its teeming population in crowded narrow streets, its forest of smoking chimneys, . . . and, unfortunately, its paupers and its slums": block on block of "dirt and garbage, and foul gutters, evidently full of fleas, dark and destitute of all conveniences."[35] A *Fūzoku Gahō* writer described Samegahashi west of the palace as an area of "damp and marshy" soil, "low eaves, walls falling down, thousands of poor homes . . . squirming when a little rain or dew falls," a "pitiful" scene; an accompanying drawing showed a child carrying a rat by the tail.[36] And the teacher Noguchi Yuka said the slum there was simply "awful":

> As soon as one slipped into the side streets with their rice wine and bean cake shops, the long wooden buildings leaned precariously, the sliding panel doors were ripped, and tenement houses lined the streets. In dirty two- and

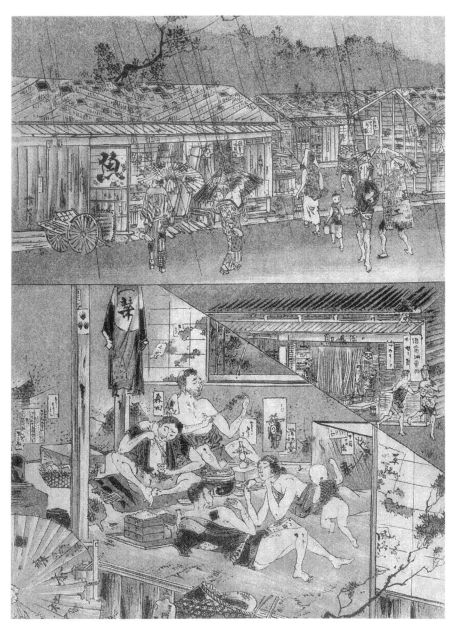

An illustrator's view of the *hinminkutsu,* or slums, in the November 10, 1898, issue of the journal *Fūzoku Gahō;* the picture of people eating and lounging inside captured the standard public view of slum dwellers then. Courtesy of University of Tokyo Graduate Schools for Law and Politics, Center for Modern Japanese Legal and Political Documents, Meiji Shimbun Zasshi Bunko.

three-mat rooms, families of five or six lived packed in together. Of course, sunlight did not penetrate these narrow streets. . . . When I thought of rais-ing children in this corrupt atmosphere, I couldn't help but shudder.[37]

The writings revealed a consensus bordering on unanimity: the late Meiji slums were sites of filth and despair—and little more.

The people who lived there, however, would have painted a different picture. Whether from Osaka's Nago-chō or Tokyo's Fukagawa ward, they lived in a world that was as varied and dynamic as it was gritty and unkempt. When the fiction writer Higuchi Ichiyō, who knew poverty from personal experience, de-scribed the depressed Daionjimae neighborhood outside the Yoshiwara pleasure quarters as a place of "shabby tenements, their eaves atilt," where "business . . . is none too good," she was quick to add, "but this neighborhood is in fact a lively place—or so the people living here say."[38] The residents of nearby Mannen-chō and the slum dwellers of Honjo and Fukagawa said the same, as did the late twentieth-century observer Edward Fowler, who found that San'ya, the day-laborer center north of Asakusa's Sensōji Temple, was "a state of mind" where the "meaning of this neighborhood is clearly not the same for the resident . . . and nonresident."[39] The *hinmin* regions may have been crowded; they may have been dirty; but they were far more than that. If they seethed, it was with energy and striving. If they shocked, it was with the unexpected as much as with the dis-tasteful. These regions were as dynamic as the people who settled there.

The first thing that stands out when one pays close attention to the materials is the cacophonous energy with which daily slum life pulsated. The *hinmin-kutsu* world was postmodern, driven by a wild, unorchestrated quality possible only in new and crowded places. By era's end, the four *shitamachi* wards had twice the population density of Tokyo overall. Two of them had more than 100,000 residents per square mile (far more than Mumbai, India, in the early twenty-first century and roughly the same as Manila, the world's most densely populated city), while each square mile of Honjo had more than 85,000 resi-dents.[40] People of every kind mingled on the streets and in the temple grounds, partly because their cramped dwellings propelled them outdoors for relaxation and partly because the public areas had so much to offer. Almost every account, even those by the stereotyping journalists, highlighted the energy: the "motley army of rickshaw pullers, day laborers, artisans, itinerant peddlers, home work-ers, and providers of all sorts of services" that filled the streets day and night.[41] One frequent visitor called Asakusa a world of "Geisha making morning visits to temples. Children going off to school. Beggars. Nannies. Day laborers. Men going home after a night on the town. Bums."[42] Yokoyama said Osaka's Nago-chō burst with the modern, the primitive, and the surprising all juxtaposed: new factories on new streets traversed by "dwarfs, cripples, and the deaf, dressed only in rags," and a woman "stark naked except for an apron being used as a substitute for undergarments."[43]

And the ever sentimental Matsubara, wandering through a Tokyo *hinminkutsu* at day's end, described a world of sweaty, worn-out men carrying pickaxes and lunchboxes, tired parents "looking for a resting place for the night," twelve- and thirteen-year-old girls counting the small coins they had collected for playing the samisen, an infirm pipe mender, a clog repairman, "women who buy empty bottles," and merchants selling everything from fruit to salmon and cuttlefish.[44] He also saw a group of children "noisily digging a hole by the toilet pit in the back to bury a dead cat, while yet another group looks like sewer rats, covered from head to toe with the clogged sewage they are trying to disgorge."[45] And then, he added, there were the "colleges of the poor" (*hindaigaku*), noted above, where *hinmin* gathered at the side of the street or in cheap bars to share survival lessons and gossip. Even nightfall brought no letup in the bustle of these "complex, intermingling places." If the politicians had their indoor clubs, the poor had the streets.

> Every day they come to exchange the secrets of the poor. . . . Carrying their boxes or their bamboo baskets, or their little buckets or their miso strainers, they squat on the club's ground, or they sit, or they stand—and across several hours, they hold their own salons (*danwakai*), talking about their daily experiences. . . . What rich material for conversations![46]

Middle-class observers might sneer about "squatting" wives "gossiping as they cooked some fish for supper on little charcoal grills"; they might chuckle

"Conference by the well" is the title of this *Fūzoku Gahō* sketch (September 10, 1898), illustrating *hinmin* mothers mixing child care, laundry, cooking, and conversation. Courtesy of University of Tokyo Graduate Schools for Law and Politics, Center for Modern Japanese Legal and Political Documents, Meiji Shimbun Zasshi Bunko.

about a motley mothers' "conference beside the well" where some of the participants were overweight and others were bare from the waist up. But to the initiated, these were lively and variegated human interactions that made middle-class neighborhoods dull by comparison.[47]

The *kasō shakai* regions also embraced a surprisingly diverse range of types of people. Even if poverty was concentrated and the slums themselves were populated by *hinmin* alone, the *hinminkutsu* neighborhoods typically contained buildings of many kinds and a broad mix of human traffic, with establishment institutions and comfortable homes intermingled with row houses and shanties. These neighborhoods abounded in temples and shrines; there were factories here (many in Fukagawa, fewer in Honjo prior to the twentieth century), along with warehouses and restaurants; there were tourist sites, villas of the rich, and pleasure boats cruising up and down the Sumida River. Sitting in his one-room tenement apartment in Daionjimae after an evening meal of watery rice gruel, a shop clerk would have heard the endless click-clacks of rickshaws taking rich men into the high-class Yoshiwara pleasure quarters next door and would have seen the brothels' "flickering lights reflected in the Oh-aguro Moat."[48] Not far away, he would have found open spaces, both planned and unplanned. When the Taishō era began in 1912, Tokyo still included more than 900 paddy fields and 13,000 meadows, along with 178 wastelands and 372 ponds and swamps, many of them in the *shitamachi* region, which was still under development in the late Meiji years. The neighborhoods around Yoshiwara had had acres on acres of wet rice paddies and dry shiso fields until the 1880s, and the area still was home to many "semirural landscapes."[49]

When the press reported in 1906 that the imperial household was considering relocating residents of Yotsuya's Samegahashi slum "because it is so near to the Akasaka palace, that filthy water from this poor quarter finds its way profusely into the palace grounds,"[50] the editor focused on the danger of contaminating the imperial family. But the implicit message in the report was that poverty and wealth intermingled; emperors and *hinmin* lived next to each other. Similarly, the sumptuous Kiyosumi gardens of Iwasaki Yatarō's family, with their quiet landscapes of artificial hills, multicolored carp, and manicured pines, sat cheek by jowl with the row houses of Fukagawa. Walls kept the poor from entering or even looking in, but they could no more have missed the comings and goings of the bushy-browed Mitsubishi founder's rich friends[51] than they could have avoided the screeches of saw blades in the area's lumber yards.[52] Honjo, home to more than 160,000 people, may have been "an expanse of one- and two-story buildings, broken only by occasional smokestacks or large factory buildings" in 1905, but it also included the "gaudy" Ekōin temple and the impressive buildings that housed the country's major sumo tournaments.[53]

No place in Tokyo exemplified this diversity better than Asakusa, a relatively compact ward along the western banks of the Sumida, which included the millennium-old Sensōji Temple, the brothels of the Yoshiwara pleasure district, the spectacular tourist-attracting twelve-story brick Cloud Scraper (Ryōunkaku), myriad theaters and parks, and more than a dozen slums, where the families of some 5,600 rickshaw pullers and 1,000 rag pickers lived in the third Meiji decade.[54] Yokoyama called it "an extremely tumultuous place," a place with heavy traffic along streets lined with tall, blue-tiled buildings intersected by slum alleys where "one would undoubtedly stumble across beggars hovering in corners or sitting in rows."[55] The journalist Fujimoto Taizō was struck by the mingling of classes there: the streets where "old and young, high and low, male and female, rich and poor" crowded together, right along with "ruffians, thieves, and pickpockets when the curtain of the dark comes down."[56] To the popular ballad singer Azembō, Asakusa was a site where "everything is flung out in the raw," where "desires dance naked," with "all races, all classes, all jumbled together forming a bottomless, endless current, flowing day and night, no beginning, no end . . . a foundry in which all the old models are regularly melted down to be cast into new ones."[57] And the novelist Nagai Kafū luxuriated in the neighborhood's variety in his late Meiji story "The River Sumida," explaining how morning walkers would find the "huge and quiet" temple grounds full of drifters and leftovers from the previous night's revelries: "several sinister-looking men, who had evidently passed the night there . . . untying the short sashes of their dirty kimonos and redoing their loincloths." The sudden "calls of crows and roosters" and a barking dog awakened by a geisha in a rickshaw invoked the nearby houses of pleasure.[58]

It was not just buildings and people that provided the cacophony; so did transportation routes, which crisscrossed each other in a maze of dirt and gravel streets, rivers and canals, bridges, and three-foot-wide alleys jammed with drying clothes, cooking fires, latrines, and playing children.[59] The petty merchants' shops and booths along roadways lined by stark telephone poles completed a scene that some found forbidding, others energizing. When Kafū's young protagonist Chōkichi wandered the area, the streets were "narrow, and so twisted that he expected to find himself up a blind alley. Mossy shingled roofs, rotting foundations, leaning pillars, dirty planks, drying rags and diapers, pots and cheap sweets for sale—the dreary little houses went on in endless disorder." The added sound of a distant flute made him sad.[60] Others found the atmosphere invigorating, even inviting. As two of the most respected Western Japan observers enthused in 1898, Asakusa was "the quaintest and liveliest place in Tokyo," not to be missed, because it provided "a spectacle than which surely nothing more motley was ever witnessed."[61]

The waterways provided a different kind of chaos and a different set of issues and attractions. In Tokyo, Fukagawa was famous for its many water channels, as well as the 140 bridges (128 of them wooden) that crossed them, while Osaka was dubbed "the city of water" because of its many canals and rivers, spanned by 253 bridges.[62] Visitors often found the waterways charming: lined with restaurants and trees, inviting places for lovers on a tryst, giving off the swishing sounds of oars and the bantering calls of boatmen. Memoirist Kaburagi Kiyokata recalled wistfully an evening under a "totally dark sky" in Tokyo's watery Tsukiji area, with human shadows flitting "thinly beneath the bridge, . . . moving along imperceptibly in the quiet waters."[63] Kafū waxed sentimental about the nighttime barges that looked like "black figures in an ink wash."[64] Locals, by contrast, remembered more troubling features of the waterways. They too experienced idyllic moments, but they had to live day-in and day-out near the blasting horns and noxious smokestacks of the boats that ferried coal and lumber to and from the shoreline warehouses, and with the pollution that permeated the waters.[65] During the late winter droughts, when the canals dried up, the refuse on their bottoms stank; in the summer and autumn, when the rains came, the low-lying slums of Honjo and Fukugawa turned into filthy lakes and mud holes. Learning that the Kabukiza Theatre was washing actors' kimono in "the filthy ditch water of Honjo," a *Tokyo Puck* artist worried lest they make the actors sick; a few years later one of his colleagues described the typical *shitamachi* canal as "an open channel for the unrestricted circulation of disease, slime and filth."[66] And in those years when the heavens turned truly angry, the flooding was lethal. In August of 1910, for example, heavy rains inundated more than four thousand Honjo and Fukagawa homes, left Asakusa Park four feet deep in water, and killed more than a thousand.[67]

The *shitamachi* skies too carried a peculiar mix of the pleasant and the ugly. It goes without saying that many noises and smells were pleasing: the evening reverberations of Osaka Shitennōji's giant temple bells, for example, or the streetside scents of skewered chicken and roasting chestnut, or the sweet aromas of early morning rains along the Sumida River in June and the "clattering of sandals in the evening cool."[68] But one of the slum areas' most onerous distinctions was the abundance of ugly sounds and aromas that reminded residents of the special price "progress" imposed on people without means. Asano Cement Company in Fukagawa and Yūkōsha Paper Mill across the Sumida in Kakigara-chō spewed out smoke clouds, creating "a really insufferable nuisance" and suffocating neighborhoods with "an unbearable foul smell."[69] Of Osaka's industrial area, an elementary school textbook noted (with a non-slum-dweller's pride) that more than eight thousand factories made the region the "Capital of Smoke." "Even on a fair day," the writer boasted, "the sky grows dull as you approach Osaka station by train, making the city appear overcast. . . . Chimneys belch smoke incessantly. With its diversity of flourishing industries, Osaka is truly Japan's greatest industrial city."[70] Nor was it the industrialists alone who fouled the air. Kaburagi talked about the stench from uncovered toilets, some of them next to restaurants with open windows.[71] Others described the smells of leatherwork, particularly in Osaka's Nishihama neighborhood of former *burakumin,* where "the stinking hides of animals, their odor combined with pungent tanning chemicals and artificial dyes, violently irritate a person's nose."[72] And writers poked fun at the fetid results when night soil collectors spilled their collections on the street. Such problems were relative, of course. Visiting foreigners often commented that Japan's poor regions had "far less offensive smells than in a London slum," since they had better ventilation, more bath houses, and fewer dirty rag piles.[73] But such comparisons hardly assuaged the housewife whose freshly washed clothes were blackened by soot when she took them off the line.

Taken in sum, the *kasō shakai* neighborhoods were simultaneously depressing and vibrant, like Kawabata's "young punk." Dirt, foul odors, litter, crowded buildings, chaotic alleys—they all were real, supporting Tanizaki's description of Asakusa as a place "where ugliness bares its essential form."[74] But the ugliness mongers told only half the story. Youths who grew up in the poor regions, as much as those who grew up in middle-class homes, looked back on their childhood with nostalgia. In part, that reflected sentimentality, but there was more to it than that, because the grim side of the poor regions was balanced by enticements available only in areas such as this. Factories were juxtaposed with some of Japan's most impressive, visitor-attracting temples and shrines, even with high-class entertainment quarters. The tumult and noise of street markets were tempered by the luxury of interesting sights and the conviviality of shared experiences. Pushed into the streets and alleys by living spaces that were too small and too hot or cold, depending on the season, people talked, cursed, napped, shared horror tales, drank, shopped, and loitered. And they did it together, creating a raw human symphony whose happier melodies were missed by better-off observers. Even refuse piles provided exciting spaces for children to play. And the proximity of the ugly factories shortened commutes. These places were poor; they were chaotic; they were variegated. It is obvious why outsiders (and insiders too) so often called the poverty neighborhoods a living hell. It may have been less obvious, but it is no less true, that these regions also were a paradise, a cacophony that many residents found melodic. As Tanizaki himself conceded, "at times ugliness shines with the luster of beauty."[75]

Housing Arrangements

If energy and variety tempered grimness in the *hinmin* setting, what about the quarters workers called home? Unfortunately, the case for a half-full glass was harder to make when it came to living spaces. Bleakness ruled. The official attitude about housing for the poor was illustrated by the government's refusal to make any provision at all for *hinmin* evicted from central Tokyo in the 1870s for the development of foreigners' residences and the Ginza Brick Street. Despite some improvements over the years, slum living quarters generally remained unregulated, crowded, flammable, and inadequate to the end of Meiji,[76] "monuments," in Sōseki's evaluation, "to . . . bottom feeding capitalists, seizing the opportunity of Tokyo's explosive but severely underfunded growth" to get rich.[77] The *Taiyō* essayist Saitō Kokubu complained in the autumn of 1901 that "landlords throw all of their capital into building as many homes as they can, then getting out all of the rental income possible, with the result that we have much construction and many crude properties." He deplored the frequent fires that resulted and warned that "if we continue this way, Tokyo will have nothing but small, crude properties. It will be simply the countryside swollen large."[78] Another critic, Takayuki Ikue, pointed out that typical homeowners built their *nagaya* or row houses so cheaply that they could recoup all of their building costs and make a 40 percent profit in a building's first year.[79] There would be no solution, said Saitō, until the government become involved with long-range planning and regulation, an unlikely possibility. A *Tokyo Puck* cartoonist captured the typical slum dweller's condition in 1910 under the caption, "The pitiful plight of a worker's home." Taking readers inside a rental home on a steaming night, it showed a sweating, naked, crimson-faced father holding up a lighted candle while his wife sat nearby, scratching her shoulder. Between them slept two children, and to the side lay a hand fan and some bedding. That tiny space constituted the whole of their home.[80]

The typical lodging was a one-room rental, usually in a barracks-like (some observers said "train-like") tenement structure called a *nagaya* (literally, "long house") or an *uranagaya* (back-street row house). At Meiji's midpoint, reported Matsubara, the average family in Tokyo's Shin'ami-chō slum lived in a single room of two or three mats—thirty-six to fifty-four square feet—with as many as six or seven "persons of both sexes, from the old grandmother down to the new-born child," living together, "scarcely sheltered from rain and wind." Even the larger apartments had less than 100 square feet of space.[81] Made of wood

The reality of tiny living quarters on a blistering hot night with nothing to cool things down is captured by a *Tokyo Puck* cartoonist on January 10, 1910. The caption, "Pitiful plight of a worker's home," illustrates the era's middle-class condescension. Courtesy of University of Tokyo Graduate Schools for Law and Politics, Center for Modern Japanese Legal and Political Documents, Meiji Shimbun Zasshi Bunko.

and owned either by factories in the neighborhood or by private entrepreneurs, the flimsy structures deteriorated rapidly. Long-term resident Arthur Lloyd, who usually looked at Japan through positive lenses, called them "squalid and mean in comparison with the courts and alleys of London, Liverpool or New York," though the absence of second stories meant that residents had ample sunlight, "which makes the life of the poor in Tokyo endurable."[82] It was a *nagaya* that a worker in Kinoshita Naoe's *Pillar of Fire* clearly had in mind when he quipped to his fellow workers about coming home to a "mansion . . . that a pig would turn its back on," a place where his wife and four children would be "wallowing in the muck waiting for me."[83]

Things improved slightly for some *hinmin* as the Meiji years progressed, and a few even moved into the shabby houses that Natsume Sōseki found multiplying in the 1910s "like flies . . . at an extraordinary rate."[84] Nevertheless, the vast majority continued to the end of the era to live in what the journal *Fūzoku Gahō* described in 1898 as abodes with "walls crumbling, a decaying threshold whose doors will not shut, and a worn roof that does not keep out the rain and dew, . . . a place like a pigsty."[85] A 1903 survey of Kobe's match factory neighborhoods reported families of four to six people living in a single three-mat *nagaya* room, sharing just two futon, which they rented for two sen a night. Another survey in 1905 found that the typical Tokyo *nagaya* still consisted of rows of three-mat apartments facing on a dirt corridor, with the families sharing a toilet at the end of the block. It was common for these families to pay their rent by the day since they could not afford a full month's levy.[86] Even in 1912, at era's end, a study of Tokyo's major slum areas revealed that three-fourths of families still lived in a single room, with a mere 1.2 percent occupying three or more rooms. The economic historian Koji Taira estimates that the average living space for poor families then was four and a half mats, or about eighty square feet. Just one of every 250 families lived in a stand-alone house; not a single one did in Asakusa.[87]

Into that small space, families crammed everything necessary to life. A tiny entry way with an earthen floor typically held the family's tools, jackets, and shoes—and often a wash basin. The room itself was used for bedding, food, and clothes, as well as the odds and ends the family members brought home each day. Sometimes, there would be a small table with a chipped lacquer bowl on it, sometimes a hibachi-like cooking stove, and occasionally a little Buddhist altar. An oil lamp might be included for light, since no one in the caverns of the poor could afford the gas heaters that were spreading through other parts of city during the last Meiji years. The floors that supported these items, said Matsubara, had a worn and shredded quality. Sometimes they sagged, and the walls holding up the wood-shingled, flammable roof were "scarcely strong enough to keep the houses from tumbling down, but somehow, like their inmates, they are so much crowded together that they keep up one another."[88] Cooking usually was done in the crowded alley behind the tenement, where laundry also was hung. Even in the early 1910s a full quarter of Tokyo's *hinmin* families still had to share toilet facilities with other households.[89]

As the Ueki family made clear, rental prices for these spaces caused endless anxiety. Until the start of the twentieth century, the majority of the poor paid their rents—which ranged from seventy sen to three yen a month—in either daily or thrice-monthly installments because they could not afford the whole monthly amount at once; at the start of the Taishō era, 25 percent of the families in Honjo and Fukagawa still paid daily.[90] And even that was too much for the poorest families; one early survey found many of Asakusa's *hinmin* taking out loans just to pay rents, then absconding to another slum when they could not repay the loans.[91] That surely was the reason landlords were among the period's most hated figures: always there, always threatening, often harsh and unsympathetic, sometimes cruel, always holding overweening power. Most owners made collection visits each morning and each evening, and while some listened when renters protested that they could not pay, others turned a deaf ear to renters' troubles, as well as to their complaints about leaking roofs or sagging doors. Laws regulating property owners were very few, and the typical contract gave owners the right to make repairs, raise rents, or evict tenants "at their own discretion." One cartoonist indicated the typical landlord's attitude in a set of four panels that depicted first, a leak in a second-floor tenant's roof; second, the tenant drilling a hole in his living room floor to let the leakage escape; third, the water falling onto the head of a smoking landlord below; and fourth, the landlord finally fixing the leak.[92] The essayist Nishikawa Kōjirō said the advantage always lay with the landlords: if wind or rain damage required repairs, they would raise rents; if a landlord wanted more money, he could increase the rent arbitrarily; if a property changed owners, rents went up. "If we valued people more than property," Nishikawa declared, "we would have better laws, which would prevent these practices. . . . If the government were the people's government, . . . it would arrest these thieves."[93] These images may not have been fair to all landlords, but they represented the situation as *hinmin* perceived it. Landlords stood for the worst in the era's class inequities, because they were the ones close at hand, the ones who came by regularly to demand payment and then ignored pleas for improvements. Many a slum dweller told visiting journalists that no other basic need, not even food, caused as much anxiety as rent.[94]

The poorest of the poor occupied the day's most notorious living spaces: the cheap lodging houses known variously as *kichin'yado* (dosshouse), *doya* ("flophouse"[95]), *anpaku* (cheap stay), and *yaki* (literally, wooden lodging). Called the "haunt of the poor" or the "gathering place for 'rogue outlaws,'" the *kichin'yado* provided refuge for the most transient and least settled people, a majority of them single: cart drawers, rickshaw pullers, day laborers, itinerant priests, seasonal temple merchants, street musicians, and the casual workers known as *tachinbō* or "loafers."[96] As might be expected, most of the cheap lodging houses were in the tenement regions. When Yokoyama studied the *kasō shakai* in the late 1890s, official figures listed 145 *kichin'yado* in Tokyo, concentrated in Honjo and Asakusa, with nearly thirteen thousand people sleeping in them each month. By 1904, there were a reported 200, with the numbers in Asakusa having declined slightly while those in Honjo had remained steady and those in Fukugawa had soared to more than 60. A police report in 1907 identified 344 *kichin'yado* throughout Tokyo, more than 85 percent of them in the three poverty wards of Honjo, Fukagawa, and Asakusa. By the end of the Meiji era, Tomikawa-chō in Fukagawa had become Tokyo's largest *kichin'yado* neighborhood, with a reported 186 houses.[97] Lodgers paid daily, even if they regarded their quarters as "quasi-tenement houses";[98] some stayed as long as nine years.

Like the *nagaya*, the *kichin'yado* were largely unregulated, and living conditions were forbidding. At the majority of establishments, the owner would provide one big room for up to a dozen clients, letting them compete for sleeping spaces. For that space, the typical Osaka lodging house charged between four and seven sen in the 1890s, those in Tokyo five to ten sen, with prices rising slightly in the early 1900s.[99] Those who paid the higher rates would be given a quilt along with the space, while those who paid less had to either rent a futon for a slight additional fee or sleep directly on the hard floor. Some of the more expensive *kichin'yado* provided "better-off" guests with *betsuma* or special rooms costing up to twenty sen a night. At the other end of the spectrum, the very poorest schemed to get in free by waiting until after midnight, when a forgetful manager might have gone to bed without locking the front door. Cheap or pricey, the flophouse rooms had a reputation for being "unclean, just like [a] hog-pen."[100] Reports of smelly bedding were standard, and stories went the rounds of quilts being "pitilessly torn away from the shivering wretches" who did not come up with the one-sen futon fee. "Any one possessed of the least humane feeling could not follow the occupation of a lender of quilts," commented one observer.[101] Stories of lice also abounded, as did tales of bedbugs, noisy neighbors, foul odors, and the theft of towels and footwear. One sleeper reported that on most nights "noise would continue until one a.m. When it was cold, if bedding was in short supply, the tips of your toes would stick out. . . . The night wind would come through the cracks and penetrate you beyond endurance." On clear days, the sleepers would leave when dawn came, but if the weather was nasty they might stay all day in the cramped quarters, often with nothing to eat.[102]

One reason so much is known about *kichin'yado* is that they were open to anyone who paid a night's fee, making them easy for journalists to observe. Yokoyama provided graphic descriptions of his own night in a tenement house, where he encountered "a horde of cockroaches marching in succession," a lodger "in soiled underwear" warming his hands over a hibachi, and a "woman of about forty, with sunburned and leathery skin," who shook her husband and accused him of lewdness in "an angry torrent of obscenity." The other lodgers applauded her, Yokoyama said, "as if a comedy performance were taking place."[103] Matsubara's descriptions in the early 1890s were even more vivid. Stopping in a flophouse late one afternoon, he found an array of traveling salesmen, entertainers, temple priests, touring groups, day laborers, rickshaw pullers, umbrella repairmen—and children. After paying three sen and removing his shoes, he was taken to a large room of perhaps 360 square feet, divided into three sections by paper sliding doors. In his section, half a dozen guests had gathered, all of them "defending their own corners." One was shaving; others were smoking or stretching their muscles. He reported himself revolted by the "terrible stench" of his dirty futon. Equally bad were the breath of an old person who had been selling candy to children and the sight of a homeless man biting insects. "Seeing him," he reported, "I could hardly bear to remain seated." Late-comers awakened him repeatedly during the night; so did the raunchy smells and the mosquitoes that found their way through holes in the mosquito net-ting. His fellow lodgers appeared to sleep soundly, however. When morning came, he went off to wash with the only implements available: a pail of murky water and a rusty dipping can, both revolting. He said he would rather sleep under the stars than experience again the "lice, the fleas, the mosquitoes, the offensive odors, the drunkenness, the stifling heat." And yet, he added, it was not hard to understand why many poor lodgers actually liked the *kichin'yado:* it offered community to people without friends or relatives. Indeed, he said, on those rainy days that prevented outside work, the big rooms would become a crazy symphony of gamblers, "noisy quarrels," saké drinking, gossip, and nap-ping. One could get used to stifling heat and foul smells more easily than to loneliness. He added that people who accuse the poor of being dirty "forget that cleanliness is a luxury that the very poor simply cannot afford."[104]

For new arrivals and a few of the most destitute, the cities also offered a handful of free lodging places (*muryō shukuhakujo*) and settlement houses, most of them with a religious tie. Japan's first settlement houses—the Jiaikan, founded in Tokyo by the Women's Christian Temperance Union, and the Okayama Hakuaikai, started by the missionary Alice Pettee Adams—provided assistance for prostitutes and bereft women and children, while the well-known but short-lived Kingsley Hall, created in 1897 by the Christian socialist Kata-yama Sen in Tokyo's Kanda Ward, sought to initiate social change.[105] Following a different path, the Higashi Honganji sect of Buddhism opened a *muryō shu-kuhakujo* in 1902 in Honjo's Wakamiya-chō area, providing sleeping quarters primarily for destitute men who had recently arrived in the city. It opened its doors at nine o'clock each evening, allowing about twenty-five men to sleep on futon in a single large room on the second floor, with an occasional woman spending the night on the first floor. On the night the journalist Fujimoto Taizō visited, the lodgers included a newcomer to Tokyo wearing tattered clothes and carrying "nothing but an old towel," a forty-year-old man wearing "a small piece of old red blanket," a brothel security guard (with a belt "made of two old towels connected together"), and a group of "porters, . . . flag-bearers for advertise-ment, . . . and pushers of hand-carts." Motivated by charitable sentiments, the Buddhist owners kept the establishment immaculate and filled its walls with admonitions not to lose one's temper, encouragements to tell the truth, remind-ers to "endeavor to work today," and announcements that drunks and people with contagious diseases were unwelcome. The overseers also prided them-selves on trying to find work for the lodgers and reported that one man had gone on to work as an editor at "a certain industrial newspaper."[106] Lodgings of this sort were not part of life's equation, however, for most *hinmin*.

The literary critic Maeda Ai described Matsubara's *hinminkutsu* as chaotic places of "dark energy" where "the boundary between life and death itself seems to dissolve," places framed by "the cycle of ingestion, digestion, and excretion." That, certainly, is the way the newcomers to the *nagaya* and *kichin'yado* of Osaka's Nago-chō and Tokyo's Fukagawa had to feel when they arrived from the village late in the 1890s. The dark energy of rural impoverishment had forced them to strike out in new directions. The unruly energy of modernity had set them down in new places where they knew no one and had neither jobs nor money for settling in. The slums in which they found themselves were the very encapsulation of chaos intensified by unfamiliarity: smelly neighborhoods filled with too many people, places where "the infant . . . sucks on skewered giblets as if it were breastfeeding," places that filled the Higuchis and their counterparts with stress and anxiety.[107] But as the foregoing has suggested, chaos was only part of the story. Hidden in the grimiest alleys were hints of something more heartening. Rural partings were heart-rending, but they also held hope for better times. Dirty and ugly as life in the *kichin'yado* was, it throbbed with bawdy humor and shared humanity. Litter-strewn streets and narrow alleys that stunk of factory fumes and sewage also bustled with playing children and shopping mothers. Indeed, at the base of the survival struggle for all but the most unfortunate lay a determination to make living spaces happier and life better. Hope may have been hard to find in those early months when resourceless newcomers faced the new maelstrom or when crises struck. But as people found jobs and settled into the process of making lives for themselves—the topics of the chapters that follow—that hope would become as important a definer of *kasō shakai* life as the chaos and stress were.

CHAPTER 2

Earning a Living
Making and Building Things

Some of them are rather wise; some have adequate resources; some are
quite funny; some are fairly literate—and they all use a variety of jobs to
fill their mouths.

—Matsubara Iwagorō, journalist[1]

I f finding a place to sleep was the first goal of migrants from the villages, locating a job was the second, and it was the more daunting task because newcomers had neither money nor time to look for *good* jobs. No work meant no
food. If nothing could be found, they faced hunger; if something was available, they took it. Asked what kinds of work those in the *kasō shakai* did, a slum
dweller's answer would have been as simple as it was complex. They did whatever
they could find, which meant any one of the thousands of jobs necessary to making life possible in a modern society, always for very low wages. While a given
area might have been home to a preponderance of certain kinds of workers—factory employees in Fukugawa, for example, rickshaw pullers in Asakusa—the caverns of the poor housed workers in a greater variety of occupations than one
might have imagined possible. A fundamental reality of capitalist modernity was
that no matter how low the pay, if a task was needed, someone would do it. To
understand the impact of late Meiji modernity on the *kasō shakai*, it is necessary
to begin with a look at the many kinds of work that put food on *hinmin* tables.

When Suzuki Umeshirō reported on his early study of 8,500 workers in Osaka's Nago-chō, he tried to keep things simple by lumping diverse jobs together
under broad labels such as "normal trades" and "entertaining," and he still ended
up with seventeen different categories, ranging from money lenders (90 of them)
and garbage handlers (105) to rag pickers (1,092) and 1,716 people with "no job."[2]
Later job cataloguers, who cared less about simplicity, came up with lists guaranteed to numb the brain. Tanizaki Jun'ichirō's memoir of his childhood years
in Tokyo's poor regions includes pot and kettle makers, attendants at saké shops,
men who sold sweet bean soup and others who sold rice crackers, rouge sellers,
ferrymen, tobacconists, wig makers, barbers, liquor dealers, and assistants at
archery clubs ("shady establishments" where "customers spent all their time

laughing and talking with the women and never seemed to get around to drawing their bows").[3] The pioneer statistician Kure Ayatoshi's 1891 list of Tokyo *hinmin* included day laborers, construction workers, rickshaw pullers, temple merchants, factory workers, people who repaired *geta,* kappore dancers, open air lecturers, clam and bait diggers, hawkers of goods hanging from shoulder poles (*botefuri*), makers of cords for tying up the hair, makers of decorative twisted paper, fish salesmen, and cart pullers.[4] The historian Kawashima Yasuyoshi took a different approach, focusing on poor women at the end of the 1800s; among the jobs he found were telephone operators, spinners, machine workers, hairdressers, shop managers, telegraphers, flower arrangers, koto players, day laborers, delivery people, child care providers, matchbox makers, cigarette rollers, paper makers, and rag pickers.[5] And Matsubara, who sometimes seemed obsessed with people doing the weird or unusual, included ash sellers and charm doctors (*majinai suru hito*), who attracted people whose lives were "so hard that they are very apt to believe in wonders."[6] An official index of Tokyo employment categories in 1898 included no fewer than 358 different kinds of workers, everything from carpenters to makers of paper cords for tying the hair, from those who chiseled teeth into saws to doll makers.[7] The lists may have invited tedium, but they made a point: jobs were as varied, numerous, and rich in content as were the people who performed them.

For those who prefer order in their categories, both Yokoyama and the economic historian Nakagawa Kiyoshi have suggested several broad groups. Yokoyama, who leaned toward Marxism, focused on the proletariat in his formal analyses, dividing 1890s *hinmin* into three major groups: (1) craftsmen (subdivided into those who worked at home and those who worked away from home), (2) weavers and workers in handicraft factories, and (3) machine factory employees. He left other workers out of the formal analyses, discussing them primarily in his more journalistic accounts of forays into the *kasō shakai* world.[8] Using a different typology, Nakagawa said the majority of slum dwellers until about 1900 belonged to two groups: physical laborers (*rikiekigata*) and miscellaneous workers (*zatsugyōgata*), with a third group—including beggars—being "close to jobless" (*mugyō ni chikai*). As industry increased late in the century, he added, the proportion doing physical labor increased.[9] Both of these organizational schemes are useful, but in an effort to cast the net as widely as possible and at the same time provide an ordered understanding of work types, I have used a slightly different approach, grouping workers broadly by the functions they performed: (1) factory workers, (2) builders, (3) transporters, and (4) servers, the first two of which will be examined in this chapter. In each category, I will focus on a few representative occupations that provided particular insights into *kasō shakai* life.

Factory Workers

General Conditions. Before leaving the lists, it bears noting that the late Meiji factories produced most everything a modern society required or wanted: beer, machine products, chemicals, tobacco, printed matter, paper, cement, fertilizer, sugar, railway cars, coke, glass, ships, and munitions, among other things. And the numbers of factories multiplied in the last half of the Meiji era—more than doubling in Tokyo between 1897 and 1907,[10] for example—causing the poverty chroniclers to pay them a great deal of attention. Factory workers did not, however, make up a majority of the period's urban poor population; Yokoyama observed that "of the many inhabitants of the slums of Tokyo only a few are engaged directly in industrial production."[11] Nor were "factories" the large, bustling institutions that often come to mind when they are mentioned. The typical factory in the 1890s had fewer than forty employees; most had fewer than ten. Figures varied depending on how one defined a factory, but government surveys at the end of the 1890s showed Tokyo with a mere 20,307 workers in factories of fifty or more employees, while the journal *Taiyō* said Tokyo had 33,577 workers in 1904. The important fact for us is that factory workers—even the great majority who worked in businesses with fewer than five employees[12]—would have made up no more than 12 percent of the *hinmin* population. The numbers were higher in Osaka, where five thousand factories gave it the moniker "Manchester of Japan," but even there they were not a majority.[13]

That did not, however, negate the crucial role factories played in defining the poverty pockets. Slums sprang up in areas such as Tokyo's Fukagawa and Honjo (where more than 12,000 factory workers lived in 1900[14]) and in Osaka's Nago-chō in large part because of the presence of factories there. Indeed, most of Tokyo's factories were in the poor regions, east of the city center, on newly developed lowlands along the rivers and bay and away from the regions where the affluent lived. As late as 1919, a study placed a third of the city's factories in the two slum wards of Honjo and Fukagawa, with another 20 percent in Kyōbashi and Asakusa.[15] And those factories influenced the lives of everyone who lived near them. Their smokestacks spewed odors and soot into the neighborhood skies. Their noises reverberated across the area, and their schedules shaped the transportation patterns and life rhythms of the shopkeepers, food sellers, and archery club women as much as of the textile weavers and spinners themselves.

The factory worker's life had a few positive aspects, and many negative ones. Income, for example, was reliable even if meager. Fellow workers provided community even if work pressures diminished the space for enjoying it. While long, endless work days and weeks left limited time for leisure, holidays generally were vacation days, and outings tended to be enjoyed to the fullest when they came. Managers even boasted that food was better for factory workers, that while *hinmin* lived off rice and pickled vegetables on the farm, "once they go to work in the factories, . . . fish and meat become the daily fare."[16] That was not, of course, the way the vast majority of workers saw things. In their accounts, the negative features of factory work were almost the whole story. Reading the literature of this era, it is difficult to find workers (or impartial observers, for that matter) who had much of anything good to say about factory work. When a journalist wrote in 1903 that "even the slightest reform in the recent factory system is welcome to us," he was expressing a consensus among nearly everyone but those with vested interest in the capitalist system.[17]

One of the hardest features of daily life for factory-working *hinmin* was the contempt in which both the owners and the public held them. To the general public, factory workers stood on the lower rungs of the social ladder, particularly in the early years of the industrial system. As a *Tokyo Nichi Nichi Shinbun* writer put it in 1892, theirs was "an occupation of the lowest grade . . . perhaps inferior to the eta [outcastes]."[18] To a major portion of officials, the workers were cogs in the national project, producers of labor who would enable Japan to increase industrial production and compete in the international world. Even to many reformers, who had begun pushing for better labor conditions by the turn of the century, the major spoken concern was to prevent labor unrest. As one put it late in the 1890s, if laborers' discontents were not addressed, "we will soon witness the onset of a virulent social disease of the type which befell England at the beginning of this century."[19] Workers, said the Osaka reform advocate Seki Hajime, were seen by most officials as "extensions of the machines that they operated," not as "producers in their own right."[20] That was the reason Japan had no laws to regulate the treatment of factory workers until 1911,[21] in contrast to Great Britain, where factory laws had been in force since the early 1800s, and the United States, where federal laws were lacking but where several states, including Massachusetts in particular, regulated factories.

If officials and the public saw workers as cogs in the industrial process, most managers regarded them as irritants or impediments: always demanding higher wages, willing all too often to shift firms, putting their own interests above those of the factory. Industrialists loved to repeat old, paternalistic litanies about the "time-honored custom and moral principles" that made Japanese employer-employee relationships better than those in the West. As an editorialist for *Tokyo Keizai Zasshi* put it in an 1891 attack on the idea of government regulations for factories, "Our employment relations are warm and peaceful because employers and workers share common moral sentiments, undefined but every bit real."[22] In truth, that commonality was anything but real. Profits were what mattered to managers, not people; a spinner's personal well-being was a concern only as it affected the bottom line. One owner told a government surveyor in 1903 that he realized that long night shifts might not be good for a tuberculosis-prone spinner's health, but they were "unavoidable because they doubled the return on capital."[23] Several scholars have pointed out that factory workers' employment hours and earnings were better than they had been back on the on farm;[24] they also were as good, on average, as those of their *hinmin-kutsu* neighbors. But life on the farm had been untenable. Factory pay was a pittance by any standard, and the work was grim, made worse by an absence of the humaneness that industrialists loved to tout.

Take wages (see table 2). Koji Taira has argued that the late Meiji industrial world had not yet gone through the "psycho-cultural revolution" that would enable capitalists to grasp the "modern" economic idea that higher wages and worker satisfaction were conducive to increased profits. Factory owners thus operated on the traditional idea that profits were possible only if one kept costs as low as possible and that every demand for a living wage should be resisted.[25] Metal workers, who were among the best-paid factory workers, averaged 52 sen a day or about 14 yen a month in 1903, while a government survey of sixteen factory workers in the Osaka area at that same time found that more than 80 percent of all workers earned less than 32 sen a day and textile factory women averaged just 20 sen daily (5.5 yen monthly). That was in a period when a bare minimum existence for a family of four required more than 20 yen a month. Three years earlier, ironworkers at the Tokyo Arsenal had averaged about 30 sen a day (7.5 yen a month), with a few getting as much as 80.[26] These wages were supplemented at many firms by small bonuses for exemplary workers. In 1900, Tokyo Gas Spinning Company, for example, promised young girls a three- to seven-yen bonus if they served out the full term for which they had been recruited when they entered the factory. It also offered rewards of five to fifteen yen for three years of continuous service. And in an indication of the suspicion with which managers tended to regard workers, it offered snitch money: a three-yen reward to anyone who reported on fellow workers who were performing badly. Fuji Spinning Company promised a bonus of one to five yen for workers showing special diligence, and one to ten yen for employees who demonstrated "irreproachable behavior."[27] Such bonuses were doled out frequently, but they amounted to very little as part of a worker's total income; ten yen for staying on the job for three years, after all, meant an increase of less than a sen a day. Such rewards made a difference when wages were so low to start with. But workers saw them for what they were: inexpensive, motivational substitutes for living wages.

Work hours, moreover, were long—almost always ten or more hours a day, as much as eighteen in some occupations—and days off were few. There was no universal pattern since factories were unregulated. But the government's 1903 survey of factory conditions, *Shokkō jijō*, reported that most companies had ten- or twelve-hour workdays. The typical day, it reported, included two shifts: 6:00 a.m. to 6:00 p.m. and 6:00 p.m. to 6:00 a.m., with a thirty-minute meal break. Some factories also gave employees two fifteen-minute breaks; some did not.[28] Another study of more than twenty industries (not just factories) in 1904 showed two, shoemakers and sawyers, working nine hours a day, one (*shōyu* makers) averaging fourteen hours, and the rest putting in between ten- and twelve-hour days.[29] And most workers got between two and four days off each month, plus a few days each year for national holidays and local festivals such as the *bon* celebration of the dead.[30] If production requirements were heavier than usual, employers felt no compunction about asking laborers to work on their scheduled free days or to work longer hours, usually at the same rate as regular work. When Yokoyama advocated "four holidays each month as appropriate," he thought himself a progressive. "If factory workers were to work the same hours as those of the general public," he added, "they would never be able to support a family."[31]

Table 2. Average daily wages (in sen) of factory jobs discussed in chapter 2

Decade of the 1890s	
Match maker: at home	
Match maker:	
child, at factory	10
Textiles-women	18
Cigarette maker	18.3
Metal worker	32
Carter	50
Match maker:	
adult, at factory	50–60
1900–1904	
Printer-female	13–35
Glass maker	17
Iron worker	18–30
Ship builder	19
Textiles-female	20
Dyer	23
Metal worker	52

Figures in this table represent averages from the sources cited in the treatment of different types of workers in chapter 2. Rough numbers intended to give a sense of comparative wages, they were obtained by averaging the available figures for specific years during the 1890s. Dyers, ship builders, and glass makers (1904) come from *Shūkan Heimin Shinbun,* February 7, 1904. For greater precision, see tables 3 and 4.

Even worse than the long hours and low wages may have been the oppressive atmosphere in factories. Managers and foremen obviously varied in approach. Some were humane and kind, but the majority, by all accounts, were harsh and insensitive. Foremen are "overbearing, and think they are performing well if they continually scold and chastise workers," reported one journalist. Overseers were notorious for shouting and humiliating workers in front of peers. It was standard to view all workers as lazy, regardless of evidence to the contrary. It also was common practice for promotions to be made arbitrarily, with no known guidelines except that "workers who excel in currying favor with their superiors tend to be advanced." Yokoyama said that when asked, "every worker harbors complaints about promotions or the lack of them."[32] And shaming was common: individual wages often were posted publicly and notes were put up on workers' machines when they received "deductions for bad work."[33] At many places, foremen refused to let employees go to the bathroom without permission and docked their pay if they made mistakes. When a worker or a loved one died, the factory provided a pittance in condolence money, sometimes nothing.

When Yokoyama visited a woodworking plant near Tokyo Bay, he found the place empty because the employees had gone to a fellow worker's funeral. The man had worked up until an "hour before his death," a guide told the journalist, but the firm had given his family no memorial money, "not . . . even one *rin*."[34]

Closely related to the grim working conditions was the transience of late Meiji laborers, especially in their early years on the job. According to one study, four of every five cotton spinners stayed less than six months at a given factory before moving on; according to another, less than half of the workers at six heavy industrial factories stayed put for a full year. Other surveys found similar patterns until the 1920s.[35] A writer in the journal *Taiyō* said in 1903 that Japanese workers "lack the spirit of concentration."[36] The reason for job hopping, said the managers, was that workers were unreliable and disloyal. In truth, the system encouraged such behavior. Company piracy was widespread, wages were too low to make workers want to stay, and factories were uninviting places. In Yokoyama's words they were "desolate buildings where money and articles are exchanged and where human feeling and moral obligations are missing."[37] Two British visitors to textile factories in Nagano, Nagoya, Kyoto, and Osaka reported that the female workers always "looked extremely apathetic and dull—even unhappy," hardly raising "their eyes to look at us."[38] And when the exceptional manager Mutō Sanji implemented more worker-friendly policies at Kanegafuchi Cotton Textile Company in the 1890s, he found that his employees stayed on, even when rival employers sent thugs to intimidate them into leaving.[39] Low wages, endless work hours, and inhumane work spaces made late Meiji factories hellish cauldrons and encouraged transience.

THE MATCH MAKERS

Few Meiji industries more clearly illustrated the symbiosis between *hinmin-kutsu* neighborhoods and factories than match making. Japanese match production had been launched in 1875 by Shimizu Makoto, a young Kanazawa man who had studied in Paris, and by the middle Meiji years he and his successors had turned matches into a crucial component in Japan's assault on the international trade front. By 1895, more than two hundred factories were turning out more than three billion matches a year, with more than three quarters of them being sold abroad,[40] and by 1910 match making had become one of the country's five leading industries in terms of production, earning Japan thirty-three million yen a year in foreign sales.[41] The crucial thing for this study is Yokoyama's observation that match making had more to tell us about the workers' livelihood and living conditions than any other industry except cotton spinning. The *Shokkō jijō* surveyors agreed in 1903, writing that "there is a singular, inseparable relationship between the match-making enterprise and *hinmin* communities."[42]

More than half of the country's 180 match factories in 1899 were in the Osaka-Kobe region, and they produced three quarters of its matches, primarily for export to China and India.[43] While the tiny sticks might have looked simple, their manufacture involved a surprising number of steps, several of which illustrated the complex relationship between industry and *kasō shakai* life. A few factories made the splints or slender sticks in-house, but most purchased them from hundreds of small splint-making firms in Hokkaido. Then, in the Osaka and Kobe area, the workers carried out the many separate processes required to turn a splint into a match, first waxing them and treating them with chemicals, then drying them, next arranging them in sets of fifty, and finally putting them into boxes, which had had friction pads and trademarks applied in still other steps. Finally, the boxes were wrapped for distribution and sale. Although quite a few Kobe firms were modern enough to do the work by machine, most Osaka factories had to do it by hand, slowly. And while a few factories were big enough to carry out the entire process under one roof, the majority specialized in just one or two tasks.[44]

The match-making process dramatized how hard *kasō shakai* families had to work to survive. In contrast to textile factory workers, match makers usually were paid by what they produced rather than by the hour, and they lived not in dorms but in the nearby shantytowns, where rents for tiny two-room apartments ran between six and eight sen a day, or two yen a month. Single people more likely lived in *kichin'yado,* paying between four and seven sen per night for a single mat space. Women at the match factories often worked at home in the morning, then came to the factory in the afternoon, little children in tow, to make the few sen that allowed them to visit the bath, rent a futon, or add a sliver of meat to the day's meal.[45] In Osaka's Nago-chō area, match workers who were too hard up to wait for monthly cash payments sometimes were given certificates for each completed case of match boxes, which they exchanged at a local shop for rice and other food products. The merchant then turned the certificates into the factory's business office for a monthly payment. A worker at Osaka's flint-making Seisui Company reported that children sometimes arrived at work at three o'clock in the morning during winter months, even though production did not start until six o'clock, in order "to escape the discomfort of their cold homes." He said that such cases had declined in the late 1890s because money from match work had enabled more families to buy blankets.[46]

Much of the match work was done outside the factory, as "by work." Indeed, more people made the match boxes at home than at the factory. Even when the work was done at the factory, it typically was done part time, as an income supplement, rather than full time. And the great majority of the match workers were female.[47] In Kobe, according to Yokoyama, most *hinmin* households had at least one member who made matchboxes as a side job. "Someone," he said, had come up with an estimate of five million matchboxes that were "scattered daily around the households of impoverished people." A Ministry of Agriculture and Commerce survey in 1896 found that 64 percent of Japan's 37,500 match factory workers were employed at home as "by workers," and well over 80 percent of the total were female.[48] A hard-working, skillful housewife might paste the paper covers onto two thousand boxes a day, earning eight sen, much less than the thirty-nine sen her husband made that day as a metal worker or even the eighteen sen her daughter made in a textile factory,[49] but enough to pay the month's rent.

The most striking indicator of how hard up match-making families were lay in the large number of children employed in this business. Yokoyama estimated that more than half of the employees in the Kansai region's match factories were aged fifteen or younger, with some only six. Indeed, he said, as many as 80 percent of those who put the matchsticks in boxes were under ten years of age, a figure rivaled only by the rug-making business.[50] And official surveys told the same story. The researchers who did the legwork for *Shokkō jijō* reported that they saw "large numbers of children who appeared to be seven, eight, or ten years old coming and going" at thirteen Osaka factories. Their data revealed that more than a thousand of the 5,330 workers at these factories were children under fourteen; nearly 200 were under ten.[51] Yokoyama described these children as "captives of the frames on which they struggle to arrange the matchsticks," children who "look about restlessly while mechanically arranging the splints in order." Distracted or not, they were relatively fast, given their inexperience. While an average adult might arrange thirty-six frames of matches a day, an eight-year-old would typically do twenty. No sooner does a child fill one box with matches, Yokoyama said, "than he picks up another in almost one sweeping, continuous motion." Children were a good deal for employers, because they were paid so poorly. Yokoyama was not particularly critical of this child labor; it was standard practice in the Japan of his day. So was the wage disparity. And he knew that without the child's work the family would have had to choose between paying rent and buying fuel.[52]

The 1903 *Shokkō jijō* survey provided snapshots of anonymous, real-life families as examples of how important the children's income was. In one case, chosen at random, the forty-two-year-old father, whose family had moved to Osaka when he was a child, worked full-time as a police assistant, for a salary of twenty-three sen a day. His wife worked two jobs—match making and rope making—and his eleven-year-old son joined her five days a week at the match factory. Together, mother and son made nineteen sen daily. A six-year-old daughter did not work. The family's budget was typically spartan: 1.2 yen a month (four sen a day) to rent a two-room apartment with about 115 square feet of total living space; about thirty-seven sen daily for rice and other food; and three sen for the children's needs. All that totaled a sen and a half each day more than the three family members brought in, which would have been bad enough without the father's failing eyesight, which required an extra yen a week (fourteen sen a day) for medicine. The survey writers left readers to speculate on how the family made up the serious difference between income and outflow. What they did make clear was that the family could not have managed without the nine daily sen the lad brought in. They also noted that "family circumstances forced the son to quit school after just one year of attendance."[53]

One other feature of *hinmin* life—sheer luck—comes through in the materials on match work. There were, of course, the uncontrollable exigencies of geography, illness, and disaster that forced people to take jobs they hated or robbed them of their source of income. Beyond that, the equally uncontrollable vagaries of managerial style determined whether an employee's work atmosphere would be bearably humdrum or tyrannically unbearable. At the Kansai region's many Social Darwinian places where employers cared about profits alone, Yokoyama found workers disengaged emotionally, staring restlessly while doing their work. At those factories where foremen barked out verbal abuse and applied draconian rules arbitrarily, he found some workers rowdy in response, belting out "vulgar or obscene songs" to pass the time. At one Kobe factory, by contrast, an earnest Christian foreman acted "like a parent," balancing his strictness with tolerance and having his workers sing hymns each morning. Yokoyama also found a Kobe firm that ran a voluntary night school for more than seventy match factory workers, providing a three-year curriculum in civics (everything from manners to lessons from Samuel Smiles' *Self Help*), reading, calligraphy, and arithmetic, as well as sewing for women. Humane places of this sort were unusual, however, so those who worked there considered themselves lucky, even if they would have felt luckier still if the humaneness had extended to paying a living wage. For all the match workers, whether favored by the gods with health or damned by the devil-bosses to torture, capricious luck seemed often to be the sole determiner of life's fortunes.[54]

TEXTILE WORKERS: WOMEN AND CHILDREN

Textile factories illustrated even more dramatically the symbiosis between *kasō shakai* neighborhoods and urban industrial life. If there were thousands of match factory workers, there were tens of thousands in the country's "big three" industries: spinning, reeling, and weaving,[55] and most of them were women and children. The story of the textile factories—and the people who worked there—has been told at length elsewhere, but a few words are needed here, since the textile workers' experiences have so much light to shed on *hinmin* life in the 1890s and 1900s. First silk, then cotton, fueled Japan's entry into the world of international trade in the early Meiji decades, and by the 1890s the textile firms accounted for more than a quarter of the nation's manufacturing output, trailing food processing but producing more than twice as much as all heavy manufacturing industries combined. Japan's raw silk production nearly quadrupled in the last twenty-five years of the era, from 7.5 million to just under 28 million pounds a year, turning Japan into the world's largest producer of silk. And cotton followed, with spinning mills spreading across the country in the 1890s and the industry launching an impressive attack on the international markets long dominated by the British, Americans, and Indians. North China, which imported a mere 3 percent of its cotton from Japan when the twentieth century began, was buying nearly 17 percent from its near neighbor a decade later.[56]

Historians spill a great deal of ink telling us about the important role the textile industry played in spurring Meiji Japan's economic growth, but the *hinmin* have a different story to relate, one equally important to Japan's modernization narrative. For them, the growth of textiles had most to do with personal livelihood: the hope for new, nonagricultural ways to make money and the hope of providing a place for women and children to earn income, balanced by dismal working conditions and low pay in an unsafe and filthy environment, as well as the brutal treatment of women. A 1903 study by the Tokyo government showed that workers in silk reeling and weaving rarely worked fewer than thirteen or fourteen hours a day; sometimes they were kept on the job eighteen hours at a time.[57] The standard workday in the cotton-weaving industry was fourteen hours. And the accounts of dirty factory floors, abusive supervisors, inadequate (and nasty) food, sexual harassment, and inhuman confinement are legion.[58] Textile factories, in other words, epitomized the way most *hinmin* saw modernity generally: it offered slivers of light shrouded by heavy layers of darkness.

The thing that most vividly set the textile industry apart was the preponderance of young—often very young—female workers.[59] Although spinning employed similar numbers of males and females in its early years, the balance had swung dramatically toward females by the 1890s, when three-fourths of the employees in the machine-cotton industry were women and girls. For the entire textile industry at the end of 1896, Yokoyama gave the figure of 57,334 men and 921,386 women (94 percent!). Across the 1890–1930 period, some 80 percent of textile workers were female. As in other countries that were developing a textile-

Kiryū Textile, Japan's largest and most modern factory when it released this photo early in the 1900s, intended to present a different image from the oppressive places with lecherous foremen that journalist Yokoyama Gennosuke had seen in Kiryū a few years earlier. Courtesy of Kjeld Duits Collection, MeijiShowa.com.

manufacturing sector, Japan's industrialists preferred to hire women because they could pay them less than men. Patricia Tsurumi points out that "companies viewed workers much as they regarded another resource in the Osaka region, raw cotton." They strove to get as much of that resource as they could, as cheaply as they could. She points out that factory recruiters were not above using floods and earthquakes as levers to induce bereft young women to work for them.[60]

Across the industrial world, women were paid less than half of what even lower-wage men made, with female weavers, for example, averaging 8.0 sen a day in 1892 while male metal workers made 25.1 sen and day laborers made 18.3 sen. Within the overall textile industry, women earned roughly half of what men did, and that was *before* a quarter of their wages were subtracted for board and lodging if they lived in the company dormitory.[61] The result was that textile salaries were regarded by families as supplementary. One exception, to both the age pattern and the consideration of textile salaries as supplemental, came in families where the wife had become the main breadwinner because of her husband's incompetence or incapacity. These women were not, unfortunately, exceptional when it came to wages; being chief breadwinner did not increase the pay. But it did make life even harder, because the era's norms made it "unwomanly" to head a household, scandalous even. Beyond the difficulty of making ends meet, such women typically had to endure scorn from neighbors and relatives. A newspaper deliveryman in Kinoshita Naoe's *Pillar of Fire* captured the attitude of the day when he gossiped with his fellow carriers about a family where the father had lost his job: "So that's what's coming: the girls all out at work to keep the men lying in luxury at home. . . . Kids all grumbling—rice grown cold—the wife away!"[62]

Child labor kept the textile industry going. The labor organizer Takano Fusatarō pointed out in 1896 that almost a quarter of female spinners were under fifteen years of age, and a government labor survey of Nagano Prefecture in 1901 showed that 17 percent of female silk workers were fourteen or younger, while another 46 percent were between fifteen and twenty.[63] Similarly, an 1897 report by the Spinners Association, Bōseki Rengō, indicated that 53 percent of its workers were under twenty, while an official survey of sixteen Kansai area textile factories three years later found 47 percent under twenty, with 2,514 (10.2 percent) of its workers under fourteen, and sixteen under ten. One of the most shocking reports, surely, was the Bōseki Rengō's finding that a thousand of its employees (1.5 percent) were under eleven and that all of its 144 factories hired girls of fifteen.[64] Even when the formal hiring age was twelve or thirteen, said one of the *Shokkō jijō* writers, most factories had many "untrained children," who accompanied their mothers and earned two or three sen a day.[65] The figures varied from plant to plant and from year to year. But every study painted the same picture: more than half of factory workers were teenagers or younger.

Behind each statistic lay a human situation, always difficult, sometimes tragic. There were the children who could not go to school, a group that will be discussed in a later chapter. There were those whose sense of self-worth was diminished by their uncontrollable work situation, like the Toyama Prefecture eight-year-old sent to a Tokyo spinning factory. "I worked there for about two years," she recalled in 1902, "but not one bit of what I earned in salary entered my hands. I suppose some middle man made off with it." She escaped once from the factory dormitory, but the police found her and returned her to the factory, where her master ripped off her clothes and beat her.[66] There also were those children who were too young either to work or to stay at home alone. It was common to find several of them loitering on the factory floor because their mothers could not afford child care. One surveyor related the account of a wid-owed mother living in a one-room apartment with three small children. She took her eight-year-old with her to the factory to spin for six sen a day (she herself received eleven sen), but on most days the factory refused to let the other two, ages three and five, come along. After several months of frustration and worry about leaving them at home with no supervision, she sent the two small ones back to her home village to live with relatives.[67]

The preponderance of teenage female workers set textile factories apart in one other way: a large percentage of the workers lived in dorms. Most of the male laborers and many of the mature women lived in their own *nagaya*, close enough to the mills to be able to trudge off to work each morning—or night—just as everyone had done in the first two Meiji decades. From the 1890s on-ward, however, as the cotton and silk industries grew, factories began building two-story dormitories inside the mill compound for the single young women workers. By 1899, three of every four female spinners (but none of the males) in Tokyo between the ages of fourteen and forty lived in a company dorm.[68] The decision to build dorms was economic and strategic. The girls and women could be controlled more efficiently there: housed and fed cheaply, kept under supervision, and prevented from running away or developing romantic liaisons. Conditions in the dorms were Dickensian. Surrounded by fences topped by barbed wire or bamboo spears, the buildings were utilitarian and without adornment. Girls were only rarely allowed to leave the quarters except to go to work. Each one was given a single three-by-six-foot *tatami* mat space, which she often shared with someone who worked another shift. Toilets were seldom cleaned. A hundred girls shared the same bath water, which "was always filthy." Food consisted of low-grade rice mixed with coarser grains, along with small quantities of pickles, soup, and occasional bits of bean curd or egg, much of it too smelly to be appetizing, according to a Ministry of Agriculture and Com-merce investigation.[69] When Takai Toshio, a girl from Gifu, went to Ogaki To-kyo Woolen Mill in 1913 at age twelve, twenty girls were assigned to her twelve-mat room. "The dining hall was filthy, dark, and gloomy," she said; "there were virtually no side dishes with meals. All we got everyday was miso soup and pickles, but even the pickled radishes were old and smelled bad." The only thing of substance in the soup was an occasional fly or cockroach.[70] Her even-tual partner, the mill hand and labor researcher Hosoi Wakizō, said that if he were asked to choose a single term for the dorms, "*pigsty* would be the word."[71]

Confronted by these conditions, factory owners typically retorted that a girl's life had been at least as bad back in the village, where she made no outside in-come at all, and that it would have been worse yet in the only other employment option: the brothel. What the owners refused to acknowledge was that here in the dormitories, there were neither relatives nor close friends to provide human succor, no mountain streams or forests to refresh the spirit, none of the festivals and community activities that made rural life bearable. The dormitories were stark. And dirty. And inhumane. On one occasion, Yokoyama ran into a factory girl from his own native region talking with a klatch of fellow textile workers. "I asked her about the activities that occupied her on holidays," he reported. "The girls, aged about fifteen or sixteen, replied that girls gather at a bridge in front of their weaving house and spend their holidays talking about their home towns. A younger girl of twelve or thirteen years broke in and said that as soon as the wind begins to blow, all the girls run into the house." He called the situation "pathetic" and said it got worse when girls stayed more than a year at the factory, because they lost their ties to home and began "descending step by step into the abyss of depravity . . . from which they cannot be rescued."[72]

A final way in which female labor set textile factories apart was suggested in Yokoyama's concluding comment: the sexual vulnerability of single young women fenced in in a profit-driven world where men held the power. One of the day's stereotypes held that factory girls were given to licentiousness, that "morals," as the *Shokkō jijō* analysts put it, were "in great disarray." Sexual liaisons on the part of dormitory girls and women were not uncommon, and the standard wisdom held that this was because girls lacked a moral conscience, having been separated from their parents too young to have received adequate training about sex.[73] The *Shokkō jijō* compilers gave no statistics but reported that factory girls agreed that sex was common: even though males were not allowed in dorms, intercourse with men working near their factory occurred often. They reported that girls who became pregnant usually left the dorm when their stomachs began to swell, at around two or three months, sometimes moving in with the father-to-be, sometimes returning home. Asked whether there were prostitutes in the dorms, the girls said that while none admitted it openly, some went "to lodgings where only male workers stay" and others, finding factory life "bitter" (*tsurai*), ran off and became prostitutes. The researchers also reported, again without statistical data, that many girls "had boyfriends" and some were taken advantage of sexually by supervisors, while other "pretty girls" were sold to brothels by dormitory heads seeing a "rare opportunity." The end for these girls, said the surveyors, invoking the day's moralizing tone, was usually tragic:

> Once submerged in the abyss of depravity, they grow listless in their factory life, but they are not allowed to return to farm work in their home villages. Abandoned even by their friends, many of them drift from factory to factory and end up in the dens of scoundrels, or among the ranks of petty street sellers, or as prostitutes or harlots. There is not a particularly great difference between the moral disorder of the spinning girls and the moral decadence found in their home villages, but back in the village, girls usually will stay home and create their own families. . . . When they come to the factory, however, there is no chance for redemption once they fall.[74]

Hosoi did not dispute the accuracy or the moralizing style of the *Shokkō jijō* account of the situation, but he found its analysis inadequate. These girls were not lacking in moral sensibilities, he argued; indeed, they were more timid and more conservative than their urban counterparts. But they were victims of an isolated life in a soulless factory compound and of a system dominated by men who took advantage of them. "Factory girls' depravity was very often due to their lack of autonomy, to crafty businessmen who seduced or kidnapped them," he argued. He pointed out that 11 percent of licensed prostitutes had been textile workers before entering the sex business and estimated that the number would rise to 30 percent if unlicensed sex workers were included. But the reason the majority moved to prostitution, he said, lay in a lack of options after they had been seduced or even kidnapped by factory men.[75] In sex, as in so many other areas, the textile workers' experience revealed, in other words, what factory work meant to *kasō shakai* culture: graphic gender disparity and victimization, inadequate income, cramped and unclean living quarters, and yet just enough income to make the *hinmin* keep going.

Builders

Our second *kasō shakai* group, the builders, illustrated how complex modernity's impact could be on whole classes of people. For some builders, the modern age provided jobs and income that would have been nonexistent in an earlier time, while for others it triggered a sharp decline in both status and wages. For some, building and creating provided stability; for others, it meant transience and insecurity. The workers whose role in society was most sharply affected by the Meiji transformation may have been the once-honored artisans, or craftsmen.

CRAFT WORKERS

Craftsmanship had a rich history in Japan, with artisans ranked from antiquity as the third of the four Confucian classes or status groups, behind the ruling warriors and food-producing farmers and ahead of merchants. They also were ahead of the priests, entertainers, and others who did not even make the status scheme. When an artisan asked how he could possibly attain enlightenment given that his trade left him no time for meditating, the seventeenth-century Zen scholar Suzuki Shōsan replied, "All trades whatsoever are Buddhist practice. . . . Without smiths, carpenters, and all the other trades, the needs of the world would never be met."[76] That sense of purpose, combined with strong money-making instincts, created a medieval world dominated by guilds that gave the silver makers, the dyers, the painters, and the carpenters a strong sense of solidarity and guarded the quality of their work; it also brought them pride. The guilds were outlawed in the Tokugawa years, but the tradition remained, with artisans and merchants at the core of the urban economy.[77] One result of this was the domination of specific crafts by certain respected families across many generations. As a scion of the commercial Mitsui family put it, "Artisans keep their families going for several generations because they would lose their livelihood immediately if they relaxed for even a day." Merchant families, by contrast, "leave things to clerks" and soon "lose their estates."[78]

The Meiji era brought an end to the status system when the government replaced the old structures with three categories: descendants of the court (*kazoku*), ex-samurai (*shizoku*), and all the rest, including the former outcastes, lumped together as commoners (*heimin*), although the ex-outcastes often were labeled "new commoners" (*shinheimin*) by local authorities. As David Howell has pointed out, in the new era "economic activity was detached from status." In an atmosphere pervaded by what he calls the "politics of the quotidian," occupations rooted in the old status system continued to give many people a sense of identity, but they did not necessarily determine how they fit into the overall economic system or how they related to the state and the public.[79] This change was positive for many people, giving them new freedom to seek their occupations in any sphere and providing fields of work unknown before. It also

A carpenter saws a huge log while children play outside his shop in this staged photo by an unknown photographer in the 1890s. The most interesting feature of the photo may be the unstaged child looking on from the inside. Courtesy of Kjeld Duits Collection, MeijiShowa.com.

made *heimin* relatively equal before the state, at least in theory. But for many of the country's artisans, the ones who made up the bulk of the Meiji era's builders, the politics of the quotidian took away all protection from the winds of capitalism and caprice, resulting in the loss of both status and income. Carpenters, or *daiku*, for example, saw the scope of their craft dwindle as masonry, representing permanence, replaced the more "temporary" wood as a hallmark of modern construction. For centuries, *daiku* had been responsible for everything from design to construction; some had assumed priestly functions, assisting in (or even carrying out) religious ceremonies at various stages of the construction project. But their responsibilities narrowed with the advent of the "modern" Meiji era. Some *daiku* adapted and operated successfully, but the majority found new professions such as architecture and masonry eating away at their work, turning them, in the words of Gregory Clancey, into "another native people sadly (but necessarily) displaced by modern change."[80] It was a fate that placed many of them squarely in the *kasō shakai* ranks.

Modernity did not undercut the *numbers* of people doing craftsman work; to the contrary, the era's massive building projects expanded the demand for such jobs rapidly. When the Tokyo metropolitan government did a survey in 1898 of small-scale businesses engaged in what once had been called artisan work, it found 107 different occupations producing jobs for tens of thousands of workers. Carpentry, plastering, sawing, and weaving each engaged more than a thousand families; tatami making, blacksmithing, kimono making, and wood cutting claimed more than five hundred families; roofing, gardening, paper hanging, and tin smithing more than three hundred; pencil making, cotton willowing, and umbrella making upwards of two hundred; and wig making, bookbinding, and embroidery over one hundred, with fewer families engaged in occupations such as making soap, knitting, figurine painting, and hairpin making. When Matsubara talked about the rich conversations he heard in the streetside "college of the poor," one of the things he had in mind was the diversity of their occupations.

The demand for workers did not, however, result in living wages. Perhaps the clearest sign that craftsmen as a group belonged in the *kasō shakai* category was their low income. A Ministry of Agriculture and Commerce survey of the 1894 earnings of thirty-one craftsman occupations (see table 3)—everything from paper hangers to plasterers, from shoemakers to woodblock printers—found an average daily income of 27.9 sen, or just under 7.0 yen a month. The salary range was large, with cigarette makers at the bottom earning 18.3 sen a day and bag makers at the top taking in almost twice that, 35.9 sen. The once-proud *daiku* placed seventh on the list, slightly above the average with 30 sen, or 7.5 yen a month. When one considers Yokoyama's estimate that it cost more than 33 sen a day for a bare minimum existence for a family of three (with rice alone consuming more than half of that), it is clear that the carpenters and other craftsmen were *hinmin*.[81] Nearly all adult male factory workers earned wages well above that, as we saw above. Nor did the craftsman's situation get better over the years. Figures at the beginning of the new century still showed *daiku*, plasterers, metal workers, and typesetters making between and 9 and 13.5 yen a month at a time when the hypothetical Ueki family with whom this book began needed twice that amount merely to exist. A 1904 study showed carpenters generally averaging less than rickshaw pullers and a little more than plasterers and carters[82] (see table 4).

Table 3. Daily wages, 1894, in selected craftsmen professions, in sen

Cigarette maker	18.3
Woodcut printer	23.1
Tailor (Japanese dresses)	24.7
Lacquer ware maker	27.8
Paper hanger	28.3
Blacksmith	28.9
Carpenter	30
Plasterer, shoemaker	30.6
Stonemason	34.6
Bricklayer	36.3
Bag/pouch maker	38.3

Wages selected from Yokoyama (Yutani), 247–248, based on Ministry of Agriculture and Commerce data.

Table 4. Daily wages in 1904 in selected *hinmin* professions, in sen

Toilet cleaner	48
Lathe operator	58
Cook	63
Gardener	63
Painter	70
Carter	98
Tachinbō	100
Brick maker	100
Plasterer	103
Railway builder	119
Carpenter	115
Iron worker	139
Rickshaw puller	150

Based on *Shūkan Heimin Shinbun,* March 6, 1904, 2. The paper gives highest and lowest wages within each profession; the chart here averages those two, which undoubtedly skews them upward since greater proportions of workers labored at the lower end of the scale. Another list of wages, for varied types of workers in Honjo and Fukagawa in 1912, is found in Hiromichi Ishizuka, "The Slum Dwellings and the Urban Renewal Scheme in Tokyo, 1868–1923" (June 1981), 181.

In many ways, the changes in status and reputation were as difficult a problem for these families as were the low wages. By the middle Meiji years, modernity had robbed many, perhaps most, of them of their sense of being artisans and had rendered them pawns in the capitalist game. "Craftsmen have also been engulfed by vicissitudes of various kinds, and find it extremely difficult to preserve their honor and dignity," Yokoyama wrote. Apprenticeships with master artisans, which once had brought promising young men to the master's home for seven or eight years of training, now lasted as little as three years and often required that they live in their own homes while they trained, with the result that "the intimate relationships which had bound master and pupil together no longer exist," a fact that left "older men . . . appalled." Contractual agreements replaced personal ties. And "pecuniary relations" took the place of the old family-like, parent-child (*oyabun/kobun*) relationship between mentors and young apprentices. The situation disturbed Yokoyama. Today, he wrote, big construction projects "fall into capitalists' hands," and "nothing matters much nowadays. As long as a craftsman does his work fast, he is good enough. . . . Craftsmen in contemporary society need neither skills nor competence. . . . We should by no means be pleased over this changed attitude."[83] It would be a mistake to put too much of a good-old-days patina on the Tokugawa-era artisan communities. Many artisans were poor then too, master-trainee relationships could be abusive, and inequalities made for hardship. But there is no gainsaying that modernity changed the class as a whole, and largely for the worse. It demolished the long-held conviction that carpenters, leather workers, book binders, and their ilk were special, even as it ate away at the craftsmen's pride in personal skills and undermined the fraternity-like ties that for centuries had bound them to other practitioners of the same trades. It made craftsmen links in the capitalist chain. And the poverty-level wages that forced them to live in tiny apartments along litter-filled, noisy alleys made the changes all the more galling.

DAY LABORERS

Worse off still were the day laborers (*hikasegi ninsoku, hiyatoi*), men (and a few women) who are included here because the great majority of them worked mainly in construction and other building tasks. On any given morning, thousands of these temporary workers would leave their lodgings in the slums either to head directly to a job site or to go to a *yoseba* (gathering place) in the poor areas of Tokyo or Osaka, where they hoped to be hired for a one-day stint at building bridges, drilling wells, dredging rivers, repairing roads and ditches, or erecting the buildings that were changing Japan's urban face. On occasion, they might be used instead to remove snow from a roadway or to carry out public service projects such as installing telephone equipment or rendering assistance at a funeral. But most of the time they were employed in construction, the foot soldiers of the huge army that was building a modern Japan.

The public image of these temporary workers was better than that of beggars or rag pickers but worse than rickshaw pullers and most other *hinmin*. People often referred to day labor as *waraji kagyō*, or the "straw sandal trade," an epithet for its lack of stability. Matsubara described the day laborers themselves as herd-like drinkers and gamblers who never thought of the future; "they live and die like animals," he sniffed.[84] Yokoyama recognized the great variety of people who filled temporary work slots but derided some of them, particularly the *tachinbō* ("loafers" or cart-pullers), as "slothful" men who stood "idly by, hands in pockets," waiting for work. He likened them to beggars, called them "cowards," and scoffed at the way they displayed their machismo.[85] Another writer mocked the way they seemed, despite their difficult straits, incapable of admitting vulnerability:

> In that world, there were a few things you just never said. One was "I'm hungry"; the others were "I'm cold" and "I'm hot." . . . It was a kind of competition to see who could bear it longest. If any of the men standing around there complained of being hungry, he'd be treated as an outsider, a slob who didn't have the guts to stick it out.[86]

When members of the *enka* singer Azembō's family started a new factory and had trouble finding men willing to work for anything other than day wages, a friend captured the public attitude toward *hikasegi ninsoku* with his comment: "All you should be giving them is salt! They aren't worth much more than that."[87]

The history of day labor in Japan stretched back to at least the late 1700s, when the Edo government would round up homeless people, convicts, and some outcastes in the major cities, house them in special areas known as *yoseba,* and force them to do construction work and other projects.[88] By the mid-Meiji years, day laborers in Tokyo usually were recruited through a contractor system in which the municipal government licensed three organizations—the Arima Group, the Nagai Commercial Firm, and the Government Construction Workers Group (Doboku Yōtashi Gumi)—to work with bosses (*oyakata*) who secured men each day to work on specific projects. Each morning, these bosses or their scouts would come to the *kichin'yado* and other slum sites frequented by day workers and announce their presence with a loud shout, rousing dozens of men to come out for that day's jobs. Those who were not selected would head back into the lodging or ramble off onto the streets to wait for another day, or until another scout showed up later with new jobs. Over the years, it became common to give recruits a small amount of money for breakfast before taking them to the job, because "otherwise they'd be too hungry to work properly."[89] The bosses received two or three sen for each worker they recruited.

Fluidity and instability—plus unusually strenuous demands—characterized *hikasegi ninsoku* labor. When rain or snow stopped construction work, both the lodging houses and the cheap eating establishments around them overflowed with the jobless. If the weather was good, the *kichin'yado* would empty out. There was no assurance, however, that the same job would last for more than a day or two. Even when a specific project continued over time, most day laborers had little compunction about switching work sites if something more attractive came up, or skipping work if they felt like it. Loyalty was nonexistent, among the laborers, among the bosses, and among the employers. So were those human feelings or *ninjō* that writers and officials liked to make so much of. The sole thing that would almost always keep a worker on a project for a longer period was a loan or a pay advance from a boss. "They could not get out of those loans," Yokoyama observed; "there were no cords, but the workers were bound, by a mere 25 or 26 *sen* of borrowed wages."[90]

Many day laborers continued in these fluid and insecure situations for years, even for a full working career, but some found ways to make their work more stable even if they could not completely escape the *hikasegi ninsoku* life. If a large construction project were underway, for example, they might tie themselves to a given *oyakata* for an extended period of time, even while getting paid daily. In some cases, a laborer would make direct arrangements with a nearby factory to work regularly but to be paid daily, in order to ensure a steady income stream even on bad weather days. And workers with special skills also contracted on occasion for longer-term work, yet daily pay, with a plastering or carpentry—or stonecutting—firm. The primary reason these workers continued as day laborers rather than opting for biweekly or monthly pay contracts was poverty; they did not have the financial margin to wait for an end-of-month check. Azembō thought cultural norms also influenced their decisions to insist on pay-by-the-day, based on his experience managing a firm south of Tokyo in which people from fishing villages "wanted day wages no matter what," while those from farms were comfortable with biweekly or monthly pay.[91]

The wages for day labor varied by the job but were never lucrative. Sometimes pay amounted to so much per worker per day; sometimes an entire labor group was given a set amount for a certain project, to be divided among them; sometimes each person was paid individually by the amount of work completed.[92] Certain kinds of work paid more than others. And the *oyakata* often played a role in determining how much a crew received. Whatever the arrangement, wages never amounted to enough to raise the day laborers out of their *hinmin* world. The average *hikasegi ninsoku* pay in 1897, according to government surveys, was 29 sen a day, or a little less than 7 yen a month, for those who worked the day-laborer average of twenty-three days. A year later, Yokoyama estimated the average daily wage at 32 or 33 sen, noting that day workers with special skills such as plastering or stone cutting might make as much as 60 sen, while road workers made a mere 27 sen and women could expect only 20 sen a day. Among the best-paid of the day laborers were the cart pullers (*shariki*), who will be discussed as a special category in the next chapter. They might receive as much as 84 sen if they pulled a specially heavy load, but their stated wages could be misleading since *shariki* often had to pay up to a fourth of their income to the *oyakata* who got them their work.[93]

What did these wages mean in terms of livelihood and life station? To understand, one needs merely to look at what the day laborers could buy with their earnings and at what other groups made. Even the highest-paid *hikasegi ninsoku* would have made only the bare minimum required for our model "Ueki" family of four. The average day worker in 1898 made less than a sixth of the starting salary of a low-level public servant. According to price charts at the end of the 1890s, a day's wages would have given him enough to buy one dish of hot rice, or one large bottle of beer, or a dish of boiled eel.[94] He could not, in other words, have supported a family on what he made, or laid away even a *rin* against the future. That is one reason so many day laborers were single. It also helps to explain why the public so often saw them as "the lowest of the low."

The most important thing the *hinmin* who made things—both the factory workers and the builders—had to tell us about *kasō shakai* life was that Japan's march toward modernity had a darker side than one sees in historical surveys. The match makers demonstrated that modern city living required the income, no matter how paltry, of *every* family member. Had the match-making family described in the 1903 government survey of factories been dependent on the father's wages alone, they would have starved. The textile workers, who made up the majority of all factory employees, made it clear that women and children bore the brunt, nay the burden, of modernization. They made up a major portion of the factory worker population, they worked for even less than men did, and their children sacrificed their own schooling as a result. If men's wages were unjustly low, the pay of women and children was inhumanly so, and the capitalist modernity project depended on that fact. The craftsmen's plight highlighted the capriciousness of modern changes, particularly for many in time-honored professions. Modernity may have offered new kinds of work in the factories, but at the same time it pushed carpenters, plasterers, and their fellows downward economically and robbed them of their old prestige. And the day laborers showed how hard it could be to resist change. They were, quite often, the ones who were too proud to say "I'm hungry" or "I'm cold"—the independent ones who would not submit to regular bosses and schedules—and as a result they also were the ones who slept in flophouses and took whatever jobs a day might or might not offer. Life was not all grimness for factory workers and builders, as subsequent chapters will make clear. But on many days modernity looked, to them, more like a cruel master than a beacon of promise.

CHAPTER 3

Earning a Living
Movers and Servers

> Many a Japanese workingman is a very fair Apollo between the ages of
> fifteen and twenty-five, and after that he becomes a respectable Hercules.
>
> —Edward H. House, American journalist[1]

It was easy for the middle class to ignore the "distasteful" factory workers and builders discussed in chapter 2, hidden away as they were in industrial plants and construction sites. Not so the movers and servers. They may have been nameless, but they were everywhere in the late Meiji cities. They served tables and poured drinks at restaurants. They gave massages and shampoos and scrubbed patrons' backs in public bathhouses. During temple festivals, they played instruments and performed acrobatic tricks. Streetside, they sold tofu to housewives and candy to children. They delivered milk at the front door in the morning and collected urine and feces from household tubs at night. For a large portion of the male population, they provided sexual favors. And wherever one looked, they were trotting along in their special garb (occasionally no more than a loin cloth), pulling people through the streets and alleys in that useful Japanese invention, the rickshaw. They may have been expected to remember their rank and "have relations . . . only within the limits carefully prescribed for them," but their presence could not be ignored, because their work infused the cityscape.[2] While factory workers and builders constructed the materials of modernity in obscurity, the movers and servers nurtured the era's human side in the open.

Movers, Not Shakers

Those *hinmin* who transported whatever needed to be moved—people, objects, human waste—received minimal attention from the list makers. The officials who studied Osaka's Nago-chō at the beginning of the third Meiji decade, for example, included beggars, rubbish collectors, and "normal trades," but no transportation workers except the rickshaw pullers.[3] Similarly, a compilation based on the Home Ministry's study of the *saimin* in 1911 includes day laborers and rag pickers along with workers in metals, woodwork, textiles, construction, and commerce, but leaves out the nonrickshaw movers.[4] It is a puzzling omission, because transportation workers were not just visible, they were numerous. The era's various data collections make it clear that the moving occupations provided jobs for at least 10 percent of the urban *hinmin*, more than commerce or public works or any other field except manufacturing. The movers' work was crucial too: assuring that vendors had goods to sell, that waste and filth were eliminated from city neighborhoods, and that people got to the places where they needed to be. Without them, Japan could not have modernized.

The representative profession among the movers was rickshaw pulling. Matsubara devoted a full third of his *Saiankoku no Tokyo* to the pullers, or *shafu*, and some scholars go so far as to call them the perfect symbol of the Meiji modernity process. Before examining *shafu* lives, however, it should be helpful to look briefly at several of the occupational groups overlooked by the list makers—the railway workers, the deliverymen, the carters, and the night soil collectors—because each has something important to say about the nature of *hinmin* work life, as well as the relationship between the mover occupations and Japan's rush toward modernity.

RAILWAY WORKERS

Railway workers provided a window into both the baffling variety of jobs demanded by modern life and the lack of congruence between a job's importance and the treatment workers received. Looking at Tokyo's Shinbashi station in 1901, the *Taiyō* writer Mandai Nanao found nearly twenty different kinds of jobs requiring greatly varied skills: station managers, ticket checkers, baggage handlers, engineers, and restroom cleaners, among others. He counted six signalmen at the station, each of whom made between thirty and sixty sen a day, and more than 160 porters who made about half that much. One sign of changing times, he said, lay in the cadre who cleaned the station and platform. In the early years of railroads, they had been "true menials" with no qualifications except a willingness to work hard; now they had to have an elementary school certificate. The most skilled rail workers, he said, were the twenty security officers who had to deal with pickpockets, quarreling passengers, disorderly drunks, stolen objects, and lost goods, always without losing their professional composure. They were not, however, paid any more than the signalmen. Then there were the ticket sellers, thirteen of them handling more than seven thousand tickets each day for riders on more than 580 trains that came through the station.[5]

The 130 train conductors provided the clearest example of the incongruence between a job's worth and the employees' work conditions. Although the conductors' direct engagement with the public required special skills and earned them slightly more than the average *kasō shakai* wage, or about seventy sen a day (eighteen yen a month), they had the era's longest work days: sixteen hours. Their work was unusually taxing too, since they had to be on their feet almost the entire time. As another journalist noted in 1903 when the conductors' workday had been cut to a *mere* fifteen hours, the work conditions entailed "too little time for sleep and extreme problems for their health"; they were treated like "cows and horses."[6] The conductors' young assistants, called "train boys," had it worse yet, doing gofer work on the trains for similar long hours and about half the pay (ten yen a month). It was their job to quiet down drunk or difficult riders, throw switches, answer travelers' questions, and get luggage on and off the trains. Despite the low pay, some young men with an individualist streak found the assistant job appealing because of the variety of the tasks it entailed and the camaraderie it provided. Offered a more "proper" job by a "gentlemen" train rider, one hard working train boy declined, confessing that while the proffered job was appealing, he liked the "irregular and wild" nature of railway work too much to make a switch.[7]

POSTAL/TELEGRAPH DELIVERYMEN

The railroad workers' occupational cousins, the Post and Telegraph Office (PTO) deliverymen, illustrated a third feature of mover work: the emotional stress entailed in pleasing the public.[8] A full century later, when things had become more "modern," a worker in the courier business commented to me in an interview that the speedy, reliable delivery service for which Japan is famous has a dark side. Supervisors, he said, apply unrelenting pressure, yelling at workers and sometimes harassing them. "It is shit work" (*kusai mitai no shigoto*), he grumbled.[9] If the deliverymen make mistakes or are not speedy enough, they can expect verbal abuse. It was even worse in the late Meiji years. Divided into three groups—*taishū taihai* (collect-and-distribute men), who delivered mail from one postal branch to another, *futsū taihai* (regular mail carriers), and *denpō haitatsu* (telegraph deliverymen)—the PTO workers typically were former students or shopkeepers who, "finding themselves at wits' end" in their old work, took the physical and written exams required in the field[10] because they wanted a more stable profession. The job's reality usually fell short of their hopes.

Deliverymen typically were single males who lived together in two-story lodges (*shukuchoku beya*) located in poor neighborhoods.[11] Their work demanded speed and precision. One challenge was the cities' byzantine address systems, in which street names generally were nonexistent and building numbers haphazard; finding locations was a nightmare for inexperienced deliverymen and getting lost was common. Another difficulty was the taxing hours they had to keep, "getting up before dawn and working until late at night, walking fast, even galloping, whether they wanted to or not." A third was the necessity of dealing with thoughtless patrons and vandals "who threw lighted matches into mailboxes or stuffed in garbage." Worst of all, however, was the unrelenting pressure to be quick. It was especially hard for the telegraph workers, who had to record the precise times when they picked up and delivered each item. If it took fourteen minutes to reach a spot that should have required twelve, the carrier would be scolded and his pay likely would be docked. The public image of postal deliverymen, said a writer for the journal *Seinenkai*, was that they were good-natured and adequately paid; the truth was that they were harried and impoverished. Salaries in 1903 averaged about thirty-five sen a day (with more opportunities for bonus pay than in most occupations), about the same as bathhouse workers and less than blind masseurs (see table 5). "Even though most of them look for other ways to supplement their low salaries," said a writer for *Seinenkai*, "they don't have a thousandth of a pence left at month's end. They're just poor and out of luck (*piipii*)." Some thrived on the hurly-burly nature of deliveryman life, but most hated the pressures that went with keeping customers happy. Short tenures were common.

Table 5. Daily wages of moving and service workers, in sen, 1900

	Reported wage	1900 wage
Performer at fair	7–10 (1899)	7–10
Female waiter	5 (1893)	7.8
Rag picker	5–15 (1895)	7.5–22.5
Shop apprentice	5–16 (1901)	5–16
Prostitute: lowest class	10–50 (1900)	10–50
Telephone operator	15–50 (1902)	14.5–48.5
Bathhouse worker	20 (1902)	19.5
Blind masseur	30 (1911)	20.5
Rickshaw: over age sixty	16.5 (1893)	25
Railway signalman	30–60 (1901)	30–60
Postal deliveryman	40 (1903)	40
Rickshaw: middle-aged	10 (1893)	47
Carter:		
employed	40–50 (1899)	40–50
self-employed	60–70 (1899)	60–70
Railway conductor	70 (1901)	70
Rickshaw: prime of life	64 (1893)	100
Prostitute: highest class	100 (1900)	100

These figures are taken from the sources cited in the discussions of each of these occupations throughout this chapter. The 1900 figures are calculated on the basis of inflation over time in the occupations for which shifting data are available; see especially Mori Kiichi, *Nihon no kindaika to rōdōsha kaikyū: kaikyūzō no rekishiteki tenkai* (1979), 73. In the case of postal deliverymen, according to *Seinenkai*, March 1, 1903, 77, workers earned around thirty-five sen but had considerable opportunity for overtime and bonus work; hence, I have used the higher figure.

CARTERS

Another delivery group, the "sturdy and robust" carters (*shariki*) whose small wagons carried everything from fruits to lumber to household belongings, illustrated a more surprising feature of *hinmin* work: the nuanced and hierarchical relationships that shaped *kasō shakai* society as much as they did the outside world. Sometimes lumped together with day laborers because many of them took work on a job-by-job basis, a full 1.7 million carters toiled on Japan's streets and roads at the end of the Meiji era.[12] One thing that divided *shariki* was ownership. Although most worked for entrepreneurial cart owners who took between 20 and 25 percent of their earnings as commission, an elite group owned their own carts and made more money. According to Yokoyama, the former made roughly the same as rickshaw pullers, between forty and fifty sen a day in the late 1890s for hauling six or seven cartloads of up to six hundred pounds each, while those who owned their own carts made as much as seventy sen. A second thing that divided *shariki* was their varying attitudes toward cooperation. While those in Kanda and Asakusa followed type and defied organization, the Fukagawa carters, who specialized in transporting rice, pioneered in organizing workers to fight for leverage and rights. They formed a "solid labor union" named Sangyō Kumiai in the 1890s to negotiate wages and provide protection against rival cart owners. The union, which had more than a thousand members at decade's end, was known for its rigorous enforcement of Kumiai regulations.[13]

The clearest example of hierarchy in the carters' world lay in the hiring of unemployed drifters, *tachinbō*, as assistants when loads were unusually heavy or the routes were steep, as at Kudan Hill in Tokyo. If carters were looked down on by general society, the *tachinbō* were despised. They usually slept in flophouses during the winter and parks during the summer; they were notorious for flouting middle-class norms; and even the *shariki* tended to regard them as lazy good-for-nothings. Noting that they boasted to officials that they never would "do such a foolish thing as working regularly," Yokoyama called them "lazy, slothful members of the lowest stratum," men who "think it clever to spend their days basking in the sun and picking the lice off their bodies,"[14] and Matsubara Iwagorō said they had "no ambition, no desire beyond the satisfaction of gross animal wants," even though he deplored society's refusal to pay them what their work actually merited.[15] An equally contemptuous image was conveyed by a *Niroku Shinpō* reporter who wrote about seven similarly dressed *tachinbō* at the Kudan slope who gruffly warned away anyone trying to do business there, claiming that they had "been asked by the police to stand watch." Their claim was a "fiction," said the writer.[16] They were blowhards as well as ne'er-do-wells.

NIGHT SOIL COLLECTORS

The movers with the most complicated public image may have been the ones who collected night soil (*shinyō shūshū*), an often maligned group who illustrated the persistence and usefulness of many premodern practices. Although they were ubiquitous on Meiji streets, going from house to house with buckets of feces and urine hanging from poles slung across their shoulders, most respectable people (including journalists) ignored them. One looks in vain for descriptions of them in the writings of Yokoyama and Matsubara, or in the columns of *Taiyō* and *Seinenkai,* or even in plebeian papers such as *Yorozu Chōhō* and *Niroku Shinpō.* The one exception was the humor magazine *Tokyo Puck,* which occasionally made jokes about their work. They were ever-present—sometimes odiferously so—but seldom seen.

Those who bought and transported human waste for use on farms had a history stretching back centuries. Unlike Europeans of the seventeenth and eighteenth centuries, who threw people's excrement into pits and rivers, the Japanese regarded fecal matter and urine as "an economic good" to be "carefully collected for use as fertilizer."[17] "The superior farmer," said a Tokugawa farming manual, "values shit as he values gold." Advised another: "Waste not a drop . . . shit nourishes the land."[18] For that reason, the buying and selling of human waste played a significant role in the pre-Meiji economy. As Harvard University historian David Howell puts it, the early modern Japanese may not have been particularly concerned about the environment or urban cleanliness, nor did they like its "stinky and yucky" texture, but they found it useful, and "that, much more than conservation or sanitation, is the story of shit in Japan."[19]

It was a story that affected urban life and provided work for the *hinmin* until the 1930s, when flush toilets and chemical fertilizers brought night soil collection to an end. Regulations regarding human waste increased after the Meiji government took power, with city officials limiting collections to nighttime and forbidding uncovered containers in order to limit odors and keep the filth away from water sources. But the numbers of night soil workers multiplied in the Meiji years. Every night (and sometimes during the day, restrictions notwithstanding), men carried their buckets along Osaka and Tokyo streets, calling out, "Night soil, night soil!" When householders responded, the collectors dipped the stinking liquids and solids out of large household barrels or tubs, filling buckets that would in turn be dumped into the vats on ox-drawn carts. The results of their collections were prodigious both quantitatively and economically. Just after the Meiji period ended, according to one study, Japan's GNP (gross national poop) amounted to five billion gallons a year (ninety-five gallons for each woman, man, and child), with urine and excrement accounting for nearly a quarter of all that was spent on fertilizers.[20]

Foreigner visitors sometimes complained about the smell of night soil collection, but they also noted its positive effects. One remarked in 1903 that Japan appeared to be well ahead of Great Britain in sanitation, partly because the "sewage and refuse of every house are collected nightly and carefully used in agriculture."[21] The locals who did take note of the *shinyō shūshū* collectors, on the other hand, found in them either humor or signs of backwardness. One *Tokyo Puck* cartoonist sketched a collector holding a bucket out toward the mother of a urinating child and quipped, "Even a baby's piss is business for him." Sometimes the writers sneered at the smells that followed collectors;

sometimes they complained about their ragged appearance and irritating shouts of *"shimogoe"* (manure) when they came down the street.[22] A former collector recalled what a nuisance these people could be when things went awry. "I upset a bucket of the stuff right in front of a restaurant—next door to the second-hand clothes shop by the canal," he said. "They made a hell of a fuss, so I hadn't much choice, I tried scooping it up with my hands and putting it back in the bucket." When the slimy goop kept slipping through his hands, he took off his kimono and used it as a cleaning rag, then jumped into a nearby canal to wash off. He cursed the neighborhood people for their rudeness in standing

The prominent photographer Kimbei Kusakabe took this shot in the 1880s of a man carrying what almost certainly were night soil buckets. Kimbei's stylized photos were taken largely for foreigners in Japan. Courtesy of Kjeld Duits Collection, MeijiShowa.com.

around and gawking.²³ Even the gawkers would have agreed, however, that while night soil collectors might be obnoxious, while their work was "premodern" and embarrassing, they performed one of the city's essential tasks. Low pay and public disdain condemned them to *hinmin* status, but as with their *kasō shakai* fellows, pay was no indicator of importance.

RICKSHAW PULLERS

If the night soil collectors were present but invisible, the rickshaw pullers were both omnipresent and omnivisible, carrying oral messages, delivering packages, sometimes committing crimes, more often helping out people in trouble on the street, and always transporting people on trips both short and long. Postal deliverers, newspaper carriers, and night soil collectors came once or twice a day; delivery agents came irregularly; railway workers and tram conductors were seen only occasionally. But the *jinrikisha* (literally, human-powered vehicles) pullers were everywhere, all the time, enlivening and polluting the atmosphere with the *charan charan* clickety-clack of their wheels and the shouts of their greetings. They were, in so many ways, the quintessential urban symbol of the late 1800s. "Their rise and fall," said the ethnographer Yanagita Kunio, "can be seen as representative of the whole Meiji-Taishō process."²⁴

It had not always been thus. As the Boston journalist Edward H. House commented when he arrived in Japan in 1870, palanquins (instruments "of hideous torture") were "the only popular vehicles in Japan."²⁵ Mostly, people traveled by foot, horse, or cart. But whether House knew it or not, a year before his arrival three enterprising Japanese had secured official approval to begin producing rickshaws, reputedly after seeing foreigners in horse-pulled carriages in Yokohama, and within three years Tokyo streets were crisscrossed by forty thousand of them.²⁶ The rickshaws were simple contraptions at first: two iron wheels topped by a wooden platform supporting a seat and four pillars covered by a cloth. Over time, they became more complex and more comfortable, with canopies, steps for getting up to a cushioned seat, advertising slogans, baggage holders, and sometimes even distance meters. In the late 1870s and early 1880s, enterprising pullers in Kyoto began heating their rickshaws with charcoal burners and some in Tokyo began providing newspapers for riders.²⁷ By mid-Meiji, however, standardization had set in, particularly in Tokyo, with owners increasingly opting against decorative peonies and dragons on the sides and toward more utilitarian, uniform black cabs. Rubber tires became de rigueur early in the 1900s, increasing speed and decreasing noise: a mixed blessing, according to the paper *Niroku Shinpō*, because while "fine gentlemen of our time would be as lost without their rubber-tired rickshas [*sic*] as without their trousers," drivers found the quietness boring, taking away the old "spirit of competition."²⁸ A foreign visitor in the 1890s thought the improved rickshaw seemed like a "comfortable, flying arm-chair."²⁹

Rickshaw use soared in the mid-Meiji years, partly because populations mushroomed and partly because the vehicle was so useful. It was, says the historian M. William Steele, the premotorization vehicle that "most immediately altered the way the majority of people in Japan . . . experienced time, distance, speed, leisure and mobility." Pulled by a muscular man likely to be under fifty years of age, the contraption provided "speeds up to 10 km in one hour, . . . shake-free," according to an early advertisement.[30] And it was cheap, even with the city taxes that were assessed after the early 1870s. Fares started at 6.2 sen per *ri* (about two and a half miles) in the early 1870s and rose by 1901 to an average charge of 3.3 sen for a ride of up to fifteen blocks (*chō*), about the cost of a visit to a public bath. Each additional fifteen blocks, up to one *ri*, cost another 7.5 sen.[31] The result was that hundreds of thousands of urbanites, rich and poor alike, used the vehicles. And that meant the rise of a huge new class of colorful *hinmin*. By 1875, Tokyo had a hundred thousand rickshaw pullers; at the peak in the 1890s, the country as a whole had more than two hundred thousand rickshaws pulled by even more men.

If middle-class citizens held generalized images of the *kasō shakai* as a class, they held vivid mental pictures of the *jinrikisha* pullers because of their constant interactions with them. The first thing that came to mind for many people was simply how important the puller was to negotiating the city. The pages of a Tanizaki short story or memoir, for example, rarely proceed more than few pages without a "rickshaw man . . . wearing a large, round wicker hat and a rain cape," or a rough-handed puller who "grasped me and lifted me into the rickshaw," or a "long line" of the vehicles outside a restaurant, "filled with our friends and acquaintances, various foremen, carpenters, and tradesmen, drunk as lords and threatening to fall from their rickshaws at any moment."[32] The British teacher Howard Swan said that the character of the roads he traversed was produced by the rickshaw. The road "has little alleys along it," he observed, "made by trundling rickshaws, twisting and curling in and out like snakes against the ever-present pebbles." Here dashed "long lines of rickshaws [one] after another, in single file, their shadows brightly outlined by the sun, meeting and constantly almost colliding." And there "the cries of 'Hi! He!' from the rickshaw men greet one at any turn, along every street, round every corner, down every little lane, and at every broad crossing."[33] The *jinrikisha* was the moving platform from which the middle and upper classes saw their cities.

Asked about the men who did the pulling, riders often used negative descriptors. Some depicted them as low-class and coarse, often scantily clad, frequently loud- (and foul-) mouthed, contemptuous of social norms and rich snobs. Matsubara bemoaned the disgusting food they ate. Novelist Nagai Kafū wrote about "evil-eyed rickshawmen" who "loitered about, pestering the relatively more prosperous-looking pedestrians for business."[34] *Enka* singer Azembō, a man of meager means and plebeian sensitivities himself, sneered about the "dimwitted rickshaw man" who trailed him tenaciously, and he commended a friend who, when "followed relentlessly" by a puller "would wheel on his feet and scream 'Idiot!'" a "patented method for repulsing the rickshaw puller's attack."[35] And there were other negative images. Poverty came to mind first for many people. It was no accident that two empty rickshaws sat outside the hovels in a *Fūzoku Gahō* drawing of "evening among the poor families of Samegahashi," one of Tokyo's "three great slums."[36] Nor was it surprising that a *Heimin Shinbun* report on the suicidal leap from a Tokyo bridge of a poverty-stricken Tokyo family added knowingly: "The father was a rickshaw puller."[37] Others described the *shafu* as dishonest, men who would take roundabout routes to get a "higher fare than they had originally agreed upon."[38] And many saw the pullers as troublemakers and petty theives.[39]

At the same time, accounts of the *shafu* also brim with positive, often romantic, pictures of men filled with skill, bravado, and gallantry. Some of the images sprang up in the vehicle's earliest years, when the glamour of the new profession attracted affluent young pullers whose soiled clothes and silk-crepe sashes became faddish as undersashes for stylish women.[40] The critic Saitō Ryokuu said he would never take any other form of transportation because rickshaw pullers were so reliable; he used the pullers even to deliver his packages.[41] And the American naturalist Edward S. Morse, who introduced the Western approach to zoology to Japan during the late 1870s, liked just about everything about *shafu*. He traversed the whole country in rickshaws, despite an initial "sense of humiliation in being dragged by a man," taking them all

In the 1880s and 1890s, rickshaw pullers carried everyone from geisha to businessmen to poor workers, occasionally in two-person vehicles such as the one pictured here. There was no standard attire, but pullers often took pride in wearing distinctive jackets. Edward Sylvester Morse Collection. Courtesy of the Peabody Essex Museum, Salem, Massachusetts.

around Tokyo, down to the Kii Peninsula, here and there in Kyushu, and along the great Tōkaidō highway. He described the transporters as unfailingly polite and congenial. When other drivers bumped them, he said, they grinned and went on, in contrast to Americans who would have started cursing. And when rebuffed over a fare dispute, the puller "smiles and retires with a kindly grin." Their speed amazed Morse too, particularly on a steamy July day in Enoshima when two pullers "kept up a good run without stopping, except at a few hills. . . . When we got to the last village they ran like fury, not showing the slightest evidence of fatigue." He was amazed that "they did not drop dead with sunstroke and fatigue."[42]

Whether negative or positive, the images often were of men bigger than life, iconic figures who loved doing the unusual. Newspapers had frequent stories about both heroism and skullduggery: one puller attempting to rape a rider, another who rushed to a screaming victim's aid,[43] or the *shafu* who got up and kept on going after falling, then died of his injuries the next day.[44] No one seemed ready to forget the eruption of popular acclaim for two pullers in 1891 who took down a fanatical police officer who had stabbed Russia's Crown Prince Nicholas while he was riding in a rickshaw in the town of Ōtsu.[45] More mundane and typical were the accounts of a puller named Tanaka Kumaichi in Shiba, who turned in to the authorities a lost purse filled with ninety-three yen (four months' wages) and of a selfless *shafu* who gave a full day's wages to a widowed mother of three after reading about her "life of semi-starvation." Then there was the *shafu* in Ueno who took under his wing an eleven-year-old printer's apprentice who had run away from a tyrannical employer in Gumma Prefecture.[46] All of these pictures reinforced the popular image of rickshaw pullers as big figures, men (always men) who acted on strong impulses, some of them bad and many of them exceptionally good.

What of the reality? Few sources give us a fuller picture of the complexities of *shafu* life than Yokoyama and Matsubara, whose 1890s articles returned repeatedly to the pullers, with the former interested in their work patterns and the latter in their human characteristics. Matsubara had much to say about the peculiarities of what they ate. The *shafu* in Tokyo's Ryōgoku region, he said, ate *mochi* (glutinous rice balls); those in Asakusa loved soba noodles in hot broth (*bukkakemeshi*); in Yoroibashi, it was something called "strength sushi" (*chikarazushi*); most everywhere, they liked *yakitori*, a kebab of chicken parts. Above all, they chose cheap foods that could be eaten on the run: "They hold their chopsticks and tea cup at the ready, keeping one eye on the people coming and going and another on their food—looking in all directions for customers." He was put off by some of their favorite foods, particularly horsemeat (the "smell assaults the nose"), beef bladder, and beef intestines (*zōfu*).[47] Even more interesting to Matsubara were the varieties of men who plied the trade. One morning near the Ryōgoku levee's *jinrikisha* stop, he said, he found "every possible human specimen" looking for riders. Two *shafu* in blue jackets and white footwear were chatting animatedly, one with ripped sleeves and tattered pants, the other wearing a soldier's cap. Ranged beside them were pullers dressed every imaginable way: a bald fellow beside someone with a round wicker hat, one with a headband, another wearing old-style gloves (*tekkō*), someone with an undershirt but no shirt, another wearing long underwear. There were sharp-eyed men and simple-faced men, chaps with cruel features, one who looked coarse, another who appeared wise, and someone with a "small nose and a cat's forehead." Some were mature and experienced; some were rank amateurs, some old ("walking like a creeping insect"[48]), some young, some honest, some dull. Surprisingly, even their physiques varied. One looked like a gentleman; another was old and feeble. One was obese "like a pig," while a nearby mate appeared poor and thin "with legs like a mosquito."[49]

One image that meshed with reality was that pullers usually were strong and individualistic, often even explosive. Freed by poverty and self-employment from social norms, many asserted themselves forcefully. Some covered their arms and legs in elaborate tattoos of "grotesque designs in blue and red, some of the designs being quite artistic; a dragon, for example, extending down the back and legs and most delicately executed." Some worked "quite naked but for the loin-cloth," particularly in the early Meiji years.[50] A few turned into dandies when off work, donning "a rustling silk kimono, such as a well-to-do merchant might wear."[51] And many of them disregarded social rules about deference. They were notorious for hassling potential customers. Matsubara estimated that seven of ten passengers rode not because they wanted to, but because the *shafu* flattered, begged, and berated them as they got off trains.[52] His percentage may have been exaggerated, but even Morse commented on their persistence.[53] Loud public displays of emotion were common too: cursing out an obnoxious rider or raging about an unfair police officer. Nor was it unknown for fights to break out among pullers over customers or choice locations. Matsubara draws on a deep well of colorful prose used by pullers angry at passengers and rival pullers: "What are you doing in front of *this* station?! . . . Blockhead! . . . Impertinent blowhard! . . . Damned asshole!" He describes two *shafu* hurling invective over a sales transaction until they were too exhausted to fight further, and then walking away, beaten in spirit. Most of this anger was individual and specific, Matsubara says, focused on momentary irritants rather than systemic problems; pullers' eruptions were unlikely to lead to activism or social disruption. But their reputation for colorful behavior was earned.[54]

Shifting from individual behavior to the broader work patterns that interested Yokoyama, one finds a surprising amount of structure in the *shafu* profession. All pullers were male, without known exception, and most worked for themselves, with 93 percent of Tokyo's *shafu* owning or renting their own vehicle at the peak of the *jinrikisha* era in 1901.[55] At the same time, pullers had to conform to a system that required significant levels of cooperation and structure. In order to be certified, they had to pass an official test demonstrating a detailed knowledge of the city's streets and locations. The regulations also mandated that they own the correct attire and equipment (cap, trousers, shirt, lantern, blanket). And they had to follow numerous traffic rules and pay operator fees.[56] Perhaps most telling, they worked in recognizable patterns, belonging to one of four informal work classes.[57] The smallest class consisted of the *okakae* (retained workers) who were employed by affluent patrons for regular rides. Some of the *okakae* actually lived in their employers' homes, while others lived independently and reported each morning for the day's assignment. One reason this group remained small was that the *okakae* were poorly paid; they lost in freedom and income what they gained in job security. At the opposite end of the spectrum, a second poorly paid group, the *yado* or *heyazumi* (hangers on), consisted of the completely unattached pullers; these were men, said Yokoyama, who lived "in a rather easygoing way," often squandering their money and relying "on their more resourceful fellow *yado* to support them" when cash ran out. A larger class, made up of pullers who preferred to balance independence and mutuality, was called *ban* because they belonged to one of many loose organizations, called *ban,* each of which operated out of its own rickshaw parking lot. To join, the *shafu* had to contribute about five gallons (ten *shō*) of saké[58] and pay a small entrance fee; after entering, they continued to pay a small monthly fee, which was used as a reserve fund for members' emergencies. In certain ways, the *ban* resembled proto-unions, but members were notorious for ignoring group rules.

The fourth class, the vast majority of whom lived in the slums, was popularly called *mōrō* or "obscure ones" because its members worked mostly in the late afternoon and evening. As Yokoyama described the daily scene:

> At about six or seven in the afternoon the city would begin to bustle, with the squeaky sounds of rickshaws and the flickering of gas lights. It was night, that boisterous time of shifting traffic. The *mōrō* came out from their lodgings then, as the day workers hurried home even while factory men and women continued to work away at their machines. This was when you saw the most rickshaws on the city streets—the time when, in some respects, the world belonged to the *mōrō.*[59]

Until at least midnight, the *mōrō* rickshaws would seek customers at transportation centers such as Shinbashi station and Ryōgoku bridge, or at pleasure quarters such as Yoshiwara. Poorly paid, most of them pulled rented rickshaws, and the poorest sometimes borrowed clothes for their work. It was said that those servicing brothels, particularly in Osaka, supplemented their low pay with tips from rich riders.[60] A subgroup of the *mōrō* was called *yonashi* (night worker) because they continued to ply the streets even after midnight, working until dawn brought their fellow *shafu* back to the streets. It was said in the early 1890s that "of the 5,000 Tokyoites who do not sleep, 4,000 are *shafu.*"[61]

All the *shafu* were poor, some desperately so, yet most pullers' families were decently fed and adequately clothed. As a class, rickshaw families lived farther from the precipice of disaster than many other *hinminkutsu* dwellers did. Although the mid-Meiji journalists made a good deal of the pullers' poverty, Ministry of Agriculture and Commerce statistics in 1896 placed their average daily wages at about fifty sen, at least three times those of the best-paid rag pickers and higher than skilled bricklayers; other data suggested that their work hours were about average for the era, roughly twenty-five days a month, or six days a week. Another survey in 1904 had the average pullers making more than most others in the *kasō shakai* but slightly less than carpenters, iron workers, and railroad construction workers, with a few of the best-paid rickshaw men topping all other *hinminkutsu* dwellers with more than two yen a day.[62] On heavy traffic days—especially the first, last, and middle days of the month—they might make as much as eighty sen. Yokoyama concluded that most "rickshaw-men lead a rather comfortable life" but conceded that they had to spend a full 80 percent of their income just for food. Displaying his middle-class bias, he accused pullers of spending too much on alcohol and wondered how they "make both ends meet."[63]

One shadow hovered over all *shafu:* the seasonal and chronological fluctuations of their working lives. During off-season months such as October and February, for example, traffic almost always was lighter, and declining fares made it hard for many to live. Moreover, pullers reaped wages only as long as their bodies cooperated. When they aged, their income fell. Matsubara observed that young men at their physical peak—"vigorous young men, single and in their prime, in good health and made of steel, as it were"—were able to carry their clients a full time and a half as far each day as their elders and to make more than twice as much income as those in the thirty to fifty age group. Pullers over sixty saw their income plummet to half that of the thirty to fifty group, and to a third that of the young *shafu.*[64] In other words, pullers could expect no more than two decades of pay at the top income levels; after that, infirmity and aging slowed down their pace and their wages. Only occasionally, said a *Kokumin Shinbun* reporter, would one find "a man of sixty-five or seventy wandering vaguely around the streets with an old broken-down rickshaw."[65] For men whose incomes were not high even in the best years, the short career span could mean decades of bleak living.

The public nature of rickshaw pulling also rendered the *shafu* particularly vulnerable to certain troubles. In a day before insurance or public assistance, for example, any accident or injury could push a family to the brink of starvation. Even more likely (often even more tragic) was the danger of an encounter with the authorities. Fines, levied for everything from improper equipment to harassing clients, had reached thirty sen per infraction by the end of the Meiji period, and if the mistakes were serious or frequent enough they resulted in license suspension.[66] A fine might mean an empty stomach for a day or two; a suspension meant disaster. "The end of work means the end of life," wrote the socialist essayist Nishikawa Kōjirō in 1904, citing the example of a sixty-year-old *shafu* who was apprehended for forgetting to light a lantern on his rickshaw at dusk one afternoon. His remonstrations and pleas about financial desperation fell on deaf ears. The municipal rule prohibited men over fifty from having a license if they committed even a single traffic offense, no mercy granted. "He will have no work after tomorrow," Nishikawa said; "he will head down the road of bare existence—and that in a household in which four people have depended on his arms." He said he knew four or five similar cases in the Asakusa district; most had resorted to begging, thievery, or suicide.[67]

In the last Meiji decade, an even more serious problem hit the *shafu* world. Modernity, which had brought the profession into existence, now threatened to wipe it out. Many writers had been uncomfortable from the beginning with the harnessing of human beings "like horses and cows . . . as an implement for transportation." It is "illogical, unequal," said one writer. "It is inappropriate."[68] A *Taiyō* writer in 1902 urged the government to banish rickshaws for moral, economic, and sanitary reasons, on the ground that market forces alone would never bring the inhuman work to an end.[69] But he was wrong about market forces, and many moralists started to have second thoughts about the issues as trains, streetcars, bicycles, and even some automobiles began to take away *shafu* jobs. The most reliable data, from Tokyo's Metropolitan Police Department, showed privately owned *jinrikisha* peaking in 1902 at roughly 46,000, then declining sharply to 26,499 in 1905 and then again to 22,000 in 1911 and to 19,000 in 1912. Within a decade, 60 percent of the city's rickshaws had vanished. And by 1932, the city had fewer than 2,000 of them.[70] In areas around train stations on the urban fringes where the streetcars had not yet come, there remained a need for pullers, but elsewhere, the situation was described by a *Tokyo Asahi Shinbun* writer who worried in mid-decade about men who "have found themselves completely without customers." Sometimes, he said, "a driver stands around all day and takes in only from five to thirty *sen*, which is not nearly enough for himself and his wife to live on." He wondered "what is to become of them."[71] Journalists spilled much ink discussing what to do about the problem. Some suggested paying *shafu* families to migrate to Hokkaido or Taiwan. More typical was the writer who bemoaned the troubles but concluded with a shrug, "The law of progress can not be arrested, but the victims of this progress need not be afraid of their fate, because as we say in Japanese, . . . 'Where there is a god who forsakes us, there is a god who rescues.'"[72]

The rescue god never showed up for most pullers. The railway workers, delivery people, carters, and even the night soil collectors continued to have ample work into the 1930s. But not the *shafu*. No late Meiji group more fully encapsulated the lifestyles of the urban *kasō shakai*. No other poor group captured the public imagination quite as vividly, with all their shenanigans and contributions. No group made people more aware, day in and day out, of how dependent Japan's middle-class citizens were on those who inhabited the *hinminkutsu*. And no occupation groups demonstrated more clearly the symbiosis between the forces of modernity and the fortunes of the urban *hinmin*. By the end of the era, the modernizing titans who had relied so heavily on the pullers left them bereft, propelling great numbers into work as peddlers, rag pickers, and trinket salesmen, or worse. One editorialist declared the situation, only partly in hyperbole, "more terrible than any disaster we have seen."[73]

The Serving Professions

Just about every member of the late Meiji *kasō shakai* was a server. What, after all, was night soil collection, or printing, or textile weaving if not service? Certain professions, however, entailed a more direct, sometimes more intimate, form of service to their customers. These included the street entertainers who brought color and gaiety to city street sides, the girls and women who served at restaurants, the bathhouse boys and blind masseurs, and those who worked in the sex trade.[74] Among all the *hinmin,* their jobs were the least examined by list makers and commentators.[75] With the exception of a couple of pages on street performers, even Yokoyama mentions such people only in anecdotal asides. It is hard to account for this omission. Perhaps it related to the difficulty of articulating neat economic categories for their work. Perhaps the serving jobs garnered too little respect to be considered in orthodox economic analyses. Indeed, it was telling that when Yokoyama described the jobs of the "wretched people" in Tokyo's slums, he analyzed three standard categories— laborers, rickshaw and cart pullers, construction workers—but listed without discussion "all manner" of other occupations: physiognomists, masseurs, beggar priests, street dancers, blind beggars, street storytellers.[76] Whatever the reason, the omission throws the researcher onto piles of anecdotes and journalistic references in the effort to understand the serving life. The effort is important though, because while the people who entertained, healed, and cleaned may have been impoverished, they were the source of much of the era's urban vitality.

BODY HEALERS

Near the bottom of the social scale in everyone's mind were the widely popular blind practitioners of acupuncture, massage, moxibustion, and shampooing: healing and soothing practices that required an intimate understanding of the human body. For at least three centuries, these people—male and female alike, many of them victims of smallpox—had been subject to wide discrimination, often regarded as mentally deficient and frequently held responsible for spreading diseases, sexual and otherwise, when they touched people's bodies. Their reputations, sadly, changed little in the modern period, even though there was scant evidence to support the slanders. The standard practice of the shampooers and masseuses was to walk the streets, particularly at night, whistling to attract clients; the masseuses offered full-body as well as head massages. Generally, these blind healers carried two items: a whistle to attract customers and a walking stick to help them find their way. Respond to the whistle, said the naturalist Morse, and "for half an hour or more the masseur will hammer, pinch, rub, and maul you in such a way that when the work is finished you feel like a new man"; they employed a hand movement "not unlike that made by the dentist's mechanical filler." And they did it all for "the sum of four cents!"[77] At evening's end, they used scents and sounds to navigate their way home. A good month's work usually brought

between five and ten yen at the end of the Meiji era, less than half of what carters made, even less than what toilet cleaners took in.[78]

Data on how many worked in these healing services are scarce, but a Metropolitan Police report in 1899 showed 919 officially blind people in Tokyo, with
more than half of them working as shampooers, while an unofficial report a
dozen years later indicated that the city had in excess of 2,000 blind masseuses.
Other accounts suggested much higher numbers of both shampooers and masseuses.[79] More frequent are the narrative accounts—almost always filled with
pity or contempt—of the difficult lives these healers led. *Seinen* reported in
1899 that the police still regarded blind acupuncturists as carriers of "contagious hereditary diseases of venereal character" because they wet their needles
with their tongues; the officers' recommendation was not for them to employ
more hygienic practices but to shift to a "harmless" profession such as music.
The same journal ran a police report several years later about a group of Fukagawa children who had mocked and stoned a blind shampooer who was
walking along, whistling for customers. When he struck back with his cane,
said the reporter, the police dragged him, not the children, off to the station.[80]
The worst of conditions was discovered by Matsubara early in the 1890s in a hot
springs area west of Tokyo. There, he reportedly found more than a hundred
blind shampooers, *hari isha* (acupuncturists), *kyū isha* (moxibustion practitioners), and "other stepchildren of nature" living in indescribable conditions under the control of a boss served by a blind wife and three blind concubines.
They lived in houses "so situated that the inmates never see the sun"; some inhabited "cellars made under the houses." The only people Matsubara could
imagine being willing to live here were those with no choice, "those to whom
the air and light are unattainable luxuries."[81] Conditions improved somewhat
after 1911, when the Home Ministry began regulating the blind healers' work,
requiring that they be certified. Their pay remained minuscule, however, and
their living conditions grim.

SHOP APPRENTICES

Just slightly better off were the apprentices (*kozō*) at city shops, another group
overlooked in most studies. As described in a *Taiyō* essay early in 1901, once a
lad had accepted a *kozō* position, he became, in effect, a kept person, required
to work from six o'clock in the morning until ten o'clock at night. The shop
provided sleeping space, food, and work clothes; in return the apprentice gave
body and soul to the owner. Visits to family were prohibited, except on "big
occasions" like the death of a parent. Trips to a barber or the local bath required special permission. And no work was too menial: cleaning toilets,
stacking boxes, serving customers, or sweeping floors. For all this, the worker
received somewhere between five and sixteen sen a day, or 1.25 to 4.0 yen a
month. Nor did the work provide prospects for much advancement, the "apprentice" label notwithstanding. A *kozō* who managed to put up with the boss'
harangues and maintain his respect might advance in five or ten years to clerk
(*tedai*), with more responsibilities and slightly better pay, but there was almost

no possibility of ever rising to the position of head clerk or *bantō*. "They are like birds in cages," sighed a *Taiyō* essayist. "They get no education. They have no savings. They are shown no mercy, no compassion—and they have not a single hope for the future." He added, "The other humans who merit similar pity are the prostitutes."[82]

BATHHOUSE WORKERS

Bathhouse workers (*sansuke*) too labored long hours for paltry wages, but their working conditions were far better. Public bathing, called Japan's "supreme pleasure,"[83] went back to at least the eleventh century and *sentō*, or public bathhouses, were spreading steadily across Japan's cities at the turn of the century, in part because of the mushrooming urban population and in part because baths were inexpensive to start and quite lucrative for owners.[84] Tokyo had perhaps a thousand *sentō* in the early 1900s,[85] and they were used by all classes, including the *kasō shakai*, who embraced regular "social bathing" not just for getting clean but for exchanging news and gossip.[86] As one foreigner observed, baths had become "a perfect passion" with Tokyoites by 1903, rich and poor alike.[87] A late night on the men's side at the *sentō* might find a shopkeeper and a factory worker alongside a carpenter "tattooed with a coloured picture of a beauty under cherry blossoms," lustily singing a popular tune, while the "noise and confusion" in the women's bath across the partition was "still greater."[88] *Hinmin* budgets almost always included a few sen a day for baths.

A typical public bath would employ two male *sansuke* and one female, meaning that at least three thousand Tokyo *hinmin* were working as bath attendants in the middle Meiji years. Most of them fit a familiar profile: urban immigrants, recruited to the city by employer agents, "sturdy young fellows" who had come from the rugged Noto Peninsula north of Kanazawa early in the era and now hailed more often from the Japan Alps region. Their work involved managing the bath, stoking the fire, scrubbing backs (for an extra *nagashi*, or "washing," fee), and keeping temperatures right for *shitamachi* people who liked their baths hot. "Nowhere," said a cheery *Taiyō* columnist,[89] is there "an occupation so easy as his." He pointed out that the attendant "does not actually need any dress, as in summer time from morning to night he has not a thing on his back, and even in winter a pair of drawers and a short thin frock constitute his whole attire." The owner provided meals, and though the pay was under five yen a month, the *sansuke* received extra fees for rubbing backs, plus five or six yen each year in bonuses. With few necessary expenses, the writer said, a frugal worker ought to be able to save most of the wages. What was more, each bath worker was given "an off-day at least once a month when he may enjoy a 'spree,' visit a theater or any other place of amusement." The bright tone of the piece cloaked a harsher reality. One free day out of thirty? Confinement always to the bathhouse? A salary below that of textile workers and postal deliverymen? Little prospect for advancement? This was hardly the "easy" life. There was, however, much to say for the convivial atmosphere in which bath attendants worked.

PERFORMERS

The thousands of performers who enlivened the late Meiji markets and festival grounds had more experience than most with bitterness. The variety of their acts was breathtaking: playing the samisen, doing handstands and acrobatic flips, singing, dancing, telling stories, making children laugh with their contorted faces, making them gasp with their magic tricks. More than perhaps any other group, the performers embodied paradox: thrilling audiences with their humor and joy, exuding color and vibrancy in public, even as they struggled with sadness, loneliness, and impoverishment at home (if they had a home). It would be hard to imagine any group whose public personas conflicted more completely with their actual lives.

On the one hand, the range of the performers' skills was stunning. Yokoyama's lists of "wretched" ones included traveling storytellers, beggar-priests, street entertainers, shrine dancers, acrobats, burlesque chanters, unlicensed (*moguri*) samisen players, and old women performing the comic dance called *kappore.* Others described jugglers, crossroad lecturers (*tsuji gōshaku*), puppeteers, lion dancers, men who "flung noodles high into the air and caught them with chopsticks," others who tossed up coins "and caught them on the tip of a straw," armless people who stood on their heads, some who leapt through tubes lined with knives, those who held the samisen on their heads while they played, and men with unusual bodies, including an Asakusa performer with his "mouth in his stomach."[90] Still others presented monkey shows or dog shows. *Tokyo Puck* devoted ink to less savory sorts too, people whose acrobatics were mental and spiritual rather than physical: "swindling wonder-workers," among whom it included "fake oracle mongers, faith-cure cheats, and . . . fortune tellers," all of them scam artists who relied on the gullibility of " brainless folks."[91] The Japanophile Lafcadio Hearn added to the list "poor blind women" who sang street ballads in contralto "tones that draw tears."[92] Some of the performers were hacks; many were virtuosos.

Virtuosity and vitality did not, unfortunately, assure prosperity and respect. Like their Tokugawa-era ancestors, the *hinin* ("non-person") *gōmune* or beggars with braided hats who staged shows at crossroads,[93] the late Meiji performers were demeaned as inferior, even by those who applauded and gave them a few sen for their acts. Why then did they choose this line of work? Some did it because they loved performing, others because it was what their parents and grandparents had done and they knew nothing else. Many chose it because of unfortunate circumstances of some kind: children, for example, pressured into the work by indigent parents or by bosses, "notoriously brutal men who forced them to dance all day while performing handstands."[94] For some, it was a lack of other skills, like Izumi Kyōka's old samisen player who began "wandering the land" after being disowned by his uncle and, on finding a cheap "old samisen, also abandoned by the floating world," strolled from city to city playing it for just enough sen to stay alive.[95] The one thing they all shared was poverty. Famous actors might get handsome salaries, but the street performers earned even less pay than respect. And the income they did receive was erratic. Many nights the samisen players at evening fairs earned no more than seven to ten sen, meaning it would take nearly two weeks to accumulate a single yen. Burlesque chanters did better; they might make a full yen, and good acrobats sometimes made a whopping six yen on busy festival days at major temples. But even for them the pay was sporadic. When the festival ended or the weather turned foul, earnings dropped or ceased.[96] Nothing told the street performers' tale better than the fact that the majority slept at *kichin'yado*, most often in Tokyo's Shin'ami-chō slum. Even they were better off than Izumi's musician who was forced, yen-less, to sleep "under the stars about half of the time."[97] Pawning household items to get through the hard times was common for entertainers, and when it rained for successive days, they put even their instruments and performance paraphernalia into hock. "If you went to Shin'ami on rainy days," said Yokoyama, "you saw many despondent performers sitting around a fireless hibachi, staring wordlessly at the sky. Poor people are always sad, but the sight of an artist's anguish under a rainy sky evokes special pity."[98]

FOOD PROVIDERS

The Meiji surveys also ignored the food workers, the vendors at those thousands of market stalls, the men who hawked their steaming soba from carts, and the women and girls who waited tables in the restaurants and *izakaya* (drinking places).[99] The omission should not be taken to mean that these people were not important in people's lives. Few grew up without warm feelings about the three thousand hawkers whose cries of *"ya-ki-i-mo-o"* (hot sweet potatoes!) brought children running. As one writer noted, Honjo and Fukagawa children might not be able to afford decent rice but they could almost always find a sen for a sweet potato, and it tasted better than the home gruel with its "half-rotten rice and little pieces of old fish-flesh mixed into dried-up vegetable."[100] For their fathers, it was the workers at "vulgar restaurants" (*katō inshokuten*) and *izakaya* who evoked the warmest feelings, for it was here that they congregated after work, sometimes to fill their stomachs and quench their thirst, just as often to share the day's gossip and troubles with fellow workers or to drink off woes. And it was here, in the cheap eating places, that the street performers and day laborers found refuge when the weather prevented work. "On rainy days," said Matsubara, "these places are crowded with jinrikisha coolies and others who make their living out of doors, so that there is a constant stream of small coins flowing in." He said the favorite winter drink was *shirouma* (unrefined saké); the summer favorite was *shōchū*, an alcoholic drink with centuries-old origins in Kyushu.[101] "Vexation at earning no money," he noted, was a good pretext for drinking.[102]

The female waiters at the "vulgar restaurants" vied with performers and rag pickers for the era's worst working situation. In their late teens, many of them had come to the city from farm or mining families; not a few had been abandoned by parents. Their work hours were like those of bathhouse attendants and shop apprentices: twenty-nine days out of thirty, from early morning until day's end. And they slept with other waiters in a single room of two or three mats "without space to spread out their arms or legs."[103] For that, they received about five sen a day (roughly what street fair performers received, enough to buy a loaf of bread[104]), plus kimono and board. They took orders, brought food, cleared tables, washed dishes and chopsticks, cleaned the restaurant (including the toilet, if the establishment had one), and, perhaps worst of all, humored patrons who ranged the gamut from the kind and docile to the flirtatious, drunk, and violent. Matsubara found many of the waiters "fresh and rosy," covered with "a more liberal than judicious use of *oshiroi* (face powder)" but gifted with "an inexhaustible stock of good nature, ever ready to burst out in a ringing laugh about anything or nothing."[105] Since most *inshokuten* were unheated, or equipped at most with a charcoal heater or two, winter work was especially bitter. Matsubara saw young women whose hands would fill with corns, chilblains, and boils from the work. Sometimes, he said, the cooking utensils were left unwashed because it was too painful to put cracked hands into the cold washing water. It was not uncommon, he added, for them to "dribble pus (*kuzoshiru*) onto the dirty tables." Not surprisingly, many of these women suffered from chronic illness. While some worked until middle age, most left after a few years, sometimes to get married, sometimes to take jobs in factories or less demeaning places.[106]

TRASH COLLECTORS

Like rickshaw pullers, rag pickers (*kuzuhiroi*) and trash collectors showed up everywhere: on streets, behind shops, in alleys, picking through litter to find anything that could be sold, much like today's urban junk collectors but without the trucks. In contrast to the *shafu*, however, they attracted little attention, except as splotches on the urban tapestry. Dressed in rags as tattered as the things they collected, often unwashed, picking up soiled and unsanitary materials—and living somewhere along the "borderline between employment and vagrancy," in the words of the economic historian Koji Taira—they were an embarrassment to most people: "of no more value than the junk they pick."[107] Life was less awkward for middle-class shoppers when they could screen them out. But they were too numerous to ignore altogether. By all counts, the *kuzuhiroi* numbered in the thousands in each of Japan's big cities. Osaka's Nago-chō alone had at least 1,100 of them in the early 1890s, and nearly 8,000 were identified in that work in Tokyo in 1889, more than 1,000 of them in the Asakusa region (particularly in the Mannen-chō slum), nearly 1,500 in Shitaya, 649 in Shiba, where the Shin'ami-chō slum was located, and more than 700 in the factory worker regions of Honjo and Fukagawa.[108] Their ranks were dominated by women and children. In Nago-chō, for example, almost 500, or 45 percent, were under age fifteen, and nearly 700 were female; only 15 percent were adult men. An 1896 report in *Jiji Shinpō* estimated that about a fifth of Tokyo's rag pickers were under age seventeen.[109]

Rag-picking work was more organized than most city dwellers probably knew. At one end of the picking process were the trash wholesalers (*tateba*); in the middle were contractors who secured the pickers' haul and passed it on to the *tateba*; at the beginning were two kinds of *kuzuhiroi*, collectors and sorters. The sorters also organized things, separating trash into saleable categories: paper (divided into Japanese paper and the less-valuable Western paper), glass, rags (*borokuzu*), and a miscellaneous category that included coal and charcoal pieces, old clogs and sandals, hairpins, discarded cans, old lamps, and even soiled loincloths. The clock and calendar imposed an additional kind of organization. Most days were divided into three rag-picking shifts. Hardier types would hit the streets before dawn, looking for things that had been discarded when the entertainment centers shut down for the night. Another group would come out when the stores and shops had finished their preparations and unpacking for the new day. And still a third began their work early in the evening, looking for the things thrown away that day. At three times of the year, however, trash collection continued all day (and night) long: at *setsubun,* the day before the formal arrival of spring, when dutiful households did a thorough cleaning; at *doyōboshi,* a midsummer period for airing clothes and doing special cleaning; and throughout the entire month of December, when people prepared for the new year by discarding the year's accumulated wastes and making things immaculate. These periods put slightly better food on the rag pickers' tables, and left them exhausted.

Life's greatest trial for rag pickers was their low income. Dependent on the recycling wholesalers who refused to pay more than a pittance, the *kuzuhiroi* at the end of the nineteenth century took in between five and fifteen sen a day, with paper paying the higher amounts, glass shards the lower. That amounted to less than four yen a month, about a third of what a bag maker earned, half what a shoemaker or factory worker made, and less even than the pay of the despised *tachinbō* or slackers who helped to pull carts.[110] Only the poorest of the street entertainers and restaurant servers made less. Such salaries were hardly surprising in an era when women and children were expected to work for crumbs, but they helped to explain why progress for rag-picker families was glacial. They also explain why the *Jiji* report in 1896 found that nearly two-thirds of rag pickers supplemented their income through "illegitimate jobs" or "stealing."[111]

The impact of these low wages was rendered even worse by public attitudes. On rare occasions, a *kuzuhiroi* was singled out for praise—as when the Shiba ragman Nozawa Tarakichi took a valuable gold ring to police in 1910 rather than keeping or selling it[112]—but even praise usually had a patronizing tone, and the standard approach was disparagement. "The contempt of the general public for ragpickers has always been deep," Taira wrote. Yokoyama, who thought of himself as empathetic, used harsh language in describing both their work and their character. While admitting that some rag pickers were "intelligent and clever," he opined that scavengers in general were "an almost subhuman species only slightly related to other human beings on this earth."[113] At the era's end, a *Tokyo Puck* artist sketched a pile of garbage being picked over by two different scavengers: "the black headed waste-picker and the red-combed chicken."[114] The most insidious aspect of this denigration surely lay in its impact on the rag pickers' own sense of self. When late Meiji government surveyors asked *hinmin* to account for their economic "predicament," about a fifth of the overall poor population blamed their own personal failings, but a full 55 percent of the rag pickers blamed themselves, using words such as laziness, gambling, lack of education, and debauchery. Only one in eight (compared to a third of the general *kasō shakai* population) blamed the economy, while a quarter cited "biological" causes such as illness and family deaths.[115] Middle-class citizens saw rag pickers as failures, and a majority of *kuzuhiroi* accepted that view. Life was poor; work was hard; society despised them: it must be their own fault.

SEX WORKERS

Societal attitudes toward a final group of servers, the urban sex workers, were as complex as the workers' actual lives were. Like all countries, Japan had a conflicted past when it came to opinions about prostitution. Amy Stanley of Northwestern University has demonstrated that "female promiscuity was not heavily stigmatized" in the Tokugawa years, even though the prostitutes themselves were usually controlled by their family, the state, or the brothels. The government licensed houses of prostitution in the major urban pleasure quarters, but by the eighteenth century a large informal sex industry flourished along the highways and in towns, defying control and uniformity.[116] The courtesans of the licensed quarters, known as *yūjo*, were celebrated in literature and painting, and the urban "culture of play" was widely accepted as a natural component of human nature, even though some writers complained about women being used as commodities, and moralists criticized the unlicensed sex centers for undermining male authority.[117] After the start of the Meiji era, officials paid increasing attention to the sex industry. In 1872, the government issued a largely unenforced law outlawing the purchase and sale of prostitutes. In 1875 it stepped backward, recognizing again the right of brothels to sign indenture agreements, and in October 1900 it issued new regulations, giving the Home Ministry responsibility for controlling prostitution and authorizing police to arrest unlicensed sex workers. Under those regulations, registration and medical examinations were called for, and a minimum age of eighteen was established for working as a prostitute, although the health checks did not become mandatory for all prostitutes until 1926, when a Bill for the Prevention of Venereal Diseases was passed.

The new laws were a response to a public debate swirling over Japan's entertainment world. On the one side, many in the male establishment defended sex work as a way of satisfying innate human needs and boosting the economy, a view buttressed by the nearly 1.8 million yen that the country's 10,172 licensed brothels contributed annually to the government in fees, and by the million-plus men who visited the 175 Yoshiwara brothels alone each year. Prostitution was a "money-making venture," which officials "did not hesitate to exploit . . . to bring in revenue."[118] Taking a slightly different tack, Prime Minister Itō Hirobumi declared in 1886 that Japan's prostitution system was a way of providing income for poor families.[119] And the head of the Bureau of Hygiene argued in

1900 that sex with a prostitute differed from that with a wife only in the location where it was carried out and in its failure to produce children.[120] Licensed brothels, said Liza Dalby, were seen by the Meiji government "as a safety valve against rape, seduction, adultery, 'unnatural vices,' and illicit prostitution."[121] The money they poured into the economy was a bonus.

On the other side of the issue was a growing number of reformers who by the 1890s damned prostitution, both licensed and unlicensed, as either a "slavery system" or a "social evil" that forced young women into unwanted and unseemly occupations. Some of these were Western Christian moralists such as the Salvation Army officer Henry Bullard, who established a rescue home in Tokyo "to receive girls sincerely desirous of forsaking their life of sin and returning to the path of virtue."[122] More of them were Japanese intellectuals, both Christian and non-Christian, who tended to make fewer moral judgments about women in the trade. The socialist Nishikawa Kōjirō repeated the axiom that "no Japanese man is without conceit or the pox," pointing out in *Heimin Shinbun* that syphilis had been a problem for centuries.[123] *Mainichi Shinbun,* edited by the parliamentarian Shimada Saburō, called the "Home Minister himself" a "perpetrator of rape" for not enforcing the 1872 regulations that would have enabled prostitutes to "emancipate themselves" when they wanted to leave the profession.[124] And in September 1900, Shimada's peer, Akiyama Teisuke of *Niroku Shinpō,* staged a dramatic "self emancipation" (*jiyū haigyō*) episode, sending two of his reporters to assist a woman who had decided to leave her Yoshiwara brothel. When they were beaten up and bloodied by brothel thugs, he publicized the violence, securing her release and setting off a wave of self-emancipations, then boasting that "Yoshiwara now looks like a dead place covered by cobwebs."[125] In October, after demands by several powerful papers, the government issued the new regulations described above.

Two things—the location of the entertainment quarters and the flourishing of *un*licensed prostitution—made the debates relevant to the urban *hinmin.* Since most of Tokyo's six licensed quarters were located near the slum areas, a symbiotic relationship existed between the poor and the entertainment centers. Yokoyama did not have much to say about sex work, but he did take notice of the proximity of the Yoshiwara quarters to the Asakusa slums and commented that brothels might be a blessing to people living near them. Houses of ill fame "must be severely criticized," he said, since they caused men to "squander their fortunes," but they "do give the poor certain advantages and jobs."[126] Indeed. As the novelist Higuchi Ichiyō made clear in the short story "Takekurabe" (Child's play), life in the grim neighborhood of Daionjimae, not far from the Mannen-chō slum, was affected deeply, often positively, by the next-door Yoshiwara quarters. Playing children mimicked courtesans and patrons. Adults typically would "live in or live off the brothels,"[127] with men doing odd jobs in the quarters and women making clothes for the prostitutes. And the local economy boomed when the neighborhood temples and shrines—whose proximity to the pleasure quarters was not accidental—held festivals. Asking why Daionjimae's "tumble-down houses" had so many colorful rake-shaped pieces of paper hanging from open windows one November day, a visitor was told that they were charms for Ōtori shrine's coming festival: "You ought to see the big-wishers buy them up!"[128] A priggish critic called the neighborhood "that most vulgar of places: an area whose residents aren't ashamed of receiving money from people who are engaged in selling sex."[129]

For poor neighborhood girls, on the other hand, the proximity to Yoshiwara provoked a mixture of fantasy and fear, particularly when their families saw the pleasure quarters as a place of potential employment for their daughters. As Higuchi told it, men leaving the brothel would notice the poor teenager Midori, the story's central figure, and quip, "I'd like to see her three years from now!"[130] Her neighborhood playmates envied her because, being pretty and quick, she would not have to worry about how to make her way as an adult: she would be a Yoshiwara courtesan, probably one of those in a third-class establishment who sat behind the latticework in a showroom "exposing their painted faces for onlookers . . . and shamelessly smoking their long bamboo pipe" but perhaps a more fortunate woman in a second-class brothel where selections were made from printed pictures. If really lucky, she might end up in an elite brothel with her own servants and clients who spent nights eating, talking, and sleeping

The gates to the Yoshiwara prostitution quarters, pictured here in the mid-Meiji years, were famous for their elegant calligraphy, as well as for the constant flow of men in and out. Courtesy of Kjeld Duits Collection, MeijiShowa.com.

with her.[131] For Midori herself, the prospect invited periods of hopelessness and depression. The future might be secure, but on many days it felt like the security of entrapment. "She hated, hated this growing up!"[132]

Sex work, for most *hinmin*, took place outside the licensed establishments. Across the country, in towns and cities, tens of thousands of poor women worked in an unlicensed, illegal, and unstoppable sex industry.[133] Hundreds of small establishments with innocuous titles and names served in Tokyo and Osaka as fronts for illicit activities. Their signboards advertised their ostensible purposes; they were billiards parlors, archery centers, small restaurants, tiny theaters, massage parlors, tea houses, beer halls. Inside, their real business was clear from the paucity of food or beer and the abundance of young women wearing makeup. In Asakusa's Rokku, or sixth district, said one visitor, one found rows of small establishments with names such as *"Meishuya* (Drinking-shops), *Shinbun jūran-sho* (Newspaper Reading Halls), and *Kitchaten* (Tea-shops), whose open occupations are to sell wine, read papers, and serve tea respectively; but their real business is taken by courtesans."[134] These shops evoked an outpouring of moralizing essays, including a 1901 piece titled "Urban Temptations" (*Tokai no yūwakubutsu*) by Kōjimachi Bō, who wrote that Tokyo's atmosphere had become "putrified" (*fuhai*), with "high and low" alike "falling into great depravity." He described six major "urban temptations" that had inundated Japan's cities: theaters, music halls and storytelling places, women workers at questionable shops, houses of ill-fame (*kashizashiki,* which included licensed brothels and tea houses), unlicensed brothels, and gaming centers. Altogether, he said, more than 10,000 businesses sold sex undercover, with Asakusa leading all regions with 1,573. At gaming centers (92 billiards shops, 67 shooting galleries, more than 150 archery halls), he noted, billiards and archery were mere covers; seductive young women were the attraction. Kōjimachi's solution was to build bigger middle-class homes. If private residences were better equipped for entertaining, he said, guests would not have to be taken to places where "various immoral things are introduced."[135]

The reformers worried most about the unlicensed prostitutes, or *inbaifu,* who operated outside the law's eye. Licensed quarters maintained an aura of respectability and were walled off from the public. They also looked after clients' health by requiring that prostitutes have regular health inspections, with infected women being sent to the Yoshiwara Hospital for treatment.[136] Unlicensed sex, by contrast, had neither cultural traditions nor official regulation to shape its practices or modulate its image. It was illegal; it provided no revenue to the government; it was cheap; it was everywhere (especially in Asakusa's Senzoku-machi entertainment area); and it was difficult for officials to control, as evidenced by the fact that fewer than three hundred unlicensed sex workers would be apprehended by Tokyo police in any given year.[137] The many incongruities of this world—including the income it brought to the poor, the way police tried to shut it down, and the health dangers it posed—were detailed in 1900 in a dozen articles in Akiyama's *Niroku Shinpō* titled "Katō baiin no jikkyō" (The actual conditions of low-class prostitution).[138]

The women in this occupation, said the series' unnamed writer, were driven to their jobs by poverty. Some were former factory workers from the Honjo slums who could not make enough in spinning or weaving to survive (April 18). Others were poverty-stricken housewives. Many had children. "During the day, they make matchboxes or cigarettes. In the evening, if they cannot make ends meet, they reluctantly do their night work. . . . Usually, they sneak out of their homes without telling their husbands. They are stronger than those cowardly husbands" (April 15). Sometimes from embarrassment, sometimes to avoid apprehension by the police, they disguised themselves, putting on "makeup so thick that it might come off if they smile" before heading out with "a scarf or towel over the head, holding the edge in the mouth to keep the face half covered" (April 18). The writer labeled the sex workers "pitiable": women who "take up hell work when they cannot earn enough to eat in their own living hells."[139]

The paper described three classes of unlicensed *inbaifu* (April 11). The cheapest worked out of doors along the river banks and shoreline quays, hiding on a mattress or crouching in the bushes along the river while a barker hustled up customers. When busy with a client, they would attach a piece of cloth to a nearby tree or entranceway to warn others away. Middle-level women worked out of a room, often in a tenement building or row house. If the room had no door, they would hang up a piece of fabric for privacy; when walls had large cracks or holes, they stuffed in paper or cloth to discourage voyeurs. The provision of a futon marked a woman as "upper class" among the unlicensed prostitutes. Even she would not offer more than a single pillow, however, because men who got too comfortable might overstay their welcome and diminish her income flow. Some women operated independently, while others worked out of brothels or for pimps. None got rich.

Income varied, depending on a worker's status, the neighborhood in which she operated, and the length of her clients' stays.[140] In expensive areas such as the Ginza, a high-class courtesan might receive a yen or more for a night of sex with a single man. If the prostitute were young, "low-class," and working in a poorer area, on the other hand, the intake from a full-night stand with one man would range from ten to fifty sen. And the more common *choi* (quick session) seldom yielded more than ten or twenty sen, sometimes as little as seven. Those on the low end "barely had the means to stay alive," said *Niroku* (April 17). It is worth keeping in mind, however, that in a period when female factory workers averaged only twenty sen a day, a time when even the highest-paid *hinmin* made less than a yen a day, the income for unlicensed prostitution was not a pittance. It is hardly surprising that more than a few women who could not feed their children or pay for medicine sought survival on the streets or along the riverbank.

Finding customers was a challenge. Unable (for obvious legal reasons) to make their whereabouts known, many women resorted to word of mouth and subterfuge. Some simply waited along popular streets where men were known to go for pleasure. Some walked about dressed as "regular" young women or housewives and struck up conversations with soldiers or students or returning factory workers who looked like potential customers. Often they concocted sad stories about deceased fathers or sick mothers to start a conversation and gain a man's heart (April 14). Others took jobs at the archery centers and billiard parlors discussed above or at tobacco shops or beer halls. And some worked at places that looked like *meishuya* or high-brand bars "with bottles of famous brands of saké lined up and cups placed on the tables." Once the potential patron had come inside and found the bottles empty, the woman would lead him to a waiting futon (April 16). Not a few of the *inbaifu* worked in tandem with barkers who wandered the streets dressed like gentlemen, looking for men out for an evening of sex. If the woman was not employed by a sex-offering establishment, the question of where to stage the liaison could be complicated. Sometimes they used unoccupied spaces in a tenement building or vacant hut, sometimes they found room in the client's *kichin'yado*,[141] and sometimes they searched for a place out of doors: in a cemetery, behind the riverside bushes, or in a secluded corner under the main hall of a temple (April 15). Some, called *yadobiki* (inn-connected), charged slightly more and took customers to a room they had secured at an inn, a practice that required a minimum of five clients a night to pay for the room rent, more if they also had to pay barker's fees (April 18).

The most frightening part of sex work for *hinmin* prostitutes was avoiding the authorities, since the police were ever on the prowl. In areas known for street prostitution, plain-clothes officers made visits most every night, causing the *inbaifu* to scatter "in every direction, like little spiders spinning their webs" (April 11). Sometimes an officer would disguise himself as a customer and arrest the woman when she got into bed with him; at other times he would take over for a neighborhood's more recognizable regular officer in order to catch women unawares. But the prostitutes and barkers were clever too. A common practice was to employ a *buraikan* ("rowdy") who would cough or whistle when an officer appeared. If the barker saw an officer about to enter the building, he might stage a scuffle with the *buraikan* to divert attention and give the prostitute time to flee; after the danger had passed, he paid the rowdy a bit for helping (April 13). As a last resort, an *inbaifu* might offer the policeman a bribe, a tactic that often worked. In one episode reported by *Niroku*, a prostitute mistook a mat maker for a policeman and handed him an envelope. Puzzled, he accepted it, had sex, and went home, where he was shocked to find a one-yen bill inside the envelope. "He was delighted and dashed to Yoshiwara" for more lovemaking, according to the report (April 17). In a less fortunate episode, police used information in the *Niroku* series to locate one of the cheap brothels, where they arrested two women and threw them in jail for ten days (April 18).

Niroku's rationale for running this highly unusual report was articulated at the beginning and the end of the series. In the first installment, the writer said people needed to know about unlicensed prostitution because of the health dangers it posed. Though widespread, syphilis had been regarded as "just another infectious disease" prior to the Meiji era,[142] but with modernity had come greater awareness of the dangers inherent in venereal diseases and, along with that, increased efforts to control STDs through health inspections of licensed prostitutes. The discovery in the 1890s that at least one of every ten soldiers had a venereal disease had fueled even greater official concerns.[143] Knowing this, the *Niroku* editors decided to "violate our own high literary standards" and detail the "actual conditions" of lower-class prostitution. While upper-class men might get medical treatment if they contracted sex-related diseases, those in "lower-class society" (*karyū shakai*) could not. But the troubles would not end there: "If we leave things as they are now, lower class society will become a sea of syphilis (*baidoku no umi*). Then the surging, dirty waves will inundate the middle class, and after that the upper classes, and eventually they will drown our entire society" (April 10). The final article, on April 25, concentrated on the health issue. In a move that suggested *Niroku*'s close identification with its large *hinmin* readership, the writer eschewed the usual middle-class approach of blaming women and focused on male clients and the impact of sexual promiscuity on families. "The price is cheap; so people buy a prostitute to satisfy their momentary lust," he said. "But that insidious moment can infect them with the frightening disease of syphilis and change their lives completely." Nor would the curse end there: "Even if a man accepts for himself the fact that he must reap what he has sown, there remain the troubles he has created for his wife and children." He explained that syphilis begins in "one's private parts and gradually spreads to the entire body" in a sinister process that remains hidden for the first month or so. After that, it causes ulcers and boils, leaving permanent marks and scars, sometimes destroying the nose or lips, sometimes rotting the teeth or causing deafness. "Not only does the man end up discrediting his family," the writer said, "he can quite literally bring an end to his family lineage."

The April 25 article concluded with possible solutions. Pointing out again that poverty was the culprit, the writer said that Japan had too few resources to provide adequate jobs for all these sex workers and acknowledged that "the total abolition of prostitution will not be easy." Rejecting the French approach of fining illegal prostitutes and the German solution of "driving the prostitutes out of our country," he urged that a "quasi-prostitute" (*junshōgi*) category be created to license poor women who took up the trade temporarily, with weekly health inspections required. To skeptics who said these measures would not eliminate sexual diseases, he responded, "No one says criminal laws are useless simply because criminals will continue to exist." To the end, the series eschewed moral judgments, focusing on the relationship between unlicensed sex work, which was endemic in the *kasō shakai*, and the economic imperatives of *hinmin* life. Poverty forced women into that work. Illegal prostitution put food on tables and saved the lives of sick and malnourished children. But it also caused humiliation and suffering. And it threatened the whole of society.

More than a century after the end of Meiji, the Uruguayan menial worker Ingrid Schmutz commented, "The rich couldn't live without us . . . the poor."[144] She could have been speaking for the movers and servers in Nago-chō or Mannen-chō at Meiji's end. Without their rickshaw rides, their waste removal, the goods they transported, their cheap entertainment, their clerking, even their sex work, the entire modernity project would have taken a far different shape, if any shape at all. As a group, they have much to tell us about modernity's hidden side, particularly about three topics that have threaded their way throughout this chapter: the poor person's public invisibility, the gendered nature of *hinmin* work, and the inadequacy of commoner wages.

There was, for most *hinmin,* a constant tension between visibility and invisibility. Rag pickers and trash haulers might be everywhere; street entertainers might draw applause, but only rarely were they seen as people by the ones for whom they worked and performed. There were, of course, exceptions such as the rickshaw pullers who charmed Morse, but poor workers were usually a backdrop, sometimes a smudge on the city surface. Nothing highlighted this invisibility more than the truism that *hinmin* were uneducated. It was a fact that most of the *kasō shakai* had limited formal schooling, but few observers ever commented on the fact that their informal, life-generated education surpassed what many in the middle classes learned in a formal classroom. Rickshaw pullers and mail deliverers could not be certified without knowing the cities' complex, confusing grids inside and out; many a masseur's grasp of the intricacies of the human body would have confounded University of Tokyo graduates; telephone operators had to understand human nature as well as complex phone systems; the knowledge required of craftsmen and carpenters could be passed down only through years of training. An observer like Matsubara might occasionally remark on the practical lessons "studied at the college of the poor"; more typical was the *Taiyō* writer's comment that "no one in the world is more pitiable than shop boys or clerks" because "they get no education."[145] It was easy to shut one's eyes to the toilers all around on the streets, easier still to ignore the detailed, specialized learning that enabled them to do what they did. No matter how impressive, the movers' or servers' knowledge remained invisible to most onlookers.

Employment patterns also revealed the importance of gender in shaping *hinmin* options and life experiences. Just as in making and building, moving and serving work was overwhelmingly divided by gender, with men dominating in transportation and women in serving. Only in a few areas such as entertainment, bathhouses, and blind healing did one find a genuine mix of men and women. The inherent nature of the work accounted for some of the differences: men dominated in jobs that required greater physical strength, women in those that required less strength and sometimes in those requiring finesse. Often, social values were more important in determining whether men or women dominated a profession. The day's norms dictated that men be household heads and that they be paid more. Thus, part-time or irregular work usually went to women, who were expected to spend most of their time at home as unpaid mothers and housewives. Females who worked full-time—as waiters or as sex workers, just as in factory labor—often were young and their wages trailed those of men. In 1903 when male metal workers averaged fifty-two sen a day and day laborers forty sen, the average female textile worker earned twenty sen and the female waiter about eight sen.[146] When one averages wages for the representative occupations shown in tables 2 through 5, the daily income differences, equalized at 1900 rates, are dramatic. The predominantly female factory worker and server categories averaged about twenty-six sen, compared to more than forty-nine sen in the male-preponderant builder and mover categories.[147] Similarly, a survey of nearly 25,000 textile factory workers in the Osaka-Kobe region in 1903 found that men's wages averaged 50 percent higher than those of women; while almost four of every ten men made more than thirty sen a day, only 13 percent of women did.[148] It would be simplistic to say that women were valued less, but the data are consistent in pointing to a single truth: gender was crucial in deciding who got which jobs at what pay levels.

The most obvious feature of *kasō shakai* work was low pay, for everyone. The economic historian Mori Kiichi says that most workers in the late 1890s had no money for cigarettes or entertainment, no funds to give children an education, and no resources to assure basic health and happiness, not because they spent too few hours working or because their work was unskilled or nonessential, but because employers did not pay a living wage.[149] A labor journal survey of more than seventy workers in the late 1890s found only ten with enough income to cover monthly expenses.[150] When the *Niroku* writer said in 1900 that it would be "futile" to talk about finding "legal occupations" for unlicensed prostitutes because employers would not hire them,[151] he could have said the same about asking employers to pay laborers what the social or productive value of their work actually warranted. And that was as true at the end of Meiji as it was at the beginning, according to the economic historian Alan H. Gleason, who found "no perceptible improvement in real wages" for the "less privileged groups" between the onset of Meiji and 1906. His data suggest that real wages actually were higher in 1885 than they were two decades later.[152] The single most anxiety-producing problem for many *hinmin* was that their ten- and twelve-year-old children could not attend school because their earnings were necessary to put food on the table. That would not have been the case if adults had been paid what their work was worth. Women may have been paid less than men, but even the men received too little to enable their families to survive.

CHAPTER 4

Making a Life
At Home

The wind at a time of crisis: cold, cold. . . . The wind that blows through this world is harsh.

—*Enka* singer Soeda Azembō[1]

Thousands of scenes unfolded each day in the late Meiji *hinminkutsu.* Children frolicked and fought along street sides and alleys; sometimes they foraged for food, sometimes they fed the birds. Day laborers gathered at recruitment sites on sunny mornings and drank at cheap bars on stormy mornings. Ambitious boys scarfed down some rice, then headed off to sell newspapers before returning to share their earnings with family members and heading to school. Young mothers mended clothes and made matchbox coverings after the others left for work, nursing their babies as they chatted with other women on the way back from buying the evening's food; some of them went out, stealthily, in the evening to do sex work. On festival days, families walked together to the nearby shrine to watch lion dancers and sample rice cakes. There was no "representative" scenario for the *hinmin* class, any more than there was for the middle class and the rich. A highly typical day for our Ueki family, however, would have followed a scenario that went something like the following.[2]

It is 5:30 on a Thursday morning, August 8, 1901, in their one-room Fukagawa *nagaya,* not far from the smoky factory district. Already the day is sunny and steamy. Noriko, the mother, is in the alley behind their apartment cooking rice gruel and shredding a strip of seaweed for breakfast. She wipes sweat from her brow and moves quietly, trying not to disturb Hidetoshi and their son Tōru. Half an hour later, they too arise, awakened by the rattling sounds of the night soil collector. They pull on pants and stumble out to the alley, where they find enough water left in Noriko's bowl to splash away the night's sweat. Back in the cluttered apartment (how could it not be cluttered, with three, some days four, people in 120 square feet?), Hidetoshi lowers himself to the low table, lights a cigarette stub from the previous night, and glances at headlines in the *Yorozu Chōhō* newspaper, which, at a sen a day, is one of the household's few luxuries.³ Too groggy for much conversation, he grunts while downing his gruel that it might be fun to go to next week's Tomioka Hachimangū shrine festival and toss water at the portable shrines. Fifteen-year-old Tōru agrees, then grumbles that what he really wants is for his foreman to "stop being a turd." Noriko is silent this morning. She is worried about the children: Why can't we scrape together enough to let Tōru quit at the print shop and go to school? Why does Eiko—only thirteen—have to live away, in the spinning factory dorm? What will happen when the children grow up without an education? This is the modern era, after all; growing up without schooling can be a real problem.

After Hidetoshi and Tōru leave for work (a fifteen-minute walk for Hidetoshi, twenty for Tōru), Noriko clears the table and sets about her morning routine. Dishes are washed with water from the well at the end of the street, the ragged futon and patched mosquito net are stacked in a corner, and what room straightening she can do in such a tiny space is finished quickly. There are not many bed clothes to worry about, since Hidetoshi and Tōru both sleep nearly naked on these stifling late summer nights. ("*Ittai!* Did it even get below eighty last night?") A two-drawer chest accommodates the family's clothes, a shelf holds their dishes and utensils, and a low table serves for eating, working, and chatting. Papers and odds and ends are in piles along the wall and in the earthen entranceway. Next, Noriko goes to the well, where she chats for a few minutes with other wives, then washes out some clothes in the alley and hangs them on rods behind the apartment. Then, for an hour, she sews patches on the sleeves of the shirt that Tōru is not wearing today and darns a pair of Hidetoshi's socks. The chores done, she begins rolling cigarettes, the side job that pays each month's two-yen rent. Today she is interrupted several times by vendors: a tofu man a little after 10:00, an umbrella mender later, and a fish monger early in the afternoon, but she always declines. She would love some fish, and the umbrella is broken, but there is no money. Her work brings in a pittance, but she worries as she rolls the cigarettes about what the family would do if she got sick—or even worse, pregnant—and had to stop the work or find a way to abort the child.

Midway through the afternoon, Noriko pushes the tobacco box under the table and heads down the street to the *nagaya*'s resident overseer (*ōya*) to pay the daily rent, wishing there were enough in the till to let them pay weekly or even biweekly like one of their neighbors has begun doing. Maybe next year. Then it is off to a leftover food shop three streets away to buy some rice and miso soup that young military trainees did not eat yesterday. Saving on that, she may be able to afford a small cube of tofu (not the fresh kind the vendor offered) or a scrap of meat to vary the evening meal. She does not have to buy as much today because Hidetoshi has to stay overnight at the firm where he does errands; she and Tōru will eat alone. The afternoon's main diversion is chatting with the line of housewives waiting for leftover food. They are not relatives, not necessarily people she would have chosen as friends, but she sees them often and they share life experiences. There are no patronizing outsiders to defer to when they talk, no need to explain the daily survival compromises. Their husbands too sneak a few things from the boss now and then.

This particular evening also brings a bit of respite. Tōru gets home at 6:30, earlier than usual, and after the quick meal, the two of them go to the public bath, where a few sen buys a soaking for sore muscles. Then, because the apartment has not cooled down from today's 91-degree humid heat, they walk to old Eitaibashi, which was rebuilt four years ago as Tokyo's first iron bridge. The streets are alive here, at the Sumida River crossing, with hundreds of stalls selling cheap things they cannot buy and acrobats and singers competing for coins. A blind man hawks massages, and a lute player diverts them briefly, until the echoes of the Fukagawa Fudō Temple half a mile say they had better head home. Back in the dusky apartment, they take their clothes off without saying much, spread out the futon, climb under the holey mosquito netting, and close their eyes. Tōru falls asleep immediately, but worries keep Noriko awake. Her mind wanders to Hidetoshi: was he able to sneak a few charcoal bricks today? There are none left at home. (*"Ittai,* have I lost all conscience about stealing?") How about Eiko? Is her foreman abusing her? Is she getting enough to eat? Exhaustion finally erases the dark thoughts. She falls asleep.

As Noriko's long day suggests, *hinminkutsu* life amounted to more than earning money. Journalists described the poor man's life as a mindless cycle: getting up, washing, having breakfast, going to work, coming home, eating, bathing (sometimes), going to sleep, starting again when the sun rose. It was a life where "every day he did the same."[4] But the reality was more interesting. Scarcity may have compelled people to spend more time than they would have liked doing—and thinking about—unfulfilling jobs, but other issues consumed them too. There were families to create, nurture, and rear. There were living spaces to secure and tend to. There were meals to cook, budgets to balance, rents and taxes to pay (and curse), education to consider, even leisure moments to plan. The *hinmin* had an expansive world away from the job, a life to be planned and ordered if work were to have any meaning. The multifarious ways in which those in the *kasō shakai* constructed the human side of life will be the focus of this chapter.

"Family" Matters

Most literature about the late Meiji poor takes family life as the norm, as does this chapter's description of the Uekis. The cities may have hosted great numbers of single *hinmin*—widows, widowers, orphaned children, and the tens of thousands of unmarried males who poured into the city from the farms—but the standard accounts placed the poor in families. It was not an idyllic view, nor did journalists expect *kasō shakai* families to conform to middle-class social and ethical norms. But the writers nonetheless pictured their "unfortunate" fellows consistently as members of family units. *Tokyo Puck's* writers were typical. *Hinmin* life attracted their interest almost weekly, and nearly all the sketches depicted some combination of mothers, fathers, and children. There were nursing mothers and chatting mothers, a couple lying together on a sweat-drenched futon, drunken fathers haranguing children, mothers holding infants while they hung out the wash, a couple teaching their child to pick pockets. One of *Puck*'s most poignant cartoons showed five children in a ramshackle house clamoring for their mother's attention, two of them at her breasts, while the father begged Cupid to stop making them produce children. Cupid responded that he had power only to make couples "intimate" (*shinmitsu*).[5] The subjects of these cartoons were poor; they usually were benighted. Sometimes they were lecherous, but they lived together as families. The Meiji Civil Code of 1898 likewise defined households as parent-child units in which the child is "subject to the parental power of his father."[6]

The evidence, however, suggested a messier reality for the *kasō shakai* world, where the married-couple-with-children unit was far from the norm. The tens of thousands of male immigrants to the city, for example, generally lived alone or with other single men, but they were not the only challenges to the stereotype. Male-female pairings often were informal and fluid, and even parent-child groupings tended to be unstable. One reason for this lay in the wide acceptance of divorce as normal. In contrast to the low divorce rates for which Japan would be known in the late twentieth century, the late Meiji rates were among the world's highest, with nearly 35 percent of marriages resulting in

A *Tokyo Puck* cartoonist (November 10, 1908) reinforced the generally inaccurate but popular notion that poor families had many children. To the father's question, "Why do you give me so many children?" Cupid replies, "My only work is to make husbands and wives intimate, not to worry about what comes after. Goodbye." Courtesy of University of Tokyo Graduate Schools for Law and Politics, Center for Modern Japanese Legal and Political Documents, Meiji Shimbun Zasshi Bunko.

divorce before the rate began to decline after 1898. In the words of one mid-Meiji European diplomat, "The knot is loosely tied and may be easily unfastened."[7] Of special relevance was that the highest divorce rates occurred among the poor, with rural regions having more breakups than urban areas and *kasō shakai* neighborhoods more than other parts of the cities. A second reason for family fluidity likely lay in the inequality of gender relationships in a world where male dominance was regarded as "natural" and husbands were excused for abusive behavior or unfaithfulness. A writer for *Yorozu Chōhō* in the spring of 1900 said the family system was imperiled by a "dark and impure" situation in which "constancy and chastity on the part of wives are strictly demanded" while "husbands are little blamed for acts of conjugal faithlessness."[8] "What is a woman but a man's plaything?" echoed a *Heimin Shinbun* writer, citing examples of a Fukagawa tenement resident who forced his wife into prostitution and a nurse who went mad as a result of male unfaithfulness.[9]

The most important cause of family fluidity was poverty itself, which, said Nakagawa Kiyoshi, caused "extreme mobility" in *hinmin* neighborhoods. Low wages undercut loyalty to jobs, and abysmal housing conditions robbed people of attachment to their living spaces, so *hinmin* "rarely stayed long in any one house," he said. Always on the move and always pressured by the demands of employers, they had a hard time nurturing steady relationships, either among peers or at home.[10] One result was that large numbers of unrelated people cohabited, sharing apartments for no reason except that fate had placed them in a given place at a certain time. It was common, said a journalist studying life in Tokyo's Shitaya area in the 1890s, for four or five people with no ties except poverty and proximity to "have their fortunes mixed together" in a shared *nagaya* apartment.[11] As late as 1908, another reporter described people living together, "two or three families in a little shabby hut in the most unhealthy manner."[12] Even when relatives lived together, they often invited one or more unrelated people to stay with them to "help offset the cost of firewood or oil."[13] It was common, in other words, for economics rather than family ties to dictate living arrangements.

Moreover, as Yokoyama found in 1899, there was a strong chance that even couples who lived together with children eschewed traditional relationships. Most couples, he said, simply cohabited without worrying about the formalities of marriage. He described one neighborhood with "scores of children . . . whose names appear only in a policeman's notebook," never in an official ward registry. Sometimes couples were too embarrassed by their circumstances to sign a local registry, and some preferred anonymity so that authorities could not find them. More often they were too preoccupied with the survival struggle to think about legal formalities; sometimes they intentionally flouted the laws of a society that treated them as outsiders.[14] The early reporter Suzuki Umeshirō blamed sexual laxity and moral failure for the fluidity; he found the frequency with which young people in the slums of Osaka had sex—and children—"uncivilized and nonsensical," too much like the "American way."[15] The percentage of stable households increased with the passing of years, particularly as factory workers in particular developed "a desire to settle into the fabric of the capital's city life and a sense of family-centredness" in the last Meiji decade.[16] Nonetheless, a full 40 percent of *kasō shakai* couples had common law marriages as late as 1911–1912.[17]

Almost every commentator saw this deviation from supposed norms in living arrangements as unhealthy. Yokoyama thought unsettled family patterns triggered household quarrels, which in turn led to breakups and made orphans of children.[18] He accused many women of showing "little care or kindness toward their husbands" and squandering money because of their lack of commitment to the family relationship; the "willful and selfish" men, he said, were just as bad.[19] In the 1890s, Tokyo Poorhouse director Adachi Kenchū contended that a major cause of juvenile delinquency was the "ease with which members of the lower class married and separated," abandoning children when they changed partners.[20] Even the sympathetic *Heimin Shinbun* saw family fluidity as destructive of human wholeness in a 1904 essay, arguing that income equality would allow couples to stay together, to concentrate on love and relationships rather than "those life problems of food and clothing."[21] These writers' worries may have been overly colored by middle-class stereotypes of what a "household" ought to look like, but there was no denying either the fluidity of household arrangements or the negative consequences that often flowed from instability. Weak commitments put "the family unit itself into distress," Nakagawa said.[22]

Children and School

Descriptions of the *kasō shakai* world overflowed with children: playing and working on the streets and alleys, spinning and sweeping up in factories, tugging at Mother's hem or sucking at her breast back at home. Middle-class writers talked much about the laxity with which *hinmin* children were reared. Two social work pioneers set the tone when they explained why they were opening a day care center at the beginning of the twentieth century: "The children roam the trashy streets from infancy. . . . Their environment is filled with evil and temptation, which increases their misfortune. When they grow older they fall into crime."[23] One of the period's more gripping *Tokyo Puck* cartoons captured the common view with its depiction of a hairy, bulbous-nosed couple on the left—the man holding a jug of wine, the mother drinking from a cup—carrying a child who screams "Right or left?" as an official on the right tries to pry him away. The caption explains that the official wants to take the child to school, but his *hinmin* parents "teach pickpocketing and pilfering."[24] The visiting British sociologist Beatrice Webb said in 1911 that the worst thing in Japan's slums was "the neglected state of the children." Too many, she said, had "sores, bad eyes, and other signs of neglect." Worst of all, so many of them did not go to school.[25]

There was truth in the accounts of parental neglect; no one denies that some parents abandoned offspring or that some families were dysfunctional. The reality, however, was a great deal more complicated. If neglected children roamed city streets, it was usually not due to parental indifference or chicanery. Most often, it reflected the lack of choices. Both parents and older siblings had to work long hours to meet the budget, relatives who would have looked after children in the village were nonexistent, and there was no money for child care even if it had been available. Parents did not have to worry that officials would remove their children to poorhouses or foster homes as the Americans might have done,[26] but life's economic realities took away their parenting options anyway. Some spinning mills allowed mothers to bring small children with them to play along the edges of the mill floor, but workers in most trades had to leave the children at home, and even the mills permitted children only in the daytime. For those working the night shift, there was nothing but to leave the children at home, where in the best situations the "children cried, wanting to go back to their village home," and in the worst, they took to the streets.[27] Sometimes, as the next chapter will show, they found crime: shoplifting, pickpocketing, grabbing grapes or sweets from street merchants, taking coins that worshipers had tossed into temple boxes. But the great majority of children neither huddled alone at home nor created trouble on the streets. They spent their hours working, sometimes at home or on the street, often at nearby factories and shops. In one survey of Osaka workers, children under the age of

If one believed the *Tokyo Puck* cartoonist (November 20, 1908), poor parents taught their children to be criminals despite the government's best efforts to get children into school. The truth was that most parents desperately wanted an education for their children, while officials, industrialists, and businessmen made school unreachable. Courtesy of University of Tokyo Graduate Schools for Law and Politics, Center for Modern Japanese Legal and Political Documents, Meiji Shimbun Zasshi Bunko.

sixteen made up a quarter of all umbrella makers, a fifth of entertainers, 45 percent of rag pickers, and a full 59 percent of match and matchbox makers. Nearly three of every five beggars also were under sixteen, children working a job that, while despised, was a job nonetheless.[28] The poverty that plagued parents plagued the children too. Once they passed the age of ten, most children worked, or the family did not eat. That left limited time for mischief.

A few of the young children found a haven in the four compulsory years of education.[29] But since enrollment was not free, most *kasō shakai* children had to forgo even that. Indeed, school was the most worrisome sphere of all for many *hinmin* families. Historians describe education as one Meiji Japan's great success stories, with good reason, given the constant rise in school attendance and literacy figures after the government's adoption of the world's first compulsory universal education system in 1872. There was justifiable pride in data claiming, for example, that by 1891 two-thirds of the nation's males and a third of its females had at least functional literacy, and that by the beginning of the 1900s, 94 percent of men and 82 percent of women could read.[30] But the brightness of such figures made the *hinmin* reality even darker, because it was their offspring who made up most of the uneducated tenth. As Yokoyama pointed out late in the 1890s, "Japanese workers cannot afford to set aside any sum for education in their living expenses, although they need to."[31] In 1902 the reporter Harada Tōfū found it "natural" that the "poor as a whole never have an education" because "they never have any leeway in matters of food and clothing."[32] And a year later, the first large official survey of conditions among factory workers, *Shokkō jijō,* reported that match factory workers, in particular, were "extremely poor and uneducated," with illiterate parents "utterly lacking a commitment to education."[33]

The *Shokkō jijō* evaluation of parents is debatable, but its data about *hinmin* illiteracy is unassailable. Until the turn of the century, Tokyo's educational figures lagged behind those in the rest of the nation, mainly because of the huge numbers of immigrants living in the city slums. Urban regulations exempted working *hinmin* children from school attendance, in part because the leaders of industry did not want to lose their cheap labor. The fact that many thousands of poor families never registered with city offices made it impossible for authorities to enforce compulsory education laws in the poverty pockets even if they wanted to. It was hardly surprising then that an army survey of twenty-year-old males in 1904 found that the Fukagawa/Honjo/Asakusa region was one of only four in the entire country where literacy rates actually had declined across the previous five years.[34] The situation was better in Osaka, but even there illiteracy rates in industrial areas were twice what they were in the city's commercial areas, and a late 1890s survey of twenty factories found more than a third of all workers wholly uneducated, with only one young worker in twenty having had four years of school.[35] As late as 1911, more than four thousand Osaka children of elementary school age were officially exempted from school attendance due to "poverty."[36] School attendance simply was not an option for vast numbers of *hinmin* teenagers until the very last years of the Meiji era.

The primary reason for nonattendance obviously was money. As the Ueki family illustrated, most *hinmin* households could not survive without their children's work income. After putting the father's and mother's incomes together at the end of a twenty-five-day work month, most *hinmin* could come up with no more than two-thirds of what they needed for food, housing, and clothing. The resultant equation was simple: everyone works or everyone starves. And even if they could have scraped by without the children's income, they still could not have afforded the school fees. The law called for every child to be in school, and the Education Ministry recommended in 1900 that education be free, but limited income and official priorities meant that Tokyo's hard-pressed schools would continue to charge each child a hard-to-pay fee of twenty sen a month in the early 1900s.[37] Yokoyama despaired of what this reality portended for the future of poor families. Without education, he predicted, the offspring will repeat the cycle and "grow up to become the poor of society. Some may become criminals."[38] He agreed, however, that families had no choice.

It was not merely *hinmin* financial difficulties, however, that kept children out of school. Official funding and commitment to class-free universal education also were lacking. A survey in 1896 concluded that ninety new schools would be needed if Tokyo were to educate all the children not attending classes and that the government lacked the means to build those.[39] Nor were many officials overly concerned about whether *kasō shakai* children received adequate schooling (or even any schooling). There was wide skepticism about whether poor children were as worthy—or as capable—as the rest of the student population. One essayist sniffed in 1899 that teaching English in particular was "not only superfluous but positively injurious" for poor children, because they could not be expected to stay in school long enough to become proficient, and English would "make them conceited."[40] There was fear too of what might happen if schooling put subversive thoughts into the heads of the masses. Many officials actually preferred to leave poor children uneducated, said Yokoyama, lest they "cultivate any political ideas." If education were to spread widely among the *kasō shakai,* he predicted, "people of the lower classes" would become "aware that they themselves are members of society" and officials would "not be able to remain as serene as they are today."[41]

The most important inhibitor probably was the ideological collusion of officials and industrialists, both of whom were committed to ensuring business profitability in order to advance Japan's economy. As David Ambaras, a student of juvenile delinquency in this period, has pointed out, even the Ministry of Education eschewed efforts to bring child labor to a halt.[42] And that was because the influence-wielding business leaders—men who actually might have gained the most from worker literacy—feared that the loss of cheap child labor would undercut profit margins. Keeping wages low, in other words, was more important than ensuring literacy. When a private educational group surveyed Osaka firms in the mid-1890s, it found that 27 percent of all workers were of school age, and 94 percent of those children had received little or no education. But the managers, it concluded, did not care. A dozen factories reported that they were trying to make some kind of education available to children, but their efforts were halfhearted and skimpy, and more than fifty failed to respond or reported no efforts at all, prompting the surveyors to exclaim, "Good heavens! Do they regard education as useless?"[43] After making his own "close and personal observations" of those same factories, Yokoyama drew a similar conclusion. He found several initiatives by reformist citizens to get education into the factory system, but management's indifference—or outright opposition—doomed all but an exception or two. Many companies, including Shibusawa Eiichi's industry-leading Osaka Spinning Mill, ballyhooed their education programs but provided scant evidence that they were offering anything other than occasional lectures on ethics or a few classes on sewing or math at the end of the boys' and girls' eleven-hour workdays. "A system of instruction for factory workers seems to exist in form only," said the crusading journalist.[44]

This was not, however, for lack of effort by reformers. An important feature of the last two Meiji decades was the energy that a few officials and private citizens put into the education problem, with results that showed both the potential of *hinmin* education and the difficulty of helping more than a small minority of poor children as long as child labor was legal and schools charged fees. Experimental projects ranged from factory-sponsored learning centers (Yokoyama's exceptions) to a few schools designed specifically for *hinmin*.[45] In the city of Sakai near Osaka, for example, four night schools were set up in the mid-1890s for rug weavers through the efforts of a chamber of commerce president who had been impressed by American education when he visited the Chicago World's Fair in 1893. Despite opposition from factory managers and workers, who resented having to go to classes at the end of twelve-hour shifts, the school was kept alive for several years by a group of idealists who persuaded government officials and grudging factory owners to provide funding; when Yokoyama made his survey in 1898, he found 1,600 workers studying math, writing, and civics.[46] In Tokyo, several private reformers created schools for poor children. In the late 1890s, for example, Shin'ami-chō was home to two private schools, one run by a church and one by an "old man named Soda Tadashi." Soda's school charged just five *rin* a day and reminded Yokoyama of a Tokugawa-era temple school (*terakoya*) because of its old-fashioned methods, while the church school offered a full curriculum (including religion) to between twenty and thirty students. Samegahashi slum also had two schools, one of them operated by the temple Hōzōji. And Mannen-chō had a "cooperative night school" run by a high school principal named Watanabe with the backing of several private philanthropists; it offered courses in reading, math, calligraphy, and civics.[47]

The most ambitious reform effort, which came at the beginning of the twentieth century, illustrated both the vision of reformers and the difficulty of reaching significant numbers of *hinmin* with education. In 1903, the city of Tokyo opened, in Mannen-chō, the first of an ambitious system of "free schools" intended to provide tuition-free education to poor children along with social services for their families.[48] Assisted by a gift from the imperial family, the school provided children with baths, clothes, school supplies, medical treatment, and limited wage-earning opportunities, in addition to their studies. Two more such schools were opened three years later, and by 1913, Tokyo had ten such schools. There were downsides to these projects: the loss of the child's factory wages, the hardship imposed on *hinminkutsu* residents when hundreds of homes were torn down to make way for the free schools, the embarrassing stigma of being in what was popularly labeled a "pauper school," and the small percentage of the city's poor children who actually were served. But for that small number, they were beacons of hope. A handful of *hinmin* day care centers also sprang up, pioneered in 1900 by Futaba Yōchien, which offered schooling to sixteen children from Tokyo's sprawling Samegahashi slum.[49] Japan had ten such programs, sometimes called "pauper's kindergartens" (*hinmin yōchien*), by 1912: in Tokyo, Kobe, and Osaka.[50] These programs trod a lonely path, but they illustrated two contrasting truths: the idealism of a cadre of reformers who took *hinmin* education seriously, balanced by the impossibility of making education available to the great majority of poor children, given the social and economic climate.

Indeed, the educational picture for most poor children remained grim to the end of Meiji, despite the pockets of progress. While official statistics had more than 95 percent of school-aged children across Japan enrolled in elementary schools by 1906, *hinmin* children remained largely uneducated. Brian Platt's studies of rural school districts show that enrollment data often provided a misleading picture of actual attendance in village schools.[51] The same was true in *hinminkutsu* regions, where working children continued to be exempted from school and where a full 40 percent of families remained unregistered even in the 1910s.[52] Impressive as special projects such as the Sakai factory school and Tokyo's free schools were, they touched a small minority of *hinmin* youths. The more common *hinmin* family experience in the late Meiji years was that of a household described in Futaba Yōchien's 1908 annual report, where three girls lived with their parents in a nine-by-twelve-foot room without plumbing. One daughter was "gravely ill and unable to work"; the other two and their mother made a total of twenty-one sen a day at a cigarette factory. Education? It was out of the question or, in the words of Nakagawa, "simply nil" (*kaimu*).[53]

Putting Food on the Table

The pioneer folklorist Yanagita Kunio identified three ways in which the changes of the Meiji era affected Japanese food consumption patterns: everyone started talking about food, hot foods became popular, and people began consuming sweets. He said the Meiji years also brought a new consciousness of nutrition, which squared in ironic ways with the growing popularity of candies, meats, and sweeter fruits. After the 1890s, he noted, "it became necessary to attach the four characters *jiyō eisei* (nutritious and healthy) to candy labels."[54] Newspapers and journals in the late Meiji years bore him out, with regular stories on food, food preparation, and nutrition. Columnists touted the virtues and science behind healthy eating with an avidity that would have made them comfortable among twenty-first-century foodies. When a 1905 *"Katei kagaku"* (home science) column at the paper *Nihon* explained the scientific difference between regular rice (*kome*) and glutinous rice (*mochi*), as well as the varied ways in which salted and dried fish could be prepared, it was following the day's standard journalistic practice.[55] Family pages and homemaking columns accompanied women into the press at the beginning of the 1900s, and food joined household management as the core content. Food, to middle-class Japanese in the early 1900s, became a conscious part of good living.

Members of *hinmin* households would have been aware of these changes because they read newspapers, but their knowledge necessarily remained abstract, because food, for them, was sustenance and little more, a necessity that took pains to acquire and provided little nourishment for the senses. A look at family budgets shows that food consumed a whopping seven-tenths of the monthly income in most poor households, not because people ate well but because their wages were so small. In the often-cited 1888 study of Osaka's Nago-chō, people spent 70 percent on food and drink; a decade later official surveys showed that the urban *hinmin* generally were spending even more, 72 percent, on food, with some occupation groups above 77 percent. In 1910, near the era's end, the figure had dropped only marginally, to 65 percent. The thing that made these figures particularly remarkable was the contrast to what Nakagawa calls the "new middle class" (*shin chūkansō*), which in both 1898 and 1910 spent a full 20 percent less of their budget on food and drink.[56] In study after study, poor families were found to spend more than three times as much on food as they did on rent, sometimes four or five times as much.

Nor did their menus contain luxury or superfluity. In the early 1890s, one report said that Honjo residents mostly ate rice gruel and *kirazu*, the leftover residue from making tofu, while those in Shitaya and Fukagawa struggled to survive on cheap foreign (i.e., inferior) rice and those tofu lees.[57] Yokoyama provided detailed budgets for a variety of late-1890s families: a rickshaw puller, an ironworker, a lathe operator, a finisher, and a performer. The lists show less variety in their eating than in their jobs. All spent more than half of their food budget on rice, about a fifth on fish, and a smattering on miso, bean paste, bonito flakes, soy sauce, vegetables, and "side dishes" such as pickled radish. That was it, except for saké or wine, which almost always occupied its own small space in the budget, a sign to middle-class pundits of profligacy, an indication to sensible souls that even hard-pressed life required respite.[58] Other observers discovered a few more items. Some mentioned sweet potatoes and tofu leavings mixed with a bit of rice, some observed the poor buying "scraps of greens from city markets,"[59] some noticed "grilled *katsura*,"[60] and some the fish entrails, smelly horsemeat, and beef bladders that rickshaw pullers scarfed down on the run. The most striking thing about the lists is their bare-bones quality. When Tanizaki described the menus in the poor middle-class home of his childhood, he waxed eloquent about fish, meats, and vegetables prepared with sauces and crusts. There was nothing of this sort on the tables of the *hinmin*. "Sardines or cod?" asked the poor folks' singer Azembō; "times are too tough for that fine fare." Instead it was "rice and raw saké."[61] And the quality was as limited as the variety, particularly when greedy merchants cut corners in preparing and selling food. A notorious example of what the *hinmin* had to face in buying food came in a 1900 scandal, when officials discovered vendors diluting cheap rice with salt and sand.[62]

The energy *hinmin* families put into finding inexpensive food said as much about their ingenuity as it did about the state of their budgets. Matsubara noticed that many poor people shopped at night, either because they had to work during the day or because prices dropped late in the day. He said that the poor were constantly on the lookout for special deals, pointing to temple staffers at Sengakuji in Takanawa who expressed surprise at the huge numbers who showed up for a giveaway of surplus rice. "I can't believe how little those benefactors knew about the *hinmin*," he quipped.[63] Nothing illustrated the intensity of the quest for affordable food better than the popularity of leftover food shops. In the early Meiji years, military schools and army barracks sometimes would give away food that their residents had not eaten; after the 1890s, they began selling the leftovers on consignment to vendors for up to forty yen a month, an amount that rose to as much as one hundred yen by the turn of the century. The vendors in turn sold the food cheaply to *hinminkutsu* residents: a *rin* for a plate of leftover vegetables, two *rin* for a bowl of miso, a sen for four bowls of leftover rice. (By way of comparison, a kilogram of standard white rice at this time averaged 1.12 yen at regular stores, a hundred grams of tea 8.3 sen, a cup of coffee 2.0 sen, a dish of broiled eel 30 sen.[64]) The journal *Fūzoku Gahō* estimated that 7 percent of slum dwellers bought from the leftover rice shops in 1898, adding that when "there was not enough of the leftover rice, they had to endure for one or two days on an empty stomach."[65]

To understand how leftover shopping worked, Matsubara took a job at one of the shops early in the 1890s for twenty-five sen a week. The store was ramshackle, he said, a few mats spread out in the front yard of a house whose eaves were "sodden and rotting," with an inner yard "littered with tubs, bottles, jars, pitchers, and anything that might serve to have refuse rice put into it." Customers came in droves. On a typical day, Matsubara said, "it was pitiful to see with what joy we who carried this stale food were welcomed by the waiting crowd." Once, when no leftover food could be secured for three days, the shoppers became desperate. When he begged managers at the military college to come up with extra food of some kind, "no matter what," they said all they had was spoiled bean paste and some old potatoes that were "really only good to feed the pigs or to be used for manure," plus a bit of rice and "some dregs of *miso*" soup. Matsubara took it and was floored by the "keen rivalry" for even that. The old rice was called "soldiers' rice" (*heitai meshi*) because of its origins, or "scorched rice" because it came from the bottom of the cooking kettle, and other leftover foods were given idiosyncratic names such as "tiger's skin" (*tora no kawa,* for the food's color) or "plant stub" (*kirikabu*). After his stint at the shop, Matsubara reflected that the "uttermost depth of poverty" lay not in shivering through a cold winter, or in having to wear rags, but in being "obliged to use the refuse of rice kitchens."[66] These shops declined in the last Meiji years, but some remained into the 1920s, providing day laborers with what the novelist Kawabata Yasunari called the "leftovers of leftovers."[67]

Hinmin did not always eat at home, particularly if they were not part of a family unit. The underclass included high percentages of unconnected people: single young men, widows and widowers, students, day laborers with no interest in marriage, wanderers and beggars of many types, and other urban "immigrants [who] in many cases ate all their meals out."[68] For them, as well as for rickshaw pullers, carters, deliverymen, and others working on the streets, survival depended on the cities' thousands of cheap restaurants, including everything from *izakaya* or grogshops, "where instead of chairs there are soy sauce barrels,"[69] to noodle stalls. Some of these were neat and clean, while others were cluttered and unsanitary; they all served cheap food. In one journalist's telling, the "lower grade" restaurants in Tokyo often were marked by "narrow sloppy yards, choked up drains, low roofs, broken windows and . . . an evil, pestilential smell"; they were places where "the mistress of the house goes about with unkempt hair and looks like a ghost, the maids look dirty, . . . and all day long there is no end of brawling."[70] Another reporter said that when one stepped into one of the cheap spots, particularly late at night, "your nose is attacked by the stinging smell of bad saké and boiling flesh," all served up by noisy "maid-servants of ugly face."[71] The food was inexpensive and plentiful, heavy on noodles, horse meat, and "other cheap dishes," often heavily spiced with red pepper "to disguise any unpleasant taste." The most surprising menu item at some cheap spots was blowfish (*fugu*), which was sold cheaply despite its savory taste because, being poisonous if not prepared correctly, it made most people "afraid to eat it." The waiters may not have been known for refinement, but visitors often commented on how many of them had an "inexhaustible stock of good nature, ever ready to burst out in a ringing laugh."[72]

None of the eating establishments were more convivial than the drinking spots near every *hinminkutsu* and factory, nor did any draw more public comment. The journalist Fujimoto Taizō was amused by one Asakusa place, which made its own brandy and whiskey and had a notice on the wall: "Up to 3 glasses . . . can be served, and Never More."[73] Observing that "throngs" of poor folks made daily visits to their favorite saké shops, "full of promises of happiness that are never kept," Matsubara quipped: "Who would begrudge them the modest dissipation in which they indulge after a day's hard work, the brief hour of recreation that separates one day's toil from that of the next?"[74] Most observers were less amused and less charitable than Fujimoto and Matsubara. Indeed, one reason the drinking establishments drew so much ink was that commentators typically saw them as symbols of moral decay. Even the urban reformer Seki Hajime, who blamed factory workers' problems on "cold-blooded industrialists," saw a moral failing in the way laborers leaving the factory each day would "gather in saké shops, where they become intoxicated on strong drink" instead of going home to enjoy "the charm of a family circle."[75] Yokoyama was particularly contemptuous of the propensity for drinking. Noting that four-fifths of the urban *hinmin* drank saké, he sniffed that poor people were more afraid of offending their wine dealer (*kabutoya*) than of being unable to pay rents or debts. "Their hardships in life result largely from drinking," he said, adding that "it may be that because they are poor, these slum dwellers seek solace in drink."[76] It is, in fact, not clear that the *kasō shakai* community consumed alcohol in greater quantities than their more affluent peers did. What is clear is that, like everyone else, they regarded saké and *shōchū*, Japan's native drinks, as essentials.[77] Most worried no more about the quality of the drink than they did about the nutrition levels of their food, nor did most of them consume large quantities of alcohol. Budgets allowed neither quantity nor quality. But in both eating and drinking, whether at home or at a restaurant, they did follow a few rules. The beverage or food had to be cheap. It had to be basic. And it had to fill the stomach. Sauces and adornment were not options except on special occasions. If the food and drinking code was rigid, it was the only one *hinmin* incomes allowed. A "good meal," said Matsubara, was a "greater festival" for poor people than a grand dinner for state guests at Japan's icon to modernity, the Rokumeikan Pavilion.[78]

Managing Income

Everything revolved around money for the urban poor: getting it, stretching it, watching it fly away, suffering when it ran out, dreaming about having more. To be classified as *saimin* or "poor people," said a 1912 Home Ministry handbook, one had to be among those "people who barely manage to support themselves day to day with their own income."[79] To comprehend fully how the urban poor experienced the struggle to make ends meet—trying to maintain a semblance of humanity even when they were "uncertain where to sleep at night, worrying all year long about food and clothing, daily on the verge of starvation"[80]—is not possible for a middle-class reader in the twenty-first century, but the effort must be made, since nothing defined everyday *kasō shakai* life more completely than the all-consuming quest for money.

BALANCING INCOME AND EXPENSES

How representative was the Ueki household, where the combined intake of all four family members fell half a yen short of each month's minimum needs? A random sample from nearly two dozen factory workers whose family situations were sketched in *Shokkō jijō* suggests that they were highly typical. Although the incomes of those Kansai area families varied considerably as a result of differences in family size, age, and health, all of them took in somewhere between 0.3 and 1.65 yen less each month than their minimum expenses.[81] A mid-1890s *Rōdō Shinbun* survey of some seventy-five workers' families showed a similar pattern. That study was less complete than the *Shokkō jijō* survey, generally reporting only on the adult male's income, but the story was essentially the same: income seldom matched basic living costs. Drawing on the *Rōdō* survey, Yokoyama provided details on the ways three of the *Rōdō Shinbun* cohort spent their money and why they had such a hard time making ends meet.[82]

One of the respondents, a thirty-six-year-old lathe operator, reported a monthly gap of 7.29 yen, with 16.25 yen coming in and 24.29 yen going out. His family was among the fortunate ones, in certain ways, because while the household had only three people (husband, twenty-eight-year-old wife, five-year-old daughter), they had an unusually large apartment for *hinmin* of the 1890s: three rooms, which rented for an expensive 4 yen a month. The rest of their budget, on the other hand, was bare-bones: rice, vegetables, fish, miso, saké, and *shōyu* for food; a small amount for clothes and sandals; nothing for household items or reading materials; a single yen for the child's expenses; and only two hygiene items: thirty-five sen a month for hairdressing and thirty sen for baths. Even so, their reported income amounted to just 70 percent of their expenses. How did they make ends meet? The survey gave no answer, but the likeliest explanation is that his wife supplemented the family budget by doing piecework or working part-time at a factory.[83] There is little doubt that they also resorted to at least some of the income stretchers that will be discussed below: pawn shops, loans, even petty pilfering.

If the lathe operator's monthly budget produced anxieties, that of his twenty-four-year-old peer who did finishing work must have caused terror. Although the finisher's monthly income (16.38 yen) was roughly the same as that of lathe worker, he had to support not just a twenty-year-old wife and a two-year-old daughter but also his mother and father, both in their sixties. All five lived in two rooms that totaled eight mats (about 144 square feet) and cost less than 2 yen a month for rent. In addition to cutting expenses on rent, they clearly did wonders in making their food stretch since they reported similar expenses to the lathe operator in the rest of their budget, except for spending forty sen on cigarettes and a relatively high seventy-five sen for soup (in addition to *miso*)—an expense that made Yokoyama wonder whether one of the parents might have been ill—as well as twenty sen for a newspaper subscription, something of a rarity among *hinmin* workers in the mid-1890s. Their monthly expenses (21.32 yen) were almost 6 yen more than their reported income. As with the lathe worker, the *Rōdō Shinbun* report failed to explain how the family made up the deficit. Yokoyama concluded simply that it must have been "pitiful and miserable" for five people, two of whom were elderly and probably in poor health, to live on so little.[84]

Table 6. Monthly budgets (in yen): Three mid-1890s families

Lathe operator's family (father, mother, five-year-old child)							
Income:		16.25 yen					
Expenditures:		24.29 yen					
rent	4	rice	7.6	fuel	2.69	vegetables	1.5	fish	1.6
wine	1	miso	0.5	hair	.35	bath	0.3	child	1
misc.	3	(annual items: clothes 6, sandals 3)					

Finisher's family (father, mother, two-year-old child, grandfather, grandmother)							
Income:		16.38 yen					
Expenditures:		20.02 yen					
rent	1.65	rice	7	fuel	1.68	vegetables	1.71	fish	1.8
wine	1.2	miso	1.4	hair	0.38	bath	1	tobacco	0.4
child	0.3	nwsp	0.2	paper	0.15	soup	0.75	assoc. fee	0.2
sugar	0.2						

Iron worker's family (father, mother, twelve-year-old child)							
Income:		25.96 yen (includes 17 yen in "miscellaneous" income: 15 from contract work, 2 from wife)					
Debt:		33.65 yen					
Expenditures:		17.6 yen					
rent	1.75	rice	6.5	fuel	1.3	vegetables	1.5	fish	0.5
miso	0.9	hair	0.35	bath	0.8	tobacco	0.5	child/school	1
misc.	2.5						

From *Rōdō Shinbunsha* survey, in Yokoyama, *Kasō shakai*, 227–230. He identifies the date only as "several years ago." Monthly expense totals are derived by adding the items listed in each worker's expense category; for the lathe operator, 0.75 has been added to the monthly total to account for the annual clothes and sandals item. Two profiles say nothing about the women's income; the iron worker's snapshot lists 2 yen a month from "wife's work."

The survey's third family, headed by a thirty-eight-year-old rifle and machine factory hand who worked an astounding twenty-eight days a month for twelve hours each day, was an outlier: relatively better off on first glance, yet filled with contradictions that showed the complexity of the *hinmin* balance sheet. When one added in unidentified "contract work" and the wife's work, the three-person family took in 25.96 yen a month, more than 8 yen more than their reported expenses. Like the finisher's family, they lived in a cheap (less than 2 yen a month) two-room apartment and spent little on tobacco. In contrast to most families, they listed no expenses for alcohol, but spent a full yen on their twelve-year-old child's education and, most remarkable of all, devoted only half of their budget to food. How well off they actually were, however, was open to question because their budget had unexplained, foreboding spots. The report failed to clarify where the "miscellaneous" income—which made up two-thirds of their monthly earnings—came from or how reliable it was.[85] Even more ominous, they reported heavy debts, owing 12 yen on a loan and having fallen 21.65 yen behind on payments to a pawn shop. Yokoyama adjudged them the "most blessed among factory workers" because they made more than they spent,[86] but the large debt suggests the tenuous quality of life in the *kasō shakai* even for those with marginally more to spend.

Taken together, the *Rōdō Shinbun* survey revealed three shared features of *hinmin* finances: one about what was in family budgets, one about what was not in them, and one about the bottom line. All the budgets included similar, unsurprising things: very low rents and spartan food lists (even though food consumed as much as 70 percent of monthly income), along with a few items that arguably could be called nonessentials such as wine, tobacco, baths, newspaper subscriptions, and haircuts. Anyone trying to find fat in the expenditure columns would have failed. The budget omissions were equally consistent, and they told us as much as the inclusions did. Nowhere, except in small "miscellaneous" categories, did one find any thought about entertainment, no budget included utensils and household items, only one mentioned clothing, none provided for health or emergencies, none mentioned transportation. Nor did a single budget make provision for savings. If an item was likely to allow anything above subsistence living, it was absent. Even with that kind of frugality, the third pattern was that income seldom matched expenses. More than 85 percent of the *Rōdō Shinbun* respondents reported spending more than they made. That meant, said Yokoyama, that "Japanese labor is priced too cheaply to support a livelihood. Labor has no dignity. It is devoid of spirit, of metaphysical meaning."[87] The lathe workers, finishers, and ironworkers might not have put it so abstractly, but they would have agreed: income did not match needs.

BUDGETS: UNEXPECTED PRESSURES

Surveys and government data were powerful indicators of general patterns, but they had little to say about how individual families' situations varied from month to month, or about the tensions parents felt when some unpredictable, unbudgeted development forced them to decide which necessity they would have to withhold from their children this month. Salaries were, of course, the fundamental building blocks of budgets, the core reason that life in the *hinminkutsu* was so difficult. But, like data, salaries did not tell the whole story. In addition to wages, a number of factors outside the family's control, none of them predictable enough to include in financial planning, put special pressures on household budgets, sometimes tearing them to shreds, sometimes sending families over the cliff into disaster. A few occurred often enough to demand special consideration.

Health was one of the unpredictables. For reasons that will be discussed in the next chapter, impoverished people had more sickness than their financially better off peers; they also were more prone to epidemics and medical disasters. Accounts of sickness and accidents taking away a family's ability to earn were legion: a toymaker in poverty-plagued Shitaya who went "insane with grief" after his wife fell ill and disappeared, a Tokyo family left bereft when a man named Yokoyama drank his employer's hydrochloric acid after sickness made it impossible to pay the bills, a rickshaw puller's pregnant wife who nearly starved to death when lung disease took him off the streets.[88] In a world without safety nets, a margin-less world where everyone already worked and there were almost no savings, even a brief wage stoppage could spell disaster. As a father in Kanagawa put it when he and his twenty-one-year-old son fell ill at the same time, "Poverty pursued us and we thought about killing our child." He tried to strangle the son with a headband after lunch one day but was stopped by his younger daughter. "The problems of existence had become too much," said the reporter covering the story.[89]

Inflation was another exigency that mocked family budgets. Economists note that Japan had a "chronic tendency toward monetary inflation" in the late Meiji years, with wholesale prices rising almost continually between 1890 and 1914, by more than 85 percent all told. The paper *Yorozu Chōhō* reported an average price rise of 90 percent on forty staples between January 1887 and January 1900, noting that life was no longer a "happy, easy-going affair" for average citizens.[90] The *hinmin* did not need economists or journalists to tell them what the impact of inflation was on daily budgets. A glance at the prices of a few goods shows its effect on daily staples. A 1.8-liter container of *shōyu* rose from twenty to thirty-two sen—60 percent—between 1897 and 1905. Monthly rent for a three-room *nagaya* (row house) in Itabashi rose 700 percent between 1899 and 1914, from seventy-five sen to 5.2 yen! Rice prices increased by nearly 60 percent between 1897 and 1911.[91] And salt more than *tripled* in cost between 1904 and 1906.[92] What such increases meant for the poor was front and center in the summer of 1906 when a one-sen increase in Tokyo's streetcar fares prompted riotous demonstrations by thousands of citizens, a significant proportion of whom were *hinmin*. Shouting that the fare increase would mean personal ruin, they threw stones "like rain" at passing cars and managed to get the increase delayed, though only for a few months.[93]

A less continuous exigency, war, had a more complex, but frequently deleterious, impact on *kasō shakai* budgets. When Japan went to war with China in 1894 and again with Russia in 1904, some *hinmin* benefited. Newspaper accounts showed new opportunities for rickshaw pullers and others called into the military, and laborers at war-related industries such as the Tokyo Arsenal found their work in heavier demand, while the overall economy received a major boost from the first of the wars, mainly because of the huge indemnity Japan received at its end. But for great numbers of the poor, the papers reported increased financial difficulties. The work of carpenters, plasterers, and gardeners dried up, as home construction went down. *Kichin'yado* lost customers in droves when single men went off to war, prompting them to raise rates for those who remained. Festival and temple dancers and lantern makers reported having to go home hungry many a night because people gave their charitable coins to soldiers instead of to them. Even prostitutes and brothels talked about "unprecedented" drops in business during the Sino-Japanese War.[94] When Japan fought Russia, thousands of weavers lost jobs as men from the poor areas went off to war in disproportionate numbers, and applications to the Tokyo Poor House soared.[95] An English-language writer for *Heimin Shinbun* commented early in the Russo-Japanese War, "The poorest part of the City is quiet and lonely and exhibits a state of absolute poverty everywhere."[96]

Taxes were a serious problem too, a problem from which (unlike war) there was no respite. While the bulk of government revenue came from a land tax, a host of levies were imposed on *kasō shakai* essentials after the middle Meiji years: sugar, liquor, and soy, for example. And a small income tax that began in 1887, combined with local taxes on everything from bicycles to rickshaws to room rentals, added to *hinmin* woes. There may not have been a tax category on *Rōdō Shinbun*'s survey of *hinminkutsu* budgets, but taxes were a flashpoint for slum dwellers, prompting much of the activism that will be discussed in a later chapter. In 1908, for example, an expansion of the commodity tax sparked a rally of ten thousand protesters in Tokyo, and one paper wrote that when the government used "such shameful means to increase taxes," people were "far from ashamed to evade them."[97] The balladeer Soeda Azembō devoted one of his popular songs to taxes, describing a life of "hell and hardships" with "the draft whistling through the paper-paneled door," all followed by "And a tax increase, tax . . ."[98]

A 1910 *Tokyo Puck* cartoon shows the *shotokuzei to iu oni,* or income tax devil, leering over a poor family in a room with cracked walls, demanding their rice, their clothes, and their medicine money, while a frightened father with a baby on his back covered his eyes and a mother tried to keep the devil from stealing her coat.[99] Taxes may have been a small part of the monthly budget but they loomed large in *hinmin* consciousness, because any increase could make the difference between hardship and desperation.

Then there was the worker-be-damned, erratic approach of unregulated employers, which imposed hardships well beyond the mere problem of low wages. Managerial favoritism and capriciousness had a major impact on both the budget and the psyche. Few were as bluntly disdainful of the poor as Furukawa Ichibei, the copper magnate from Ashio, who responded when asked to buy tickets for a famine-relief concert that it would be "a matter of annoyance to buy them. I therefore return them."[100] But in an unregulated era, arbitrary treatment of workers was the norm and it wreaked havoc with budgets. Yokoyama complained about the lack of standards, which allowed factory owners to reward or punish workers by whim. He described one unidentified firm that changed prices monthly and adjusted wages downward whenever it cut prices, throwing employees "into a panic." He said the company's only clear pay standard was "that workers who excel in currying favor with their superiors tend to be advanced."[101] Nor was there any recourse when employers decided to fire someone or cut their wages arbitrarily. One paper described the empty tenements and unhealthy crowding caused in 1908 by cuts in employment and wages: "Suicide, robbery, petty theft and murder are the headlines of the daily press painted in the most brutal fashion!"[102] And the mental toll was exacted on everyone, from the lowly Fukagawa man (named Yamada) found wandering the streets with nothing but soup and flour to eat after he was fired from his job[103] to the labor activist Uchida Tōshichi, who said his bosses' favoritism and arbitrary treatment left him "psychologically on the verge of exploding."[104] Low wages were, without a doubt, the biggest source of budget anxiety. But a wide range of exigencies—health crises, inflation, wars, rising taxes, capricious employers—always loomed, threatening to tear the budget to shreds.

MAKING ENDS MEET

After teaching for six years in the mountain town of Komoro along the Chikuma River, the novelist Shimazaki Tōson commented, "I went out as a teacher; I came back as a student."[105] A few of the more insightful reporters said the

Hinmin would have agreed with this February 10, 1910, cartoon in *Tokyo Puck,* which shows the merciless tax devil stealing food and clothing even though there was no money to repair the cracking walls or care for the sick grandfather. Courtesy of University of Tokyo Graduate Schools for Law and Politics, Center for Modern Japanese Legal and Political Documents, Meiji Shimbun Zasshi Bunko.

same thing about their experiences with the urban *hinmin*. If those families had one thing to teach, it was how to stretch a sen into a yen and a yen into a livelihood, not without anxieties, not without occasional desperation, but with ingenuity and determination. A small percentage of these families managed to balance budgets on a regular basis, even putting a small amount away in savings. The vast majority fell short of that standard, with wages that failed to match life's daily needs. But even they found ways to get by, leaving only a small number to fall into actual destitution. How they made a go of it is one of the most important lessons of this study.

The unlikely twins of theft and charity helped some *hinmin* survive. The errand man Hidetoshi, for example, was far from alone when he stole those charcoal bits from his shop. And charity was important in more than a few *hinmin* lives. Assistance usually came from private sources, since there were no government aid programs for the poor in the Meiji years except the Relief Act (*jukkyū kisoku*) of 1874, which called for "mutual aid and friendship among the people" and provided public assistance only to those "who are completely dispossessed and completely without recourse to other forms of aid."[106] Rich families like the Iwasakis (those who built the grand gardens in Fukagawa) occasionally provided "poor relief,"[107] as did the emperor and empress after disasters. Newspapers sponsored "charity parties" for destitute children on holidays. And a number of charitable institutions were created, by both government and private groups: the Tokyo Poorhouse, the Hakuaisha (forerunner of Japan's Red Cross), the Okayama Orphanage (whose goal was to provide "child relief through communal labor"[108]), several Buddhist lodging houses for urban indigents, a Salvation Army shelter in Hana-chō, the Japan Poor Men's Hospital in Honjo, and the Futaba Nursery School described earlier.[109] Yokoyama also discussed several charitable institutions set up by individual philanthropists such as Ono Tasaburō, an "exceptional" Kanazawa man who went about "clad in soiled, short, closefitting trousers and an equally dirty single undershirt" while creating houses for the blind, aged, and infirm.[110] And the *Shokkō jijō* survey described erratic assistance programs at a few factories.[111] Systemic forms of relief, however, were opposed even by most liberally minded intellectuals as policies that would undermine self-reliance and Japan's economic vitality.[112]

Relief thus was a help for a few, but, like petty pilfering, its impact on the *hinmin* generally was minimal. Individual organizations providing relief were just that: isolated projects that provided help in scattered doses. Yokoyama described the general lack of public concern about poor people in an 1899 complaint about the Diet:

> Money is scarce. Complaints about business depression are heard everywhere. Yet, the Imperial Diet, which ought to provide the country with relief, has been indifferent and has passed a bill to increase land taxes. It has raised postal rates and increased taxes for soy sauce. . . . Among members of the Diet, there is no one who stands by his principles; each pursues his own selfish interests.[113]

In Great Britain and the United States, the two countries Japan looked to most as models of modernity, public discussions of assistance were vigorous. While neither of those countries had adequate relief programs, both did have a public commitment to providing aid to the "truly poor," with a special focus on children. Not so in Japan, where a study found that between 1895 and 1910 an average of only 128 people a year—about half of them aged or infant—received official assistance in the entire city of Tokyo.[114] As the last Meiji decade began, Tokyo had just four schools for poor children, each accommodating fewer than 150 students.[115] Not until 1911, notes Sally Hastings, did officials begin to pay serious attention to the idea of official aid to the poor, and then only because the Great Treason trial, which found several socialists guilty of a plot against the emperor, produced calls for "welfare work to alleviate the social conditions that might generate such opposition."[116] A number of efforts at official poor relief resulted, including labor exchanges in slum areas and a gift of 500,000 yen from the emperor (who lamented that some of his subjects could not "find the means for obtaining medical aid and on that account have to die prematurely") to establish a medical relief agency, the Saiseikai, or Life-saving Society.[117] Until the last year of Meiji, however, *hinmin* understood that to be poor was to have no safety net.

How then did households stretch income to cover needs? The fundamental answer lay in the practice already discussed: relying on spouses and children to supplement the household head's wages. The things that wives made at home to bring in money were beyond enumeration: lampshades, brushes, fans, charcoal briquettes, straw sandals, candle wicks, handkerchiefs, and envelopes. They also sewed *tabi* (digitated socks) and sandal soles, twisted paper strings, colored lithographs, and rolled cigarettes. Some did evening sex work or, if they lived near the pleasure quarters, washed the clothes of prostitutes and their patrons. Classism compounded by sexism meant that their work brought in only a fraction of what their husbands made—for example, a day spent making six thousand match containers paid twelve sen while male day laborers took in twenty-seven sen a day—but those paltry figures made the difference between paying the rent and taking out new loans.[118] The same was true even more of children, who suffered additionally from ageism. If male cotton spinners earned twenty sen a day in the early 1900s and women as little as eleven, female children received six.[119] Yet without those six sen, the family could not have gotten by. That was why one Tokyo educator commented in 1912 that "the children of the slums are truly filial."[120] Their sacrifices enabled families to survive.

That reality also helps to explain one of the era's more perplexing issues: why there was so little public opposition to child labor well into the twentieth century. Certainly it had opponents. The labor leader Takano Fusatarō wrote in 1896 that there was no excuse for imposing harsh labor conditions on "children of tender years" and called child labor "a mockery to our national integrity and a blot upon our civilization,"[121] and six years later Terada Yūkichi discussed the tragedy of rickshaw pullers who knew that the "children they loved" needed an education, yet "had to put them to work . . . due to the difficulty of making a living."[122] But agitation to end child labor was muted, even among the Christians and socialists who might have been expected to champion children's causes.[123] The Ministry of Education called in 1900 for factories to "provide education to the children in their hire through simple, convenient methods," but it did not come out against hiring the children.[124] Ironically, the cotton industry's trade association, Dai Nihon Bōseki Dōgyō Rengōkai, was one of the few organizations to advocate a reduction in children's employment, arguing on economic grounds, late in the 1890s, that child workers spent 80 percent of their time playing and thus stood "in the way of making factories run efficiently."[125] But theirs was a minority voice until 1911, when the Diet finally passed a loophole-laden factory law outlawing the hiring of most children under age sixteen.[126] To the end of Meiji, child labor continued unabated, because children's work was cheap for employers and crucial for family budgets.

The other measures that *hinmin* took to meet budgets demanded the ingenious, often contorted, and sometimes unwise manipulation of household resources. They used most goods until their utility was gone and then used them longer still: sewing patches on already-patched work clothes, handing clothing down to second and third children, buying quilts and furniture from shops that specialized in discarded goods (including items left behind by "people who died an unnatural death").[127] They also shared, borrowing small items and bits of food from neighbors when the pantry was lacking. A number of observers commented on the generosity of the poor in helping out friends and neighbors with special needs. A *Fūzoku Gahō* reporter observed in the late 1890s that it was "not unusual" for people to borrow food "each night and morning" in the *hinminkutsu*, satisfying their stomachs and creating a sense of community at the same time.[128] When they needed bigger items or when the other stretching was not enough, they turned to moneylenders, entering a poorly regulated world that could be wild and dangerous. The government had enacted a law in 1877 limiting annual interest rates for loans under a hundred yen to 20 percent. But enforcement was, in William Lockwood's phrase, "a dead letter,"[129] and it was the *hinmin* who suffered most. The kinds of loans available in *kasō shakai* neighborhoods varied depending on the borrower's situation, but they all involved small amounts, short terms, and exorbitant interest rates. Most common was the *hinashi*, or daily installment loan, typically a one-yen loan to be repaid in daily installments of four sen until the borrower had paid 1.2 yen, for an annual interest rate of 240 percent. Another was the *tsukihashiri* (literally, gallop away in a month), in which the borrower received eighty sen, then paid back a full yen within a month (annual interest rate: 300 percent). And a third, *karasugane* (crow's money), used especially by entertainers, demanded repayment the evening of the day it was borrowed.[130] At year's end, when people needed special clothes or food for the New Year celebrations, it was not unusual for lenders to charge sixty sen for a three-day loan of fifty sen, an annual interest rate of 2,400 percent![131]

Matsubara and Yokoyama both had strong words for the lending world, which the former said was inhabited by people with fancy homes who eschewed personal risk themselves but never hesitated to defraud other people "of millions." His harshest criticisms were reserved for a special breed of lenders who would entice people to take out second (and third and fourth) loans on funds that they knew they could not pay back, until the borrower had paid seven or eight yen for a one-yen loan: "a wonderful example of multiplication indeed," he quipped. "The rats in a house are said to multiply in the same way, but nothing else in the world does."[132] Yokoyama talked about a world where *hinashi* lenders allowed "disqualified" people to borrow, heaping loan upon unpaid loan until they "cannot within their lifetime rid themselves of shackles." The lenders were "relentless"; they were "merciless"; they were unregulated; they were usurious. And they terrorized debtors with arbitrary collection methods. As a result, "the poor people's livelihood, which is already irregular, is made all the more disorderly." Yokoyama's solution was the creation of better lending institutions. The *hinmin* needed nothing, he argued, more than government-guaranteed savings and loan banks that would assure regularized, fair lending policies. He predicted that his calls for reform would be ignored. And he was right.[133]

A final option was to turn to the pawn shop, or *shichiya*, one of the era's most pervasive institutions. As in most countries, these establishments had a long history. They started in the Kamakura period (1185–1333) and were ubiquitous in Edo of the 1860s, with almost every block holding a pawn shop run by someone on "the lower fringes of the merchant class."[134] The Meiji government placed no limitations on who could start such a business, so *shichiya* multiplied right along with the *kasō shakai* in the 1880s and 1890s, reaching a national peak of perhaps 25,000. According to a common saying, "Banks serve the country, but pawnshops serve poor people."[135] According to understated government figures, Tokyo had nearly 1,000 such shops in 1885, 1,169 in 1908, and 1,230 in 1912. From 1884 on, they were regulated by national laws that limited interest rates and forbade trade in stolen goods; after 1895, annual interest rates were capped at 48 percent for loans of less than one yen, 36 percent for those between one and five yen, 30 percent for those between five and ten yen, and 12 percent for those between ten and twenty-five yen.[136] Enforcement was uneven but stricter than for bank loans; in 1894, for example, officials brought 1,158 charges against pawn shops and levied punishments in all but 52 cases.[137]

It would have been hard to find a poor neighborhood in the last Meiji decades without one or more *shichiya,* and it was almost as hard to find a family that did not use them, a fact indicated by one late Meiji survey that showed 63.5 percent of poor households currently in debt to a pawn shop.[138] The heavy use was also clear in municipal statistics that showed Tokyo's pawn shops making no fewer than four million loans, worth 18,373,834 yen, in 1912, with nearly half of the loans going to residents of the four "poverty wards": Asakusa, Honjo, Fukagawa, and Shitaya.[139] Heavy use and lucrative profits did not, unfortunately, equate with sophisticated or ethical business practices. The typical shop, according to observers, was dingy and unattractive, with a dark blue curtain at the front entrance. Inside, a manager would be seated at a desk behind a wooden rail, probably studying an account book while two or three clerks worked nearby. If it was in a middle-class neighborhood, the shop might have an assortment of furniture and art objects on its shelves, perhaps even some old swords and tortoiseshell combs; in the *kasō shakai* areas they were filled with thin cotton shirts, tools, underwear, mosquito nets, and, possibly, faded bedding, although shop owners disliked futon because they consumed too much space. If times were especially hard, there also would be an assortment of cheap kitchen objects and work essentials, including rice tubs, low tables, kettles, sandals, and tobacco pipes. And in the direst periods, when everything else had been hocked, there might be plants, stray cats, canaries, and even the family mortuary tablet. It was not unheard of for a puller to pawn the wheels of his rickshaw or for a washerwoman to pawn some of her client's clothes, hoping to get them back before the client returned.[140] So desperate were *hinmin* needs on some days.

It was said that pawn shops never experienced hard times, because the poorer people were the more they needed *shichiya,* those places, said a *Taiyō* writer, where "usurers . . . gratify their insatiable thirst for gain wrung from people in misfortune."[141] The shop owner probably would have flinched at that characterization, because his life was full of challenges too, including both officials who watched for every possible illegal move and conniving customers, who haggled over loans (with wits bright enough to "dazzle the eyes of a bank president") or absconded without paying.[142] But while the pawn shop tango was complex, with shrewd and desperate clients on the one side facing shrewd and conniving money makers on the other, the advantage lay with the owners. For that reason, few institutions illustrated more vividly the stressful nature of the *hinmin*'s daily struggle to stretch means in order to get by. "There is a simple but terrible logic in the lives of the poor," said Matsubara. "The pawnshop furnishes money with which the pangs of hunger may be staved off, and the shop that lends quilts helps to keep out the cold."[143] That sometimes meant pawning a quilt for two sen in the morning, and then getting it back in the evening by repaying half a sen and pawning a jacket for the other sen and a half. All the while, the shopkeeper heaped up profits. Where would the money come from to retrieve the pawned jacket? That was a question for tomorrow morning, or tonight's sleepless hours.

"How, then, do we live?" asked the Jewish prophet Ezekiel.[144] The residents of a late Meiji *hinminkutsu* would have answered that they did whatever they had to on any given day, at any given moment. Survival methods were as varied as were their life patterns. If living units encompassed every imaginable configuration—singles, couples, related people, unrelated strangers, one generation, two generations, three generations—so did the schemes for making daily existence manageable. If some marriage arrangements were fluid, some illegal, and increasing numbers traditional, so were the ways of making and spending money. If about 5 percent managed to put away a tiny amount of savings and some stayed out of debt by eating skimpily or devising schemes to bring in extra money, others went dangerously into debt, some so much so that the stress drove them to suicide. Daily life, in other words, was as varied as it was hard. But two patterns were common enough to merit comment.

One—widespread enough to endanger our No-Universals Rule—was that *hinmin* found the challenge of creating a vibrant life excruciatingly (and constantly) difficult. Few of the activities examined in this chapter show that more vividly than the cycle that entrapped slum children. Welfare and support programs were unavailable. So was child care. Nor could parents have taken advantage of child care if it had been offered, because the only way to balance the monthly budget was to have the children—at least those over ten—employed at a paying job. School beyond the first three or four years thus was not an option; even in the child's early years it frequently was unavailable because parents could not afford the fees. As a result, the majority of poor children—a million of them nationwide by official count in 1903[145]—would be exempted by poverty from school attendance. And the same enervating cycle affected every other life endeavor: the search for food, the desire for a little rest or leisure, the struggle for decent housing or clothing, the fight to make income cover expenses and keep creditors away. Pawning a futon in the morning, then trading in a jacket to get it back in the evening: could anything speak more loudly? A *Tokyo Puck* cartoonist understood that when he sketched the way eighteen different groups of people saw coins in 1906; for the poor, he offered a single image: a coin with wings.[146]

But difficulty was only part of the picture, because the very immensity of the struggles helped to create the second pattern: namely, that given the choice between being resilient and falling into destitution, the vast majority of *hinmin* chose resilience. That was obvious in the housewives who turned second-hand food from the urban military schools into a "good meal." It was clear in the carefully planned theft of those little charcoal bits from the boss' fuel pile. In the tens of thousands of women who simultaneously managed the household, cared for children, and did factory work. In the way total strangers formed living communal units in order to save on rent. And in the wily juggling of items between pawn shop and home. Their activities were not always respectable, few in the middle class found them admirable, and no one would have chosen such complicated ways of making do. But the urban poor not only endured but shaped the messiest, most difficult situations into meaningful and liveable lives. One of the first to study the *hinmin* seriously, Matsubara, had plenty to say about how hard it was to be poor; he oozed middle-class condescension. But he was awed at the same time by the determination and ingenuity of poor families. "I would like to learn from them how to make do for so many on so little," he said. "That is the first subject to be studied in the college of the poor" (*hindaigaku*). Again: "Poverty keeps a terrible school. One must graduate with honors from it or die."[147] *Hinmin* families studied poverty's lessons a thousand different ways in late Meiji Japan, not always successfully. They knew every nuance of the word "difficulty." But the great majority of them brought a gritty, ingenious persistence to life-making that rendered middle-class lives bland by contrast.

CHAPTER 5

Shadows and Storms
Endurance

> We never saw so many empty houses and shops in the city as at the
> present. . . . Suicide, robbery, petty theft and murder are the headlines
> of the daily press.
>
> —*Shūkan Shakai Shinbun*, March 22, 1908

L ife offered no breaks to the Ueki family, whose story has illustrated so much of this study, but their experiences were, at least, bearable. Not so the hardships that the days meted out to the Tokyo cabinet maker Tanaka Kanji. It was on the first morning of August in 1898, a beastly hot month, when a rickshaw puller happened upon him sleeping on an Asakusa Park bench, cradling the lifeless body of his ten-year-old son. Awakened by the puller's approach, Tanaka took off, fleeing "in trepidation," then stopping for a drink, and then another, to calm himself. When police found him that evening, drunk, he told them he was on the way to the station to confess what had happened. He had killed his son. Ten days before, he said, he had left his wife, despondent over troubles too hard to endure. He and his son had wandered about for more than a week, hungry and homeless, and last night they had fallen asleep on the bench where the rickshaw puller found them. About midnight, Tanaka said, he had awakened and, "on a momentary impulse," decided to act on one of night's dark thoughts. He would wrap his kerchief around the boy's throat and "free himself of the cumbrous care of the child." After strangling the boy, he fell back asleep, "the corpse in his arms," and slept until the rickshaw puller startled him.[1]

What could lead a father to kill his son? Life had enough redeeming moments for most poor people—enough hope—to keep them toiling on through the dark times. The journalist Yokoyama was impressed by the resilience most *hinminkutsu* residents showed in their mutual sharing, particularly during times of special crisis. And Nakagawa Kiyoshi found statistical evidence of an upward economic trajectory, however glacial, that kept most *hinmin* families going, as the following chapter will show. But cabinet maker Tanaka's despondency was not unique. When the middle-class pundits painted their dark portraits, they may have exaggerated but they were not fabricating things. The consequences of economic deprivation often were dire. When nature unleashed torrents of wind and rain, when an alley stove tipped over and ignited a fire, when rats spread the plague or a petty mistake cost a worker her job, slum dwellers had little margin, either financial or spiritual, for dealing with the results. As a result, even ordinary crises in the *kasō shakai* world had the potential to precipitate tragedy. These special difficulties of the poverty-mired life, the tempests that assailed the cities' poor families in unique ways, will be the focus of this chapter.

The Downward Spiral

One of the pernicious features of *hinmin* society was the lack of buffers, the near-total absence of savings, communities, or structures to insulate life against the unpredictable. Thus when a major illness or a firing or a recession occurred, ordinary difficulties were inflated. For a small but not insignificant number, the result was a downward spiral to despair beyond hope. The Christian socialist Kinoshita Naoe summarized the pattern, as he had seen it, citing a possibly fictitious newspaper article: A skilled tobacco factory worker, whose wife fell ill after childbirth and lost their child, was struck by tuberculosis. Penniless and desperate, he sold his nine-year-old daughter to a geisha house, and then, when he still could not put food on the table, he began thinking the unthinkable: "Maybe his wife and kids'd stand a better chance of keeping body and soul together if he were out of the way—folk'd take pity on them and see they didn't starve." So he wrote a note asking neighbors to look after his wife and daughter and then drowned himself in the Kanda River.[2] In the early 1890s, said the journalist Matsubara, most people who suffered a downturn due to a calamity or crisis recovered within a year or two, but a few started down a grimmer road. The first year, the struggling man used up any accumulated savings; the second, he sold off family furnishings; the third, finding friends unwilling any longer to offer a hand, he lived off loans; after that, idleness and pauperdom became his "everyday normal."[3]

Those who reached this bottom layer were the most likely to experience one of poverty's most severe threats: homelessness. Observers made frequent, often belittling references to the *higenjūnin,* or transients, who cluttered the city scape, snoring away the afternoon on a park bench or drunk and passed out on the street corner. One reason the vagrants drew the ire of respectable people was that there were enough of them to make them noticeable, even if they constituted a small minority of the *hinmin* population. Home Ministry surveyors at the end of the era found more than 2,300 of these people in Tokyo's four poverty wards (Honjo, Fukagawa, Asakusa, Shitaya), a modest number compared to the 11,000 homeless in East London when William Booth wrote, but nonetheless roughly 11 percent of those officially classified as paupers (*saimin*). Although males predominated, some 45 percent of the *higenjūnin* were female; in Asakusa, which had the smallest number of transients among the four wards, girls and women formed a majority.[4] The survey's most striking finding may have been that vagrancy was heaviest among ten- to twenty-five-year-olds. Children and young people, in other words, paid the heaviest price for poverty.[5] When the public thought of homelessness, the stereotypical image was *Tokyo Puck*'s drunk being pulled off the street by an angry officer, or the slumbering gray-haired man beside the street, with a police officer yelling, "You can't sleep in the gutter! Get up, you bastard!"[6] The more frequent reality lay in the hundreds of children and teenagers who shivered in the midnight chill beneath temple porticos or alongside empty buildings.

Just who were these people at the bottom of the downward spiral? Some were long-term, unclassifiable vagrants with no means of support. Most, however, had some sort of low-paying work. Many *tachinbō*, or cart pullers' assistants, were homeless. The journalist Yokoyama commented that "even impoverished people have a regular place in which to rest, but *tachinbō* have no place they can call home,"[7] and Matsubara bemoaned the injustice that left them doing crucial work yet unable to afford lodging places. He said the fault was partly their own, because many of them led "a wild existence." But the public's "failure to value their labor" was equally responsible. Without them, farmers would not be able to get their goods to market, nor would ships be able to offload their cargoes. When people saw them crouching "by the wayside" without food or shelter, Matsubara said, they should "give thought to the ten or hundred yen in your pocket and remember that five or fifty rightfully belongs to them."[8] The homeless population also included substantial numbers of rag pickers, more than half of whom were teenagers and children.[9] And the other major group was the beggars (*kojiki*), whose ranks included two-thirds of Tokyo's urchins. The American geologist Edward Morse insisted that "no street beggars are seen," but while his view may have pointed to a relative paucity of begging in comparison with that in major Western cities, he was wrong. The journalist Fujimoto Taizō said that no matter how often the police tried to drive them away, "they come back like flies."[10] Beggars were almost universally regarded as the lowest of the low, "the worst of what poverty creates," in the words of one journalist.[11] Many routes led people to that line of work. Some adults began begging when illness or a broken marriage threw them out of their homes. Some parents sent their children to the streets to supplement family income. Some *hinmin* got too old to work and, having no savings, went into panhandling. Some children, particularly those without families, signed on with agents or patrons to seek money from festival goers or streetside shoppers. And a few *kojiki* were eccentric opportunists, like the educated English-language speaker who told a journalist that he begged because it brought him as much as fifty sen a day, more than what a railway porter or bathhouse attendant earned.[12] What most beggars had in common was the lack of permanent housing. It was not unusual, said Fujimoto, to find as many as sixty "beggars and outcasts" sleeping uncovered under the Asakusa Sensōji temple's veranda floor on a typical morning, many of them with their arms wrapped around each other for warmth.[13]

Most striking among the *kojiki* were the family-less juvenile beggars (*kojiki kozō*) whose situation was discussed in a *Jiji Shinpō* series in the fall of 1896.[14] Some three hundred of them operated across the city, particularly in popular regions such as Asakusa, Ueno Park, Shinjuku, and around the various pleasure quarters, including Yoshiwara. Some of them were runaways, others had been thrown out of the family, still others had lost their parents to death. A typical eight-year-old, Okamoto Fuku from Mannen-chō who ended up at the Tokyo Poorhouse, was described by poorhouse manager Adachi Kenchū as twice-discarded, first by her parents with whom she had lived in a cheap inn and then by an aunt and uncle who abandoned her "like a flower on the garbage dump" when she fell ill. Fuku told Adachi that her father had made and sold *tabi* and her mother had played the samisen while Fuku danced and begged. When both parents died within a year of each other (for reasons unexplained), her aunt and uncle took her in and had her continue dancing and begging. When she got sick, however, they threw her into the streets, where she was found by a police officer and taken to the poorhouse. Asked by Adachi what her parents' names were, she said she did not know.

No matter what took them to the streets, the *kojiki kozō* rarely worked alone. To enter the begging world, they had to seek out a group of other child beggars, headed by a young *oyabun* or boss, who decided where the group would work and who would do what, as well as what remuneration each child would receive. Some bosses provided a percentage of the intake; some required a daily fee, with the child retaining everything above that. Any child who tried to operate alone would be bullied or otherwise persuaded into joining one of the groups in the region; the bravest or most ingenious occasionally formed new bands of their own. For most of the children, begging went hand in hand with petty thievery: pickpocketing during festivals, taking cash from temple boxes when the priests were asleep at night, sneaking sundries, cigarettes, or dried squid from shops along the street. Most of the time, the children did their thieving in small groups, with one or two watching out for police, one creating a diversion, and another carrying out the theft. When not begging or stealing, they often spent their time picking over refuse: fish entrails, food thrown out by shopkeepers, and things that could be scavenged from trash cans.

What were their lives like? A few made enough money to eat decent food and pay at least occasionally for nighttime lodging. Most, however, slept under bridges, in alleys, under the overhanging eaves of houses, or beneath temple verandas, wherever they could find a place. If it was cold, said the *Jiji* writer, they covered themselves with rags or old bags. When it rained or dew was heavy, they got wet. For sustenance, the majority of *kojiki kozō* ate what people gave them in their begging or what they could rummage during the day, either the refuse thrown out by shopkeepers or food they had pilfered. And almost all of them smoked, often the butts of Western-style cigarettes. When they reached the age of fifteen or sixteen, according to the series, many left begging and became rag pickers, although that did not necessarily mean an end to their homeless status. To the question of why more of the children were not taken, like

Fuku, to the poorhouse or an orphanage, or why they did not voluntarily seek out such a place, one answer is that such facilities were scarce. Another is that the reputation of the poorhouse for harsh rules and for humiliating its residents frightened most children. Still a third is that many *kojiki kozō* liked the challenges and camaraderie that street life offered. One child told Adachi in 1906, "There is no life as easy as that of a beggar. If you only give five sen a day to the boss, no one bothers you. In fact, many people take pity on kids like us and give us not just food and drink but also money."[15] So when authorities tried to apprehend them, they slipped away, "hiding here and appearing there; suddenly gathering, suddenly scattering—like floating water plants that never stay put." There was no gainsaying the difficulty of homeless life, either for children or for adults, nor was society inaccurate in placing homelessness at the bottom of the economic spiral. For many *kojiki kozō,* however, freedom and the challenge of finding whatever survival required had an exhilarating quality that offset poverty's hardships, at least while they remained young.

Felled by Illness

Illness ranked near the top of the problems that lurked in *hinmin* doorways during the late Meiji years. By world standards, Japan's cities were quite clean and sanitary at the start of the twentieth century. Night soil collectors removed polluting wastes from city neighborhoods, even poor families bathed often, local governments took health-related policies seriously, relatively litter-free streets prompted a British visitor to note in 1903 that "the Japanese seem to be further advanced in sanitation than the inhabitants of the British Islands."[16] But none of that negated the worry that health and hygiene caused in the *hinmin-kutsu* across this modernizing period. Not until the last year of Meiji did Tokyo even lay out plans for a modern sewer system. Unregulated factories spewed smoke into the skies and toxic wastes into city streams and canals, while untreated water caused dysentery and cholera. Popular awareness of what it meant to eat healthily was limited, and even if it had not been, there was no money for nutritious foods. Physical ailments were a never-ending source of concern for rich and poor alike, but for the poor those concerns were overwhelming.

Almost everything about the slum districts invited diseases, and then heightened their impact when they came. The concentration of factories in the poor areas, the lack of money for health care, the crowding, the absence of plumbing and private toilets, the constant tossing of dirty water—what one journal called "muddy water" (*doromizu*) and "bowel water" (*harawatamizu*)[17]—into the alleys where children frolicked, they all were unavoidable in poor regions, and they all bred illness. The weekly *Shūkan Heimin Shinbun* pointed out in 1904 that the crowded tenements, where seven people shared three-mat apartments and ate "leftovers from prisons," invited diseases to "spread violently."[18] And the Futaba teachers said that the *hinmin*'s "hot, cramped, and dirty" living quarters and inability to get medical care meant that "the weak ones quickly die,"[19] a point backed up by government surveyors, who found repeatedly that while *hinmin* illness rates were only marginally higher than those of other Tokyo-ites,[20] the poor died much more often once they got sick. For 1898, for example, they found significantly higher per capita rates of death due to infectious diseases in Tokyo's *shitamachi* regions where the poor were concentrated than in other parts of the city.[21] A survey of major illnesses in 1902 showed that while per capita cases of cholera, dysentery, intestinal diseases, and diphtheria were not much different in the four poverty wards than they were elsewhere in the city, a substantially higher percentage of sick people there actually died.[22] Official disease reports revealed the same pattern again in 1912, when residents of these wards made up just 29 percent of those who became sick with major illnesses but more than 36 percent of those who died from them.[23]

The range of illnesses and health problems that stalked the *hinminkutsu* neighborhoods was broad: stillborn births, bouts of influenza, lice and worm epidemics, a "rather rampant" scourge of scarlet fever in Tokyo in 1902, repeated outbreaks of the plague and beriberi,[24] in addition to the frequent scourges of cholera and tuberculosis that garnered more public attention. One of the serious problems, which the *kasō shakai* shared with the broader society yet felt in special ways, was venereal disease. Some studies indicated that one in every ten Japanese had at some time had syphilis or gonorrhea and that sexually transmitted diseases were as prevalent as tuberculosis in the early 1900s; other studies put the STD rate even higher.[25] The problem was especially serious in the military (the navy in particular), where doctors treated thousands of men each year for chancroid, gonorrhea, syphilis, and other sex-related diseases that produced blisters and blotches, ate away at the nose and brain, and sometimes led to death. STDs also were rampant in the poor neighborhoods' sex-work communities, despite the regular examinations of women in licensed brothels. In 1914, one exam found a fifth of prostitutes ill with syphilis or gonorrhea, a finding that many observers thought to be on the low side.[26]

Data do not make clear how much more prevalent sexually related illnesses were in the *hinmin* communities than in the larger society, but there is no question that they were a severe problem there. The essayists and reporters were convinced that STDs were widespread among the poor. Even compassionate pundits used pejorative language in describing the sexual practices of the *kasō shakai*: they "know only lust"; they procreate like "lower animals."[27] Yokoyama talked a good deal about the frequency with which people in the slums flaunted sexual norms.[28] The writers of a 1908 series on the "sexual problem" (*seiyoku mondai, seimondai*), which ran in the mass-oriented newspaper *Yomiuri Shinbun*, contended that while "the sexual nature of relationships among the working class . . . seemed far less clear" than that of the middle classes, they were sure that female factory workers in particular were given to promiscuity and "indecency," including the "phenomenon of lesbianism," which was "quite common," and frequent masturbation, which was "stimulated by living in small, crowded housing."[29] These evaluations must be read in the context of limited data and the era's social conventions, but no one would question that the *hinmin* were particularly vulnerable to sexually transmitted diseases. As earlier pages showed, poor women dominated the sex trades. They also made up the majority of factory workers, where sex-related diseases were prevalent. The 1903 government survey of Kansai region textile mills reported sixty-five cases of venereal disease a year, about half of the number of tuberculosis cases, and a three-year study of spinning factories a decade later ranked venereal disease along with tuberculosis at the top of diseases afflicting employees.[30] If poor workers found themselves with STDs, the results often were dire because they could expect no help from support networks, either medical or governmental. When the government's Bureau of Health and Sanitation drew up a plan for worker's illness insurance in 1898, bureaucrats killed it.[31] At the factory level, there was a good chance that the worker would be fired, with no appeal or recourse. A late Meiji study found that roughly half of all women (and roughly a quarter of men) who contracted an STD or TB were dismissed. And for a majority, that was a death sentence, because skilled or professional treatment was simply unavailable.[32] One resident of the Fukagawa poor regions said that when he contracted syphilis and went to a doctor, patients "were spilling outside from the entrance hall" and treatment was primitive. The "elderly doctor with a beard" had "three great brutes of assistants" and threatened: "Listen—this is going to hurt a bit, but you're not to move. . . . You struggle, and you might find yourself with something important cut off." Operating without anesthetics, the doctor "took a great slash at me with the knife right next to the balls, then twisted it sideways." The doctor sent him home with pills that caused vomiting and bleeding and left him feeling as if his body were afire. When he survived, the doctor called him "a tough fellow."[33]

Officials worried a great deal about these sexually related diseases, particularly those contracted by prostitutes, because of their potential for infecting middle- and upper-class patrons, but they worried even more about epidemic-causing diseases such as tuberculosis, diphtheria, dysentery, influenza, cholera, smallpox, and typhoid. Like the STDs, they affected all of society harshly but the poor neighborhoods doubly so. In 1898, for example, when 364 residents of the four poverty wards were struck by dysentery, more than 43 percent died, in contrast to the rest of Tokyo, where less than a quarter of patients died, and while cholera was not a widespread problem anywhere that year, nearly two-thirds of those poverty ward patients who contracted it died.[34] Few pages are more chilling in the official and journalistic reports than the accounts of deaths from epidemics, year upon year upon year. In 1898, smallpox took a monumental 40,971 lives (more than a quarter of all who contracted it) across Japan. In 1901, 42 died in Yokohama's poor neighborhoods from flu. In 1902, 619 died of TB, while diphtheria and foot-and-mouth diseases took large numbers of lives in Tokyo. In 1905, smallpox ravaged Osaka and diphtheria struck more widely. In 1908, another plague of smallpox took the lives of nearly 6,000 people nationwide. And on it went.[35] Numbing as the figures may be, the novelist Nagai Kafū reminded us that each death involved a human tragedy. In "The River Sumida," he spins the tale of Chōkichi, the grandson of a pawnbroker in an "unflourishing neighborhood" in Tokyo's *shitamachi* area. The young man went walking, coatless, not far from Asakusa one evening as spring was turning to summer. When a seasonal torrent let loose, he decided to walk on, splashing "through mud and water from evening on into the night," excited by the sight of flooding in the low-lying regions. It was a reckless decision; he caught a cold, and at the story's end he is dying of typhoid. His house is nearly empty, the walls are peeling, the shutters are drawn, and the rooms reek of disinfectant spread by ward officials. An uncle's declaration—"No matter how ill you may be, you are not to die"—heightens the despondency.[36]

The most pernicious of the infectious diseases was tuberculosis (commonly called consumption), a disease of the lungs that caused coughing, fever, bloody mucous, weight loss, and the death of more people than all the other infectious diseases combined. Although TB had been present in Japan from its earliest centuries, it became epidemic only in the mid-Meiji years, propelled by the onrush of industrialization and the explosion of transportation networks, which allowed people (and pollutants) to move with ever greater freedom and speed. While Japan's overall mortality rate fell between 1886 and 1898, the death rate from TB doubled in those years. In 1904, one journalist, deploring the "phenomenal increase in the number of TB patients," remarked that ads for curing tuberculosis now were appearing daily in Tokyo's major newspapers.[37] Particularly hard hit were what William Johnston calls "a who's who of modern Japanese literature"[38]: novelists Mori Ōgai, Kunikida Doppo, and Futabatei Shimei; the great chronicler of *hinmin* life Higuchi Ichiyō; and the poets Masaoka Shiki and Ishikawa Takuboku, who wrote in 1912, not long before he expired, "If die I must, in my village let it be."[39] Even Yokoyama, the great chronicler of *hinmin* life, died of TB in 1915 at age forty-five, having told his lover Ozaki Tsuneko, "I have lived a lonely life. . . . I am a human being utterly alone in this world."[40] By 1909, the government statistician Nikaidō Yasunori found that nearly one in eight of all Japanese deaths came from that disease. And TB deaths increased in each succeeding year in Tokyo, passing 7,000 in 1912. By the late 1910s, when the disease peaked, mortality rates approached 300 per 100,000 in the overall Japanese population.[41] As the populist paper *Yorozu Chōhō* said in a 1900 report on more than 130 cases in Tokyo's elementary schools: there is "nothing more dangerous!"[42]

If TB was pernicious in the population at large, it was devastating for the *hinmin*. Repeated studies showed a close connection between poverty and tuberculosis. Pollutants filled the lungs of people in or near factories with fibers and dirt, and long work hours weakened the body's resistance to disease. Two standard factory practices intensified the problem. First, most firms charged workers a fee for visiting a physician. Second, companies fired a high percentage of those who contracted the disease, a practice that helps to explain a 1912 study in Tokyo, which found that people who were no longer working made up more than half of the 2,101 who died of TB.[43] For other *hinmin*, the problems lay in crowding, poor nutrition, and lack of sanitation, as well as the stressful anxieties that accompanied poverty. The socialist pioneer Nishikawa Kōjirō called lung diseases such as TB "artificial" illnesses because they were largely preventable. "You cannot but detest the sins of greedy landlords who deprive workers of adequate sunlight and fresh air, or the sins of capitalists who make their laborers work too hard," he said. "If we want to decrease these human-created diseases, first we must get rid of the landlords and capitalists."[44] *Hinmin* vulnerability was increased too by their lack of access to medicine. In 1892, the German expatriate physician Erwin Baelz deplored the absence of facilities in Tokyo for poor people with epidemic diseases. "A scandalous state of affairs," he fumed. "Not one hospital for such epidemic cases where the poor wretches are as well cared for as a horse in a good stable!"[45] As Johnston notes, "When entire families are crowded into confined, poorly ventilated rooms, infants and young children are easily infected, and those who become infected at early ages generally have a greater chance throughout their lives of dying from tuberculosis." Slum conditions, he said, "bred disease, especially tuberculosis."[46]

The end result was that death felt ominously close for anyone in the slums who had contracted TB, so close that people "would not go near the sick. Every family tried to hide the fact that a family member had TB."[47] A government statistician identified tuberculosis as the cause of 12 percent of Japan's total deaths in 1909, but 32 percent of textile workers' deaths. Another study, carried out in 1910 by Ishihara Osamu of the Ministry of Agriculture and Commerce, showed that young women who worked in textile factories died at nearly five times the national rate and that roughly half of their deaths were from tuberculosis. Ishihara also discovered, to no one's surprise, that the young girls (and men) who were fired because of TB spread the disease even more widely once they returned home. In one village of two hundred families, a single male TB victim was said to have caused the deaths of thirty people. The same thing happened in the *hinminkutsu*. According to an 1890s survey, poverty-plagued Asakusa had Tokyo's highest mortality rates from TB: 530 per 100,000.[48]

When the thirty-six-year-old novelist Kunikida Doppo lay in bed, poverty-stricken and battling TB late in the summer of 1907, he wrote to a friend, "I have wasted away to a bag of skin and bones. If you saw me you would be shocked and if you were honest with me you would tell me I don't have long. . . . I frequently weep profusely, wondering if I am about to die." Unfortunately, he was. Almost as heart-rending as the early death of a brilliant writer was what his postscript revealed about late Meiji attitudes toward his disease: "By the way, don't tell anyone I have pneumonia catarrh. I'd hate to be treated immediately like a consumptive."[49] Few scourges brought greater pain to the *hinmin* community than tuberculosis. It pushed impoverished men and women from the realm of the excruciating into the region of the impossible. Kunikida was bankrupt when TB struck, but at least he could afford a doctor. For those in the *kasō shakai* world, there was no money even for that. As a popular axiom had it, "The rich recover from tuberculosis but the poor do not."[50]

Tuberculosis was not, however, the most dramatic of the illnesses that struck the poor in a special way. While it may have caused the most deaths across time, its effects were relatively steady from year to year. Some illnesses were more notorious because they came in unpredictable waves, afflicting small numbers most years, hitting with paralyzing force in another. Dysentery was one of those, causing more than 41,000 deaths in 1893 and nearly 7,000 deaths in 1909.[51] Cholera, another of the "modern" epidemic diseases, took even more lives when it hit. Spread by contaminated food and water, it caused terrible diarrhea and vomiting and killed a third or more of those who contracted it. Japan first had been plagued by it as cities grew and foreign ships entered Japanese waters in the early nineteenth century, with an initial appearance in 1822 and epidemics causing the deaths of as many as 200,000 people between 1858 and 1860, another 105,786 in 1879, and 108,405 in 1886.[52] The visiting foreign geologist Edward Morse reported that cholera was "killing thirty or forty a day" when he arrived in the town of Shizuoka during an 1882 epidemic and that all of the major inns had been shut down to prevent the spread of the disease.[53] The *enka* singer Azembō recalled the constant passage of coffins along the road in his town during the 1886 epidemic: "Here three coffins, there five, until the number grew alarmingly large," all headed for the crematory. His aunt told him, "Don't watch that, stay inside," but he could not take his eyes away. "During a single evening," he reported, "I saw seven or eight coffins go by in a row."[54] As late as 1902, cholera claimed more than 9,000 lives, with two-thirds of those who contracted the disease dying.[55]

The government's efforts to prevent cholera and dysentery sometimes were enlightened, sometimes draconian. Ships arriving from abroad were inspected and quarantined if cholera was discovered aboard.[56] Public education campaigns about water and food were mounted. Laws were promulgated, one after another, culminating in a comprehensive infectious diseases law in 1897.[57] And from that year on, all corpses were required to be cremated.[58] At the draconian end of the spectrum, after an 1878 epidemic the government developed harsh quarantine policies that hit poor neighborhoods with special force. Isolation hospitals were built, with the single goal of removing patients from neighborhoods where they could infect others. By the last half of Meiji, more than 1,500 such institutions had been opened, many of them without a doctor to care for patients. Sometimes referred to as "dump sites," they ran counter to the traditional practice of caring for patients at home and provoked a number of violent confrontations between citizens and the authorities, with some of the protests taking on the style of traditional peasant risings and a few resulting in the deaths of unpopular officials or doctors.[59] As might have been expected, *hinmin* were the ones most likely to be found in the dumps. On the enlightened side, cities across the country poured resources into developing sanitary water and sewage systems. Yokohama launched the country's first city waterworks in 1887; Osaka followed, and in 1893, an audience of three thousand gathered at Yodobashi to witness the ground breaking of Tokyo's first modern water system, a project designed to "reduce the fear of epidemics and allow people to eat and sleep without anxiety." The Tokyo system had been completed by 1900, and an expanded waterworks was begun in 1908. The result was that by the early 1900s, Japan had reduced its cholera mortality rates to roughly the same as those in Great Britain, even though the English were five times as wealthy as the Japanese. By the 1920s, cholera was no longer a serious threat.[60]

Throughout Meiji, however, cholera remained a fearsome specter. And the *hinmin* feared it even more than other people did, for two reasons. First, they lived in the crowded neighborhoods most susceptible to epidemics, low-lying places where water contaminated by feces and other foul matter was most likely to overflow the canals and embankments. Reporter Suzuki Umeshirō noticed the disease's prevalence in Osaka's Nago-chō slum in the 1880s before the sources of cholera were fully understood and blamed the food in cheap stores where "every item sold . . . was a powerful cholera-causing material."[61] By 1911, when research had made cholera's causes clear, *Tokyo Puck* was reporting that "every canal or river, large or small, *running through the . . . densely populated wards* is only a large repository of household refuses,"[62] in other words, a source of cholera. Second, as was apparent in the discussion of TB, factory owners and officials followed health policies guaranteed to make things worse for *hinmin*. The owners' lack of attention to health issues was highlighted repeatedly in the 1903 factory report *Shokkō jijō*. At match factories, the surveyors reported, workers were expected to go directly from the plant floor where they had been handling noxious chemicals to the dining room without washing or taking any hygienic precautions. Tobacco factories made their employees work and eat in narrow, packed rooms that swirled with dust and germs. None but the largest firms provided doctors or plans to deal with work-time injuries or illnesses. Left unregulated, the vast majority of smaller plants provided health care "in name only." The system, said the *Shokkō jijō* writers, left workers completely vulnerable.[63] Looking at cholera specifically, labor activist Hosoi Wakizō said that when workers fell ill, foremen first tried to hide the sickness, then, if it spread, they placed patients in hastily constructed isolation barracks where they lay, several to a mat, beneath a red hot roof of galvanized metal, while a single overworked doctor passed out the same medicine to everyone. Those who died were taken to a corpse room (*shitaishitsu*), put in crude boxes, and transferred to a crematorium. He said the cholera victims in one factory were handled "like slaughtered cows," in another "much like a family throwing away silkworm droppings." Watching factories treat patients, he said, "I truly learned the meaning of hell."[64] And if the patients happened to make it home alive, they were the first sent to the "dump sites" called isolation hospitals, where "there was little hope that the patient would return."[65]

One other epidemic disease—the plague, or the pest (*pesuto*) as it was called in Japan—claimed a relatively small number of lives and, in contrast to other epidemics, had positive as well as negative effects in *hinminkutsu* communities. But its history and dramatic nature ensured that it drew a great deal of attention. Carried by fleas on rats, it had not affected Japan as it had Europe, India, and China in earlier periods. But its international infamy, added to its terrible impact on victims—chills, seizures, vomiting of blood, excruciating pain, delirium, quick death—assured that officials and reporters would pay close attention whenever it appeared in Japanese port cities. In late 1899, for example, when the other parts of Asia were struggling with the disease, *Taiyō* ran extensive coverage of its entry into Japan and the rigorous efforts of the government to keep it from spreading, with a detailed list of a score of victims: names, dates on which they fell ill, and when they died (often the day the symptoms appeared).[66] The press' special interest in *pesuto* was illustrated by *Yorozu Chōhō*'s repeated stories in 1900 about the plague in Osaka, despite the relatively small number of deaths. The first account, on January 7, was about a doctor who had died from the disease. In April, May, and June, the paper reported regularly on new cases, most of them fatal: five new cases the week of April 29, two the week of May 6, three the week of June 3, three more June 10. In mid-May, it ran the story of an official reprimand to the governor of Osaka for slow action that enabled the disease to spread. In late July, the paper announced that *pesuto* had been eradicated. Two months later it was back again, causing eleven new cases in mid-September.[67] Only fifty cases occurred in Osaka across that entire period, but the disease's reputation, combined with its potential for disaster, kept it in the news.

The main reason the plague's impact was not greater lay in the diligence officials showed in fighting it, a diligence that affected *hinmin* communities positively as well as negatively. As with cholera and dysentery, officials were more concerned about eradication than about the fate of sufferers. When infected rats appeared in Osaka in 1902, for example, the police began requiring worker inoculations, over the vehement objections of factory managers who worried that the fever caused by the shots would keep workers away from work for two or three days.[68] When the disease was discovered in Yokohama that same fall, the *New York Times* reported that "when the residents of that district, several blocks in area, awoke the next morning they found themselves walled in by a substantial board fence, eight feet high, closely guarded." The officials evacuated the neighborhood and set fire to the 162 "unsubstantial" and "wickware" homes there"; they also began inspecting passengers as they disembarked from trains and ships in the region, and they made people stop going barefoot. Similar evacuations recurred repeatedly in the early 1900s, almost always in the regions of the *hinmin*, with impressive results in terms of disease prevention but a great deal of dislocation and isolation for poor citizens.[69] A less disruptive fighting technique involved financial incentives to get rid of rats. As soon as a case of the plague was discovered, officials would begin encouraging people to turn in rats at specified centers for five sen each. The purchases would continue until the epidemic was over, at which point announcements were made that "the pest has been stamped out" and no more rats would be bought.[70] The policy was effective. Five sen was a significant sum—a quarter of the daily wage of a bathhouse worker in 1902 or more than half of what a restaurant waiter made each day—and it evoked a vigorous response in both poor and middle-class neighborhoods.[71] On the first day of rat purchases in Tokyo in 1900—ironically, the Year of the Rat—people brought in about 4,000 rats; on June 10, 1901, Yokohama residents turned in 1,375 rodents. In a single month at the beginning of 1900, Tokyo residents reportedly sold 110,073 rats at a cost to the city of more than 5,500 yen. "Discarded rats turn into money," said a *Fūzoku Gahō* writer;

"it's as if the Year of the Rat has turned into a profit."[72] The *Tokyo Puck* humorists commented repeatedly on what a boon rat sales could be, with one cartoonist placing a rat on the crest of a fictitious family made rich by rodent sales and another showing Osaka police feasting on rat kebabs.[73]

Dark humor may have lightened some spirits, but for those who lived in the *hinminkutsu,* illnesses were not matters for joking. Sickness was always in the shadows, threatening to turn difficulty into tragedy, or worse. Epidemics reserved the worst of their attacks for poor, polluted neighborhoods where malnourishment made resistance doubly difficult. When illness came, there were no funds, no social networks, no public services to help. Indeed, what public responses there were often increased the troubles for the *hinmin* victims. As the paragraphs below will show, the press overflowed in these years with accounts of people for whom illness was the final blow, the hammer that broke up households or crushed hope. The Shitaya toymaker's wife who disappeared when she got sick, leaving her octogenarian husband "insane with grief," was not uncommon. Neither was the sobbing, middle-aged mother whom police found on an Ebisu bridge late in the summer of 1898, urging her three crying children to jump because death would be better than the "semistarvation" that had become their reality after her husband died of an illness a few weeks earlier. Sickness had killed hope.[74]

A *Tokyo Puck* wit illustrated rumors that the government's purchase of rats to eliminate the plague had become a boon for Osaka police, who were using funds from rats to buy udon noodle dishes and even feasting on the rats themselves (January 20, 1908). Courtesy of University of Tokyo Graduate Schools for Law and Politics, Center for Modern Japanese Legal and Political Documents, Meiji Shimbun Zasshi Bunko.

Hit by Disasters

If it was not disease that overwhelmed the *hinmin* family, it was accident or disaster, often natural, often manufactured. Sometimes there were everyday accidents: the cart puller crippled when his fish-laden wagon "got out of control" and smashed his legs; the Asakusa sandal dealer who stuck his head out of an open train window and was killed when the car passed an electric pole; the many people injured and killed when a bridge railing broke during an 1897 festival alongside the Sumida River.[75] There also were freakish furies of nature such as the March 1908 dust storm blown up by "dry wind . . . like gunpowder smoke" and a blizzard the next month that downed phone lines and caved in roofs, depriving small shopkeepers of days of crucial income.[76] Typhoons and earthquakes struck too, including the 1891 Mino Owari quake that leveled textile mills and killed more than seven thousand people in the Nagoya region, and the Tokyo quake that killed thirty-one in 1894.[77] There were even the ravages of war: children lost to faraway battles, wives who struggled to support families while their husbands were gone, the "thousands of weavers" in Kyoto who were thrown out of jobs and forced to live "on a gruel of rice" when the silk market plummeted during the war with Russia, even the twenty people killed in the spring of 1904 during a stampede touched off by a demonstration supporting Japan's soldiers in Manchuria.[78] But the disasters that most terrified the *hinmin* were the two Fs: floods and fires.

That floods were a regular part of the seasonal cycles made them no more bearable. Heavy rains caused minor floods and turned poor households into musty, soaked bins every two or three years in the last two Meiji decades, and they brought major deluges in 1885, 1893, 1896, 1902, 1907, and 1910. Tanizaki remembered days when "everything was blotted out by the din of the driving rain" and nothing was visible but "the lamps placed here and there above utility-pole advertisements."[79] The American visitor Eliza Scidmore said of the 1885 flood in Osaka that "only the castle and a few business streets were left above water." Nearly 150 bridges were washed away, factories were "paralyzed," and "the suffering and destitution were terrible."[80] And the 1896 inundation, among the worst in modern times, destroyed or damaged 20,981 towns and cities across Japan, sweeping away nearly 89,000 bridges, taking 1,250 lives, and causing losses in excess of 113 million yen.[81] A national River Law, passed as a result of that flood, significantly lessened the damage from nature's watery assaults, but flood disasters continued to plague the *hinmin* regions until the Great Kantō Flood of 1910 caused officials finally to draw up Japan's first thoroughgoing flood control plan.[82] One sign that flood control made a difference was that a 1912 typhoon, which unleashed "the severest rainstorm that had . . . been known for the past ten years," bringing heavy downpours to the poor regions of Fukagawa and Shitaya and causing "great terror" among women in the entertainment quarters, actually caused less damage than many of the earlier floods had.[83]

The mid-August 1910 flood illustrated the *hinmin's* special vulnerability when the skies loosed their downward-facing geysers. A *Tokyo Puck* writer had warned in early July that

> We are again in the rainy season, when everything gets musty; when the very sky hangs low, as if mildewed and ready to crumble down; when everyone feels depressed in heart, heavy in head, and drooping in body; . . . when the sun himself looks as if he were in eternal mourning."[84]

As if on cue, an "incessant downpour of rain" let loose on August 8 and continued for three days without letup. By the time it was finished, most of eastern Japan was a "scene of disasters," with 709 homes and 45 bridges washed away in Tochigi Prefecture north of Tokyo and 3,500 houses flooded in Ibaraki to the northeast. Riverbanks were washed away, and damaged communications systems frustrated relief efforts.

Tokyo's low-lying slum regions were hit hardest, in part because they rested in the city's low areas, which once had been marshland, and in part because they were so densely populated. *Taiyō* reported that riverside sections in Tokyo's *kasō shakai* areas were "almost entirely submerged, the water in some places being several feet deep in the streets." Honjo, where humorists had long quipped that "even its famous mosquitoes take a boat,"[85] became a 200-square-kilometer lake in which a reported 170,000 buildings were destroyed. Asakusa Park was under four feet of water, and portions of Fukagawa, Shitaya, and

During the Great Kantō Flood, photographed here on August 11, 1910, people in the poor regions along the Sumida River often had to be rescued from their homes by boat; more than 1,300 lost their lives. Courtesy of Kjeld Duits Collection, MeijiShowa.com.

Asakusa were inundated too. Firefighters, it was said, were "no longer firemen but watermen" who rowed their boats along streets and down alleys, searching for people and animals in trouble. All told, more than 3,000 homes in Honjo and another 1,000 in Fukagawa were at least partly submerged. *Puck* showed people wading knee deep in water and naked men urinating in the "lake." And *Seinen-Rising Generation* reported that green grocery prices rose as much as 70 percent because of the vegetable scarcity. By the end, more than 1,300 people were dead or missing, even more than in the massive 1896 flooding.[86] And psychological effects continued for months. When a less devastating Saturday night downpour two years later inundated "all the houses in the lower part of Fukagawa . . . as usual," a reporter noted that "the inhabitants packed up their goods and fled, fearing a repetition" of 1910.[87] The only saving grace for the *hinmin* when floods came may have been their poverty: they had so few material goods that restoration did not take long.

Fires, on the other hand, took away everything, raging through neighborhoods in a few unpredictable minutes or hours of flames that filled the skies with eerie and gorgeous glows and turned everything to cinders. Once labeled the "flowers of Edo" because they were "as much among the great sights of the city as the cherry blossoms on the south-east bank of the River Sumida,"[88] they continued across the Meiji years to terrorize people who lived in Tokyo's densely packed, flimsily built houses despite improvements in firefighting techniques and increased water supplies. A single fire in 1881, memorialized in four prints by the woodblock artist Kobayashi Kiyochika, lasted more than sixteen hours and consumed more than 10,600 Tokyo homes including that of Kiyochika himself.[89] In 1892, one fire leveled 4,000-plus dwellings. Indeed, a list of Tokyo fires between 1885 and 1898 showed only two years when fewer than 1,000 homes burned to the ground; more than 2,000 were destroyed in each of five years. The year 1898 was particularly bad, with some 3,517 homes going up in flames: 502 in a January 3 fire in Shitaya, 126 in an Asakusa fire late in February, 1,478 in a March 23 Hongō blaze that killed two men. The total economic loss from fires that year was 810,946 yen.[90] Things got better after the turn of the century, but municipal reports for the twelve months from October 1909 to September 1910 described 454 Tokyo fires, or 37.8 a month, with 62 set intentionally, 40 caused by chimneys, 84 by lamps, 32 by the *kotatsu* used to keep warm in winter, and 23 by cigarettes. The year 1911 saw another eruption, with 6,535 homes destroyed in more than 440 fires.[91] And in Osaka, which traditionally had fewer fires, a day-long, wind-fanned conflagration on July 31, 1909, touched almost a third of the city, destroying as many as 20,000 buildings and causing half a million yen's worth of damages. The paper *Yorozu Chōhō* called it a "great fire almost unprecedented in all the world," noting that the citizens of Osaka were demanding the removal of the mayor who reportedly partied while the fire "was at its hottest."[92]

It has become tedious to hear that the poor experienced disaster's terrors most intensely, but that does not diminish the statement's truth when it came to fires. While conflagrations occurred everywhere, the dangers were greater where housing materials were most combustible[93] and residences most tightly packed together. It did not help that *hinmin* had only cheap and unstable lamps for light (and for killing mosquitoes) and kerosene stoves or charcoal burners for heat. The common quip was that rent was a form of fire insurance because "landlords building new houses or tenements to let could count on losing their entire property to fire every three to five years."[94] The row houses of the *hinminkutsu* were often nicknamed *yakiya,* or burn-lodgings. "It is so easy to burn down a wooden house," said the Meiji journalist Inouye Jukichi. "A rag soaked with kerosene is enough to destroy any number of houses and is the favourite means with incendiaries who hope to steal household goods which are brought out in confusion into the street whenever there is a fire in a neighborhood."[95] Few records show the vulnerability of the poor regions more clearly than Tokyo's 1914 Statistical Yearbook, which reported that in 1912, the four poverty wards had had 32 percent of the city's fires but a monstrous 92.6 percent of its "wholly burned" houses. A decade earlier, the respective figures had been less dramatic but similar: 41.2 percent of the fires and 64.9 percent of the homes destroyed. When a fire broke out, slum environments made disaster a near certainty.[96]

Studying Tokyo city records in the 1890s, Ogi Shinzō found arson to be the single greatest cause of fires, sometimes as a result of youthful deviltry (a lad, for example, caught setting fires in Shitaya in 1910 because it was fun to watch flames[97]), sometimes to get rid of debt records, sometimes to trigger alms-giving, sometimes as occasion for looting, and sometimes to create work opportunities in the reconstruction that followed a big fire.[98] Police records suggest that arson occurred no more often in the *hinmin* neighborhoods than elsewhere, but more damage was done when it happened in the poor regions.[99] The second and third causes of fire were lamps and hibachi, with cigarettes, bath heaters, and candles following behind.[100] The worst fire of the decade in Tokyo was caused by a candle sitting near a paper door. That is why, said Inouye, "the inhabitants, as they go to bed, are never sure, especially in crowded quarters, of still having a roof over their heads next morning." He said the frequency of fires made some people numb. The "dreaded triple peal of the alarm-bell" signaling a nearby fire might send them fleeing to the streets, but the double peal indicating a fire in the next district barely roused them from sleep.[101] When fire actually struck, the scene was more likely to be the one described by the memoirist Saga Junichi: a woman "clinging to the roof and screaming" while her sister cried "Jump!" and "the whole place was in a complete panic, with people rushing around through the bits of drifting fire, all of them shouting like mad."[102]

Factories too were the sites of frequent fires, some of them deadly. In the early 1880s, small conflagrations occurred regularly—indeed nightly—at many factories after they introduced night shifts with oil lamps for illumination. The installation of electric lights in the mid-1880s decreased the fires but it did not end them. Among the worst was the 1892 fire at Osaka Spinning Mill, which broke out at dawn on December 30 and spread "like a fire train" along the belts and ropes that ran between floors and sections. Workers on the second and third floors heard the screams but could not escape through the "sea of flames below," according to Hosoi. Because the few escape ladders were too narrow to be helpful, some jumped from third floor windows, often to their death. By the time the flames were controlled, the factory complex was largely gone, as were thirty-four residences nearby. Ninety-five workers were dead, twenty-two were maimed, and uncounted numbers were injured. People were mistaken when they referred to fires as "natural disasters" (*tensai*), Hosoi lamented; they were "mass murders" (*gyakusatsu*), the result of capitalist owners' unwillingness to pay for any safety measure that might reduce profits.[103] It was the *hinmin*, of course, who died.

Among the most spectacular *shitamachi* conflagrations during the Meiji era was the Shin Yoshiwara fire of 1911, which destroyed Tokyo's elite prostitution center. In a matter of hours on Sunday, April 9, most of the quarters' establishments, more than two hundred in all, were burned to the ground. Military units were brought in along with firefighters, but, as *Tokyo Puck* lamented, "neither steam pumps nor water supplies were of any use." The actual number killed remained undetermined but was said to include many prostitutes; the scores of injured ranged in age from four to fifty. Photos of the aftermath showed a scene not unlike that of the Great Kantō Earthquake a dozen years later: a few walls and small tea houses standing in a vast expanse of debris and ashes, with smoke still rising from a leveled plain, what *Puck* called "wild scenes of Hell upset." The humor magazine predicted that while moralists might rejoice in the destruction of so many brothels, "hell never dies."

The Shin Yoshiwara fire in 1911 left Tokyo's famous prostitution quarters destitute, destroying more than two hundred buildings and taking many lives; it did even more damage in the surrounding neighborhoods of the poor. Courtesy of Kjeld Duits Collection, MeijiShowa.com.

Needed as a "safety valve" for human drives, Yoshiwara would rise "phoenix-like out of its own ashes."[104] The magazine's prediction was right about the rebirth, but the quarters never recovered their former status. Less attention was paid to the impact of the fire on the surrounding *hinmin* communities, where more than six thousand homes and shops also were turned to ashes, and shopkeepers, cleaners, washerwomen, and flower shop workers lost their sources of livelihood for a considerable period of time. For the thousands of *hinmin* living in the sprawling area, the fire was a painful reminder that disasters *were* respecters of persons.

Crime and the Poor

So was crime. The late Meiji papers were filled with stories of crime and moral failure, organized into two categories. In the first were upper- and middle-class indiscretions: the sexual affairs of nearly five hundred political and business leaders who turned their wives into "playthings," the corruption of officials, the hypocrisy of commercial giants such as the Ashio copper mine's Furukawa Ichibei, who despoiled the landscape and took advantage of workers, and the moral decline of young people.[105] Opinion leaders wrung their hands a great deal over the failings of young people, both the thousands of minors apprehended for various forms of juvenile delinquency[106] and great numbers of students whom journalists saw as exemplifying the moral dangers of modernity. Young couples holding hands in parks worried some writers. Bullying drew its share of ink. Many wrote about the financial and sexual laxity of students living in unsupervised urban boarding houses, where the "moral depravity of youth is extremely deplorable."[107] Student smoking, banned for teenagers in 1900, also became a target.[108] And student gang fights were "savage things,"[109] bemoaned as moral lapses, with the *Niroku Shinpō* commenting after a fight involving several "promising" sons of famous politicians that "it is regrettable that they gave into anger and strayed into youthful impetuosity."[110] As the *Niroku* tone suggests, the reports on elite misbehavior typically were couched in terms of moral failure; miscreants were fallen men and youths who succumbed to greed or sexual drives, descending, as one writer put it, "to occasional despondency and . . . to vice and dissoluteness, without shame."[111]

The second category, *hinmin* crime, evoked a different tone. The vices of the poor were not so much moral failings as the natural results of being in the underclass, behaviors to be expected of lower beings. Some essayists worried lest *hinmin* failings infect the values of the upper classes; a few saw them as a threat to middle-class safety and security. But crime in the urban poverty areas generally was viewed as the deplorable—but colorful—problem of a world to be observed but not worried about overly much. The New Year 1900 issue of *Yorozu* might feature a grim miscellany: a theft, the suicide of a poor middle-aged man who burned his own house down, a woman sentenced to death for killing her husband, the murder of three lovers in Yokohama, a fire that separated wives from husbands, and another murderer who took three lives. On another day that year, April 13, the widely read *sanmen kiji* (Page Three articles) might include a fire, an infant suffocation, a burglary, a piece on gambling, a description of violations of the new anti-smoking law, and an account of bullying. On still a third day, March 25, the tale would be of Suzuki Mikizō, the wayward son of a Honjo sweets shop owner, who took the shop's earnings to buy unlicensed prostitutes in Asakusa instead of banking the money as he had been instructed to do.[112] And *Yorozu*'s counterpart, *Niroku*, would report on the thirty-six-year-old "bad rickshaw puller" who raped one of his riders at eight o'clock the previous evening, and on the "The Quick Turnaround of a Priest" who had come to the city to raise money for his temple but turned to extortion when his travel funds dwindled.[113] The accounts were multitudinous and endless, but they lacked the outrage, the sense of departure from an expected norm, that pervaded the stories of elite crime. Page Three features were simply news, subscriber-inducing glimpses into what Matsubara called the "deep darkness" of life among the lower classes.[114]

The data tell a nuanced, sometimes counterintuitive story about crime in the *hinminkutsu* regions. Tokyo's official surveys suggest that violent crimes and theft occurred at heightened levels in the poor regions, at least in some years, but that the difference generally was less than public perceptions of it. In 1900, for example, police statistics showed that rickshaw pullers made up more than 9 percent of all those convicted of crimes in Tokyo that year, even though the pullers constituted just 3 percent of the total population.[115] Similarly, city records in 1912 showed that exactly half of Tokyo's sixty murders and 63 percent of its counterfeiting cases occurred in the four poverty wards of Shitaya, Asakusa, Honjo, and Fukagawa, where only 39.3 percent of the population lived.[116] But other crime categories and other years showed a different pattern. In most of the twentieth century's first decade, for example, the murder rates in the poverty wards were about the same as those across the entire city.[117] And crimes such as arson and extortion were committed less often by citizens in the poor wards than by those in the city at large. Even in the high-murder year of 1912, overall criminal cases per capita in the *hinminkutsu* regions closely mirrored those elsewhere, with Shitaya, Asakusa, Honjo, and Fukagawa accounting for 39.2 percent of the crimes, while they were responsible for only 21 percent of the city's stolen money (see table 7).[118] One may argue about the nuances, but the data undermine any categorical claims about the *hinmin* being particularly crime-prone. When a Chōfu villager named Kinzō fled to Asakusa and then to Fukagawa after murdering two women in 1900, he may have been trying to hide among the throngs,[119] but if he was merely seeking the company of fellow law breakers, he made a mistake: there were no more of them there than in the more affluent Kanda, Nihonbashi, Kyōbashi, and Shiba wards.

Table 7. Tokyo: Selected crime categories and population, 1912

	Population	Murder	Theft	Arson	All Crimes
Entire city	2,009,980	60	13,369	62	19,454
4 poverty wards	789,998 (39.3%)	30	5,395	17	7,630 (39.2%)
4 better-off wards	600,666 (29.9%)	19	4,356	15	6,539 (33.6%)

The poverty wards are Shitaya, Asakusa, Honjo, and Fukagawa; the "better-off" wards are Kanda, Nihonbashi, Kyōbashi, and Shiba. Sources: For crime, *Dai jūichi kai Tokyo shi tōkei nenpyō: 1914*, 362–363. For population: *Tokyo shi tōkei zuhyō* (1914), chart 5 (pages unnumbered). Other crime categories in the report are counterfeiting, extortion, fraud/intimidation, miscellaneous, and "violations outside the formal laws" (a category with small numbers).

That did not mean that crime was not a serious issue for people living in poverty. The official crime categories in the late Meiji years included homicide, arson, extortion, counterfeiting, gambling, indecency, breaking and entering, rape, prostitution, fraud, official corruption, and obstructing officials, and it is clear that great numbers of *hinmin* were involved with all but the last two. Sometimes their crimes were petty or amusing, as when a seventeen-year-old wife used a milk bottle to hit the milk deliveryman who had quarreled with her husband. Sometimes they reflected camaraderie: groups of boys shoplifting, the extorting "brotherhoods" of novelist Kawabata Yasunari's *Scarlet Gang of Asakusa,* or the clever plots of a group of *enka* singers who "degenerated into a nest of hooligans" and perfected the art of drinking and eating without paying. A distressing number of the crimes involved arson. And all too often they constituted violence *against the poor* by outsiders: an adult bully in Kōjimachi giving a street roamer a red hot coin just to see his reaction, Ashio mine agents abducting boys in Asakusa Park in the summer of 1912, student gangs bullying beggars, a pederast who lay in wait "for little boys in some dark corner" when Tanizaki was a child.[120] But the majority of the *hinmin*-connected crimes fell into a few categories related to theft and murder.[121]

Theft seemed unavoidable to many *hinmin,* as Ueki's charcoal and coin pilfering suggested. Yokoyama described textile pieceworkers in the Kiryū region "appropriating waste threads" in order to survive on wages too low for survival. It was estimated, he said, that as much as two hundred yen worth of thread and cloth was pilfered each day from the region's textile factories; industry officials reported "extreme concern" over workers who only "care about reaping their own selfish profits." Such practices were common in the Tokyo and Osaka firms too. Yokoyama also described the theft of small personal items—footwear, towels, umbrellas—at flophouses and from streetside shops in the *hinminkutsu* regions. And in the moralizing tone that was typical of him, he suggested that rag pickers "have a disposition toward stealing," which makes them "appear to be a quasi-human species."[122] Ushiyama Saijirō of the newspaper *Jiji Shinpō* provided

numerous instances of worker theft, including one Osaka factory where depart-
ing employees were searched daily for copper pieces, and a brush-making plant
in the same city where "factory girls expose themselves to a scandalous scene
when they leave the factory because supervisors inspect their clothes and ask if
they may have taken brushes or toothpicks."[123] Many writers argued that a propensity for gambling turned some poor people into thieves.[124] Very few took
note of the fact that most of the stolen items were petty goods needed to survive.

Pickpocketing may have been the most irksome form of *hinmin* theft for
those in the middle classes, though it was hardly the most damaging. Data on
the numbers of pickpockets is spotty, but one report in 1902 estimated that 350
or 360 were operating regularly in Tokyo, about 200 of them on trains.[125] If one
added the boys and girls who stole sporadically or by whim from passersby, the
number would be much higher. While some made a fairly decent living from
their work, the sums they took from individual victims were usually small: a
foreigner's watch, some eggs or fish snitched from a shopper, ten yen grabbed
from the rickshaw rider Nakamura Fukusuke on a February evening in 1900.[126]
But small or not, those sums were a source of public consternation. The 1908
Tokyo Puck cartoon described earlier, showing parents teaching their son to
pickpocket, captured the popular image. So did Matsubara, who described juvenile *suri* (pickpockets) and shoplifters (*manbiki*) as "sharp-faced boys from
about twelve to fifteen years of age who move as swiftly and as lightly as swal-
lows and are as agile as monkeys," rifling the pockets of unwary festival-goers
in an "easy game which scarcely anybody but a detective can spoil." He estimated that Shin'ami-chō had thirty or forty of them in the early 1890s.[127] In the
public mind, they were bad boys who mostly worked by themselves in crowded
areas, and their targets were upstanding citizens who felt vulnerable and violated. In truth, the effective pickpockets often were organized and sophisticated in their work, operating under an older boss. In the mid-Meiji years, a
woman known as "Granny" gained notoriety by leading a group of pickpocketing and thieving boys in the Asakusa area, avowedly wanting to help them
avoid "becoming criminals" even as she made a profit off their crimes. Adachi
described a lad at the Tokyo Poorhouse in the early 1900s who had worked for
a Honjo boss who taught his young troops to beg first, then to steal, giving the
best of them stylish clothes and gold watches for good work.[128] One of the era's
most notorious—and revealing—pickpocketing episodes came in 1909, when
the theft of a gold watch from a well-known politician aboard a train caught
the public imagination. Until then, Tokyo police had most often treated pickpocketing fairly benignly, but in response to the uproar they launched a major
roundup of the city's suspected pickpockets. A tailor named Ginji, found to
have been leading a band of petty *suri* for nineteen years, was arrested, along
with eight of his followers. He was sentenced to ten years of penal servitude
and fined two hundred yen.[129]

The targets of pickpockets were primarily the affluent, in contrast to the
crime of murder, which more often found the poor themselves victimized. The
papers were full of graphic, sometimes lurid, accounts of blood and violence in

the late Meiji years. Sometimes the murders occurred in the more affluent areas. But at least as often they were carried out in the poor regions, where they involved violence both by and against the poor. Many of them were murders of passion, triggered by a combination of poverty, alcohol, and sex. An umbrella repairman named Toyama who lived in a shabby row house near a horsemeat shop, for example, was already desperate because of the lack of customers during a summer drought when his wife ran off with "one of those men with a little stall on wheels who used to go around cleaning out the tiny pipes that people smoked tobacco in." When Toyama found her with the pipe cleaner a few days later, he lost his temper, hit her, knocked her against a gravestone, and "the first thing I knew, she was dead." He said he later found himself standing beside the gravestone, holding a bloody umbrella and unable to remember what had happened. Sentenced to six years in prison, he reported that when she came to him in dreams, she was "always in a good mood," making him suspect "that deep in her heart she was glad I killed her."[130] Or there was the dead-drunk soldier who murdered a geisha in Asakusa in the spring of 1900. Or the inebriated, peeping tom gardener called Debakame who grabbed a twenty-four-year-old woman in March 1908 as she left a bath and killed her in a nearby vacant lot.[131] And there was the typical story, told in *Yorozu*, of half a dozen "merrymakers" who began quarreling at an Asakusa restaurant early in 1900. When the fight got serious, a man named Kiichi, who had consumed large quantities of saké, ran to a nearby street stall, got a knife, and came back to take on his antagonists. The fight turned bloody and at least one person died. Taken to a hospital after collapsing, Kiichi was in "precarious" condition at the time of the *Yorozu* report. Accompanying the article on his fight were several other murder accounts.[132]

Pure desperation also precipitated some *hinmin* murders. Stories such as that of the cabinet maker Tanaka Kanji, whose strangling of his son introduced this chapter, appeared so often in the press as to lose their sense of drama. Breadwinners looked at crying, underfed children or at enfeebled old parents and, knowing no way to help them, decided death was the only way out. In the spring of 1900, *Niroku* reported with little comment on the case of a man named Uehara, who choked his sick mother to death as "an act of mercy." A few weeks later, it told the story of a fifty-five-year-old father who tried to strangle his sick, young adult son with a towel but was foiled by a younger daughter who heard her brother's gasping. The story's tag read, "Pursued by poverty, I thought of killing my child." *Heimin Shinbun* repeatedly told similar tales. On the day it described a weeping father who killed his starving four-year-old child because that seemed kinder than letting the child live without food, it also told two different tales of couples who tried unsuccessfully to kill themselves—and, in one case, their child—by jumping off bridges.[133] The nuances of acts such as these will be discussed later in this chapter; they are mentioned here to make it clear that murders in *hinmin* communities resulted as often from desperate circumstances, even from compassion, as from heinous motives. Whether produced by drunken passion or by desperation, most murders were rooted in poverty.

The more prosaic truth was that crime did not factor largely in the lives of the great majority of *hinmin,* except perhaps for the petty thievery that made daily life possible and the gossip that gave it color. The majority of slum families exemplified the values of the schools and the middle class, working their endless hours and aspiring to creep up the financial and class ladders. Because they had so little money and so few possessions, they generally were not the targets of pickpockets and other thieves. And they were as aghast (or titillated) as their better-off peers at the sensational accounts of robbery and murder. But that did not keep them from being touched by crime. The crime rates in their streets were on the high side of average, they were denigrated and punished as a class for thefts at factories and shops, public perceptions of "*hinmin* crime" added to their psychic burdens. And it was on their neighborhoods that police concentrated, especially at night, evoking Kawabata's quip that there seemed to be "more police detectives than ordinary people wandering around Asakusa after one-thirty in the morning."[134] They also were thus likely to feel police wrath even when they were law-abiding. "If you were walking alone late at night you were bound to get stopped," said one Fukagawa resident.[135] A *Niroku* writer agreed, noting that the police had a "hateful" habit of focusing on less-educated people, "especially women," and ignoring "those who are able to protect themselves with legal terms, whether right or wrong."[136]

One of the ironies was that most police were themselves quite poor—"the poor sod's no different from us," was the way one old pauper put it[137]—inadequately paid public servants who had to enforce order on their peers. They might put on a respectable front, noted a *Tokyo Puck* cartoonist, but away from public eyes they committed the offenses for which they apprehended their impoverished fellows: abusing wives and children, poaching fruit from neighborhood yards, gambling away earnings.[138] The tension of upholding a public standard while living by another, added to their own difficulty in making ends meet, likely triggered the officers' reputation for special roughness in dealing with *hinminkutsu* suspects. The Fukagawa police "were really something to be scared of," said one gambler. "If they thought there was anything at all suspicious about you, you were hauled straight off to a police box." He called the police "a bunch of arrogant bastards in those days." They abused slum dwellers endlessly, sneering at one, "the little bastard fancies himself a real yakuza," then shouting at another, "D'you think we've got shit for brains?"[139] The result was that even law-abiding members of the *kasō shakai* found it hard to escape an acute consciousness of crime. Perpetrators or not, *hinmin* were unavoidably splattered in one way or another by crime's bristled brush.

Mind and Spirit: The Worst Storms

The effects of crime were terrible; so were the ravages of sickness, fire, and flood. None of these produced a deeper darkness, however, than the shadows of the mind and spirit that took some *hinmin* families unawares. Disasters, crimes, and sickness were external, incapable in themselves of making life unlivable. But for some in the *kasō shakai*, they became the precipitating tragedy that opened the door to despair. For others, finances triggered the watershed moment. And for some, the tipping point was the loss of the communal networks that had embraced them before the move to the city. Whatever the cause, the worst darkness of all lay in those catastrophes of the spirit that pushed certain people into the ultimate pit, an abyss from which there was no escape.

The research of an international group of scientists demonstrated early in the twenty-first century that poverty "reduces cognitive capacity," not because of anything inherent in the skill sets or behaviors of poor people but "because the very context of poverty imposes load and impedes cognitive capacity." Studying both rural and urban poor populations, the scholars found that "poverty-related concerns consume mental resources, leaving less for other tasks."[140] It is not, they found, innate intelligence or behavior patterns that reduce cognitive capacity but the environmental factors in which the poor are forced to live. As George Orwell put it, so much more pithily, "hunger reduces one to an utterly spineless, brainless condition, more like the after-effects of influenza than anything else."[141] The experiences of the late Meiji *kasō shakai* make that clear. A recurring theme of the studies of the *hinmin* world is that poverty placed so many pressures on people that rational thinking and behavior became more difficult. Many of these pressures—the low salaries, the crowded living conditions, the inadequacy of food, the necessity of having children work for pay—already have been examined. A few others, which had a particularly strong impact on the spirit, need yet to be highlighted.

For thousands, the demands of having to work twelve-hour night shifts (with only one day off in seven) posed a special threat to emotional equanimity. The 1903 *Shokkō jijō* survey of factory workers found that "night time taxes the spirit a great deal more than day time does"; night workers got ill more often and females on the night shift almost always lost weight, while those on the day shift gained weight or lost less.[142] For others, the isolation of city living, away from old family and village ties, laid an unusually heavy burden on the spirit: "These lonely girls are homesick," said Yokoyama when he saw a group of girls huddled around a hibachi at New Year; they "yearn for their dear parents, brothers, and sisters."[143] And for many thousands, an emotional tipping point was created by the calculating "culture of free competition" that governed city work patterns. Cutthroat capitalist competition did more than anything else (even low wages), argues the labor historian Kumazawa Makoto, to undermine coping skills. He said that factory girls did not mind even the excruciating hours and low wages as much as they did the worker-against-worker environment created by employers: the performance ratings, the ostracism of anyone who showed individuality, "the cold, inhumane treatment of the employer when their health broke down." And they had to bear it "while cut off from home communities whose cultural traditions might have provided grounds to resist."[144]

Worst of all probably was the way the *hinmin* environment caused poor people to blame themselves for their troubles, the way the poverty pocket turned into what the University of Tokyo sociologist Nishizawa Akihiko calls a "zone of self abnegation."[145] Hearing the constant middle-class critiques, many *hinmin* came to accept the idea that responsibility for their financial troubles lay not in luck or in unjust societal patterns but in their own inadequacies. Paulo Freire has called "self-depreciation" a "characteristic of the oppressed, which derives from their internalization of the opinions the oppressors hold of them. So often do they hear that they are good for nothing, know nothing and are incapable of learning anything . . . that in the end they become convinced of their own unfitness."[146] Evidence that he was right is overwhelming in the late Meiji *hinminkutsu*. Sometimes it showed up in self-doubt, as when the prostitute Masuda Sayo decided that her difficulty in understanding some things was "because I'm not really a human child; that's why I don't understand."[147] Most often it showed up simply in the readiness of slum dwellers to look at failures and blame themselves, as Yokoyama found in Tokyo's Samegahashi slum early in 1897. He was moved by a woman's discussion of her miserable marriage. She regretted her husband's heavy drinking, his harangues, his sloth, and she said he "is poor because he wants to be poor." Then she turned on herself, telling the reporter that she wanted to divorce her spouse but did not have the strength to do so because:

> I . . . think that perhaps I continue to live with him because of the Karma effects. Don't laugh at me! . . . I have had previous experiences of not being able to break up, I am afraid that I may be no better this time than before. What do you think of me? I have become weary of this world.[148]

A host of external factors influenced her troubles: the unavailability of jobs, illiteracy, an absence of support systems. But none of those occurred to her. And she was typical. When officials asked nearly five thousand people in Asakusa, Shitaya, Honjo, and Fukagawa in 1911 why they were poor, the majority blamed themselves or their families, with a full quarter saying they lacked adequate physical or mental capabilities, and 6.5 percent calling themselves morally deficient. Only a little over a third cited external economic conditions such as unemployment and low wages.[149] In a similar survey in 1910, 55 percent of rag pickers had said that personal failings such as drinking, debauchery, and inadequate skills were responsible for their poverty, with a mere 16 percent blaming acts of God or external economic factors, prompting Koji Taira to comment, "If the general community regards ragpickers as of no more value than the junk they pick, ragpickers themselves tend to accept this lowly status and social role." Taira's further conclusion—that rag pickers had "lost the bounce, energy, and stamina required to rise above poverty"—is debatable,[150] but there is no denying that self-blame was pervasive.

The emotional depths to which both self-blame and financial desperation were capable of dragging *hinmin* was clear in the endless accounts of suicide that appeared in the papers during the late Meiji years. *Seinen-Rising Generation* reported a steady increase in Tokyo suicides generally at the turn of the twentieth century, from 7,658 in 1897 to 8,582 in 1901, and the papers made it clear that a significant percentage of those were in the poverty pockets.[151] Annual police reports told the same story, in data that understated the total numbers of suicides but showed the preponderance of such deaths in the poor regions. In 1900, for example, Fukagawa, Honjo, Asakusa, and Shitaya reported thirty-four suicides per ward, nearly four times the average numbers for the other wards (excepting Shiba, where the Shin'ami-chō slum was located). That same pattern held across all the late Meiji years, with the poverty wards annually having two or three (in some cases eight or nine) times the numbers of suicides reported elsewhere in the city.[152] These official reports listed "spiritual confusion" (*seishin sakuran*) as the cause of nearly half of all suicides in the late 1890s, with despair over illness, distress about work, and romantic passion (*chijō*) following far behind.[153]

The cold reality suggested by these studies was fleshed out on the human level in continuing stories in the press. The weekly *Heimin Shinbun* reported on three apparent suicides on a single page late in 1903: an Asakusa carpenter named Tanaka who strangled himself because he could not pay the family bills, a factory girl who "fell into a pathetic state of degeneracy" and was killed by a train as she tried to escape, and a man named Watanabe who could not feed the nine residents of his household even with the extra matchbox work with which he supplemented his income. A week later, it described two cases: a Mr. Yokoyama of Kyōbashi who was thrown into poverty by illness and killed himself by drinking hydrochloric acid, and a Gunma pauper who threw his children in a well when he could not feed them. Two issues after that, under the heading "fate of the poor" (*hinja no unmei*), the paper reported on an insolvent worker named Ishikawa who strangled himself after his wife was hospitalized for insanity. And four issues later still, there was the tale of a woman, driven to insanity by poverty, who choked herself to death.[154] The details differed but the story was the same in plebeian *Niroku*'s May 1900 account of the forty-two-year-old Miyata Genjirō, a musician from Shiba Ward who had played in a naval band until inflation made things so bad that he could not keep up with bills. "Everything went wrong," the report said, "and from this April, he was struck with stomach problems. Then his wife went insane from worry." Despondent and panic-stricken, he carried a can of kerosene to the toilet, poured it over himself, and lit a match. His neighbors came rushing when they heard his screams as the fire engulfed his body. They rushed him to a hospital but it was too late; he died that night. The caption of the story said it all for Miyata: "Pressed by poverty, he set his body on fire."[155] Scarcity had sent him into an emotional spiral from which there was no escape.

"There is always grist for gossip," wrote Higuchi, recounting the tale of a twenty-year-old blind masseuse who killed herself in Ueno Park's Mizunoya Pond: "The details are tedious, but the stories make the rounds."[156] One of the tragedies of the late Meiji years was that while frequency made accounts of death boring, each story was about a real person, an individual whose experiences were excruciating, and gripping. Matsubara wrote in 1893 that the poor "lay themselves down at night, some to sleep and some to die."[157] That the vast majority of the *hinmin* fell into the former category—surmounting life's injustices, determined not just to struggle on but to transcend the struggle itself—says powerful things about the human survival instinct and the shrewdness of the late Meiji *hinmin*. At the same time, the fact that other thousands fell victim to the era's shadows and storms does more than just dramatize how serious the ongoing threats were in the *kasō shakai* neighborhoods; it also clarifies several of the era's less salubrious characteristics.

Most obvious among these was the fact, so constantly detailed in the preceding pages, that life's tempests hit the *kasō shakai* most harshly. Natural disasters, illnesses, and even mental depression were problems in every class, but if they created discomfort in the broader society, they created chaos in the *hinminkutsu*. When abnormal rains fell, the lowlands where factories and poor people commingled were inundated first, and most extensively. When TB or typhoid fever struck, factory owners most often fired the workers and sent them back to neighborhoods or villages that lacked medical care. When tragedy struck, there were no networks of family and friends in the poor regions to provide succor or help. The list was endless and the cycle was vicious. Inadequate income led to overwork; overwork weakened resistance to disease; sickness meant lost income, hunger, and new stresses; on and on it went. And official policies frequently made matters even worse for those in the *kasō shakai*. When a case of the plague was found in a poor neighborhood, officials cordoned off the area and burned it, with no provision for those who lived there. When cholera spread, it was primarily the poor who were sent to the "dump sites" called isolation hospitals. Dark clouds may have engulfed everyone in times of disaster and epidemic, but none so overwhelmingly as the poor. As Matsubara put it: "The law that governs the lives of the poor is want." "Want," he said, "makes all other burdens harder to bear."[158]

A less obvious characteristic of the late Meiji years relates to crime. While it was widespread and often violent, and while it invaded *hinmin* neighborhoods, it had less impact on general society than middle-class accounts led one to believe. Murders were, as a rule, isolated affairs, committed against others in the *kasō shakai* world, either people connected to the perpetrator or those who happened to be in the spot where a drunken man lost control of himself. Premeditated assaults on outsiders were rare. The more ubiquitous crimes—petty theft, shoplifting, and pickpocketing—inflicted economic and emotional pain on individuals but rarely disrupted society more generally. Perhaps the most important point to be made about crime is comparative. Shocking or irritating as *hinmin* abuses were, they were mosquito bites compared to the epidemics of inequality and poverty unleashed by the elites. Inhumanly low wages, disregard of workers' health, the complete absence of public social safety nets; these capitalist patterns may not have violated written laws, but they condemned great numbers of people to a subhuman existence in a way that can only be called criminal. George Orwell sneered that the well-off classes in Paris of the 1920s looked at poor workers and said, "So, dear brothers, since evidently you must sweat to pay for our trips to Italy, sweat and be damned to you."[159] So it was in late Meiji Japan. The system-wide misery the elites brought to the *kasō shakai* dwarfed what theft and pickpocketing did to the middle classes. The discrepancy drew little comment—except for the occasional remark by someone like Matsubara that "charity" was "a cloak for former robbery"[160]—but avoidance of the issue did not negate the massive disparity in impact between the narrow criminal acts of the *hinmin* and the broader transgressions of the middle and upper classes.

It needs finally to be reiterated that the roots of this darkness lay not in qualities inherent in poor people but in the environment that engulfed them. Of course the *kasō shakai* included people who were lazy, antisocial, or criminal. But those were as much exceptions as dysfunctional people were aberrations in the middle classes. Most who succumbed to desperation would have succeeded had circumstances not conspired forcefully against them; many of them succeeded anyway, as the next chapter will demonstrate. Taken as a whole, the poor worked harder than those in the middle class. There is no evidence that they were less intelligent. They showed impressive survival skills and ingenuity. But circumstance assailed them, sometimes with an intensity that made survival impossible. The suicides were not, as a rule, carried out by people who were inclined toward self-destruction; they were the result rather of multiplying assaults that in the end made suicide seem like a rational choice. One should blame not weakness so much as the cumulative effects of empty tables, unpayable bills, stomach ailments, and a spouse's insanity for making the musician Miyata opt for self-immolation. So too with many of the murders described in the day's papers. Killing a child or a starving spouse "as an act of mercy" was a crime, but within the moral rulebook penned by poverty, it often made sense. Assaults from without, intensified by an absence of material or social resources, made for a tragic, often deadly, combination. But the causes of these tragedies lay less in inherent *hinmin* characteristics than in the attacking forces that took away humane options.

CHAPTER 6

The Sun Also Shone
Embracing Life

"Step by step, slowly by slowly"

—Handwritten on the eaves of a home in

Mondesa Township, Swakopmund, Namibia[1]

Whispers of spring had begun lifting spirits by the third week of March 1901, when *Niroku Shinpō* announced plans for a special event for poor people. On April 3, when cherry blossoms were to be in bloom, the paper would sponsor a viewing party in the *hinmin* region, at Shirahige Shrine in Mukōjima on the eastern side of Tokyo's Sumida River, not far from Asakusa's grand Sensōji Temple. "Come, Laborers!" cried the paper. "We seek the poor, the workers who never enter the abodes of the rich" for a Social Gathering of Japanese Workers (Nihon Rōdō Konshinkai).[2] To be held "rain or shine," the event was not intended "to have any particular meaning but simply to let people play together on a relaxed spring day and wash away the year's gloom."[3] There would be music, games, raffles, a pig chase, food, alcohol, soft drinks, fireworks, and talks by *Niroku* writers and labor leaders. The cost? Just ten sen a person, less than a day's wages for a bathhouse worker. Tickets could be purchased at designated locations across the city.

The following days demonstrated what Tokyo's workers thought of the idea of a celebration. As word of the event spread, people flocked to the ticket sites. With a reported seventy thousand entrance passes purchased by the end of March, *Niroku* announced that special trains would be used to get everyone to Mukōjima and back.[4] City officials, for their part, began to worry. What about the potential for disruption? What was the event's real meaning? The paper's comment in a March 22 article that there was a "possibility" that, in addition to providing a chance to party, the gathering "might serve as an inducement to awaken both workers and capitalists from their long night's slumber"[5] gave the authorities pause. As a result, the Tokyo police issued a set of guidelines, prohibiting attendees from bringing saké into the shrine grounds, forbidding anything raucous, and limiting attendance to five thousand; they also forbade attendance altogether by workers at government institutions such as the

Koishikawa Arsenal and the Printing Bureau. The paper, for its part, bought back thousands of the tickets. But the enthusiasm could not be dampened. Participants began camping out near the shrine on the evening of April 2; by dawn on the 3rd, more than the prescribed five thousand already had shown up; and when the gates opened at 7:00, no fewer than twenty thousand entered, police prohibitions notwithstanding.[6]

It was a lively and, on the whole, peaceful day. "The reluctant Mukōjima cherry blossoms were about 40 percent in bloom and 60 percent in bud," reported *Niroku*. "It felt as if one were moving in a tunnel of white clouds." Because the Shirahige grounds were small, the crowds became "congested to the point that people could not open their mouths."[7] Sabre-holding police, stationed everywhere, acted roughly at times, but revelry and joy pervaded. Drink and food disappeared in great quantities, performers did sword dances and played melodies on the *koto, rakugo* performers amused the crowds with stories of traditional life, thousands of small items were raffled off, and merchants gave away towels advertising their establishments. When a much-anticipated pig chase was announced, the frightened animal headed for the river, prompting outsiders who had not been able to get into the shrine grounds to join the chase. They also "liberated" some other pigs from nearby shops, igniting a melee and getting into a fight with police that damaged the shrine gate and some adjoining properties.[8] The day's most notable speech was delivered by the labor pioneer Katayama Sen, who praised laborers for their "sweat-drenched work" and called for the government to "protect laborers," give them the vote, and provide them with adequate schools.[9]

"Japan's first May Day," declared Akiyama, was a great success, "a celebration of what is human" (*hyūmanitei no tachiba kara omatsuri*).[10] And its spirit sent ripples across eastern Japan. In May, the newspaper *Jiji Shinpō* reported on similar friendship events in the cities of Tochigi and Ashikaga north of Tokyo, drawing in excess of a thousand workers each. In the fall, more than three thousand showed up for a similar gathering in Matsumoto to the west.[11] That these events were peaceful and joyous was not enough, however, to placate the authorities. Nervous about the implications—and potential for disruption—of large worker gatherings, they decided that one friendship celebration was enough for Tokyo. When *Niroku* announced a successor event the following March, the police banned it. The paper mocked the prohibition, proclaiming "Tears for the Police interference! Cheers for the coming reunion!" But in the end Akiyama called the event off and urged people to stage smaller flower viewings on their own. The police also brought charges against several *Niroku* writers for their defiant articles, and when they were acquitted, the editor celebrated with a keg of beer for his employees. Huge gatherings would occur again, repeatedly, across the next decade, but as "spontaneous" political demonstrations rather than as worker celebrations. As Akiyama recalled, "it became impossible after that to hold large gatherings of this sort."[12]

The political implications of *Niroku*'s celebration were important, but equally significant was the light the Mukōjima event shed on aspects of *hinmin* life that have been largely overlooked. For one, the Konshinkai made it clear that poor people in the late Meiji cities were more than supine objects; they were self-conscious agents, people who responded to an invitation for fun with alacrity and refused to stay away from a celebration even when told to. For another, it demonstrated a *hinmin* proclivity for activism, a willingness to participate in the public square even if that activism was not yet highly organized. Most of all, it illustrated the eagerness of poor workers to attack life, to experience it in its fullness and to seek joy where it could be found. It demonstrated that shadows and storms were only one part of the *hinmin* life's equation. Celebration, merrymaking, and resistance were important too. While the disasters, dysfunctions, and despair described in the previous chapter were real, so were the joys and the expressions of fully fledged humanity. Without understanding the place those brighter elements took in daily life, it is impossible fully to understand the *kasō shakai* class.

Agency on the Job

The focus on the *hinmin* plight—on the "miserable lot" of all poor people and the conviction that many of them accepted life "in tranquility like fetid pigs"[13]— blinded contemporaries to the take-charge way most of those in the *kasō shakai* world lived. Even an egalitarian activist like Paulo Freire argued a century later that the "oppressive reality" of poverty and the capitalist system tends "to submerge human beings' consciousness."[14] One reason for this interpretation undoubtedly lies in a tendency of observers and activists alike to focus on the political and social spheres, to assume that people who do not fight for themselves at the systemic level are not acting as agents. But if one understands agency at its fundamental level, as an indication of the ability and determination of people to make conscious, rational choices in response to their own social and physical environment, it is clear that most of the *kasō shakai* were active agents. When Ueki stole his pieces of charcoal, when an iron worker dressed in a gentleman's clothes for a Sunday stroll through Ueno Park, when a Samegahashi family gave food to a neighbor whose mother had died, they were asserting agency. The novelist Nagai Kafū had it right when he trumpeted the conscious rationality of a once "respectable" *hinmin* who decided to withdraw from working society and give himself over to pleasure, sex, and poverty, to eschew the old pattern of "jumping out of bed and putting on Western clothes at the sound of the alarm clock on a winter morning, . . . playing by turns the enemy, the rival, the obsequious underling, the malevolent detractor, in the process of what was known as gathering for friendly social intercourse."[15] The man's actions may have appeared bizarre. Certainly he was atypical. But one could not have denied the intentionality of what he did. Poverty may have gotten in the way of the observers' ability to see agency in *hinmin* behaviors, but it had no power to eviscerate it.

Nowhere was *hinmin* agency more pronounced than in the workplaces where so many injustices occurred. One need not doubt the factory girl's declaration that life on the shop floor was "like working in a prison" or the reporter's observation that railroad companies treated their conductors "like cows and horses"[16] to understand that oppression and darkness were only part of the story. Even the workplace had compensating features for large numbers of *hinmin*. Searching among the accounts of life in the factory and on the street, one finds repeated bits of evidence that many laborers felt a dignity and sense of accomplishment in their work that brutal managers could not take away. In the early 1990s, Edward Fowler described day laborers who would look at buildings they had helped to construct and "utter with conviction, 'We have built Japan.'"[17] Writing about worker life decades earlier, the novelist Nakagami Kenji described the digger Akiyuki, slaving away so hard that "sweat ran down like water," and experiencing pure pleasure in doing so: "Damn, he liked to work hard with his body like this. It was the purest form of work."[18] Matsubara found similar sentiments in these workers' late Meiji counterparts. Often, he said, illiterate workers would ask him to write letters for them, a task that gave him "much insight into their character." Writing those letters convinced him that a full eight out of ten workers, even those living at flophouses, had "succeeded in their goals" and found fulfillment in doing so. In contrast to most rich folks, he said, they had "clean souls"; anyone who could not understand the sense of artistry they experienced in making clogs or plastering a broken pot to make it into a hibachi was simply "ignorant."[19] Putting it slightly differently, the orphaned newspaper delivery boy in Hara Hōitsuan's 1892 novel *Shinnen* (New year) declared that he felt like Benjamin Franklin, who "published his own newspaper, and then walked the streets selling it. . . . Those lazy fellows who do nothing but play," he exclaimed, "it is they who ought to be ashamed of themselves!" The lad added that when it came to doing productive work, he saw no difference between the prime minister and himself.[20]

If significant numbers embraced this kind of pride in their work, even greater numbers—indeed, the vast majority—harbored hopes for advancement. Matsubara told his readers that one reason the inhabitants of "poverty street" used fortune tellers was that they had "a firm belief that better days must be coming" and, "weary waiting for them," they wanted "to know *when*."[21] Several of the outside observers found substantial reason for this optimism, reporting that while massive numbers of people were feeling the bitterness of poverty at any given time and while progress usually was glacial, improvement over time was the norm, not just in dreams but in reality. Looking at Osaka's Nago-chō slum in the mid-1890s, Yokoyama said that income from the match-making industry had enabled the area "to overcome its former notoriety"; in neighborhoods where residents once "were all clad in rags" and where quarrels had "wreaked unmentionable violence," people still were poor but tranquility generally reigned now and people wore decent clothing.[22] In Tokyo's Asakusa region, recalled another observer, the slum areas "with the wives squatting outside their shoddy little tenements" had been replaced in the 1910s by poor people living in cramped but decent housing.[23] Social scientists found the same pattern. While more than 70 percent of *hinmin* wives worked outside the home in 1911, only 44 percent did in 1920. And less than a decade after the end of the Meiji era, the proportion of children under fifteen who had to work for an income had declined to 13 percent.[24] Poverty persisted, but the general pattern for individuals and families was upward, supporting folklorist Yanagita Kunio's observation that when one looked at the Meiji-Taishō years as a whole more people succeeded in new jobs than fell into poverty.[25]

It was not unusual to hear reformers and industrialists repeat the success stories of individual *hinmin,* stories that surely proved the middle-class truism that anyone could make it by working hard. The magnates and reformers were not impressed, however, by another kind of worker behavior that demonstrated agency in its own way: the spontaneous, sometimes crude way laborers stood up for their rights on the factory floor and in the neighborhood. Yokoyama criticized ironworkers as "rude" and boiler workers as having "rowdy manners," and he was appalled by Shin'ami-chō slum dwellers "who speak flatteringly but who will make faces and stick their tongues out when the other person's back is turned."[26] Boorishness and bad manners bespoke inferiority to middle-class outsiders. With another set of lenses, however, observers might have seen those behaviors as signs of the self-assertion and independence that lie at the heart of human agency. The insistence on taking breaks, the cursing, and the ribald joking around with fellow workers were signs of humanity, evidence that laborers were ready to be either obsequious or rude, depending on what the situation required. So too were the acts of petty theft. The Kiryū Union of Commerce and Industry might complain about the loss of thousands of yen a year from the scraps of threads stolen by pieceworkers. But to the pieceworkers, that theft represented a kind of protest and an affirmation of personal initiative, an unspoken assertion that if employers were going to rob them of living wages, they would find ways to put food on the table.[27] As Kinoshita Naoe said in *Pillar of Fire,* "Nobody steals for the fun of it. . . . if a man's got more of anything than he needs, it's his duty to share it." The "real thief" is the one who lives in plenty while others starve.[28] Yokoyama was being critical when he said that workers would "get together in a corner, talk privately, and become frolicsome" when supervisors were absent.[29] What he did not notice was the community-building humaneness that such out-of-sight frolicking demonstrated.

Few behaviors revealed human agency more clearly than the bravado and brashness of the rickshaw pullers to whom Matsubara gave so much ink. Picking up the journalist's chapter on what it would take for "the underclass to erupt" (*kasō shakai funka sen*), one expects a discourse on social movements but finds instead a description of the things that cause rickshaw pullers to lose their tempers and strike out at personal tormentors and oppressors. His tone is dismissive as he explains that *shafu* or pullers never can be expected to organize or form a political movement. "If they get thirty-five *sen* a day in wages, they do not worry about whether Tokyo moves forward or backward," he says. "They do not have ringleaders or chiefs. They are extremely weak when it comes to spiritual movements or to institutional things such as organizing, preparing manifestoes, holding meetings, or forming groups."[30] Then he proceeds to describe the things that trigger a *shafu* outburst. Confronted by police officers who arrest them for minor offenses or by inconsiderate clients, he says, they blow up, cursing out their enemies in language too coarse for polite ears. Matsubara regrets that such outbursts are always personal and unplanned, but he leaves no doubt that the expressions of outrage are intentional, that *shafu*, pushed to the limit, refuse to simply take it. They take on their oppressors, expressing themselves in language that puts fear into the hearts of middle-class riders. This may not have been an appealing sign of agency but it revealed agency nonetheless, a worker agency that was highly effective in achieving its quotidian goals.

Yokoyama employed the word *isamihada* (chivalrous disposition or, literally, "daring skin") to denote the kind of agency he wanted to see in *hinmin* workers. Drawing on a phrase used by late Tokugawa fiction writers to suggest a combination of masculine strength and empathy, he argued that workers should possess the *isamihada* of old-time artisans.

> I am not referring to cheekiness or wildness; I definitely am not talking about being noisy and clamorous. To put it simply, I mean having the spirit of a worker, nurturing a passionate desire to improve one's skills, respecting one's masters, and being fervent about treating one's fellows kindly. Those who exhibit these qualities are the true exemplars of the worker's *isamihada*.

For Yokoyama, the mid-Meiji working class did not measure up; *isamihada* was an aspiration rather than a reality, because the *kasō shakai* workers had descended a long way from the behavioral standards of those bare-chested artisans of Tokugawa days. But even though *isamihada* remained an ideal "for the future," he said that when finally realized it would enable *hinmin* workers to "nurture first-class knowledge, maintain a secure life position, and achieve power politically."[31] Had the journalist been able to remove the blinders that middle-class values forced on him, he would have seen an abundance of *isamihada* in his own time. He would have seen that even the noisiness and cheekiness he abhorred (to say nothing of the workers' constant scheming and planning to move forward in the most difficult circumstances) signified "daring skin" of the first order. Their behavior may not have appeared chivalrous to him, but it overflowed with intentionality and resilience, with agency.

Communal Agency: The Activists

The newspaper *Yorozu Chōhō* reported on the morning of January 12, 1900, that fifty-three Japanese strikers at the Yokohama Steam Laundry Company had been replaced by thirty Chinese workers. The writer said the police were protecting the new employees—who "are doing the business much better and quicker than the Japanese workers ever did"—from violent attacks by the men on strike. Japanese laborers, complained the article, "lack those fine qualities in a workman, namely obedience and responsibility."[32] Consciously or unconsciously, the writer of the article had identified another facet of *hinmin* agency: the readiness of Japan's urban poor to fight jointly—and publicly—for improvements in the quality of their lives. Organized unions and widespread strikes may not have been possible in the late Meiji environment, but the era's last two decades produced more *kasō shaki* activism and popular protests than generally has been recognized.

Individual acts of protest and self-assertion were part of a broader pattern of intentional noncompliance with public policies and practices. When the Tokyo government outlawed smoking by minors in 1900, for example, parents widely ignored the law and let their children smoke indoors, away from police eyes. When the Osaka government began taxing bicycles, barely 10 percent of riders actually paid. The same happened in Tokyo. Said one sympathetic journalist, "As the government tries shameful means to increase taxes, so people are far from ashamed to evade them." And when *kichin'yado* owners raised prices in the mid-1890s during the Sino-Japanese War, small groups of renters made news by refusing to pay until prices were lowered again.[33] A dramatic example of individual action against the system came in response to the *jiyū haigyō* (self-emancipation) campaign launched at the turn of the century by *Niroku's* Akiyama. After the bloody episode described in an earlier chapter in which Ayaginu fled the pleasure quarters, large numbers of prostitutes took their own initiative, often against heavy pressure, to free themselves. It was not unusual for police, parents, and owners to cooperate in intimidating the women, trying to keep them from leaving the profession. Yet within a month of Ayaginu's act, more than a hundred had left their brothels and by the following spring a reported 1,100 Tokyo prostitutes had emancipated themselves.[34] Every one of those *jiyū haigyō* actors, just like every young smoker and every rent protester, acted intentionally, defying norms and customs or laws.

Hinmin agency was more obvious still at the communal level, in the public demonstrations and riots that peppered the last Meiji years, most of them "centered in the housing districts of the poor."[35] Nine major incidents rocked Tokyo alone between 1905 and 1918, each providing evidence of the increasing connection poor people felt with the public sphere. Similar episodes occurred in Osaka and elsewhere. The opening event—when for "the first time . . . the crowd acted as a political force"[36]—began at Hibiya Park in Tokyo in September 1905 and resulted in three days of rioting, with tens of thousands of enraged citizens overturning street cars, burning newspaper offices, and destroying hundreds of police stations in protest against Japanese diplomats' failure to secure greater gains in the negotiations that concluded the Russo-Japanese War. The Hibiya rioters also killed seventeen people, and their protests were replicated in Osaka, Kobe, Yokohama, and forty other towns and cities. By the time the Meiji emperor died seven years later, three other uprisings also had sparked riots, and the half dozen years after his death produced another five major urban protests and riots. Added to hundreds of smaller public rallies and protests in the late Meiji years, the unrest was enough to cause elder statesman Yamagata Aritomo to express a private fear "that if Japan continued on its present course, it would head for a fall."[37] Scholars have labeled this the Era of Popular Violence (*minshū sōjō ki*).[38]

One reason so much attention has been paid to these rallies is that they marked a transition in the role commoners played in Japan's political life. Labor historian Andrew Gordon describes this as a period when, for the first time, commoner demonstrators "unequivocally articulated a vision of the political order at odds with that of the elite," a time when commoners began insisting that ministers of state had a responsibility to act in keeping with the *"expressed will of the emperor and the people."*[39] It was a period, I have argued elsewhere, when average citizens—both the *kasō shakai* of the slums and Nakagawa Kiyoshi's slightly better off "new middle class" (*shin chūkansō*)—became a conscious, participating part of the public sphere, imbued with a sense of being members of a larger political whole, or state.[40] Fueling their new activism was a powerful consciousness of *kasō shakai* agency.

Official records make it clear that the *hinmin* were major participants in the period's biggest demonstrations. The majority of the 308 people tried for violence after the Hibiya tumult of 1905 were identified by police records as factory workers and craftsmen, rickshaw pullers, shop workers, and people with no occupation.[41] If one includes artisans, nearly 70 percent of those arrested in the combined riots of 1905 and 1906 were from *kasō shakai* occupations.[42] Similarly, a full two-thirds of the 600,000 to 800,000 Osaka participants in the 1918 rice riots were workers and other poor people.[43] Okamoto Shumpei, a student of Russo-Japanese War diplomacy, says the Hibiya "rioters were overwhelmingly . . . 'lower-class people'" who "had a low degree of political consciousness."[44]

Demonstrators, a majority of whom were *hinmin,* ravaged Tokyo in early September 1905, protesting Japan's settlement terms in the Russo-Japanese War. Here, *Tokyo Riot Graphic* shows them setting fire to a streetcar on the night of September 6. *Japan Graphic,* No. 56, September 18, 1905. Courtesy of Andrew Gordon.

His characterization of their political consciousness is disputable, as the following paragraphs will show, but his assessment of their economic backgrounds is not. While the vast majority of the participants were male, thanks in part to laws that forbade women from taking part in political meetings, photos and sketches of the rallies also include occasional shots of females, including one of a woman running from the police. It should not surprise us that 5 percent of those apprehended in the 1905–1906 disturbances were rickshaw pullers, given the *shafu*'s flexible work hours, which made it easier for them to participate, and their reputation for strong opinions.

The heavy *hinmin* involvement in the late Meiji disturbances sprang primarily, though not exclusively, from the economic nature of the issues. Although the Hibiya riots focused on "populist nationalism,"[45] most of the other uprisings dealt primarily with pocketbook issues such as streetcar fares and taxes. Even the Hibiya protests, which were ostensibly about Japan's "weak" diplomacy, had an important economic tinge, with protesters incensed that their war taxes had not produced greater territorial gains and worried that the lack of an indemnity from Russia would mean higher taxes. Prime Minister Katsura Tarō wrote to his political mentor Yamagata on September 2 suggesting that the "people," who had been "making quite a bit of noise about the peace agreement," were incapable of separating their personal economic and social concerns from the national "political" issues. Ever the class-conscious elitist, he blamed journalists and political activists for "inciting the minds of the lower classes," with the result that "the lower-class people have mixed up social problems with politics, and people like rickshaw men and petty merchants are making noise without understanding the pros and cons of the problems." He said the government needed to find a way "to separate this from social and economic questions and make it exclusively a question of politics."[46] The disdain that the political leaders and the writers had for the intelligence of *hinmin* demonstrators is neither surprising nor well-founded. But they were right in their assessment that *kasō shakai* activism was closely tied to the matters of putting food on the table, affording a ride to work, and securing livable housing.

Three key points surface when one looks closely at the popular disturbances of the last Meiji decade. First, the *hinmin* acted consciously, as people with a clear sense of the political principles that lay at the heart of their demands. There may have been an element of truth in the officials' dismissal of the poor as easily manipulated by outside agitators. Certainly some people attended mass rallies for their entertainment value; these were, after all, street dramas of the highest order. But the evidence suggests that most *hinmin* came to the rallies of their own volition, with a distinct understanding of the political and economic issues. When the mass-oriented *Yorozu Chōhō* invited its readers to the Hibiya demonstration on September 5, 1905, it cried out, "Come! Come! Come! A national assembly to protest the treaty is going to be held today at Hibiya. . . . Come, those who have backbones. . . . Come, those who know justice. . . . Come and all together raise a voice of opposition to the humiliating and shameful peace."[47] The words were emotional, but the issues were thoughtful. A year later when the "maverick activist" Matsumoto Chiwaki asked a crowd of several thousand people whether they wanted to "do some smashing" to prevent streetcar fare increases, only a minority followed his protest march to the Home Ministry; the majority preferred to wait to see if the government would pay heed to their protests.[48] They were people with individual minds, not the spontaneous, impassioned mob the officials were wont to describe. Even more telling, the language invoked most often in calling these demonstrations was that of constitutionalism and the officials' responsibility to pay attention to citizen demands. As a *Yorozu* editorialist wrote in the summer of 1911 when the issue was public ownership of streetcars, everyone "who agrees that the constitutional system belongs rightfully to us" should gather for the next day's rally at Hibiya Park. At least ten thousand, perhaps twenty thousand, showed up.[49] Emotional speech making and overreaction by police may have turned some rallies into riots, but there was no denying that an awareness of the impact political policies had on their own lives was instrumental in bringing *hinmin* to the public square.

Second, the rallies and riots bespoke a transition in the public consciousness of the urban poor. The late Meiji protests showed a growing understanding among the urban masses that they belonged to a city-wide and national whole that was greater than their own family or *hinminkutsu* circles, a public sphere that owed them certain things in return for their taxes and fees. Demonstrators in the Tokugawa years had usually focused on the local merchants or the nearby village heads who made their lives miserable. Activists in the political rights movements of the 1880s gained only limited support from the still-small urban poor populations. Matsubara's and Yokoyama's accounts of "dark Tokyo" in the 1890s show only meager pockets of activism in a world where the term "explosion" connoted a rickshaw puller spewing invective on a nasty rider. By the onset of the Era of Popular Violence in 1905, however, vast numbers of the *hinmin* had begun to see themselves as citizens. Papers referred to them more often now as *kokumin* or *shimin* (citizens). "This is a world," said a journalist in 1901, "in which even rickshaw pullers take newspapers."[50] When those pullers, or their factory-working counterparts, felt abused or threatened by rising prices and increased streetcar fares, they were increasingly likely to vent their frustrations in a public space and to speak in the language of citizens whose "constitutional rights" allowed them to hold officials' feet to the fire.[51]

Third, these *hinmin*-centered protests had considerable impact, both positive and negative, immediate and long-term. Beyond the physical and human destruction they caused, they precipitated policy changes. In 1906, for example, demonstrators got officials to postpone (though not cancel) a proposed increase in streetcar fares. And three years later, the very threat of public uprisings prompted officials to reject new fare increases. The labor activist Abe Isoo commented, after the railway companies agreed late in 1903 to establish uniform three-sen fares following a public outcry, "The influence of public opinion should not be passed unnoticed. . . . The private companies surrendered at last after showing much obstinacy."[52] The weekly *Heimin Shinbun* agreed, calling the companies' response "a signal triumph for the popular demand, and a great advantage for the majority of people."[53] There also is evidence on the darker side of the ledger, suggesting that the demonstrations pushed officials to begin adopting more stringent speech-control policies, which increasingly limited expression and restricted publication in the decades that followed Meiji. When Katsura made his often-quoted statement that "socialism is today no more than a wisp of smoke, but if it is ignored it will some day have the force of wildfire,"[54] he had the French Revolution and Japan's restive urban masses in mind. A major theme in a series of letters between Yamagata and the conservative journalist Tokutomi Sohō in the early 1900s was the question of how to control "the people." "The present political situation and the temper of the people are extremely volatile, so I am praying that you will devise an appropriate and correct policy. . . . Please destroy this letter," wrote Tokutomi in 1915. Yamagata, on another occasion, said, "There is nothing more fearful than unthinking courage; because when people open their eyes to reality after thrashing about in blind courage, it is too late, and by that time the nation is beyond rescue."[55] Frightened, officials went down the road of increasingly heavy-handed censorship and thought control in the years following Meiji's death. When the *kasō shakai* took to the streets, they were exhibiting not just agency but a capacity for influence that generally has been overlooked by journalists and scholars.

Another thing that cries for attention is that *hinmin* activism went beyond rallies and demonstrations. If the protests involved minimal organizational work on the part of the participants, other types of activities showed that significant numbers of the urban poor were conscious of the need to work together, in an organized fashion and over the long haul, to improve their situation. The prevailing view has been that *kasō shakai* society was, for many reasons, incapable of organization: poor people were iconoclastic and independent minded, long hours and desperate finances made organized activities impossible, low literacy rates meant low levels of political interest, people without agency do not organize. Early in the 1890s, Matsubara said explicitly that personal idiosyncrasies made cooperation impossible for rickshaw pullers. In 1899, Yokoyama drew a similar conclusion about factory workers, observing that "until now, unity has been noticeably missing among our laborers"; most workers, he said, were "too timid to fight back."[56] Two years later, a *Yorozu* advocate of labor unions talked about systemic problems such as employers' incentive systems and long, enervating work hours that made it difficult for iron horse tram workers to join cooperative organizations.[57] And a few years after that, the socialist pioneer Kōtoku Shūsui despaired over the workers' prospects for organizing, arguing that the capitalist system kept laborers from looking after their own interests even as "the capitalists were getting better and better at cruel struggle."[58] The truth, however, was that these conventional views obscured a more complex—and engaged—reality.

While widespread unionization would not come until the post-Meiji decades, the 1890s and early 1900s provided what must be seen as a remarkable amount of organized *hinmin* activism, given the factors militating against it. As

Gordon has noted, actions varied significantly from place to place and from one worker group to another, but workers both in and out of factories "gradually learned to carry on labor disputes of increasing sophistication," creating in the process "important traditions of protest even before the advent of self-identified union organizers." Chapter 3 of this work showed the propensity of Tokyo carters to form proto-unions and of the notoriously independent rickshaw pullers to engage in cooperative endeavors in the 1890s. And they marked only the beginning. Workers in several of the more traditional crafts and services—from cloth dyers to construction workers, from geisha to prostitutes—created localized union-like organizations to fight for better work conditions in that same decade. Shipbuilders in Tokyo launched the short-lived Union for Industrial Progress in 1889, and an ironworkers' union founded in 1897 lasted for more than two years before collapsing in the face of official pressure and the co-optation of labor leaders. Railroad workers too were effective as early as 1892 in organizing at individual plants to fight for better wages and fairer treatment, and by the end of the 1890s they were carrying out highly organized strikes, largely without support from a broader union. Indeed, by 1900, roughly 200,000 Japanese workers had affiliations with some kind of union-style labor organization. These efforts did not last, but they showed a propensity to agitate collectively that flies in the face of *hinmin* stereotypes as beings without agency.[59]

Japanese laborers generally avoided the machine-smashing protests of early British workers; indeed, a historian of the Nagoya region sees "political quietism" as a key ingredient in Japan's "smooth political transition from agrarianism to industrialism."[60] But they did stage hundreds of strikes and protests in the last half of the Meiji era. According to one compilation, Tokyo alone had 170 labor disputes between early Meiji and 1916, by artisans, printers, factory laborers, transport workers, and others. Another study found 234 worker actions across the whole of Japan in the eleven years from 1897 to 1907, involving 41,539 laborers.[61] Although the great majority of struggles related to wages, it was not unusual for workers to fight over issues such as the length of the work day, sick leave, and demeaning work environments. The year 1897, when rising prices overwhelmed many families, saw more than thirty disputes: by forty-four silk reeling girls in rural Shimane Prefecture, by sixty-nine miners in Hokkaido, by trainmen at Shimbashi Station in Tokyo, and by a miscellany of brick makers, salt field laborers, stone masons, tobacco curers, pottery makers, sawyers, and charcoal makers. The strikes ranged from a few hours to more than three weeks in length, and most of them resulted in at least partial victories for the workers. They represented, in the words of Yokoyama, "outcries against the hardships of maintaining a living." The venerable journalist insisted that workers generally were too quiescent; he repeatedly accused laborers of "playing at striking" and begged them to organize more actively, but he had to admit that, whether adequately organized or not, large numbers of *hinmin* "were thoroughly prepared to fight."[62]

A random sample of press items early in the 1900s gives some sense of how many different fields were touched by this kind of *kasō shakai* activism. On February 25, 1900, the establishment-oriented *Seinen-Rising Generation* expressed satisfaction over the stamping out of Tokyo's latest plague epidemic, then reported with concern on a strike by more than 1,800 Tokyo umbrella makers for better wages. A month later, *Yorozu Chōhō* relayed the news that Sumida River barge workers had begun "making a fuss" after learning that a recent wage increase was far less than the new profits the company was making; "they are stubborn enough even to go on strike if the situation continues," said the writer. Mid-decade stories in *Shūkan Heimin Shinbun* included a work stoppage by 121 women in a Saitama Prefecture tea factory, a concession-inducing, four-day strike by more than 600 Tokyo brick makers, and 900 women temporarily shutting down a Kofu silk filature factory. In April 1905, Yokoyama described an action by the workers at Koishikawa Army Arsenal who refused to work and held a festival on the factory grounds. *Tokyo Shakai Shinbun*'s many protest accounts in mid-1908 included one story about 800-plus striking dyers in Nagaoka and another on more than 100 Tokyo *hinmin* demanding lower rents. *Shūkan Shakai Shinbun*'s work stoppage reports that same summer included 100 Yokohama train conductors demanding both better wages and an end to the use of "slavish language," newspaper employees at the *Japan Gazette* opposing rules about tardiness, and 60 trolley carpenters seeking better work conditions. And *Seinen* wrote about 2,000 Tokyo streetcar workers who shut down the city's whole system on New Year's Eve, 1911, refusing to return to work until well into New Year's Day, when several former company directors agreed to forgo their year-end bonuses and distribute the savings to the workers.[63] The point of such a list is that while workers may have been slow in organizing, they were anything but docile, anything but mute. They did more than complain to dormitory roommates; they fought back as agents, with energy and ingenuity.

And like their peers in the street demonstrations, they had an impact. One indication of that lay in the hard work officials put into curtailing their activism. The draconian Public Order Police Law in 1900, for example, forbade workers from organizing or striking and prohibited women from joining political groups, while a string of other administrative and legal measures restricted "radical" speech and actions in the following years. An even clearer indication showed up in the results of the worker actions. More often than not, the strikers and protesters got much (or all) of what they demanded. Of the thirty 1897 strikes that Yokoyama described, only five were clear failures; two-thirds yielded all or part of the workers' demands. Sometimes, strike leaders were fired as sacrificial lambs, but even in those cases the wage increases usually were forthcoming. Indeed, the most common notation in the strike reports was "Demand for pay increase. . . . Wages raised."[64] Another study of 107 strikes by more than 20,000 workers between 1903 and 1907 found that while thirty (28 percent) failed to produce improvements, seventy-one resulted in either significant wage increases or shorter hours.[65] Typical was the crusade of 600 Tokyo brick makers who refused to work for four days in March of 1904, then went back to work after accepting a compromise roughly halfway between their demands and management's offer. Just as typical were the *Japan Gazette* strikers who won a total victory when they insisted that the paper drop a new policy of docking workers an hour of pay for being five minutes tardy.[66]

The majority of the *hinmin,* of course, worked quietly and avoided public protests; so did most middle- and upper-class citizens. But there is no gainsaying that a vocal, energetic minority of the urban *kasō shakai* followed the activist route. Writing in the early 1890s, Matsubara had predicted a time when the "great hungry beast" of the slum dwellers "will learn its strength, and . . . need no longer hunger and suffer to provide luxury and ease for its keepers." On that day, he said, a "soul will be born unto the beast, a soul of passion whose fire will devour its rags and its filth." But for now, he sighed, "The beast is blind."[67] One doubts that he would have written the same thing a decade and a half later. By then, tens of thousands of *hinmin* were participating in the protests that had turned Tokyo's and Osaka's streets into news spots. Thousands were taking direct action in the workplace, led most often by organizers from their own ranks. It is not surprising that a *Taiyō* writer referred to them as "passionate plebeians."[68] They may have been less violent than their Western counterparts, but they were not passive. Nor were they ineffective. They secured better wages and working conditions; they gave officials and factory owners sleepless nights. And all the while they provoked the increasingly heavy hand of official restrictions, which became such an important part of Japan's public scene in the decades that followed. They lived and acted, in short, as agents, not simply as objects.

Daily Life: Not All Shadows

In standard depictions of *hinmin* homes, darkness filled every corner and the center of the room too: eaves drooped, rips disfigured the shoji paper on sliding doors, wooden walls rotted, stray cats pooped on the floor. As a *Tokyo Pakku* cartoonist said of a poor wife preparing food for New Year, "she truly is miserable."[69] To some elites, this was a comforting view, highlighting the distance between "us and them." To others, it was a disturbing picture of how far Japan remained from modernity. To progressives, it confirmed the need for charity and legal reform. Had those observers been able to change the direction of their vision, however, they would have seen that shadows occurred only in contrast to the light that was at the core of *hinmin* lives. Real and frequent as the squalls and troubles were, life was filled with compensating pleasures and hopes that made things bearable, often even joyous. One of Kinoshita's *Pillar of Fire* activists encapsulated the nuanced whole when he reacted to his selfish father's description of miners as "a hairy mob, like bears." "They're not bears" replied the son. "They're human, they're our brothers."[70] Indeed. The accounts of daily life in the Asakusa alleys and the Fukagawa *kichin'yado* yield endless nuggets of evidence that the *hinmin* pursued daily life zestfully, with an optimism that often defied logic. Much of this evidence is anecdotal, since it fell outside the surveyors' categories, but the stories are too numerous to ignore.

One thing that emerges is quiet determination and pride. A visiting novelist from Indonesia remarked that even when drunk, Japanese commoners "never forgot themselves; and jolly as they were, they were never rude," in contrast to what she had seen in Europe. The Boston zoologist Edward Morse commented on how "immaculate" even Japan's poorest people and cheapest shelters were "in comparison with . . . similar quarters in nearly all the great cities of Christendom."[71] And Futaba Day Care teachers liked to tell the story of a rickshaw puller who went blind. Did he take to begging or depend on others for assistance? No. He and his daughter became street vendors, selling boiled beans in the day and deep-fried sweets at night. He would carry the produce and, leading him, she would make the sales, "day in and day out for the whole year, with no days off, braving rain and snow."[72] Beneath all of this, for many workers, lay personal pride. As a *Niroku* writer pointed out after watching people in a park one weekend, "They do not cry when they see rich people; they are not envious; they certainly do not worship them. . . . Many are the laborers (*shokunin*) who toil untiringly in their oil-stained clothes every day, then stroll through the park in top hat and frockcoat on Sundays."[73] One of the most poignant accounts was the *Seinen* description of a beggar with a "rather aristocratic bearing" and considerable skill in English, who lived at a flophouse but, when given two yen, bought himself an old overcoat, a morning coat, and a hat, then spent the rest on cakes for the poor children near his *kichin'yado*.[74] These were people who knew how to work and stretch yen; they also were people with a sense of self-worth.

Among the less predictable *hinmin* proclivities when it came to chasing away shadows was newspaper reading. The success of plebeian papers such as *Niroku Shinpō* and *Yorozu Chōhō*—which had become Tokyo's two biggest-selling papers by 1903 with a combined circulation of almost 230,000—rested on their ties to the *kasō shakai*.[75] When *Yorozu* editor Kuroiwa Shūroku declared in 1892 that Japan needed a paper that the "average person" could read, he had in mind the potential markets in the poor working classes. Such a paper, he said, should be cheap and interesting, with simple, clear writing; it should "make it easy for the average masses to know the times thoroughly at a glance"; and it should be "read by wives, read by clerks, read by youngsters, read by manservants, and read by woman servants."[76] The elite editors sneered at his ambitions and at the cheap red paper on which he printed the daily *Yorozu*, and they called him "Shūroku the pit viper" for his attacks on the establishment. But they hardly could have criticized the balance of materials he published. *Yorozu* and *Niroku* may have specialized in stories about salacious events, but they covered serious news too, and vigorously. A typical *Yorozu* front page, chosen at random from the fall of 1909, included articles on political tumult in Spain, tax-reduction schemes, a research society studying military balloons, a university reform plan, the winners of a haiku competition, the assassination of a military officer in England, and the announcement of several new novels and plays.[77] Foreign events were routinely covered in depth. And when the plebeian papers' circulation soared, the old *ōshinbun* (prestige papers) began emulating the poor people's press with their own "Page Three" feature sections to attract readers.

The press historian Ono Hideo said that Kuroiwa "wanted to think as the general public did, to feel anger with them and solve problems with them. He wanted to help the poor, the weak."[78] That likely was the reason that from the 1890s onward the denizens of poor neighborhoods subscribed to his paper by the tens of thousands. The influential essayist Uchimura Kanzō said in 1900 that he was interested only in what two papers, *Yorozu* and *Tokyo Asahi Shinbun*, had to say because they were the only ones "read by the great numbers of workers, craftsmen, and farmers—the so-called lower reaches of society (*iwayuru karyū shakai*)." A Police Bureau survey backed up his impression of *Yorozu*, finding that a full third of its 105,000 subscriptions were taken by the "lower classes," with another third going to students; where he got his opinion of *Asahi* was less clear, since that paper sold a measly 5 percent of its copies to the *kasō shakai*.[79] One of the vignettes that captured the fancy of the day's writers was the sight of rickshaw pullers on street corners, or prostitutes in doorways, reading newspapers as they awaited clients. And a small percentage of the plebeian readers were *writers* too. When the urban press began to solicit postcard essays from readers late in the 1890s—a sort of early "voice of the people"—the response was overwhelming, with workers and students contributing more cards than teachers or businessmen did. Press historian Yamamoto Taketoshi says "the period's chief characteristic was the fact that this correspondence came from the lower classes," from maids, factory workers, and soldiers.[80] *Taiyō* in 1903 called *Yorozu* and *Niroku* the "representative spokesmen of the mass of Tokyoites, . . . favorites of the largest section of the public."[81] The most remarkable thing about that evaluation was its unconscious assumption that the *hinmin* should have a public "spokesman." Even for the *Taiyō* elites, the urban masses had become participants in public life.

If newspaper reading showcased the positive side of this zest for living, the acts of cunning and conniving showed a darker, equally impressive, side. The cartoonists and reporters had great fun passing on tales of the naughty, whimsical things slum dwellers did to survive—or to get revenge. A *Puck* artist portrayed a jealous chimney sweep pouring his soot on a couple standing beneath the roof. Multiple writers passed on stories of women and men in the slums playing tricks to get even with tormentors. One young woman broke a milk bottle over her unwanted pursuer's head (his "first present of the new year"); another, in a cartoon labeled "revenge of the deliveryman," struck the head of her husband's rival milk deliveryman with a bottle of her own, hitting him hard enough to cause a concussion. One of *Puck*'s subjects wiped his dirty feet with a Christian tract, eliciting the cartoonist's observation that the tract had "saved him" by providing something to "clean his sole." A 1907 set of cartoons showed different ways that *hinmin* foiled their bill collectors: they pretended to be mad when the agent came; they tried to hypnotize him; or they urinated on the street in broad daylight, trying to get themselves thrown in the slammer until collection day had passed.[82] One should not make too much of these accounts. They were jokes. But they demonstrated the gutsy, gritty ways people coped with life's daily challenges.

It also is hard to miss what a cartoonist called the *"sōshi sōai"* (mutual love) that permeated *kasō shakai* life. One *Puck* sketch has two couples strolling on a beach, one of them dressed smartly, the other wearing rags and carrying night soil buckets. The sketcher's only comment is the caption: *sōshi sōai*. Economics did not matter when it came to affection; if anything, it was the poor couple whose affection appeared to be stronger.[83] Togetherness and mutuality show up often in descriptions of *hinminkutsu* homes, balancing the contrasting reality of absent parents and dysfunctional households. The poor geisha Masuda Sayo, for example, tells us of her interactions "with an exceedingly poor person" with yellowed teeth and "an apron so grimy it was impossible to tell if it had ever been white." The woman's appearance "disoriented me," Masuda said; she was "wretched." Yet the woman was obviously happy, because she loved her children with a heart "made rich . . . by the hopes and peace of mind she could look forward to when her children grew up."[84] More concrete still was the story of a geisha named Tokiko, known for her purity, who spent twenty yen a month in 1910 to keep her brother in middle school despite the disapproval of her brothel mistress, who saw the expenditure as "a sheer waste of good money."[85] The folk singer Azembō found a similar example of compassion in *hinmin* parents—too poor to "afford sardines or cod"—who said farewell to "beloved children" as they headed out for a life on their own:

Although they conceal it, these parents weep inside
Bear the chill and don't catch cold . . .
We will be waiting here for the day you return.

Elsewhere, he described the departed child who wanders astray in the company of bad companions, then remembers that farewell, and "a cold sweat trickles down his back."[86] Even the judgmental reformers at Futaba Day Care Center saw evidence of family bonds. Teacher Noguchi Yuka may have criticized parents for using their own little ones for child care, but she was impressed by the affection they showered on them. When there were disputes among parents at Futaba, the antagonists always took the side of their own children. If their children were sick, they worried. If parents had a day off work, they kept the children home so the family could spend that day together. And they gave the children "a generous slice of their meager daily incomes for pocket money." The children may have been malnourished; they may have been incorrigible. But it was clear to Noguchi that they were loved.[87]

Mutual affection was obvious outside the family unit too, in sharing among individuals and households unrelated by anything except proximity and circumstances. After discussing his own eagerness to get away from the filth of the *kichin'yado*, Matsubara pondered why so many poor people continued to stay there, even in summer, instead of sleeping in the cleaner air outside. The answer came quickly and obviously: human companionship was wanting outdoors, where one had "only the stars for companions"; inside there was "the sound of the human voice," which made the flophouse "a better place to sleep in for coolies, vagrants and other poor single people."[88] Even beggar children had communities, according to *Jiji Shinpō*'s 1896 series on the Tokyo poor, "creating hidden societies—their own dens—beyond the law and hidden from the police."[89] Yokoyama's tales of camaraderie confirm these pictures. Slum dwellers joke together. They swap stories of daily trials. They quarrel and yell at each other. They come to each other's assistance. They go together to religious meetings. In the words of one *hinmin*, "They'll put their own head in the noose for you." Even after calling a neighbor a nasty name in a bitter argument, an Osaka slum resident would go to the police to demand the neighbor's release when he was thrown in jail.[90]

Socially, some *hinminkutsu* neighborhoods came to resemble the old village communities as the years passed, with mornings finding mothers talking around alley wells and evenings bringing neighbors to the nearby baths. When a family rented a room, one of its first acts would be to give presents to the people who lived nearby, thereby establishing the family's place in the community of which it hoped to be a part.[91] Reciprocity made the Mannenchō slum a "good place," said one Taishō-era youth. When his aunt lacked food, he said, she "goes to the flat next door and gets something from them. It's a mutual thing." And when the neighbors felt the need, they helped themselves to his aunt's pickles. It was "like everybody's family."[92] The journalist Hita Sei expressed surprise in 1898 at the degree to which the people in Tokyo's row houses "show mutual care for each other. They help each other as neighbors; they show mutual compassion. It is not unusual for them to borrow food from each other night and morning, almost as if they were blood relatives."[93] Whether in a tenement or a *kichin'yado*, whether as individuals or as family units, the *hinmin* gradually came to form what Nakagawa calls "quasi communities" (*gijiteki na kyōdōken*), in which groups of families cooked, reared children, washed, gossiped, bathed, and cared for children together, sharing "mutual relief in tribulations and mutual rejoicing in pleasures."[94] Postwar scholars would lament the way authorities attempted early in the 1900s to control urban energy by imposing the restrictive features of traditional village life, creating what Kamishima Jirō called *gisei dai ni no mura,* or fictive second villages that undermined democratic impulses.[95] Within the cities' poverty pockets themselves, however, the democratic, communal sides of village life evolved naturally, in caring expressions of mutual support and assistance.

The "relief in tribulations" was an important part of this connectedness. Matsubara saw this early in the 1890s when a woman who "seemed to have much experience in 'Poverty Hall'" encountered a young flophouse lodger struggling to mend his torn shirt sleeve. "As soon as she saw it she snatched the poor garment from his hands and in a few minutes had it neatly repaired." The "*kichin'yado* had become a home" to the woman, he said, adding that "such trifles as these, . . . light as snowflakes, sometimes change the whole current of a man's life."[96] A few years later, Yokoyama saw similar acts in Tokyo's sprawling Samegahashi slum. People might gossip and quarrel, he said, but "they take days off from their work to assist at funerals of their neighbors. These poor people provide assistance to others despite the fact that if they do not work even one day, their livelihood will immediately be in jeopardy."[97] A recurring theme in discussions of factory workers was their readiness to help fellows when the company turned a blind eye, responding like the coworkers of the man in *Pillar of Fire* who was ignored by company officials when a machine took off his arm; the "workers themselves got up a fund—though none of them could really spare a single sen—so that he could go to hospital."[98] *Niroku* noted that even quarrelers cared for each other, citing the case of a teenage worker at a saké stand who bloodied his fellow's eye in an argument, then took him straightaway to a doctor, "even though he was an enemy."[99]

One might argue that acts of kindness like this are unexceptional, no more than what might be expected of anyone. But that is the point: compassion ran as deeply in the poor neighborhoods as it did anywhere. Often it ran even more deeply, as the middle-class father of a little girl found when his child was nearly trampled to death in a crowd of worshipers during a year-end fair at Tokyo's Kanda Myōjin shrine. The man wrote to *Yorozu Chōhō*:

> At first, I stretched my arm around the little girl and protected her as well as I could. . . . After several minutes, my strength began to leave me, and our position became critical. . . . I was at a loss. . . . Suddenly, a strong man, who appeared to be a workman, and who was also struggling to escape from the crowd, turned back and shouted: "Don't kill the child!" And he stretched out his arms and helped me in keeping back the pushing throng. . . . At last, a little crevice was opened in the crowd, as we three succeeded in getting out. . . . My little girl and I will bless our unknown hero to our dying day.[100]

The anthropologist Victor Turner has said that "communitas breaks in . . . at the edges of structure, in marginality; and from beneath structure, in inferiority. It is almost everywhere held to be sacred or 'holy,' possibly because it transgresses or dissolves the norms that govern structure and institutionalized relationships." The ones most likely to experience "comradeship and equality," he said, are those "at the bottom of the pecking order."[101] Anyone spending time in the *hinminkutsu* would have understood what Turner was talking about.

Even when it was not apparent on the surface, most *hinmin* also lived with hope. Walking through a slum, it was easy to conclude, with Matsubara, that poor children "will always remain near the gutter, there is no getting away from it."[102] The truth actually was not that dark. Difficult as the storms and budget pressures were, most people lived in the expectation that tomorrow—or next year, or some future day—would be better. Many placed their hope in children who appeared to have potential. Some looked to the lucky break that might change their fortunes. And the great majority believed, simply, that today's efforts would improve things over time. *Seinen-Rising Generation* loved to trumpet one form of these hopes: the success stories that "proved" the middle-class truism that hard work and ambition could take anyone to the top. And there were many stories to be trumpeted, some of them about exceptional children, others about determined adults. There was the twelve-year-old Itō Hitoshi, for example, a Hokkaido native living with his Tokyo grandparents who sold sundries at a "poor booth." Worried about their poverty, Hitoshi began traveling to Hongō each morning before school to buy twenty packages of *nattō* (fermented soybeans), which he would resell for a profit of six yen a month. About 40 percent of his earnings went to Grandma and Grandpa, part went to his school necessities, and the rest went into savings. At school, he ranked at the top of his class and was tardy just once in four years.[103] Then there was Takasu Takehiko, a teenager who had come to Tokyo after being orphaned in Shizuoka. Finding lodging in a cheap Fukagawa flophouse, he too bought and sold *nattō*— with money from his own used clothes—and before long he was attending night school and living with a neighbor who was so impressed by his work ethic that he offered him free lodging. At the time of the report he was balancing study and work, clearly on his way up.[104] And there were more, almost always linked to education: a Kyoto rickshaw puller and his wife who scraped together enough funds to send their bright son to middle school and then on to the elite Kyoto University; a young man whose parents were willing to "pinch themselves to the utmost" to find money for him to go to school and then start on a civil servant's career; an ambitious Tokyo telegraph operator named Tamura who studied at home, using the toilet for privacy, and eventually passed the bar.[105] Such stories represented exceptions, but they also expressed an ideal that resonated not just in middle-class publications but in those conversations beside *kasō shakai* wells.

Looking at things from the other end of the life path, it was hard not to be impressed by the numbers of people of renown whose lives demonstrated that hope was not pointless, whether success brought financial stability or not. Literary giants such as Tanizaki Jun'ichirō and Higuchi Ichiyō used lowly beginnings as fodder for their writings. Even during her peak writing years Higuchi remained poor, surviving only by taking out loans and selling cheap candy in a shop near the Yoshiwara prostitute quarters. "We get poorer all the time," she wrote in 1891, five years before her death. When her mother went off to seek loans to buy food, she asked, "What will we do when we can't borrow more money? . . . Who wants to talk to someone down on his luck?"[106] Several of the era's prominent journalists came from poverty. Both Matsubara and Yokoyama, for example, spent their early Tokyo years as *hinmin.* For several years, Yokoyama, the son of an unmarried fisherman and housemaid, "led an aimless and gloomy life," staying sometimes in Buddhist temples, sometimes in the homes of friends, and often in the flophouses that he eventually would write about.[107] *Niroku Shinpō*'s Akiyama grew up poor too, a fact that he said influenced his activist preference for the poor as an editor. "My misfortunes were a great benefit," he said in his memoirs. "They made me a greatly blessed child."[108] Poverty also nurtured several political figures, particularly those on the left who fought for workers' rights and progressive causes. The labor activist Takai Toshio was born into rural poverty, then recalled walking "everywhere, from one end of Tokyo to the other," trying to find work when she migrated to the city. She said Tokyo's rivers surprised her because "if you walked upstream, there would be a whole bunch of factories lined up on the left side of the river."[109]

Poorer still was Kaneko Fumiko, the famous anarchist whose father was an alcoholic wife beater and whose mother lived with serial partners, all of them poor. The poverty and dysfunctional family convinced her that the only "absolute, universal law on earth . . . is the reality that the strong eat the weak"[110] and led to her support of philosophical anarchism, which in turn caused officials to send her to prison, where she committed suicide in 1926.

Several points demand attention regarding these people who achieved influence despite early (and sometimes continuing) poverty. First, they were exceptional. The overwhelming majority of Meiji Japan's modern leaders came from samurai homes or from relatively affluent merchant or farmer families where educational opportunities were abundant and personal connections lubricated the path toward prominence. Second, most of them made their way upward by gaining access to education, frequently at considerable personal sacrifice. It is clear that the era's success in creating schools for the great majority of children opened otherwise unimaginable doors for bright and ambitious children. Third, the most important key to success lay in the ambitions and talents of the achievers themselves. The nation's education system helped them along, but ambition and talent were present already when they were young, carving out the spaces that allowed hope to penetrate their *nagaya* abodes. Fourth and most important, the exceptional qualities possessed by these future leaders differed only in degree from the energies and attitudes that kept most of their more ordinary peers going every day. While the writers and leaders may have represented the *peaks* of the poor experience, their aspirations and persistence were emulated across the *hinminkutsu* alleys, by neighbors who toiled daily in the belief that life would get better.

The Meiji data have convinced Nakagawa that improvement was constant for the majority of the late Meiji *hinmin.* As the early twentieth century began to unfold, the "lower-class" stratum became more differentiated, with factory workers and a "new middle class" developing slightly more stable, better-off lives. More of the residents of the Osaka and Tokyo *hinminkutsu* were paying *monthly* rather than daily rents by 1910, fewer were using pawn shops, more families were living by themselves as single units, no longer having to share space with other families. While new urban immigrants kept coming, holding down the *kasō shakai* averages, significant numbers of the earlier slum dwellers were themselves living better than they had in the 1880s and 1890s. Indeed, one machinist said in 1910 that it was hard to find older master workers at plants because "the skilled and experienced among them . . . are either running their own factories or have saved some capital and have turned to some agricultural or commercial venture."[111] The most dramatic changes in lifestyle did not come until the later 1910s and 1920s, but by the last Meiji decade the foundations for those greater changes were well laid.

It is important to note, moreover, that these changes were not merely a result of evolving economic structures; they came largely as a result of the conscious efforts of poor individuals to improve their personal lives. Nakagawa cites the case of a copper-stretching factory worker who immigrated with his family of four to Osaka in 1906. He came to the city with a goal of making enough money to get his children into secondary school, because "he himself had never been to school" and "thus felt strongly that education was necessary." By the time a government surveyor talked to him sixteen years later, he had decided that in another decade he wanted to start his own small business too. Great numbers were like him, Nakagawa says, motivated by "a desire to distance themselves from lower-class people and to move closer to those of a higher status." They may have lived in cramped quarters with spartan meals; they may have shared in the mutuality of impoverishment. But they distinguished themselves by rising ambitions, family centeredness, and thoughtful budgeting.[112] For an impressive number of families, the hopes that sustained life during the dark times yielded quantifiable improvements as the years stretched into decades.

Celebrating: Streets, Parks, and Temples

Matsubara observed of the *hinmin* in the 1890s that "the desire for a little pleasure . . . is still strong and pleasure is sought in spite of the distress that the next day threatens." It did not matter that they might not have dress clothes, he said, because "no appearances have to be kept up."[113] Matsubara was more attentive than his peers to this aspect of *kasō shakai* life, but even he understated the situation, just as he missed the fact that many of them cared about appearances. Slum dwellers who were determined to assert agency at work and to agitate on the streets for lower streetcar fares also were determined to make merry when they were off work. If the *kichin'yado* had an open space, they used it to sing sentimental or ribald songs, a cure for "the fatigue of their day-work." If the neighborhood had a piece of unoccupied ground, they shed their clothes and staged sumo wrestling bouts. One of the largest slums, Shin'ami-chō, was said to put on sumo matches every summer evening, with neither "the army of mosquitoes" nor the stench of rotting food in nearby alleys able to keep away crowds.[114] Shop boys may have slaved away six or seven days a week, but that did not keep them from celebrating holidays with a zest that belied life's difficulties. Nor did most families hesitate about devoting a few sen to the little amenities that made life human: the daily visits to the bath, the regular visits to shops for having hair cut or styled. No wonder Tokyo's municipal records showed Honjo with more bathhouses than any other ward, or that Shitaya, Honjo, Asakusa, and Fukagawa were among the five wards with the most hairdressers.[115] More than twenty profiles of worker families drawn up by government researchers at the outset of the twentieth century showed a universal determination to do little things to soften life's hard edges. Invariably, an otherwise grim profile ended with a phrase such as "head of household: drinks saké if there is money for it"; "household head academically inclined, teaches children"; "drinks one *gō* (.384 pints) of saké each evening."[116]

Joy and energy were never more obvious than on the streets, particularly in the markets for which Tokyo and Osaka long had been known. In Osaka, the street market in front of Yasaka Shrine was famous for the crowds it attracted each morning, not just on festival days but all year long. One central Tokyo market with more than 350 shops and stalls drew fifty thousand people a day in the early 1890s, with crowds so thick that "if a coin were thrown up it would not fall to the ground."[117] In both cities, many of the liveliest markets were on river bridges or intersections near the row houses and *kichin'yado* where the *hinmin* lived and shopped for food. Along Tokyo's Sumida River, the Ryōgoku Bridge reportedly had done three thousand *ryō* of business a day in pre-Meiji years, a third in its morning vegetable markets, a third throughout the midday hours, and a third "from the bustling evening crowds."[118] Now, as the late Meiji years gave birth to all those modern factories with their surrounding mazes of human habitation, the markets grew larger and busier still. Carts would arrive continuously at the morning markets, starting at about two o'clock, with carriers bringing products beyond numbering: dried fish, household goods, toys, tofu, soy paste, candies, and the green vegetables and fruits sold by 240 different vendors at the Kanda Tamachi market alone.[119] The stall-keepers yelled out for customers to buy their wares. In the spring, there were strawberries, new potatoes, cucumbers, and lettuce. In the summer they offered eggplants, lotus, watermelons, beans of all kinds, sprouts, even corn. In the fall, housewives could find nashi, squash, and persimmons. And the early winter months produced *mikan*, bamboo shoots, and the sour citrus fruit *yuzu*. Always, there were seafoods: mackerel, bream, salmon, crocodile (*wani*), bonito, yellowtail, cod, herring, sea bass, and that low-nutrition fish that made novelist Nagai nostalgic, pike. Some vendors offered bean jam in buns, some cigarettes, some sandals, some tops, balloons, and squeaking toys. Others sold candied fruits, others still paper fans, rosary beads, cheap woodblock prints, toothpicks made of shaved wood that left "your mouth full of little bits and pieces of the brush,"[120] and dolls that sometimes fell off of the cluttered tables. At the eating booths, one could get *kushi dango* (sweet rice balls on skewers), bowls of soba, shaved ice, boiled tofu with soy sauce, kebabs of horse entrails, fried noodles, and *sashimi* and sushi of every sort. One visitor professed to love the sardines. "Good it was, too. Sometimes we'd have them raw. You pulled on their guts with your fingers so that they came out evenly, then took off the heads with your fingers. . . . Then you'd slice them up thin and eat them dipped in soy sauce."[121]

If the products created a riot of color, the people provided a riot of activity and noise. Every summer night, recalled Nagai, as "summer twilight would be giving way to night, . . . the street would be coming to life, with the nasal songs of artisans, the clatter of their wooden sandals, bits of conversation."[122] And the daytime hours were lively too. Peddlers announced their goods with full and raspy voices, competing in the accents of their home regions; acrobats, dancers, and singers performed for a fee, sometimes awkwardly, sometimes comically, sometimes brilliantly; storytellers, puppeteers, and Buddhist lecturers drew klatches of onlookers, some of whom wore kimono, some work clothes, and some very little at all; vendors attracted circles of children by modeling their pastries into every imaginable object and blowing glutinous rice candies "into various fantastic shapes," much "like bubble gum,"[123] while beggars and rag pickers worked the edges and pickpockets sought their prey. Rickshaw pullers waited at the street and alley corners, smoking and chatting, sometimes grabbing a bite of food, with their eyes casting about for potential customers. Most of them added to the verbal clamor by harassing people for business, sometimes rudely and raucously. Buddhist monks held begging bowls beneath their huge straw hats. And then there were the gathered crowds, come to shop, to chat, to stroll, or just—in novelist Kawabata Yasunari's words—to watch "the modern-style dancing of . . . powdered naked bodies."[124] Pilgrims in the city for a temple festival jostled against shoppers looking for scraps of cheap fish and against tourists who had come to see Asakusa's dramatic twelve-story Ryōunkaku ("cloud scraper"): "that huge, clumsy pile of red bricks" that could be seen "from the roof of every house," a place from which despondent women and men jumped to their death on occasion.[125] Neighborhood housewives chatted as much as they shopped, discussing "all manner of secrets and stories . . . with much gusto, and no doubt with many an embellishment."[126] And they all were joined, said the painter Kaburagi Kiyokata, by hosts of young frolickers (*zomeki*), prowlers (*jimawari*), and quite a few window shoppers.[127] If ever there were a cacophony, it was here.

Nor should one forget the pleasures of the flesh, which attracted the *hinmin* as much as they did those in the middle class. These pages already have examined the amount of time workers spent in bars and entertainment centers, as well as the omnipresence of sexual activities, both in and away from the brothels. A government report from that time said that after work, typical laborers "gambled, went to the whorehouse, or went to entertainment halls," and Eiji Yutani concluded, after surveying the *kasō shakai* literature of the 1890s, that the journalists' image of the typical worker was that of a "hard drinking, gambling hedonist, with little concern for saving for tomorrow."[128] The moralistic tone of their evaluations may raise doubts, but there is no disputing that most *hinmin* balanced their daily drudgery with alcohol or other worldly pleasures. As Tanizaki made clear, the search for titillation was part of what made the street scenes so lively. Describing a street fair at the beginning of the 1900s, the memoirist recalled the excitement he felt as a poor youth on the street below as "the shadows of people dancing wildly on the second floor of the Kinseirō restaurant seemed close enough to touch" and as "crowds of young men from the rice traders' street, girls from the archery booths, . . . and other men and women sauntered back and forth in droves along both sides of the street."[129] The streets were enlivened by vice venues as much as by food shops and temple acrobats. The essayist Kōjimachi Bō's essay on "urban temptations" that "trespassed every nook and cranny," discussed in chapter 3, described nearly 10,000 shops and centers in Tokyo's shadowy demimonde world: some 350 gaming places (including those "archery booths"), nearly 300 vaudeville venues (which averaged 300 daily visitors each), more than 7,500 houses of ill fame (which took in more than 3.6 million yen a year), and hundreds on hundreds of unlicensed brothels, the greatest number of them in Asakusa and Shiba, where the *hinmin* street scene was most lively.[130] If Kōjimachi found all of this "putrid," most of the participants found more pleasure than guilt. When Matsubara saw street crowds listening to a storyteller, he commented, "Some great fun must be going on there, just listen to . . . how the people laugh; it does one good to hear them."[131]

No one who ventured into the urban markets could miss yet one more thing that made street life so lively: children. They were uninhibited and unavoidable. "Tokio is the children's city," said one foreign observer. "The Japanese child is everywhere. . . . Every other woman one passes has one enthroned on her back; in every shop, every house-front, they are to be seen playing; one trips over them in the streets." He also saw them in the parks near the markets, "balancing on a tree-trunk swinging horizontally and trying [to see] who can knock off the others."[132] And if the children were numerous in the areas foreigners visited, they overflowed the poor regions, where tiny living spaces and absent parents (usually off working) made street life a necessity for many a little one. Yokoyama found their ubiquity disturbing, a painful reminder that *hinmin* children were not getting the education or parental care they deserved; so did the visiting sociologist Beatrice Webb. And Matsubara lamented all the children engaged in unsavory play: burying a dead cat, eating refuse, sweeping gutters for fun.[133] But no one denied the energy that these children brought to the streets as they played together "around candy stores enviously ogling the merchandise."[134] "To a child, poverty is not a source of misfortune," noted *Niroku*'s Akiyama, thinking of his own youth.[135] Every sales booth was an invitation for the children, every trash pile an opportunity, every third-rate acrobat a delight. At one corner, a sly lad would be snatching a piece of candy from the table of a preoccupied seller. A few feet away a gentle girl would be holding her mother's hand, grinning at the monkey grinder across the street. At the temple gate, a mud-streaked lass with a tattered blouse might be begging, while nearby a clumsy tyke was knocking a ceramic toy off a vendor's booth. Sometimes the children fought in small gangs, often they played games—marbles or Chinese checkers (*jūroku musashi*) or tangrams—on the street, sometimes they bought candy or a paper doll, and most of the time their dirty faces and sticky fingers bore witness to what they had been doing. Their uninhibited romps made the marketplace wilder and more interesting.

Children were especially evident on the festival days that have framed the Japanese calendar for a millennium. Each urban open space took its turn in hosting public celebrations during the late Meiji years, attracting as many people from the impoverished neighborhoods as from affluent areas. When an official national celebration was called for, to publicize the opening of a new street or to welcome soldiers home from war—or when firemen put on their seasonal climbing and acrobatic shows—the event was likely to take place at a municipal park, perhaps at the one opened in Tokyo's Hibiya grounds in 1903, perhaps in Osaka's first public park, Nakanoshima, which had opened in 1891, perhaps at the venerable Ueno Park near Asakusa.[136] For viewing cherry blossoms, hundreds of temples, shrines, and parks invited the faithless and faithful alike. For a school excursion, the Tokyo teachers were likely at least once a year to choose the zoo at Ueno, which had been open since 1882. For the annual fireworks display, hundreds of thousands of people would make their way to the millennium-old Tenjin Festival at Osaka's Tenmangū shrine or to the banks of Tokyo's Sumida River near Asakusa. And poor neighborhood children always made up a big part of the crowd. They "swarmed" to the events, in the words of one *Taiyō* writer. They came in "droves," in the recollection of Tanizaki, "streaming into the garden through an open gate on the side street."[137] If there was a day off, or something to be celebrated or worshiped, the children were there, bringing their parents and neighbors with them.

No public spaces offered brighter respite to the *hinmin* than Buddhist temples and Shintō shrines on festival days. Taking note of the enthusiasm with which Japanese religion embraces both the secular and the profane, the poet Noguchi Yonejirō commented in 1910 that "we . . . do not forget pleasures of the senses even in religion." Temples, he said, specialized in "freedom which let the joy hunters follow after their own purpose."[138] Indeed. The drinking and pouring of saké was central to Shintō practice, naked festivals combining alcohol and testosterone-driven competitions attracted visitors to temples across the country, ribald dancing and the sale of sexually oriented items was common outside temple and shrine grounds, and festivals were unabashed money-making events,

A *Fūzoku Gahō* artist sketched the massive crowds—*hinmin* and middle classes all mixed together—that gathered for a fireworks display at the Ryōgoku Bridge in *shitamachi* in its February 25, 1898, issue. Courtesy of University of Tokyo Graduate Schools for Law and Politics, Center for Modern Japanese Legal and Political Documents, Meiji Shimbun Zasshi Bunko.

intended as much to bring money to the priests as to provide spiritual succor to attendants. As Higuchi said of the protagonist priest in her short story "Child's Play": "His holiness was the busy one. Loans to collect, the shop to oversee, funerals to arrange, not to mention all the sermons every month. . . . Prayers in the morning, accounts at night."[139] It was hardly surprising then that a week rarely passed when a large urban temple or shrine was not hosting masses of people— *hinmin* and rich alike—in a *matsuri*, or festival, where the priests' prayers were drowned out by the hundreds of vendors "eager to make business with people who came . . . to pray" and by every imaginable kind of magician, rickshaw puller, puppeteer, acting monkey, beggar-priest, and performer of "dances and rude comic farces" of every kind.[140] Festival time in Asakusa's leading temples, said the eminent scholars Basil Hall Chamberlain and W. B. Mason, provided "a spectacle than which surely nothing more motley was ever witnessed within the precincts of a religious edifice." Crowds were biggest on Sunday afternoons.[141]

A significant portion of those crowds were *hinmin* who, like their richer peers, were more interested in the festivities than in pieties. The winter healing festival at Fukagawa's Fudō Temple illustrated the drawing power of one kind of festival: the weeks-long event with a specific focus. Held across thirty days in the middle of winter, it invited supplicants dressed in white to immerse themselves in water for the healing of sick family members. Up to 1,500 came daily, according to the journalist Fujimoto Taizō, most of them from Fukagawa, Honjo, and neighboring wards. The great majority were craftsmen—"young and high-spirited employees of carpenters, plasterers, cabinet-makers, mat-makers, masons, roofers, brick-layers, sawyers, and hoopers"—who came at night because they had to work all day. Fujimoto estimated that a third genuinely sought healing, while the rest (including not a few children) came "half in fun," interested primarily in tasting the sweet, heated saké that was given out free.[142] Higuchi's "Child's Play" describes two of the more typical festivals, shorter periods of religious merrymaking that took place in the poverty wards: the local late summer festival of Senzoku Shrine and the November Cock's Fair at Ōtori Shrine next to the Yoshiwara quarters. As Senzoku's celebration approached, groups of children excitedly made plans to build floats. "The saucy things they dream up will give you goose bumps," said Higuchi. When the day itself came, "children under fifteen or so weren't satisfied until they had accumulated all the trinkets they could carry—Daruma dolls, owls, dogs of papier mâché."[143] The only other day that held as much excitement for them, Higuchi said, was the Cock's Fair, dedicated to the money god Ōtori Daimyōjin. That fair began at midnight, when the temple gates opened to let in a "grand mass of visitors crammed up before the gate . . . pressed up so densely that nobody could move." Inside the grounds, vendors welcomed them "in a state of craziness."[144] "They are pilgrims," said Higuchi, "but, ah, the roar of young laughter is loud enough to rend the pillars holding up the heavens." Crowds "keep pouring in," people from all walks of life. A rickshaw puller's tattered son nicknamed Bucktooth is there, selling steamed potatoes at one of the booths, while his friend "Donkey" hawks dumplings. Other vendors sell the *kumade*, or ornamental rakes, for which the festival is famous, along with a hundred other foods and trinkets.[145] *Hinmin* life grim? Not on this day.

The *hinmin* also took a lusty part in Japan's seasonal rituals and holidays—cherry blossom viewing in the spring, *obon* or the Festival of the Dead in late summer, New Year's festivities in January—when poor and rich commingled in city parks, along river banks, and in public squares. The fervor with which outdoor seasonal excursions engaged even the *kasō shakai* communities was illustrated in July 1909 by the climbing excursion of two dozen blind shampooers on Mount Fuji. *Yorozu* announced on July 14 that the group had decided on "quite a record breaking" activity: to climb the sacred mountain. Their plans captured the public imagination, and over the next two weeks the paper covered their expedition avidly. On July 18, it ran a sketch of the group, dressed in pilgrims' straw hats, clutching a rope behind their leader and feeling their way cautiously around rocks. They left the mountain's sixth stage at three o'clock that morning in heavy fog, serenaded by the "beautiful tones of an old nightingale that was still singing long after spring has passed." After stopping at a tea house for refreshments an hour after sunrise, they went on, chanting, "With all our hearts, we move forward up Mt. Fuji. Mountain climbing! For sure!" By midafternoon, they had reached the seventh stage, where they were met by newspaper reporters. And so it went until they made the tenth stage at the summit. They were blind shampooers, regarded as the most pitiable of the pitiable. But as they themselves put it in another of their climbing ditties, "Our very blindness brings us a lot more sympathy than others get! All said and done, blindness . . . it's a blessing."[146]

At *setsubun,* the last day of winter on the old calendar, people tossed beans in their homes and *nagaya* apartments to drive away the evil spirits. In the spring, they took part in a hundred different kinds of flower festivals. Summer brought the massive fireworks displays at Tenmangū and along the Sumida, as well as the *bon* festival, which commemorated the annual visit of dead spirits to their ancestral homes. No events, however, compared to the year's two major times for playing and socializing: New Year and blossom viewing. The *shōgatsu,* or New Year, festivities took place in homes and shrines alike, pulling every class and age group into a stock set of activities. The weeks before December 31 crammed in enough activities to make New Year's Day itself an afterthought: year-end markets called *toshi no ichi,* the settling of debts and cleaning of apartments so as to enter the new year with a clean slate, the making and buying of decorations to ensure a successful new year, parades and performances by neighborhood fire fighters, gift giving, food preparation, year-end parties. Then, as the old year ended, temple bells tolled 108 times to cleanse each of the human passions. At precisely midnight, shrines and temples opened their gates, and for the next three days throngs of people poured through, to throw a coin or two into the box in front of the main hall before clapping their hands, saying prayers, and buying amulets to assure good luck in the coming months. Away from the shrine, people would spend the three holidays eating all the specially prepared foods, playing card games, participating in seasonal sports (particularly battledore, which young girls played in their narrow streets and alleys "utterly regardless of the crowded traffic"[147]), and making calls on relatives and friends. Everything commercial stopped for these three days; only celebration, commemoration, and rest were allowed.

And—most important—everyone participated. The *hinmin* may not have had money for the expensive battledores but they stretched their budgets in order to participate as fully as possible. For some, the holiday brought extra cash. Even before the *toshi no ichi* season, poor peddlers began hawking new year calendars, and the year-end markets offered endless opportunities for selling the cheap goods reputed to go particularly well in December "because the sellers look so pitiful" and shoppers were sympathetic.[148] Cleaning occurred in poor neighborhoods just as it did in the middle-class homes. Slum dwellers and their children joined the throngs of shrine visitors and amulet purchasers; a good luck charm might have taken a higher percentage of their income, but they felt the need for it even more acutely. They too listened to the bells; enjoyed the days off work; grilled goby, the poor man's fish, on the hibachi; and devoured it "with a bit of salt . . . as a special treat on New Year's Day."[149] More than a few managed to make their way back to their home regions every year or so. Poverty undermined the joy for some: those factory girls who could not go home, the truly destitute whose loneliness was intensified by all of the merrymaking, those who had to work so others could play. But the dominant reality for most poor families was that the new year was a time to rest from work and celebrate along with their compatriots.

The great spring festivity, *hanami,* or cherry-blossom viewing, provided less time off from employment but even livelier celebrations. If New Year was a time to rid oneself of old pollutions, *hanami* betokened everything new. Following a tradition that extended back a millennium, the whole populace came out to celebrate when the cherry blossoms opened in early April. Laying blankets and oil cloths on every empty space of earth, particularly on weekend days, people spent hours in the tree-filled parks, soaking in sun, drinking and eating with friends, singing raucous folk melodies, and throwing social strictures to the winds. "Great crowds are gathered," exclaimed one writer watching a blossom-viewing afternoon along the Sumida River, "their hearts are gladdened, their faces brightened. . . . Everybody seems to have forgotten the past sorrows." He called the cherry blossom "the queen of flowers, . . . respected, admired and loved" by all, "the beautiful emblem of the true sons of . . . Yamato's land."[150] This was, above all, the commoner's holiday. Both "high and low, more especially the latter," came out to "forget the year's toil," sometimes "to the extent of jarring the sense of delicacy and respectability," said another writer.[151] One reason the *hinmin* participated so actively in the *hanami* parties of low-city Tokyo was that their neighborhoods had the best sakura groves. The journal *Fūzoku Gahō* said the "champion for the perfect sakura blossoms in Tokyo is the Sumida area," home to the great parks, temples, and shrines of Ueno, Mukōjima and Asakusa—and to so many *hinminkutsu.*[152] Moreover, the usual behavioral constraints, both legal and customary, were thrown to the winds at this time, just

In this *Tokyo Puck* cartoon titled "Seven flower days when the authorities wear masks" (April 15, 1912), the cartoonist captures the sometimes raucous and even illegal citizen celebrations that police officers ought to ignore during the joyful cherry blossom season. Courtesy of University of Tokyo Graduate Schools for Law and Politics, Center for Modern Japanese Legal and Political Documents, Meiji Shimbun Zasshi Bunko.

like the falling blossoms. A *Tokyo Puck* cartoonist captured the atmosphere during the 1912 season with a sketch of people of every class partying under clouds of blossoms while police stood by wearing blindfolds labeled "great leniency" (*daikan*). The caption said that "investigators wear a covering over their eyes for the seven days of blossoms."[153] As at New Year, the poor also bore the brunt of the work that had to be done to make the partying possible. According to the caption accompanying a *Niroku* sketch of a man sweeping up dung in 1900, "If there are people who view cherry blossoms, there also are those who sweep away the horse shit; it is the way of this world."[154] The season's overriding tone, however, was joy.

Few stereotypes clung more tenaciously to the *kasō shakai* than the idea that poor people were pitiful and passive. Even reformers painted them most often as angry or angst-ridden over the troubles fate had given them but unable or unwilling to change things. And large numbers of the *hinmin* themselves accepted that characterization as accurate. "Be self-conscious, honorable rickshaw pullers!" admonished a left-wing activist at *Heimin Shinbun* in an essay suggesting that they were incapable of managing their own destinies. He said their "right to a living was being trampled on every day"; modernity was "bringing poverty, pain, and shortages to the family, causing you to lose heart." Train workers, said a fellow *Heimin* writer, were "treated like cows and horses," and like horses and cows, he implied, they remained mute.[155] One reason for the persistence of the image lay in the fact that some poor people were indeed passive. Another was that tropes about *hinmin* docility served the status quo, justifying low salaries and rendering the "lower classes" less of a threat to the current order. Even charitable reformers often found understandable, if subconscious, pleasure in being able to help the "helpless." These pages have demonstrated, however, that images of widespread passivity and muteness were simply inaccurate. Life was hard—desperately hard—for the poor, but only for the most extreme did that fact constitute the whole story. Nor did it render them helpless.

In the workplace, rickshaw pullers and factory girls alike took charge, sometimes in an organized way, using their wits to make employment more bearable and a little more profitable. Rickshaw patrons and plant managers who complained about self-centered and assertive employees seemed not to notice the contradiction when they said in the next sentence that workers did not care enough to change their situations. On the streets and in the public square, the urban *hinmin* confronted both their overlords and their own fates ferociously in the last Meiji years. When Prime Minister Katsura warned about the danger of socialism taking on "the force of wildfire," he had in mind the capacity of *kasō shakai* protesters for disrupting things. In daily life, mothers, fathers, and single folk alike took charge of their own personal affairs with survival strategies propelled by hope, giving us example after example of planning and sacrificial acts that would enable their children and friends to have a better life. The parents who would "pinch themselves to the utmost" to provide education for their child were hardly passive, nor was the telegraph operator who studied in the only space available: the toilet. And then there was all of that pleasure seeking. Whether stopping at the bar after work, grappling with neighbors in the sand lot, chatting with other housewives while nursing the baby, or heading to the year-end market to buy New Year's food, the *hinmin* sought pleasure and companionship with as much abandon as anyone else in the cities. That was why Akiyama could declare *Niroku*'s 1901 friendship gathering a "celebration of what is human." And it was the reason officials found the event too much of a threat to allow a repeat the next year even though nothing untoward had happened. The *hinmin* were agents, avid, all of them, in seeking pleasure and a better personal life. They were determined, in impressive numbers, to improve the system for their peers too. Their wholehearted engagement with life may not have erased the stereotypes of passivity—facts alone rarely change narratives— but that engagement was obvious enough to frighten everyone whose interests depended on maintaining the status quo.

CHAPTER 7

Poverty on the Farm
A Comparative Look

Their life appears to be extremely gray and austere, but I have no idea of
how many layers there are in that gray.
　　　　　　　　　—Novelist and schoolteacher Shimazaki Tōson[1]

Okamoto Jitsuo, a chipper octogenarian, had nothing concrete to say
about Meiji Japan as we sipped tea in his modest but comfortable
Oritachi living room, tucked into one of those deep river ravines
that define Totsukawa. We were only fifty miles from the city of
Nara, but it had taken three hours to drive the mountain road to the village; it
would have been a two-day walk from the nearest train station in the Meiji
years. Okamoto had nothing to say, because he was not born until 1919, seven
years after the Meiji emperor died. He lacked no confidence, however, in making assumptions about what late Meiji life would have been like on the farm,
because rural customs persisted across generations, and his parents had passed
on what villagers thought and did. There were no cars then; only a few rich
homes even had bicycles. There were no paved roads, no electricity, not much
rice. The mountain slopes were too steep and the village too remote for electric
lines to reach it. Often, he said, families made do on *chagayu,* a gruel made by
putting rice kernels in a pouch and dipping them into salted tea water. There
was lots of timber work, however, with thick-muscled men felling trees, which
were floated down the Totsukawa and Kumano rivers for shipment to Osaka,
Kobe, and Tokyo, where they became part of those new factories and row
houses. And there was a school, where discipline trumped everything. "Teachers and policemen were the scariest things in the world to us kids," Okamoto
chuckled. "If we quarreled or didn't 'get it,' the teacher scolded us. If we were
noisy, he hit us. And if my father found out what the teacher did, he yelled at me
too. . . . Today's teachers are soft; kids don't listen."[2]

One thing Okamoto made abundantly clear: he and his fellow townspeople
were poor, probably as poor as the tenement dwellers in Samegahashi and
Nago-chō. But the deprivation he described sounded different from that in the
cities. It was hard and soul-taxing, but its contours felt softer, its exactions

slightly less frightening. Perhaps the difference was a matter of memory; time may have erased some of the bitterness. But it appeared to be more than that. Okamoto and his friends described a kind of poverty that felt qualitatively different from that of the Ueki family in Fukagawa. The more I talked with Totsukawa villagers the more convinced I became that a full understanding of urban poverty demanded at least a cursory examination of its cousin: economic hardship in the rural areas. For one thing, Totsukawa was the kind of place from which the Uekis and their *hinminkutsu* neighbors had come to the city; here I would find the roots of the great urban migration. Even more important, if rural poverty was not the same as that in Osaka and Tokyo, an understanding of the differences should help to clarify what was distinct and what was universal about economic deprivation in the cities.

There was no typical Japanese village. The historian Simon Partner divides villages into four broad types: those on the plains, where rice cultivation dominated and income was relatively stable; mountain villages, where rugged terrain required more varied types of agriculture and rendered life harder; northern villages, in which the bitter climate made survival itself hard; and fishing villages, where most people engaged in small-scale agriculture on the side.[3] When one moves beyond broad categories, the writings about late Meiji villages stagger the imagination with the variety of their descriptions and interpretations. Focusing on functions, folklorist Miyamoto Tsuneichi describes rice-farming villages, hunting villages, fishing hamlets, towns of foresters, silk-growing villages, carpenters' hamlets, abalone-diving communities, and villages that specialized in tea. Looking at culture, sociologist Fukutake Tadashi argues that the stereotype of farm families as "backward . . . was by no means mistaken," in contrast to Tōson, who declares the mountain dwellers of Komoro "poor on the surface but rich underneath."[4] Historian Gary Allinson argues that late Meiji farm incomes "compared favorably with those of their urban counterparts,"[5] even as Miyamoto talks about Shikoku locales where householders ate foultasting spider lily cakes because they had no other food.[6] A medical worker in Sendai wrote that farmers in his region "may walk upright, but most of the time their spirit crawls along the ground."[7] All the descriptions are correct, at least for some farmers. Poor, rich, passive, entrepreneurial, solitary, energetic, ugly, picturesque; every imaginable adjective fit villagers somewhere in the late Meiji years.

This dictates that our examination of village hardship be sweeping and skeletal. The best that can be attempted in a single chapter is to delineate salient patterns that provide insights into *urban* poverty. To that end, these pages will focus on the writings of a group of the era's more sensitive memoirists and novelists, supplementing their observations with farmer interviews and analyses by scholars and journalists. Not every literary type will be used equally, since prominent novelists like Mori Ōgai and Natsume Sōseki wrote about villagers but gravitated toward stereotypes.[8] More reliable are four literary giants—Tōson, Nagatsuka Takashi, Tayama Katai, and Inoue Yasushi[9]—who spent years in the countryside themselves, either as children or as adults, and wrote from perspectives that were at once informed, critical, and sympathetic. Inoue was reared by his grandmother in the mountainous Izu Peninsula south and west of Tokyo; Katai grew up in Tatebayashi village in Gunma Prefecture to the capital's north and used a rural teacher's diary as the main source material for one of his most important works[10]; Nagatsuka was a farmer himself[11]; and Katai's friend Tōson, who hailed from mountainous Nagano, spent six years as a teacher in Komoro and later lived in Sendai in the far northeast. Of his time in Komoro, Tōson said, "I went out as a teacher; I came back as a student," not a surprising sentiment, perhaps, given his friendship with the pioneer ethnographer of Japan's villages, Yanagita Kunio.[12] Few writers understood the pulse of rural Japan in the late Meiji years better than these men.

Rural Japan: An Overview

One would hardly guess from reading standard histories of the late Meiji era that four of every five Japanese lived in a small farming or fishing village. A typical farm family's total holdings in these years amounted to no more than four acres (1.5 *chō*), and as late as 1910 more than 70 percent of farm families had less than two and a half acres. The likelihood was that they grew rice, a crop that demanded at least a hundred days of back-breaking labor each year: from bending over and planting seedlings in muddy water in the spring to guarding the plants against insects and birds all summer, and on to cutting the yellowed plants in the fall, then winnowing and bagging the ripened kernels, and fighting with merchants for a fair price. The work was all done by hand.[13] Muraoka Koremitsu recalled the planting process as exhausting and communal when he was a lad in Kyushu early in the 1900s. To assure uniform spacing, he said, planters would stretch a rope the length of the field, with "red yarn . . . tied as a marker at one-foot intervals" to indicate where seedlings should go.[14] Because the plots were small and scattered, neighbors shared tasks, whether they liked each other or not.[15] And the work entailed long hours and tired muscles, particularly at harvest time. Of particular concern to this study is that this combination of shared fieldwork and back-breaking labor on tiny plots nestled among forested mountains gave peasants a different understanding of hardship from that experienced by their urban relatives.

The ancient proverb, "the mountains are high and the emperor is far away," still held sway in China at the turn of the twentieth century, but not so in Japan. By the middle of Meiji's reign, government policies were changing village life. Determined to make Japan an international power, officials in Tokyo extended their arms into almost every aspect of local life after the 1870s, requiring children to go to school, drafting boys into the army, encouraging farmers to produce silk and cotton for foreign export, promoting factories that would hire village girls, building railways across mountain valleys, and taxing rural lands to balance central budgets. Scholars argue about the degree to which these policies changed late Meiji peasant life, but two results are indisputable. On the positive side, villagers experienced an uneven but steady increase in productivity and real wages across those years, with average rural income rising at least 1 percent a year. Richard Smethurst of the University of Pittsburgh argues persuasively that the living standards of both tenant farmers and those who owned part of their land and rented the rest "clearly improved" in the late Meiji years, while the Oxford University historian Ann Waswo notes that regardless of wage fluctuations, late Meiji farmers "appeared to believe that the future held brighter prospects than the past did." They had better seeds, new tools, richer fertilizers, and improved ways of controlling insects and disease, resulting in "a mood of vitality rather than stasis."[16]

On the other side of the ledger, few farmers were able in these years to rise out of the poor living conditions that had plagued villages for centuries. As Smethurst adds, "I do not intend to portray them as absolutely well-off. . . . Farmers could be *more prosperous*, but *still poor*."[17] The data bear this out. It was a great depression, of course, that sent hundreds of thousands of rural emigrants to the cities in the 1880s. And Nakagawa Kiyoshi shows that late Meiji farm families, year-in and year-out, had no more than 70 percent of the income to spend that urban families did, even though they had more children.[18] The anecdotal evidence, moreover, is filled with accounts of villagers pressed for food, children wearing clothes too tattered to hold the patches, and the old Tanohata woman telling her interlocutor that "whatever stories they tell, . . . all we did was survive."[19]

Few things made the difficulties clearer than the great number of farmers who lost their land during the middle and late Meiji years. The journalist Yokoyama Gennosuke "noticed" in the late 1890s that "old farming houses are decreasing in number while the number of tenants is increasing." He said that bad weather and crop failures "delighted" some landlords who knew that natural disasters would push their cash-starved neighbors to sell their land.[20] Indeed. When the era began, just over a quarter of Japan's farmers were tenants; by 1908, 45 percent were.[21] In one hamlet in Yamanashi Prefecture west of Tokyo, nearly half of farmers who took out loans in the 1880s and 1890s had to default, and ninety-five families lost their land through forfeiture between 1888 and 1907.[22] Similarly, a visitor to the Chiba region in 1904 found that the greater portion of Shirahama village's six hundred households' land had been bought up by twenty rich families, some of them local and some of them outsiders.[23] When they lost their land, villagers also lost most of their bargaining leverage with landlords. "When crops were poor owing to storms or drought or insect damage," said Mori Giichi, "tenant farmers would meet in secret," in the forest, to discuss how much relief they could ask from their landlords; then they would approach the landlord individually, as supplicants, powerless to do anything but curse if he refused.[24] Only after the 1910s did collective action improve the situation.

The Village Setting

Most of Japan's 5.2 million village households in this period had a sense of what was going on in the broader world. Literacy was rising as fast in villages as it was in the urban areas, sometimes faster, and it was not uncommon for a household head (or his daughter) to remove the day's fish from its newspaper wrapping and then read the soiled paper to the family. Nonetheless, the national trends were primarily a backdrop. Too many things impinged on daily life to permit much attention to the world beyond: too many hours in the field, too many mountains and valleys inhibiting contact with other villages, too little money for travel, too all-encompassing a village culture to make outside contact necessary. The village viewpoint was grounded in the local setting, and nothing defined that setting more than the surrounding natural world. Animals lolled in farmhouse entrances; outdoor smells wafted indoors, unobstructed; children shuddered when they had to go outside "in the total darkness" of night to pee beside the old plum tree.[25] No one talked more vividly about nature than Tōson. In the afternoon, he would sit on a bale of hay, chatting with a tenant farmer who knew nature as well as any scholar knows history. The man "tells me about everything from 'male' and 'female' grain heads to the fact that it is impossible to grow good rice on the lower slopes of Mt. Asama, because there is so much gravel." He describes which birds destroy crops, which soil is suitable for barley, and why north/south furrows produce better grain.[26] At night, says Tōson, "the voices of all kinds of insects blend in with the sound of flowing water to fill the entire valley," while dogs bark and a farmer sings.[27] And he is awed by nature's seasonal impact. In summer, farmers stuff "leafy branches into the backs of their clothes to make a bit of shade."[28] In autumn, they shudder as the wind howls and hurry "to finish their work before the first snowfall."[29] Winter pushes their spirits to the edge: days are short; food supplies dwindle; snow brings "a fathomless, melancholy whiteness . . . that makes one shiver to look at it."[30] And then spring comes, a time "overflowing with flowers," a time of the plum, then the cherries, then damson plums, apricots, and oleasters, a time that "brings intoxication to our hearts."[31]

The natural world was important in the lives of urban *hinmin* too, but not in the same way. There it was a backdrop most of the time, something one cursed or praised, then forgot. In the village, the powers of nature were a matter of life and death, all the time. One worked *with* and *within* nature or one did not live. In some places, mountains soared on the horizon; in others, they enfolded the village, with farmhouses scattered along the banks of a sharply falling stream that eased children's sleep with its gurgling and occasionally took a little one's life. The sun determined when hamlet residents slept and when they rose. The rains and winds dictated when they went to the fields. Those able to secure land that was "to the south and got very good sunlight," as one farmer put it, usually lived well.[32] If, on the other hand, their paddies were shaded, or if it rained too much, crops failed and food was scarce. When temperatures dropped too low in late spring or early fall, the harvest would suffer, as it would if locusts invaded or diseases attacked a field. If the rain and temperatures were favorable, harvests and income would be plentiful and cellars would be stacked with enough apples, pickles, and rice to get a family through the winter. Nature, in other words, was the Big Determiner: sometimes the cause of poverty, sometimes of plenty, sometimes of pain, sometimes of joy, usually of succor. It connected villagers to life's elemental forces in a way that city dwellers knew only in times of typhoons and earthquakes.

Physically, variety ruled. Sometimes locales that were identified officially as a single hamlet or *mura* actually consisted of several small groupings of households scattered across a large mountainous region. Sometimes a *"mura"* was made up of a string of houses stretched beside the beach or along a mountain path. More often than many city residents knew, there was no cluster of homes, but just what Katai described as "a house here, a house there, a few houses over by some cryptomerias, another house over beyond the fields, and so on and so on."[33] Most frequently, however, villages consisted of a concentrated group of perhaps fifty or sixty—sometimes a hundred or more—houses in the center of a farming area, where each family had its own collection of small, scattered paddies and fields, along with a grove of mountainside fruit trees if they were fortunate. At Inoue's grandmother's place, the cluster included a wooden clog shop, a barber, a post office, a sweets shop, a tinsmith, a dressmaker, a pharmacy, and a general store with "hardware items and an array of sundries . . . crammed so tightly within its walls they looked as if they might overflow the earthen floor and spill out the entrance."[34] Once Katai's "country teacher" had passed the disconnected homes, the road revealed "a dirty-looking barber's shop, a disreputable-looking café, and a cheap sweet shop with a crowd of children around," as well as a one-story school building where a "white dappled dog searched lazily for scraps of food." There also was an inn selling soba and udon, near a thatch-roofed village office and an umbrella stall.[35] The two staples of a typical village, in other words, were clustered households and a set of basic shops.

Another staple was the dirt road that people took to and from the countryside. Highway improvement was largely nonexistent in rural Japan in these days, as was telephone or telegraph. Roads were "mostly narrow, muddy, and unpaved."[36] In the rare places where the newfangled train stopped, the population soared and the village became a town or small city. But few Meiji villagers had personal experience of trains. The well-off rode horses or took carriages; a few used a bicycle or hired a "tottering old rickshaw-man" to make the bumpy roads easier.[37] Everyone else walked, with an umbrella to shield them from summer heat or a jacket to hold off the February cold, and nothing but straw sandals to protect their calloused soles from the stones and gravel of the road. For children, the daily trip to school might take two hours each way, at least part of it in darkness during the winter months, a darkness made blacker by the absence of any artificial lights. "On rainy days," recalled one traverser of the countryside, "it was awful. Country roads back then were hell to walk along. The whole road would be more like a paddy field—or a river, if the rain was heavy—with the mud splashing right up to your ass. If you had tall clogs on, the mud got stuck between the cleats and dragged down on your feet."[38] Rural travel was hard.

Houses, by contrast, were usually much larger than those in the city slums. There were, of course, exceptions. Tōson visited a mountain watchman's hut that had just two rooms: one with soot-stained walls, where the family ate, entertained, and stored tools; another that doubled as a bedroom and a sitting room. In mining communities, even the best homes had just two rooms with a total of ten mats (about 180 square feet).[39] Even those were as large as the typical urban *nagaya* apartment, however, and the majority of village abodes were relatively spacious. Housing seven or eight, sometimes as many as fifteen, people, they would usually have at least four or five rooms: a kitchen, a living room, one or more sleeping rooms where they would lie on futon or straw, and a room at the front for animals. In the main room, there would be an *irori*, or sunken fireplace, surrounded by "timber framing and filled with sand to within an inch or so of floor level"; because there was no chimney, the fire would fill the room with smoke, stinging the eyes as it warmed the bodies and cooked the food. Often a carved wooden figure of some sort would hang above the fireplace to hold teakettles and cooking pots. The main room of the village's most affluent families might have a small tatami-mat area atop a concrete or bamboo floor, but floors were earthen in most homes. Rooms would be separated by translucent *shoji* paper, likely grimy and marked with holes where children had poked their fingers. One wall might support a family altar, and a soot-darkened mask of a protective deity would hang from one of the pillars, while a paper amulet from a local shrine hung from another "to guard against robbers."[40] In the autumn, an assortment of dried persimmons, onions, and peppers was suspended from the eaves, while potatoes and apples might be stored (possibly buried in the earth) in one of the rooms or in a root cellar.

This village home never lacked odors or country sounds. There was the "delicious fragrance of the wood smoke" when one walked in on a winter evening,[41] balanced by the mixture of aging cedar beams, a nearby toilet, and, in summer, human sweat. Outdoor aromas—burning leaves, newly cut hay, rain, the "holding tank for night soil," spruce trees, seasonal flowers—wafted through the open partitions and doors all year long. And most households smelled of animals, which had their own quarters at the front of the house itself, separated from the main room by *shoji* paper or a door that did not shut tightly. Tōson was "struck by the way in which the lives of human beings and of cattle are all blended together." It was common, he said, for a family to have two or three cows in the front space and to know their cows as well as they knew the weather: which moo or bawl indicated hunger, which one signaled sickness, which one came from a heifer in heat. Most families in his area also kept a horse or two for riding or extra cash, as well as chickens, both the roosters that woke people up in the morning and the hens that laid eggs. And in Komoro they might have pigs, which made horrible noises on butcher day. "I go out into the courtyard to see the fat white short-legged pig raising its tragicomical voice and running desperately around the courtyard in search of a way out," he said. "I become quite upset as it begins to cry out even louder right before my eyes."[42]

While some of the implements like rice bowls and kettles might be purchased, farmers' food and clothes were almost all homemade, home grown, or home-caught.[43] Clothes were functional, with little concern about fashion or style, although most people had a single dress-up kimono stored away for weddings and festivals. Wearing something until it became tattered, then mending holes repeatedly with discarded fabrics, was the norm, as was using rice straw to make sandals or raincoats and grasses from the hillside to make fieldwork hats. When Tōson criticized the conversational skills of a local field watchman, he said they were like his clothes: "shaggy" and "unkempt." And he praised the many uses villagers made of light cotton hand towels: on the head as a kerchief, around the forehead as a sweatband, in the bath as a washcloth or a towel, or "dangling from the hip, one corner tucked into the sash" as an all-purpose handkerchief.[44] In homes where every sen made the difference between hunger and comfort, functionality trumped form and style.

It did so with food too, where the goal was simply to fill the stomach. It should be no surprise that variety ranked near the bottom of the list of culinary values. Although the seasons brought some differences to the table—apples in fall, berries in spring, greens in summer—menus were like those in the cities in terms of being much the same, morning to evening and season to season. In-oue, whose family was relatively well off, blamed the sameness on the fact that his grandmother "was not one to put a lot of effort into cooking." So it was miso soup, pickles, and rice every meal; "the only difference between breakfast and lunch or dinner was that for the later meals some cooked cabbage would be added."[45] In most households, the blame lay on the lack of available foods and the lack of money. For breakfast, it always was "wheat-rice," miso and pickled vegetables, with a little boiled fish added at noon and in the evening, recalled Okano Kame of her childhood on a Yamaguchi farm early in the 1900s. In the summer, they would pickle enough radishes (*daikon*) in a "big barrel to last us a year," then "every day for a year, we would take some out and eat it." They were too poor to eat anything else. In the fall, they would stack up thirty or forty bags of rice, to be eaten every day until the next harvest or, if things got bad, until the harvest two years hence[46] "We didn't eat meat," she said. One Yama-guchi farmer said that the few animals they owned were more like farm hands than animals. "Cattle were considered treasures," he said. "Farmers wouldn't eat cow or horse meat. They wouldn't invite people who ate meat into their houses. . . . The cattle were part of the family and eating them was like eating their own children."[47] Sameness and simplicity, rice and fish bits, miso and year-old pickled radishes, with some seasonal fruit or greens, that was mealtime in the poor farm home.

Nothing stands out more vividly in writings about the countryside—or in sharper contrast to descriptions of city life—than the influence of the seasons that so intrigued Tōson. Nature's patterns shaped rural living. Early spring had a bitter side because most of the food stored up six months before was depleted and the new sprouts were only sprouts. But for most people, the bitterness was whisked away by hope, by the days when "the sunlight grows steadily warmer," when "the blossoms on the alder trees begin to dance" and all the frogs "open their throats and proclaim to the sky their return to life." It was a season too of soul-stretching hard labor, said Nagatsuka Takashi's protagonist, farmer Kanji, when "people, too, . . . are once more standing upright on the soil like needles in the grip of a powerful magnet," when "everyone, whether careworn or carefree, was back at work,"[48] turning the paddy soil, mulching it with grasses, smoothing it out, fertilizing it, filling it with nine inches of water, then wading "into the cold and leech-ridden water in bare feet and . . . for a final breakup," all before transplanting rice seedlings one by one, with feet "numb from the cold water."[49] Spring meant cherry blossoms and a return of warmth for urban slum dwellers. It meant that for the rural poor too, but it also meant redoubled village work schedules.

Then came summer, which continued spring's hard toil, but without the inspiration of newness: a dawn breakfast of rice and miso, a day of back-breaking planting, hoeing, weeding, plowing, and, in some regions, applying animal or human feces (called *shirimochi* or "butt rice cakes" in some regions[50]) to the crops, a hasty bath and short meal after sundown, possibly half an hour talking with friends outside a village shop, and a short night's sleep with aching muscles

Farmers in the mid-Meiji years cooperate in transplanting rice seedlings into a flooded paddy. Broad straw hats shaded them from the sun, while boots protected them from the filth and contamination of the muddy soil. Edward Sylvester Morse Collection. Courtesy of the Peabody Essex Museum, Salem Massachusetts.

before it began again. Summer meant heat. And humidity. In July, recalled Katai, "the heat suddenly became very intense, and at night in that country town benches were put out in the shop entrances, and groups of people could be seen fanning themselves."[51] Even more back-breaking and intense was the labor of autumn, the season when rice and trees turned golden. Edible, reddish gold mushrooms began cropping up in the forests around Komoro. Nights grew chillier. And every family sharpened their scythes and sickles for harvest. First, the yellowed stalks were cut. Then bundles were tied together with straw ropes. Next, said Osame Manago of her childhood in Fukuoka, "I carried the rice stalks on my shoulder to this place where there was something like a table with holes," where the women would pound the stalks to remove the grain. Once the rice was threshed and the wind had blown away the hulls, "we sisters measured the rice and put it into sacks, tying each with a rope" before stacking the sacks on a cart and going home.[52] *Hinminkutsu* dwellers might go to Ueno Park to revel in the yellowing ginko trees. On the farm, Manago and her family glanced at the foliage while working, or not at all. Otherwise, harvesting would not be finished before the snows came, which would mean disaster.

One morning, indeed, families would awaken to a white landscape. Snow might come later in the south, but everyone would experience it, and from central Honshu north it would be bone chilling. By mid-November in Nagano, the "frost-blasted leaves" were blowing "back and forth across the mulberry field that has already been stripped bare," and red-cheeked, red-eared, red-nosed men on the street were "wrapped in raw silk or flannel cloths," the women working "with hand towels over their heads and their hands hidden in their sleeves. Everyone . . . sniffling, red-eyed and weeping."[53] Winter drew more ink than any other season, perhaps because there was more time to write now. This was the season when "banks of snow . . . built up along the streets" and the people of Kosugi in the "snow country" of the northeast felt isolated and lonely, "their hands full just keeping the main paths open in the hamlet."[54] It was the time when children went to school while their elders stayed indoors as much as possible, mending tools and clothes, using up the stored food, chatting over the open hearth, and coughing up the hearth smoke that filled rooms already darkened by closed doors and thick shutters. This also was the season of many rural tragedies: two Niigata wood cutters swallowed up by a violent late-March storm in 1902, 199 soldiers frozen to death on military maneuvers on northern Mount Hakkōda the same year, 24 Hida mountaineers killed in a 1908 snowdrift.[55] It was not all grim: hot wine and a "wonderful fire" made the novelist Izumi Kyōka nostalgic for his old home in Kanazawa.[56] Tōson, despite "the violence of the climate," considered winter the "most interesting and pleasurable time," a season when "the onion fields white with frost" produced an "almost piercing sense of joy."[57] By any measure, however, winter was the most challenging season.

Then spring started the cycle all over. Many things set villagers and the urban *hinminkutsu* dwellers apart, but few more so than the ways each perceived the seasons. Only people who worked the soil or fished the coastal waters could appreciate the meaning of seasonal change in its fullness. Only those who depended on food from their own fields for daily subsistence could understand, at the stomach level, the difference between summer's abundance and winter's empty cellar. Only those whose homes and workplaces allowed the natural forces to flow right through them, those who lived in valleys that funneled raging winds and flooding spring streams, could understand in their bones the differing meanings of fall, winter, and spring. Natural disasters came to both city and village; seasons helped to frame the annual narrative in both; rural people and city people alike observed the season-based calendar of festivals and celebrations. But nature was moderated by "civilization" in the city in a way that it never could be in the rural regions. That is why the seasonal variations fill rural writings, even more than jobs, food, and homes do.

Daily Life

Life followed a more singular pattern in the villages than in the cities. People in the *hinminkutsu* might work in the daytime or at night, they might collect night soil or they might build buildings or connect telephone callers, they might live in a cramped apartment or sleep under a temple veranda. Variety was infinite. In the countryside, by contrast, almost everyone worked toward a single purpose. Their goal, honed over centuries, was to produce (or make it possible to produce) the rice, fish, and fibers necessary for human existence. This means that anyone wanting to know how the urban *hinmin* experience was distinct must look at the patterns of daily *mura* life, at the kinds of work villagers did, the customs that circumscribed each day, and the way women, men, and children related to each other.

WORK

Like the urban slums, Japan's villages included people and jobs of many kinds. Farmers and fishermen may have dominated, but the accounts of rural life are filled with oil and medicine peddlers, rickshaw pullers, blind masseuses, roof thatchers, ex-samurai who loaf and fish, geisha, and night soil collectors who, according to the local joke, must have "a bunch of onions or something else . . . at the bottom of each of those buckets," along with the blind beggar who would sing "cheerful songs, somewhat out of tune," to solicit money, the dead priests whose "moss-covered gravestones . . . appear to weep" when it rains, the midwife with an "interfering sort" of mother, and the slovenly woman whose establishment "was known as the 'Lousy Tōfu Shop.'"[58] There were elites too: the wealthy farmers and headmen, who had bigger houses and shared their baths with other villagers. Sometimes the headman was "just a vulgar farmer with a bit of money, an impudent lout;" sometimes he was generous and kind; always he was the village's primary contact with the broader world.[59] And then there were the teachers, whose stories peppered village accounts. Komoro, for example, had the teacher who served as the model for the "bachelor of science" in *Chikuma River Sketches*: a "kindly, honest" heavy smoker with a drinking problem, who was "completely indifferent to his appearance but passionately involved in his teaching." It also had a school principal named Kimura Kumaji, who had graduated from Hope College in Michigan.[60] Mountainous Iiyama had Ōe Isokichi, the inspiration for Tōson's complicated hero in *Broken Commandment* who created a sensation by revealing his own outcaste origins when villagers began discriminating against his low-caste students.[61] And a village in Shikoku had a whole cast of eccentric teachers who made Natsume Sōseki's novel *Botchan* popular.

It was the poor farmers and fishermen, however, who dominated village life, in a way that no single group ever could in the *hinminkutsu*. And it was their grueling fieldwork and boatwork that ruled the rural calendar. Because they had to do almost everything by themselves—pulling in fish, mending nets, breaking up and watering the soil, weeding, fertilizing, harvesting, winnowing—without the aid of machines or animals, the work was more than exhausting; it was physically damaging. "Try catching 150–250 pounds of sea bream in a day. Your fingers and arms start to hurt," said the Tsushima fisherman Kajita Tomigorō; he said hauling in a fish was like "persuading a woman who hates you."[62] A Kyushu worker said that weeding in the days before chemical weed killers meant "we had to weed by hand and soon lost our fingernails."[63] It all demanded workdays even longer, if that were imaginable, than those of their city cousins, especially in planting and harvest seasons. Tōson observed that laborers spending the night in a mountain hut left for work at about three o'clock in the morning, much like the lad from Hiroshima Prefecture who told an interlocutor that he would always head for the fields "in the morning when it was still dark" and stay there "until late at night." At harvest time, he said,

> we had no time to sleep; once my sister even told us to just squat down for a while until dawn and nap in the shed without taking a bath. . . . Usually we worked until twelve o'clock, one o'clock, or two o'clock in the morning. By the time we went to take a bath, the water would be cold. . . . We'd have to start again early in the morning.[64]

The recollections were backed up by data. As late as 1933, when machines and chemical fertilizers had alleviated some of the work, a nationwide survey found farmers between the ages of thirty-one and fifty averaging sixty-five hours a week on the job, and that was across the year's full fifty-two weeks. If one had taken out the winter months, when fieldwork was light, the weekly hours would have surpassed eighty.[65]

THE WOMAN'S PORTION

If the male head of household's work was heavy and hard, his role generally was clear and simple. He was expected to run the farm: plan the crops, supervise the fields, do the heaviest paddy work, arrange for the sale of whatever was harvested, and represent the household within the village. Women occupied a more complicated place in the rural structure. To start with, even though the state's "good wife/wise mother" (*ryōsai kenbo*) preachments suggested that the woman's role was in the house, they actually spent 60 percent as much time in the fields as men did in the 1933 survey, 77.3 percent if they belonged to the crucial thirty-one-to-fifty age category.[66] When there were small children, there often was no choice but to take them along. "Once you put your baby on your back," recalled one mother of her days in the fields, "you could not put him down until your work was done," even when he peed. A typical village woman's kimono in this period was threadbare in the upper back, "the result of . . . carrying her child on her back." Work was filthy too. "It was very hard," remembered an eighty-four-year-old Iwate Prefecture grandmother, "like weeding in the fields, especially during that time of the month. . . . I was often waist deep in mud. . . . What was so terrible was that after working like that all day, at night you would suffer an unbearable itchiness around your bottom, but you couldn't very well scratch there, you know."[67]

Women also did most of the housework: they rose first, to make breakfast and pack lunches for the fields; in the afternoon they left the paddies a "little earlier to prepare the food";[68] and they squeezed in time in the evening or during daytime breaks to mend clothes, clean house, wash the apparel, shop for necessaries, carry water, and do everything else required by daily life. There also were children to be delivered and reared, a task Waswo calls "a very great burden," because in an era of high infant mortality young wives were "almost constantly engaged in childbirth or childrearing."[69] And then there was the supplemental work in which most all families engaged to stave off the worst of

Here, in about 1890, a woman cooks on a range in front of the house in a poor mountain village; outdoor cooking of this sort had largely vanished by the last Meiji decade. Edward Sylvester Morse Collection. Courtesy of the Peabody Essex Museum, Salem Massachusetts.

poverty: making everything from tobacco pouches to straw sandals, taking in the neighbor's wash, delivering milk or sweets, sewing, weaving cotton on a hand-powered home loom. Both sexes did supplemental work, but women did more than the men. In a 1915 Niigata prefectural report, the adult women in two or three households put in more workdays than the adult men did, spending more than half as much time as the males in the fields, while the men spent very few hours in household tasks.[70]

Rural women took sole responsibility for such nonfield jobs as midwifery, textile work, and diving. Although self-deliveries of babies were common in the villages until the end of the Meiji era, most hamlets had one or more midwives, or at least a "delivery granny" (*toriagebāsan*), who came to a home when a mother went into labor to "push on the mother's stomach" and pull the baby out, then, after the birth, to bathe the newborn, wash the "dirty things," and burn the bloody straw mat on which the mother had lain.[71] In the coastal villages of central Japan, the supplemental work—sea diving—often brought in as much money as the male fishermen earned. Part-time female divers, or *ama*, who plunged into the cold Pacific waters to bring up abalone, seaweed, and oysters, were famous for their toughness and aggressive approach to life. Typically, they would make breakfast, clean the house, care for children, do the wash, and collect the firewood, in addition to making two diving trips a day. Known for being cunning in business, the *ama* also had a reputation for wild spending. "This is a place where the women support the men," said a diver born in the late Meiji years. If a spouse died, she said, sea-diving widows would get along fine, but their widowers would "have many problems."[72]

The most prevalent nonfarming jobs for village women were related to textiles. Thousands of girls and women worked in textile factories: more than twelve thousand in mountainous Nagano Prefecture's 613 silk factories in 1898, for example, and another fourteen thousand in the country's next five leading silk-producing rural prefectures.[73] Precise figures are unavailable, but a significant proportion lived at home and commuted to the factory, turning their earnings over to the family.[74] Thousands more lived in families where textiles accounted for a significant part of the household income. In 1896, according to Yokoyama, Japan had a total of 637,525 "weaving households," meaning that "more silk weaving was carried out at home than in factories."[75] In vast numbers of families, silkworms and weaving provided peripheral but crucial side work, most of it done by females. The historian Simon Partner recounted how silkworms literally took possession of a Kosugi household at peak times in the spinning season. A box of twenty thousand silkworm eggs looking like a "mass of white foam" would arrive each March and September, roughly sandwiching the rice-growing season. By the time the worms reached maturity, they were eating huge amounts of mulberry leaves—more than 1,300 pounds in total—making it "all that the family could do to harvest enough leaves to feed the voracious creatures." The work was exhausting now: "no school for these kids during the last week." Every hand and every hour was needed to bring in the mulberry leaves, spread out the leaves, arrange the worms in rows for the spinning, carry away their feces, and take the spun silk to market. When the process was finished, they would put the discarded cocoons to use too, making their family's own silk thread from the remains, or using empty cocoons as fish bait. Sometimes they ate the unsavory pupa. The work robbed already busy families of a great deal of sleep, but the extra yen got them through those late winter months when food supplies dwindled.[76]

INTERACTIONS

Few things revealed the heart of rural living more vividly than the way people interacted, both within families and across households. One the one hand, interpersonal relations in the village were no more idyllic than human interactions anywhere. The wife of the rice farmer "Zenji" in far northern Yamagata Prefecture, who ran off with a young male employee in 1910, was not unusual.[77] Inoue Yasushi was shipped off to the village as a child, to be reared by an unrelated "Granny Onui" who had been his great-grandfather's mistress; when his mother visited she was abusive to Granny Onui and called him "a skinny thing" and a "regular lump of grime."[78] When Katai's fictitious (but reality-based)

Much of the silk work went to women such as these who are selecting silk worms, which they will transfer to the shelves behind them, where the worms will attach themselves to twigs and spin their cocoons. Edward Sylvester Morse Collection. Courtesy of the Peabody Essex Museum, Salem, Massachusetts.

schoolteacher Seizō visited his brother's grave two years after his death, he found no marker on the plot; "it looked as though his parents hadn't visited for some time, for the flower vase was cracked."[79] Stories of uncaring parents, of sexual infidelities, of jealousy and intrigue, and of absconding mates were common in families challenged by the same grueling schedules and material scarcity that their cousins knew in the cities.

The hamlet also resembled the city in the prevalence of informal socializing among neighbors. Katai's account of "steamy" village bathers gossiping about the strange death of a local fisherman and Nagatsuka's picture of farmer Kanji's naked neighbors splashing about in much-used tub water "covered with scum" differ only in detail from stories of neighborhood baths in the *hinmin-kutsu*.[80] And the abalone divers gathered around the village bonfire (a place with no "higher or lower status attached"), "breast-feeding small babies and raising their children together as a group," sound very much like the reporters' accounts of a "back alley council" of poor Tokyo women chatting while the children drank their mother's milk.[81] The village accounts are filled too with men drinking together on the way home from the fields, children playing ball in empty fields, and boys smoking together along a pathway, all in the spirit of Tōson's favorite buckwheat noodle establishment, Agehaya, "where the lowliest laborers, the teamsters, and the poor farmers round about come to have their saké warmed."[82] Humanity trumped locale when it came to human connectedness.

At the same time, several structural features of village life set rural relationships apart from those in the city's poor regions. First, there was the impact of time: villagers had lived together for generations, nurturing traditions that dictated how people should relate to each other. Some traditions were comforting and womb-like, and some were suffocating. Always they were inescapable. Second, there was geography: both the isolation and the lack of protection from forces of nature forced people to work together in distinctive ways. Third, there was scale: villages were small. When a few hundred people live together in isolated spaces across generations, their interactions necessarily take on a family-like character that is impossible in the city. When the nonagenarian Kaneko Yukie talked about her childhood in the northern Kyushu village of Ōyama, she could describe the different families—who was poor, who was rich; who was lazy, who was hard-working; who was bright, who was not; who left to go abroad, who stayed—with a detail unimaginable for a child of the ever-changing urban poverty neighborhoods.[83] That was true not because she had a gifted memory (though she clearly did) but because of the size and isolation of her village. The same combination of scale and chronology enabled Partner to comment about the child Toshié in Kosugi village: "What was notable about her was her complete acceptance of, and by, the hamlet and society that surrounded her." He said her friendships "would stay with her for the rest of her life."[84]

One reason villagers interacted so intensely lay in the way they shared work and decision making. Because fields were scattered and resources scarce, residents from different households worked together a great deal. This was especially true in growing rice, which required cooperation not just in deciding who got how much paddy water and when they got it but in transplanting the seedlings. A typical village image from this period—labeled "bottoms up" by some wags—had eight or ten neighbors stretched in a line across a paddy, all of them bent over from the hips as they inserted seedlings into the muddy rows. "We did the paddy tilling as a community," recalled Gotō Hideyoshi of Ōkubo village in Aichi Prefecture, "because the work was just too hard to do alone." They would sing as they worked, partly to make the work go faster and partly to keep their minds off the blisters that formed on their hands.[85] Beans brought neighbors together too; Komoro farmers, for example, went into the fields every June in "teams of four: one to spade up the ground, one to plant the beans, one to add the fertilizer, and one to smooth out the ground." If there were not enough hands to get it all done, relatives from another village would come to help.[86] Villagers also had to make joint decisions about the use of natural resources. Water and forests, in particular, were usually under the control of the entire village, with hamlet-wide meetings to decide how water levels would be maintained in ponds or cisterns, how water disputes should be settled, when each family could go into the forest to gather wood or grasses, and how much wood a household would be allotted to cremate a body. And the village council decided on dues and collective work assignments. The control of communal property, said the sociologist Fukutake, "made the hamlet a community-like self-sufficient society."[87]

The communal nature of this sharing meant that late Meiji villages operated according to a set of behaviors as predictable as the passing of the seasons. Gift giving, for example—fish or pears for the sick, hillside mushrooms when supping at a neighbor's home—was ritualized in every village, with the poorest feeling a sting of embarrassment if they could not afford to give something. Match making too followed established rules that a young woman or man defied at great personal risk. "It was Mother who decided my marriage," reported one young villager. "Not much used to be discussed with the person who was getting married."[88] Ages-old rules governed the way children treated parents, the way youths treated elders, and the way village heads made their baths available to poor neighbors. Most hamlets had voluntary (in actuality, not so voluntary) groups of housewives, or young men, or veterans, or altruistic farmers to help with funerals, ditch repairs, festivals, policing, and all the other activities that individuals could not accomplish by themselves. And most also had at least one "mediating granny" (*sewayaki babbaa*), "an old woman with a fairly settled life who knew village affairs well and worked insidiously at helping others." Miyamoto cited instances of these old women calling on troubled neighbors to solve problems in the middle of the night or taking food to households having an especially hard time.[89] One village in Gunma Prefecture even had a "secret virtue plowing society" (*sentoku junkōtai*), which prepared the fields of needy families under cover of darkness so that the family would not feel an obligation to return the favor.[90] The web of communal norms could be oppressive and exclusionary, but for most villagers it provided stability and mutual sustenance, things the cities' tenement districts could not duplicate.

HIERARCHY

A strong sense of hierarchy accompanied the sharing, with one's place determined by a mix of age, gender, wealth, length of residency, and land holdings. There was no concept of class in the modern sense, but there was a keen awareness of who stood where on the ladder of respect, accompanied by intricate codes dictating when one should use polite language, when one bowed and how low, and whose opinions carried weight. Within families, the elder was superior to the younger, except when an elder son was too lethargic or weak to assume family leadership, in which case a younger (or adopted) son might become household head. In Toshié's village, Partner found a division into three general status levels that had existed for centuries: the chief families, the little peasants, and the water drinkers (landless residents). When the chief families talked to the peasants and water drinkers, they used familiar, diminutive language; the peasants responded with formal, polite speech.[91] Individual villages were ranked too, with communities of outcastes, or *burakumin,* at the bottom, even though individual *burakumin* might be financially well-off. Residents of *burakumin* villages typically were denigrated by those in neighboring hamlets as "tramps," "dog eaters," or "savages."[92]

There also were rankings by gender. No matter which group it was, women were regarded as subordinate to men. In some villages, shrine priests would paint the character for small on a newborn girl's forehead and big on a boy's.[93] As children grew, they were given an intricate set of gender rules: girls were not supposed to play "rough"; girls had responsibilities for "purity" that were not applied to boys; women cared for children and the household, regardless of what duties they had in the fields or in the shop; women were to keep quiet in public and avoid any pretense of interest in community leadership roles. And women in traditional villages had to remove themselves during their time of menstruation. Ogasawara Shiu of Yashirowaki hamlet in Aichi Prefecture told Miyamoto that in the 1890s "women were at a disadvantage" because during "the monthly hindrance" all females in her village had to move to a *himaya* or separate shed because "it was said that if we ate with the family, the family would be defiled." That custom had largely died out in Aichi by the last Meiji decade, but the menstrual cycle itself remained a mark of impurity—and thus inferiority—far into the twentieth century.[94] Thinking back to her childhood in Hiroshima Prefecture, Bun Kobayashi Yoshimori said "it was not our place" to have ambitions. "We were only made to do farm work, and when we became adults people would come from here and there to ask for our hands in marriage."[95] Exceptions abounded; stories of strong and powerful women running businesses or taking the initiative in sexual affairs were common. But the time-honored behavioral norms resulted in condemnation of most assertive women. It was hardly surprising that women seeking help from the midwife Shibahara Urako in Hiroshima Prefecture often would ask: "Why were we born women? Nothing is more miserable than coming into this world as a woman."[96]

The hierarchical norms made a nuanced puzzle of village life, a puzzle in which harmony trumped individual desires. Schoolteacher Tōson found this out when his headmaster "got carried away" and criticized the "fecklessness of physicians" in a speech. The area's doctors demanded an apology, the police chief was selected to mediate, and Tōson (the subordinate) was ordered to stand in for the headmaster at a meeting with the Komoro Medical Association. In his account of the episode, he declines at first to apologize, saying he does not know what the headmaster actually said, whereupon the police chief "leaps to his feet and, for the sake of peace in the town, turns toward the assembled group and makes a deep bow." Tōson concludes that he has no option but to make his personal puzzle piece pliable and offers an apology: "I make my bow and leave the second floor of the restaurant, reflecting on what distasteful duties may fall to the lot of a country school teacher."[97] Harmony is restored. Nagatsuka depicts farmer Kanji in *The Soil*, by contrast, as paying a heavy price for refusing to bend to his fellow villagers. When he takes some "illicit oak stumps" from the forest for firewood, villagers demand that he apologize. When he insists that he has done no wrong, they turn on him, calling the police, who humiliate him in front of his peers. Similar episodes occurred repeatedly in Kanji's life because conformity was not in his nature. Ann Waswo, the translator, says, "It is chiefly Kanji's violation of community norms and values . . . that accounts for the low opinion that others have of him. He will not do the 'proper' thing."[98]

Viewed from a twenty-first-century egalitarian perspective, the hierarchical system left much to be desired. It preferred some groups over others. Men received more advantages than women, rich people reaped rewards that poor farmers could barely dream of, those who went along found life easier than nonconformists (who might be shunned or even banished if they were too recalcitrant[99]). It was a rigid and unchangeable system, too deeply rooted in centuries of custom to be affected much by the modernizing policies of the Meiji government. But most villagers—poor as much as rich—valued it as a good way of ordering life. Custom and hierarchy made things easy as long as one accepted one's place or "fate," which helped people know where they stood in relation to everyone else, assured them of help when special troubles occurred, and lubricated social and conversational interchanges. When *hinmin* families in the Nago-chō or Samegahashi slums sat, lonely, beside the hibachi at New Year, or when they felt the arbitrariness of a factory manager who fired one of their children for simply getting sick, they tended to remember the old village system—hierarchy and all—more as a warm comforter than as an entrapping web.

CHILDREN: AT PLAY AND AT SCHOOL

Children's roles also were different in the village, where they almost always were seen as blessings. Drawing on the diary of Kobayashi Shūzō, Katai had his morose village teacher comment that the only time he had "no complaints, no grievances" was when he was with children: when they "wrestled on the sand, chased grasshoppers in the bushes, or splashed around the water's edge."[100]

Inoue's youngsters were always staging sports events, "chasing tiny pale creatures that floated like bits of cotton" in the evening sky, or swimming nude in the river, then "warming their bodies on the sun-drenched boulders scattered along the streambed."[101] Children hiked in the mountains; they stole persimmons from neighbors' groves; they made missiles out of bamboo sticks. In the summer, they played "something which somewhat resembled baseball—nothing with strict rules." In the fall, they flew kites. In winter they had snowball fights and used aluminum hot water bottles as sleds. And in spring, they caught cicadas. "We had lots of *bu* (military play) in our village when I was a child," said Ōno Toshio who grew up in the Totsukawa mountains; "one of the most fun things" was going mushroom hunting. When the children in Inoue's Ise village heard of someone's death, they would play "the funeral game, running around . . . and chanting '*Jam-bon, jam-bon*' in approximation of sounds they had heard at funerals."[102]

When not in the fields or in school, village boys often went fishing in the local river, with nets, buckets, and even rough spears. Holger Rosenberg Collection, National Museum of Denmark. https://tinyurl.com/y84ofwcg

The play was not always joyful but neither was it seen as dysfunctional. Okano Kame never got over the day her little brother Benzō drowned while they were trying to catch shrimp, swept away by a rain-swollen river.[103] Sometimes the play turned crude (Katai's teacher complained that "children of seven and eight picked up extremely lewd songs and sang them openly in school"[104]) or mean (Inoue was perversely satisfied when a timid classmate threw a rock at his tormentors[105]). And Tōson talked repeatedly about how rough children could be with each other. Every day, he said, he saw this kind of scene near the school: First, one little boy stuffed grass into a playmate's mouth. Then his victim yelled "'Damn you!' at the top of his lungs." Then he screamed "Bastard!" And things escalated from there. Most telling in Tōson's account, however, was his comment that while Tokyoites would have called these children "savages," he found their roughhousing "completely innocent," even stimulating.[106] While urban reports about *hinmin* children focused on absent parents and incorrigibility, rural observers invariably found child play natural and buoyant, no matter how pugilistic. Why the difference? Clearly, the variant pictures had less to do with behavior and poverty than with the fact that children were integrated into the village fabric in ways that were impossible in the *hinminkutsu*. In the city, small children had to bring in income, and there were no extended families or communal systems to look after the tykes when the parents were away at work. That meant that impoverished city children were more likely to be alienated from support communities, whether their behavior was delinquent or good. In the village, even the poorest and most wayward child had a place, a communal context that was absent for city children.

By the second half of the Meiji era, village children also had ties to an institution that was unavailable to most slum children: the public school. The most important thing about schools may have been that the great majority village children actually attended them, regardless of their family's economic status, particularly after 1900, when tuition was abolished. There is no denying that rural areas faced special challenges in getting children into the classroom. Early on, farmers resisted the idea of losing their children's field labor during class hours and questioned the value of formal schooling. One Kumamoto native recalled that most of his fellow villagers opposed the new schools on the grounds "that education makes one dislike farming,"[107] while the father of a girl in Fukuoka said, "What good does it do to get more education for working in the fields or for business? If you can sign your name, that's enough."[108] Other parents resisted schools because they needed their children to look after infants while they themselves were in the fields. Planting and harvest seasons presented particular problems, and absenteeism soared in the spring and fall; in some mountainous regions, classes actually were cancelled during silkworm season. Scale was a challenge too, with children from small hamlets having to walk as much as four or five miles each way to and from school, through "pine forests or along the railroad tracks or beside the banks of the Chikuma River" in Komoro, along a road bordered by "a dirty-looking barber's shop, a disreputable-looking café, and a cheap sweet shop" for Katai's "country teacher" in Saitama, climbing steep mountain paths in many parts of the country.[109]

Despite the obstacles, however, rural areas did better than cities in getting poor children into schools, with more than 90 percent attending for at least four years in most regions by 1900 and a province like Yamanashi able to boast 98 percent attendance by 1905.[110] With local hamlets determined to have new schoolhouses "in no way inferior to those of the other towns,"[111] the schools that rural regions nurtured were, by and large, impressive places that introduced new worlds to millions of village children. Curriculums were basic, focusing on reading, writing, and math, plus practical classes in sewing or homemaking. Teachers were at least relatively well educated, and they were known for their strictness, much like Okamoto's "scariest thing in the world" at the beginning of this chapter. Most, though, were not as harsh as Inoue's classroom "ogres" who were prone to rapping miscreants on the head or slapping them across the face before dragging them by the ear to the hallway and making them stand there for long periods of time.[112] If a child's hijinks were reported to the parents, there would be hell to pay at home, perhaps a spanking or an evening without food, even the application of a burning coal.[113] At the end of each school day, children in most schools would clean their own classrooms.

The schools' most important influence on village children—and on the way they experienced poverty—probably lay in opening their minds to new worlds, both spatially and intellectually. For one thing, the village school brought them into contact with new peers. Because most schools included children from a number of hamlets spread out across the region, students had to mix with youngsters from other valleys and from areas that had hitherto been rivals or enemies. Classmates from different hamlets "showed hostility towards all the others," said Inoue, "sometimes subtly, sometimes not so subtly. . . . Sometimes rocks were thrown for no apparent reason."[114] Nonetheless, they had no choice but to interact, and rivalries often turned into friendships. The local school also confronted children with a sense of nation and world, something that had been missing for most of their parents and grandparents. And at the intellectual level, the new education challenged ages-old village beliefs, including the idea that fate alone determined one's life chances. While private schools in the Tokugawa years had provided some challenge to fatalism, most rural children did not attend the pre-Meiji schools. Now, with compulsory education, the local school became a place where "generally speaking . . . a meritocracy (of scholastic ability, athletic prowess, or wit) founded on the idea of equality took hold," a place where "girls found they were not inferior to boys and even surpassed them."[115] When young Kosaku's Granny Onui learned in *Shirobamba* that a commoner classmate was wearing fine clothes to school, she was aghast, exclaiming, "If people don't know their place, nothing good will come of it!" By contrast, Kosaku, a boy drawn directly from Inoue's own childhood, found her ideas old-fashioned. School had given him a new set of values.[116] Neither schooling nor the close community interactions inoculated these village children against the ravages of poverty, but both gave them a framework for dealing with financial hardship that was different from that of urban slum children.

Spaces for Meaning and Pleasure

Farmers worked hard, but life involved more than work. To a degree that made emigrants to the city nostalgic, village traditions provided endless spaces for social and religious activities, which leavened daily life and balanced the economic troubles. As was clear above, children played everywhere, all the time. So did adults, though not as often: on national and local holidays, in communal baths, during shrine and temple festivals, and in social interactions, both sexual and platonic.

THE BATH

One of the most important diversions was the bath. Japan's bathing traditions were as prevalent in the countryside as in the cities. In contrast to the cities, where baths were in nondescript buildings with piped-in water, rural baths often (though not always) were natural and beautiful. Hot mineral springs abounded in the mountains; river sides provided gurgling backdrops and abundant water; bathing under the sky was not unusual. Notorious for his condescension toward things rural, Natsume Sōseki would say of Shikoku, "Every other thing made a very poor comparison with things in Tokyo, but as to the hot spring, it was just splendid."[117] Almost everyone went to the communal baths regularly. Those who could not afford tubs at home used either the large baths of rich hamlet families or cheap public baths; some bathed in a nearby river. Toshié's affluent family in Kosugi made its bath available to village residents, who typically would come weekly, "their hands . . . hard and callused, their fingernails black with dirt." By the end of the evening, Toshié reported, the water would be "the color of vegetable soup," with a "thick scum of human detritus—skin, hair, and drowned lice" at the bottom of the tub.[118] If the hamlet was large enough or well enough endowed naturally, entrepreneurial types would construct a bathhouse, sometimes just a "simple roof with a dressing area in one corner." Tōson liked to visit a little spring-fed bath in the mountains above Komoro, the "kind of place where people from the countryside round about bring their own rice and miso and come up to forget their miseries."[119]

Sociability was at the heart of bath culture. People may have loved the clean, embracing feel of soaking, but, as in the city, they cared more still about the human atmosphere, talking animatedly in a place where neither rules of propriety nor dress codes inhibited free interaction. When the schoolchildren in *Shirobamba*'s Nishibira hamlet on the Izu Peninsula headed for the bath after school, they invariably "raced to undress, jumped into the tub, and set about splashing and rough-housing, sending up sprays of water." Their parents may have splashed less when they came after work, but they were just as exuberant in enjoying each other's company. No one worried much about gender separation. The children "would dash out naked," and even the parents, whose large bathing tub sported a wooden slab to separate male and female sections, had "no fast rules as to which was which and no one paid any attention."[120] The government had prohibited mixed bathing in 1869, concerned about Westerners who regarded it as "licentious," but the prohibition was widely ignored in countryside baths. As the historian Hirota Masaki notes, "a sense of propriety or modesty" dictated that people not stare, but "in the poorest strata of society, there existed social spaces where nudity was considered unavoidable and accepted."[121] Bathing meant cleanliness, relaxation, conviviality, and freedom from rules about modesty.

SEX

Freedom from inhibitions in the bath did not indicate any particular attitude toward sexual behavior, only that dress norms there had nothing to do with sexuality. The late Meiji ethnographers and novelists portrayed villages where sexual activity outside the baths was common and attitudes toward sex were casual, if complex. Katai complained of "loose morals" in the Saitama Prefecture village of Hotto, where newspapers reported on male homeowners who seduced female workers and children who sang bawdy songs. And he showed teacher Seizō embarrassed but hardly scandalized when he chanced "this evening . . . upon the priest and his wife 'being friendly together,' in their little bath," while the priest himself gave "a nonchalant laugh" and quipped, "A fine time to be seen!" Sumii described an adolescent boy in Nara Prefecture who experienced his first awakenings when a girl's secretive hand squeeze caused "a pain in his chest, as if he were suffocating." She said that every village was full of gossip about "what some girl had been up to, or about some married woman having an affair with someone."[122] Men in Aichi boasted to folklorist Miyamoto about how uninhibited they were with young village women during the late Meiji years. "When night came, you'd call on her. She wouldn't refuse you," said Kaneda Shigesaburō of Inosawa. If he was worried that the parents might raise a fuss, he would "pee on the runners, and the door slid open without a sound. . . . When you got under the futon, unlike these days, the girls weren't wearing panties. That's how we all played, because there were no other pleasures to speak of."[123] Visits to brothels were commonplace too, as the sociologist Bernice Webb was told when she inquired about an unidentified group of houses in Nagano Prefecture in 1911. They constituted a "not very 'highclass'" settlement of "public prostitutes for the whole neighborhood," her hosts told her, a village "resorted to chiefly by the peasant cultivators, the coolies, and some of the visitors to the bath-villages." Police officers saw to it that the women were inspected twice weekly for diseases and provided free treatment if they were found with venereal diseases.[124]

One characteristic of rural sexual practices was the freedom with which people discussed them. Hirota notes that the "civilized" classes applied the epithet "barbarian" to villagers because of their "much more frank and free sexual morals," a condescension he calls "hypocritical."[125] When the anthropologists Ella Lury Wiswell and her famous husband John Embree lived in a hamlet near

Sue in northern Kyushu two decades after the end of Meiji, they found an unrestrained quality in sexual discussions that left them "by turns amused, startled, and exasperated."[126] "Frankness," they reported, "was common." Embree wrote in his journal that "no chance to make an indecent gesture or joke is ever passed up." Village women were graphic in talking with Wiswell about intercourse, using words like *kara-imo* (sweet potato) for penis and explaining that "having intercourse twice in one night is quite usual, especially on long evenings when you go to bed early and if you are still young. Three times is not really unusual." They insisted "that women enjoy intercourse just as much as men. 'Why should they bother otherwise?'" Brides, they said, rarely were virgins. And many men had multiple partners. Nor were children innocent, since they constantly "eavesdropped . . . and listened in on adult conversations." Mothers used the child's word for penis, "*chin-chin,*" constantly around their children: "What is that I see? Is it your *chin-chin*? Don't run around here naked showing your *chin-chin.*" And parties "involved dancing, singing, eating, and heavy drinking, and almost invariably considerable sexual joking and play." Even at temples, it was common for a priest to give a sermon and then leave, urging them to "enjoy themselves," whereupon drinks flowed, dances turned erotic, and sex flourished. None of the evidence suggests that Sue was greatly different from other villages across Japan, either in the 1930s or in the late Meiji years.

All was not pleasure, however, nor were villagers above judgmentalism, particularly in regard to prostitutes. Though visiting brothels was common, working at one was not respectable. Daughters who went off to work as overseas prostitutes (*karayuki*) sometimes carried a certain cachet, particularly when they returned years later wearing fine clothes and giving out money to support local shrines and build homes.[127] But as a rule, brothel work evoked shame or pity. Horikiri Tatsuichi, a student of early twentieth-century rural life, calls the brokers who persuaded farm families to send their daughters to brothels "slick and merciless, people who were capable of viewing other humans as if they were mere cows and horses."[128] Katai says his teacher Seizō shed "tears of sympathy" over "the ill-fated life of a geisha, unable to preserve her own chastity and body."[129] Villagers generally saw rural prostitutes as worse off than the girls who went off to textile factories. Their pay might be slightly better, but they had no more freedom from their bosses and their work carried a moral stain. The Tokyo editor Kuroiwa Shūroku insisted in 1898 that the practice of regarding women as "playthings of men" was a *national* "problem in male/female morals (*danjo fūzoku mondai*)," not just a rural one.[130] But the sense of disrepute that clung to rural sex workers was particularly heavy because there was so little anonymity in the rural setting. Everyone knew who the brothel workers were, and the best of the emotions that most people reserved for them was pity.

FESTIVALS AND CELEBRATIONS

Villagers across Japan particularly enjoyed three things on their free days—celebrating, worshiping, and partying—and the distinction between the three was ambiguous. Religion, which was ubiquitous, took many forms. One center of religious practice was the nearby temple or shrine, which provided space to meditate and celebrate. Some locales, like the mountain town of Iiyama along the Chikuma River, swarmed with temples and ceremonies, causing Tōson to wonder if "something in the snowbound lives led during long winters . . . inclines most of these people toward religion," while others had just a small worship place or two, with priests who "seemed little different from . . . the laymen of the region."[131] Another space for religious practice was the roadside, where thousands of small statues, sacred rock piles, and Buddhist images invited "pious wayfarers, who pause before every Buddhist image on their path to repeat a brief prayer."[132] A third center was the farmhouse. It would have been hard to find a hut or home without Buddhist or Shintō worship objects: a charm on the door post to keep out illness, hanging relics to please the gods of wealth, a spirit shelf (*kamidana*) to appeal for help from ancestors. And still a fourth center was the faraway, famous shrine or temple to which many villagers went on pilgrimage every few years, partly, said one woman from the Inland Sea, because "in the old days, no one would marry a girl who didn't know the world." She herself traveled with girlfriends to prominent temples in Shikoku.[133]

Celebrations were not restricted to religious institutions, however. As in the cities, the national holidays were occasions for festivities in every hamlet and town, in individual homes as well as in public spaces. "We would plan for about three days straight" at New Year, recalled a farmer from Yamaguchi. "The big thing . . . was the *mochi* [rice cake] pounding. We would pound about one bag of *mochi* and put big pieces . . . up on the shelf to dry. We would put it all in bags. . . . Then we would get some out from time to time and cook and eat it."[134] In a typical village on the Inland Sea island of Ōshima, the whole village would turn out for the evening *bon* dances in the summer and to listen the toothless old farmer Miyamoto Ichigorō sing ballads. Once his singing began, "a hush would come over the dancers," causing them to dance "quietly, as if in a dream." After performing until late into the night the year he was eighty-one, Miyamoto came home and collapsed; three days later he died.[135] In Muraoka's Kumamoto village, people eschewed the dancing at *bon* but "visited the graves and temples" and "made a bit of a feast" at home, wearing new clothes "as much as possible."[136] Inoue said that the national holidays prompted even old Granny Oshina in his household, a solitary woman "who usually stayed cooped up in her back room," to join the family at dinner, "her body doubled over as if she were trying to lick the tatami mats on the floor."[137]

Each region also had its own special celebrations and traditions. The villages of eastern Nagano staged an annual *monozukuri* (creating things) festival in mid-January, hanging up cocoon-shaped rice flour balls to bring good fortune in the silkworm season; they followed this in February with a day of placing straw horses and rice cakes on the "tiny roadside shrines of the gods so beloved by children." In late summer, Komoro would put on its own version of Kyoto's Gion festival, with farmers walking five miles into town to ring the Kōgakuji's temple bell and watch worshipers pull a heavy portable shrine down the street. After the parade, the shrine bearers would begin "getting drunk" and "running about and shouting like madmen," turning at last "into a sort of mob" and nearly tipping the shrine over.[138] On May 8 each year, the people in Tottori Prefecture's Daisenji region dressed up their cows, ascended the mountain, and held "a large cow fair right there in front of the temple." In Kawame far to the north, villagers held a raucous ceremony each year to dedicate the spears they had used during the hunting season and to memorialize the spirits of the bears they had killed.[139] The Niihama miners on Shikoku Island had an annual mountain festival when locals insisted that the "Forty-Seven Rōnin" be performed.[140] And in Muraoka's Kyushu village, there was an annual sumo festival, when wrestlers received gift boxes with auspicious rice dishes after several days of competition.[141] A locale without an annual festival would have been unthinkable.

Ask almost any elderly Japanese farmer for the best childhood memories and the answer will be the annual temple or shrine *matsuri* (festival). Muraoka waxed enthusiastic about the "Jizō-san and Kannon-san" festivals, when locals walked miles to enjoy the booths filled with trinkets and games. "Going there was one of the pleasures for the farmers," he said.[142] Lloyd Sugimoto from Hiroshima said of his village's September shrine festival, "Oh, it's a big thing. . . . Everybody comes out. Not only the kids, you know. The whole family."[143] The octogenarians interviewed in Totsukawa Village said the same thing. Ōno Toshio, a former schoolteacher born in the Taishō years, said the festivals at the two-thousand-year-old Tamaki Shrine of the ancient Kumano region were the two best things to happen each year. More than five hundred villagers would climb for three hours to the 3,500-foot-high sacred spot, to venerate the local mountain spirits and Japan's creator *kami*. At the top, they would watch as male celebrants, dressed as young girls, played musical instruments and danced. And they all would socialize, eating box lunches, sampling the *manjū* (steamed yeast buns) and Wakayama fish, drinking saké, dancing along with the carriers of portable shrines, and buying little toys. "We walked back down the mountain in the dark," Ōno said, "always with our parents, not with the other children."[144]

What made the festivals so special, and what did they have to do with the rural experience of poverty? One answer surely lies in the human need for celebration and joy, another in the respite they provided from the drudgery of work and the anxieties of budget stretching. "Otherwise, it was all just farming, day in and day out," said Hawaiian émigré Tanima Kazo about his days in Yamaguchi.[145] The *bon* festival "atmosphere was one of forgetting the cares of the world to make the most of a night of freedom," said Katai.[146] Indeed. Writing about the silk farmers of Nagano, Tōson captured the soul of the situation with a comment that his reader never would be able to understand "the joy which the Gion festival brings unless you first think of the dark frames on which the worms are raised, the awful stench, the worries about the pupation of the worms, the endless hauling of mulberry leaves, and the times when men and women labor desperately throughout the night."[147] Exhausted from back-breaking work and soul-breaking anxieties, farmers needed revelry and respite, be it in the cleansing bath, in physical intimacies, or in the *matsuri*. What anthropologist Robert J. Smith said of the villagers of Sue he could have said of rural people everywhere in late Meiji Japan: They "were always ready for a party, and one cannot but be impressed by their seemingly limitless capacity to find occasions for them."[148] Whether this set them apart from their city relatives is not entirely clear; there is no question, however, that the merrymaking and the hardships were part of a complex rural tango in which the merrymaking made the dark days a little less dark.

Hardship

Villagers were not all poor. Nearly every hamlet boasted a few affluent households, along with several who were poor but comfortable. Katai said of his village, "There were opulent houses with encircling hedges of tall oaks, but then again there were also tumbledown houses with rough plaster walls fronted by a dirty-looking, stagnant ditch."[149] The reality for the greatest numbers of villagers, however, was serious economic deprivation. As the labor leader Takano Fusatarō pointed out late in the 1890s, tenant farmers across Japan averaged 13.8 yen a month, less than any of the urban workers whose monthly budgets have been examined in this work. "As a rule," he said, "living conditions prevalent among peasant proprietors and tenant farmers represent the lowest type of Japanese life," and fishing villages were poorer yet than farm villages.[150] Yokoyama, a friend of Takano, reported on Niigata farmers who ate "grasses to stave off hunger," Yamagata peasants who made cakes from bracken (*warabi*), and villagers in Aomori who lived "from hand to mouth with dried strips of potatoes and radishes." He added, "One need not stretch one's imagination to realize how these people spend the New Year's days."[151] A poor sex worker in Suwa observed that "pets at geisha houses ate better than the parents of many geisha."[152] Sometimes the story had the ultimate ending, as in the report from a Miyagi farmer who heard a moaning voice coming from a neighbor's home early in 1902: "I think I'm dying." The farmer gave his neighbor some rice cakes but it was too late. Village officials said the moaner and his wife died from "prolonged lack of food."[153] If field work was hard, the task of stretching income to feed and shelter a family was, for a majority of farmers, harder still. Was it, however, harder than the survival struggle in the urban *hinminkutsu*? To answer that, several facets of village poverty demand a closer look.

WHY FARMERS WERE POOR

Few of rural poverty's causes were more particular to the middle and late Meiji years than the sharp rise in tenancy outlined at the outset of this chapter. While four of every five farmers owned the land they tilled in the late Tokugawa years, just over half did by Meiji's end. Moreover, the rents people had to pay consumed on average half of a family's annual production; in some cases, they took a full 80 percent, in contrast to the 10 or 15 percent of income that most urban *hinmin* paid in rent.[154] The painful process by which this transfer of ownership occurred in one region west of Tokyo was described by Partner: when farmers lacked cash for food or seeds, they would turn to the rich neighbor Aizawa Kikutarō for a loan, pledging land as security. Then, when they could not pay the loan, he would visit their homes and explain that "although it is inconvenient, we must honor our promises and pay off our debts." If the debtor complained that he had no collateral left, that "his land and even his home are rented," Aizawa likely would give an extension. But if the debt remained, he would take the land and the debtor would become a renter.[155] The cycle resulted in endless tension, with landlords and tillers blaming each other for irresponsible or heartless behavior. Aizawa wrote in his diary that tenants had a "lack of sincerity," and the proprietor-priest in Katai's *Country Teacher* called tenant farmers who schemed to pay lower rents "absolutely hopeless!" The farmers retorted that landlords were "self-important," or cold-hearted manipulators. When farmers admitted to finagling and cheating on rents, it was in a tone of righteous indignation. One tenant told Tōson on rent day that his fellows, who put stones or damp grains in the rice sack to inflate its weight, were simply carrying out "minor strikes."[156] Tōson's sympathies lay with the tenant farmers, but regardless of where guilt lay, all would have agreed that the necessity of paying half of one's earnings in rent played a major role in keeping farmers poor.

There were, of course, other causes, including those cases that the middle classes liked to trumpet: people pushed into destitution by profligacy or undisciplined habits. Yasumatsu Toshio, for example, grew up on a tobacco farm where solvency turned to desperation because "my father liked to drink so he lost it all."[157] But personal failings were exceptions, not rules. More often, guilt lay in a market system that left farmers in continual uncertainty over how things would be in the next season: how much seed and fertilizer prices would rise, whether interest rates would go up, what their produce would sell for, when their landlords would use rising taxes as an excuse to jack up rents. When the Russo-Japanese War sent taxes—and then rents—soaring,[158] the young farmer Morihara Usaku from Yamaguchi Prefecture decided that the uncertainties of the economy gave him no choice but to leave the farm. "There is nothing as foolish as being a farmer," he later declared. "Why? Because farmers do not price their own goods. The . . . company decides on the price of their products." He said "people who remain farmers are . . . dumb.[159] The mass migrations away from Japan's farms in the late Meiji years made it clear that he was not alone in that thinking.

Then there were the unpredictable whims of nature, which sent tens of thousands over the financial cliff in these years. Seldom were they more devastating than the 1889 flood that wiped out much of Totsukawa village in Nara Prefecture, killing 255 people, destroying or damaging a third of the area's homes, and forcing nearly 2,500 people to migrate en masse to Hokkaido, where for several years they nearly starved.[160] Or the Tōhoku famine of 1905–1906, which left 280,000 in Miyagi Prefecture destitute and prompted 1,512 Fukushima farmers to emigrate to Hawai'i.[161] Or an 1898 famine in Iwate in which insects devoured 80 percent of two villages' rice fields, compelling people "to hunt for plants, shrubs, and any sort of herb they can render available for food."[162] But it was not just the dramatic disasters—Nature Writ Large—that threatened farmers. As Nagatsuka's *Soil* showed, Nature Writ Small poured out its own troubles nearly every year: a fire whipped by wind into a raging inferno, a minor drought that prevented crops from maturing, a murderous late-spring frost, an attack of aphids or cutworms that killed "one plant after another." "Poor farmers were caught up in a vicious circle," he wrote. Lacking money for fertilizer or for disease-resistant seeds, they produced inferior crops. The poor crops brought low prices, and the low prices left them too little money to pay for rent and food, or for fertilizer. And that meant, of course, that "they had to find other work in order to obtain the food they needed," and thus lacked the time needed for regular weeding, which propelled the cycle. Thus, "at the end of the harvest season poor farmers withered up like the vegetation around them." Invariably, Nagatsuka said, "a time would come when they had nothing left to eat."[163] He may have exaggerated, but only slightly. Folklorist Miyamoto said that on his walks across rural Japan, he "often heard stories of people who, having run out of food, had left their homes to wander here and there."[164] Both nature's whims and the vagaries of the economic system left all but the affluent few aware in their bones of what social activists a century later would call "precarity": an existence without security or predictability.

HARDSHIP AND CHARACTER

Scarcity intensified some people's personal weaknesses. Attacking them where they were most vulnerable, it drove them to antisocial behaviors that they normally would have found unthinkable. In Saitama, the parents of Seizō, the teacher, moved from their home under cover of darkness and absconded on their bills, not, in Katai's construction, because they were immoral but because they were too desperate to be able to pay what they owed. Similarly, when villagers outside Komoro used baited fishhooks to steal their neighbors' chickens, they did it not because of an evil inner nature but because they had nothing to eat. When farm wives in Hiroshima Prefecture had too many children (as many as thirteen in a single household) and then neglected them, it was "a question of economics" and "exhausted bodies," not of moral callousness: mortality rates were high, hands were needed in the fields, and the mothers had to spend every waking hour peddling goods or digging in the paddies. As in the city slums, the pressures of living with what Tōson called "the almost unbearable misery of . . . poverty"[165] pushed a certain number of rural families into destructive behaviors that reinforced the journalists' stereotypes of "those unlettered peasants."

For most rural folks, however, the hardship nurtured something more impressive: an ability to endure, with little complaint, in the worst of circumstances. The journalist Yano Sōrō, visiting half a dozen villages near the Besshi copper mines in Shikoku in 1904, found deplorable conditions: mine refuse "piled up like a mountain, then dumped into the sea," where it killed fish and seaweed; shrubs and conifers "withering . . . half yellow, half green"; houses red from mine pollution "as if painted with lipstick"; harvests "declining every year," with people gargling constantly and breathing with difficulty, their "bowels and stomachs going bad." And yet they persisted, he reported, going to the fields and mines each day, complaining to each other and fighting with their employers, yet working with steely stoicism. When someone suggested that life might be better elsewhere, they objected, insisting that "nothing was so clean or beautiful as the mountains." Here, they told the visiting reporter, they would "bury their ashes."[166] This combination of stoicism and practicality marked the response to scarcity everywhere. In Tanima Kazo's Yamaguchi village, when money was in short supply, fishermen simply turned to barter, "asking to trade fish for potatoes" or offering neighbors trinkets in exchange for rice.[167] It was the same mix that Katai was trying to portray when he described the aftermath of Seizō's death of tuberculosis. Having no money, his family held the simple funeral procession at night as "insects sang noisily in the hedgerows" and deposited the body in an open grave filled with "muddy red water at the bottom." His old mother grieved bitterly for a while, then went back to sewing because they "had to work to feed themselves." There was no money for a marker, but she faithfully kept flowers on the grave.[168] Stoicism and practicality: her firewall against despair.

VILLAGE AND NATION

Hardship also affected the way villagers thought about their nation. One of the significant features of the Meiji era was the regime's systematic effort to bring every neighborhood and *mura* into the national project. The tax system was rooted in rural land ownership, schools celebrated national holidays and taught about the emperor, patriotic hamlet organizations were created to assure loyalty.[169] The impact of these nation-creating policies was particularly apparent in wartime, when townsmen were expected to celebrate and assist the local men and boys who were off fighting, then hold parades when they came home. It was no surprise that Okano Kame recalled, probably with more nostalgia than accuracy, that "everyone" in her Yamaguchi village "was happy to be a soldier" during the Meiji years, in contrast to later times when "you can say, 'If I go into the army I shall die, so I won't volunteer.'"[170] Waswo notes that "rural residents almost certainly participated more consistently than did their urban counterparts in the observances of Emperor Jimmu's accession, Army Day, Navy Day, and Japan's victories over China in 1895 and Russia in 1905."[171]

Village patriotism nonetheless was complicated by the close relationship between war and hardship. War entailed higher taxes and rents, along with inflated food prices that hurt farmers as consumers more than they helped them as producers. It also meant the loss of labor in the fields when fathers and sons were drafted. Many observers have pointed out that young farmers—called "one and a half sen soldiers" because that was the cost of the call-up postcard[172]—were less likely to get exemptions and more likely to serve at the front than their city counterparts. As an old Chichibu villager put it in Kinoshita Naoe's *Pillar of Fire,* "It's always the poor they take for soldiers. You can see why: they're working so hard always, they're bound to be the strongest."[173] The result was that village responses to war were often negative, particularly after the number of draftees began to soar and casualties multiplied in the Russo-Japanese War of 1904–1905. Aizawa's diary had described scores of enthusiastic villagers sending young men off to the front in the 1894–1895 war with China, shouting banzais "so loudly that they whipped up a wind on the platform," but he mentioned send-offs in the war with Russia matter-of-factly, with little comment.[174] Reading local newspapers, military historian Stewart Lone concluded that during the latter war villagers in Gifu Prefecture had "a healthy cynicism . . . towards elites or propaganda, as well as a readiness to express discontent rather than suffer in silence." One reader complained in a letter that the elites in mountainous Takayama would "attend funerals of those from wealthy families but rarely made an appearance at those of the poor."[175] Sometimes, resentments were expressed in tragic ways. *Heimin Shinbun* reported on a Kumamoto woman who collapsed and died when her husband received a draft notice. The husband asked the village office for aid for the two children he would have to leave behind. When he was "brusquely" turned down, he "killed his two children with his own hands and then went to report for military service."[176] Villagers may have borne their situation "patiently and stoically," as the historian Irokawa Daikichi has suggested,[177] but there is scant evidence, except in formulaic official documents, that they participated in national causes out of patriotic conviction. They sent their men to war because they had to; they participated in patriotic events as required. But for most poor farmers, the bottom line was that war (and national projects generally) brought more obvious hardship than benefits, hardly a cause for joy.

REDUCING FAMILY SIZE

One of the most difficult responses to poverty—the decision to improve the budget by getting rid of family members—linked urban and rural hardship together directly, since the majority of those who left did so as part of the great urban migration chronicled in this work. It was hardly surprising that when government surveyors collected sketches of Kobe and Osaka factory workers in 1903, they reported where each laborer had come from, assuming the worker had grown up elsewhere, likely in a village.[178] The first thing to be noted about the decision to have children leave is that it almost always was rooted in economics. Despite the "heir and a spare" culture noted in the introduction, farm families averaged between five and six members, and 40 percent of households included three generations,[179] meaning that when the economy turned downward, it became a challenge to feed everyone. Although a few left home to avoid the military draft, most were like Ōtani Matsujirō, the son of a fisherman on Ōshima Island in the Inland Sea, who decided to depart when he "heard how many people, seeing no future in this solitary island, left."[180] Desperate conditions at home made distant places appealing.

A second feature of the decision was that it often was made not by the emigrants themselves but by the desperate family. As Bill Mihapoulos writes in a discussion of farm daughters sent off to Southeast Asia for sex work, the ultimate moral failing for any rural family was to disgrace ancestors by "the failure to secure the prosperity and longevity of the household." That meant that no matter how much one cherished children, they must be "shed when the consumption of the household had to be reduced during times of scarcity,"[181] as fifteen-year-old Muraoka Koremitsu found out when his Kumamoto family decided he should go to Hawai'i to make money for his impoverished family. He did not want to go and was overjoyed when he failed the required eye test. But his father insisted that he get his eyes treated and try again. The next time, Koremitsu passed and left, never to return. Emigration "wasn't something which I had hoped for," he recalled years later. "It was forced on me."[182] Studying the urban *hinmin*, Nakagawa found that second sons "often were, quite literally, pushed out of their villages by their families and or the whole village, because they were a drain on village finances."[183] A third feature of the family reduction decision lay in the influence gender and poverty levels had on who left and where they went. Nearly all emigrants' families were, of course, poor. But even destitution has degrees, and those degrees influenced choices. Single-daughter emigrees, who tended to come from the very poorest families, almost always went to factories or to brothels. Young men had more options, but money influenced their choices too. If the family was poor but not destitute, if it had enough to pay for transportation and entry fees, there was a chance that the sons would go abroad, since work on foreign coffee or sugar plantations usually offered more money and more opportunity to return home if things did not work out. If, on the other hand, the family truly was destitute, the chances were strong that the young man would head for a city in Japan or for one of the country's thriving mines, where the cost of getting there was low and settling in seemed a little less daunting.

DECLINING VILLAGES

The numbers who left the villages in the late Meiji years were staggering: 160,000 Japanese in North America or Hawai'i by 1910, 90,000 in Taiwan, 146,000 or more in Korea, and several million in Japan's own cities. Even sparsely populated Okinawa had sent nearly 9,000 to Hawai'i by the end of the Meiji era.[184] The impact of that kind of outflow on the village psyche could be sobering. In 1910, a lad named Yamasaki Toyosada in Western Honshu's Nakatsubo village began crying as he read an article about how the people of Tasmania were vanishing, because he saw the same kind of thing happening all around him, in rural Japan. All but one of the thirty houses of the village where he had spent his first years had disappeared, lost, "one by one," to the depredations of poverty; "no one remained to look after the graves." His fears were not unfounded. From the beginning of the Meiji period in 1868 until the onset of World War II, Japan's farm population remained stagnant, while the country's overall population more than doubled, from thirty-five to seventy-two million.[185] By the Taishō years, the diminishing of the village population had become a concern to opinion leaders. The *Kahoku Shinpō* in northeastern Sendai ran a series in the autumn of 1918, demanding, "Stop the concentration of young men in the cities; it is creating a shortage of farm labor!" And *Tokyo Asahi Shinbun* ran a ten-day series in 1922 titled "Villages on the verge of destruction," arguing that the young men and women moving to the cities were robbing the rural communities of leadership. The writers generally ignored the economic reasons for emigration and blamed youthful hedonism, partly because Taishō writers were preoccupied with decadence and moral decline and partly because modernity had begun stimulating cosmopolitan dreams among rural youths by the late 1910s. The *Kahoku Shinpō* writer said the emigrating youth suffered from three illnesses: "the lazy disease (*honeoshimibyō*), the get-rich-quick disease (*narikinbyō*), and the faddishness disease (*haikarabyō*)."[186]

Even if the writers missed key reasons for leaving, they spoke to a serious reality: villages had been losing their human reservoirs since the 1880s. "This generation was different from earlier farm village generations," says urban historian Ōkado Masakatsu: "It was a generation quite free from the old village order."[187] That was not all bad. It meant poor villagers had options not available to their ancestors: they could move to the city or even take work abroad. But the exodus brought a sense of loss to almost every late Meiji village. To the problems that for centuries had been accepted as a normal part of the farmer's and fisherman's life—inadequate food and health care, vulnerability in the face of nature, the necessity of working the human body harder than it was designed to be worked—was now added something new: *human* scarcity. Not only did the nation demand new taxes, it took children out of the fields for schooling and sent men off to war, even as the forces of economic modernity conspired to pull people away to the factories, the slums, and the foreign coffee fields. When Tōson sat around the hibachi with fellow teachers in Komoro at the beginning of the 1900s, smoking and talking about how traditional life in the mountains was, he saw continuity. He was right: traditions persisted across generations. But even as the teachers talked, the Komoro region was changing more than they realized. Young people were leaving, depleting the hamlets' human pool and undermining old norms as they went. By the 1910s, the problem would be seen as a crisis.

Was Village Poverty Different?

Inoue's young village protagonist Kosaku was overwhelmed when he first visited a city in the 1910s. Children all wore shoes and "much nicer clothes." Bustling streets stretched on forever. There was a cinema. His inn served "fried eggs, dried fish and dried seaweed . . . all at once," along with "miso soup in beautiful lacquer bowls." And he was given a "yellow gelatin dessert" that "looked so beautiful he hesitated to insert his spoon." This was "totally foreign territory"; it left him "feeling utterly outclassed." When he visited again, a playmate called him a "country bumpkin" and warned him not to show his ignorance because "they'll laugh at you."[188] All this echoed the standard late Meiji motif about what Katai called "irredeemable oblivion in the countryside,"[189] a motif repeated by villagers as well as city dwellers. Urbanites and villagers were wholly different types: the former modern and open to change but aloof and unfriendly, the latter warm and friendly but backward and hidebound. Such stereotypes were simplistic and unfair, but they were important because they framed the images that most Japanese had of themselves and their compatriot Others. Although it is beyond the reach of this study even to try to understand the complex realities behind these images, the book's central question—what urban poverty was like in the late Meiji years—demands reflection on one central point of comparison: how the experiences of being poor in hamlet and city compared with each other. Did villagers and urbanites experience deprivation the same way, and if not, why not?

As the beginning of this chapter made clear, economic data about the income levels of farmers are subject to various interpretations. Some scholars emphasize the general improvement made by rural Japanese across the Meiji years; others argue that rural economic conditions were grim, with tenant farmers representing "the lowest type of Japanese life."[190] Both arguments can be supported by statistics. What most studies fail to address is the way village impoverishment *felt* in comparison to impoverishment in the city. Many of the themes of this chapter—the natural setting, the isolation of villages, the character of village culture—make it clear that scarcity had a distinctive coloration in the countryside. They suggest that the environment, both natural and human, made poverty a different phenomenon in the *hinminkutsu* than it had been in the mountainside hamlet.

The natural setting was the first reason for the difference. The immediacy of forests, mountains, or seas sometimes made things worse. Typhoons wiped out entire fishing villages; volcanic eruptions did the same to mountain hamlets; drought brought famine and caused starvation among rural families on a scale not seen in the city. Late winter months regularly depleted rural pantries and rendered stomachs hungrier than they ever were in even the poorest urban neighborhoods. Moreover, the isolation of mountain villages meant separation from modern assistance and knowledge, which was particularly problematic in crisis times: no trains to bring help, limited communication channels, few modern medicines, no licensed physicians, only poorly educated doctors who diagnosed tuberculosis as "debility" to be cured by "drinking wine" or treated fevers with wolf droppings filled with hair and bone "because wolves eat rabbits and birds."[191] It was little wonder that in 1911 the visiting British sociologist Beatrice Webb found "neglect of infantile health and child development in rural Japan" to be "the most serious defect that we have noted so far."[192] According to one 1899 study, rural areas had only one modern doctor for every ten thousand people, one-tenth as many per capita as the cities had.[193] The natural setting gave rural hardships the potential for being even worse than those in the city when sickness, famine, or disaster occurred.

Day-in and day-out, however, nature was more often a source of succor. Even when the money pouch was empty, poor villagers usually could find something to eat. Trout swam in the rivers; greens, mushrooms, and wild grapes grew on the mountainside; rabbits scampered across the fields. There were frightful exceptions, during catastrophic droughts or in those late-winter months when the land was frozen and the pantry bare, but in most times and most places, nature's bounty meant that the lack of money alone would not cause serious hunger. The natural setting also offered spiritual respite: bamboos and spruces swaying in the breezes along the side of a ravine, gurgling streams with gentle rapids, a white crane sitting atop a cedar, splashes of pink azaleas, white sakura and yellow daffodils, an occasional roadside tombstone or a statue of a Buddhist deity, fireflies and cicadas competing for attention.[194] Seizō, Katai's country teacher, was deathly ill in the spring and summer of 1904, yet his journal identified more than thirty flowers on the Tone River bank and another twenty flowers in the nearby fields. There also were "ants and bees and beetles, and at night unknown insects would sing their noisy songs, as the frogs also did."[195] Off in Komoro, Tōson wrote in his sketch book:

> The sound of the stream keeps me awake and I get up to enjoy more of the special quality of the moonlight here. As I lean against the high railing, the voices of all kinds of insects blend in with the sound of flowing water to fill the entire valley. There are other sounds down in the bottom of the dark swamp: people locking up their doors, others talking on into the night, dogs barking, and a happy-sounding farmer's song.[196]

Nature did not prevent Tōson from moving to the city, but the mountains and fields nourished his spirit in ways that were unavailable in the treeless slum alleys.

The human environment also affected the rural experience with hardship. A negative impact was the insularity that left hamlets behind in incorporating knowledge about the broader world and made life difficult for anyone not well integrated into the local systems. A key feature of village culture was a strong insider/outsider (*uchi/soto*) mentality that lubricated interactions among insiders but held others at arm's length. If this was comforting to old-timers, it could be excruciating for newcomers and for anyone with an independent streak, as the charcoal maker's daughter Takai Toshio found when she went to school in rural Gifu. She ranked first in her class academically but because her family had no roots in the village, classmates continued to taunt her as "the little monkey girl from the mountains."[197] Just as farmer Kanji demonstrated earlier in this chapter when he refused to bow to village norms in Ibaraki, poverty's pain became more bitter still when one was branded a misfit—an outsider—by a community where everyone else embraced each other.

On the other side of the ledger, the insiders—the vast majority—found great comfort in the village's close human relationships and time-honored behavior structures, which made life's rules easy to understand and thus less stressful, even when poverty stalked. A village, says Thomas Smith, was above all a "repository of tradition,"[198] a place where common practices and beliefs had held sway for so long that everyone regarded them as natural, as determined by fate rather than by conscious design. That meant that people knew the nuances of behavior without being told: how marriage partners were to be found, which *kami* spirits merited honor at the local shrine, how to speak to and treat each other. They knew that one should not dress too brightly, that women should not wear makeup lest they be "pointed at and reprimanded as prostitutes,"[199] that one should not argue with one's parents even if the parents were wrong. And they knew that if authorities behaved arrogantly, villagers should act like the Tōhoku villagers who, when ordered to host peacetime soldiers on maneuvers, gave "excessively generous welcomes" with "smiles on their faces," even while "in their hearts they wept."[200] The traditions might feel constraining, but their clarity and pervasiveness gave even the poorest villagers a sense of security. One knew one's place; one knew one's neighbor's place; one even knew that people with greater means were required to help out in time of need. In contrast to the urban *hinminkutsu,* where everything was in flux, the village traditions insulated farmers and fishermen from many of the external pressures and changes that made poverty so intense in the city.

Most significant of all, the rural setting enabled poor villagers to experience hardship as part of an embracing community. Being part of a group of insiders provided people with a sense of both obligation and belonging. And it meant that when troubles arose, others would be there to help. As the emigrant Morihara Usaku recalled of his own Yamaguchi village, "Your neighbor is more helpful than the cousin in Kyoto. . . . When you got sick they wouldn't worry about you, but your neighbor would. . . . We took care of each other."[201] Even iconoclastic Kanji found neighbors giving him mats and household essentials when he had a fire, and when his father-in-law Uhei was needy, the friends in Uhei's "prayer group took turns supplying him with decent food." When Kanji and Uhei quarreled violently, a neighbor tried to mediate, commenting, "Like I said before you're family."[202] What was more, the neighbors most often were poor too. One's hardship was shared with almost everyone in one's world, to a degree that could not be replicated in the city where rich and poor commingled. Nakagawa goes so far as to argue that "there was no sense of poverty (*hinkon*) in the village. Of course, you could be cold or hungry, but it was not conceptualized as poverty, only as a lack."[203] A very few villagers had sufficient means even in hard times. The rest did not, and in that fact there was mutual comfort and shared dignity.

There was nothing noble about economic hardship; hunger still hurt. But the *uchi* womb of village life gave poor farmers and fishermen a network of support in dealing with their hardships. In the trenchant words of Sally Hastings, "In the countryside, one could starve, but family were nearby and one's housing was on a long-term basis. Moreover, if one is reduced to eating leaves and tree bark, it is better to live near trees."[204] As time passed, the *hinminkutsu* residents too began to develop communal networks, eventually turning the slum into "its own world within the broader city."[205] But those human networks grew gradually; they had yet to form during the 1890s and much of the early 1900s, and that added a starkness to urban poverty that villagers did not have to worry about. When the Meiji-Taishō farmer Tanaka Umeji from Shimane Prefecture lauded farming as the peak of professions, he was thinking partly that the work was "interesting and enjoyable," partly that farms were important because they produced the food people needed, and partly that nature's rhythms allowed time for relaxation by the indoor fire in winter after the intense seasons in the fields. But he also had in mind the village's communal interactions and the "intimacy with nature's beauty" that surrounded people tilling the fields. "Our first sons, the ones who carry on the family, must by all means continue farming," he insisted. "We have to make them remember that the farmer's tireless toil (*ryūryū shinku*) is sacred work (*tenshoku*)."[206] In his sentimentality, he captured an essential difference between rural and urban poverty: no resident of an Osaka slum, no lodger in a Fukagawa flophouse, ever was heard to speak of hardship in lyrical terms.

CHAPTER 8

Poverty Abroad
Hawai'i's Sugar Fields

It was pretty hard work for us. We'd get up at about 4:30. Only time to rest

or have friendship: in *ofuro* or on long route to fields.

—Yano Toraji, 1906 immigrant to Hawai'i[1]

S itting on the patio of their Waialua home, an hour's drive from Honolulu, George and Willa Tanabe look across their neighbors' heliconia-
and hibiscus-filled gardens to lush fields of taro, corn, and bananas. And
beyond those, to Mount Ka'ala. As the sun sets and chickens roost in the
surrounding trees, the Tanabes sip drinks. The scene exudes gentle prosperity,
spiritual as much as material, the kind of life to which eminent University of
Hawai'i scholars like the Tanabes *ought* to be entitled. It has not always been
that way, however. When George's grandfather came to the archipelago from
Yamaguchi Prefecture in 1898, he joined a rough cohort of Japanese who had
left farm work back home to toil in Hawai'i's sugar plantations. These were ad-
venturous people, courageous people, poor people—more than 200,000 of
them eventually—who wanted to make money for a few years in the middle of
the Pacific before resuming life in Japan. Their courage surpassed their prog-
nostication skills. Few would have predicted that only a third of their fellow
emigrants ever would return home, and fewer still would have foreseen the
prominent roles that so many of their grandchildren and great grandchildren
would, like the Tanabes, come to play in Hawaiian society.

That these emigrants belonged on the lists of the Meiji downtrodden is without dispute; nearly all of them were very poor, some near destitution, when they
sailed from home, and significant portions remained poor for a generation and
more. Beyond that they were poor, however, what did their experience have to
do with urban poverty in late Meiji Japan? The differences between *hinminkutsu* dwellers and sugar workers certainly were numerous: leaving Japan required a different kind of courage than moving to Osaka; once on the job, the
emigrants inhabited a wholly foreign, rural setting; they worked mostly for big
companies that provided housing and determined the parameters of their lives;
the very foreignness of their new setting made most of them feel more Japanese

than their *hinminkutsu* counterparts did. The list of differences is long. But the similarities are striking too. Scarcity and survival framed the lives of plantation workers as much as they did those of the urban *hinmin;* both groups felt keenly the way their bosses and poverty restricted personal freedoms; they fought equally against the temptation toward despair by working hard and looking to a better day. The important thing for this study is that the differences and similarities alike shed a great deal of light on both the unique aspects and the universal qualities of the urban *hinmin* experience.[2]

Emigration: A New Phenomenon

Emigration was not in the Japanese blood. Although officials began directing foreign policy outward immediately after the Meiji Restoration in 1868, setting up a "colonization office" for Hokkaido and engaging in diplomatic and military efforts in Korea and Taiwan, almost no one thought in terms of individuals leaving the archipelago. Foreign travel of any kind had been forbidden during the 250 years of Tokugawa control, and after two ill-conceived 1868 efforts to export Japanese farmworkers to Guam and Hawai'i, the Meiji government forbade such forays. Nor were people inclined to venture abroad on their own. Even within Japan, citizens resisted limited government attempts to get them to relocate. When the Meiji officials offered a variety of inducements in the 1870s to encourage farmers and former samurai to settle the sparsely populated island of Hokkaido, the results were disappointing, prompting one observer to comment, "Only the poorest and least motivated seemed to want to migrate to Hokkaido." Echoed the Hawaiian official W. N. Armstrong in 1881, "The Japanese are not an emigrating people."[3]

Attitudes began to change in the 1880s, however, as the movement toward modernity, reinforced by the decade's dire economic conditions, caused people to begin thinking in new ways about the rest of the world. One reason for the change lay in the nation's expanding view of its place in the world. By the second Meiji decade, Japan was pushing commercial ties with Korea, claiming territory in the Ryūkyū Islands to the south, and making acquisitions in the Kuril Islands of the north. Commentators began talking about potential growth farther away and the resettlement of fellow countrymen in those distant regions. European nations had developed colonies by resettling their own people; perhaps Japan should do the same. At the same time, a labor shortage nearly four thousand miles away, in Hawai'i's sugar industry, caused plantation owners to turn their eyes toward poor Japanese farmers. When the forty-five-year-old King David Kalākaua visited Japan on a world tour in 1881, he lobbied for a pro-emigration policy, suggesting as an inducement that his five-year-old niece Ka'iulani be given in marriage to the imperial prince Yamashina Kikumaro. Japanese officials declined the marriage proposal but took the ideas about sending Japanese to Hawai'i seriously. The most important impetus for the change in attitudes was the same as that for the great domestic migration of the 1880s: the economy. The financial downturn that caused farm families to begin sending their sons to Osaka and Tokyo and their daughters to the factories left bureaucrats frightened, worried not only about the widespread suffering but about the potential for peasant unrest. As a result, they began contemplating the idea of exporting poverty right along with silk and coal. Could the emigration of farmers strengthen the country's broader modernization program? Might it provide additional capital (in the remittances emigrants would send back home), even as it lessened the numbers of mouths to feed? Answering in the affirmative, the government began, for the first time in Japanese history, to encourage people to seek fortunes across the oceans.

The emigration program began in February 1885, with 944 contract laborers, most of them farmers, heading for Honolulu on the ship *City of Tokio*. An even larger group went in June, and the following January the Tokyo government signed a convention with the Kingdom of Hawai'i, establishing a "system of free and voluntary emigration" under the supervision of the governor of Kanagawa. The convention provided that immigrant workers would be given three-year contracts, with transportation costs borne by the government of Hawai'i (which in turn would charge the plantations), and government-paid inspectors and physicians charged with ensuring that the immigrating farmers were treated well.[4] With the spigot opened, Japanese farmers began to go abroad in great numbers, so great, in fact, that in 1892 the American minister in Tokyo declared it a Japanese "national characteristic to wander about in search of new scenes to gratify their love of sightseeing."[5] By 1900, more than twenty thousand Japanese were toiling in the archipelago's sugar fields. They constituted a larger group than the immigrants from all other countries combined.[6]

The emigration rules changed repeatedly across the next quarter century. For the first nine years—the "government contract period" (*kan'yaku jidai*)—workers were contracted directly by the government of Hawai'i, which assigned them to specific plantations on arrival. During these years, Japanese officials attempted to control the process and to assure as good a deal as possible for the émigrés. The struggle for fairness was a difficult one, however, since Hawaiian planters and officials were concerned primarily with their own financial ledgers. In 1887, for example, after the arrival of the first four shiploads of workers, the kingdom began charging each emigrant a transportation fee of $65, to be subtracted in installments from wages. The planters' expenses for a typical worker's shippage dropped from $52.11 to $1.77, but for the workers the change was disastrous: shipping charges now ate up as much as a quarter of their monthly wages across the entire three-year contract period, an abuse to which the Japanese government vigorously objected.[7] A second era, the "private contract period" (*shiyaku jidai*), began in April 1894, when Japan started licensing private companies to handle immigration, with workers typically required to sign three-year contracts as a condition of emigration.[8] This was a particularly difficult period for the migrants, because most companies charged exorbitant fees for the contracts, which workers had no choice but to pay since the Hawaiian government turned away anyone without either a signed contract or a $50 deposit as insurance against becoming a burden on the state. In 1897, island officials denied entry to more than a thousand arrivals, nearly all of whom had come in good faith.[9]

Congress' decision in 1898 to annex Hawai'i brought immigration policy directly under the U.S. government and initiated the "free immigration period" (*jiyū imin jidai*), when contract labor was outlawed and workers were allowed to come to the islands on their own. Freed legally to move between plantations and occupations, some laborers gravitated to new jobs such as strawberry picking, shopkeeping, and fishing; a few even bought their own coffee or taro farms. And they used the greater freedom as a lever to agitate for better wages and working conditions. Freedom was not the new norm, however, because plantation owners worked assiduously to limit worker initiatives and keep the cost of growing sugar low. An example of the system's inequity came in 1908 when President Theodore Roosevelt negotiated the Gentlemen's Agreement in response to racism in California. From that year on, the only workers allowed into the United States—including Hawai'i—were previous emigrants and family members of workers already here. The resultant "picture bride" phenomenon, which brought to Hawai'i thousands of women who married men without ever meeting them, made the 1910s colorful but created excruciating difficulties for thousands of mismatched couples. Immigration of all kinds ended in 1924, when the Johnson-Reed Act barred East Asians from entry.

The Japanese came to Hawai'i in impressive numbers during the late Meiji years. Government agents hoped for several hundred volunteers when they first solicited applications in 1884, but more than 25,000 sent in their names. Across the next decade, twenty-six shiploads brought an average of more than 1,100 wealth seekers each.[10] By 1890, five years after the arrival of the first group, some 12,000 Japanese made up 14 percent of Hawai'i's total population. Two decades later, nearly 80,000 made up more than 40 percent of the total, in contrast to the native Hawaiians, who had decreased in the same period from 35,000 to 26,000.[11] And in 1908, before the Gentlemen's Agreement, seven of every ten people producing Hawai'i's half-million tons of sugar were Japanese.[12] This was not merely a *Japanese* migration, however; it was a western Honshu/Kyushu phenomenon. Across the first decade, the great majority of plantation workers came from just four poverty-ravaged prefectures targeted by the powerful Meiji official Inoue Kaoru: Hiroshima and Yamaguchi in Honshu, and Kumamoto and Fukuoka in Kyushu. By 1894, indeed, nearly 95 percent of all the arrivals had come from there.[13] The late Meiji years also would see significant numbers from Okinawa, but to the end, Hawai'i's sugar fields were worked primarily by people from a relatively small swath of Japanese soil.[14]

The reasons for this concentration illuminate the way local conditions and national policies worked together to shape emigration. After deciding early on that farmers would adapt better to plantation work than other Japanese would, officials declared that "under no circumstances" should people be recruited from urban areas or "from among persons engaged or trained in pursuits other than agriculture."[15] The mountainous lands of western Honshu and northern Kyushu—poor regions where residents already were known as sea rovers—

provided an abundance of people needy enough and sufficiently skilled in field-work to be open to recruiters' offers. What was more, those regions largely had been overlooked in earlier campaigns to recruit factory workers. Once the emigration process got under way, momentum took over as people began talking to each other about the opportunities overseas. Alan Takeo Moriyama, a historian of immigration companies, found that once a few early emigrants sent money back to their relatives on the sweet-potato-raising island of Ōshima, for example, "rumors quickly spread throughout the island; everyone's imagination was seized with the idea of emigrating to Hawaiʻi to make money."[16] One young man from Ōshima, Ōtani Matsujiro, said that when he heard reports in 1907 of the money a fellow villager was making on Hawaiʻi's Big Island, "my heart was moved. I decided to go to Hawaiʻi."[17]

With the free immigration period well under way by then, Ōtani gravitated toward fish selling, but the vast majority settled on sugar plantations, often near others who had migrated from their own regions. Sugar, after all, was the core of the islands' economy and it was where the recruiters put their energy. The cane had been grown on the islands for centuries, typically on communally owned lands. But after a series of midcentury acts known as the Great Mahele (land division) legalized private ownership, a relatively small group of Caucasian entrepreneurs, most of them from missionary families, began acquiring great swaths of land, the first step toward owning three-fourths of Hawaiʻi's land and eventually stealing its independence. A combination of abundant water and warm temperatures made those lands ideal for growing sugar. As a result, after midcentury some eighty thousand acres were turned into more than sixty plantations, spread across all the islands. To work such vast fields, these foreign owners needed more human power than was available locally, so they turned to immigration, and by the mid-1880s as many as fifty thousand Chinese had come. When those numbers were still inadequate, the plantation owners began thinking about Japan.

The reason so many workers were needed was that sugar farming was labor-intensive, as a look at the huge plantation ledger books makes clear. Across the top of a page of a typical ledger—for Kauaʻi's Lihue Plantation, March 1904—one finds the categories by which plantation managers classified their workers: Officers, Chinese, White *lunas* (supervisors), Colored *lunas*, Portuguese, Natives, Italians, Chinese, Japanese, Women, Boys, Mules, and others. Down the side are listed thirty-five broad categories of jobs.[18] There were workers who maintained water channels (called flumes), men who maintained wharfs, some who cleared fields, women who hoed cane rows, others who planted or re-planted the sugar, and still more who plowed, cut cane, stripped the leaves from cane, loaded it onto carts, or hauled the carts to the mill. Beyond the fields, some maintained roads and bridges, others gathered firewood for furnaces, and some cared for cattle and sheep. And that was just a sampling of the outdoor jobs. There also were myriad indoor positions: blacksmiths, harness makers, millworkers, bakers, and office clerks, as well as *lunas* who worked both indoors and outdoors. And after that there were variations within each category. The "roads and bridges" column, for example, included builders and repairmen along with those who kept the dirt roads passable, and still others who carried heavy ties to build railroads. The miscellaneous category included people who rang bells and people who stood watch. "If any place get fire," recalled Mitsugi Muraoka in the rough English of an immigrant, "well, he goes down and then ring the bell"; he also rang a wake up bell at 4:00 each morning and a depart-for-the-fields bell at 5:30.[19] And the flume category encompassed everything from the men who dug water tunnels to Lloyd Sugimoto's mother, who did "*hanawai*—irrigation work" before taking over a supervisor's laundry.[20] Most of the Japanese did mill work, hoeing, or cane cutting, but significant numbers also toiled in the stables, stripped cane, or hauled cane. A few even worked in management.[21]

The sugar workers' experiences dramatized the influence a setting can have on a person's failures and successes, shedding nearly as much light on the lives of slum dwellers in Japan as on the plantation experience. During the early Hawai'i years, the sugar workers lived in slave-like conditions, with daily life marked by instability, despair, and high crime rates. By the 1890s, however, the Japanese community was growing more stable and the immigrants were being singled out by the plantation owners as hard workers with high skill levels and common sense (though some of them were feared as troublemakers). And by era's end, the Japanese had forged a success story as the archipelago's largest, most dynamic worker community. While the speed of the plantation workers' advances appears to set them apart from their fellow *hinmin* in Osaka and To-kyo, it is clear that the differences had more to do with context than with qual-ities inherent in the immigrants and *hinmin* themselves. It is clear too that the plantation immigrants simply created a more rapid version of what was hap-pening more slowly in the urban slums. How then did they get to Hawai'i and what happened once they arrived?

Getting to the Plantations

The villagers of southwestern Japan may have had a reputation as "sea rovers," but that term was relative. In truth, they had been home-bound for centuries, living along the same dirt paths for generations, never roving beyond their own fishing waters. Sociologists working in the southwestern prefecture of Okayama in the 1950s found that a family whose ancestors had lived for three centuries in the village of Niiike was still considered "a relative newcomer to the region"; many villages in the region were populated by people whose forebears had set-tled more than a thousand years earlier.[22] While stereotypes of farmers as hide-bound and simple-minded were inaccurate, images of villagers as people who stayed put were not. A farm family might have sent second sons to the city when faced by starvation. It might not have been surprising for a few adventur-ous types to strike out on their own. But for great numbers of eldest sons and household heads to set sail for unknown places thousands of miles across the Pacific would have been unimaginable.

The fundamental cause of their migration, as should be clear by now, was economic. The national recession of the 1880s did not spark the protests and uprisings that it did north and west of Tokyo, but the southwestern areas were hit just as hard. Faced with hunger, many on the Inland Sea islands or in northern Kyushu simply decided that they had had enough: enough of eating out of the same pickled *daikon* barrel for a year, enough of facing miso and rice gruel three times a day, 365 days a year.[23] Often, a family crisis or an unforeseen personal circumstance (always related somehow to economics) forced people to make unthinkable decisions. For Torahichi Tsukahara of Kumamoto, the precipitating event was the financial hardship that followed his father's death. When his elder brother, the heir, began spending wildly on alcohol and luxuries, he and his mother had to sell property to pay off the rising debts, and before long he found the humiliation too much to bear. "I had to listen to what all the kids would say to me, like this land used to belong to your family. . . . I was ashamed," Tsukahara said. So "I asked my mother to send me to a foreign land, to Hawai'i, . . . And she gave me permission without hesitation, saying, 'Go, if you want to go.'"[24] He planned to stay for three years, but he never went back. For Kazo Tanima from Yamaguchi, the prompt was inadequate finances at home to support his ambitions. When both his school principal and his town mayor urged him to go to middle school, his mother said no, the family had no money for that. So he decided that the only chance for a better life was in Hawai'i, where his father already had gone. "I was disappointed," he said, "but I had been born poor, and there was nothing I could do about that. I thought it was probably god's discipline."[25]

As these cases suggest, financial difficulty was rarely the only reason for the move. In contrast to the urban migrants for whom survival was the whole story, most of the emigrants to Hawai'i had more than one motive. They were not, for one thing, the poorest of the poor, since they had to have enough funds, particularly after the late 1880s, to pay passage costs and the arrival fees in Hawai'i. One inducement was aggressive recruitment by immigration agents. From the earliest days, a host of people, from plantation owners and Hawaiian officials to ship owners and commercial agents, worked assiduously to persuade the farmers of the southwest to emigrate. At the top of the recruitment system in the early years was Robert Walker Irwin, a great-great-grandson of Benjamin Franklin, who represented Hawai'i's government in Japan as a recruiter for the plantations. During the 1885–1894 government contract period, he was promised a five-dollar commission, plus even larger broker's fees, for each adult male émigré, a deal that made him more than $3,000 on the initial shipload alone.[26] (When the British sociologist Beatrice Webb visited his "charming" mountain home outside Tokyo in 1911, she found him a "garrulous bore" who "professes to be very pro-Japanese."[27])

Observing his success, a plethora of agents turned recruitment into an industry in the late 1880s and 1890s. Both companies and individuals published guidebooks, some of them serious about helping émigrés, some of them designed merely for profit. They included practical details about the English language, advice on how to obtain travel permits and negotiate bureaucratic mazes, information on what to take on the journey, and descriptions of life in Hawai'i. One of the earliest recommended that workers take "three sets each of ordinary wearing apparel, a short-sleeved kimono, a pair of tight fitting trousers, a set of summer nightwear, summer bedding and mosquito netting."[28] Others described Hawai'i as a paradise. The more effective ran into many editions. The recruiters themselves came in two guises: itinerants who traveled from village to village, and locals—usually a headman or a landowner—paid by emigration companies to recruit fellow villagers. Like the notorious agents who scoured the countryside elsewhere for factory and brothel workers, many emigration recruiters concocted fantastical tales. Lloyd Sugimoto described those who came to his Hiroshima village early in the 1900s: They "talk as though you just go to Hawai'i and the money will just rake it in. See? Everyone." His parents listened to the recruiters with a healthy dose of skepticism but were persuaded anyway.[29] Recruitment efforts intensified after 1894 when the government contract period ended and the plantation owners began paying the emigration companies a direct fee for each employee they secured. A Japanese law to protect workers from unfair exploitation by these companies took effect in mid-1896, but enforcement was lax.

Other factors that prompted emigration were discussed less but were hardly less important. As the years went along, for example, personal connections played an increasing role. A group of fishermen from the Niojima region near Hiroshima City was typical. After settling in 1888 at Paauhau Plantation some fifty miles from Hilo, they sent continual letters and gifts back home, along with invitations to join them, and within two decades one of every seven Niojima residents had done just that. Some localities sent off as many as a third of their inhabitants, a few up to half.[30] One of the more remarkable examples of friend-influenced emigration came in Okinawa, where the educator Tōyama Kyūzō personally persuaded more than forty fellow villagers to go with him to Honoka'a Plantation on the Big Island, where he gave pep talks each Saturday aimed at creating a stable community.[31] After the 1890s, the most important social inducement probably was marriage, as single émigrés began seeking young women to help them establish families. A certain number also headed to Hawai'i for individual and idiosyncratic reasons. Some talked about the allure of adventure. Some wanted to get away from rigid social structures. One woman, Saka Chika, hoped a new setting would cure her husband of his drinking habit.[32] And after the mid-1890s, quite a few admitted to taking advantage of the draft law's exemption for émigrés. Said the Okinawan emigrant Higa Toden, "I was still in Okinawa when the Russo-Japanese War began. My parents were afraid that I would be drafted if I stayed in Okinawa. So that is why my parents asked me to go to Hawai'i."[33] In contrast to those who went to Japan's cities, few emigrated for a single reason. Empty cupboards were important inducements, but the recruiters' portraits of beauty and riches lured many, while others emigrated as wives, or village comrades, or draft evaders.

Once the decision to emigrate was made, the path to the plantation was daunting enough to hold back anyone without courage and a bit of luck. It began with making arrangements to leave, a process that had grown complicated and expensive by the mid-1890s, when twenty-three-year-old Mizunaka Rinzuchi from Yamaguchi Prefecture secured travel document No. 100424, allowing him to "pass freely without hindrance" and assuring him "such protection and assistance as he may be in need of."[34] First, one needed to get an agent to sponsor the travel, which could be expensive, as Ōtani found when he went to the local office of the Bōchō Emigration Company in 1907. The attendant "nodded politely and asked if I had a wife. I said no. He cut me off sharply, saying that was bad; this company didn't handle single people." Asking around and finding that the company's real reason was pecuniary (couples paid twice the application fee), he offered a bribe and got his papers.[35] Next came the trip to the departure port. For Kumamoto native Kuwahara Shigeru, the journey took two weeks: a train ride to Nagasaki, ten costly days at a local hotel because the boat to Yokohama "was overcrowded," and another four days of waiting in Yokohama before the ship left for Honolulu.[36] Ōtani said that he found himself "choked up" on the train ride to Kobe as he mulled over his father's teary farewell: "In Hawai'i, you don't have a single relative; you don't have a single friend. How lonely! But you must persevere." His "tough" mother simply told him to "give it your all and take whatever comes your way."[37] Worst, for many, were the barriers when they reached the port of disembarkation. Hotels overcharged for crowded and dirty rooms. Agents delayed permits in order to squeeze out more money. And officials terrorized emigrants with a battery of physical tests. First, recollected one, they studied the eyes, then they examined the throat, then they tested for broken legs by having men jump over a box. "Then, of course, they will examine your bowel movement." If worms were found, "No pass." One young woman reported regular trips to a doctor for several months to have medicine applied to her eyes so that she would pass the test.[38]

The voyage to Honolulu provided a two-week respite, if not always a tranquil one. A typical ship carried a thousand passengers, with men and women sleeping separately, on individual cots "in rows like silkworm racks. . . . one place for each person."[39] Many found ship life convivial. Ōtani said he felt "sort of sad" as he lost sight of "sacred Mt. Fuji" but even when the ocean was stormy he was "too excited to be sick."[40] Some worked for food; many socialized with émigrés from their own regions; small klatches sang songs such as Azembō's "Rappa bushi" (The bugle song), which was popular at the time of the Russo-Japanese War; many smoked and played games. And almost everyone but Ōtani got seasick. The singing ended when the seas got rough, said Tsukahara, "since everybody was vomiting."[41] One passenger noted that many sufferers "barely made it to the toilet."[42] And Kame, who was pregnant, said she became so nauseated that "for eleven days I didn't eat anything, I just drank water."[43]

In Honolulu, the process was straightforward for some and tortuous for others, particularly after the government contract period ended. First, officials checked their papers, making sure they had the required work contract or fifty dollars. Next, inspectors carried out a medical check. Then, if they passed that, they were ready to be taken to their plantation or to begin the search for work. Customs agents were notorious for their rudeness, like the "nasty-looking" interpreter who threw Sōga Yasutarō's money back at him in 1896, shouting that he was too busy to count bills.[44] For some, rudeness was the least of the problems. Most years, several hundred were sent directly back to Japan because they lacked sufficient money or had a serious infectious disease such as syphilis or trachoma; on one March 1897 shipload alone, 183 were returned.[45] If the inspectors discovered a less serious disease, the new arrivals and those around them were quarantined in a nondescript hall on Sand Island, usually for two weeks or more. When Ōtani arrived, he breathed a sigh of relief when the inspector waved him through, only to be told that someone else on the ship had smallpox. He and 150 fellow passengers "had to put our heavy wicker trunks on our backs and walk the long wooden bridge and road to the crude lodging called the *sennin goya* (thousand-person barracks), where we would stay." He spent his quarantine "watching automobiles going over the bridge."[46] Once ashore, in an unfamiliar city with tangled streets and strange names, newcomers had to scrounge money for as much as two weeks' board and room while they waited

After arriving in Honolulu, probably in 1899, the Japanese on the dock here await a ship to take them to a new sugar plantation on the Big Island of Hawai'i, where they have contracts to work for at least three years. Courtesy of Bishop Museum.

for a boat to come from the island on which they had contracted to work. After the contract system ended in the early 1900s, things got much more complicated for many people, as they were forced to find jobs on their own. The greater freedom increased individual opportunities but for many it also increased the bewilderment of those early weeks.

Working the Fields

Any visions of an idyllic life that had not been disgorged with the seasickness were shattered when Japan's emigrant farmers reached the plantations. The vistas and nearby beaches may have been lovely, but living conditions usually were wretched and the work left little time for savoring natural beauty. Even at era's end, recalled Yosoto Egami, whose parents arrived in Kona in about 1905, "it was sort of rough." Coming ashore, his family's landing apparatus was engulfed by a large wave, leaving everyone "soaked." The first night the newcomers began itching and the next morning they awakened with swollen faces, arms, knees, and necks, the result of bedbugs. And that was only the beginning. Refused any time for settling in, they were sent to the fields immediately for days of "at least ten hours" under the supervision of *luna,* who treated them "just like dogs," shouting "the mules are more valuable than you guys" and pulling out whips if they moved slowly.[47] And their experience was typical. With chilling consistency, newcomers reported that the initial years on the plantation came closer to hell than to paradise.

The framework of plantation life was set by the Hawaiian Sugar Planters' Association (HSPA), a cooperative of the sixty-plus sugar estates, created in 1885 to "apply scientific methods to solving problems, develop new varieties of cane, and make improvements in sugar farming."[48] Working through a subsidiary on each island, the association managed every aspect of the industry, allocating immigrants to the plantations, lobbying for tax breaks and proplantation policies, keeping the records of the individual plantations, and making recommendations about everything from "proper" charitable contributions to what kinds of housing should be built. The association even handled workers' savings deposits. Nothing affected the Japanese workers' lives more than the HSPA's single-minded focus on efficiency and profit. Sanford Dole, the first governor of the Territory of Hawai'i, told a group of owners in the 1880s that the chief aim must be "plantation profits," adding that "the prosperity of the country, the demands of society, the future of the Hawaiian race only come secondarily if at all."[49] He and his compatriots were gilded-age capitalists who worked with the titans of public life to secure dominance and riches. Soil depletion, water diversion, low wages, cramped housing, even the annexation of Hawai'i to the United States over the opposition of the majority of Hawaiians: all were part of the pursuit of profit. When challenged, owners sometimes would argue that workers got better wages than they might have received back home, but they did not waste much time defending themselves.

This approach had profound implications for the immigrants' everyday experiences in the fields. Before receiving compensation, a worker injured on the job was required to sign a bond, promising to make no further claims. If a local manager suggested giving bonuses to more productive workers, HSPA officers invariably urged caution, to avoid "destroying the incentive to hustle"; minimum wage proposals evoked the retort, "there will be no incentive to work a full month."[50] The association refused to allow the hiring of assistants to carry workers' meals to the fields "unless such lunch men are paid by the men themselves."[51] Two 1909 cases illustrated the singularity of the profit fixation. In the first, when the Chinese consul in Honolulu asked support for the widow of a Chinese employee who had been "found burnt to death while working in the sugar cane field at Waipahu," the HSPA responded simply that such requests must be directed to the Oahu Sugar Company (OSC) and it would not recommend assistance.[52] In the second, when the local Salvation Army chapter asked for a $10 monthly contribution at Christmas time, Oahu Sugar replied that the Salvation Army's work was "of little value"; since the firm already had "refused to assist the Native and Methodist Korean Churches," it would refuse this request too.[53]

This profit fixation also justified the owners' practice of playing national and ethnic groups off against each other in pay scales, housing arrangements, and even punishments. Internal plantation correspondence and reports were filled with racial and ethnic generalizations about workers from different nations and the importance of keeping them separate, in part to prevent groups from colluding with each other and in part to balance the alleged strengths and weaknesses of different nationalities. A 1909 OSC report to the U.S. Immigration Commission listed national characteristics as if they were simply indisputable fact. Chinese were "the most desirable labor"; Japanese were "probably the most progressive"; Portuguese and Spanish were unable to work together "amicably" and were "either unable or unwilling to do some classes of hard work"; Koreans were "mostly addicted to excessive use of intoxicants, and . . . do not work over 50 percent of their time"; and it was "practically impossible to harvest the cane without the Asiatic labor, as other races show a distinct aversion to loading as well as stripping cane."[54] A student of the Kipu-Huleia plantation on Kaua'i concluded that national origins played "the dominant role in a person's place in the plantation hierarchy": *haoles* (Caucasians of British or American background) came first, followed by Germans, Portuguese, Hawaiians, East Asians, and "Filipino bachelors."[55] Wages followed the same pattern. In 1902, "skilled" workers from America and northern Europe were paid a daily average of $4.22, compared to $1.69 for Portuguese and $1.06 for Japanese.[56]

Contracts with the companies set the basic features of daily work for the Japanese immigrants. A typical contract on January 26, 1885, the first year of emigration, provided that thirty-three-year-old Saka Shoshichi of Kanagawa Prefecture would be paid $9 a month plus lodging, medical care, "cleaned rice" for a maximum of five cents a pound, and free cooking fuel. In return, he would work three years, for ten hours a day (twelve if his work was in the "sugar house"), twenty-six days a month. A quarter of his salary ($2.25) would be deposited automatically in a savings account from which he could not make withdrawals unless the Japanese consul in Hawai'i approved; he would be exempt from taxes for three years.[57] Unlike the majority of the early immigrants, Shoshichi brought his wife and two sons along, and the contract provided that if his wife decided to work, she would be paid $6 a month for the same work. They were required to provide their own bedding. Wages gradually improved across the years, with a promise of a minimum amount of living space (typically 900 cubic feet for a family of four) and time off on legal holidays.[58] By 1899, Miyashita Haruemon from Niigata Prefecture was promised $15 a month ($10 for his wife Soyo "if she works"), with $2.50 placed automatically into savings. His work hours remained the same, however, and he had to promise to "work at night and rest during the day" if management demanded it and to work overtime at ten cents an hour (seven cents for Soyo). The holidays were stipulated: New Year, Christmas, November 3, Sundays, and American national holidays.[59] Conditions improved after the end of contract labor in 1900, when workers had greater freedom to shift jobs, but hours remained long and pay low,[60] a fact that even the HSPA officials occasionally admitted privately. As one HSPA officer wrote to a plantation owner in 1906, "In times past we got too much in the habit of treating the Japanese and Chinese as if they were more animals than men."[61]

In the fields, the work broke backs and depleted souls. Hours followed hours, sometimes far into the night. Days of blazing sun were followed by days of bone-chilling rain. A report by a writer sympathetic to the plantation owners described the work before the Japanese arrived as "severely taxing the energies and strength of man and beast," commenting that each man "toiled at the risk of his life." Once the Japanese had arrived, this same writer said, they were particularly good in the heavy work because Japanese "are indifferent to weather conditions, rain and exposure seeming to keep them in a healthy condition, while white men, similarly exposed, would be disabled by rheumatism and other ailments."[62] The workers themselves usually remembered not resilience but the difficulty of the work. Their recollections repeatedly begin with the six-day-a-week schedule: women up at 4:30 (or 4:00) to make breakfast and prepare lunches; the waking up whistle; a 5:45 gathering for the trek to the field in groups of twenty or thirty, carrying their lunches and heavy work tools; a 6:00 starting time followed by ten and a half hours in the field, with a ten-minute mid-morning break and a thirty-minute lunch. Lights went out at eight. On the week's other day, Sunday, "they had to work on the firewood," recalled Mitsugi Nishihara of his late Meiji childhood: "Our fathers really worked hard. Yeah, just imagine, boy. Six days a week, ten hours a day."[63] It was not unusual in busy seasons to work four straight weeks without a single day off. And the work was hot, partly because of the sun and partly because even on the most blistering days they had to wear multiple layers of shirts and pants, plus long stockings and *teoi* (elbow-to-knuckles mittens) if they were women, all as protection against the sharp, rough cane leaves. "If you were working on the plain," recalled one worker, "it was so hot you would drink water and the sweat would just come pouring out of you."[64] Even lunch had its pitfalls. It was not unusual, according to Koga Noriyu, to "open the lunch so eagerly" and find it covered with red ants. "You no can eat, eh. Hoo, boy, goddam, no can do nothing."[65]

Women who worked in the fields, most often in hoeing, faced even stiffer challenges. Like their counterparts back in Japan, they were the ones responsible for preparing the family's meals before and after work, they did most of the laundry and housework, they cared for the baths and sewed, and they bore the burden of child care. Most young mothers had no choice but to take their small children along to the fields, sometimes strapping them on their backs, more often placing them in boxes or on mats beside the cane rows. One plantation worker recalled the day when his infant brother wandered off into the dense, tall cane rows, sending his mother into a panic because of the open reservoir nearby. When another worker found the baby safe, "she . . . run up to him, oh she was so happy to see that."[66] Breastfeeding mothers sometimes had to fight the dreaded ants; one recalled taking her three- or four-month-old to a tent for nursing and finding "so many red ants swarming there, biting the baby."[67] And always the work was back-breaking. William Yamanaka, who studied sugar plantation work in Huleia on the island of Kaua'i, concluded that "the women folks were even busier than the men. It was endless toil every day, seven days per week. . . . Only later, when the children were grown up, would the ladies relax and enjoy some leisure."[68] One reason the Japanese were aggressive in opening schools during the last Meiji decade was that someone was needed to look after children while they were in the fields.[69]

People who did the supportive jobs—the barbers, cooks, deliverymen, and construction workers—were sometimes envied for having easier work. But their work was demanding and enervating too, as the seventeen-year-old Ōtani from Ōshima found when he took a job on Maui as a horse rider. His assignment was to ride from plantation to plantation delivering goods. The work was heavy, he said. Lunch often consisted of a single hard biscuit, the horse could be stubborn, daylight hours most often bled into the blackness of night. One night, the horse suddenly balked as he was galloping along on a hillside. He whipped it, he dug his feet into its belly, he recited Buddhist chants, he tried gimmicks that he had used on the farm in Japan, all to no avail. When the horse finally relented, it threw him off. By the time he got home and to bed, it was 2:00 a.m. And at 4:30, the morning bell rang, rousing him to get up and start the process all over again. "I kept quiet about my unhappiness though," he said. "I just stuck with it."[70] In that, he emulated most of his compatriots.

Workers lessened the drudgery by singing together *hole hole bushi*, or "melodies of the cane leaves" that gave words to the facts and the soul of immigrant life. Some described how hard the work was:

My husband cuts the cane stalks / And I trim the leaves,
With sweat and tears we both work / For our means.

Others bemoaned the futility of the immigrant life:

Those who came on First and Second Ships / And still don't go back to Japan
Will become fertilizer at the end / For the poi plants.

Still others spoke of the secret sides of life away from home:

Though I checked what's written / On my passport,
It doesn't say a word that I can't have / A secret lover.[71]

And the greatest number talked about struggle, including the sharpest irritant of all: the *lunas,* who so often were "brutes" or "watchdogs of hell":

Neither earthquake nor thunderstorm do I dread
But just to hear the *luna's* voice makes me shudder.[72]

Like the girls in the factories back home, the sugar workers found solidarity in singing and a way to articulate what they were afraid to put into writing.

The most consistent complaint about *lunas* was their harshness and cruelty. There is no disputing that many supervisors were fair-minded, but the ones who drew the workers' comments yelled at those who rested for a moment or beat those who were too slow. Some sent workers home without any pay for the day if they found them slacking a few minutes before quitting time, and many mocked those who complained of illness. The callousness of which overseers were capable was encapsulated in an 1885 case in which several workers at Pā'ia plantation in Maui died after the *lunas* ignored their illnesses. Fellow Pā'ia workers blamed the deaths on "a combination of sickness and cruel treatment,"

Tropical heat notwithstanding, Japanese women had to wear heavy protective clothing in the fields when this unnamed irrigator's photo was taken in Maui in 1912. Hoes were used both to dig out weeds and to remove debris and keep water running freely in the ditches. Photograph by R. J. Baker. Courtesy of Bishop Museum.

and after investigations, the Board of Immigration backed them up.[73] Nor was this was an isolated incident. When Sōga Yasutarō went into the fields as an interpreter a decade later, he saw numerous such cases, including a worker from Yamaguchi Prefecture who died after being forced to work with a high fever.[74] The abusive treatment sometimes crossed the boundary into criminality. In the fall of 1889, for example, an immigrant Japanese shopkeeper named Goto in Honokaa on the Big Island, a man known for assisting plantation workers with their problems, was found hanging from a telephone pole, prompting an outcry among the Japanese community that led to an investigation and manslaughter convictions for three plantation supervisors. In 1891, a *luna* on Maui killed a worker by pushing him into a bonfire. And in 1892, a *luna* who shot a Japanese worker in the leg "for no cause at all" was sentenced to six months in jail, then released after he bribed the judge.[75]

It would be easy, reading the accounts of cruel treatment and worker perseverance, to conclude that the Meiji immigrant was a docile sort, the kind of person described by chief recruiter Irwin in 1888 as always "satisfied with his employer," someone whose "health was generally good," someone gifted by "universal prosperity."[76] Certainly that was the image Japan's own officials worked to preserve, in the spirit of the country's Immigrant Bureau Director in Honolulu, who advised mistreated workers at He'eia plantation on O'ahu that they "should realize that they were nothing but mere contract laborers" and keep their mouths shut.[77] Such a conclusion would be wrong, however. While the Japanese were hard-working, most of them showed the same toughness and feisty resolve that their cousins in the *hinminkutsu* did. They fought back, sometimes with careful forethought and sometimes impulsively. It was not unheard of for a man to drink soy sauce in the morning to speed up his heartbeat in the hope that the plantation physician would excuse him from work. Exasperated cane strippers sometimes "paced" their work to slow things down. Pushed, laborers occasionally struck back verbally at their abusers or clogged the gears of field machinery. Then there was the case of the 220-pound Kashiwabara Kihachi, whose *luna* ("a brute of a man of German ancestry, armed with a sidearm [pistol] and a whip") ordered him out of a sickbed and kicked him. The proud Kihachi, in the telling of his grandson, "turned around, grabbed the startled overseer, lifted him, and threw him to the ground," yelling, "Now, you can kill me if you want to!" The overseer treated him with respect after that.[78]

One of the more common forms of resistance was desertion, as evidenced by both official data and a sampling of plantation reports, which were filled with items such as a request for money to cover the expense of capturing "the Japanese deserter Tarakichi" (April 29, 1890)[79] or a clarification about "Japanese laborer #6375 Suzuki Yahachi," who had been reported as a deserter the previous November but still was on the books as receiving a salary (April 13, 1900).[80] It was not unusual for as many as a thousand workers to run away a year. In 1898, for example, 140 had left the single plantation of Paauhau already by summertime.[81] Of the 450 people who deserted in 1895, a full 90 percent were Japanese.[82] While the plantation owners cursed the absconders as irresponsible deviants,[83] the workers themselves saw desertion as pure practicality. Some-times, they ran away to evade gambling debts or to escape a punishment for misbehavior; more often they were getting away from a *luna*'s cruelty, fleeing unfair contracts, or seeking more livable wages at a distant plantation. They were, in other words, asserting the right to live decently. The early journalist Sōga told the story of the amateur wrestler Watanabe Masaji at Wai'anae plan-tation on O'ahu, who "despised being driven like a cow or a horse" and ran away repeatedly, only to be recaptured each time. Finally, after his corpulent supervi-sor had locked him in a room and whipped him bloody with a leather strap, he sneaked away a final time, on his hands and knees, and disappeared forever. Rumors had it that he had found a place on the Big Island.[84] When University of Hawai'i ethnographers interviewed former plantation workers in the 1970s and 1980s, a surprising number invoked the desertion refrain: "He ran away." "He traveled at night. He was afraid of being caught during the day." "They must have thought of the workers like cats or dogs . . . so he ran away."[85]

Organized resistance also occurred among those who stayed on the planta-tion, more often in per capita terms, it would appear, than among the urban *hinmin* back in Japan. In the first year of immigration, for example, 156 Japa-nese struck Papaikou plantation on the island of Hawai'i, refusing to work over-time without compensation. And when a *luna* at Pā'ia plantation on Maui beat a worker for not knowing how to yoke two oxen, his fellow laborers refused to work until ordered to do so by a sheriff. When *luna* abuses continued at Pā'ia, resistance continued too, and several workers were sent to a jail thirteen miles away, where they were "whipped and kicked" by guards, resulting in several hospitalizations and one death. The resistance was so strong that the Japanese government sent Inoue Katsunosuke, the son of the oligarch Inoue Kaoru, to investigate, and when he found that "unwarrantable and frequent acts of vio-lence . . . have been perpetrated upon the Japanese by overseers on many of the plantations," all the workers were removed from Pā'ia. Negotiations following the episode resulted in a new agreement with the Hawaiian government, pro-viding for regular inspections of plantations by officials.[86]

Planters worried about the potential for wider resistance when it became clear that the contract system would end in June 1900. The Japanese "are per-haps more skillful in getting up labor combines than any other nationality," an officer at the plantation agent Hackfeld & Company wrote to the OSC manager a month before the new system came into effect. Warning that they were "very likely to take every advantage of their present position by demand-ing higher wages or other concessions and getting up strikes on a large scale," he recommended firm resistance lest higher wages "take away a considerable portion, if not all the profits now made by the plantations."[87] And he was right to worry, because during the first six months after the contract system ended, workers carried out what a proplanter historian called an "epidemic of strikes." Hawai'i's labor commissioner recorded twenty-two labor disputes in that period, focusing on issues as varied as wages, *luna* behavior, forced holi-day work, and the care of injured workers. All but two were led by Japanese.[88]

In early May 1904, some three hundred went on a three-day strike at Waipahu in O'ahu after a *luna* named Patterson whipped a worker, prompting the *Hawaiian Gazette* to write:

> The Japanese are getting more self-confidence; they are losing their superstitions about white men; they are beginning to realize that even in the Hawaiian canefields they have rights. If treated well, they will stay here because they are poor and need work. But it will be hard to keep them if badly governed, and they will not be tractable in the meantime.[89]

The *luna* was dismissed, as were several lesser supervisors. A year later, in May 1905, fourteen hundred Japanese workers staged a "near-riot" at Lahaina plantation in Maui after a Polish *luna* mistaken for a Russian beat a Japanese worker named Iwamoto. Security guards attacked a gathering of several hundred strikers, killing one and injuring three, and before the strike was settled several days later, the government had sent in more than a hundred troops. The years 1904 and 1905 produced a total of ten strikes, all of them local and short-lived.[90] Then, in 1909, an archipelago-wide campaign saw seven thousand Japanese workers on O'ahu go on strike while laborers on the other islands assisted the strikers financially. That strike will be discussed in some detail later; for now it serves as evidence of both the harsh conditions the Japanese immigrants faced in the sugar fields and the workers' increasing willingness to fight for better conditions.

Life in the Camps

If the fields devoured the workers' days, camp life framed their sense of self. On arrival, they were assigned by employers to either a shack or a space in a longhouse, almost always constructed as cheaply and efficiently as island regulations would allow. Here, they slept, ate, bathed, washed their clothes, and formed whatever sense of community was possible. Some, like Alice Yoshiko Ohashi, looked back on camp life in the latter Meiji years with nostalgia, remembering a "peaceful and quiet" place "where the mules cry, mynah birds chatted, the doves cooed, and crickets chirped at night and frogs croaked at night and during the day."[91] More of them—indeed most all of them in the early years of immigration—found the spartan living conditions difficult on the best days, hellish and life-threatening on the worst. The plantation owners lived in mansions graced by grand pianos in the parlor, art from Tokyo and Berlin on the walls, bookcases filled with French philosophers and New York humorists, and exquisite gardens beyond the picture windows. Not so the workers.

The quality of the "free" housing required by the official agreements differed from plantation to plantation, with some of the better owners providing materials for immigrants to build their own thatched roof homes, and with nearly all housing improving over time. Most of the owners provided clusters of cheaply built homes and barracks in which the workers lived communally, at poverty levels. In the early years, when a preponderance of males came without wives or families, barracks-like longhouses dominated; as the years passed, the numbers of small single- and multiple-family dwellings increased, often with a cloth or a "thin wall between families" in the latter, allowing everyone to hear what everyone else said.[92] The Puna Sugar Company, founded in 1900 on the Big Island, provides an example of the way housing evolved. At the beginning, Puna had two camps, one with a single long barracks, the other with "four tenement buildings" occupied mostly by Filipinos. In 1907, a third camp was built with ten single-family homes, mostly for Japanese families, and three longhouses for single Filipino men. By the mid-1910s, three more camps had been constructed with a combination of cottages and longhouses.[93] To era's end, workers said their lodgings "gave us the illusion of being in a prison cell." They were nondescript places where "at night mosquitos kept us awake and other poisonous insects such as scorpions and centipedes came into our room and stung us. . . . Miserable."[94]

Camps generally were divided by ethnic groups, in keeping with the owners' divide-and-conquer approach. If the plantation was large enough, the Chinese had their own camp, the Filipinos theirs, and the Japanese theirs. In smaller plantations, each nationality group was assigned its own section of a camp. People of all ethnicities shared a few things: the bell that woke them up and summoned them to the fields; a plantation store, which might be supplemented by immigrant-owned shops as the community grew; a huge rubbish or trash dump for throwing away refuse; and in some camps large water-storage tanks and a communal outhouse. But the separation of living quarters was pervasive, with Europeans ("non-Asiatics" in the planters' lexicon) assured better housing than their peers. Even at era's end, the Oahu Sugar Company managers reported to the government that they provided bunks for Chinese, a room for each group of two to four Japanese men, and a single room for each Portuguese man. The company also gave "non-Asiatics" plots for gardening.[95] The system discouraged immigrants from different countries from forming united fronts against the owners, but it also created resentments for which the owners eventually would pay a price in labor unrest.

Barracks-style living was particularly bad, offering neither space nor privacy. According to an 1899 inspector's report, one plantation required six families each to live jointly in 360-square-foot houses without partitions or a kitchen, while "at other plantations several hundred persons of both sexes are also mixed up and kept in one large square house without any partition in it." He concluded that housing overall was "very unsatisfactory."[96] At one plantation, workers slept on thirty-five- or forty-foot-long "shelves of rough wooden boards" stacked six or eight rows high "like silkworm cocoons,"[97] with couples assigned to the bottom shelves and single men to the upper ones. When babies cried at night, the inspector said, mothers took them to the cane field so as not to awaken other residents.[98] One observer described the barracks as "pig stys"[99]; another said the quarters he shared with fifty others in 1903 were so small that when he was washing "the wives of others stepped over me matter-of-factly as if I were a dog or cat in their path. I remember cold drops from the ends of their hair falling on my back."[100] It was no surprise that one late Meiji visitor looked at the houses and exclaimed, "I never dreamed that Japanese could come to this!"[101] Even individual family homes, which varied more, were spare and cramped. Typically, they were built of boards twelve inches broad and one inch thick, painted a nondescript cream or brown and topped by a corrugated galvanized roof. Most houses were not much more than the legal minimum of 300 cubic feet of "air space" per adult.[102] Floors were covered with straw mats, and newspapers often served as wallpaper. Since there was no electricity until the 1930s, most families cooked and heated water with wood and used kerosene lamps for light. The ceiling, if there was one, was a canvas or cloth sheet stretched beneath the rafters.

Water was a special concern for a people who had come from a land of baths and water-based Shintō worship. In the more advanced plantations and in places where rainfall was abundant, such as Puna on Hawai'i, individual homes had their own wooden water tanks for drinking, cooking, and bathing, although filtering the tadpoles and red silt out for drinking could be a problem. In other camps, such as Kōloa in Kaua'i, people had to carry water in buckets from a tank shared by the entire camp.[103] The bath situation varied by camp and by period. In the early days, many camps had no baths. As the years passed, however, most plantations gave in to the incessant demands of the workers and the communal bath, or *ofuro*, became a fixture in Japanese camps. Then there were the toilets. A few families had their own outhouse; more often, the camp shared an outhouse, about fifty feet away "and partially secluded by some kind of plant." Newspapers and magazines served for wiping, and lime was used as a disinfectant. On occasion, someone "fell through the rotten floor . . . and had to be fished out . . . quite a mess." Many a child shuddered years later at the memory of having to use an outhouse at night: "located far in the corner of the yard, among the banana trees, in pitch dark, in a thundering winter storm."[104]

When families complained about their housing, the plantation owners' typical response was that housing was as good as what the workers had had back home. It was an ignorant or disingenuous response, because most of the farm houses in Hiroshima or Kumamoto had been quite large and fairly comfortable, even if they were old and decaying. In 1906, near the era's end, the HSPA trustees finally recommended "that the accommodations for Asiatic laborers in camps be improved, especially . . . in view of what is being offered to Portuguese immigrants." They called for "more spacious" quarters, better facilities, greater privacy for individual families, and space for raising "vegetables and garden truck."[105] The HSPA motives had less to do with the journalist Karl K. Kawakami's observation that bad housing leads to "a certain sense of disappointment which easily develops into depression and indifference"[106] than with growing worker activism. But the recommendation provided another piece of evidence about how bad housing conditions indeed had been.

From the first, gender-related issues had a great effect in the camps. When the sugar growers began to recruit Japanese farmers, they discouraged women from coming, worried that wives would be less productive in the fields and that families might distract men. To make it hard for families to come, they levied a $40 surcharge on any man accompanied by a woman.[107] As a result, nearly 84 percent of the 1,931 arrivals that first year were adult men, and seven years later, 88 percent of the 3,125 immigrants were male. Across the entire first decade fewer than one-fifth of those who came were female.[108] The impact of that imbalance on the sugar camps was profound. Without the balancing influence of women or families, camps became centers of decadence. Andō Tarō, the Japanese consul general in Hawai'i between 1886 and 1888, informed Tokyo that "the reputation of the Japanese is not too good." Although the majority of men were hard-working and law-abiding, he reported, the accounts of "immoral" behavior were widespread. "Out of sheer loneliness," he said, many men sought "solace in gambling, drinking and the companionship of women with questionable morals." Night-long gambling sessions were "common" and men shirked their work.[109] By 1895, several hundred Japanese men also were participating in gangs, and "racketeering, intimidation, extortion, and fraud were common practices."[110] A Buddhist priest who came to the islands in 1900 was appalled. He said that "plantation laborers were extremely wild. Since there were no recreational facilities, the only outlet after returning from long hours of hard field labor was drinking and gambling." Camp life felt like a "cave of

The Wainaku plantation camp on the island of Hawai'i in the 1890s received water through a wooden flume (right side) from the mountain; the center building with banners probably was the camp bath. Photograph by J. A. Gonsalves. Courtesy of Bishop Museum.

tigers and wolves or . . . water full of sharks and crocodiles." His analysis of the cause: "Lack of women."[111]

Prostitution was a particular issue.[112] The 1886 convention said that "Japanese subjects in Hawaii, who may . . . encourage dissipation of any kind among the emigrants" would be returned to Japan, and Inoue Kaoru had written that year to the emigration agent Irwin that Japan would not countenance "immorality, drunkenness and gambling" among the sugar workers. But little effort was made by the authorities to enforce the prohibition, and a combination of economics and the male composition of the camps led to a quick rise in the sex trade. Some of those few women who came on the early ships were attracted by sex-worker pay, which was higher than field-work salaries, and some men sold their own wives to pimps or gangs. As a "cane leaf song" had it, "If I work at stripping *hole hole*, all I'll earn is 35¢. If I sleep with a Chinaman, I'll make $1.00!" One sex worker told the Christian minister Okumura Takie: "Doesn't a big, healthy man on the sugar plantation get only $14 a month? I'm far better off, for in this work I can save up and send back $200 a month to my home in Japan. Am I not a real patriot who enriches our country?"[113] Much of the prostitution occurred in Honolulu's brightly lighted Chinatown, where hundreds of women, many them Japanese, worked in "shed-like buildings" with glass windows facing onto the streets.[114] But a great deal of it occurred in the camps themselves, where each payday saw the arrival of "cart-loads" of gamblers and women. "New hay and blankets would be spread on the stable floors," says the University of Hawai'i historian Joan Hori, "and blankets would be hung in front of the stalls for the women to conduct their business."[115] Statistically, Japanese crime rates in the camps were not particularly high—less than half that of the Chinese community and lower than that of other immigrant groups, except the Portuguese[116]—but the womanizing and the gambling gave the camps a sordid reputation and worried Japanese officials and plantation owners.

By the late 1890s, however, camp life was changing, as was the gender balance. When the missionary educator Sidney Gulick surveyed fifteen plantations at the end of the Meiji era, he was surprised by the stability of the Japanese communities, as well as by the improvements in housing. A major reason for this, he concluded, lay in the development of families. In contrast to the early years, plantations owners now were opting for couples over singles, because men with spouses were "more contented, more steady, more diligent, and more free from venereal diseases."[117] The data bore him out. According to census figures, the number of Japanese women in Hawai'i doubled between 1896 and 1900, from 5,079 to 10,684, while the numbers of children increased more than 800 percent, from 1.2 percent of the islands' Japanese population to nearly 10 percent. As the early 1900s unfolded, that trend accelerated.[118] Tadao Kawamoto, who had four brothers and lived on the McBryde sugar fields in Kōloa, explained his understanding of the owners' motivations:

> They found that the Japanese workers are very conscientious and honest workers. And in order to keep them they had to figure out some way so that

they can keep them longer instead of only for three years contract. . . . So what they did was ask each worker there, if they are married, "Do you want your wife to come over here to work?"

Say, "Oh yeah, sure." . . .

They knew that when they start having kids they are going to be stuck here, anyway.

There was no more such thing as birth control. Every two years you get one child. They all had big families, see.[119]

Signs soon were everywhere of the new tone the wives brought to the camps. They cooked, sewed, did laundry, and created households. They also improved most men's financial situations, not only by reducing profligate behavior but by handling budgets (as they had done in Japan) and by making money on their own. Yamauchi Tsuru recalled earning extra cash by getting up at 3:30 every morning to wash and iron the clothes of several workers. "I did the laundry by hand," she said; to heat the water, she used a fireplace made of steel train rails. Another immigrant, Hanako Ishiyama Gushiken, said her mother and step-mother sewed clothes to bring in money.[120] And a third recalled that his mother cooked for single men in the camp. "You know, in those days," said Mitsugi Muraoka, "they get lot of single people, eh? And then, some people, you cook, and then they come and eat at your place. . . . I think, lot of guys, they never even pay."[121] Most important, the wives turned the camps into family-centered communities in which couples produced children (often prolifically), who in turn inspired adults to prefer stability and discipline over mere pleasure. One grandmother in a Kona region that had no midwives recalled delivering "117 babies."[122] Gushiken, speaking in her distinctive English/Japanese mix, said her mother gave birth *"nani toshi-go toshi-go"* (year after year).

> I used to stay home from school for weeks to help her. And then the following year, she had again. Fourth one, third one *ga shinda no* (died). Second is a girl. Third *ga* boy. And then, that [third] one *shinde* (died). . . . *Daibun atta, kodomo ga, no?* (There were quite a few children, weren't there).[123]

Nothing illustrated the changed attitude toward women more clearly than the picture bride (*yobiyose*) phenomenon that followed the 1908 U.S.-Japanese Gentlemen's Agreement. Since it precluded almost everyone but family members from coming to the United States, the young men on the sugar plantations began asking close relatives in Japan to help them exchange photos with potential wives. Once a couple (or family) had reached an agreement by mail, a ceremony would be held in Japan without the presence of the new husband, and, in accordance with Japanese law, the bride would live with the groom's family for at least six months prior to sailing. When she arrived in Honolulu, there would typically be a harried time as the unacquainted man and woman tried to find each other by looking at the photos. Then, in keeping with American requirements, there would be another wedding ceremony, conducted by a Christian minister for as many as a hundred couples at a time. If things went well, that might be followed by a day or two in a Honolulu hotel, and the couple would head for the plantation. The fact that four thousand picture brides had come by the end of the Meiji era (more than fourteen thousand by the mid-1920s) dramatized how much plantation norms had changed since the early days.[124]

The abnormality of this process made for endless difficult experiences. Sometimes photos bore little resemblance to the new husband or wife; sometimes personalities were incompatible; some brides took the next ship back to Japan or ran away, convinced they had been misled; frequently new brides "cried as they worked in the tall sugarcane fields."[125] Most of the time, however, women plunged into their new lives stoically, committed to creating a stable family whether they found their spouse satisfactory or not. The experience of Bun Kobayashi Yoshimori at Kōloa Plantation was typical in its complexity and its outcome. Many of her companions on the ship felt trapped, she recalled, when introduced to men far older than their photos had suggested. They "would cry and cry that it was the wrong person," and often they would separate. Fortunately, her own husband turned out to be near her in age, "well-built and at the peak of his health, . . . an earnest and faithful person." But that did not make the adjustment painless. During the early months, she often felt despair over the life she had chosen. She did not know how to sew the kinds of pants and shirts required in the sugar fields and spent a great deal of time at the sewing machine learning. "I thought I should never have come to such a place. I even cried." But life back in her Hiroshima village had not been easy either. She had not had the freedom even there to choose a mate of her own liking, so she decided that she would see things through, come what may.[126]

The biggest worry of all for most plantation workers, just as for the urban *hinmin* back in Japan, was the struggle to make ends meet. Even at era's end, when options had increased and pay had improved, most sugar workers remained very poor. Accounts from those years abound with comments like those of Torahichi Tsukahara, who made a relatively lucrative $22 a month early in the 1900s but found it consumed entirely by expenses: "I spent it all. I didn't save any."[127] It was not quite that bad for every family, but few of them had much margin. A report in Sōga's *Nippu Jiji* late in 1908 described a typical worker's average budget since the turn of the century: a monthly income of $14.60, with expenses of $12.33 for food, laundry, tobacco, baths, raincoat (and raincoat oil), heating oil, shoes and socks, postage, haircuts, work clothes, and contributions of 25 cents a month. That left $2.27 a month for savings or anything else.[128] The "anything else" for most families included a remittance to the family back in Japan, either to repay the loan that had financed the voyage to Hawai'i or to alleviate the farm family's own poverty. Nothing better illustrated how tight budgets were than the struggle that most families engaged in to find even the tiniest supplements to their plantation salaries. A few took their children out of school, just like their cousins in the Tokyo *hinminkutsu* did, because they needed their field earnings. Wives cooked, sewed, and did laundry for the single men in the longhouses. Children sold crabs and catfish. Some of the more enterprising adults brewed beer for sale. One Kipu-Huleia worker recalled "a young child carrying two 5-gallon soda cracker cans full of tofu, balanced on a stick on his shoulders, walking along the railroad track . . . to sell tofu."[129] Another, on Oʻahu, recalled his mother taking in laundry, then raising chickens and ducks for sale, and barely having time to sleep each night: "you know, two hours, sometimes three hours, sometimes one hour."[130] Even still, most of them barely scraped by. The historian Alan Moriyama says that for nearly every family, the wife's income supplement made the difference between solvency and debt.[131]

Nonetheless, and despite the persistence of poverty, the Hawaiʻi immigrants' experience was marked almost always by steady, noticeable improvement, particularly after the camps became more family-centered, a fact that set them apart from their *hinmin* counterparts in Japan. On the material side of life, daily clothes remained utilitarian but people described more variety as the years passed. The early accounts took note almost exclusively of hand-me-downs, mended again and again, "men's working clothes with patches over patches," pants with "more patches than the original fabric."[132] Everything was badly wrinkled. "Coarse stiff" footwear made by local Chinese cobblers was purchased when shoes had too many holes to be worn any longer. By the onset of the 1910s, however, increasing numbers of families had the wherewithal to supplement their wardrobes with special things for public occasions: a "new *heko-obi* (waist band) for a boy or a *yukata*" for the summer *bon* festival, said Muraoka; "as much as possible, . . . we changed into something new." The journalist Kawakami was impressed in 1914 by the numbers of Japanese women on a holiday wearing kimono "made of costly silk evidently imported from Japan." The women to whom he referred appear to have been in the cities but even their presence there spoke to growing mobility, an aspect of the evolution that will be discussed below.[133]

Mealtimes showed even more noticeable improvements. In the early days of longhouses and $9-a-month salaries, mess halls were the norm, with *ōgokku* or "big cooks" preparing meals of rice, miso broth, noodles, and small pieces of pickled radish (*takuan*), supplemented by a boiled egg or slice of fish once a week, a diet not unlike that served in the notorious factory dorms at home. Malnutrition was common, as was bad eyesight. Even plantation owners worried about poor health from inadequate eating; one immigration official suggested in 1889 that all the pickled dishes the Japanese ate might be responsible for malnourishment, with "frequently fatal results."[134] Over time, however, most families saw their mealtime fare improve significantly, partly because of better wages but mostly because of the changes in the way camp communities operated: the stability that came with having families, the appearance of peddlers with weekly truckloads of vegetables, fruit, and other staples, and the appearance of private stores run by Japanese grocers who imported rice, soy sauce, and a hundred items from the homeland. By the onset of the twentieth century, most families also had begun cultivating vegetable and fruit gardens, which gave them the advantages of the farm back home without the pantry-depleting problems of a Japanese winter. Hiroo Sato on the Big Island recalled his family's harvests of daikon, carrots, beans, green onions, cabbage, ginger root, shiso, and various herbs, along with ginger flowers that were sliced and eaten with a soy sauce/vinegar dressing. They also grew the Hawaiian staple, taro, as well as *fuki* (bog rhubarb), *mitsuba* (Japanese wild parsley), and *shun-giku*, sometimes called chrysanthemum greens. Others described the fruits that gave each season a distinct flavor: bananas (which "seem to grow and taste best when grown around outhouses"), mangoes, pears, oranges, lemons, papaya, and breadfruits, along with the mountain apples and guava that they picked in the wild. There also were bamboo shoots. And a sugar cane snack was "always available for those with strong teeth and jaws."[135] One of the more notable changes was the growing accommodation to the American practice of eating meats. William Yamanaka recalled people in his Kipu-Huleia camp eating every kind of meat, including *opu* or tripe, "the low point in poor man's food."[136] And Minoru Inaba said of the Kono plantations in the 1910s:

We had pigs all the time. . . . We had chickens running around in the yard. Every time we wanted to eat the chicken, we'd catch one. There were no chicken coops or anything like that. They were running around in the yard there. . . . And fish. Every so often, the peddler would come from Kailua on a donkey. He used to peddle his fish in the community. We used to buy fish from him.[137]

Poverty had not lost its grip on most families, but by Meiji's end even poor households enjoyed better food than their 1880s predecessors could have imagined.

As the appearance of fruit peddlers and immigrant-owned stores suggests, camps increasingly evolved into vibrant communities as the years passed, with the emergence of social institutions that replicated—or even improved on—village life back home. The most fundamental institution may have been the bath. At first, owners resisted demands for baths, but the Japanese were insistent, and by the onset of the twentieth century, most plantations had installed "large wooden tubs capable of accommodating six to eight persons,"[138] and some had built even larger baths. They were a far cry from what the workers remembered (not always accurately) back home. Many were grimy and dirty. Often they were too small, with nothing but a low partition dividing the male and female halves of a single large tub, allowing mischievous boys to play tricks on unsuspecting women and girls. Koga Noriyu particularly recalled how unsanitary the early bathing was. "You were in the same water," he said. "If you did work like *hapai ko* [carrying sugar cane], you were really filthy. After work when you got to the bath, there was no more hot water so you had no choice. . . . A lot of people used that water. Even if you felt the water was dirty, you had no choice."[139] The filth did not keep workers away from the baths, however, because above all, they were places to socialize, to talk with neighbors while soaking tired muscles. By the end of the Meiji years, nearly all camps had installed some kind of central bath, and many had put in separate rooms, with improved washing facilities, for men and women.

One institution that changed camp life after the 1890s was the temple or church. In the eyes of many officials and religious leaders, the plantations' early disorderliness sprang at least partly from a lack of religion. A Buddhist priest who visited Hilo late in the 1880s said workers appeared to be "wandering, as sheep not having a shepherd."[140] Another priest, Imamura Yemyo, reported in the late 1890s that the workers still were "extremely wild," which he blamed at least partly on the lack of religion: "Even when I managed to talk to some of them, I was afraid of violent attack by roughnecks to prevent my religious talk."[141] One can question whether debauchery was as serious as Imamura thought and whether the lack of priests caused it. What one cannot question is that the volatility of early camp life prompted both Buddhist and Christian groups to begin sending representatives to the plantations and that by the early 1900s temples and churches had assumed central roles in the camps.

Christianity was introduced by the Methodist evangelist Miyama Kanichi, who began making trips through the islands in 1887, preaching human dignity and abstinence from alcohol. Miyama reportedly did not push conversion, but Japan's consul general Andō Tarō became a Christian under his influence and, after swearing off liquor himself, actively urged sugar workers to convert to the Western faith. The immigrants did not do so in great numbers, but the Methodists and the Congregationalists set up Hawai'i missions in the 1890s, with churches, schools, and homes for women and troubled children. The Congregationalist Sokabe Shiro started a boarding school on the Big Island in 1894 for boys whose parents "were often too tired to give their children full parental care,"[142] while the Methodists created the Susannah Wesley home for poor families and orphans in rural O'ahu in 1899, and Salvation Army missionaries made regular visits to many of the camps.[143] The Buddhists, who arrived in 1889, were even more active, despite early problems with several scoundrels who promised to build temples or perform death rites, then ran off with the workers' money. Japan's major Pure Land sects began sending priests in the mid-1890s, and by 1907 the islands had twenty-two Hongwanji temples and another eleven Jōdo centers, with more than eighty temples across the islands by the Taishō years.[144] Even camps without a priest were visited by itinerants, and in some camps laymen held services. A "very religious" old man named Taketa in Hōlualoa plantation on Hawai'i, for example, would hold Shingon sect services on the twentieth of each month. One lad said he and his friends went to the services because "we knew that he used to have refreshments."[145]

The temples played a particularly important role in turning the camps into communities. In addition to providing religious services, the Buddhists built schools, sponsored festivals, and created youth and women's groups. By the turn of the century, most of them promoted seasonal celebrations with *mochi* pounding for New Year, bean throwing for *setsubun*, flowers to celebrate Buddha's birth, and special ceremonies when children were born. They also staged funerals and maintained cemeteries, including one at Pāhoa with the remains of "young bachelors killed during mishaps while dynamite blasting . . . to lay the railway tracks."[146] In late summer, some temples brought in special generators to provide lights for lively *bon* dances honoring the spirits of the departed. "No one has seen the dead return to eat the food at the graves," remarked one celebrant, "but in a day or so, all food was gone. Maybe, just maybe . . ."[147] By the early 1900s, the owners were encouraging the Buddhists with gifts of land for temples and money to operate them.[148] After the strike at Waipahu began in 1904, one priest reported that "plantation authorities" asked him to go to the plantation to encourage workers to eschew violence. "So I went there and spoke before the excited audience," he said. "I spoke entirely from the religious standpoint to calm them. . . . I felt the great power of Buddha." He took credit when the strikers returned to work.[149]

Not everything about Buddhism was positive. The church was no freer from personal agendas than Christianity was. Different sects competed for followers, sometimes bitterly and unfairly, and the journalist Karl Kiyoshi Kawakami accused temples of undermining island education by resorting "to all means in trying to take pupils out of the non-religious schools and enroll them in their own." Even worse, he said, they squeezed money out of adherents ($100,000 by his account) in ways that could only be labeled "corrupting." Calling the head Hongwanji temple in Kyoto a "hotbed of financial troubles and factional feuds," he commented sarcastically that "water cannot rise above its source."[150] Nonetheless, most would have included the religious institutions, both Buddhist and Christian, among the forces that brought social health to the worker camps. Writing about the first-generation immigrants, the historian Dennis Ogawa said, "The plantation worker's great thirst for common social bonds" was crucial in making camp life stable. "Without a wife, children, the Bible, sutras, *mochi, kōden, kami, odaisan*, or the *bon* festival," he said, "the Issei would forever be the sojourner."[151] His list left out one other key institution: the bath.

Transcending Circumstances

It would have been as hard in 1890 to imagine the disorganized sugar workers creating a labor movement as it was for Matsubara to think of rickshaw pullers organizing. Yet that is exactly what they did, within a generation. Nothing illustrated the evolution of the Japanese population more clearly than the strike of 1909, which involved the coordinated efforts of workers across the entire archipelago. Momentum for the labor action began building in 1908, when two of the islands' Japanese newspapers launched an editorial war, with the proworker *Nippu Jiji* of Sōga Yasutarō decrying the low wages of Japanese workers and the probusiness *Hawaiian Shinpō* calling Sōga's supporters "agitators." In an August article, *Jiji* pointed out the discrepancy between the wages of Japanese immigrants and those from most other nations, noting that sugar owners had earned a 35 percent profit that year, more than $22 million.[152] In November 1908 the activists met in Honolulu to create the Higher Wages Association (HWA), selecting the heavily bearded druggist Fred Makino as president and University of California law graduate Motoyuki Negoro as secretary. The entire Japanese community in the islands debated, with old-timers generally preaching conciliation while newer workers and a group of highly educated supporters pushed unionism.[153]

As support for the activists spread, the owners grew worried. In January 1909, a Hackfeld official wrote letters urging the plantation owners to watch the newspapers in their camps and "let us know immediately, in case you hear anything." Fearing that the HWA wanted to secure "parity with the European laborers employed upon the plantations," he asked the owners to submit information about wages and "conditions existing upon his plantation," in order to counter HWA charges of inequity.[154] In a bit of wishful thinking, he also opined that the unrest "originated with and is carried on by, irresponsible agitators in nowise connected with the laborers."[155] The planters also prepared a study showing that in contrast to the $18.50 a month wage figure cited for Japanese workers, the average was $23.19 when one included skilled laborers, managers, and people on special contracts.[156] By April, Hackfeld was writing that "the Higher Wages Association is . . . a danger, and one difficult to control," and warning that if the plantations offered any raises, the workers would just ask for more. When the strike began on May 11, the Hackfeld agent reminded owners that they could make no deals without HSPA approval and that *lunas* should "at no time attempt to precipitate violence and bloodshed."[157]

The workers struck first at Oʻahu's Aiea and Waipahu plantations, with a manifesto focusing on wage equity:

> The demand for higher wages is based on the efficiency of our laboring class. . . . If a labourer comes from Japan and he performs the same quantity of work of the same quality within the same period of time as those who hail from the opposite side of the world, what good reason is there to discriminate one against the other?[158]

Japanese at the other Oʻahu plantations quickly joined the work stoppage, prompting a threat by the owners to evict them from their homes if they had not returned to work by May 22. The HWA set up temporary housing for five thousand Japanese laborers in response, mostly in Honolulu hotels and parks. And the owners began hiring strike breakers at a rate of $1.50 a day, more than twice the 69 cents the Japanese had been receiving.[159]

The strike lasted for nearly three months and was notable for the discipline of the Japanese, as well as the efficiency with which the HWA cared for the strikers. At the same time, it sparked acrimony and infighting within the broader Japanese community. On one side, all the Japanese papers except *Nippu Jiji* and *Kona Hankyo* opposed the activists. On the other side, some of the more bellicose strikers committed acts of violence against the strike breakers and those Japanese who stayed on the plantations. Lloyd Sugimoto, a ten-year-old on Ewa plantation at the time, remembered the fierce criticism his father received for attempting to negotiate a deal to allow his family to remain in their plantation home if he promised to return to work at the end of the strike. The other workers berated him, Sugimoto said, saying, "Sugimoto got bribed from the plantation. . . . So, we going to kill him." When an angry group came to the house, his mother confronted them: "If anybody is brave enough, step over here, come in. See what happen." Nobody accepted her challenge.[160] Except for reporting localized disputes of this sort, however, observers on both sides echoed the post-strike finding of the territory's Commissioner of Labor that the strikers were "perfectly law abiding in the sense of refraining from violence and destruction of property." Even the antistrike *Semi-Weekly Star* reported in early June that "there was no drinking, no loud talking, no argument, no agitation and nothing of a disturbing nature whatever."[161]

The owners refused to bend, and on August 5 the HWA halted the strike, acknowledging that its $40,000 cost had stretched them to the limit and that support among the strikers was dwindling.[162] The mood within the Japanese community was dark at the strike's end; one journalist called the episode "a complete fiasco for the strikers." Not a single demand had been met.[163] But as the months passed, that evaluation changed. By 1910, the planters—who complained continually to the HSPA about the inferior work of the replacement laborers and estimated their own losses at more than $2 million—had gone beyond the strikers' original demands, raising Japanese wages to $20 a month, improving housing and sanitary conditions, and adding a bonus system for effective work. Some also began to provide recreation facilities, and a program was launched to plant thousands of trees around the barren camps. Even more important, the owners lost their aura of invulnerability as new, aggressive leadership emerged in the Japanese community. And increasing numbers of Japanese families were liberated from the plantations psychologically and financially, as evidenced by those who turned to other work: starting shops, taking up trades, becoming small farmers or fishermen, moving to jobs in the cities. To call the strike revolutionary would be too much. Changes already were underway when it occurred, and the basic pattern—long and brutal workdays with inadequate pay—continued. *Lunas*, while more diverse and generally more attuned to worker sensitivities, still ruled the fields. Families and individuals still had trouble stocking the cupboards. But, in Ogawa's analysis, "a bridgehead had been won. The Japanese had insisted that they were equal to the other nationalities, and the Planters had spent two million dollars to prove them wrong."[164]

The scale of the changes under way was described by a Buddhist cleric who visited several plantations a year before the strike. "I have made a tour around these islands lately, and have found the standard of life of Japanese laborers by no means low," he said. "They are consuming beer, whiskey, and wine. They also eat fresh fish. This is quite a change as compared with conditions of several years ago."[165] He was not alone in this evaluation. By the end of the Meiji period, the accomplishments of large numbers of Japanese were attracting increasing attention. The family successes of the scholar George Tanabe, referred to at the outset of this chapter, were on their way to becoming more typical than exceptional. Certainly, the majority of people on the plantations continued to experience hardship; indeed, Tanabe recalls that his "grandparents and parents were poor" decades after the end of Meiji. But he also recalls that "most, if not all, people had homes, and most, if not all, had enough to eat."[166] While the community's post-Meiji successes lie beyond the boundaries of this study, it would be a mistake not to note a few of the key indicators of vibrancy, which by era's end had become central to the Japanese sugar plantation workers' story.

One indicator was the large flow of money to needy relatives back in Honshu, Kyushu, and Okinawa. Like the girls who went off to textile factories, emigrants headed for Hawai'i with a promise to send part of their earnings home, and by all accounts the majority followed through, typically sending a few yen each month, first through the Japanese consulate in Honolulu and later through Japanese banks. One survey found nearly three-fourths of the emigrants from Hiroshima sending remittances, and an 1892 study reported that the thirty workers from one Hiroshima village averaged a little over four yen a month each in remittances, enough to cause one recipient to exclaim, "In America there must be trees which bear money."[167] One striking thing about these remittances was the regularity with which they were sent, even when times were hard in the camps. Another was the steady increase in their amounts. Across the first decade of immigration, the annual total sent back by all Japanese immigrants in Hawai'i averaged 382,609 yen, and after that the amount soared. The journal *Taiyō* reported nearly ten million yen sent home in 1903 by workers abroad, the majority of whom were in Hawai'i, and the Honolulu consulate estimated that more than six million yen was sent from Hawai'i alone in 1908.[168] Letters from homeland relatives often asked for help with highly specific needs: farm tools, a pilgrimage, a new roof for the house.[169] The amounts declined after the end of the Meiji era as American restrictions reduced the number of Japanese coming and the emigrant families themselves identified increasingly with Hawai'i as a permanent home. But the steadily rising amounts until then spoke to the increasing ability of plantation workers to set aside money for things other than life's necessities.

A second indicator of vibrancy was the movement of workers into more diverse jobs after the late 1890s. For Kashiwabara Kihachi, an 1889 arrival notorious for being able to "hoist aloft a 100-pound sack of rice with one arm and twirl it around in the palm of his one hand," improvement meant moving to Honolulu in 1896 to start a construction business and launch a Japanese-language school.[170] For Hazama Etsuo, whose parents came in 1902, improvement meant buying his own truck and eventually hiring three employees of his own. Decades later, he commented, "When I left Japan as a teenager, I didn't think that Hawai'i would be home for the rest of my life, but I'm happy here. I have my children, grandchildren, and even great grandchildren."[171] For Yano Toraji, the improvements entailed the freedom to go to work at a store in Maui in 1912 and a few years later to open his own dress shop.[172] The journalist Kawakami observed in his 1914 survey that Japanese were working in nearly every industry: building trades, plumbing, taxicabs, dry goods stores. "In Hilo," he said, "I saw a Japanese merchant erecting a building which when completed promised to be one of the largest business buildings in the city." Even on the plantations, he added, they "fill highly responsible positions."[173]

The range of occupations and business ventures pursued by immigrants bordered on breathtaking by the early 1900s. At Kukui'ula on Kaua'i, Kingoro Matsunaga set up a barber shop. At Wai'anae near Honolulu, Sōga Yasutarō worked in a "miniature department store," where he gave advice and helped illiterate clients write letters before launching a career in Honolulu as an activist journalist. On several islands, Okinawan immigrants gained both sneers and profits by pioneering the raising of hogs. And at Pāhoa on the Big Island, some Japanese started billiards parlors and blacksmith shops, while others peddled fish, worked as "neat and meticulous" carpenters, opened fish markets, entered the liquor business, and ran small hotels, as well as theaters, candy stores, and tofu shops.[174] By the mid-1890s, plantation owners had begun complaining that their company stores could not sell their American and British goods because "these people are demanding their own wares from Japan." Said one, "Japanese junk shops and stores are springing up all over, and anyone who is not blind should see where we are drifting."[175] By the turn of the century, more than two hundred Japanese stores dotted the plantations.[176] And they were supplemented by new institutions, including half a dozen Japan-language newspapers, the Japan Mutual Aid Association, the Japanese Association of Kona, and the Japanese YMCA. Most of the social organizations were headquartered in the cities, but they served the plantation workers too. By the early 1900s, league sports competitions—from sumo wrestling to baseball—also had become common ties across each island.

And health care improved. Primitive (or nonexistent) medical facilities made plantations sound like the Japanese *hinminkutsu* during the first years as tuberculosis, diphtheria, broken bones, beriberi, ulcers, syphilis, and measles ravaged the camps. Cholera was reported in 1895; in 1897 nearly sixty workers died of some "strange endemic epidemic," soon after a new plantation opened on Lanai.[177] One worker called the medical system "good-for-nothing as far as we immigrants were concerned."[178] But the situation improved almost yearly. By the 1890s, peddlers were selling traditional Japanese medicines from camp to camp, and by the start of the 1900s, Japanese doctors were setting up practices on many plantations, often with a small attached hospital, where "anytime, we have little bit *pilikia* [trouble] . . . we run over there."[179] By the last Meiji decade, almost every camp of any size had a hospital or a dispensary that provided medicines, ointments, prenatal and postnatal assistance and had treatment for the most common problems. The gradual expansion of Lihue Hospital, which opened on January 3, 1899, on Kaua'i with connections to several plantations, was typical. The hospital saw only 102 patients the first year, in part because it was "difficult . . . to persuade patients to go to the Hospital" since "it was looked on as certain death," and in part because plantations resisted the twenty-five cents a day they had to pay when their workers were admitted. Half a decade later, in 1905, 200 were treated, more than 85 percent of them from plantations and more than half of them Japanese. The hospital built a cottage for TB patients in 1908, followed by four private rooms, a wash house, and an operating room, and by 1911, more than 400 patients were being served annually. One doctor noted in the hospital's 1910 report, "The Plantation people are learning more and more each year to appreciate the advantages you have given them in an up to date hospital." Appropriate health care had become the expected norm.[180]

The most important institution may have been the school, which pulled camp communities together and turned young Japanese into "Americans." During the first decade when conditions were desperate and schools were scarce, parents (the majority of whom were themselves literate) often made exceptional efforts to see that their children received at least some education. In 1898, about half of the archipelago's roughly five hundred Japanese children were attending public schools, and after the removal of attendance fees in 1899 and the U.S. annexation of Hawai'i the following year, attendance rose rapidly. In 1910, seven thousand were attending public school. At least as important for community building was an explosion during the last Meiji years of Japanese-language schools, most of which were created as supplements to the public schools. The first of these opened on Maui and on the Big Island in 1895; by 1900, there were eleven across the islands, and by 1907, 120 of them provided instruction for nearly five thousand children.[181] The result was that by the mid-1900s, almost all school-age children were in classes all day long, Monday through Friday: morning and early afternoon in the public school, late afternoon for two hours in the Japanese-language school. Many also spent part of Saturday at the Japanese school.

Even decades later, these schools maintained a vivid hold on the immigrants' memories, telling evidence of how important education was in shaping the camp communities. Interviewed by scholars in the last half of the twentieth century, seniors invariably harked back to school as key in framing their lives. One memory was of the walking, miles and miles each day, carrying books and a lunch of rice balls, salty plum (*umeboshi*), and small bits of dried fish or vegetables. "Barber" Kawamoto in Kōloa said he walked thirty or forty minutes each way, along the local railroad tracks. Sato in Pāhoa admired his classmates for "walking barefoot six miles each day," and some recalled the streams they had to ford.[182] Many also remembered the strictness of teachers who made them shave their heads (one principal warned that if boys wore long hair, "the nourishment of the food that you eat will only go to the hair, whereas, if you are baldheaded, the food nourishment will all go to the brains"[183]) or the tedium of repeating America's flag pledge and Japanese vocabulary words. Some old women talked about how useful the Japanese-school sewing classes were, and a number praised the ethics classes for teaching "etiquette, proper manners, proper attitudes, respect for others."[184] The topic that usually drew the liveliest comments was the interaction with classmates. Reactions were mixed about the way the Japanese schools made them work together in cleaning classrooms and washing toilets. But nearly everyone enthused about playtime pranks and games: marbles, tops, rocks-scissors-paper, and mumblety-peg.[185] Jiro Suzuki remembered playing cowboy on the way home, when boys would "act grown up by making pipes from papaya stems" and smoking the crushed papaya leaves: "a real torture, with coughing and gagging as a result."[186] Playing or studying, female or male, the children illustrated what sociable places the plantation camps had become by the end of the century's first decade.[187] The schools not only taught skills and facts, they fostered a sense among the children and their parents that they were parts of a bigger whole with a future worth investing in.

Taken in its entirety, across a third of a century, the Hawai'i sugar plantation workers' story shed almost as much light on *urban* poverty in late Meiji Japan as on life in the fields and camps. The plantation experiences resembled those of the city *hinmin* in the early years of immigration. The settlers were overwhelmingly male and single, they came from impoverished Japanese farms, they were forced into foreign and hostile living situations, life was grim. In the words of one laborer, "it was endless toil every day, seven days per week," with "holidays and vacation . . . practically unheard of, except for New Year day."[188] Within a few years, however, the slums and the camps had begun to head in different directions or, more accurately, to change at different paces. Women started coming to Hawai'i in increasing numbers, and families began to form. Institutions such as temples and schools grew steadily, sponsoring activities and programs that turned camps into communities. With them came commercial activities, and then health facilities and schools, all of which led to increased economic opportunity: more diverse work opportunities, worker activism, labor organization, better working conditions, and higher wages. Not everyone shared equally in the progress; a major portion of the plantation community still found life harsh when the Meiji emperor died in 1912. But by then, an unmistakably sharp contrast had emerged between plantation camps and *hinminkutsu*.

The reasons for the difference will be discussed in the conclusion. Suffice it to note here that they were more structural than human. The early journalist Ushiyama Saijirō was writing with blinders when he argued that young factory workers in the late Meiji cities were poor because, as "the children of poor families from agricultural villages," they lacked discipline.[189] Had his vision encompassed Hawai'i, he would have found that the sugar plantation workers were "children of poor families from agricultural villages" too. They worked hard and showed discipline, but no more so than their cousins back in Japan. Nor were they more intelligent or ambitious. But the scale and environment of the two places were vastly different; cities were more populous, more sprawling, and more difficult to shape. The urban *hinmin* lived in a wilderness, a world without institutional support for family development, for health care, or for children's education. In contrast to their Hawaiian counterparts, they inhabited a challenging new sphere with almost no familiar jobs, no ties to families back home, and no recognizable customs or social groups. And they generally were paid even more poorly than their peers in Hawai'i.[190] When Freire claimed that "the humanization of the oppressed signifies subversion," he meant that when poor people come to understand that they are fully human, that they are as capable as people with more means and luck, they are no longer easy to control.[191] The sprawling wilderness of the urban slums and factory dormitories made such a self-recognition more difficult to inspire in the city, and that in turn made urban progress slower.

Poverty ... You thought it would be quite simple; it is extraordinarily
complicated.

—George Orwell, *Down and Out in Paris and London*[1]

If it is not clear by now that the *kasō shakai* merited more attention than
history has given them, this book has failed. The urban poor of the late
Meiji years performed most of the tasks that made Japan's modern transformation possible. They turned out the factory goods that clothed people
and propelled Japan onto the international market; they built Ginza's brick
town and Osaka's 250-foot Tsūtenkaku Tower; they prevented epidemics by removing human wastes from the cities; they pulled the rickshaws that got people
to work and to play. And they did more than merely support the modern forces:
they shaped them, through activism that held down streetcar fare increases
and toppled prime ministers. They also provided much of the color and hubbub
that observers found so appealing and irritating in modern city life: the clickety
clacks of rickshaw wheels on pebbled streets, the hawking and squawking in
public markets, "the smell of roasting pike" and yet-to-be-collected urine on
"poor back streets," the flickering paper lanterns and "indecent pictures" in
Ryōgoku's entertainment byways, the temple acrobats and festival storytellers.[2]
If Meiji modernity was a cacophony, the urban poor made it so.

What then was daily life like for them, not as an abstract element in an economic or social system, but as they lived and felt it? It is a simple question without simple answers, a question complicated in part by the sparseness of their
own writing and in part by the multifaceted nature of their experiences. There
are, however, several salient features that every *hinmin* would have acknowledged as true, the most obvious of which is that material life was difficult, often
excruciating. Most of the *kasō shakai* population in the late Meiji years came
from impoverished households on the farm. Sometimes they had moved to the
city of their own volition, seeking new opportunities; just as often, they had
been pushed out by families too poor to feed them. If villages once had been
safety valves to which cities could send their surpluses in hard times, the re-
verse became true during the onrush of modernity: cities offered a safety valve
for the starving villages. For the emigrants themselves, however, the early urban reality was more storm than respite. Their new surroundings were unfamiliar and uninviting. Jobs were hard to find and paid inhumanly low wages.
The old human networks were replaced by bosses and city officials who talked

paternalism but offered neither succor nor material aid. Comforting mountain vistas and gurgling streams became haunting memories.

Two things demonstrated the ferocity of poverty's winds most forcefully: the ugliness of their living spaces and the paucity of their income. While some poor people lived in nearly every part of the cities, the *kasō shakai* were increasingly concentrated after the late 1880s in sprawling *hinminkutsu*, or slums, that rivaled the London and New York slums in their crowding and grimness. Whether home was in Osaka's Nago-chō or Tokyo's Shin'ami-chō, it was shared with thousands of equally impoverished *hinmin* crowded together, three to six (or more) people each, in one-room, three- or four-mat apartments with neither indoor toilets nor cooking spaces. Alleys were narrow and littered, nearby waterways smelled of filth and factories belched out smoke, rains turned slums into lakes, disease stalked. Even a cramped apartment was beyond the reach of the thousands who could afford no more than the single futon on the hard *kichin'yado*, or flophouse, floor. These were "dark, dismal caverns of hunger and cold," said Matsubara, places too often "devoid of the sun's warm embrace."[3] They were places, moreover, where days were driven by uncertainty about whether there would be enough money to get through to next week. If Japan's *hinmin* had heard George Orwell's remark that "the mass of the rich and the poor are differentiated by their incomes and nothing else," they would have nodded in agreement.[4] Too often, they paid rents by the day because there were not enough yen to pay for a week at a time. Only the simplest, most boring food could be put on the table. Sometimes, bedding was hocked in the morning with the hope of having enough money to redeem it before nighttime. Children above the age of ten (sometimes six or eight) had to go to work rather than to school. Even little ones accompanied their mothers to the factory; otherwise, ends could not be met. At the era's end, food still consumed two-thirds of the average slum dweller's monthly income, and as late as the 1920s, significant numbers got their meals from the scraps available at leftover food shops. The musician who set himself on fire to escape life's pain may have been an exception, but all *hinmin* understood what caused him to do that.

If paucity and privation framed the poor person's outer world, what about the inner sphere? What did it *feel like* to experience endless economic challenges? As the look at rural life demonstrated, there had been little sense of poverty (*hinkon*) in the villages, even when there was keen awareness of hardship, because difficulties were shared and social networks were vibrant. What of the city cousins? One answer that shows up repeatedly in the stories and the studies is that urban *hinmin* felt like outsiders, like inhabitants of a world set apart physically and spiritually from their better-off fellow citizens. The physical separation was undeniable, whether they lived in factory dormitories surrounded by fences, hid from police while engaging in sex work, watched rich people entering the Iwasaki's Kiyosumi gardens in Fukagawa, or simply lived in that "dismal space proliferating unceasingly": the slums.[5] Clothes, food, transportation modes, entertainment, they all set the poor apart visibly. And the separation from families and communities back on the farm often was total in this era before easy communication. Lonely girls in the dorm may have dreamed at New Year of returning to the village; for many slum dwellers, even such dreams were impossible. The anthropologist Yamaguchi Masao has argued that "those who have been forced to assume a recessive, secondary position in society are likelier to form intense communitarian affiliations almost in inverse proportion to the marginalization they have been forced to endure."[6] He is backed up by the way slum neighborhoods developed their own sense of intra-*hinminkutsu* community across the late Meiji years. But the reason they formed such communities was that they were separated so sharply—both physically and materially—from the society around them.

The separation also was emotional and mental. Certainly, the more affluent classes saw those in the *kasō shakai* as "different." The cabinet minister Kaneko Kentarō may have had poor prisoners in mind when he said that he would not mind having workers "fall dead from . . . hard labor" because that would "decrease the number of their kind of people,"[7] but his vision of the poor lay at the heart of his callousness, differing only in degree from the editor of *Seinen: The Rising Generation* who admonished a correspondent who complained about how hard it was to be poor to stop acting "like an old woman."[8] The poor, in other words, were different; they had themselves to blame for their plight. While villages spawned little consciousness of poverty, the spreading urban slums turned *hinkon* into a major topic. And the *hinmin* not only knew about these attitudes, they imbibed them. They felt the gibes of neighborhood children about their clothes or manners. They heard their bosses' disparaging comments about their "laziness" or sexual behavior. They read the newspapers, where depictions of otherness were a staple in the Page Three stories that focused on poor peoples' crimes and health scourges. When one of the characters in Natsume Sōseki's unfinished novel *Meian* (Light and darkness) is irritated by a poor visitor's frankness, she says that the main trouble with the man is that he did not understand his place as a *hinmin*. Other poor people she had met "had known very well that there were differences in rank, and they all had dared have relations with her only within the limits carefully prescribed for them." To be a *hinmin* was to be aware that one was an outsider.[9]

One other reason the poor felt their otherness so keenly was that separation was institutionalized. Those in the poor communities knew that infrastructure improvements would come to their neighborhoods last, if at all. When epidemics broke out, their neighborhoods would be quarantined first, and they would be the ones sent to isolation hospitals or "dump sites" to die when cholera struck. They were aware that they would be fired and sent home if they got seriously sick at work. And they knew that when tragedies occurred, they would be excluded from support systems that might be available to people who were better-off.[10] Everything about modern institutions told them they were outsiders. The reason that, even at Meiji's end, nearly half of all *hinmin* still ignored the requirement that they register at a local ward office lay, surely, in the knowledge that the institutions of modernity largely left them out. If they did not belong, why should they register? When the prostitute Masuda Sayo said of her difficulties, "It must be because I'm not really a human child,"[11] she was expressing a sense of separateness shared by many in the *hinmin* world.

No institution made *hinmin* families feel the outsider status more sharply than the schools. Every urbanite, poor or rich, knew that education was crucial in the modern world. Farm households might discourage "too much schooling with the rationale that education makes one dislike farming,"[12] but such an attitude was untenable in the cities, where the evidence was everywhere that success without education was no longer possible. Yet school attendance continued to lag among the urban poor until well after the turn of the century, for the simple reason that children had to bring in income. If the ten-year-old did not work for wages, the family did not eat. The evidence makes it clear that this plight inflicted considerable pain on *kasō shakai* families, heightening their sense of being excluded from the rules that framed life for everyone else. Terada Yūkichi wrote in *Taiyō* in 1902 that rickshaw-pulling families "shed tears" when they could not send "the children we love" to school "due to the difficulty of making a living."[13] That the government formally accepted poverty as a reason for exempting children from the compulsory education system heightened the sense of separateness; so did the resistance of profit-driven factory owners to efforts to get school-aged employees into the educational system. Even the occasional attempts by reformers to create special "paupers' schools" for *hinmin* children trumpeted separation. It hardly is surprising that many poor parents said they would not be humiliated by putting their children in such schools.

At the same time, the feelings of humiliation and anger about being kept on the outside provided a glimpse into another side of the slum dwellers' lives. That they resented their exclusion dramatized the degree to which they had come, by the late Meiji years, to identify with modern society. The urban poor saw themselves as builders of the modern world, as participants in the transformations going on all around them. One reason for this surely lay in the fact, demonstrated so often in this study, that they did much of the work that made modern urban life possible: spinning silk for export, serving strong drinks at restaurants, punching train tickets. Modernity changed the kinds of jobs open to them; their work in those jobs changed the shape of modern society. No group illustrated the symbiosis between *hinmin* work and modernity more vividly than the rickshaw pullers, whose occupation was called into being by the need to move crowds around expanding urban spaces quickly. The world's first rickshaws are thought to have been built in Japan at the start of the Meiji era, and by the mid-1870s, some forty thousand *shafu* in Tokyo alone defined city life by getting people and materials wherever they needed to go. But modernity also doomed the pullers. By the turn of the century, essayists were worrying about what would happen to rickshaws with the spread of electric trams and trains. When the emperor died in the summer of 1912, the city had less than half as many rickshaws as it had had little more than a decade and a half before, and by the early 1930s, all but a few pullers had found new work or joined the ranks of the jobless. *Shafu* were, in other words, both the carriers and the victims of modernity. To have told any *shafu* that he was not an important component of modern urban society would have drawn a sneer (or curse).

The members of the *kasō shakai* saw themselves as more than builders of the modern society, however. They considered themselves participants in its frenzied life. That was apparent, most obviously, in the way they engaged in all the activities, petty and large, that any modern city dweller is expected to carry out. Gathering in front of the leftover food shop to talk with other women about colicky children and nasty foremen, stopping by the *izakaya* to "have a drink, take a puff, and eat a bit of vegetable" on the way home from work,[14] even sneaking a couple of pieces of charcoal from the boss' pile for the home hibachi: these were the normal activities of typical urbanites, and they defined the daily regimen of *hinmin*. So did most of their other activities. The poor worker with oil-stained knuckles wearing the silk frock coat in Ueno Park on Sunday rubbed shoulders with leisure seekers from the middle class. The poor children loved the monkey grinders and lion dancers no less (and no more) than the rich children who got to go to school every day. The workman who saved the little girl from being trampled at Kanda Myōjin Shrine was doing what middle-class citizens hoped they themselves would do but inwardly feared they might not.

But being a part of the broader society involved more than merely doing standard things. The late Meiji poor helped to *change* society, taking their own active part in the influential political and economic movements of the day. I have argued elsewhere that the newspaper press played a key role in turning the "people" or *minshū* into citizens during the Meiji years, giving a sense of Japaneseness to commoners who previously had had little emotional or intellectual connection to a public sphere.[15] One of the surprises in doing the research for this study was the discovery that *hinmin* made up a significant share of the *minshū* whose evolution from isolated personhood to citizenship originally convinced me of the press' influence. When a *Taiyō* essayist urged police in 1903 to investigate rumors about discontent among Osaka rickshaw pullers, who, he said, would become "a big problem for society" if they organized, he was talking about *hinmin* activism.[16] The tens of thousands who responded to journalists' calls for antigovernment rallies in the last Meiji decade were, to a significant degree, members of the *kasō shakai*. So were the women who won repeated labor settlements at silk-spinning factories in the 1890s and early 1900s. And who were the demonstrator-rioters who created the "ghastly scene" as Tokutomi Sohō's newspaper offices burned down in September 1903?[17] They too, to a surprising degree, were *hinmin*, angry that Tokutomi had supported the government's alleged sellout in the negotiations ending the Russo-Japanese War. Even the poorest urbanites felt enough of a stake in society to engage in public activities designed to force changes in the body politic. They may not have lived as comfortably as their middle-class peers; they certainly felt excluded and discriminated against. But that did not keep them from seeing themselves as integral parts of the urban whole.

Before turning to a final question that has propelled this work—whether the *hinmin* were "ordinary" people—another comparative issue demands a brief detour. To wit: what can be learned about the late Meiji *hinmin* by comparing their experience with the new poverty that has captured journalists' and scholars' attention in recent decades? Poverty largely vanished from public discourse during Japan's period of high growth following the mid-1960s. Prosperity seemed permanent, riches were for everyone, Japan had become egalitarian. Then the markets crashed at the beginning of the 1990s. The bubble burst, and a quarter century of economic downturn swept away the euphoria. While the causes and extent of the downturn are beyond the scope of this study, there is no gainsaying the re-emergence of poverty as a fact. Lifetime employment declined after the 1990s, labor regulations were curtailed, "nonregular" part-time or contractual labor soared. An international study in 2006 found that "the rate of relative poverty in Japan is now one of the highest" among OECD (Organization for Economic Cooperation and Development) countries, noting that nonregular employment had doubled in a decade to more than 30 percent of the workforce. In 2009, only seven of the thirty-five OECD countries had greater income gaps between rich and poor. And by 2014, contractual and part-time workers topped 40 percent. "Working poor" had become a standard category in economic discussions.[18]

The new poverty resembled late Meiji hardship in numerous ways. Divorce rates rose after the 1990s, to levels approaching the late Meiji years. As in Meiji, children and young employees were among the hardest hit, with nearly 55 percent of children in single-parent families living in relative poverty in 2012; a full thirty thousand children had no health insurance, even though Japan boasts universal health coverage.[19] Homelessness reappeared, with street dwellers consigned to "a jail without bars" in urban parks and station stairways. The gap between the working poor and the more affluent classes rose, and with it the sense of separateness that had marked the Meiji slums. Nishizawa Akihiko of Tōyō University argues that the official and corporate establishment worked consciously, as it had a century earlier, to "nihilate" the poor, keeping indigents invisible. Official policy, she said, amounted to "nihilation by dispersal, segregation, and image manipulation" designed to give Tokyo a "civilized appearance."[20] Another observer, Scott North of Osaka University, echoed the words of the Meiji city reformer Seki Hajime when he saw in the new poverty-inducing policies an imposition of "the common sense of the capitalist class upon the workers."[21]

At the same time, twenty-first century *hinkon* provided contrasts that make dramatically clear just how stark Meiji slum life was. For one thing, there are no sprawling Meiji-style slums today. Most *hinminkutsu* had disappeared by the 1930s, partly because many original residents had moved out, toward better lives, and partly because officials designed policies to eradicate slums, especially after the 1923 earthquake. Although poverty concentrations and cheap inns exist today and tent camps of homeless people appear at times,[22] there are no Nago-chō or Samegahashi-style slums. The government's nihilation philosophy has combined with economic forces to keep today's poor more dispersed. For another, basic schooling is now universally available. Impoverished children may not be as likely as their peers to get an advanced or quality education, but neither are they likely to be illiterate; in the twenty-first century, roughly 90 percent of poor children went on to high school compared to 98.4 percent in the overall population.[23]

Today's welfare system handles the poor differently too. There was no safety network in late Meiji cities for any but the wholly destitute and family-less. Even today, welfare programs are limited, focusing on making sure a person has exhausted every avenue for finding work and granting assistance primarily to the elderly, the sick, and children. But while the working poor receive limited help, the contrast to the Meiji years is sharp. Not only is there a welfare (*seikatsu hogo*) act, there are numerous social assistance programs in the form of child care, pensions, and national health insurance. As Iwata Masami of Nihon Joshi University puts it, the postwar system is based not on specific genres of "lonely souls" but on the concepts that "the poor in general are to be judged only by their living standards" and that assistance should be applied universally. A Homeless Self-Reliance Support Law in 2002 provided for shelters and significantly reduced the numbers of official homeless from 25,296 in 2003 to 7,508 in 2014.[24]

The most important departure from Meiji norms may be the shift in public attitudes toward class and poverty. It has been clear in this study that class-based stereotyping was nearly universal in the *hinmin* era: poor people were unworthy. The term *kasō shakai* itself announced that some classes were less worthy than others. The defeat in World War II, the influence of the 1947 constitution, and the egalitarian orientation of postwar education appear, however, to have fundamentally changed national attitudes. Stereotypes have not disappeared, nor has class consciousness. But poverty is less likely today to be seen as someone's just due than as a failure in the system or bad luck. The postwar years have produced a lively civil society, with ideas such as equality and citizen rights kept at the forefront by the schools and more than eighty thousand citizen-led nonprofit organizations. One danger in these attitudinal changes, argues Abe Aya of Tokyo Metropolitan University's Research Center for Child and Adolescent Poverty, is a citizenry "blinded to poverty by the myth of equality." But it is encouraging nonetheless that, as the political scientist Jeff Kingston notes, the public discussions of the newly poor—the "winners" and "losers"—have provoked "considerable turmoil" in "a society that values egalitarian ideals."[25] Poverty is taken seriously today as a public problem to be solved, not ignored as the victim's fault.

A final question revolves around the questions of ordinariness. Were the late Meiji *hinmin* a different breed of people or were they simply ordinary people down on their luck? The answer seemed clear in the era's popular images: they were different. And a great deal of evidence backed up that view. Rickshaw pullers did commit more crimes per capita than average urbanites. Parents did teach their children how to pickpocket or beg. Poor people did live in dismal places that filled "the air with noxious odours."[26] Claims that factory workers engaged in "extremely lustful activities" were not figments of the imagination; neither were Yokoyama's "lazy, slothful members of the lowest stratum."[27] Dysfunctional people, psychopaths, or homeless people were fairly easy to find. So were those exemplary types who "proved" that anyone who studied and worked hard enough would get ahead. No matter the stereotype, there was evidence to support it.

Anecdotes do not in themselves sustain broad social patterns though. For every *hinmin* failing, one could have found equivalents in the middle class. If petty theft and pickpocketing abounded among slum dwellers, more substantial crimes such as corruption and the refusal to pay living wages prevailed in the rich classes. The writers who damned the "lustfulness" of factory workers early in the 1900s also bemoaned sexual wantonness among "young and hot blooded" male students who, in Kinoshita Naoe's words, "easily fall into the temptation and seek very unhealthy forms of love."[28] The irritating hijinks of rag pickers' children along city thoroughfares were no more damaging to social order than the delinquency of middle-school gangs at the turn of the century.[29] And on the coin's other side, the charity of a rickshaw puller helping out a hapless boy from the provinces and of needy *hinminkutsu* families giving food to even more needy neighbors had their counterparts in middle-class benefactors who devoted their lives and money to charity. Neither stereotypes nor extremes provided much insight into the question of whether the *hinmin* as a class were ordinary Japanese or something wholly other.

To pursue that question, one must turn away from anecdotes and focus on the commonplace, the day-in and day-out lives of the majority of the cities' poor. There the answers abound. The one way *hinmin* were not like their more affluent peers was economic. By definition, hardship set them apart from those who monopolized the public narratives. In most other aspects of life, the experiences and attitudes of the *kasō shakai* replicated those of the rest of the population, often to a surprising degree. They worked as hard as their affluent fellows, sometimes harder. They read newspapers, joined demonstrations, flocked to markets and festivals, shopped for the cheapest goods, and celebrated holidays, just as everyone else did. Their world, in the view of Miyamoto Tsuneichi, "was surprisingly expansive."[30] And their skill in finding ways to survive in desperate circumstances, in what Matsubara called the *hindaigaku,* or college of the poor, from which one must "graduate with honors . . . or die,"[31] suggested intelligence levels at least on a par with their more comfortable peers. Even the causes of their poverty mirrored the factors that made the middle classes better off; in both cases, economic realities sprang more from external conditions like birthplace and labor opportunities than from individual worth.

The best illustration of ordinariness probably lay in the aura of hope and progress that permeated most *hinmin* households on most days. Living in a blindered present, the early poverty journalists failed as a rule to recognize this. For them, the *kasō shakai* constituted a static class, a largely intractable creation of industrialization and urbanization. When Matsubara waxed eloquent about the *hindaigaku,* he was talking about survival within the slums, not about escape or transcendence. But as these pages have shown repeatedly, the longer look revealed a poor population moving forward, even if not at the speed of their sugar plantation relatives. In Nakagawa's view, change was possible because most people in the *kasō shakai* saw themselves not as lower-class but simply as poor, meaning they did not accept their situation as unchangeable. Many fought to get their children into school; even more scrimped to save a few sen a month; families worked out plans to buy small appliances; they dreamed of better days and their outlooks became increasingly family-centered as the years passed. The result was that within a decade after the end of the Meiji era, the majority of wives no longer worked away from home. And by then surveyors had begun using "*yōhogo setai*" (primary family) rather than "*hinminkutsu*" as the basic unit for studying poor neighborhoods, a sign of an evolution in the structures and worldview of the very poor.[32] Even Yokoyama, who had focused at first on how different *hinmin* were from other Japanese, was ready to declare in an article on New Year's celebrations in 1909 that "there is no difference" between *hinmin* and others. During this season, he said, poor families might limit their meals to two a day or eat just a pair of *mochi* rice cakes instead of three so that they could get a kimono from the pawn shop for their child. Why did they make such a choice? "It would have seemed strange to a baldheaded landlord," he said, "but from the standpoint of parental love, it was not surprising at all," because, after all, "*hinmin* are no different at New Year than ordinary people."[33]

Another way of putting this is to emphasize that being poor or destitute did not rob the vast majority of the *hinmin* of their basic humanity. Dehumanizing insults from their middle-class fellows stung but they did not kill. Inhumanly low incomes created anxiety and depression, sometimes even crime, but they also inspired persistence and creativity. Poor people knew the pain of not being able to give children the education they merited, as well as the anguish of having too little space and not enough food. They feared grasping landlords, mean-spirited bosses, untreatable illnesses, and capricious authorities. Day upon day, they wondered, in Matsubara's words, if "the gods have forsaken the poor."[34] But their reactions to all these things were impressively, yet predictably, human. The bottom line was that most of them simply refused to give up or to remove themselves from society, even in the short run. They kept working, changing jobs when something potentially better showed itself, finding little ways to save a few yen and to fight the system. On holidays, they celebrated. They faced the constant hardships and occasional triumphs with a resilience that defied stereotypes. Like ordinary human beings, they took what life gave them, and, across the years, they moved slowly forward. They were, in other words, quite ordinary, though often in an extraordinary way.

Introduction

1. Anonymous inscription, wall of Elmina slave castle, Ghana, observed by author, September 15, 2011.

2. Yokoyama Gennosuke, *Meiji fugō shi* (2013), foreword.

3. The term *kasō shakai* was used by officials and some scholars in the 1890s but not by society generally; it included all of the various poor groups. See Nakagawa Kiyoshi, "Senzen ni okeru toshi kasō no tenkai, jō," *Mita Gakkai Zasshi* (June 1978), 68.

4. Yokoyama Gennosuke, in Eiji Yutani, "'*Nihon no Kaso Shakai*' of Gennosuke Yokoyama" (1985), 184–185 (hereafter cited as Yokoyama (Yutani)). The book was initially published in 1899. Yokoyama's first article at *Mainichi*, on December 8, 1894, was about the failure of the Sino-Japanese War to benefit rural workers. His relationship with *Mainichi* is unclear after 1899; he said he remained a "friend of the paper" (*shayū*) until the mid-1900s, but his byline ceased after 1899. Tachibana Yūichi, *Hyōden Yokoyama Gennosuke* (1977), 41–45, 64.

5. "Historical Statistics of Japan," Population Chart 2–5, Statistics Bureau, Ministry of Internal Affairs and Communications, Government of Japan, http://www.stat.go.jp/english/data/chouki/02.htm.

6. Data for this paragraph from Andrew Gordon, *Labor and Imperial Democracy in Modern Japan* (1991), 18, 70, and Sheldon Garon, *The State and Labor in Modern Japan* (1987), 9.

7. Aoyagi Junrō, ed. *Meiji kyūjūkyūnen: sesō jiken* (1935); the stories about electricity and telephones are on page 90.

8. Takeo Yazaki, *Social Change and the City in Japan: From Earliest Times Through the Industrial Revolution* (1968), 363.

9. Sally Ann Hastings, *Neighborhood and Nation in Tokyo, 1905–1937* (1995), 15.

10. His work is described as a model for social science researchers in Chubachi Masayoshi and Koji Taira, "Poverty in Modern Japan: Perceptions and Realities," in *Japanese Industrialization and its Social Consequences*, ed. Hugh Patrick and L. Meissner (1976), 401. They are referred to as "poverty explorers" by Koji Taira in "Urban Poverty, Ragpickers, and the 'Ants Village' in Tokyo," *Economic Development and Change* (January 1969), 156.

11. Sakurada and the *Jiji* and *Chōya* works are reprinted with slight revisions in Nishida Taketoshi, ed., *Toshi kasō shakai: Meiji zenki rōdō jijō* (1949). Also see Kida Jun'ichirō, *Tokyo no kasō shakai: Meiji kara shūsen made* (1990), 31–38, for material on Sakurada. The *Jiji* series (October 11, 18, 25, and November 1, 22, 29, 1896) and *Hōchi* series ("Sakkon hinminkutsu," 20 installments, November 13—December 11, 1897) are available in Nakagawa Kiyoshi, ed., *Meiji Tokyo kasō seikatsu shi* (1994), 90–187, as are extensive excerpts from Sakurada, 37–76. For a regional report on poverty, see Tsuchida Hirotoshi, *Hinmin kyūjo ron* (Asahimachi: Tsuchida Hirotoshi, 1902). For a list of the early works on poverty, see Tachibana, *Hyōden*, 100.

12. Kida, *Tokyo no kasō shakai*, 39.

13. For Matsubara, see analysis of Tsubouchi Yūsan in Matsubara Iwagorō, *Saiankoku no Tokyo* (2015 reprint), 160. Yokoyama has been called the founder of the "literature of realism" (*riarizumu bungaku*). Tachibana, *Hyōden*, 5.

14. For the former ("unimaginable"), see Anon., "Fuka hinmin no shinkyō," *Chōya Shinbun* (March—April 1886), reprinted in Nakagawa, ed., *Kasō seikatsu shi,* 14; the series said the poor ate "food that ought to be for animals" (28). Nakagawa sees Matsubara as typical of the human-but-pitiable state of reporting.

15. Nakagawa Kiyoshi, *Gendai no seikatsu mondai* (2011), 3–35 (quote, 35).

16. Sōseki Natsume, *The Miner* (1988), 93.

17. Tanizaki Jun'ichiro, *Childhood Years: A Memoir* (1988), 137, 50, 133.

18. David Ambaras, *Bad Youth: Juvenile Delinquency and the Politics of Everyday Life in Modern Japan* (2006), 2, 33, 63. Ambaras' new "middle class," which had as much an intellectual role as an economic one, differs from the more purely economic *"shin chūkansō"* that Nakagawa sees emerging in the early 1900s.

19. Nakagawa Kiyoshi, ed., *Nihon no toshi kasō* (1985), 354.

20. See his incomplete *Bimon gimon joron* (1888), 11, discussed in Maeda Ai, "Utopia of the Prisonhouse: A Reading of *In Darkest Tokyo,*" in *Text and the City: Essays on Japanese Modernity,* ed. Maeda Ai (2004), 48.

21. Maeda, "Utopia," 50, 46.

22. See Nakagawa, *Nihon no toshi,* 63, and Tsubouchi Yūsan in Matsubara, *Saiankoku* (2015), 163. "Wretchedness": William Booth, *In Darkest England, and the Way Out* (1890), preface.

23. Naoya Shiga, *A Dark Night's Passing* (1976), 16.

24. Matsubara, *Saiankoku no Tokyo* (1893, 1988), 25, 9.

25. Jun'ichirō Tanizaki, "The Secret," *The Gourmet Club: A Sextet* (2001), 49.

26. Kaburagi Kiyokata, *Meiji no Tokyo* (1989), 118.

27. Ambaras, *Bad Youth,* 5.

28. *Yorozu Chōhō,* January 4, 1900, 3; April 13, 1900, 3.

29. *Niroku Shinpō,* 1900: murder of young woman (February 5), blind man (February 23), "bad priest" (February 10), pickpocketing (February 8), attempted rape (April 9), series on prostitutes (April 10–18), musician's suicide (May 13); all were on page three.

30. The persistence of this equation of poverty and crime can be seen even in the Japanese library classification system, which places social pathologies in section 368, lumping together such topics as Mafia, rape, prostitution, crime, evil deeds, juvenile delinquency—*and poverty*; for the Nippon Decimal Classification system, which was developed in 1956, see http://www.asahi-net.or.jp/~ax2s-kmtn/ref/ndc/e_ndc3.html#ndc36.

31. Matsubara Iwagoro, *Sketches of Humble Life in the Capital of Japan* (1897), 71. This is an abridged translation of Matsubara's *Saiankoku no Tokyo,* true to the spirit of the original but not always to the exact wording.

32. W. Dean Kinzley, "Japan's Discovery of Poverty: Changing Views of Poverty and Social Welfare in the Nineteenth Century," *Journal of Asian History* (1988), 8.

33. Yokoyama (Yutani), 178.

34. Ambaras, *Bad Youth,* 27, 38.

35. Kathleen Uno, *Passages to Modernity: Motherhood, Childhood, and Social Reform in Early Twentieth Century Japan* (1999), 63.

36. *Yorozu Chōhō:* March 25, 1900, 3 (troublesome son); July 18, 1900, 2 (carpenters).

37. Yokoyama (Yutani), 199 (drinking husband), 180 (rickshaw pullers), 268–269 (textile workers).

38. Hastings, *Neighborhood and Nation,* 20. Japan's earliest efforts included a public relief agency (*kōseikai*) in Osaka in 1912; in 1918, the city began a plan that assigned volunteers to the city's poor neighborhoods to identify those most in need of assistance; see Kingo Tamai, "Images of the Poor in an Official Survey of Osaka, 1923–1926," *Continuity and Change* (2000), 102–103.

39. Ronald P. Loftus, *Telling Lives: Women's Self-Writing in Modern Japan* (2004), 34.

40. *Seinen: The Rising Generation,* December 1, 1905, 110 (hereafter *Seinen RG*).

41. All these examples come from *Shūkan Heimin Shinbun,* April 10, 1904, 2.

42. *Seinen RG,* July 15, 1906, 175.

43. Robert Lyons Danly, *In the Shade of Spring Leaves: The Life of Higuchi Ichiyō With Nine of Her Best Short Stories* (1984), 262. The story title, "Takekurabe" in the original, also has been translated as "Growing Up."

44. Yokoyama (Yutani), 200–201.

45. See Ambaras, *Bad Youth,* 61.

46. Paulo Freire, *Pedagogy of the Oppressed* (2007), 131.

47. Harada Tōfū, *Hinminkutsu* (1902), 109.

48. Yokoyama (Yutani), 183.

49. Sōseki, *Miner,* 40.

50. Fukuzawa Yukichi, *An Encouragement of Learning* (1969), 19.

51. English comment, *Tokyo Pakku,* October 20, 1909, 178.

52. Taira, "Urban Poverty," 156.

53. Tanizaki, *Childhood Years,* 3.

54. *Yorozu Chōhō,* March 1, 1898, in Kanzō Uchimura, *The Complete Works of Kanzō Uchimura,* vol. 6 (1973), 215.

55. Jeffrey E. Hanes, *The City as Subject: Seki Hajime and the Reinvention of Modern Osaka* (2002), 183, 185.

56. Shimazaki Tōson, *Chikuma River Sketches* (1991), 80.

57. Yokoe Tesseki, in Michael Lewis, *A Life Adrift: Soeda Azembō, Popular Song, and Modern Mass Culture in Japan* (2009), 65.

58. *Yūbin Hōchi Shinbun,* February 28, 1880, quoted in Kinzley, "Discovery of Poverty," 12.

59. Quoted in Hanes, *City as Subject,* 141, 140.

60. Matsubara, *Saiankoku,* 104.

61. Ibid., 33, 30.

62. A mine owner in Naoe Kinoshita, *Pillar of Fire* (1904, trans. 1972), 57.

63. Kinzley, "Discovery of Poverty," 24.

64. Teruhito Sako and Suzanne K. Steinmetz, eds., *Japanese Family and Society: Words from Tongo Takebe, A Meiji Era Sociologist* (2007), 140.

65. Among others, see Kagawa Toyohiko, *Hinmin shinri no kenkyū* (1915); Yanagita Kunio, *Meiji Taishō shi sesō hen* (1993); E. Patricia Tsurumi, *Factory Girls: Women in the Thread Mills of Meiji Japan* (1990); Mikiso Hane, *Peasants, Rebels, Women, & Outcastes: The Underside of Modern Japan* (1982, 2016); Nimura Kazuo, *The Ashio Riot of 1907* (1997); Hastings, *Neighborhood and Nation*; Lewis, *Life Adrift*; Irokawa Daikichi, *The Culture of the Meiji Period* (1985) and *Shinpen Meiji seishin shi* (1973).

66. Typical is Juro Teranishi's *Evolution of the Economic System in Japan* (2005), which lists "the rapid impoverishment of the rural sector" (150) among the failures of the Meiji-Taishō economic system but is silent about urban poverty. Similarly, E. Sydney Crawcour's "Economic Change in the Nineteenth Century," in volume 5 of the authoritative *Cambridge History of Japan* (569–617), has next to nothing to say about poverty or commoner-level economics. Deborah J. Milly, *Poverty, Equality, and Growth* (1999), an exception, concentrates on the post—World War II era. She notes, as background, that two principles guided Japan's welfare policies early in the 1900s: (1) the state itself was responsible for "programs that addressed severe need," and (2) a "very uncompromising distinction" was made between "able-bodied and non-able-bodied poor," resulting in only in-kind support for the working poor, 21.

67. Nakagawa spent his career first at Keiō University in Tokyo, then at Dōshisha University in Kyoto. His most pertinent works for this study include *Nihon no toshi kasō*, 1985; "Senzen ni okeru toshi kasō no tenkai, jō," *Mita Gakkai Zasshi*, June 1978, 58–104; *Gendai no seikatsu mondai* (2011), "Ambitions, 'Family-Centredness' and Expenditure Patterns in a Changing Urban Class Structure: Tokyo in the Early Twentieth Century," *Continuity and Change* (2000), 77–98; and *Meiji Tokyo kasō seikatsu shi* (1994). For a journalistic treatment of the Meiji *kasō shakai* and analyses of Yokoyama and Matsubara, see Kida, *Tokyo no kasō shakai*, as well as his *Tokyo kasō shakai* (2000).

68. For a discussion of Booth's and Marx's categories, see Masami Iwata and Akihiko Nishizawa, *Poverty and Social Welfare in Japan* (2008), 4–5. Also see Booth, *Darkest England*, 24.

69. From the last Meiji years onward, the poor came more often to be called *saimin*, a term that had more derogatory connotations, but *hinmin* was most often used in the period of our study. Another term for the poor was *kasōmin* (lower-class people). All of these terms, including *kasō shakai*, were used vaguely, without clear differences in their meaning or delineations of specific poor groups; the term *kasō shakai* also was used by Matsubara. See Yokoyama (Yutani), 27–28.

70. Nakagawa, "Senzen ni okeru, jō," 68–69, gives 12.7 percent in 1900. Also see Harada, *Hinminkutsu*, 8, and Hiromichi Ishizuka, "The Slum Dwellings and the Urban Renewal Scheme in Tokyo, 1868–1923" (June 1981), 187. In *Gendai no seikatsu mondai* (47), Nakagawa estimates that a tenth of Tokyoites in the 1890s lived in the slums. Using government surveys, Chubachi and Taira estimate that by 1920, just 11 percent of Tokyoites were truly poor, with the "ghettoized poor" constituting roughly 4.2 percent of the population. "Poverty in Modern Japan," 400. The Meiji scholar Maeda Masana estimated in 1883 that 57 percent of all Japanese were in the lower classes, in contrast to 43 percent in upper and middle classes. Milly, *Poverty*, 212–213.

71. Nipponbashi, located in the old Nago-chō, today is a shopping district known for electrical goods. Just south of the Namba area, Kamagasaki in Nishinari-ku is a center today for day laborers, the homeless, and the poor.

72. A fourth, Yamabushi-chō in Shitaya, sometimes was included; see Hita Sei, "Hinminkutsu," *Fūzoku Gahō* (November 10, 1898), 9.

73. Kagawa, in *Hinmin shinri*, quoted in Edward Fowler, "The Buraku in Modern Japanese Literature: Texts and Contexts," *Journal of Japanese Studies* (Winter 2000): 13.

74. Survey of Nago-chō, 1888, in Nishida, *Toshi kasō shakai*, 231–232.

75. For charts on work types, see Nakagawa, "Senzen ni okeru, jō," 88–90; Mori Kiichi, *Nihon no kindaika to rōdōsha kaikyū: kaikyūzō no rekishiteki tenkai* (1979), 73.

76. Yokoyama, *Nihon no kasō shakai*, 187.

77. By way of comparison, surveyors estimated that London had 20,000 "out-of-works" in 1888, which amounts to about 2 percent of the 993,000 people whom Booth counted as "very poor" or worse. *Darkest England*, 22, 32–34.

78. Surveys in Nakagawa, "Senzen ni okeru, jō," 75, 103. The former were taken in 1899 and 1902; he bases the latter on the Home Ministry's surveys *Saimin chōsa tōkeihyō* (1912), 93–94, and *Saimin chōsa tōkeihyō tekiyō* (1912–1913), 144–145. See also Taira, "Urban Poverty," 165. A Taishō-era study in Osaka found illness as the main cause of dire poverty. Tamai, "Images of the Poor," 113.

79. *Taiyō*, November 5, 1901, 5–6.

80. In the 1912 Home Ministry survey, only 5 percent of the poor blamed low wages for their plight. Nakagawa, "Senzen ni okeru, jō," 103.

81. Ibid. In the same 1912 study, 6.7 percent of the poor cited large families as the main cause of poverty.

82. Ibid., 70 (1880s and 1898), 82 (late Meiji data); also see his "Ambitions," 80.

83. Kawashima Yasuyoshi, *Fujin kateiran kotohajime* (1996), 64.

84. Fabian Drixler, *Mabiki: Infanticide and Population Growth in Eastern Japan, 1660–1950* (2013), 23 ff, 130–132; Drixler argues that wide acceptance of infanticide and abortion played a major role in holding down Japan's population during the Tokugawa era, with infanticide in eastern Japan not dropping substantially until after the turn of the twentieth century. As late as 1890, 30 to 50 percent of babies were "still-born" in some rural areas (233–234).

85. Matsubara, *Saiankoku*, 26.

86. Nakagawa, "Senzen ni okeru, jō," 85–86.

87. Material on food from Matsubara, *Saiankoku*, 143–144 (horsemeat and soba, which cost 1.5 sen a bowl), 116 (drink and puff), 43 (scuffles); *Taiyō*, November 5, 1901, 5–6 (low-quality rice); Yokoyama (Yutani), 193 (bonito flakes, drinking).

88. Anon., "Fuka hinmin no shinkyō," *Chōya Shinbun*, 1886, in Nakagawa, *Kasō seikatsu shi*, 24.

89. Nakagawa, "Senzen ni okeru, jō," 93.

90. Ibid., 91.

91. *Shūkan Heimin Shinbun*, December 3, 1903, 2.

92. *Taiyō*, "Omise kozō tedai no genjō," February 5, 1901, 205–208.

93. Matsubara, *Saiankoku*, 57, 115.

94. Nakagawa, "Ambitions," 78, 84. He argues that by the early 1900s, the *kasō shakai* of the 1890s had become differentiated into three groups: old poor, an expanding factory-worker class, and the new middle class. This point is corroborated by the salary charts in Mori, *Nihon no kindaika*, 81. For a discussion of housing changes precipitated by the rise of heavy industry in late Meiji, see Ishizuka, "Slum Dwellings," 178, 185.

95. Nakagawa, "Senzen ni okeru, jō," 101.

96. For Osaka, Richard Torrance, "Literacy and Literature in Osaka, 1890–1940," *Journal of Japanese Studies* (Winter 2005), 35. For Tokyo, Yamamoto Taketoshi, "Meiji sanjūnendai zenhan no shinbun Nihon no dokusha sō," *Shinbun Gaku Hyōron* (March 1967), 123, drawing on *Teikoku tōkei nenkan*. Official figures are regarded by scholars as likely to have been inflated.

97. Tokyo formally ended fees for schools in 1898, but it took several years for the proscription to be enforced. By 1906, the city had four night schools to facilitate those who had to work during the day; by 1912, the number had increased to twenty-one. Nakagawa, *Nihon no toshi*, 184.

98. Just four years were required until 1907.

99. Nakagawa, "Senzen ni okeru, jō, " 85; Torrance, *Literacy and Literature*, 43.

100. It bears noting that much of the primary literature used in this study came from people influenced by Marxism. Matsubara had socialist leanings; Yokoyama considered himself a socialist; the *Heimin Shinbun*, which provided regular reports on poor people, was Japan's first avowedly Marxist paper.

101. As late as 1920, the rural areas made up more than 80 percent of the Japanese population; see "2–9 Population of Cities," "2–5 Population by Prefecture and Sex," "Historical Statistics of Japan," Statistics Bureau, Ministry of Internal Affairs and Communications, Government of Japan: http://www.stat.go.jp/english/data/chouki/02.htm.

102. James Lasdun, "Diary," *London Review of Books* 28, no. 3 (February 9, 2006): 34.

103. Nakagawa, "Senzen ni okeru, jō," 72. He says their mutuality was captured in the phrase *dōrui sōai*, which translates as kindred or mutual love.

104. Simon Partner, *Toshié: A Story of Village Life in Twentieth-Century Japan* (2004), xiii.

105. See Irokawa Daikichi, *The Culture of the Meiji Period* (1985), 191.

106. Cited in Barbara Ehrenreich, *Dancing in the Streets: A History of Collective Joy* (2006), 2–3: from W. O. E. Oesterley, *The Sacred Dance* (Cambridge: Cambridge University Press, 1923), 128–129.

107. Matsubara, *Saiankoku*, 49–50.

108. See Sakurada Kurabu, ed., *Akiyama Teisuke den*, vol. 1 (1977), 157–159, 246.

109. Shimazaki, *Chikuma River*, 161.

110. Edward Fowler, *San'ya Blues: Laboring Life in Contemporary Tokyo* (1996), 47.

111. James C. Scott, *Domination and the Arts of Resistance: Hidden Transcripts* (1990), 3–4 (public v. hidden transcripts); v (farts).

112. Freire, *Pedagogy of the Oppressed*, 14, 32, 156.

113. Ibid., 43, 40.

114. Ibid., 48.

115. Ibid., 74.

116. The core of this criticism was captured in Karel van Wolferen, *The Enigma of Japanese Power* (London: Papermac, 1990), but the ineptness of government has been a major theme of historians in every era, a point elaborated in Cameron McLauchlan, "Interview with James Huffman: Incompetent Leaders No Hindrance to Progress," *The Daily Yomiuri*, January 1, 2011, 8.

Chapter One: The Slum Setting

1. Yasunari Kawabata, *The Scarlet Gang of Asakusa* (2005), 30, 44.

2. The names here are fictitious, but the work and economic details are factual, derived from the description of an unnamed but actual *kozukai* family in *Taiyō*, November 5, 1901, 5–6, and December 5, 1901, 5–6. When suppositions are made, based on facts about similar families, the sources of those suppositions are cited.

3. See Nakagawa Kiyoshi, "Senzen ni okeru toshi kasō no tenkai, jō," *Mita Gakkai Zasshi* (June 1978), 91.

4. *Taiyō*, April 5, 1902, 4.

5. Description of dock workers in Tokyo's Fukagawa region. Junichi Saga, *Confessions of a Yakuza: A Life in Japan's Underworld* (1991), 16.

6. A sen was a hundredth of a yen.

7. For a discussion of this improvement, see especially Kiyoshi Nakagawa, "Ambitions, 'Family-Centredness' and Expenditure Patterns in a Changing Urban Class Structure: Tokyo in the Early Twentieth Century," *Continuity and Change* (2000), 77–98.

8. Kawabata, *Scarlet Gang*, 44.

9. See George De Vos and Hiroshi Wagatsuma, *Japan's Invisible Race: Caste in Culture and Personality* (1966), 39, 100, 115–125.

10. Takeo Yazaki, *Social Change and the City in Japan: From Earliest Times Through the Industrial Revolution* (1968), 391.

11. Nagatsuka Takashi, *The Soil: A Portrait of Rural Life in Meiji Japan* (1989), 48.

12. Ian Takeo Moriyama, *Imingaisha: Japanese Emigration Companies and Hawaii 1894–1908* (1985), 4–5.

13. Eiji Yutani, "'Nihon no Kaso Shakai' of Gennosuke Yokoyama" (1985), 327–328 (hereafter Yokoyama (Yutani)).

14. Yokoyama (Yutani), 475.

15. *Seinen: The Rising Generation* (hereafter *Seinen RG*), December 1, 1905, 110. For further discussion of these movements, see Yanagita Kunio, *Meiji Taishō shi sesō hen* 2 (1976), 77ff.

16. *Dai jūichi kai Tokyo shi tōkei nenpyō: 1914* (1914), 94–95.

17. *Tokyo shi tōkei zuhyō* (1914), chart 2 (pages unnumbered). The "poor wards" were Honjo, Shitaya, Fukagawa, and Asakusa. Asakusa, which already was huge, saw a smaller increase; the other three wards grew by an average of 411 per thousand.

18. Nakagawa Kiyoshi, "*Toshi seikatsu no tenkai: hen'yō to risuku,*" in Fujita Hiroo and Urano Masaki, eds., *Toshi shakai to risuku: yutaka na seikatsu o motomete* (2005), 75–78. For further discussion of gender concentrations, see Nakagawa, "Ambitions," 79. In each year after 1898, births rates were higher than deaths, and the gap grew steadily, if erratically; by 1912, the city's 53,216 live births exceeded deaths by more than 15,800. Some scholars question whether these figures exaggerate the imbalance, but Nakagawa argues that at the very least they show a trend of male statistical preponderance early on and more marriages as the years passed. For further birth/death data, see *Tokyo shi tōkei zuhyō* (1914), chart 8 (pages unnumbered).

19. Inoue Yasushi, *Shirobamba: A Childhood in Old Japan* (1991), 61, 66.

20. Matsubara Iwagorō, *Saiankoku no Tokyo* (2015 reprint), 55–56.

21. Nakagawa, interview, March 27, 2014.

22. Yanagita, *Meiji Taishō shi,* vol. 2, 164; he gave two reasons for emigration from the village: the quest for a larger world and economic need. See also Kamishima Jirō, *Kindai Nihon no seishin kōzō* (1961), 32.

23. Yokoyama (Yutani), 384.

24. Makoto Kumazawa, *Portraits of the Japanese Workplace* (1966), 26.

25. English column, *Yorozu Chōhō,* January 1, 1900, 2.

26. See Shibamura Atsuki, "Kyodai toshi no keisei," in Narita Ryūichi, *Toshi to minshū* (1993), 157–158, and Suzuki Hiroyuki, *Toshi e, Nihon no kindai* (1999), 161–179.

27. Nakagawa Kiyoshi, *Gendai no seikatsu mondai* (2011), 47.

28. Jeffery E. Hanes, *The City as Subject: Seki Hajime and the Reinvention of Modern Osaka* (2002), 182, from Suzuki Umeshirō, "Osaka Nago-chō hinminkutsu shisatsu ki," *Jiji Shinpō,* 1888. Suzuki's work is reprinted in Nishida Taketoshi, ed., *Toshi kasō shakai: Meiji zenki rōdō jijō* (1949). Also see Yokoyama (Yutani), 539.

29. Nakagawa Kiyoshi, ed. *Nihon no toshi kasō* (1985), 28. For a chart of these slums, see Hiromichi Ishizuka, "The Slum Dwellings and the Urban Renewal Scheme in Tokyo, 1868–1923," *The Developing Economies* (June 1981), 174.

30. The term *shitamachi,* which has no precise geographical demarcations, dated back to the Tokugawa centuries, when the artisans and merchants lived in Edo's lowland areas to the east of the castle, while the more aristocratic classes lived in the hilly areas (Yamanote) west of the castle. While the nature of *shitamachi* changed in the second half of Meiji, when it became home to so much of the new laboring class, the term itself continued to be used, as it does to this day. For a colorful summary, see Edward Seidensticker, *Low City, High City: Tokyo from Edo to the Earthquake* (1983), 8–11.

31. Data largely from Nakagawa, "Senzen ni okeru, jō," 68, 77–78. The wards made up 39 percent of Tokyo's population. Not surprisingly, homeless people also were concentrated in these wards, with the numbers of homeless people compared to those with lodgings ranging from 9.7 percent in Fukagawa to 20.8 percent in Asakusa. Population data (1912) from *Tokyo shi tōkei zuhyō* (1914), chart 19 (pages unnumbered); automobile data (April 1, 1913) from *Dai jūichi kai Tokyo shi tōkei nenpyō: 1914,* 761. Rickshaw pullers from 1907 police report: *Keisatsuchō tōkeisho: 1907* (1907), 259. As Koji Taira notes, the slum areas changed again after the end of Meiji, as rising city housing costs pushed poverty regions to the edges of Tokyo. Following the Great Kantō Earthquake in 1923, the three largest Meiji slums—Mannen-

chō in Shitaya, Shin'ami-chō to its south, and Samegahashi just west of the palace—were destroyed and city officials prevented the poor from moving back to those areas: "Urban Poverty, Ragpickers, and the 'Ants Village' in Tokyo," *Economic Development and Change* (January 1969), 157–159.

32. From *Garasudo,* quoted in Marvin Marcus, *Reflections in a Glass Door: Memory and Melancholy in the Personal Writings of Natsume Sōseki* (2009), 45.

33. Yokoyama (Yutani), 159–160.

34. Matsubara Iwagoro, *Sketches of Humble Life in the Capital of Japan* (1897), 39–40; this is a slightly abbreviated, loose translation of Matsubara's *Saiankoku no Tokyo.*

35. Beatrice Webb, Diary, September 14, 1911, London School of Economics Digital Library, 148.

36. *Fūzoku Gahō,* October 25, 1903, 25.

37. Kathleen Uno, *Passages to Modernity: Motherhood, Childhood, and Social Reform in Early Twentieth Century Japan* (1999), 57–58.

38. Maeda Ai, "Their Time as Children: A Study of Higuchi Ichiyō's *Growing Up (Takakurabe),*" trans. Edward Fowler, in Maeda Ai, *Text and the City: Essays on Japanese Modernity* (2004), 119.

39. Edward Fowler, *San'ya Blues: Laboring Life in Contemporary Tokyo* (1996), 14.

40. *Tokyo shi tōkei zuhyō* (1914), chart 6 (pages unnumbered); Tokyo's four densest wards in 1912 were Kanda (717,459 per square *ri*) Asakusa (700,941), Nihonbashi (699,847), and Shitaya (632,616); next were Kyōbashi (509,841), Honjo (505,900), and the more recently developed Fukagawa (356,364); a *ri* equals 2.44 miles, a square *ri* 5.95 square miles. Also see William Johnston, *The Modern Epidemic: A History of Tuberculosis in Japan* (1995), 65.

41. Kumazawa, *Portraits,* 31.

42. Kawabata, *Scarlet Gang,* 21.

43. Yokoyama (Yutani), 169.

44. Matsubara, *Sketches,* 3–4.

45. From his *Saiankoku no Tokyo,* Maeda translation, "Utopia of the Prisonhouse: A Reading of *In Darkest Tokyo,*" in Maeda, *Text and the City* (2004), 50.

46. Matsubara, *Saiankoku,* 7, 49–50.

47. Saga, *Confessions,* 249; Kurosaki Shūsei cartoon, *Fūzoku Gahō,* September 5, 1900, frontispiece.

48. Higuchi Ichiyō, *Growing Up,* in Maeda, "Time as Children," in Maeda, *Text and the City* (2004), 119.

49. Maeda, "Time as Children," in Maeda, *Text and the City* (2004), 121–124 (landscapes); Yazaki, *Social Change,* 450 (paddy fields).

50. *Seinen RG,* March 11, 1906, 260.

51. See Kozo Yamamura, "The Founding of Mitsubishi: A Case Study in Japanese History," in *Critical Readings on the History of Industrialization in Modern Japan,* vol. 2, ed. Christopher Gerteis (2013), 826.

52. The 1902 government survey, Inumaru Giichi, ed., *Shokkō jijō,* vol. 2 (1998), 198, reported that there was "essentially no separation between match factory labor and the poor people's neighborhoods (*buraku*)."

53. Sally Hastings, *Neighborhood and Nation in Tokyo, 1905–1937* (1995), 25–26; Seidensticker, *Low City, High City,* 217.

54. Nakagawa, "Senzen ni okeru, jō," 68, 69; his rickshaw puller/rag picker figure is from city data for 1889.

55. Yokoyama (Yutani), 160–161.

56. Taizo Fujimoto, *The Nightside of Japan* (1915), 1.

57. Quoted in Kawabata, *Scarlet Gang*, 30.

58. Kafū Nagai, "River Sumida," in *A Strange Tale from East of the River and Other Stories* (1965), 21–22.

59. Saga, *Confessions*, 36.

60. Nagai, "River Sumida," 42–43.

61. Basil Hall Chamberlain and W. B. Mason, *A Handbook for Travellers in Japan* (1898), 131, 128.

62. Fujimoto, *Nightside*, 222

63. Kaburagi Kiyokata, *Meiji no Tokyo* (1989), 117.

64. Nagai, "River Sumida," 15.

65. See Aoyagi Junrō, ed., *Meiji kyūjūkyūnen: sesō jiken* (1935), 69.

66. *Tokyo Pakku:* June 1, 1908, 251 (kabuki), May 20, 1911, 230 (circulation of disease).

67. *Taiyō*, September 1910, 23.

68. Nagai, "River Sumida," 20.

69. *Tokyo Pakku*, February 20, 1911, 89; *Seinen RG*, March 1, 1911, 251; Jun'ichiro Tanizaki, *Childhood Years: A Memoir* (1988), 38.

70. Hanes, *City as Subject*, 195.

71. Kaburagi, *Meiji no Tokyo*, 118.

72. Noma Hiroshi, *Seinen no wa*, in Edward Fowler, "The Buraku in Modern Japanese Literature: Texts and Contexts," *Journal of Japanese Studies* (Winter 2000), 38.

73. Webb, Diary, September 14, 1911, 152, regarding slums in Osaka. The slum she visited had a communal bath house (154) and one home had a wooden bathtub outside the front door, with a place under it to heat the water.

74. Ken K. Ito, *Visions of Desire: Tanizaki's Fictional Worlds* (1991), 67.

75. Ibid.

76. The first regulations of buildings for Tokyo's poor finally came in 1907, in a law that limited *nagaya* to twelve apartments per building and set minimum standards for ventilation, water disposal, lighting, and toilets, with penalties for violators; a building code for Tokyo was adopted in 1919. Ishizuka, "Slum Dwellings," 186, 189.

77. From *Sore kara*, quoted in Maeda Ai, "In the Recesses of the High City: On Sōseki's *Gate*," in Maeda, *Text and the City*, 334–335.

78. Saitō Kokubu, "Shiku seigen no yō," *Taiyō*, October 5, 1901, 205–208.

79. Ishizuka, "Slum Dwellings," 191.

80. *Tokyo Pakku*, July 10, 1910, 35.

81. Matsubara, *Sketches*, 40.

82. A. Lloyd, "Yume no Tokyo," *Taiyō*, April 1, 1904, 11. Matsubara disagreed, arguing that the poor were cut off from sunlight. *Saiankoku*, 34.

83. Naoe Kinoshita, *Pillar of Fire* (1972), 59.

84. Sōseki Natsume, *And Then* (1997), 65.

85. Hita Sei, "Hinminkutsu," *Fūzoku Gahō* (November 10, 1898), 9–10.

86. Inumaru, *Shokkō jijō*, vol. 2, 199; rents averaged two yen a month, or six to eight sen a day. Description of 1905 *nagaya*: Nakagawa, *Gendai no seikatsu*, 55.

87. Nakagawa, "Senzen ni okeru, jō," 85. Nakagawa notes that twenty years earlier, it was unheard of for any of the poor to have more than one room, so there was improvement (86); Taira, "Urban Poverty," 161.

88. Matsubara, *Sketches*, 17. Also see Susan B. Hanley, "Urban Sanitation in Preindustrial Japan," *Journal of Interdisciplinary History* (Summer 1987), 23.

89. Nakagawa, "Senzen ni okeru, jō," 86.

90. See Yokoyama (Yutani), 194; Nakagawa, "Senzen in okeru, jō," 62, 77, 86. By the end of Meiji, most Tokyo *saimin* paid between 1 and 3.5 yen a month for rent. Also see Ishizuka, "Slum Dwellings," 183.

91. Kure Ayatoshi, "Tokyo fuka hinmin no jōkyō," in Nakagawa Kiyoshi, ed., *Meiji Tokyo kasō seikatsu shi* (1994), 78.

92. *Tokyo Pakku*, March 1, 1906, 70.

93. *Shūkan Heimin Shinbun*, February 7, 1904, 5.

94. Matsubara, *Saiankoku*, 63.

95. Fowler argues that "flophouse" is a misleading translation of *doya* because it "fails to suggest the *doya* occupant's role as a contributor to—as opposed to a parasite on—the economy." *San'ya Blues*, 44.

96. Masami Iwata and Akihiko Nishizawa, *Poverty and Social Welfare in Japan* (2008), 47. For a description of *kichin'yado* in Osaka's Fukiai region, see Inumaru, *Shokkō jijō*, vol. 2, 199.

97. Yokoyama (Yutani), 204; Aoyagi, *Sesō jiken*, 120. The 1907 figure is from *Keisatsuchō*, 237; the end-of-Meiji figures are from Fujimoto, *Nightside*, 43, which says the second and third largest concentrations of *kichin'yado* were in Asakusa-machi (Asakusa) and Hana-chō (Honjo), respectively. These figures should be taken as rough estimates, since definitions of *kichin'yado* varied. Contending that official surveys understated the real numbers, Yokoyama estimated that the *kichin'yado* averaged 432 sleepers per night, while the police report (*Keisatsuchō*, 223) put the average in the years between 1896 and 1900 at more than 700 a night. Either average suggests that most lodgers stayed for extended periods of time.

98. Kōtoku Shūsui, *Tokyo no kichin'yado*, cited in Yokoyama (Yutani), 58.

99. For Tokyo figures, Aoyagi, *Sesō jiken*, 120; for Osaka, Inumaru, *Shokkō jijō*, vol. 2, 199; the latter notes that three-mat rooms could be obtained in Tokyo for ten to fifteen sen.

100. Fujimoto, *Nightside*, 44–46.

101. Matsubara, *Sketches*, 51.

102. Aoyagi, *Sesō jiken*, 121.

103. Yokoyama (Yutani), 206–208.

104. Matsubara, *Saiankoku*, 7–10, 25; see also his *Sketches*, 8–13. Description of rainy day in Fujimoto, *Nightside*, 45–46.

105. There were few settlement houses until the late 1910s; those that existed largely were run by Western missionary organizations. Konomi Ueki, "The Woman's Movement and the Settlement Movement in Early Twentieth-Century Japan: The Impact of Hull House and Jane Addams on Hiratsuka Raichō," *Kwansei Gakuin University Humanities Review* (2012), 85–92. For the Jiaikan, see Elizabeth Dorn Lublin, *Reforming Japan: The Women's Christian Temperance Union in the Meiji Period* (2010), 21–25.

106. Fujimoto, *Nightside*, 48–52; Hastings, *Neighborhood and Nation*, 29, describes a shelter in Honjo's Wakiyama-chō, which housed "sixty women and children whose husbands and fathers had deserted them."

107. Quotes from Maeda, "Utopia," 50.

Chapter Two: Earning a Living

1. Matsubara Iwagorō, *Saiankoku no Tokyo* (1893), 61–62.

2. See chart in Nishida Taketoshi, ed., *Toshi kasō shakai: Meiji zenki rōdō jijō* (1949), 231–232. He found that 45 percent of rag pickers and 60 percent of matchbox makers were children under the age of fifteen, and that *all* rickshaw pullers were males *over* fifteen.

3. Jun'ichiro Tanizaki, *Childhood Years* (1988); for archery shops, 17.

4. Gu Ayatoshi, "Tokyo fuka hinmin no jōkyō," *Sutachisuchikku Zasshi* (January 20, 1891), in Nakagawa Kiyoshi, ed., *Meiji Tokyo kasō seikatsu shi* (1994), 85.

5. Kawashima Yasuyoshi, *Fujin kateiran kotohajime* (1996), 114–115.

6. Matsubara Iwagoro, *Sketches of Humble Life in the Capital of Japan* (1897), 23; this is a slightly abbreviated, loose translation of Matsubara's *Saiankoku no Tokyo.*

7. *Tokyo fu tōkeisho* (1901), 384–390.

8. See Eiji Yutani, "'Nihon no Kaso Shakai' of Gennosuke Yokoyama" (1985), 23–30 (hereafter Yokoyama (Yutani)). He also included farmers as a broad *kasō shakai* category.

9. Nakagawa Kiyoshi, "Senzen ni okeru toshi kasō no tenkai, jō," *Mita Gakkai Zasshi* (June 1978), 72. Nakagawa also argues that begging was itself a kind of work (interview, March 27, 2014).

10. Takeo Yazaki, *Social Change and the City in Japan: From Earliest Times Through the Industrial Revolution* (1968), 457.

11. Yokoyama (Yutani), 174.

12. See Ann Waswo, *Modern Japanese Society, 1868–1994* (1996), 60.

13. Yokoyama (Yutani), 394, citing tables from the Bureau of Industrial Affairs (Kōmukyoku); *Taiyō,* February 1, 1905, 14. Yokoyama's figures are for factories with more than fifty employees; the *Taiyō* report does not define factory. Also see Yazaki, *Social Change,* 353. For the number of Osaka factories and "Manchester of Japan," Beatrice Webb, Diary, September 14, 1911, London School of Economics Digital Library, 148.

14. "Katō baiin no jikkyō," *Niroku Shinpō,* April 18, 1900.

15. Yazaki, *Social Change,* 457–458.

16. Ariga Nagafumi (1897), quoted in Andrew Gordon, *Labor and Imperial Democracy in Prewar Japan* (1991), 22.

17. *Shūkan Heimin Shinbun,* January 13, 1903, 1.

18. In "Kōjō junshiki," *Tokyo Nichi Nichi Shinbun,* cited in Yokoyama (Yutani), 34.

19. Soeda Juichi, in Sheldon Garon, *The State and Labor in Modern Japan* (1987), 26.

20. Evaluation of Jeffrey E. Hanes, *The City as Subject: Seki Hajime and the Reinvention of Modern Osaka* (2002), 125.

21. The Factory Law of 1911 limited workdays for children under fifteen and for women to twelve hours, set twelve as a minimum work age, established safety standards, and provided for compensation for accidents, among other things. Implementation was weak and loopholes were many.

22. *Tokyo Keizai Zasshi,* August 22, 1891, quoted in Koji Taira, "Factory Legislation and Management Modernization During Japan's Industrialization, 1886–1916," in *Critical Readings on the History of Industrialization in Modern Japan,* vol. 2, ed. Christopher Gerteis (2013), 614.

23. William Johnston, *The Modern Epidemic: A History of Tuberculosis in Japan* (1995), 81, citing *Shokkō jijō* (1903).

24. See Garon, *State and Labor,* 15; Gary D. Allinson, *Japanese Urbanism: Industry and Politics in Kariya, 1872–1972* (1975), 41.

25. Taira, "Factory Legislation," 611–613.

26. Mori Kiichi, *Nihon no kindaika to rōdōsha kaikyū: kaikyūzō no rekishiteki tenkai* (1979), 73. For the sixteen factories, see Inumaru Giichi, ed., *Shokkō jijō,* vol. 1 (1903, 1998), 114 (hereafter *Shokkō jijō*).

27. *Shokkō jijō,* vol. 1, 127–134.

28. *Shokkō jijō,* vol. 1, 11, 35, 174. Meal and break times were staggered at most factories, so that machines would not have to be idled. Work hours in tobacco factories ranged from ten to

fourteen hours, with similar vacation arrangements, though one factory was known for giving workers a break every Sunday: *Shokkō jijō*, vol. 2, 238–239.

29. *Shūkan Heimin Shinbun*, January 31, 1904, 2; railway conductors, who were not included in the survey, worked up to sixteen hours a day. *Shūkan Heimin Shinbun*, December 13, 1903, 2.

30. See Webb, Diary, September 3, 1911, 92.

31. Yokoyama (Yutani), 409.

32. Ibid., 428, 411.

33. Webb, Diary, September 14, 1911, 146.

34. *Shūkan Shakai Shinbun*, March 8, 1908, 1; memorial money, Yokoyama (Yutani), 434. A *rin* was a thousandth of a yen, a hundredth of a sen.

35. Yokoyama (Yutani), 84–87; the second study was carried out by the Ministry of Commerce and Industry. See also Allinson, *Japanese Urbanism*, 48.

36. *Taiyō*, July 1, 1903, 14.

37. Yokoyama (Yutani): monthly days off, Tokyo Arsenal wages, 408–409; promotions, 411; overbearing supervisors, 428; "desolate buildings," 435.

38. Webb, Diary, September 3, 1911, 106. In Osaka, they found "the same dull, brutalized operatives," with men in a "blowing room full of cotton dust working nearly naked" (September 14, 1911, 150). Some of the women in a Kyoto silk spinning mill worked in 100-degree rooms (148).

39. The episode, which turned bloody, occurred in 1897; see Taira, "Factory Legislation," Gerteis, 629–630. Mutō persisted and his firm became one of Japan's four largest textile factories in the early 1900s. Taira describes several other progressive factories but concludes that "one should not infer the generality of modernization from the achievements of the select few" (634).

40. Yokoyama (Yutani), 302–304.

41. *Brisbane Courier*, March 6, 1924; http://trove.nla.gov.au/ndp/del/article/20683707.

42. Yokoyama (Yutani), 302; *Shokkō jijō*, vol. 2, 198.

43. Yokoyama (Yutani), 302–304; *Shokkō jijō*, vol. 2, 165–166. Tokyo had seventeen factories, which produced 9.7 percent of the nation's matches. A year earlier, 1898, a different study had shown it with twenty factories. The difference may be a matter of reporting methods, but match making was declining in the Tokyo region in the late 1890s. The Tokyo factories produced 10.2 million matches (valued at ¥207,040) in 1898, a decline of 35 percent from the 15.7 million matches (¥279,000) in 1894. *Tokyo fu tōkeisho* (1908), 381–382.

44. Detailed in Yokoyama (Yutani), 302–317.

45. Description from *Shokkō jijō*, vol. 2, 173, 199.

46. Yokoyama (Yutani), 310–311.

47. *Shokkō jijō*, vol. 2, 169; this 1903 report on thirteen Osaka match factories found 3,996 women and 1,334 men doing match work; some 59 percent of the workers were under twenty years of age. In a study of ten Kobe factories, 83 percent of the 3,000 workers were female; a quarter of these workers were under age sixteen (171).

48. Yokoyama (Yutani), 311. At the factories, 9,000 of the workers were female, 4,500 male; nearly all who worked at home were female.

49. Wage figures, which are for 1897, come from Mori, *Nihon no kindaika*, 73. It bears noting that wage differences resulted not only from gender and age but from whether a person worked at home for lower pay or at the factory for higher pay. A chart of match factory wages is found in *Shokkō jijō*, vol. 2, 180.

50. Yokoyama (Yutani), 313–314.

51. *Shokkō jijō*, vol. 2, 170.

52. Yokoyama (Yutani), 314.
53. *Shokkō jijō*, vol. 2, 203–204; the father's eye problems were due to syphilis.
54. Yokoyama (Yutani), 315–317.
55. Yazaki, *Social Change*, 408. See comparative data, for example, in *Taiyō*, February 1, 1905, 14.
56. William Lockwood, *The Economic Development of Japan: Growth and Structural Change 1868–1938* (1954), 27–29.
57. *Shokkō jijō* (1903), cited in Yokoyama (Yutani), 48. Also see Chushichi Tsuzuki, *The Pursuit of Power in Modern Japan: 1825–1995* (2000), 147.
58. See especially E. Patricia Tsurumi, *Factory Girls: Women in the Thread Mills of Meiji Japan* (1990), 132–160. For cotton industry hours, Johnston, *Modern Epidemic*, 78.
59. Printing also hired large numbers of women. The Tokyo Printing Bureau, for example, employed two thousand women at the beginning of the twentieth century, paying them between thirteen and thirty-five sen a day, depending on their age and rank; work conditions there were among the best in Japan for females. Nihon Bank and the telephone industry also hired significant numbers of women. See *Taiyō*, January 5, 1901, 201–205.
60. Tsurumi, *Factory Girls*, 106–107; Yokoyama (Yutani), 256; see also Kawashima, *Fujin kateiran*, 118. For the longer period: Garon, *State and Labor*, 13.
61. Tsurumi, *Factory Girls*, 107, 105, 150. For figures on the amounts subtracted for room and board, see Webb, Diary, September 14, 1911, 134, 150. The gender gap was reduced slightly in the late Meiji years.
62. Naoe Kinoshita, *Pillar of Fire* (1972), 60. I have not found data for how many female-headed households there were; they show up enough in the literature to suggest that the numbers were substantial.
63. Tsurumi, *Factory Girls*, 178, 87; Takano Fusatarō, "Labor Problems in Japan," *American Federalist* (September 1896), in Yokoyama (Yutani), 51.
64. *Shokkō jijō*, vol. 1, 20–21, 29. Among workers under age twenty in the Kansai study, 10,254 were girls and 1,311 were boys. A full sixty Spinning Association factories hired girls of thirteen and under, while a dozen hired children of ten or eleven; two reported hiring them at any age.
65. *Shokkō jijō*, vol. 2, 170.
66. Allinson, *Japanese Urbanism*, 48.
67. Tsurumi, *Factory Girls*, 156.
68. *Shokkō jijō*, vol. 1, 22. All the 367 male workers lived on their own, away from the factory.
69. Tsurumi, *Factory Girls*, 133–134.
70. Takai Toshio, "Changing Consciousness," in Ronald P. Loftus, *Telling Lives: Women's Self-Writing in Modern Japan* (2004), 89.
71. Cited in Tsurumi, *Factory Girls*, 133.
72. Yokoyama (Yutani), 272, 273.
73. *Shokkō jijō*, vol. 1, 210.
74. Ibid., 211–214.
75. Hosoi Wakizō, *Kōjō aishi* (1982 reprint of 1925 edition), 330–332; quote on 332.
76. Wm. Theodore de Bary, Carol Gluck, and Arthur E. Tiedemann, comp., *Sources of Japanese Tradition*, vol. 2, part 1 (2006), 438.
77. See Ian Neary, "Class and Social Stratification," in *A Companion to Japanese History*, ed. William M. Tsutsui (2007), 390. Also George Sansom, *A History of Japan: 1334–1615* (1961), 186–187.
78. Mitsui Takafusa, "Chōnin kōken roku," in de Bary, Gluck, and Tiedemann, *Sources*, 277.
79. David L. Howell, *Geographies of Identity in Nineteenth-Century Japan* (2005), 46–47.

80. Gregory Clancey, *Earthquake Nation: The Cultural Politics of Japanese Seismicity 1868–1930* (2006), 31; see his discussion, 14–15, 28–31. Andrew Gordon argues that another problem for craftsmen was that the ages-old guilds had not been interconnected or supple enough in the late-Tokugawa years to maintain their control in an increasingly urban economy. *The Evolution of Labor Relations in Japan: Heavy Industry, 1853–1955* (1985), 23–25.

81. Yokoyama Gennosuke, *Nihon no kasō shakai* (1899, 1949), 86–87, provides annual wages; the translation in Yokoyama (Yutani), 247–248, converts the averages to daily figures, which I have used since they compare more easily with other wage figures I have used. For living costs, see Yokoyama (Yutani), 190.

82. 1900 study in Mori, *Nihon no kindaika*, 73; 1904 study, *Shūkan Heimin Shinbun*, March 6, 1904, 2; this study noted that both wages and prices had risen since the recent start of the Russo-Japanese War. Monthly figures are based on an average of twenty-five days of work a month.

83. Yokoyama (Yutani), 228 (vicissitudes), 245 (intimate relationships), 237 (capitalists' hands), 238 (nothing matters).

84. Matsubara, *Sketches*, 74.

85. Yokoyama (Yutani), 178–179.

86. Junichi Saga, *Confessions of a Yakuza: A Life in Japan's Underworld* (1991), 37, talking about day laborers in the mid-Taishō years.

87. Michael Lewis, *A Life Adrift: Soeda Azembō, Popular Song, and Modern Mass Culture in Japan* (2009), 97.

88. See Brett De Bary, "Sanya: Japan's Internal Colony," in *The Other Japan*, ed. E. Patricia Tsurumi (1988), 113–114; also Edward Fowler, *San'ya Blues: Laboring Life in Contemporary Tokyo* (1996), 40.

89. Saga, *Confessions*, 36–37.

90. Yokoyama (Yutani), 29.

91. Lewis, *Life Adrift*, 97.

92. See Matsubara, *Saiankoku*, 108.

93. For 1897 wages, see Mori, *Nihon no kindaika*, 73; for workdays per month, Nakagawa, "Senzen ni okeru, jō," 91; for later wages, Yokoyama (Yutani), 170–175.

94. *Nedan no Meiji Taishō Shōwa fūzoku shi* (1981): vol. 2, 157 (low-level official's salary); vol. 1, 115 (rice), 181 (beer), 215 (eel).

Chapter Three: Earning a Living

1. Edward H. House, "Little Fountain of Sakanoshita," in *Japanese Episodes* (1881), 9.

2. Sōseki Natsume, *Light and Darkness* (1971), 152.

3. Nishida Taketoshi, ed., *Toshi kasō shakai: Meiji zenki rōdō jijō* (1949), 231–232. The "pullers" category here appears not to include carters, the men who pulled small wagons laden with vegetables, rice, lumber, bricks, and such. The carters were even more numerous than rickshaw pullers, and their numbers continued to increase after 1903, when rickshaws began to decline. See Shibusawa Keizō, ed., *Japanese Life and Culture in the Meiji Era* (1958), 173 ff.

4. Nakagawa Kiyoshi, "Senzen ni okeru toshi kasō no tenkai, jō," *Mita Gakkai Zasshi* (June 1978), 91, based on the Home Ministry's "Saimin chōsa tōkei hyō" (Statistical survey of the poor, 1912), 25–26, 33–36. In a different chart (p. 88), Nakagawa includes a category for *nigurumahiki* (cart pullers) and *unsō ninpu* (transport carriers), drawing on the same survey, 9–16, and on the Home Ministry's "Saimin chōsa tōkei hyō tekyō" (Statistical survey of the poor: a summary), 44–67.

5. Mandai Nanao, "Tetsudō ekifu" (Railway workers), *Taiyō*, December 5, 1901, 194–202.

6. Ibid. for salary; the other reporter's article was summarized from "a Japanese newspaper" in *Shūkan Heimin Shinbun,* December 13, 1903, 2.

7. Taizo Fujimoto, *The Nightside of Japan* (1915), 209.

8. Material on the postal workers comes largely from Shakai kishi (society reporter), "Yūbin haitatsu," *Seinenkai,* March 1, 1903, 74–78.

9. Suzuki Kantarō, Wittenberg University student who later became a journalist, conversation, Tokyo, spring 2007. He and his fellow employees at a Tokyo *takkyūbin* firm worked from 7:00 p.m. to 7:00 a.m. daily in the summer of 2006, often getting only five hours of sleep. He said such working conditions were illegal but common.

10. The written exam focused on postal regulations.

11. By contrast, most telephone operators were female. The Tokyo Telephone Exchange Offices required that employees be single and between thirteen and twenty-three years of age. They had to pass a comprehensive exam unless they had completed the third year of higher primary school; salaries in 1902 ranged from eighteen to fifty sen a day, with five sen extra for night work and year-end bonuses. See *Seinen: The Rising Generation* (hereafter *Seinen RG*), March 1, 1902, 8.

12. Shibusawa, *Japanese Life,* 173. "Sturdy and robust": Eiji Yutani, " 'Nihon no Kaso Shakai' " of Gennosuke Yokoyama" (1985), 177, hereafter cited as Yokoyama (Yutani).

13. Yokoyama (Yutani), 177–178; he notes that some *shariki* made as much as eighty sen a day.

14. Ibid., 179.

15. Matsubara Iwagoro, *Sketches of Humble Life in the Capital of Japan* (1897), 70; also see Matsubara Iwagorō, *Saiankoku no Tokyo* (1893), 102. *Sketches* is a slightly abbreviated, loose translation of *Saiankoku no Tokyo.*

16. Shibusawa, *Japanese Life,* 183–184.

17. Susan B. Hanley, "Urban Sanitation in Preindustrial Japan," *Journal of Interdisciplinary History* (Summer 1987), 14.

18. Both quotations are in David L. Howell, "Fecal Matters: Prolegomenon to a History of Shit in Japan," in *Japan at Nature's Edge: The Environmental Context of a Global Power,* ed. Ian J. Miller, Julia A. Thomas, and Brett L. Walker (2013), "values gold," by Miyazaki Yasusada (1697), 138; "waste not," seventeenth-century farmer's manual, 140.

19. Ibid., 148.

20. Tsubame Sakuta, *Shimogoe* (Night soil) (Tokyo: Yūrindō, 1914), 24, 6, in ibid., 141; GNP is Howell's phrase; he notes that after the mid-1910s, Tokyo's mushrooming population caused an oversupply of night soil, and the city began paying the collectors to take it to the countryside (15–16).

21. E. W. Cole, "Japan as Observed by a Foreigner," *Taiyō,* November 1, 1903, 9.

22. *Tokyo Pakku,* April 15, 1911, 172 (piss); August 20, 1911, 85, says people knew it was 6 a.m. when they heard the manure man.

23. Junichi Saga, *Confessions of a Yakuza: A Life in Japan's Underworld* (1991), 19.

24. Yanagita Kunio, *Meiji Taishō shi sesō hen shinsōban* (1993), 201.

25. House, "To Fujiyama and Back," in *Japanese Episodes,* 85.

26. See Yanagita, *Meiji Taishō shi,* 201. Also M. William Steele, "Mobility on the Move: Rickshaws in Asia," *Transfers* (Winter 2014), 90.

27. See Shibusawa, *Japanese Life,* 178.

28. *Niroku Shinpō,* September 12, 1909, quoted in Shibusawa, *Japanese Life,* 181–183.

29. Eliza Ruhamah Scidmore, *Jinrikisha Days in Japan* (1891), 8.

30. Steele, "Mobility," 89 (quote), 91 (ad).

31. See Fūzoku Shi Gakkai, ed., *Nihon fūzoku shi jiten* (1979), 332, for fees and general data; for numbers of pullers, Takeo Yazaki, *Social Change and the City in Japan: From Earliest Times Through the Industrial Revolution* (1968), 445, and *Taiyō*, April 5, 1902, 32; for cost of bath, *Nedan no Meiji Taishō Shōwa fūzoku shi*, vol. 1 (1981), 91.

32. Jun'ichrō Tanizaki, "The Secret," in *The Gourmet Club: A Sextet* (2001), 62, 63; Jun'ichiro Tanizaki, *Childhood Years: A Memoir* (1988), 35.

33. Howard Swan, "Flashes," *Taiyō*, June 5, 1902, 6.

34. Kafū Nagai, "River Sumida," in *A Strange Tale from East of the River and Other Stories* (1965), 30.

35. Michael Lewis, *A Life Adrift: Soeda Azembō, Popular Song, and Modern Mass Culture in Japan* (2009), 92.

36. *Fūzoku Gahō*, October 25, 1903, 24 ff.

37. *Shūkan Heimin Shinbun*, March 13, 1904, 2.

38. Shibusawa, *Japanese Life*, 187; in 1882, Osaka required that pullers begin posting their fares on the *jinrikisha* steps.

39. See, for example, "Jinriki shafu dōmei kyūgyō," *Taiyō*, July 1, 1903, 229.

40. Shibusawa, *Japanese Life*, 186.

41. Kenneth G. Henshall, *Literary Life in Tōkyō, 1885–1915: Tayama Katai's Memoirs (Thirty Years in Tōkyō)* (1987), 84.

42. Edward S. Morse, *Japan Day by Day*, vol. 1 (1917): 5 ("dragged"), 44 (smiles), 140 (speed).

43. *Niroku Shinpō*, April 9, 1900, 3.

44. *Yorozu Chōhō*, December 28, 1901, 3.

45. Hailed in the press, the *shafu* were given large pensions by both the Japanese and Russian governments. See George Lensen, "The Attempt on the Life of Nicholas II in Japan," *The Russian Review* (July 1961), 232–253. For Japanese press coverage, Nakayama Yasuaki, ed. *Shinbun shūsei Meiji hennen shi*, vol. 8 (1982), 84–92.

46. Purse, *Seinen RG*, February 15, 1910, 226; widow's plight, *Seinen RG*, August 15, 1898, 21; runaway, *Shūkan Heimin Shinbun*, January 17, 1904, 2.

47. Matsubara, *Saiankoku*, 143–146.

48. Ibid., 129.

49. Ibid., 132, 139.

50. Morse, *Day by Day*, vol. 1, 124–125 (tattoo), 58 (naked).

51. Scidmore, *Jinrikisha Days*, 206.

52. Matsubara, *Saiankoku*, 136, 140.

53. Morse, *Day by Day*, vol. 1, 4–5.

54. Matsubara, *Saiankoku*, 139–142; 140 (invective).

55. Metropolitan police statistics, in Shibusawa, *Japanese Life*, 190. Only 2,919 pulled for others.

56. Annual police records recorded the pass/fail rates; in 1900, for example, 92.4 percent of the 34,224 who took the rickshaw certification test passed. *Keisatsuchō tōkeisho: 1907*, 261. Also see Fujimoto, *Nightside*, 197–198.

57. Material on the four groups comes from Yokoyama (Yutani), 180–182. The early twentieth-century journalist Taizo Fujimoto divided pullers into three categories: mature men with families to support, young bachelors who spent their income on alcohol and gambling, and the better off, salaried employees of specific affluent families. *Nightside*, 196.

58. One shō equals approximately 1.8 liters or .476 of a gallon.

59. Yokoyama Gennosuke, *Nihon no kasō shakai* (1899, 1949), 35–36.

60. Shibusawa, *Japanese Life*, 192.

61. *Yonashi* is an abbreviation of *yonabeshi*, which means "night worker"; see Matsubara, *Saiankoku*, 119; also J. E. De Becker, *The Nightless City or the History of the Yoshiwara Yūwaku* (1971), 170.

62. Yokoyama (Yutani), 38 (for early 1890s), 188, 247–248 (for other material). See Mori Kiichi, *Nihon no kindaika to rōdōsha kaikyū: kaikyūzō no rekishiteki tenkai* (1979), 73, for comparative figures. For work hours, Nakagawa, "Senzen ni okeru, jō," 91, based on Home Ministry surveys at the end of the Meiji era. For 1904, see *Shūkan Heimin Shinbun*, March 6, 1904, 2.

63. Yokoyama (Yutani), 182–183. For confirmation and detail regarding the figures on food consumption, see Chūbachi Masayoshi, *Gendai Nihon no seikatsu taikei* (1975), 111.

64. Matsubara, *Saiankoku*, 152–154. He estimates these wages on a good day:

younger workers	64 sen for traveling 177 *chō*
middle-aged puller	30 sen for 106 *chō*
sixty-year-old	16.5 sen for 71 *chō*

65. *Kokumin Shinbun*, 1892, quoted in Shibusawa, *Japanese Life*, 193; the unnamed writer likely was Matsubara Iwagorō.

66. Fines are discussed in Fujimoto, *Nightside*, 201.

67. Nishikawa Kōjirō (Sei), "Eigyō teishi," *Shūkan Heimin Shinbun*, January 3, 1904, 2.

68. "Jinrikisha haishi ron," *Taiyō*, May 5, 1901, 198–202.

69. *Taiyō*, June 6, 1902, 3; also see Terada Yūkichi, "Tokyo shimin to jinrikisha," *Taiyō*, April 5, 1902, 32.

70. Figures from Nakagawa Kiyoshi, ed., *Nihon no toshi kasō* (1985), 293; Shibusawa, *Japanese Life*, 190. Another official survey, *Tokyo shi tōkei zuhyō*, chart 19, found 22,403 rickshaws in 1911, and still a third, *Dai jūichi kai Tokyo shi tōkei nenpyō: 1914*, 760–761, found 20,342 in April 1913. All showed the same decline. It bears noting that rickshaws continued to be popular in other parts of Asia; combined with bicycles to create pedicabs or cyclos, they are widely used even today; see Steele, "Mobility," 100–102.

71. Undated 1904 issue of *Tokyo Asahi Shinbun*, in Shibusawa, *Japanese Life*, 195.

72. Article from *The Railway Times*, in *Taiyō*, December 1, 1903, English column, 15. The phrase in Japanese is *sutsuru kami areba, sukuu kami arii*.

73. *Shūkan Heimin Shinbun*, February 7, 1904 (new jobs), December 13, 1903 (disaster).

74. I avoid the phrase "service industries" in order to focus on the lives of those who served rather than looking primarily at their economic and systemic roles, as social science literature tends to do in discussions of the service or tertiary sector. One other category of poorly paid servers was schoolteachers, whom I omit because, despite low pay, the profession carried a certain respect that removed it from the *kasō shakai* in public discussions. Journalists pointed out that teachers often received less pay than rickshaw pullers; see *Yorozu Chōhō*, April 23, 1900, 2.

75. One exception, an early study of Nago-chō in Osaka, has a category for entertainers (*yūgei*) and others for food/drink, and confectioneries, as well as one for rag picking; it deals with the middle-late 1880s; see Nishida, *Toshi kasō shakai*, 231–232.

76. Yokoyama (Yutani), 163–164. Even the meticulous folklorist Miyamoto Tsuneichi paid scant attention and gave little respect to the performers and beggar priests who, he says, showed up in great numbers in the late Meiji cities, in contrast to the deep respect he showed to other members of poor society. Miyamoto Tsuneichi, *The Forgotten Japanese: Encounters with Rural Life and Folklore* (2010), 297–301, especially 301.

77. Morse, *Day by Day*, vol. 1, 20 ("pinch, rub"), 220 ("mechanical filler").

78. Fujimoto, *Nightside*, 161–162 (7.5 yen would equal approximately thirty sen a day); for comparisons, see *Shūkan Heimin Shinbun*, March 6, 1904, 2.

79. *Seinen RG*, May 20, 1899, 18; June 7, 1902, 1; Fujimoto, *Nightside*, 162. Morse said there were "thousands and thousands" of them (*Day by Day*, vol. 1, 20). The latter *Seinen* article indi-

cated that Japan had 4,680 blind children of school age, with 399 (3.7 percent) of them taking lessons at a middle school level. At the end of the Meiji era, Tokyo had one school for the blind, with 75 students studying acupuncture, massage, and music, and one for the deaf, with 270 students. *Dai jūichi kai Tokyo shi tōkei nenpyō: 1914*, 230–231.

80. *Seinen RG*, April 20, 1899, 8 (acupuncturists), April 1, 1910, 2 (stoning).

81. Matsubara, *Sketches*, 65–66; also page 23 for another description of slum-dwelling shampooers and moxibustion practitioners.

82. "Omise kozō tedai no genjō," *Taiyō*, February 5, 1901, 205–209.

83. Fujimoto, *Nightside*, 70–71.

84. "Sociological Mirrors," *Taiyō*, February 5, 1902, 6. A *sentō* could be launched for less than six thousand yen capital; monthly water fees for two large tanks were two sen; an income of five or six yen a day assured a reasonable profit.

85. E. W. Cole, "Japan as Observed by a Foreigner," *Taiyō*, November 1, 1903, 9; "Sociological Mirrors," *Taiyō*, February 5, 1902, 5–6, gives a figure of eight hundred.

86. See Scott Clark, *Japan, A View from the Bath* (1994), 67. On changing attitudes toward nudity and mixed bathing, see Hirota Masaki, "Notes on the 'Process of Creating Women' in the Meiji Period," in *Gender and Japanese History*, vol. 2, ed. Haruko Wakita, Anne Bouchy, and Ueno Chizuko (1999), 200–201.

87. Cole, "Japan as Observed," 9.

88. Fujimoto, *Nightside*, 74.

89. "Sociological Mirrors," *Taiyō*, February 5, 1902, 5–6.

90. Yokoyama (Yutani), 185–187; Maeda Ai, "Time as Children," in Maeda Ai, *Text and the City* (2004), 128; Edward Seidensticker (drawing on Okamoto Kida's *Record of Hanshichi's Arrests*), *The Snake that Bowed* (2006), 121–123. For *gōshaku*, see Matsubara, *Sketches*, 22; Natsume Sōseki, *Garasudo*, in Marvin Marcus, *Reflections in a Glass Door: Memory and Melancholy in the Personal Writings of Natsume Sōseki* (2009), 42. For socialists, see *Tokyo Shakai Shinbun*, June 25, 1908, 1. For mouth in stomach, see Yasunari Kawabata, *The Scarlet Gang of Asakusa* (2005), 26.

91. *Taiyō*, October 20, 1909, 178.

92. Quoted by Kanzō Uchimura, *Yorozu Chōhō*, March 1, 1898, in Kanzō Uchimura, *The Complete Works of Kanzō Uchimura*, vol. 6 (1973), 124.

93. George De Vos and Hiroshi Wagatsuma, *Japan's Invisible Race: Caste in Culture and Personality* (1966), 19.

94. David R. Ambaras, *Bad Youth: Juvenile Delinquency and the Politics of Everyday Life in Modern Japan* (2006), 35.

95. Izumi Kyōka, *In Light of Shadows: More Gothic Tales* (2005), 57–58.

96. Yokoyama (Yutani), 186–187; the wages are for the late 1890s.

97. Izumi, *In Light of Shadows*, 58.

98. Yokoyama, *Kasō shakai*, 40.

99. An exception is the 1888 study of Osaka's Nago-chō in which Suzuki Umeshirō, using local government reports, includes categories for food and drink, confectioneries, and entertaining. Nishida, *Toshi kasō shakai*, 231–232.

100. Fujimoto, *Nightside*, 167.

101. See Christopher Pellegrini, *The Shochu Handbook: An Introduction to Japan's Indigenous Distilled Drink* (2014), 3–9.

102. Matsubara, *Sketches*, 69–70.

103. Matsubara, *Saiankoku*, 151.

104. *Nedan no Meiji Taishō Shōwa fūzoku shi*, 265: 1894 price for a pound loaf.

105. Matsubara, *Sketches*, 57.

106. Matsubara, *Saiankoku*, 150. For a study of serving women in the early Taishō years, see Chiku Seitarō, *Hensō tanbō setai no samazama* (1914); also see Kida Jun'ichirō, *Tokyo kasō shakai* (2000), 31.

107. Koji Taira, "Urban Poverty, Ragpickers, and the 'Ants Village' in Tokyo," *Economic Development and Change* (January 1969), 163, 168.

108. Tokyo data from Nakagawa, "Senzen ni okeru, jō," 69; Yokoyama (Yutani), 165, described the Mannen-chō area as "extremely unsightly and dirty."

109. Nishida, *Toshi kasō shakai*, 232 for Nago-chō; "Tokyo no hinmin," *Jiji Shinpō*, October/November 1896, in Nakagawa Kiyoshi, ed., *Meiji Tokyo kasō seikatsu shi* (1994), 134 for Tokyo. Also see Kawashima Yasuyoshi, *Fujin kateiran kotohajime* (1996), 114.

110. Yokoyama (Yutani), 187–189.

111. In Nakagawa, *Meiji Tokyo*, 134.

112. *Seinen RG*, May 15, 1910, 75.

113. Taira, "Urban Poverty," 168; Yokoyama (Yutani), 185.

114. *Tokyo Pakku*, December 1, 1909, 245.

115. Taira, "Urban Poverty," 166; 2,607 people were surveyed. Some 3 percent of the rag pickers blamed acts of God (flood, fire, etc.); 26 percent blamed biological problems such as family deaths, illness, or family size; 55 percent blamed their own personal failings; and 6 percent gave a miscellany of other reasons. Taira ("Urban Poverty," 167) suggests that the self-blame resulted from "personality problems," arguing that "pride alone would induce anyone to blame his difficulties on society in general or, at best, on forces of circumstances beyond his control." I disagree and would argue that the impact of poverty and overwhelming social denigration would cause almost all normal people to struggle with ideas of self-worth. Self-abnegation is not an indication of "personality problems."

116. Amy Stanley, *Selling Women: Prostitution, Markets, and the Household in Early Modern Japan* (2012), 4. Stanley argues that the prostitute system evolved across the Tokugawa years, with women under the control of their families and the patriarchal system in the early years, then under a state-operated system that gave them more autonomy, and by the nineteenth century under control of the market, which caused them to be seen as a threat to traditional norms.

117. Ibid., 191.

118. National data and quotation from Elizabeth Dorn Lublin, *Reforming Japan: The Women's Christian Temperance Union in the Meiji Period* (2010), 105; De Becker, *Nightless City*, 359. For the number of Yoshiwara brothels, see Fujimoto, *Nightside*, 21; he estimates that "more than three thousand" prostitutes worked there in the 1910s.

119. Yoshitake Oka, *Five Political Leaders of Modern Japan* (1986), 37; Patricia E. Tsurumi, *Factory Girls: Women in the Thread Mills of Meiji Japan* (1990), 182.

120. Sheldon Garon, *Molding Japanese Minds: The State in Everyday Life* (1997), 101.

121. Sabine Frühstück, *Colonizing Sex: Sexology and Social Control in Modern Japan* (2003), 47.

122. Letter by Henry Bullard in *Yorozu Chōhō*, July 19, 1900, 2.

123. Nishikawa Kōjirō, "Byōki seizō no kōnin," *Heimin Shinbun*, June 19, 1904, in *Heimin Shinbun*, vol. 2 (1954), 359.

124. Haga Eizō, *Meiji Taishō hikka shi* (1924), 124.

125. Muramatsu Shōfū, ed., *Akiyama Teisuke wa kataru* (1938), 185. The episode is recounted in my *Creating a Public: People and Press in Meiji Japan* (1997), 255; also see Garon, *Molding Japanese Minds*, 89. For "dead place," see *Niroku Shinpō*, September 13, 1900, quoted in Yumoto Kōichi, *Zusetsu Meiji jibutsu kigen jiten* (1998), 164.

288 | Notes to Pages 91–98

126. Yokoyama (Yutani), 162. The British sociologist Beatrice Webb said her "only unpleasant impression of Japan" was the Yoshiwara, "a Zoological Garden of Human Beasts being visited by human beasts." Diary, undated, 176.

127. Phrase of Maeda Ai, discussing *Takekurabe,* "Time as Children," in Maeda, *Text and the City* (2004), 113.

128. Higuchi Ichiyō, "Child's Play," in Robert Lyons Danly, *In the Shade of Spring Leaves: The Life of Higuchi Ichiyō With Nine of Her Best Short Storie*s (1984), 254. The fair, held each November at Ōtori Shrine, features decorative rakes.

129. Maeda, "Time as Children," in Maeda, *Text and the City* (2004), 129.

130. Higuchi, "Child's Play," 259.

131. Fujimoto, *Nightside,* 22–26.

132. Higuchi, "Child's Play," 285.

133. See Sabine Frühstück, "Then Science Took Over: Sex, Leisure, and Medicine at the Beginning of the Twentieth Century," in *The Culture of Japan as Seen Through its Leisure,* ed. Sepp Linhart and Sabine Frühstück (1998), 66.

134. Fujimoto, *Nightside,* 3.

135. Kōjimachi Bō, "Tokai no yūwakubutsu," *Taiyō,* March 5, 1901, 200–206. Nearly every issue of *Taiyō* in the spring and summer of 1901 addressed the issue of moral reform.

136. Fujimoto, *Nightside,* 128. The two-story hospital was painted white but inside rooms were "dark and shut up"; Fujimoto reports that the patient load was usually between twenty and thirty women.

137. In 1900, Tokyo apprehended 284 unlicensed prostitutes, nearly half of them in the poverty wards of Asakusa, Honjo, Fukagawa, and Shitaya. *Keisatsuchō tōkeisho: 1907,* 251.

138. "Katō baiin no jikkyō," *Niroku Shinpō,* April 10–25, 1900. Unless otherwise cited, material in this section comes from this series, with article dates in parentheses.

139. "Katō baiin," April 17, 1900. The writer was punning. Slums frequently were referred to as "hells" (*jigoku*); a slang phrase for low-class prostitution was "hell work" (*jigoku eigyō*).

140. Income figures are interspersed throughout the "Katō baiin" series, from April 12 to April 21.

141. Fujimoto, *Nightside,* 45.

142. Susan Burns, "Bodies and Borders: Syphilis, Prostitution, and the Nation in Japan, 1860–1890" (1998), 11; she says syphilis appears not to have occurred in Japan until Portuguese traders came in the 1500s (9).

143. See Frühstück, *Colonizing Sex,* 25–27, 35.

144. Oliver Balch, "A Gilded Ghetto, But for How Long?" *The Guardian Weekly,* February 5, 2016, 30.

145. College, Matsubara, *Saiankoku,* 35; no education, "Omise kozō tedai no genjō," *Taiyō,* February 5, 1901, 209.

146. Mori, *Nihon no kindaika,* 73. Also table 5.

147. Figures obtained by averaging wages for the jobs listed in tables 2 through 5 (in sen): factory workers 25.2, servers 26.8, builders 44.3, movers 54.6. As in table 5, 1894 wages were figured at 64 percent of 1900 wages, based on ibid.

148. Inumura Giichi, *Shokkō jijō,* vol. 1 (1903, 1998), 114–115.

149. Mori, *Nihon no kindaika,* 76.

150. *Rōdō Shinbunsha,* in Yokoyama (Yutani), 425.

151. "Katō baiin," April 25, 1900.

152. Alan H. Gleason, "Economic Growth and Consumption in Japan," in *The State and Economic Enterprise in Japan: Growth and Structural Change 1868–1938,* ed. William Lockwood (1954), 357, 407–409.

Chapter Four: Making a Life

1. Michael Lewis, *A Life Adrift: Soeda Azembō, Popular Song, and Modern Mass Culture in Japan* (2009), 264.

2. This material represents a composite based on working *hinmin* families generally. Specific jobs and income information are drawn from the *kozukai* family described in *Taiyō* 7, no. 13 (November 5, 1901, 5–6) and no. 14 (December 5, 1901, 5–6). Items in the daily schedule also draw on *Tokyo Pakku* cartoons "Osando nijūyonji," May 1, 1906, 141, and August 20, 1911, 85.

3. Newspaper reading varied by region, with reports in some slum districts that only one in nine household read daily papers in the 1910s, while surveys of most poor regions showed upwards of half of households taking daily papers by the late Meiji years. See Shimonaka Kunihiko, ed., *Nihon zankoku monogatari*, vol. 5 (1959–1960), 49; Mikiso Hane, *Peasants, Rebels, Women, & Outcastes: The Underside of Modern Japan* (2016), 327–328, note 64, for the lower figure; also see Andrew Gordon, *Labor and Imperial Democracy in Prewar Japan* (1991), 19. For the *Yorozu* subscription price, see Yamamoto Taketoshi, *Kindai Nihon no shinbun dokusha sō* (1981), 96.

4. Kenji Nakagami, *The Cape and Other Stories from the Japanese Ghetto* (1999), 20.

5. *Tokyo Pakku*, November 10, 1903, 232.

6. *The Civil Code of Japan*, trans. Ludwig Lönholm (1898), 214, 230.

7. Harald Fuess, *Divorce in Japan: Family, Gender, and the State, 1600–2000* (2004), 3, 5. A quarter of the divorces took place in the first year of marriage, 46 percent within the first two years. Divorces per 1,000 people totaled 3.39 in 1883, compared to 1.98 per thousand in 1999 (65).

8. *Yorozu Chōhō*, May 10, 1900, 2.

9. *Shūkan Heimin Shinbun*, February 14, 1904, 2.

10. Kiyoshi Nakagawa, "Ambitions, 'Family-Centredness' and Expenditure Patterns in a Changing Urban Class Structure: Tokyo in the Early Twentieth Century," *Continuity and Change* (2000), 79.

11. Saitō Kanejirō, 1895, cited in Nakagawa Kiyoshi, "Senzen ni okeru toshi kasō no tenkai, jō," *Mita Gakkai Zasshi* (June 1978), 70.

12. *Shūkan Shakai Shinbun*, March 22, 1908, 1.

13. Matsubara Iwagorō, *Saiankoku no Tokyo* (1893, 1988), 158.

14. Eiji Yutani, "'Nihon no Kaso Shakai' of Gennosuke Yokoyama" (1985), 198 (hereafter Yokoyama (Yutani)). Nakagawa, "Ambitions," 83, supports Yokoyama's assessment, noting that even in the 1910s 40 percent of poor families were unregistered; by the 1930s, that figure had dropped to 10 percent.

15. Reporting on Nago-chō, Fuess, *Divorce in Japan*, 58.

16. See Nakagawa, "Ambitions," 77–98.

17. Nakagawa Kiyoshi, *Gendai no seikatsu mondai* (2011), 51.

18. In 1912, the Tokyo Poorhouse (Tokyo Shi Yōikuin) was home for 653 orphaned children, ages one through thirteen, 285 of whom were girls. The numbers had increased each year from 1907. See *Dai jūichi kai Tokyo shi tōkei nenpyō: 1914*, 398–399.

19. Yokoyama (Yutani), 198–199.

20. David R. Ambaras, "Social Knowledge, Cultural Capital, and the New Middle Class in Japan, 1895–1912," *Journal of Japanese Studies* (Winter 1998), 27.

21. *Shūkan Heimin Shinbun*, February 21, 1904, cited in Kawashima Yasuyoshi, *Fujin kateiran kotohajime* (1996), 127.

22. Nakagawa, "Senzen ni okeru," 71.

23. From Tokyo's Futaba Yōchien purpose statement, 1901, Kathleen Uno, *Passages to Modernity: Motherhood, Childhood, and Social Reform in Early Twentieth Century Japan* (1999), 55.

24. *Tokyo Pakku*, November 20, 1908, 231. The child's tears form the characters for "To the right or to the left?"

25. Beatrice Webb, Diary, September 14, 1911, London School of Economics Digital Library, 154.

26. For the American system, Michael B. Katz, *In the Shadow of the Poorhouse: A Social History of Welfare in America* (1986), especially 117–184.

27. E. Patricia Tsurumi, *Factory Girls: Women in the Thread Mills of Meiji Japan* (1990), 156. Also see David R. Ambaras, *Bad Youth: Juvenile Delinquency and the Politics of Everyday Life in Modern Japan* (2006), 36–43.

28. Survey of Osaka's Nago-chō, 1888, in Nishida Taketoshi, ed., *Toshi kasō shakai: Meiji zenki rōdō jijō* (1949), 231–232.

29. In 1907, compulsory education was extended from four to six years.

30. Yamamoto Taketoshi, "Meiji sanjūnen zenhan no shinbun dokusha sō" (March 1967), 123. Richard Rubinger, "Who Can't Read and Write: Illiteracy in Meiji Japan," *Monumenta Nipponica* (Summer 2000), 183–184, maintains that by 1909 only areas on Japan's fringes had more than 10 percent illiteracy.

31. Yokoyama (Yutani), 419.

32. Harada Tōfū, *Hinminkutsu* (1902), 103.

33. Inumaru Giichi, ed., *Shokkō jijō*, vol. 2 (1903, 1998), 190 (hereafter *Shokkō jijō*).

34. Rubinger, "Who Can't Read," 181. The survey was looking for illiteracy rather than literacy. The region, labeled Hongō by the researchers, also included Kanda and the University of Tokyo, meaning that the negative impact of the *hinminkutsu* regions was even more pronounced.

35. Ibid., 186–187; Yokoyama (Yutani), 68–69.

36. Webb, Diary, September 14, 1911, 154, citing "public statistics."

37. Ambaras, *Bad Youth*, 59.

38. Yokoyama (Yutani), 545.

39. *Seinen: The Rising Generation* (hereafter *Seinen RG*), October 15, 1898, 6. The article said that the 1896 survey discovered 69,964 Tokyo children between the ages of six and fourteen who were avoiding school, with more than three-fifths citing poverty as their reason.

40. *Seinen RG*, May 20, 1899, 1.

41. Yokoyama (Yutani), 548.

42. Ambaras, *Bad Youth*, 41–42.

43. Yokoyama (Yutani), 365–369 (quote on page 369).

44. Ibid., 372; he also reported on Tokyo Kanegafuchi Spinning, where nearly two hundred studied in night classes, 370–371.

45. *Niroku Shinpō* (April 23, 1900, 1) also called for "an evening higher school if not a University . . . for those students who have to work for their livelihood in daytime," a project that appears never to have materialized.

46. Yokoyama (Yutani), 387–381.

47. Ibid., 201–203.

48. The project is described in Ambaras, *Bad Youth*, 58–63. For a Tokyo plan to launch free night schools in several wards, see *Seinen RG*, June 1, 1906, 103.

49. See Uno, *Passages to Modernity*, especially chapters 3–4 (47–88); for numbers of centers, 90.

50. Ibid., 54. A few factories also pioneered on-site day care in the 1890s to free mothers up for machine work; during the Russo-Japanese War (1904–1905) patriotic organizations operated many temporary centers for children of absent parents.

51. Brian Platt, "Educational Reform in Japan (19th c.)," *Children and Youth in History*, Item 125, http://chnm.gmu.edu/cyh/teaching-modules/125 (accessed June 19, 2013); he notes that actual attendance sometimes amounted to only 45 percent of official enrollment.

52. See Nakagawa, "Ambitions," 83.

53. Working family: Uno, *Passages to Modernity*, 59; "nil": Nakagawa, "Senzen ni okeru," 75.

54. Yanagita Kunio, *Meiji Taishō shi sesō hen* (1993), 64 (three ways), 84–86 (sweets), 89 (meat, nutrition).

55. See Kawashima, *Fujin kateiran*, 139–40; for a typical discussion of why electric lights were superior to oil lamps, see *Yorozu Chōhō*, January 2, 1900, 1.

56. Nakagawa, "Ambitions," 88. The 77 percent figure is for rickshaw pullers in 1897, in Nakagawa, "Senzen ni okeru," 74. The figures for the new middle class were 51 percent in 1898 and 41 percent in 1913. Also see Nakagawa, *Gendai no seikatsu*, 49. Per capita figures for the entire nation in 1910, which show 60 percent of income being spent on food, likely are influenced by the poverty of the rural regions, which made up the majority of the population; see Charles Yuji Horioka, "Consuming and Saving," in Andrew Gordon, ed., *Postwar Japan as History* (Berkeley: University of California Press, 1993), 267.

57. Kure Ayatoshi, "Tokyo fuka hinmin no jōkyō" (January 20, 1891), in Nakagawa Kiyoshi, ed., *Meiji Tokyo kasō seikatsu shi* (1994), 77, 79.

58. For examples, Yokoyama (Yutani), 188 (rickshaw puller), 190 (entertainer), 418 (iron worker), 420 (finisher), 422 (ironworker), 423 (lathe man).

59. Kawashima, *Fujin kateiran*, 62–63.

60. The Japanese Judas Tree, whose flower can be edible, Matsubara, *Saiankoku*, 44.

61. In Lewis, *Life Adrift*, 65.

62. *Niroku Shinpō*, April 16, 1900, 3. *Niroku* followed with a lengthy series on the rice/sand scandal.

63. Buying at night, Iwagoro Matsubara, *Sketches of Humble Life in the Capital of Japan* (1897), 74; temple handout, Matsubara, *Saiankoku*, 51. *Sketches* is a slightly abbreviated, loose translation of *Saiankoku no Tokyo*.

64. Yokoyama (Yutani), 192–193 (leftover shops), 172 (coffee price). For other prices, *Nedan no Meiji Taishō Shōwa fūzoku shi*, vol. 1 (1981): 115 (rice), 145 (tea), 215 (eel).

65. Hita Sei, "Hinminkutsu," *Fūzoku Gahō* (November 10, 1898), 10.

66. Matsubara, *Sketches*, 25–30.

67. For references to the leftover food in the late Meiji and early Taishō years, see Uno, *Passages to Modernity*, 49; Yasunari Kawabata, *The Scarlet Gang of Asakusa* (2005), 44.

68. Shibusawa Keizō, ed., *Japanese Life and Culture in the Meiji Era* (1958), 90.

69. From Azembō song, Lewis, *Life Adrift*, 65.

70. Matsubara, *Sketches*, 68.

71. Taizo Fujimoto, *The Nightside of Japan* (1915), 4.

72. Matsubara, *Sketches*, 57, 67–68.

73. Fujimoto, *Nightside*, 7. Fujimoto reported that one night a ten-year-old girl came into that Asakusa shop, looking for her father. Finding him "somewhat intoxicated," she said that "Mamma and I" would not eat supper until he came home, whereupon he paid his bill and went home (8).

74. Matsubara, *Sketches*, 7–8.

75. Jeffrey E. Hanes, *The City as Subject: Seki Hajime and the Reinvention of Modern Osaka* (2002), 163–164, 142 ("cold-blooded").

292 | Notes to Pages 113–119

76. Yokoyama (Yutani), 193.

77. *Shōchū* can be distilled from many products, including sweet potatoes, rice, wheat, barley, and brown sugar. Beer was introduced to Japan in early Meiji; by the 1890s a large native beer industry had developed. It was not until the early 1900s that the poorer classes began drinking much beer.

78. Matsubara, *Sketches,* 16.

79. Quoted in Deborah J. Milly, *Poverty, Equality, and Growth: The Politics of Economic Need in Postwar Japan* (1999), 210; as noted above, the term *saimin* had generally supplanted *hinmin* by the end of Meiji.

80. Harada, *Hinminkutsu,* 8.

81. *Shokkō jijō,* vol. 2, 200–224; samples on 200–201, 204–205, 212–213, 218. Expenses in these profiles included only rent, bedding, rice, and other foods; one (204–205) included children's pocket money. Another (218) added four sen for saké "if there was money"; I did not include that in the family's expenses.

82. Reported in Yokoyama Gennosuke, *Nihon no kasō shakai* (1899, 1949), 227–230. Also see Mori Kiichi, *Nihon no kindaika to rōdōsha kaikyū: kaikyūzō no rekishiteki tenkai* (1979), 77–78.

83. Women who worked part-time usually made two to five yen a month; see *Shokkō jijō,* vol. 2, 200–201, 204–205, 212–213, 218, 219; also this book's chapter 2, table 2.

84. Yokoyama (Yutani), 421.

85. The most likely explanation for this unusual income may be that the father did some contract work in addition to (or as part of) his regular job. It probably did not come from his wife, since the "miscellaneous" category includes two yen a month from "wife's work"; Yokoyama, *Kasō shakai,* 229.

86. Ibid., 230.

87. Ibid., 232.

88. Shitaya toymaker: *Seinen RG,* May 1, 1910, 50; suicide, rickshaw puller: *Shūkan Heimin Shinbun,* December 13, 1903, 2.

89. *Niroku Shinpō,* May 29, 1900, 3.

90. Economists, William W. Lockwood, *The Economic Development of Japan: Growth and Structural Change 1868–1938* (1954), 299–300; price rise, *Yorozu Chōhō,* April 10, 1900, 2.

91. *Nedan no Meiji Taishō Shōwa fūzoku shi,* vol. 1: rice, 115; rent, 151; vol. 2: *shōyu,* 28.

92. *Tokyo shi tōkei zuhyō* (1914), chart 20 (pages unnumbered); rice prices jumped nearly 13 percent in 1906–1907, then fell, and then jumped a full 58 percent between 1910 and 1912.

93. Coverage in *Jiji Shinpō,* September 6–12, 1906, *Tokyo Asahi Shinbun,* September 6, 1906, and *Nihon,* September 10, 1906, summarized in James L. Huffman, *Creating a Public: People and Press in Meiji Japan* (1997), 332–334.

94. From articles gleaned by Aoyagi Junrō, ed., *Meiji kyūjūkyūnen: sesō jiken* (1935), 98.

95. *Taiyō,* July 1, 1904, 19, reported seven thousand Tokyo recruits five months into the war, with the largest number coming from Asakusa.

96. *Shūkan Heimin Shinbun,* April 17, 1904, 2.

97. *Tokyo Shakai Shinbun,* May 25, 1908, 1.

98. Azembō, in Lewis, *Life Adrift,* 131.

99. *Tokyo Pakku,* February 10, 1901, 80.

100. *Yorozu Chōhō,* July 19, 1900, 2.

101. Yokoyama (Yutani), 410–411; he pointed out that employers often held up to 6 percent of wages in a special account, purportedly to help workers save but actually to keep them from quitting; if they quit while under contract, they forfeited the 6 percent (381).

102. *Shūkan Shakai Shinbun,* March 22, 1908, 1.

103. *Shūkan Heimin Shinbun,* January 17, 1904, 2.

104. Quoted in Gordon, *Labor and Imperial Democracy*, 96.

105. Shimazaki Tōson, "At the Foot of Mt. Asama II," *Chikuma River Sketches* (1912, 1991), 135.

106. The fundamental premise underlying relief was that "few people actually needed public assistance" because of the Japanese family system. Hiromichi Ishizuka, "The Slum Dwellings and the Urban Renewal Scheme in Tokyo, 1868–1923," *The Developing Economies* (June 1981), 190. "Completely dispossessed," from 1875 government guidance regarding the Relief Act; see W. Dean Kinzley, "Japan's Discovery of Poverty: Changing Views of Poverty and Social Welfare in the Nineteenth Century," *Journal of Asian History* (1988), 6.

107. Kawashima, *Fujin kateiran*, 57.

108. Tanya Maus, "Ishii Jūji, the Okayama Orphanage, and the Chausubaru Settlement: A Vision of Child Relief through Communal Labor and a Sustainable Local Economy, 1887–1926" (2007).

109. Tokyo city records listed "the principal charitable institutions in the city" at the end of the Meiji era, seventeen in all. They included everything from orphanages to hospitals, from rescue shelters to the Tokyo Municipal Asylum; two of them provided free lodging for indigents. *Dai jūichi kai Tokyo shi tōkei nenpyō: 1914*, 386–387.

110. Yokoyama (Yutani), 210–215. Yokoyama also described a negative example: a self-promoting Osaka area philanthropist, Kobayashi Jusanjo, who created a vocational center for the poor that was filthy, foul smelling, filled with children whose heads were "covered with rashes," and guilty of prison-like conditions (218–223).

111. See, for example, *Shokkō jijō*, vol. 2, 251.

112. See Kinzley, "Discovery of Poverty," 14.

113. Yokoyama (Yutani), 500.

114. Based on chart in Nakagawa, *Gendai no seikatsu*, 65. The situation was largely the same in Osaka, Kyoto, and other cities. Significant change came only after 1932 when the country's first modern relief law took effect.

115. See *Shūkan Heimin Shinbun*, November 15, 1903, 4.

116. Sally Ann Hastings, *Neighborhood and Nation in Tokyo, 1905–1937* (1995), 30. For a discussion of debates, beginning in the 1890s, over the proper role of government in dealing with poverty, see Kojita Yasunao, "Teikoku toshi to 'jichi,'" in Narita Ryūichi, *Toshi to minshū* (1993), 125–127.

117. Hastings, *Neighborhood and Nation*, 34, from *Japan Times*, February 14, 1911. When Beatrice Webb visited Japan in 1911, Prime Minister Katsura Tarō boasted about the generosity of wealthy private donors in quickly raising twenty-five million yen after the emperor asked for gifts for the poor. Diary, August 23, 1911, 84; she noted (September 14, 1911, 154) that the Osaka government had recently offered free rice to starving families but "it had not come to much" because people were "ashamed to apply."

118. Job list and income figures from Yokoyama (Yutani), 191; washing from Junichi Saga, *Confessions of a Yakuza: A Life in Japan's Underworld* (1991), 27.

119. See Tsurumi, *Factory Girls*, 156; *Shūkan Heimin Shinbun*, January 31, 1904, 2.

120. Ambaras, *Bad Youth*, 41.

121. Takano Fusatarō, "Labor Problems in Japan," trans. from *Taiyō*, July 5, 1896, 73–78.

122. Terada Yūkichi, "Tokyo shimin to jinrikisha," *Taiyō*, April 5, 1902, 32.

123. An example of the lack of priority that even socialists put on this issue is in *Shūkan Shakai Shinbun*, March 22, 1908, 1, which takes note of the long hours that children were working, but only in the context of an economic downturn that affected women and children equally. Even Naoe Kinoshita's novel *Pillar of Fire*, which focuses on social inequities, shows children working but does not make child labor an issue.

124. Ambaras, *Bad Youth*, 41.

125. Yokoyama (Yutani), 339.

126. Loopholes in the law meant that in many cases children as young as ten could still work.

127. Matsubara, *Sketches*, 58–59.

128. Borrowing, Hita, "Hinminkutsu," 10; growing sense of community, Nakagawa Kiyoshi, interview, March 17, 1914.

129. Lockwood, *Economic Development*, 288.

130. Yokoyama (Yutani), 196–197.

131. Matsubara, *Sketches*, 50.

132. Ibid., 22, 46, 49.

133. Yokoyama (Yutani), 542–543, 540.

134. Edward Seidensticker, *The Snake that Bowed* (2006), 5, 8.

135. Yokoyama (Yutani), 196.

136. Data from *Tokyo shi tōkei zuhyō*, chart 22 (pages unnumbered) and Ryūichi Shibuya, "The Emergence of Private Pawn Shops: Japanese Government Policy," *Japanese Experience of the United Nations University Human and Social Development Program Series* (1983), http://d-arch.ide.go.jp/je_archive/society/wp_je_unu59.html (accessed August 5, 2015).

137. Shibuya, "Emergence," Table 26; twenty-two of the punishments were "major."

138. Nakagawa, "Senzen ni okeru," 102; 95.7 percent reported no savings.

139. *Tokyo fu tōkeisho*, table 4, in Shibuya, "Emergence"; while 47.1 percent of the city's loans went to people in those four wards, only 38.9 percent of the yen total went there, an indication of the region's poverty.

140. Descriptions in this paragraph are from "Sociological Mirrors," *Taiyō*, April 5, 1902, 5–6; the list of pawned items also draws on Matsubara, *Sketches*, 47, 50, 53.

141. "Sociological Mirrors," *Taiyō*, April 5, 1902, 5.

142. Matsubara, *Sketches*, 48.

143. Ibid., 51–52.

144. Ezekiel 33:10.

145. Ambaras, *Bad Youth*, 41.

146. *Tokyo Pakku*, November 10, 1906 (Kitazawa Rakuten, ed., facsimile ed., vol. 2, 370).

147. Matsubara, *Saiankoku*, 36, 48.

Chapter Five: Shadows and Storms

1. Experience recounted in *Seinen: The Rising Generation* (hereafter *Seinen RG*), August 15, 1898, 16. The name alone is fictitious. *Epigraph*: *Shūkan Shakai Shinbun*, March 22, 1908, p. 1.

2. Naoe Kinoshita, *Pillar of Fire* (1972), 60.

3. Matsubara Iwagorō, *Saiankoku no Tokyo* (1893), 89–90.

4. Home Ministry surveys *Saimin chōsa tōkeihyō* (1912) and *Saimin chōsa tōkeihyō tekiyō* (1912–1913), in Nakagawa Kiyoshi, "Senzen ni okeru toshi kasō no tenkai, jō," *Mita Gakkai Zasshi* (June 1978), 78. The survey found 2,345 homeless people in those four districts, with homeless people as a percentage of all *saimin* ranging from 9.7 in Fukagawa to 20.8 in Asakusa; the overall percentage was 11.2. The ratio of men per 100 women ran from 97.6 in Asakusa to 130.2 in Honjo, with an overall ratio of 119.6. For London, William Booth, *In Darkest England, and the Way Out* (1890), 22.

5. See Nakagawa, "Senzen ni okeru," 80, for graphs based on Home Ministry surveys.

6. *Tokyo Pakku,* May 15, 1906, 153 (drunk); Junichi Saga, *Confessions of a Yakuza: A Life in Japan's Underworld* (1991), 39 (gutter).

7. Yokoyama Gennosuke in Eiji Yutani, "'Nihon no Kaso Shakai' of Gennosuke Yokoyama" (1985), 179 (hereafter Yokoyama (Yutani)).

8. Matsubara, *Saiankoku,* 103 (value labor), 101 (wild existence), 104 (wayside).

9. Nishida Taketoshi, ed., *Toshi kasō shakai: Meiji zenki rōdō jijō* (1949), 231–232. Also David R. Ambaras, *Bad Youth: Juvenile Delinquency and the Politics of Everyday Life in Modern Japan* (2006), 38; he notes that in 1896, newspapers said Tokyo had fewer than 500 urchins in total, 60 percent of them beggars, 35 percent rag pickers; see 32–44 for an excellent discussion of homeless children.

10. Edward S. Morse, *Japan Day by Day,* vol. 1 (1917), 21; Taizo Fujimoto, *The Nightside of Japan* (1915), 30.

11. "Tokyo no hinmin," *Jiji Shinpō,* October/November 1896, in Nakagawa Kiyoshi, ed., *Meiji Tokyo kasō seikatsu shi* (1994), 98.

12. *Seinen RG,* July 17, 1902, 17; September 17, 1902, 17 (different articles on the same person).

13. Fujimoto, *Nightside,* 5.

14. Material in this section is from "Tokyo no hinmin," in Nakagawa, *Seikatsu shi,* 90–128, 102 ("garbage dump," "did not know)," 107 ("floating plants").

15. Ambaras, *Bad Youth,* 37.

16. E. W. Cole, "Japan as Observed by a Foreigner," *Taiyō,* November 1, 1903, 9.

17. *Tokyo Pakku,* June 1, 1908, 250.

18. *Shūkan Heimin Shinbun,* June 12, 1904, 2; the paper also reported that nearly 10 percent of Tokyo's April births had been stillborn.

19. Kathleen Uno, *Passages to Modernity: Motherhood, Childhood, and Social Reform in Early Twentieth Century Japan* (1999), 59; the teachers added that "the children who survive are relatively healthy."

20. Nakagawa "Senzen ni okeru," 84. Using data from *Saimin chōsa tōkeihyō* (1912) and *Saimin chōsa tōkeihyō tekiyō* (1912–1913), he notes that at any given time less than 6 percent of *hinmin* (about a percent more than Tokyoites generally) were ill.

21. William Johnston, *The Modern Epidemic: A History of Tuberculosis in Japan* (1995), 64–65; data from *Tokyo fu tōkei sho.* The infectious mortality rate per 100,000 was 98.9 in the affluent *yamanote* (high city) region and 143.0 in *shitamachi* areas; in outlying areas it was 100.5. According to *Tokyo fu tōkeisho: 1898,* 168–169, the four poverty wards had more than half of the city's deaths from cholera and dysentery, and nearly 40 percent of its deaths from diphtheria.

22. *Dai ni kai Tokyo shi tōkei nenpyō: 1902* (1904), 185–187. These four wards had 37.7 percent of the city's 610 deaths from these diseases that year, but only 30.5 percent of patients who survived the diseases.

23. *Dai jūichi kai Tokyo shi tōkei nenpyō: 1914* (1914), 330–333; people from the four wards made up 38.29 percent of deaths from cholera, 40.4 percent of those from dysentery, and 45.2 percent of those from diphtheria.

24. The poor regions had the largest numbers of stillborns: *Dai jūichi kai Tokyo shi tōkei nenpyō: 1914,* 125. For scarlet fever, *Seinen RG,* May 27, 1902, 1. Beriberi, which some called Japan's "national disease," affected as many as 90 percent of Japanese men in the Sino- and Russo-Japanese Wars; see Alexander R. Bay, *Beriberi in Modern Japan: The Making of a National Disease* (2012), 87–89.

25. Sepp Linhart and Sabine Frühstück, eds., *The Culture of Japan as Seen Through its Leisure* (1998), 65–66.

26. Data on military and prostitutes from Sabine Frühstück, *Colonizing Sex: Sexology and Social Control in Modern Japan* (2003), 35, 46–47.

27. Adachi Kenchū, in Ambaras, *Bad Youth,* 27, 38.

28. See, for example, Yokoyama (Yutani), 198–199, 358–361.

29. Frühstück, *Colonizing Sex*, 58, 72.

30. Inumaru Giichi, ed., *Shokkō jijō,* vol. 1 (1998, originally 1903), 143–144 (hereafter *Shokkō jijō*); Mori Kiichi, *Nihon no kindaika to rōdōsha kaikyū: kaikyūzō no rekishiteki tenkai* (1979), 86.

31. See Sheldon Garon, *The State and Labor in Modern Japan* (1987), 27; the failed plan had been promoted by Gotō Shimpei, who went on to head colonial administrations in Taiwan and Manchuria. For Osaka's first efforts at relief, see Kingo Tamai, "Images of the Poor in an Official Survey of Osaka, 1923–1926," *Continuity and Change* (2000), 99–116.

32. Mori, *Nihon no kindaika,* 86. According to the survey, 56.5 percent of spinning factory women who had TB or venereal disease were fired; death rates among those fired ranged as high as 53.3 percent for women and 36.4 percent for men.

33. Saga, *Confessions,* 32–34.

34. *Tokyo fu tōkei sho: 1898,* 167–168; while 43.4 percent of dysentery patients in the four wards died, 24.8 percent of 609 patients in the rest of the city succumbed. For cholera, 19 in those wards contracted it and 12 died.

35. National smallpox figures are from Irwin Fairfax, "Smallpox in Japan," *Public Health Reports* (1910), 1206. Also see reports in *Seinen RG*: March 27, 1901 (flu), February 8, 1902 (TB), January 18, 1902 (foot-and-mouth, diphtheria), February 1, 1905 (diphtheria), February 21, 1905 (smallpox). On December 7, 1902, *Seinen RG,* 2, reported that Japanese government entities had spent 8,802,600 yen that year fighting epidemics.

36. "River Sumida," in Kafū Nagai, *A Strange Tale from East of the River and Other Stories* (1965), 43–46.

37. Nishikawa Kōjirō, "Byōki seizō no kōnin," *Heimin Shinbun,* June 19, 1904, in *Heimin Shinbun,* vol. 2, 358.

38. Ibid., 124.

39. Takuboku Ishikawa, *Romaji Diary and Sad Toys* (1985), 184. He was twenty-six years old, still in Tokyo; his wife died a year later, also from TB.

40. Yokoyama (Yutani), 8.

41. Annual Tokyo increases, *Tokyo shi tōkei zuhyō* (1914), chart 13. Johnston, *Modern Epidemic,* 61 (overall increases), 39 (1919 peak) (both from *Dai Nihon teikoku tōkei nenkan*), 231 (Nikaidō study).

42. *Yorozu Chōhō,* March 26, 1900, 3.

43. *Dai jūichi kai Tokyo shi tōkei nenpyō: 1914,* 142–143.

44. Nishikawa Kōjirō, "Jinzōbyō," *Heimin Shinbun,* December 20, 1903, in *Heimin Shinbun,* vol. 1, 128.

45. Erwin Baelz, *Awakening Japan: The Diary of a German Doctor* (1974), 98. Baelz was speaking particularly of cholera, typhoid, and smallpox; his observation held true for tuberculosis too. In a 1902 speech at the Tokyo Medical Congress he said the "main things" in treating TB were avoiding "noxious influences" and strengthening "the patient's powers of bodily resistance" (159), both of which were rendered more difficult by poverty.

46. Johnston, *Modern Epidemic,* 32–33, 64.

47. Hida resident, in Mikiso Hane, *Peasants, Rebels, Women, & Outcastes: The Underside of Modern Japan* (2016), 192.

48. Johnston, *Modern Epidemic,* 231 (1909 study), 83–86 (Ishihara study; the death rate was for females under the age of twenty four), 65 (Asakusa mortality rate).

49. Kunikida Doppo, *Kunikida Doppo zenshū*, vol. 5, 513–514, quoted in ibid., 135. Pneumonia catarrh and tuberculosis are so closely related that one often was diagnosed as the other.

50. Johnston, *Modern Epidemic*, 225.

51. For 1893, *Yorozu Chōhō*, March 19, 1900, based on a study by American physician Stuart Eldridge; for 1909, "Japan in 1909," *British Medical Journal* (May 18, 1912), 1140.

52. See Andrew Bernstein, "Fire and Earth: The Forging of Modern Cremation in Meiji Japan," *Japanese Journal of Religious Studies* (Fall 2000), 326. An 1882 epidemic claimed 33,784 lives. Some 9,876 of the 1886 victims were in Tokyo; see Maeda Ai, *Text and the City: Essays on Japanese Modernity* (2004), 24.

53. Morse, *Japan Day by Day*, vol. 2, 244.

54. Michael Lewis, *A Life Adrift: Soeda Azembō, Popular Song, and Modern Mass Culture in Japan* (2009), 7.

55. Dunlop Moore, "Japan: Report from Yokohama," *Public Health Reports (1896–1970)* (December 5, 1902), 2770.

56. Foreign diplomats and ship captains sometime refused to cooperate with quarantine demands, citing extraterritoriality provisions in the binational treaties; in one notorious episode, a cholera epidemic in Yokohama claimed thousands of lives after officers on the German ship *Hesperia* defied quarantine orders; see *Tokyo Times*, August 9, 1879.

57. The first infectious disease law, issued in 1877, was followed by numerous amendments and provisions, culminating in an 1897 Law for the Prevention of Infectious Diseases; see Akihito Suzuki and Mika Suzuki, "Cholera, Consumer and Citizenship: Modernisations of Medicine in Japan," in *The Development of Modern Medicine in Non-Western Countries: Historical Perspectives*, ed. Ebrahimnejad Hormoz (2009), 187.

58. Bernstein, "Fire and Earth," 326. For general control measures, see "Brief Review of the Operations of the Home Department (of Japan) in Connection with the Cholera Epidemic of the 18th Year of Meiji (1885)," *The British Medical Journal* (1878), 1046. Also Baelz, *Awakening Japan*, 47, for a July 16, 1879, academic conference on dealing with cholera.

59. Susan L. Burns, "Contemplating Places: The Hospital as Modern Experience in Meiji Japan," in *New Directions in the Study of Meiji Japan*, ed. Helen Hardacre (1997), 708–709. Patients with leprosy, TB, syphilis, and mental illness also were sent to these quarantine hospitals. Suzuki and Suzuki, "Cholera," 188, describes a violent uprising by a thousand Niigata farmers in 1879 and, in another example of resistance to new medical practices, the killing of a doctor in Chiba who "had been extremely unpopular because of his practice of digging up corpses for the purpose of anatomical study."

60. Yumoto Kōichi, *Zusetsu Meiji jibutsu kigen jiten* (1998), 166–167, quote by Yoshikawa Kensei. Also see S. Ryan Johansson and Carl Mosk, "Exposure, Resistance and Life Expectancy: Disease and Death during the Economic Development of Japan, 1900–1960," *Population Studies* (July 1987), 219–221. In December 21, 1901, *Seinen RG* attributed a sharp decline in cholera and dysentery epidemics—from an average of 3,586.5 a year to just 661.3 that year—to improved drinking water (2).

61. Suzuki Umeshirō, writing in *Jiji Shinpō*, quoted in Suzuki and Suzuki, "Cholera," 198. He quoted one slum resident as saying, "When we try to buy proper food, we find that we cannot make ends meet unless we engage ourselves with illegal activities."

62. *Tokyo Pakku*, May 20, 1911, 230. Emphasis mine.

63. *Shokkō jijō*, vol. 2, 195–197, quotation, 196. Tobacco factories treated in vol. 1, 250. For several companies' official compensation policies for workers who became ill, as well as a chart of what was paid to victims in 1896, 160–178; the policies were followed inconsistently.

64. Hosoi Wakizō, *Kōjō aishi* (1982), 245–247.

65. Burns, "Contemplating Places," 708.

66. *Taiyō*, "Pesuto ihō," December 5, 1899, 269–270; December 20, 1899, 268–269.

67. Reports in *Yorozu Chōhō*, January 7, April 22 and 29, May 6, 13, 17 (account of reprimand), and 20, June 8, 10, and 18, July 1 and 29, September 23, 1900.

68. *Shokkō jijō*, vol. 2, 196.

69. "Bubonic Plague in Japan," *New York Times*, October 19, 1902; according to the article, only five cases occurred after prevention methods were employed; Moore, "Japan: Report from Yokohama," 2770, said another case occurred on October 24, bringing the total to six. For another report on examining train and ship passengers, see *Seinen RG*, February 10, 1900, 3. Additional reports of disinfecting, isolating, and/or burning infected areas in Fukagawa, Honjo, or Asakusa are in *Seinen RG*, January 17 and 27, 1903, and March 11 and June 1, 1905.

70. *Seinen RG*, February 25, 1900, 2.

71. Data from *Dai jūichi kai Tokyo shi tōkei nenpyō: 1914*, 308–309 make it clear that rat sales were fairly evenly spread among neighborhoods, irrespective of economic status. In 1910, for example, Asakusa ranked third in the city in rats killed (155,446), behind Nihonbashi (170,455) and Kanda (162,696); Honjo collected only 94,654, making it eighth among the fifteen wards.

72. For wages, chapter 2, table 2. Rat purchases, *Seinen RG*, January 25, 1900 (4,000 rats), June 17, 1901 (Yokohama purchases), and *Fūzoku Gahō*, March 10, 1900, 32 (month's totals), February 10, 1900, 12–13 ("discarded rats"). *Yorozu Chōhō*, January 21, 1900, reported that since the outbreak of the epidemic 2,219 rats had been purchased as of January 15; it said on February 11 that 79,846 had been purchased.

73. *Tokyo Pakku*, February 10, 1908, 71 (rat crest), January 20, 1908, 39 (kebabs).

74. *Seinen RG*, May 1, 1901, 50 (toymaker's wife), August 3, 1898, 21 (mother).

75. *Seinen RG*, December 21, 1905, 131 (fish-laden wagon), April 15, 1910, 27 (sandal dealer). For the river festival, see Aoyagi Junrō, ed., *Meiji kyūjūkyūnen: sesō jiken* (1935), 146.

76. Dust storm, *Tokyo Pakku*, April 1, 1906, 100; blizzard, *Shūkan Shakai Shinbun*, April 26, 1908, 2.

77. Earthquakes were not a major problem for the urban *hinmin* from the mid-1890s to the end of Meiji. Tokyo averaged 120 quakes a year from 1903 to 1912, but none caused major damage; see *Dai jūichi kai Tokyo shi tōkei nenpyō: 1914*, 23–24.

78. *Heimin Shinbun*, in *Heimin Shinbun*, vol. 2: "The Problem of the Unemployed," April 17, 1904, in "Eibun kiji ran," 9; the stampede: May 22, 1904, 14; the May 22 article blamed newspapers for calling for the demonstration and stirring up the crowd.

79. Jun'ichiro Tanizaki, *Childhood Years: A Memoir* (1988), 62.

80. Eliza Ruhamah Scidmore, *Jinrikisha Days in Japan* (1891), 332.

81. Statistics Bureau, Ministry of Internal Affairs and Commerce, "Historical Statistics of Japan," 29-1 (Damage by Flood, Tide-water and Storms, 1875–1935).

82. The 1910 catastrophe also is called the Great Meiji Flood; the flood control plan, issued in 1911, created the twenty-two-kilometer long Arakawa Drainage Canal, which greatly reduced flood damage; see Edward Seidensticker, *Low City, High City: Tokyo from Edo to the Earthquake* (1983), 57–58.

83. *Yorozu Chōhō*, September 24, 1912, 1.

84. *Tokyo Pakku*, July 1, 1910, 2.

85. *Tokyo Pakku*, July 10, 1909, 22.

86. Material largely from *Taiyō*, September 1910, 23–24. Also see *Seinen RG*, September 1, 1910, 243 ("incessant downpour," grocery prices), and *Tokyo Pakku*, August 20, 1910 (people knee deep, urinating).

87. *Seinen RG*, September 15, 1912, 357. A twelve-hour storm days later left "extreme damage" in its wake, submerging 400 homes in Fukagawa, 500 in Honjo, and 490 in Shitaya. *Yorozu Chōhō*, September 24, 1912.

88. Jukichi Inouye, *Home Life in Tokyo* (1910), 29.

89. Fire details in Ogi Shinzō, *Tokyo shomin seikatsu shi kenkyū* (1979), 97. Also Henry D. Smith, "From Sketch to Print: Kiyochika's Ryōgoku Fire and Hakone-Shizuoka Prints" (1991), 1–5.

90. Ogi, *Tokyo shomin*, 92, and chart on 99. The 1898 total resulted from 307 fires; 194 fires in 1892 destroyed 6,674 homes. That year also produced extraordinarily heavy rains in Tokyo, with more than six inches falling on June 5 and 67.4 inches across the year; see *Tokyo fu tōkeisho*, vol. 1 (1901), 5.

91. Fujimoto, *Nightside*, 138–139 for 1909–1910; *Tokyo shi tōkei zuhyō* (1914), chart 16 for 1912.

92. *Yorozu Chōhō*, August 2, 1909 (quotations), August 3 (losses). *Tokyo Pakku*, August 10, 1909, 66, estimated buildings lost at 11,000. On August 7, p. 3, *Yorozu* reported that the emperor and empress had given twelve thousand yen to the fire's victims. The fire helped prompt Osaka to create its first public relief agency (*kōseikai*) in 1912. Across time, Osaka had a quarter or less of the fires per capita that Tokyo had. Jordan Sand and Steven Wills, "Governance, Arson, and Firefighting in Edo, 1600–1868," in *Flammable Cities: Urban Conflagration and the Making of the Modern World*, ed. Greg Bankoff, Uwe Lübken, and Jordan Sand (2012), 45.

93. Yutani says landlords were notorious for using materials cheap (and flammable) enough to enable them to recover building costs with three years of rents. Yokoyama (Yutani), 60–61.

94. Hiromichi Ishizuka, "The Slum Dwellings and the Urban Renewal Scheme in Tokyo, 1868–1923" (June 1981), 181.

95. Inouye, *Home Life*, 30–31.

96. 1912: *Dai jūichi kai Tokyo shi tōkei nenpyō: 1914*, 380–381; 1,695 homes were destroyed and another 326 partially destroyed in these four wards. The records also show that fires more frequently spread to other homes in this part of Tokyo than they did in the rest of the city. For 1902: *Dai ni kai Tokyo shi tōkei nenpyō 1902*, 224–225; equally telling is that the burned properties in these four wards in 1902 represented only 29.5 percent of the *value* of buildings lost.

97. *Seinen RG*, April 15, 1910, 27.

98. Ogi found arson to be the leading cause between the mid-1880s and the end of the century, accounting for nearly 6,500 destroyed homes and several deaths (*Tokyo shomin*, 98–99); government records suggest that it declined as a cause in the last decade and a half of Meiji.

99. See, for example, *Dai jūichi kai Tokyo shi tōkei nenpyō: 1914*, 380–381: in 1912, only 27.4 percent of Tokyo's arson cases occurred in Shitaya, Asakusa, Honjo, and Fukagawa, though those wards made up 39.3 percent of the population.

100. Ogi, *Tokyo shomin*, 98–99.

101. Inouye, *Home Life*, 30–31.

102. Saga, *Confessions*, 28.

103. Hosoi, *Kōjō aishi*, 241–242; also see E. Patricia Tsurumi, *Factory Girls: Women in the Thread Mills of Meiji Japan* (1990), 44.

104. Material from *Yorozu Chōhō*, April 10, 1911, 1, 3; *Tokyo Pakku*, April 20, 1911, 198–199; T. Philip Terry, *Terry's Japanese Empire: A Guidebook for Travelers* (1914), 222.

105. *Yorozu Chōhō*, July 7, 1898 ("playthings"); *Niroku Shinpō*, April 29—July 25, 1900 (hypocrisy); Ashio discussed in James L. Huffman, *Creating a Public: People and Press in Meiji Japan* (1997), 247–259.

106. Ambaras, *Bad Youth,* 35, 45, notes that the number of minors jailed rose from about 9,000 to 27,000 between 1882 and 1894; the early 1890s typically saw more than 20,000 juveniles a year in jail.

107. Yokoi Tokio, "Seinen no seishinteki daraku," *Seinenkai,* November 1, 1902, 35, argued that youth lacked honesty, diligence, toughness, and self-reliance. For an account of student lodgers not paying bills, see *Niroku Shinpō,* March 1, 1900, 3.

108. See reports in *Yorozu Chōhō,* February 25, 1900, 2; March 11, 1900, 2; May 8, 1900, 2; and May 24, 1900, 2.

109. Sakura Momo, "Kisha mōsu," *Shōnen sekai,* February 15, 1900, 99.

110. *Niroku Shinpō,* February 5, 1900, 3.

111. Words of education minister Makino Nobuaki, reported in *Seinen RG,* July 1, 1906, 149. A different tone was taken by the Christian socialist Kinoshita Naoe, who blamed not money-grubbing lodging-home owners but an absence of adult female nurturers for young men at "a time when spirit and flesh are very active." *Seinenkai,* December 1, 1902, 16.

112. Taken from *Yorozu Chōhō,* January 1, 1900, 4–5; April 13, 1900, 3; March 25, 1900, 3.

113. *Niroku Shinpō,* April 9, 1900, 3 (rape), February 10, 1900, 3 (priest).

114. *Saiankoku no Tokyo* (1893), usually translated "Darkest Tokyo."

115. Terada Yūkichi, "Tokyo shimin to jinrikisha," *Taiyō,* April 5, 1902, 31–32.

116. *Dai jūichi kai Tokyo shi tōkei nenpyō: 1914,* 362–363. The murder rate of roughly three per 100,000 meant that Tokyo, even in the late Meiji years, was a remarkably safe city.

117. *Keisatsuchō tōkeisho: 1900* (1901), 144–145. Combined murder rates in the four wards were 1896, 40; 1898, 73; 1900, 63, all similar to figures for the rest of the city. For 1904, *Keisatsuchō tōkeisho* (128–129) reports seventy-seven murders in the city, with Asakusa having the second highest figure (eleven, after Kanda's thirteen) and Fukagawa the fifth lowest (four).

118. *Dai jūichi kai Tokyo shi tōkei nenpyō: 1914,* 362–363, 370 (money stolen). Exactly a third (25 of 75) of the city's police stations and 33.2 percent of its 4,225 police staff were in these wards, compared with the 39.3 percent of the population who lived there; page 368 shows that 43.9 percent of the individuals apprehended for law violations in 1912 were in the four poor wards. For population, *Tokyo shi tōkei zuhyō* (1914), chart 5.

119. *Yorozu Chōhō,* July 18, 1900, 2.

120. *Niroku Shinpō,* May 28, 1900, 3 (milkman); Yasunari Kawabata, *The Scarlet Gang of Asakusa* (2005), 48; Ambaras, *Bad Youth,* 74 (enka singers); Tanizaki, *Childhood Years,* 64 (pederast; Tanizaki said he was taken off himself once by a military officer and saved from violation only when a policeman happened to show up (44–45)); *Seinen RG,* June 7, 1903 (silver coin), July 15, 1912 (Asakusa abductions).

121. For crime categories, see Statistics Bureau, "Historical Statistics of Japan." For example: 28–2 (Offenders Arrested of Offenses under Penal Code by Type of Crime, 1909–2004); 28–18 (Defendants Convicted by Type of Crime in Ordinary First Instance Cases, 1908–2004). The data do not distinguish the wards of offenders.

122. Yokoyama (Yutani), 57, 282–285 (pieceworkers), 185.

123. Ushiyama Saijirō, *Kōjō junshiki,* in *Meiji Bunka Zenshū 16* (Nihon Hyōronsha, 1959), quoted in Yokoyama (Yutani), 82. See *Seinen RG,* July 15, 1910, 272, for a story about a shoplifters ring led by a book lender and his wife, and Ambaras, *Bad Youth,* 36, for a report from *Shin Kōron* (1911) on boys stealing from local shops.

124. Lewis, *Life Adrift,* 189–190; Saga, *Confessions,* 16–18, 29.

125. *Seinen RG,* September 27, 1902, 1.

126. *Seinen RG,* June 20, 1899, 4 (watch); *Niroku Shinpō,* February 8, 1900, 3 (rickshaw rider).

127. Iwagoro Matsubara, *Sketches of Humble Life in the Capital of Japan* (1897), 42; this is a slightly abbreviated, fairly loose translation of Matsubara's *Saiankoku no Tokyo*, which gives the Shin'ami-chō numbers on 62.

128. Ambaras, *Bad Youth*, 36–37.

129. Aoyagi, *Sesō jiken*, 127; the watch reportedly had once belonged to the oligarch Itō Hirobumi. For another pickpocketing case in which a boss was given a fifteen-year sentence and his twenty-one followers lesser sentences, *Seinen RG*, November 1, 1910, 50.

130. Saga, *Confessions*, 169–171.

131. *Yorozu Chōhō*, April 5, 1900, 3; Aoyagi, *Sesō jiken*, 123.

132. *Yorozu Chōhō*, January 4, 1900, 3.

133. Strangulation accounts, *Niroku Shinpō*, May 3, 1900, 3; May 29, 1900, 3. Child, jumping from bridges, *Shūkan Heimin Shinbun*, March 13, 1904, 2.

134. Kawabata, *Scarlet Gang*, 12.

135. Saga, *Confessions*, 45.

136. *Niroku Shinpō*, May 11, 1900, 1.

137. Kinoshita, *Pillar*, 84.

138. "Life of a Policeman," *Tokyo Pakku*, May 15, 1906, 158.

139. Saga, *Confessions*, 89.

140. Anandi Mani, Sendhil Mullainathan, Eldar Shafir, and Jiaying Zhao, "Poverty Impedes Cognitive Function," *Science* (August 30, 2013), 980, 976.

141. George Orwell, *Down and Out in Paris and London* (1933), 38.

142. *Shokkō jijō*, vol. 1, 45 (quotes), 47–49 (weight studies). In two studies, night shift employees had lost between 0.8 and 1.4 pounds after a week of work, while day workers had gained weight at two of the factories and lost between 0.3 and 0.8 pounds at the third.

143. Yokoyama (Yutani), 326.

144. Makoto Kumazawa, *Portraits of the Japanese Workplace* (1996), 27.

145. Masami Iwata and Akihiko Nishizawa, *Poverty and Social Welfare in Japan* (2008), 243.

146. Paulo Freire, *Pedagogy of the Oppressed* (2007), 63.

147. Sayo Masuda, *Autobiography of a Geisha* (2004), 21.

148. Yokoyama (Yutani), 200.

149. Nakagawa, "Senzen ni okeru," 103.

150. Taira, "Urban Poverty," 167–168.

151. *Seinen RG*, September 17, 1903, 1.

152. *Keisatsuchō tōkeisho: 1900* (1901), 242. Shitaya and Fukagawa had 35 suicides each, Honjo 33, and Asakusa 32, while the average for the other wards was 8.6; for similar figures, see *Keisatsuchō tōkeisho: 1907*, 123. The exception to the pattern was Shiba, site of the Shin'ami-chō slum, which had 38 suicides in 1900.

153. *Keisatsuchō tōkeisho: 1900*, 136, for figures from 1896 to 1900. "Spiritual disorder" accounted for 46.4 percent of suicides in 1896, 42.1 percent in 1899. Comparative figures in 1896 were 10.4 percent for illness, 13.1 percent for work issues, and 4.6 percent for love.

154. *Shūkan Heimin Shinbun*, December 6, 13, 20, 1903, and January 17, 1904, all on p. 2.

155. *Niroku Shinpō*, May 13, 1900, 3.

156. Higuchi Ichiyō, "Child's Play" (Takekurabe), in Robert Lyons Danly, *In the Shade of Spring Leaves: The Life of Higuchi Ichiyō With Nine of Her Best Short Stories* (1984), 277.

157. Matsubara, *Sketches*, 5.

158. Ibid., 19.

159. Orwell, *Down and Out*, 119.

160. Ibid., 40, cited in Sally Ann Hastings, *Neighborhood and Nation in Tokyo, 1905–1937* (1995), 30.

Chapter Six: The Sun Also Shone

1. Observed by author, Swakopmund, Namibia, April 6, 2015.

2. *Niroku Shinpō*, March 13, 1901 ("Come, Laborers"), March 23, 1901 ("we seek"), reprinted in Sakurada Kurabu, ed., *Akiyama Teisuke den*, vol. 1 (1977), 157, 248.

3. *Niroku Shinpō*, March 22, 1901.

4. *Niroku Shinpō*, April 1, 1901; Uchikawa Yoshimi and Matsushima Eiichi, eds., *Meiji nyūsu jiten*, vol. 6 (1983–1986), 799.

5. *Niroku Shinpō*, March 22, 1901, reprinted in Suzuki Kōichi, *Nyūsu de ou Meiji Nihon hakkutsu*, vol. 7 (1995), 33. The political motive is suggested too in Akiyama's later recollection of the event as "the first big demonstration in the history of the Japanese labor movement." Sakurada Kurabu, *Akiyama Teisuke den*, vol. 1, 159.

6. *Meiji no kurashi no kan, Me de miru Edo Meiji hyakka*, vol. 5 (1996), 102.

7. *Niroku Shinpō*, April 4, 1901, in Suzuki, *Nyūsu*, 34. Photos of the event ran in the magazine *Fūzoku Gahō*, April 15, 1901, following 32.

8. *Meiji no kurashi no kan*, 102. *Niroku* accused the police afterward (April 6, 7) of overuse of their power and labeled them "enemies in the eyes of labor." Sakurada, *Akiyama Teisuke den*, vol. 1, 159.

9. *Niroku Shinpō*, April 4, 1901; Uchikawa and Matsushima, *Meiji nyūsu jiten*, vol. 6, 800–801. Also see James L. Huffman, *Creating a Public: People and Press in Meiji Japan* (1997), 254.

10. Sakurada, *Akiyama Teisuke den*, vol. 1, 95.

11. Suzuki, *Nyūsu*, 38, from accounts in *Jiji Shinpō* (May 6, 12, 1901) and *Niroku Shinpō* (October 29, 1901).

12. Sakurada, *Akiyama Teisuke den*, vol. 1, 161. For second prohibition, *Jiji Shinpō*, March 17, 1902; for "Tears," *Niroku Shinpō*, March 21, 1902.

13. Eiji Yutani, "'Nihon no Kaso Shakai' of Gennosuke Yokoyama" (1985), 79 (hereafter cited as Yokoyama (Yutani)).

14. Paulo Freire, *Pedagogy of the Oppressed* (2007), 51; Freire also argued that poor people should "be their own example in the struggle for their redemption" (54).

15. Kafū Nagai, "Coming Down with a Cold," in *A Strange Tale from East of the River and Other Stories* (1965), 60–61.

16. Mikiso Hane, *Peasants, Rebels, Women, & Outcastes: The Underside of Modern Japan* (2016), 185 ("prison"); *Shūkan Heimin Shinbun*, December 13, 1903, 2 ("cows").

17. Edward Fowler, *San'ya Blues: Laboring Life in Contemporary Tokyo* (1996), 229.

18. Kenji Nakagami, *The Cape and Other Stories from the Japanese Ghetto* (1999), 25–26.

19. Matsubara Iwagorō, *Saiankoku no Tokyo* (1893), 57–58, 30.

20. Maeda Ai, "Their Time as Children," in Maeda Ai, *Text and the City* (2004), 114. Maeda notes the stereotyping in this story, pointing out that this sense of self-reliance "is exactly what the adults in the Meiji state expected" (115). The frequency with which stories of ambitious young workers appeared suggests nonetheless that the boy's sentiments were shared by significant numbers of *hinmin*.

21. Iwagoro Matsubara, *Sketches of Humble Life in the Capital of Japan* (1897), 23; this is a slightly abbreviated, loose translation of Matsubara's *Saiankoku no Tokyo*. Emphasis in original.

22. Yokoyama (Yutani), 310.

23. Junichi Saga, *Confessions of a Yakuza: A Life in Japan's Underworld* (1991), 249.

24. Data from Kiyoshi Nakagawa, "Ambitions, 'Family-Centredness' and Expenditure Patterns in a Changing Urban Class Structure: Tokyo in the Early Twentieth Century," *Continuity and Change* (2000), 83.

25. Yanagita Kunio, *Meiji Taishō shi sesō hen, shinsōban* (1976), 144.

26. Yokoyama (Yutani), 407, 166.

27. Discussed in Yokoyama (Yutani), 277–285.

28. Naoe Kinoshita, *Pillar of Fire* (1972), 111.

29. Ibid., 336.

30. Matsubara, *Saiankoku*, 135, 138.

31. Yokoyama Gennosuke, *Naichi zakkyo go no Nihon* (1954), 107, 106. Although Eiji Yutani (Yokoyama, Yutani), 119–121, is mistaken in claiming that Yokoyama coined the word, its use spread after his time; today it generally is translated "gallantry" or "being spirited or dashing."

32. *Yorozu Chōhō*, English column, January 12, 1900, 2; the original misspells obedience "obeidience."

33. *Yorozu Chōhō*, May 8, 1900, 2 (smoking); *Tokyo Shakai Shinbun*, May 25, 1908, 1 (bicycles); Aoyagi Junrō, ed., *Meiji kyūjūkyūnen: sesō jiken* (1935), 98 (*kichin'yado*).

34. Figures from *Jiji Shinpō*, October 31, 1900, in Uchikawa and Matsushima, *Meiji nyūsu jiten*, vol. 6, 314, and C. William Mensendiek, "Protestant Missionary Perceptions of Meiji Japan," *Kyōkai to Shingaku* (March 1986), 243. Also see Huffman, *Creating a Public*, 255–256, and Sheldon Garon, *Molding Japanese Minds: The State in Everyday Life* (1997), 94.

35. Hiromichi Ishizuka, "The Slum Dwellings and the Urban Renewal Scheme in Tokyo, 1868–1923," *The Developing Economies* (June 1981), 169.

36. Yoshino Sakuzō, "Minshū no seiryoku," *Chūō Kōron*, April 1, 1914, 87, quoted in Andrew Gordon, *Labor and Imperial Democracy in Prewar Japan* (1991), 33.

37. Yamagata to Tokutomi Sohō, January 27, 1914, in Itō Takashi and George Akita, "The Yamagata-Tokutomi Correspondence: Press and Politics in Meiji-Taishō Japan," *Monumenta Nipponica* (Winter 1981), 420.

38. See Gordon, *Labor and Imperial Democracy*, 26–62, especially 26.

39. Ibid., 27, emphasis in original. See page 344 for a chart of more than seven thousand assemblies and rallies in 1905–1912, some requiring permits and even more not needing permits.

40. Huffman, *Creating a Public*, especially 310–358.

41. Shumpei Okamoto, *The Japanese Oligarchy & the Russo-Japanese War* (1970), 214–215.

42. Chart compiled by Gordon, *Labor and Imperial Democracy*, 37, from Miyachi Masato, *Nichiro sengo seiji shi kenkyū* (University of Tokyo Press, 1973), 227. Of the 327 people arrested or tried, 82 were artisans, 28 did outdoor labor and building work, 29 (including 16 rickshaw pullers) were in transport, 44 were factory workers, and 20 were unemployed. For female participation—including the speech of the teenager Ōno Umeyo in a 1913 Hibiya rally—see Gordon, *Labor and Imperial Democracy*, 36, as well as the photos in *Tokyo Sōjō Gahō* 66 (September 13, 1905), especially 5, 8, 27. Also Andrew Gordon, "Social Protest in Imperial Japan: The Hibiya Riot of 1905," *Asia-Pacific Journal* 12, issue 29, no. 3 (July 20, 2014).

43. Kingo Tamai, "Images of the Poor in an Official Survey of Osaka, 1923–1926," *Continuity and Change* (2000), 102.

44. Okamoto, *Japanese Oligarchy*, 215.

45. Gordon's phrase, *Labor and Imperial Democracy*, 32.

46. September 2, 1905, in Okamoto, *Japanese Oligarchy*, 185.

47. Quoted in ibid., 207.

48. Gordon, *Labor and Imperial Democracy*, 40–41.

49. *Yorozu Chōhō*, July 8, 1911, in Uchikawa and Matsushima, *Meiji nyūsu jiten*, vol. 8, 566.

50. *Yomiuri Shinbun*, July 3, 1901, quoted in Yamamoto Taketoshi, *Kindai Nihon no shinbun dokusha sō* (1981), 193.

51. This point is discussed in Huffman, *Creating a Public*, especially 378–380.

52. Abe Isoo, *Taiyō*, January 1, 1904, 7.

53. "Tram Car Fare Question," *Heimin Shinbun,* November 29, 1903, in "Eibun kiji ran," *Heimin Shinbun,* vol. 1, Osaka: Sōgensha, 1953, 6.

54. Kenneth Pyle, "The Emergence of Bureaucratic Conservatism in the Meiji Period," *Undercurrent* (March 1983), 26–27.

55. Itō and Akita, "Yamagata-Tokutomi Correspondence," June 19, 1915, 411 (extremely volatile), January 27, 1914, 420 (unthinking courage).

56. Yokoyama (Yutani), 528, 128–129.

57. *Yorozu Chōhō,* October 24, 1900, 1.

58. *Yorozu Chōhō,* April 9, 1904, in Suzuki, *Nyūsu,* 36.

59. Gordon, *Labor and Imperial Democracy,* 64 (quotation), 80–81 (early unions), 68–69 (railway workers). For the 200,000 workers in unions, see Chushichi Tsuzuki, *The Pursuit of Power in Modern Japan: 1825–1995* (2000), 148; he notes that a labor stoppage by one hundred female silk workers in Kōfu in 1886 is usually called Japan's first strike.

60. Gary D. Allinson, *Japanese Urbanism: Industry and Politics in Kariya, 1872–1972* (1975), 44.

61. Former figures from Aoki Kōji, *Nihon rōdō undō shi nenpyō* (1968), in ibid., 66; latter figures from Mori Kiichi, *Nihon no kindaika to rōdōsha kaikyū: kaikyūzō no rekishiteki tenkai* (1979), 101.

62. Yokoyama (Yutani), 521–527.

63. *Seinen: The Rising Generation* (hereafter *Seinen RG*), February 25, 1900, 2 (umbrella makers), December 1, 1905, 99 (filature workers), January 15, 1912, 227 (New Year's Eve shutdown); *Yorozu Chōhō,* March 25, 1900 (barge workers); *Shūkan Heimin Shinbun,* December 6, 1903, 1 (tea factory), April 10, 1904, 2 (brick makers); *Tokyo Shakai Shinbun,* June 5, 1908, 2 (dyers, renters); *Shūkan Shakai Shinbun,* June 15, 1908, 6 (conductors, journalists, carpenters). The Yokoyama report, Andrew Gordon, *The Evolution of Labor Relations in Japan: Heavy Industry, 1853–1955* (1985), 28.

64. Yokoyama (Yutani), 521–524; results of five of the strikes were listed as unclear. More than 4,230 workers went on strike in these episodes. Their occupations included brick making, spinning, stone cutting, railway track work, conducting on trains, paper making, running water mills, silk reeling, mining, silk dyeing, ship carpentry, salt curing, cutting tobacco leaves, construction, carrying coal, hemp work, sawing, charcoal making, electric light work, and pottery making.

65. Mori, *Nihon no kindaika,* 101.

66. *Shūkan Heimin Shinbun,* April 10, 1904, 2 (brick makers); *Shūkan Shakai Shinbun,* June 15, 1908, 6 (*Japan Gazette*); the journalists also won a promise of year-end bonuses and a cap of eight hours of work on Sundays.

67. Matsubara, *Sketches,* 54.

68. *Taiyō,* August 1, 1903, 13 (English column).

69. *Tokyo Pakku,* January 1, 1910, 11.

70. Kinoshita, *Pillar of Fire,* 106.

71. The novelist, identified as Dé Lilah (*Niroku Shinpō,* June 7, 1900, 1), appears to have been Lucie van Renesse, who had been born in East Java; E. S. Morse, *Japanese Homes,* 4–6, in Susan B. Hanley, "Urban Sanitation in Preindustrial Japan," *Journal of Interdisciplinary History* (Summer 1987), 23.

72. Kathleen Uno, *Passages to Modernity: Motherhood, Childhood, and Social Reform in Early Twentieth Century Japan* (1999), 66.

73. *Niroku Shinpō,* March 22, 1901, in Suzuki, *Nyūsu,* 32.

74. *Seinen RG,* July 17, 1902, 17.

75. Huffman, *Creating a Public,* 387.

76. *Yorozu Chōhō*, November 1, 1892, in Okano Takeo, *Meiji genron shi* (1974), 113.

77. *Yorozu Chōhō*, August 2, 1909, 1. The bottom third of the page was filled with ads, including one for transcripts of cooking lectures.

78. Ono Hideo, "Kuroiwa Shūroku," in *Sandai genronjin shū*, vol. 6 (1962), 28.

79. Yamamoto, *Shinbun dokusha sō*, 129; also see page 96. Uchimura's essay is in *Yorozu Chōhō*, October 6, 1901; it bears noting that *Niroku* did not publish between 1895 and 1900.

80. Yamamoto, *Shinbun dokusha sō*, 359.

81. *Taiyō*, August 1, 1903, 13.

82. *Tokyo Pakku*, April 1, 1909, 155 (chimney sweep); *Tokyo Pakku*, January 1, 1910, 11 ("first present"); *Niroku Shinpō*, May 28, 1900, 3 ("revenge"); *Tokyo Pakku*, September 1, 1909, 103 (tract); *Tokyo Pakku*, December 20, 1907, 263 (bill collector).

83. *Tokyo Pakku*, October 1, 1911, 154.

84. Sayo Masuda, *Autobiography of a Geisha* (2004), 141–142.

85. *Seinen RG*, November 15, 1910, 83.

86. Michael Lewis, *A Life Adrift: Soeda Azembō, Popular Song, and Modern Mass Culture in Japan* (2009), 66, 42.

87. Uno, *Passages to Modernity*, 70.

88. Matsubara, *Sketches*, 15–16.

89. From *Jiji Shinpō* series "Tokyo no hinmin," Oct. 11–Nov. 19, 1896, reprinted in Nakagawa Kiyoshi, ed., *Meiji Tokyo kasō seikatsu shi* (1994), 107.

90. Masuda, *Autobiography*, 120 (head in noose); Tamai, "Images of the Poor," 103 (demanding release).

91. Takeo Yazaki, *Social Change and the City in Japan: From Earliest Times Through the Industrial Revolution* (1968), 366.

92. David R. Ambaras, *Bad Youth: Juvenile Delinquency and the Politics of Everyday Life in Modern Japan* (2006), 64.

93. Hita Sei, "Hinminkutsu," *Fūzoku Gahō* (November 10, 1898), 10.

94. Nakagawa Kiyoshi, "Senzen ni okeru toshi kasō no tenkai, jō," *Mita Gakkai Zasshi* (June 1978), 72.

95. See Kamishima Jirō, *Kindai Nihon no seishin kōzō* (1961), 58–71.

96. Matsubara, *Sketches*, 11–12.

97. Yokoyama (Yutani), 200.

98. Kinoshita, *Pillar of Fire*, 97.

99. *Niroku Shinpō*, May 30, 1900, 3.

100. *Yorozu Chōhō*, December 23, 1900, 2, English-language column. At least eleven people were killed in the stampede.

101. Victor Turner, *The Ritual Process: Structure and Anti-Structure* (1969), 128, 202.

102. Matsubara, *Sketches*, 41.

103. *Seinen RG*, June 20, 1899, 18.

104. Ibid., June 27, 1902, 15.

105. Ibid., September 27, 1900, 13 (rickshaw puller); January 11, 1902, 9 (civil servant); May 27, 1902, 14 (telegraph operator).

106. Robert Lyons Danly, *In the Shade of Spring Leaves: The Life of Higuchi Ichiyō With Nine of Her Best Short Stories* (1984), 44, from Higuchi's diary, July 21, 1891. The popular poet Ishikawa Tokuboku would not have been considered part of the *kasō shakai* because of his fame, but, like several writers, he was a *hinmin* financially; a friend said that a few days before his death, "he asked me to find a publisher for his book of poems, as he was penniless." Takuboku Ishikawa, *Romaji Diary and Sad Toys* (1985), 34.

107. Yokoyama (Yutani), 2.

108. Sakurada, *Akiyama Teisuke den*, vol. 1, 45.

109. From Takai Toshio, *My Own Sad History of Female Textile Workers*, in Ronald P. Loftus, *Telling Lives: Women's Self-Writing in Modern Japan* (2004), 94.

110. Mikiso Hane, ed., *Reflections on the Way to the Gallows: Voices of Japanese Rebel Women* (1988), 121. See also Kaneko Fumiko, *The Prison Memoirs of a Japanese Woman* (1991).

111. Gordon, *The Evolution of Labor Relations in Japan*, 29.

112. Nakagawa, "Ambitions," 78, 85 (Osaka worker), 96 ("desire to distance").

113. Matsubara, *Sketches*, 43–44.

114. Taizo Fujimoto, *The Nightside of Japan* (1915), 47 (singing), 86–96 (sumo wrestling), especially 94–95.

115. *Dai jūichi kai Tokyo shi tōkei nenpyō: 1914* (1914), 312–313; figures are for 1912. Honjo had 117 bath houses, Asakusa 109; Shiba came next with 78. Asakusa had 1,023 hair dressers, more than 150 more than any other ward—hardly surprising given its many entertainment establishments.

116. Inumaru Giichi, ed., *Shokkō jijō*, vol. 2 (1903, 1998), 221, 216, 213.

117. Yazaki, *Social Change*, 354; Matsubara, *Sketches*, 91 ("Crowds so thick").

118. Moriyama Shōichi, *Shitamachi no hishi* (1943), 152.

119. Market features of these two paragraphs gathered from Matsubara, *Saiankoku*, 5, 91–96; Matsubara, *Sketches*, 40, 61; "Tokyo-shi chūsei watarigusa: sono ichi daidō monouri" (Medieval ways of subsisting in Tokyo: selling goods on one street), *Fūzoku Gahō*, April 5, 1909, unnumbered front pages; Yazaki, *Social Change*, 439–441.

120. Jun'ichiro Tanizaki, *Childhood Years: A Memoir* (1988), 123.

121. Saga, *Confessions*, 83.

122. Nagai, "River Sumida," in *A Strange Tale*, 9.

123. Tanizaki, *Childhood Years*, 29–30.

124. Yasunari Kawabata, *The Scarlet Gang of Asakusa* (2005), 31.

125. Playwright Kubota Mantarō, in Edward Seidensticker, *Low City, High City: Tokyo from Edo to the Earthquake* (1983), 71. The tower is described in Yumoto Kōichi, *Zusetsu Meiji jibutsu kigen jiten* (1998), 416–417. A 1908 death leap, by Tomioka Riyo, is described in *Yorozu Chōhō*, July 22, 1909, 2; the paper described hers as the third such suicide from the tower. A 1911 death leap is described in Fujimoto, *Nightside*, 4; he also describes Osaka's 250-foot tower, the Tsūtenkaku (225), built in 1912 as Asia's second tallest structure. Also see Suzuki Hiroyuki, *Toshi e, Nihon no kindai* (1999), 243–245.

126. Matsubara, *Sketches*, 82.

127. Kaburagi Kiyokata, *Meiji no Tokyo* (1989), 123. His recollections centered on the Ginza area, which drew its own share of *hinmin* onlookers, as well as beggars, street vendors, and rickshaw pullers.

128. Yokoyama (Yutani), 84.

129. Jun'ichirō Tanizaki, "The Children," in *The Gourmet Club: A Sextet* (2001), 38.

130. Kōjimachi Bō, "Tokai no yūwakubutsu," *Taiyō*, March 5, 1901, 200–206.

131. Matsubara, *Sketches*, 8.

132. George Lynch, *Taiyō*, May 1, 1905, 9.

133. Matsubara, *Sketches*, 41.

134. Yokoyama (Yutani), 545. Also Beatrice Webb, Diary, September 14, 1911, London School of Economics Digital Library, 154.

135. Sakurada, *Akiyama Teisuke den*, 45.

136. On May 8, 1904, during a mass rally to mark Japan's Russo-Japanese War victory at the Yalu River, twenty died in a stampede of celebrants trying to get into the imperial palace gates after a march from Hibiya Park. In the words of one scribe, "We may easily imag-

ine how great the confusion was when we understand that two thousand pairs of wooden clogs . . . were found at that place the next morning." *Shūkan Heimin Shinbun*, May 22, 1904, 2. For a list of Tokyo's fourteen public parks, see *Tokyo fu tōkeisho: 1904* (48–49) and *1908* (45).

137. Noguchi Yone, *Taiyō*, January 1, 1910, 14 (swarms); Tanizaki, "The Children," 17 (droves).

138. *Taiyō*, January 1, 1910, 14; Noguchi was father of the sculptor Isamu Noguchi (14).

139. Higuchi, "Child's Play," in Danly, *Spring Leaves*, 274–275.

140. Tanizaki, *Childhood*, 65.

141. Basil Hall Chamberlain and W. B. Mason, *A Handbook for Travellers in Japan*, 4th ed. revised (1907), 128.

142. Fujimoto, *Nightside*, 151–154.

143. Higuchi, "Child's Play," in Danly, *Spring Leaves*, 256–261.

144. Fujimoto, *Nightside*, 125–127.

145. Higuchi, "Child's Play," in Danly, *Spring Leaves*, 281; Sangorō had a second nickname, Mannenchō, which was the name of Tokyo's largest slum.

146. *Yorozu Chōhō*, July 14, 1909, 2 ("record breaking"); July 18, July 20, 3 (climb); July 26, 2 (reaching summit).

147. *Seinen RG*, January 1, 1910, 146.

148. Kawabata, *Scarlet Gang*, 11.

149. Saga, *Confessions*, 83.

150. I. Suzuki, English column, *Niroku Shinpō*, April 14, 1900, 1.

151. *Seinen RG*, April 20, 1899, 21–22.

152. *Fūzoku Gahō*, April 10, 1900, 18–32.

153. *Tokyo Pakku*, April 15, 1912, 188.

154. *Niroku Shinpō*, April 18, 1900, 3.

155. *Shūkan Heimin Shinbun*, December 6, 1903, 1 (self-conscious); December 13, 1903, 2 (cows and horses).

Chapter Seven: Poverty on the Farm

1. Shimazaki Tōson, regarding the mountainous Komoro region, *Chikuma River Sketches* (1912, 1991), 60.

2. Okamoto Jitsuo, interview, Totsukawa, April 27, 2006. After World War II, Okamoto became a traveling salesman. He bought a refrigerator and put it in his truck, making it Nara Prefecture's first "refrigerated truck." Another Totsukawa resident, Tamaki Kisaku, interviewed the same day, said *chagayu*, which is "delicious," still is used by locals to treat colds.

3. Simon Partner, *Toshié: A Story of Village Life in Twentieth-Century Japan* (2004), 7.

4. Shimazaki, *Chikuma River*, 81; Tadashi Fukutake, *Japanese Rural Society* (1967), 205.

5. Gary D. Allinson, *Japanese Urbanism: Industry and Politics in Kariya, 1872–1972* (1975), 41; Richard J. Smethurst, *Agricultural Development and Tenancy Disputes in Japan, 1870–1940* (1986), 228–229, agrees, arguing that the Meiji farmer, "whether rich or poor, was not merely a pawn to be buffeted by an unjust market system" but "a positive actor, an 'economic animal,' a small entrepreneur, if you will."

6. Miyamoto Tsuneichi, *The Forgotten Japanese: Encounters with Rural Life and Folklore* (2010), 218, 225.

7. Mikiso Hane, *Peasants, Rebels, Women, & Outcastes: The Underside of Modern Japan* (2016), 35; the medical worker said peasants "all have common, vulgar faces" and some

"would have been better off had they not been born." His impression of farmers improved as he worked with them.

8. For examples of their condescension, see Mori Ōgai, "Youth," *Youth and Other Stories* (1994), 395; Natsume Sōseki, *Botchan* (1968), 126. One *Taiyō* writer commented that its readers tended to "give the epithet 'provincial' to everything that is not of Tokyo": August 1, 1903, 10.

9. Certain famous novelists are typically known in Japan today by their given names. In keeping with that custom, the body of the text refers to Shimazaki as Tōson and to Tayama as Katai, while the others are referred to by their family names.

10. Tayama Katai, *Country Teacher* (1984), dust jacket.

11. His writing about village life has been described as "very realistic." Ann Waswo and Nishida Yoshiaki, eds., *Farmers and Village Life in Twentieth-Century Japan* (2003), 8.

12. Shimazaki, *Chikuma River,* 135, xviii.

13. Fukutake, *Japanese Rural Society,* 5. According to Chart 2–7, Statistics Bureau, Ministry of Internal Affairs and Commerce, "Historical Statistics of Japan," 11.7 percent of the population lived in urban areas in 1898, while 16 percent did in 1908. Rice constituted more than half of Japan's agricultural production in the late Meiji years.

14. Muraoka Koremitsu, interview, April 8, 1987, Center for Oral History, *Kōloa: Oral History,* vol. 3 (1988), 1334.

15. For data, see Hane, *Peasants, Rebels,* 29; Ann Waswo, "The Transformation of Rural Society, 1900–1950," in *Cambridge History of Japan: The Twentieth Century,* ed. Peter Duus (1988), 541; Smethurst, *Agricultural Development,* 107 (plot size); Fukutake, *Japanese Rural Society,* 6. According to Takeo Yazaki, *Social Change and the City in Japan: From Earliest Times Through the Industrial Revolution* (1968), in 1908, 89.4 percent of Japan's farm area was in farms of less than two *chō* (roughly five acres).

16. Smethurst, *Agricultural Development,* 12; Waswo, "Transformation," 566–567. Smethurst notes that taxes as a proportion of the farmers' income fell steadily after the mid-1880s (51).

17. Smethurst, *Agricultural Development,* 282, emphasis his.

18. Nakagawa Kiyoshi, ed., *Nihon no toshi kasō* (1985), 93.

19. Jackson Y. Bailey, *Ordinary People, Extraordinary Lives: Political and Economic Change in a Tōhoku Village* (1991), 51.

20. Eiji Yutani, "'Nihon no Kaso Shakai' of Gennosuke Yokoyama" (1985), 440 (hereafter Yokoyama (Yutani)).

21. Waswo, "Transformation," 543.

22. Smethurst, *Agricultural Development,* 281. He argues that while market economics caused increased tenancy, the primary cause of rising tenancy was "land reclamation and the liberation of farmers from feudal semi-bondage on large estates" (29).

23. Nishikawa Kōjirō, "Kyūjūkyū ri no kyūmin," *Heimin Shinbun,* April 24, 1904, in *Heimin Shinbun,* vol. 2, 179.

24. Mori Giichi, *Kosaku sōgi senjutsu* (Strategy and tactics of tenancy disputes, 1928), 4–5, in Waswo, "Transformation," 576.

25. Yasushi Inoue, *Shirobamba: A Childhood in Old Japan* (1991), 107.

26. Ibid., 60.

27. Ibid., 38.

28. Ibid., 34.

29. Ibid., 52, 62.

30. Ibid., 91.

31. Ibid., 119 note 55, 114.

32. Kazo Tanima, interview, October 10, 1980, *A Social History of Kona,* vol. 4 (1981), 750.

33. Tayama, *Country Teacher*, 6.

34. Inoue, *Shirobamba*, 25, 11.

35. Tayama, *Country Teacher*, 6, 7.

36. Simon Partner, "Peasants into Citizens? The Meiji Village in the Russo-Japanese War," *Monumenta Nipponica* (Summer 2007), 179.

37. Tayama, *Country Teacher*, 52.

38. Junichi Saga, *Confessions of a Yakuza: A Life in Japan's Underworld* (1991), 153.

39. Shimazaki, *Chikuma River*, 44; Haruko Wakita, Anne Bouchy, and Ueno Chizuko, eds. *Gender and Japanese History*, vol. 2 (1999), 424.

40. Shimazaki, *Chikuma River*, 116 note 15, 43; also see Partner, *Toshié*, 12–14.

41. Naoe Kinoshita, *Pillar of Fire* (1972), 175.

42. Shimazaki, *Chikuma River*, 49 (holding tank, horses), 10 (blended lives), 83–84 (pigs). For a discussion of the role small animals such as cats, dogs, and chickens played, see Yanagita Kunio, *Meiji Taishō shi sesō hen* (1993), 163–167.

43. 1900 survey in Kanagawa Prefecture; Partner, *Toshié*, 21.

44. Shimazaki, *Chikuma River*, 45, 116 note 14.

45. Inoue, *Shirobamba*, 20.

46. Kame Okano, interview, November 1, 1980, *Social History of Kona*, vol. 1, 593–594; also Miyamoto, *Forgotten Japanese*, 67.

47. Usaku Morihara, interview, November 6, 1980, *Social History of Kona*, vol. 2, 844.

48. Nagatsuka Takashi, *The Soil: A Portrait of Rural Life in Meiji Japan* (1989), 35–36.

49. Partner, *Toshié*, 21–23.

50. Michi Kodama-Nishimoto, Warren Nishimoto, and Cynthia Oshiro, eds., *Hanahana: An Oral History Anthology of Hawaii's Working People* (1984), 149. "Shirimochi" normally is used in a reference to falling on one's rear, but laborer Osame Manago said her family used the word for dried human dung that was applied to crops.

51. Tayama, *Country Teacher*, 185.

52. Osame Nagata Manago, interview, in Kodama-Nishimoto, Nishimoto, and Oshira, *Hanahana*, 150.

53. Shimazaki, *Chikuma River*, 55.

54. Shimazaki, *Chikuma River*, 90; Partner, *Toshié*, 5.

55. *Seinen: The Rising Generation* (hereafter *Seinen RG*), April 12, 1902, 2 (Niigata); *Shūkan Heimin Shinbun*, March 15, 1908, 1 (Hida). Nitta Jirō, *Death March on Mount Hakkōda* (1992), recounts the military disaster fictitiously.

56. Izumi Kyōka, *In Light of Shadows: More Gothic Tales* (2005), 14.

57. Shimazaki, *Chikuma River*, 56.

58. Ibid., 188 (shop lady), 18 (night soil); Tatsuichi Horikiri, *The Stories Clothes Tell: Voices of Working-Class Japan* (2016), 70 (blind beggar); Tayama, *Country Teacher*, 83 (priests); Ochiai Emiko, "Modern Japan Through the Eyes of an Old Midwife," in Wakita, Bouchy, and Chizuko, *Gender*, vol. 1, 239 (midwife).

59. Tayama, *Country Teacher*, 8 (vulgar farmer); Partner, "Peasants into Citizens?" 198 (broader ties).

60. Shimazaki, *Chikuma River*, 18–19, 157, 131. Also William E. Naff, *The Kiso Road: The Life and Times of Shimazaki Tōson* (2011), 188–190, 609–610. Kimura also founded Meiji Jogakkō, in Tokyo.

61. Shimazaki Tōson, *The Broken Commandment* (1974), 4.

62. Miyamoto, *Forgotten Japanese*, 54.

63. Osame Nagata Manago, interview, in Kodama-Nishimoto, Nishimoto, and Oshiro, *Hanahana*, 149.

64. Shimazaki, *Chikuma River*, 72; Bun Kobayashi Yoshimori, interview, Center for Oral History, *Kōloa*, vol. 3 (1988), 1307.

65. Waswo and Nishida, *Farmers and Village Life*, 40; survey by Imperial Agriculture Association.

66. Men in the thirty-one to fifty age category, by contrast, did just a quarter of the housework; when all ages were included, males did 29.6 percent of the housework. Waswo and Nishida, *Farmers and Village Life*, 40.

67. Horikiri, *Stories Clothes Tell*, 17, 22, 73–74.

68. Lloyd Kenzo Sugimoto, interview, October 1, 1980, *Social History of Kona*, vol. 1, 212.

69. Waswo and Nishida, *Farmers and Village Life*, 41.

70. Ibid., 42, surveying three farm households in 1915. Females over sixteen years old in these two families put in 55 percent of the workdays; in the third household, adult males put in 55 percent of the workdays.

71. Ochiai, "Modern Japan," in Wakita, Bouchy, and Chizuko, *Gender*, vol. 1, 251–253. Fabian Drixler, *Mabiki: Infanticide and Population Growth in Eastern Japan, 1660–1950* (2013), estimates that until about 1920 half of babies were born without help from a licensed midwife (214, 342–343 notes 32, 33).

72. Anne Bouchy, "The Chisel of the Women Divers and the Bow of the Feudal Lords of the Sea," in Wakita, Bouchy, and Chizuko, *Gender*, vol. 2, 382–384.

73. Data from Inumaru Giichi, ed., *Shokkō jijō*, vol. 1 (1998, 1903), 222; the rural prefectures with the largest numbers of silk factories were, in descending order, Nagano, Gifu, Yamanashi, Mie, Gunma, and Fukushima. Aichi, which included the city of Nagoya, was the fourth largest silk-producing prefecture.

74. Ibid., 273, points out that while large factories provided their own housing, workers at small factories usually commuted. In Nagano, 150 of the workers were under age ten; two-thirds were under twenty (224). According to Yokoyama, Japan had 946 factories with fifty or more employees in 1896 and 1,952 smaller than that; 36 had more than five hundred workers. Yokoyama (Yutani), 318.

75. Yokoyama Gennosuke, *Nihon no kasō shakai* (1899, 1949), 144. On the economic impact of sericulture in Yamanashi Prefecture, see Smethurst, *Agricultural Development*, 161–166 and 184–231.

76. Partner, *Toshié*, 17–20; the family's income from silk ranged from one hundred to two hundred yen in the 1920s.

77. Waswo and Nishida, *Farmers and Village Life*, 9.

78. The move to Granny Onui's is described in Yasushi Inoue's autobiographical *Chronicle of My Mother* (1982), 15–17; the mother's behavior and comments appear in his fictitious (but autobiographical) *Shirobamba*, 160.

79. Tayama, *Country Teacher*, 46.

80. Ibid., 114; Nagatsuka, *Soil*, 103–104.

81. Bouchy, "Chisel," in Wakita, Bouchy, and Chizuko, *Gender*, vol. 2, 368.

82. Shimazaki, *Chikuma River*, 67; when visited by the author in 2006, the restaurant still displayed a sign painted by Tōson.

83. Interview with author, March 23, 2014.

84. Partner, *Toshié*, 53.

85. Miyamoto, *Forgotten Japanese*, 70.

86. Shimazaki, *Chikuma River*, 12; Sué Sumii, *The River with No Bridge* (1989), 54.

87. For quotation, Fukutake, *Japanese Rural Society*, 90. Also see Waswo, "Transformation," 546–547; Richard Beardsley, John W. Hall, and Robert E. Ward, *Village Japan* (1959), 126–127, 133–138, 278–279.

88. Ochiai, "Modern Japan," in Wakita, Bouchy, and Chizuko, *Gender*, vol. 1, 251.

89. Miyamoto Tsuneichi, *Wasurerareta Nihonjin* (1984), 39. *"Sewayaki"* typically is translated "meddlesome," but Miyamoto makes it clear that he is referring to women whose intrusions were helpful; Jeffrey Irish translates *sewayaki babbaa* as "mediating grandmother." Miyamoto, *Forgotten Japanese*, 228.

90. Partner, "Peasants into Citizens?" 201. Also Richard J. Smethurst, *A Social Basis for Prewar Japanese Militarism: The Army and the Rural Community* (1974) for detail on such groups, especially 7, 28, 126.

91. Partner, *Toshié*, 32.

92. See Takagi Fukusaburō, "Outcasts," in Junichi Saga, *Memories of Silk and Straw: A Self-Portrait of Small-Town Japan* (1987), 51–53. Also Sumii, *The River*. These villages sometimes were omitted from official records, even though the "outcaste" category was officially eliminated in 1871.

93. Hirota Masaki, "Notes on the 'Process of Creating Women' in the Meiji Period," in Wakita, Bouchy, and Chizuko, *Gender*, vol. 2, 218.

94. Miyamoto, *Forgotten Japanese*, 59, 63.

95. Interview, Center for Oral History, *Kōloa*, vol. 3 (1988), 1308.

96. Fujime Yuki, "One Midwife's Life: Shibahara Urako, Birth Control, and Early Shōwa's Reproductive Activism," in Wakita, Bouchy, and Chizuko, *Gender*, vol. 1, 301.

97. Shimazaki, *Chikuma River*, 111–112.

98. Nagatsuka, *Soil*, 51–53, 201, xiv.

99. Shunning, or *mura hachibu*, is discussed in Inoue, *Shirobamba*, 15, where Granny Onui, after being shunned by her village because of her prostitute past, sees her grandson "as a valuable pawn in her efforts to consolidate her precarious position within the family."

100. Tayama, *Country Teacher*, 88.

101. Inoue, *Shirobamba*, 9, 39–40.

102. Activities culled from interviews with Ōno Toshio, Totsukawa, April 27, 1906; Muraoka, April 8, 1987, Center for Oral History, *Kōloa*, vol. 3, 1335 (baseball); Lloyd Kenzo Sugimoto, October 1, 1980, *Social History of Kona*, vol. 1, 218. Sledding described in Kanzawa Toshiko, *Mukashi mukashi obaachan wa* (1985), 135–161. Funeral play and pipe, Inoue, *Shirobamba*, 153, 163.

103. Interview, November 1, 1980, *Social History of Kona*, vol. 1, 597.

104. Tayama, *Country Teacher*, 13.

105. Inoue, *Shirobamba*, 34–36.

106. Shimazaki, *Chikuma River*, 13–14.

107. Muraoka, interview, April 8, 1987, Center for Oral History, *Kōloa*, vol. 3 (1988), 1335.

108. Osame Nagata Manago, interview, in Kodama-Nishimoto, *Hanahana*, 151.

109. Shimazaki, *Chikuma River*, 5; Tayama, *Country Teacher*, 6.

110. See, for example, discussion in Andrew Gordon, *A Modern History of Japan from Tokugawa Times to the Present* (2003), 68; Waswo, "Transformation," 560; Smethurst, *Agricultural Development*, 139 (Yamanashi statistic). In Hashimoto village, where Aizawa lived, nearly 100 percent of school-aged children were attending classes by 1900. Partner, "Peasants into Citizens?" 204. In 1907, compulsory education rose from four years to six years.

111. Shimazaki, talking about Komoro, *Chikuma River*, 96; also 197.

112. Inoue, *Shirobamba*, 29, 32.

113. Tanima Kazo from Yamaguchi recalled that when reported for misbehavior, his mother would tie his hands with a towel and apply a burning coal until "it burned all brown and yellow." Interview, October 10, 1980, *Social History of Kona*, vol. 4, 756.

114. Inoue, *Shirobamba*, 22.

115. Hirota, "Process of Creating Women," in Wakita, Bouchy, and Chizuko, *Gender,* vol. 2, 209.

116. Inoue, *Shirobamba,* 32. See page 5 for the correlation between protagonist Kosaku and Inoue himself.

117. Natsume, *Botchan,* 49.

118. Partner, *Toshié,* 16. The public bath Katai's Seizō frequented was not hygienic either; it "wasn't cleaned very thoroughly and had an unpleasant greasy feel." *Country Teacher,* 38.

119. Shimazaki, *Chikuma River,* 36.

120. Inoue, *Shirobamba,* 27.

121. Western criticism by Anglican Bishop of Hong Kong George Smith, who visited Japan in 1860. Scott Clark, *Japan, A View from the Bath* (1994), 35. Hirota, "Process of Creating Women," in Wakita, Bouchy, and Chizuko, *Gender,* vol. 2, 200–201.

122. Tayama, *Country Teacher,* 118 (Hotto's looseness), 83 (priest); Sumii, *The River,* 278 (adolescent boy), 122 (gossip). For punishment, Hotto's bawdy children were "made to stand holding a cup brimful of water."

123. Miyamoto, *Forgotten Japanese,* 74; see 87–88, 110–113 for other discussions of the "popular" practice of "visiting young women under the cover of night," and 116–127 for accounts of a blind Tosa cattle trader's affairs with several women; he comments, "I fooled a lot of people, but the cows were never fooled" (127).

124. Beatrice Webb, diary entry, September 3, 1911, London School of Economics Digital Library, 96; she commented, "The unsophisticated native regards the satisfaction of their appetite exactly as he does that of other appetites."

125. Hirota, "Process of Creating Women," in Wakita, Bouchy, and Chizuko, *Gender,* vol. 2, 218.

126. Robert J. Smith and Ella Lury Wiswell, *The Women of Suye Mura* (1982), 61. Subsequent references from 62 (frankness, twice in one night), 68 (indecent gesture), 63 ("women enjoy intercourse," brides), 67 (multiple partners), 65 (eavesdropped), 69 (*chin-chin*), 73 (parties), 76–77 (temple parties). The tendency of women to talk graphically about sex is discussed in Miyamoto, *Forgotten Japanese,* 103–107.

127. Morikuri Shigekazu, "*Karayuki-san* and *Shigintori:* Prostitution and the Industrial Economy in Amakusa at the End of the Edo Period," in Wakita, Bouchy, and Chizuko, *Gender,* vol. 1 (1999), 331. For the story of a rural Nagasaki woman who returned, "well dressed," to recruit others for work in Hong Kong, see Bill Mihapoulos, "Women, Overseas Sex Work and Globalization in Meiji Japan," *The Asia-Pacific Journal* (August 27, 2012).

128. Horikiri, *Stories Clothes Tell,* 106.

129. Tayama, *Country Teacher,* 55.

130. *Yorozu Chōhō,* July 7, 1898.

131. Shimazaki, *Chikuma River,* 94–95.

132. Lafcadio Hearn, *In Ghostly Japan* (1971), 26.

133. Miyamoto, *Forgotten Japanese,* 94. Miyamoto notes that male villagers in northern Akita Prefecture had almost all made pilgrimages to the Ise and Kumano shrines hundreds of miles away (303).

134. Kame Okano, interview, November 1, 1980, *Social History of Kona,* vol. 1, 595.

135. Miyamoto, *Forgotten Japanese,* 143.

136. Muraoka, interview, April 8, 1987, Center for Oral History, *Kōloa,* vol. 3, 1333.

137. Inoue, *Shirobamba,* 16.

138. Shimazaki, *Chikuma River,* 93, 111, 27–30.

139. Miyamoto, *Forgotten Japanese,* 172 (cow fair), 243 (hunters). Kawame residents also created an Inari Shrine in late Meiji and initiated an annual festival day (March 3) for the express purpose of improving community cohesion (254–255).

140. Yano Sōrō, "Besshi dōzan," *Seinenkai*, June 1, 1904, 106.

141. Muraoka, interview, April 8, 1987, Center for Oral History, *Kōloa*, vol. 3, 1333.

142. Ibid., 1334; Jizō were Buddhist guardian deities who protected children; Kannon was the Buddhist deity of mercy.

143. Interview, October 1, 1980, *Social History of Kona*, vol. 1, 220.

144. Interview with author, April 27, 2006.

145. Interview, October 10, 1980, *Social History of Kona*, vol. 1, 756.

146. Tayama, *Country Teacher*, 128.

147. Shimazaki, *Chikuma River*, 27.

148. Smith and Wiswell, *The Women*, 73.

149. Tayama, *Country Teacher*, 33.

150. Takano Fusatarō, "Japanese Farmers," *American Federationist* (November 1898), in Yokoyama (Yutani), 40. For fishing villages, see Yanagita Kunio, *Meiji Taishō shi*, 102.

151. Yokoyama (Yutani), 327–328.

152. Sayo Masuda, *Autobiography of a Geisha* (2004), 6.

153. Irokawa Daikichi, *The Culture of the Meiji Period* (1985), 219–220.

154. John Whitney Hall and Richard K. Beardsley, *Twelve Doors to Japan* (1965), 554; Hane, *Peasants, Rebels,* 103. For comparable figures, see Yokoyama (Yutani), 41. Also Alan Takeo Moriyama, *Imingaisha: Japanese Emigration Companies and Hawaii 1894–1908* (1985), 5.

155. Partner, "Peasants into Citizens?" 199.

156. Ibid., 195 (diary entry, January 30, 1905); Tayama, *Country Teacher*, 96 (Seizō); Shimazaki, *Chikuma River*, 100.

157. Toshio Yasumatsu, interview, February 26, 1985, *Waikīkī, 1900–1985: Oral Histories*, vol. 2 (1985), 828.

158. In 1905, Aizawa and his fellow landlords increased rents by 50 percent when taxes rose due to the Russo-Japanese War. Partner, "Peasants into Citizens?" 195.

159. Usaku Morihara, interview, November 6, 1980, *Social History of Kona*, vol. 2, 849.

160. For details on the flood, see Tabata Shigekiyo, Mizuyama Takahisa, and Inoue Kimio, "Kōu ni yoru ten'nen damu no keisei to kekkai," *Ten'nen damu to saigai* (2002), 86–104; Shimonaka Kunihiko, ed., *Nihon zankoku monogatari*, vol. 4 (1959–1960), 146–160, and Miyamoto, *Forgotten Japanese*, 264–284 (274 for data). The emigrants named their Hokkaido settlement Shintotsukawa (New Totsukawa); a lack of knowledge of northern agriculture contributed to early difficulties there, but by the mid-1890s, they had formed a stable community.

161. Irokawa, *Culture of the Meiji Period*, 219 (Miyagi); Yukiko Kimura, *Issei: Japanese Immigrants in Hawaii* (1988), 33 (emigrants).

162. *Seinen RG*, August 15, 1898, 10.

163. Nagatsuka, *Soil*, 66 (insects), 47–48 (vicious cycle).

164. Miyamoto, *Forgotten Japanese*, 293.

165. Shimazaki, *Chikuma River*, 198.

166. Yano, "Besshi dōzan," 102–103, 106.

167. Tanima Kazo, interview, October 10, 1980, *Social History of Kona*, vol. 4, 759.

168. Tayama, *Country Teacher*, 104, 205–206.

169. See Smethurst, *Social Basis*, 8–9, on patriotic organizations. These organizations grew rapidly during and after the Russo-Japanese War; by 1906, there were four thousand of them, by 1910 more than eleven thousand. The Home Ministry became active then in making Shintō shrines "sites for ceremonies related to the emperor and the state." Waswo and Nishida, *Farmers and Village Life*, 67–68.

170. Interview, November 1, 1980, *Social History of Kona*, vol. 1, 509.

171. Waswo and Nishida, *Farmers and Village Life*, 287.

172. Partner, "Peasants into Citizens?" 200.

173. Kinoshita, *Pillar of Fire*, 171.

174. Diary entry, September 1, 1894; Partner, "Peasants into Citizens?" 188.

175. Stewart Lone, "Remapping Japanese Militarism: Provincial Society at War 1904–1905," *Japanese Studies* (May 2005), 62 (Takayama, letter in *Gifu Nichi Nichi Shinbun*, April 23, 1905), 54 (Gifu deaths). Lone says Gifu locals displayed "a healthy cynicism and satire towards elites or propaganda, as well as a readiness to express discontent rather than suffer in silence" (53).

176. Partner, "Peasants into Citizens?" 200–201. For a similar, fictitious episode in Chichibu, see Kinoshita, *Pillar of Fire*, 171.

177. Irokawa, *Culture of the Meiji Period*, 221; Irokawa argues that some villagers expressed "vitality and recalcitrance" but without conceptualization or clear articulation (224–230).

178. Inumaru, *Shokkō jijō*, vol. 2, 200–213.

179. Figures for 1920, Fukutake, *Japanese Rural Society*, 35.

180. Ōtani Matsujirō, *Waga hito to narishi ashiato: hachijūnen no kaiko* (1971), 2–3; after working odd jobs, he opened a successful fish market.

181. Mihapoulos, "Women, Overseas Sex Work."

182. Interview, April 8, 1987, Center for Oral History, *Kōloa*, vol. 3 (1988), 1337.

183. Interview with author, March 27, 2014.

184. Waswo and Nishida, *Farmers and Village Life*, 179; for Korea figures, see *Taiyō*, April 1, 1910, 23; Waswo and Nishida give 170,000 that year in Korea. For Okinawa, see Kimura, *Issei*, 53. Another report showed 847 Japanese working as geisha or hostesses in the Dalian, Manchuria, region in 1911. *Seiro*, April 1912, in Morikuri, "*Karayuki-san* and *Shigintori*," 330.

185. Waswo and Nishida, *Farmers and Village Life*, 94 (Yamasaki), 4 (population); Waswo gives a figure of 5.5 million households with an average of about five families per household. Thomas C. Smith, *The Agrarian Origins of Modern Japan* (1966), 210, generally ignoring the decline of farming as part of the larger Japanese economy, says the rural population of about 27 million "was almost perfectly stable."

186. *Kahoku Shinpō*, September 6–13, 1918; *Tokyo Asahi Shinbun*, October 21–30, 1922, in Ōkado Masakatsu, "Nomura kara toshi e," in *Toshi to minshū*, ed. Narita Ryūichi (1993), 175. Partner, "Peasants into Citizens?" 31, notes that a 1915 Tokyo employment exchange report said that 95 percent of rural emigrants in the early Taishō years came to the cities for education, not jobs.

187. Ōkado, "Nomura kara toshi e," 176.

188. Inoue, *Shirobamba*, 61, 65, 81, 185.

189. Tayama, *Country Teacher*, 25.

190. From Takano, "Japanese Farmers," Yokoyama (Yutani), 40; Yazaki, *Social Change*, 356, points out that government figures in the mid-1880s placed 95 percent of fishermen in the lowest income class, compared to 80 percent of industrial workers in that class.

191. Tayama, *Country Teacher*, 193 (debility); Shimazaki, *Chikuma River*, 110 (droppings).

192. Diary entry, September 3, 1911, London School of Economics Digital Library, 94.

193. *Seinen RG*, May 20, 1899, 6.

194. All from observations on a walk in the village of Musashi Itsukaichi, April 4, 2014.

195. Tayama, *Country Teacher*, 172.

196. Shimazaki, *Chikuma River*, 38.

197. Ronald P. Loftus, *Telling Lives: Women's Self-Writing in Modern Japan* (2004), 85.

198. Smith, *Agrarian Origins*, 208.

199. Yokoyama (Yutani), 438.

200. Nitta, *Death March*, 61.

201. Interview, November 6, 1980, *Social History of Kona*, vol. 2, 843.

202. Nagatsuka, *Soil*, 190, 159–161.

203. Nakagawa Kiyoshi, interview with author, March 27, 1914.

204. E-mail correspondence to author, May 16, 2014.

205. Nakagawa Kyoshi, interview with author, March 27, 1914.

206. Quoted in Miyamoto, *Wasurerareta Nihonjin*, 279–280.

Chapter Eight: Poverty Abroad

1. Yano Toraji, *Ohchō hachijūgo nen: omoide tenten*, Ms. Group 187, Bishop Museum, back page.

2. A word about methodology in this chapter: While I have used a standard combination of primary and secondary sources in reconstructing the picture, I have filled out that picture through reliance on the impressive oral history projects of the Ethnic Studies Program and Social Science Institute of the University of Hawai'i–Mānoa. In the cases of individuals who were born or reached consciousness after the end of Meiji, I have used their recollections only if what they had to say clearly would have applied to the late Meiji years. Because of the problems inherent in oral history—forgetfulness, romanticization, a proneness to shape things to fit one's predilections—I have used these recollections to get at the tone and atmosphere of the plantation workers' lives rather than to reconstruct the factual experiences.

3. Ann B. Irish, *Hokkaido: A History of Ethnic Transition and Development on Japan's Northern Island* (2009), 119 (observer). Hilary Conroy, *The Japanese Frontier in Hawaii, 1868–1898* (1953), 59 (Armstrong).

4. The convention is summarized in Alex Ladenson, "The Japanese in Hawaii" (1938), 50–51, and reprinted in its entirety in Franklin Odo and Kazuko Sinoto, *A Pictorial History of the Japanese in Hawai'i 1885–1924* (1985), 24–26.

5. Frank L. Coombs to secretary of state John W. Foster, October 7, 1892, U.S. Department of State: Despatches from United States Ministers to Japan, 1869–1901: RG 59, National Archives, microfilm.

6. See chart, Alan Takeo Moriyama, *Imingaisha: Japanese Emigration Companies and Hawaii 1894–1908* (1985), 96.

7. Conroy, *Japanese Frontier*, 76; also see Ladenson, "Japanese in Hawaii," 61. Negotiators eventually reached a compromise whereby workers were charged roughly $15 for passage.

8. For a summary of emigration company practices during this period, roughly 1894–1905, see Yokoyama Gennosuke, *Meiji fugō shi* (2013), 182–187.

9. Dorothy Ochiai Hazama and Jane Okamoto Komeiji, *Okage Sama De: The Japanese in Hawai'i: 1885–1985* (1986), 23.

10. Figures from Japanese consulate records, in Odo and Sinoto, *Pictorial History*, 43.

11. Romanzo Adams, *The Peoples of Hawaii* (1933), 8; also see Kihara Ryukichi papers, Ms. Group 175, Box 5, Bishop Museum.

12. Moriyama, *Imingaisha*, 96–97.

13. James Okahata, ed., *A History of Japanese in Hawaii* (1971), 177; Moriyama, *Imingaisha*, 13. Kanagawa also sent 214 on the first shipload but few after that.

14. Odo and Sinoto, *Pictorial History*, 50. For comparison, records of the number of Japanese geisha and hostesses in Dalian, China, in 1912 show that just over a quarter came from western Honshu and Kyushu. Haruko Wakita, Anne Bouchy, and Ueno Chizuko, eds., *Gender and Japanese History*, vol. 2 (1999), 331.

15. Moriyama, *Imingaisha*, 16.

16. Ibid., 26.

17. Ōtani Matsujirō, *Waga hito to narishi ashiato: hachijūnen no kaiko* (1971), 2–3.

18. Labor Statistics, March 1904, Lihue Plantation Company, PV 80, Hawaii Sugar Planters' Association Plantation Archives, University of Hawai'i–Mānoa Library (hereafter HSPA).

19. Mitsugi Muraoka, Center for Oral History, *Kōloa: An Oral History of a Kaua'i Community*, vol. 1 (1988), 332–333.

20. Lloyd Kenzo Sugimoto, interview, *A Social History of Kona*, vol. 1 (1981), 216.

21. Labor Statistics, March 1904, Lihue Plantation Company, PV 80, HSPA. The only category listing no Japanese was plowing.

22. Richard Beardsley, John W. Hall, and Robert E. Ward, *Village Japan* (1959), 28, 51.

23. Kame Okano, interview, *Social History of Kona*, vol. 1, 593.

24. Torahichi Tsukahara, interview, *Social History of Kona*, vol. 2, 1262–1263.

25. Kazo Tanima, interview, *Social History of Kona*, vol. 4, 753.

26. Patsy Y. Nakayama, "Plantation Days," *The Hawaii Herald* (May 18, 1990), 16; also, in the same issue, Aaron Hara, "Issei Experience," 9.

27. Beatrice Webb, Diary, August 24, 1911, London School of Economics Digital Library, 90.

28. Foreign Ministry brochure, December 1884, quoted in Hazama and Komeiji, *Okage Sama De*, 15.

29. Sugimoto, interview, *Social History of Kona*, vol. 1, 215.

30. Moriyama, *Imingaisha*, 160.

31. Yukiko Kimura, *Issei: Japanese Immigrants in Hawaii* (1988), 51.

32. Hara, "Issei," 8.

33. Moriyama, *Imingaisha*, 88.

34. August 1897, Mizunaka family documents, Ms. Group 270, Acc. 1984.262, Bishop Museum.

35. Ōtani, *Waga hito*, 5–6.

36. Hiroo Sato, *Pahoa Yesterday* (2002), 142.

37. Ibid., 10–11, 13.

38. Sugimoto, *Social History of Kona*, vol. 1, 222 (bowel movement and other tests); Kame Okano, *Social History of Kona*, vol. 4, 599 (repeated eye tests). The hotel situation improved after new regulations in 1906 established minimum space and sanitation requirements.

39. Kame Okano, interview, ibid., vol. 4, 601.

40. Quoted in Kimura, *Issei*, 114.

41. Tsukahara, interview, *Social History of Kona*, vol. 2, 1264. For Soeda Azembō's account of writing "Rappa bushi," see Michael Lewis, *A Life Adrift: Soeda Azembō, Popular Song, and Modern Mass Culture in Japan* (2009), 115–116.

42. Muraoka Koremitsu, *Kōloa: An Oral History*, vol. 3, 1338.

43. Okano interview, *Social History of Kona*, vol. 1, 601–602.

44. Sōga Yasutarō, *Gojūnen no Hawai'i kaiko* (1953), 7.

45. Discussed in Moriyama, *Imingaisha*, 111–113; the 1897 episode resulted in the arrest of two agents of the Kobe Immigration Company who were held responsible for many of the failed immigrants' monetary problems. After considerable controversy, the Hawaiian government provided compensation to those who had been sent back as well as to the immigration company.

46. Ōtani, *Waga hito*, 17.

47. Yosoto Egami, interview, *Social History of Kona*, vol. 1, 263.

48. William H. Dorrance and Francis S. Morgan, *Sugar Islands: The 165-Year Story of Sugar in Hawai'i* (2000), 5.

49. Francis du Plessix Gray, "Profiles: The Sugar-Coated Fortress," *The New Yorker*, March 4, 1972, 66.

50. Correspondence from H. Hackfeld & Co. to Lihue Plantation Company, December 10, 1909, HSPA-LPC 3/1.

51. George Fairchild for Kauai Planters' Association to Lihue Plantation Company, April 6, 1904, HSPA-LPC 20/1.

52. Tseng Hai to H. Hackfeld & Co., August 23, 1909; W. O. Smith (HSPA secretary) to Tseng Hai, August 25, 1909, HSPA-OSC 2/14.

53. Oahu Sugar Company (OSC) to H. Hackfeld & Co., December 15, 1909, HSPA-OSC 2/16.

54. OSC report to U.S. Immigration Commission, October 23, 1909, HSPA-OSC 2/15.

55. William K. Yamanaka, *Kipu-Huleia: The Social History of a Plantation Community, 1910–1950* (1996), 17–18.

56. Gray, "Sugar-Coated Fortress," 72.

57. Shoshichi and Chika Saka papers, Fms. Group 280, Acc. 1981.503, Bishop Museum.

58. Ladenson, "Japanese in Hawaii," 67.

59. Inouye family documents, Ms. Group 297, Acc. 1986.641, Bishop Museum.

60. The impact of the contract system in keeping wages low is clear from the fact that in 1899, when about a third of the Japanese labor force had begun working out their own agreements, the "free laborers" averaged nearly $19 a month, more than 20 percent more than their contracted peers. Kimura, *Issei,* 13.

61. Okahata, *A History,* 170.

62. Carol Wilcox, *Sugar Water: Hawaii's Plantation Ditches* (1996), 57, 142.

63. Mitsugi Nishihara, interview, *Kōloa: An Oral History,* vol. 2, 762.

64. Kazo Tanima, interview, *Social History of Kona,* vol. 4, 760. *Teoi* discussed in Sato, *Pahoa Yesterday,* 84.

65. Interview, in Waialua-Haleiwa, Ethnic Studies Oral History Project, quoted in Hazama and Komeiji, *Okage Sama De,* 39.

66. Tadao "Barber" Kawamoto, interview, *Kōloa: An Oral History,* vol. 1, 52–53.

67. Koga Noriyu, in Waialua-Haleiwa, Ethnic Studies Oral History Project, quoted in Hazama and Komeiji, *Okage Sama De,* 67.

68. Yamanaka, *Kipu-Huleia,* 27.

69. Kiyoshi K. Kawakami, *Asia at the Door: A Study of the Japanese Question in Continental United States, Hawaii and Canada* (1914), 226. For material on children's nurseries and the need for them, Kawamoto interview in *Kōloa,* vol. 1, 52; Hazama and Komeiji, *Okage Sama De,* 67; Kimura, *Issei,* 165.

70. Ōtani, *Waga hito,* 24–25.

71. From a collection by Yukuo Uyehara, *Social Process in Hawaii,* quoted in Hazama and Komeiji, *Okage Sama De,* 38.

72. Kimura, *Issei,* 7. In 1905, Japanese made up 62.8 percent of the plantation workers but 14.3 of the *lunas*; their monthly pay averaged $31.33 in contrast to the Caucasians' $84.36. Moriyama, *Imingaisha,* 117. "Watchdog of hell" is the phrase of Yonashiro Kasaku, in Kimura, *Issei,* 54.

73. Conroy, *Japanese Frontier,* 67; the proplanter *Pacific Commercial Advertiser* smirked that the immigrants in this case were "making beri beri deaths into manslaughter."

74. Sōga, *Gojūnen,* 27–28.

75. Gaylord C Kubota, "The Lynching of Katsu Goto," *Waimea Gazette,* February 1998, 12–16; Okahata, *A History,* 125–126.

76. Moriyama, *Imingaisha,* 224.

77. Okahata, *A History,* 125–126.

78. Dr. Sidney Kashiwabara, Kashiwabara Collection, Ms. Group 210.1, Bishop Museum.

79. Correspondence from H. Hackfeld & Co., April 29, 1890, HSPA Collection 2/5.

80. Correspondence from H. Hackfeld, April 13, 1900, HSPA–Oahu Sugar Company Collection 5/6.

81. Moriyama, *Imingaisha*, 118.

82. Sharlene K. Watanabe, *Japanese Immigration: Abstracts of Articles from Hawaiian Planters Records, 1884–1896* (1975), 34.

83. An exception was George Wilcox of Grove Farm on Kaua'i who would not try to recover deserters because "he did not want any man who did not want to work on his plantation." Wilcox forbade his *lunas* from whipping workers and was known for permitting a smoke break at the end of a row; see Okahata, *A History*, 129.

84. Sōga, *Gojūnen*, 18.

85. For examples, see Mitsugi Muraoka, interview, *Kōloa: An Oral History*, vol. 1, 338; interviews in *Social History of Kona*, vol. 2: Usaku Morihara, 856; Torahichi Tsukahara, 1270; Minoru Inaba, *Social History of Kona*, vol. 1, 330.

86. Roland Kotani, "A Trouble at Paia," *Hawaii Herald*, 11, no. 10 (May 18, 1990), 41–45. The convention also assured free steerage for those under contract, as well as the hiring of interpreters and doctors for the workers; a supplement provided that women would make up 30 percent of those who came. It was revised unilaterally a year later when planters usurped much of King Kalākaua's power. See Odo and Sinoto, *Pictorial History*, 22–23; the 1886 convention is reprinted on 24–26.

87. Correspondence from H. Hackfeld to Mr. Aug. Ahrens, May 15, 1900, HSPA-Oahu Sugar Company Collection 1/7.

88. Katharine Coman, *The History of Contract Labor in the Hawaiian Islands* (1903, 1978), 47.

89. *Hawaiian Gazette*, May 6, 1904, in Ernest K. Wakukawa, *A History of the Japanese People in Hawaii* (1938), 132–33; the strike is described in 130–131.

90. See Wakukawa, *History of the Japanese People*, 133; also Ladenson, "Japanese in Hawaii," 122. Japan was at war with Russia at the time.

91. Yamanaka, *Kipu-Huleia*, 50.

92. Recollection of Etsuo Hazama, in Hazama and Komeiji, *Okage Sama De*, 65. Several couples slept in the same room when her parents arrived in 1895; by 1911, the partition had been put in.

93. Sato, *Pahoa Yesterday*, 65–68. In 1905, Puna was bought out by the larger Olaa Sugar Company; the name was changed back to Puna Sugar Company in 1960.

94. Suzuki Masajiro, describing life among Fukushima emigrants to O'ahu, from Takahashi Kanji, *Fukushima minshi: Hawai'i kikansha no maki* (Fukushima shi: Fukushima Hawai'i Kai, 1958), 316, in Kimura, *Issei*, 33.

95. OSC report to U.S. Immigration Commission, October 23, 1909, HSPA-OSC 2/15.

96. Reported in Moriyama, *Imingaisha*, 106.

97. Usaku Morihara, interview, November 6, 1980, in *Social History of Kona*, vol. 2, 855.

98. Moriyama, *Imingaisha*, 106.

99. Sōga, *Gojūnen*, 114.

100. Shigeta Ko, in Moriyama, *Imingaisha*, 114.

101. Kawakami, *Asia at the Door*, 216.

102. Conroy, *Japanese Frontier*, 92.

103. Nishihara, *Kōloa: An Oral History*, vol. 2, 760.

104. Sato, *Pahoa Yesterday*, 63 ("partially secluded"); Yamanaka, *Kipu-Huleia*, 22 ("winter storm" and "fell through").

105. HSPA correspondence, Hackfeld letterhead, to Kehaka plantation, May 4, 1906, HSPA Kehaka Collection.

106. Kawakami, *Asia at the Door,* 217.

107. Joan Hori, "Japanese Prostitution in Hawaii During the Immigration Period," *The Hawaiian Journal of History* (1981), 115.

108. Taken from *Immigration Report,* in Ladenson, "Japanese in Hawaii," 53. In 1900, three of every four Japanese in Hawai'i were male. By 1910, the percentage was down to 68.7; by 1920, it was 57.3. See Kimura, *Issei,* 145.

109. Okahata, *A History,* 122.

110. Kimura, *Issei,* 146.

111. Imamura Yemyo in ibid., 153–154.

112. The material on prostitution comes largely from Hori, "Japanese Prostitution," 113–124; also see Odo and Sinoto, *Pictorial History,* 26 (Convention, Article IX), 114 ("immorality"), 117 (earnings statements).

113. Dennis M. Ogawa, *Kodomo no tame ni—For the sake of the children: The Japanese American Experience in Hawaii* (1978), 62.

114. When Chinatown burned in 1900, most of the brothels moved to the Iwilei dock district; see Kimura, *Issei,* 150, and Okahata, *A History,* 158, as well as Hori, "Japanese Prostitution," 117–120.

115. Hori, "Japanese Prostitution," 117.

116. See, for example, an 1896–97 study by the chief justice of Hawai'i, in Conroy, *Japanese Frontier,* 117; the figures showed 17.36 percent of the Chinese population were convicted of a crime that year, compared to 7.94 percent of Japanese, 7.85 percent of Hawaiians, 3.49 percent of Portuguese, and 12.44 percent of "other" immigrant groups.

117. Sidney L. Gulick, *Hawaii's American-Japanese Problem: A Description of the Conditions, A Statement of the Problems and Suggestions for their Solution* (1915), 8.

118. See charts in Ladenson, "Japanese in Hawaii," 69, 128.

119. Tadao "Barber" Kawamoto, interview, *Kōloa: An Oral History,* vol. 1, 51, 38.

120. Hanako Ishiyama Gushiken, interview, *Kōloa: An Oral History,* vol. 3, 1389.

121. Mitsugi Muraoka, interview, *Kōloa: An Oral History,* vol. 1, 338.

122. Yukiko Kimura, interview, August 1, 1959, *Issei,* 127.

123. Gushiken, interview, *Kōloa: An Oral History,* vol. 3, 1890.

124. See Hazama and Komeiji, *Okage Sama De,* 66; Moriyama, *Imingaisha,* 139. After 1912, new regulations allowed couples to be married by a priest or minister of their own choice.

125. Sōga, *Gojūnen,* 183–185.

126. Bun Kobayashi Yoshimori, interview, *Kōloa: An Oral History,* vol. 3, 1310.

127. Interview, *Social History of Kona,* vol. 2, 1267.

128. *Nippu Jiji,* December 4, 1908; Moriyama, *Imingaisha,* 107.

129. Yamanaka, *Kipu-Huleia,* 32, 34, 78.

130. *Waikīkī, 1900–1985: Oral Histories,* vol. 2, 726.

131. Moriyama, *Imingaisha,* 109.

132. Sato, *Pahoa Yesterday,* 86 (also 81).

133. Kawakami, *Asia at the Door,* 223–224.

134. Moriyama, *Imingaisha,* 114. Also Kazo Tanima, interview, *Social History of Kona,* vol. 4, 763.

135. Sato, *Pahoa Yesterday,* 75–77; quotations from Yamanaka, *Kipu-Huleia,* 35.

136. Yamanaka, *Kipu-Huleia,* 35.

137. Minoru Inaba, interview, *Social History of Kona,* vol. 4, 332.

138. Ladenson, "Japanese in Hawaii," 111.

139. Koga Noriyu, interview, from Waialua-Haleiwa, Ethnic Studies Oral History Project, 678, quoted in Hazama and Komeiji, *Okage Sama De,* 70.

140. Ogawa, *Kodomo*, 45.

141. Kimura, *Issei*, 153–154.

142. Ibid., 163–164.

143. Yamanaka, *Kipu-Huleia*, 29. As in Japan, relatively few immigrants became Christian; Christians numbered four hundred, or 1.6 percent of the islands' Japanese population, in 1894. See Hazama and Komeiji, *Okage Sama De*, 78.

144. Ogawa, *Kodomo*, 49–51; Kimura, *Issei*, 156; Shintō developed less of an institutional base; its first Hawaiian shrine was built in Hilo in 1898; another was built in Honolulu in 1905. Overall figures from Ladenson, "Japanese in Hawaii," 133.

145. Minoru Inaba, *Social History of Kona*, vol. 1, 338.

146. Sato, *Pahoa Yesterday*, 336, 424.

147. Yamanaka, *Kipu-Huleia*, 28.

148. In 1909, the Oahu Sugar Company reported that it provided two large lots for Buddhist temples and free water for government schools and for a Roman Catholic mission. OSC report to U.S. Immigration Commission, October 23, 1909, HSPA-OSC 2/15.

149. Kimura, *Issei*, 155.

150. Kawakami, *Asia at the Door*, 230.

151. Ogawa, *Kodomo*, 57. *Kōden* were monetary gifts to spirits of the dead; *odaisan* were temple or shrine visits made on behalf of someone else.

152. *Nippu Jiji*, August 25, 1908, summarized in Okahata, *A History*, 173. Sōga never discontinued his activism; imprisoned on the day Pearl Harbor was bombed, he remained in jail until the end of World War II.

153. Ogawa, *Kodomo*, 135. Negoro was in the law school's first graduating class, 1903.

154. Letters from H. Hackfeld to E. K. Bull, January 7, 11, 1909, HSPA-Oahu Sugar Company Collection 2/11.

155. H. Hackfeld to F. Weber, manager, Lihue Plantation Company, January 11, 1909, HSPA-LPC Collection 01/1. Similar letters went to all Oʻahu plantations.

156. Oahu Sugar Company to H. Hackfeld, January 12, 1909, HSPA-Oahu Sugar Company Collection 2/11.

157. Letters from H. Hackfeld to Oahu Sugar Company, April 9, May 11, 1909, HSPA-Oahu Sugar Company Collection 2/11.

158. Kawakami, *Asia at the Door*, 211.

159. Ogawa, *Kodomo*, 150. Also see Correspondence from H. Hackfeld, June 18, 1909, HSPA-Oahu Sugar Company Collection 2/13.

160. Sugimoto, interview, October 1, 1980, *Social History of Kona*, vol. 1, 231.

161. Tetsuo Toyama, *Eighty Years in Hawaii* (1964), 38 (commissioner's report); *Semi-Weekly Star*, June 1, 1909, Ladenson, "Japanese in Hawaii," 139.

162. See Kimura, *Issei*, 94; Sōga, *Gojūnen*, 220–221. Another sign of the divisions in the Japanese community came after the strike's end when an activist stabbed the editor of the antistrike *Hawaiʻi Shinpō*, prompting Honolulu authorities to bring trumped up co-conspiracy charges against three strike leaders. The attacker was sentenced to two years in prison and deportation to Japan on release; the three leaders, including Negoro and editor Sōga, received ten-month sentences and $300 fines but were released after three months following a massive petition drive signed even by the president of the HSPA.

163. Toyama, *Eighty Years*, 9.

164. Ogawa, *Kodomo*, 174.

165. Ladenson, "Japanese in Hawaii," 134.

166. E-mail to author, April 9, 2016.

167. Moriyama, *Imingaisha*, 124, 24, 68.

168. Ibid., 25 (first decade), 122 (1908 remittances); *Taiyō*, December 1, 1904, 16 (1903 data).

169. See Irvine Collection: Inouye Family, Ms. Group 297, Acc. 1986.641, Bishop Museum, which contains about a hundred letters, mostly from a later period, the majority of which either request or give thanks for money from Hawai'i workers.

170. Sidney Kashiwabara, Kashiwabara collection, Ms. Group 210.1, Bishop Museum. Kihachi was known across the islands for his sumo skill. His son was the first person of Japanese ancestry to become a captain in the Honolulu Police Department. In 1914 his grandson Shigeru became the first Hawaiian Japanese to enter sumo professionally in Japan.

171. Hazama and Komeiji, *Okage Sama De*, 64–66.

172. Yano, *Omoide tenten*, 3.

173. Kawakami, *Asia at the Door*, 222.

174. *Kōloa: An Oral History*, vol. 1, 61 (Matsunaga) (his son Spark became a U.S. senator in 1976); Sōga, *Gojūnen*, 21 (Sōga); Kimura, *Issei*, 55 (Okinawans); Sato, *Pahoa Yesterday*, 164–209 (Pāhoa).

175. Conroy, *Japanese Frontier*, 100.

176. Kimura, *Issei*, 176–177.

177. Okahata, *A History*, 124.

178. Yonashiro Kasaku, quoted in Kimura, *Issei*, 54.

179. Haida Katsugoro quit work as a plantation laborer to get a medical degree and set up a practice. See comments of Seiya Ohata, in Dawn E. Duensing, ed., *Pā'ia: Evolution of a Community* (1998), 355. For "run over there," Sugimoto, interview, *Social History of Kona*, vol. 1, 228.

180. Material taken from HSPA-LPC V.82 (Lihue Hospital Corporate Records, 1898–1923): rules and regulations of Lihue Hospital, January 3, 1899; March 9, 1904, annual report; February 19, 1906, annual report; and February 13, 1919, report by Dora Isenberg.

181. Odo and Sinoto, *Pictorial History*, 127–128; 1898 percentage comes from charts in Adams, *Peoples of Hawaii*, 7, and Ladenson, "Japanese in Hawaii," 69. Kimura, *Issei*, 186, says there were 140 Japanese schools and seven thousand students by 1910.

182. *Kōloa: An Oral History*, vol. 1, 38 (Kawamoto); Sato, *Pahoa Yesterday*, 107 (Sato and lunch details).

183. Sato, *Pahoa Yesterday*, 310.

184. *Social History of Kona*, vol. 1, 341.

185. Jiro Suzuki, "My Autobiography" (1981), 6.

186. Ibid., 6–7.

187. The Japanese-language schools became controversial late in Meiji, with American chauvinists claiming they undermined American patriotism. This prompted the Hawai'i legislature to restrict the schools' curriculums, but the U.S. Supreme Court struck down the restrictions in 1927. For an example of the chauvinists' fears, see Gulick, *Hawaii's American-Japanese Problem*, 11.

188. Yamanaka, *Kipu-Huleia*, 26.

189. Ushiyama Saijirō, *Kōjō junshiki* ("Visits to factories"), in *Meiji Bunka Zenshū*, vol. 16 (Nihon Hyōronsha, 1959), in Eiji Yutani, "'Nihon no Kaso Shakai' of Gennosuke Yokoyama" (1985), 78.

190. Wages varied by locality and job, and differences in exchange rates make comparisons difficult. Nonetheless, while middle-aged rickshaw pullers made roughly twelve yen a month in Japan in 1900, for example (table 5 in chapter 3), plantation workers were averaging about twenty-two yen ($15) a month then.

191. Paulo Freire, *Pedagogy of the Oppressed* (2007), 59.

Conclusion

1. George Orwell, *Down and Out in Paris and London* (1933), 16–17.

2. Kafū Nagai, *A Strange Tale from East of the River and Other Stories* (1965), 68 (pike); *Heimin Shinbun* (English column), August 4, 1901, 1 (indecent pictures).

3. Matsubara Iwagorō, *Saiankoku no Tokyo* (1893, 1988), 1.

4. Orwell, *Down and Out*, 120.

5. Maeda Ai, "Utopia of the Prisonhouse: A Reading of *In Darkest Tokyo*," trans. Seiji M. Lippit and James A. Fujii, in Maeda Ai, *Text and the City* (2004), 33.

6. Quoted in ibid., 51.

7. Quoted in Suzuki Hiroyuki, *Toshi e*, in *Nihon no kindai*, vol. 10 (1999), 327.

8. Letters to the Editor, *Seinen: Rising Generation*, January 21, 1906, 188.

9. Sōseki Natsume, *Light and Darkness* (1971), 151–152. The *Meian* character herself often had little money, but her class was higher than that of the irritating stranger.

10. As late as 1907, only 18,000 Japanese *altogether* received any kind of public assistance, in a world where the *hinmin* of Tokyo and Osaka alone totaled perhaps 700,000. Nakagawa Kiyoshi, "Senzen ni okeru toshi kasō no tenkai, jō," *Mita Gakkai Zasshi* (June 1978), 76.

11. Sayo Masuda, *Autobiography of a Geisha* (2004), 21.

12. Muraoka Koremitsu from Kumamoto, interview, April 8, 1987, Center for Oral History, *Kōloa: Oral History*, vol. 3 (1988), 1335.

13. Terada Yūkichi, "Tokyo shimin to jinrikisha," *Taiyō*, April 5, 1902, 32.

14. Matsubara, *Saiankoku*, 116.

15. See especially *Creating a Public: People and Press in Meiji Japan* (1997).

16. "Jinriki shafu dōmei kyūgyō," *Taiyō*, July 1, 1903, 229.

17. Shumpei Okamoto, *The Japanese Oligarchy & the Russo-Japanese War* (1970), 210.

18. OECD report reprinted in Jeff Kingston, *Japan in Transformation 1945–2010* (2011), 126–127. For 2009, see Abe Aya, "Child Poverty, the Grim Legacy of Denial," Nippon.com (2016). For nonregular employment in 2014, see Scott North, "Limited Regular Employment and the Reform of Japan's Division of Labor," *The Asia-Pacific Journal: Japan Focus* (April 13, 2014).

19. Figures from Ministry of Health, Welfare, and Labor, in Abe, "Child Poverty." A 2013 UNICEF study found that for families with children, Japan was thirty-fourth in income equality among the world's forty-one richest countries; see Tomohiro Osaki, "Hidden Poverty Growing under Abe, Particularly among Young and Single Mothers," *The Japan Times*, April 26, 2016. http://www.japantimes.co.jp/news/2016/04/26/national/social-issues/hidden-poverty -growing-abe-particularly-among-young-single-mothers/#.V_-WiaNh2T8.

20. Masami Iwata and Akihiko Nishizawa, *Poverty and Social Welfare in Japan* (2008), 242 (jail), 49 (nihilation).

21. North, "Limited Regular Employment."

22. For a prominent example of a tent village at the end of 2009, see Toru Shinoda, "Which Side Are You On? Hakenmura and the Working Poor as a Tipping Point in Japanese Labor Politics," *The Asia-Pacific Journal: Japan Forum* (April 4, 2009), http://apjjf.org/-Toru-SHI-NODA/3113/article.html. On skid-row areas, see Tom Gill, "Skid Row, Yokohama: Homelessness and Welfare in Japan," Nippon.com (2014), as well as Gill's *Yokohama Street Life: The Precarious Career of a Japanese Day Laborer* (Lanham, MD: Lexington Books, 2015).

23. Yuki Hagiwara and Isabel Reynolds, "In Japan, 1 in 6 Children Lives in Poverty, Putting Education, Future at Stake," *Japan Times*, September 10, 2015.

24. Gill, "Skid Row." In addition, the Childhood Poverty Act, adopted in 2013, attempts to reduce child poverty through school-based policies. See Abe, "Child Poverty."

25. Abe, "Child Poverty"; Kingston, *Japan in Transformation*, 100; see 104 regarding NPOs.

26. Iwagoro Matsubara, *Sketches of Humble Life in the Capital of Japan* (1897), 65.

27. Sabine Frühstück, *Colonizing Sex: Sexology and Social Control in Modern Japan* (2003), 179 ("lustful"); Eiji Yutani, "'Nihon no Kaso Shakai' of Gennosuke Yokoyama" (1985), 178 ("slothful").

28. Kinoshita Naoe, "Geshukuya ni taisuru iken," *Seinenkai*, December 1, 1902, 15–16.

29. See Sakura Momo, "Kisha mōsu," *Shōnen sekai*, February 15, 1900, 99.

30. Miyamoto Tsuneichi, *The Forgotten Japanese: Encounters with Rural Life and Folklore* (2010), 303.

31. Matsubara, *Saiankoku*, 48.

32. Nakagawa Kiyoshi, *Gendai no seikatsu mondai* (2011), 35, 55–57 (surveyors' units). Nakagawa expressed his view that slum dwellers did not see themselves as lower class in an interview with the author, March 27, 2014. Also see his "Ambitions, 'Family-Centredness' and Expenditure Patterns in a Changing Urban Class Structure: Tokyo in the Early Twentieth Century," *Continuity and Change* (2000), 77–98.

33. Yokoyama Gennosuke, "Hinmin no shōgatsu" (1909), in Nakagawa Kiyoshi, ed., *Meiji Tokyo kasō seikatsu shi* (1994), 250, 248.

34. Matsubara, *Sketches*, 40.

Collections

Bishop Museum Library and Archives, Honolulu, Hawaiʻi.

Edward Sylvester Morse Collection. Phillips Library, Peabody Essex Museum, Salem, Massachusetts.

Hawaii Sugar Planters' Association (HSPA) Plantation Archives, Hawaiian Collection, University of Hawaiʻi–Mānoa Library.

Kokubungaku Kenkyū Shiryōkan, Tokyo.

Journals and Newspapers

Chōya Shinbun

Fūzoku Gahō

Heimin Shinbun (see *Shūkan Heimin Shinbun*)

Jiji Shinpō

Kokumin Shinbun. Facsimile edition. Nihon Tosho Sentā, 1988.

Niroku Shinpō. Facsimile edition, 7 vols. Fuji Shuppan, 1992 (both original and facsimile were used).

Seinen: The Rising Generation

Seinen Kai

Shōnen Sekai

Shūkan Heimin Shinbun. Rōdō Undō Shi Kenkyūkai, ed. *Meiji Shakaishugi shiryōshū*, special vol. 3, 1962. Also reprinted as *Heimin Shinbun,* 2 vols. Osaka: Sōgensha, 1953–1954.

Shūkan Shakai Shinbun. Rōdō Undō Shi Kenkyūkai, ed. *Meiji Shakaishugi shiryōshū*, 7, 1962.

Taiyō

Tokyo Pakku. Kitazawa Rakuten, ed. Facsimile edition. 8 vols. Ryūkei, 1985–2000.

Tokyo Shakai Shinbun. Rōdō Undō Shi Kenkyūkai, ed. *Meiji Shakaishugi shiryōshū*, 8, 1962.

Yorozu Chōhō

Yomiuri Shinbun

Published and Unpublished Sources

Japanese works are published in Tokyo unless otherwise noted.

Abe Aya. "Child Poverty, the Grim Legacy of Denial." Nippon.com, February 12, 2016. http://www.nippon.com/en/column/g00341/.

——. "Poverty and Social Exclusion of Women in Japan." *Japanese Journal of Social Security Policy* 9, no. 1 (March 2012): 61–82.

Adams, Romanzo. *The Peoples of Hawaii.* Honolulu: Institute of Pacific Relations, 1933.

Akiyama Kenjirō. *Gendai Nihon to teihen* (The lower classes in modern Japan). San'ichi Shobō, 1960.

Allinson, Gary D. *Japanese Urbanism: Industry and Politics in Kariya, 1872–1972.* Berkeley: University of California Press, 1975.

———. *Suburban Tokyo: A Comparative Study in Politics and Social Change.* Berkeley: University of California Press, 1979.

Ambaras, David R. *Bad Youth: Juvenile Delinquency and the Politics of Everyday Life in Modern Japan.* Berkeley: University of California Press, 2006.

———. "Social Knowledge, Cultural Capital, and the New Middle Class in Japan, 1895–1912." *Journal of Japanese Studies* 24, no. 1 (Winter 1998): 1–33.

Aoyagi Junrō, ed. *Meiji kyūjūkyūnen: sesō jiken* (Ninety-nine years of Meiji: Times and events). Orionsha, 1935.

Baelz, Erwin. *Awakening Japan: The Diary of a German Doctor.* Bloomington: Indiana University Press, 1974.

Bailey, Jackson Y. *Ordinary People, Extraordinary Lives: Political and Economic Change in a Tōhoku Village.* Honolulu: University of Hawai'i Press, 1991.

Bay, Alexander R. *Beriberi in Modern Japan: The Making of a National Disease.* Rochester, NY: University of Rochester Press, 2012.

Beardsley, Richard, John W. Hall, and Robert E. Ward. *Village Japan.* Chicago: University of Chicago Press, 1959.

Bernstein, Andrew. "Fire and Earth: The Forging of Modern Cremation in Meiji Japan." *Japanese Journal of Religious Studies* 27, no. 3–4 (Fall 2000): 297–334.

Booth, General (William). *In Darkest England, and the Way Out.* London: Funk and Wagnalls, 1890.

"Brief Review of the Operations of the Home Department (of Japan) in Connection with the Cholera Epidemic of the 18th Year of Meiji (1885)." *The British Medical Journal,* May 14, 1878, 1046–1047. http://www.jstor.org/stable/20211631.

"Bubonic Plague in Japan." *New York Times,* October 19, 1902. http://query.nytimes.com /mem/archive-free/pdf?res=F10E16FA345F12738DDDA00A94D8415B828CF1D3.

Burns, Susan L. "Bodies and Borders: Syphilis, Prostitution, and the Nation in Japan, 1860–1890." *U.S.-Japan Women's Journal* 15 (1998): 3–30.

———. "Contemplating Places: The Hospital as Modern Experience in Meiji Japan." In *New Directions in the Study of Meiji Japan,* ed. Helen Hardacre, 702–718. Leiden: E. J. Brill, 1997.

Center for Oral History (formerly Ethnic Studies Oral History Project), Social Science Research Institute, University of Hawai'i–Mānoa. *Kōloa: An Oral History of a Kaua'i Community.* 3 vols. September 1988.

Chamberlain, Basil Hall, and W. B. Mason. *A Handbook for Travellers in Japan.* 4th edition revised. New York: Charles Scribner's Sons, 1898; 8th edition revised. London: John Murray, 1907.

Chiku Seitarō. *Hensō tanbō setai no samazama* (Aspects of society: From a journalist in disguise). Isseidō, 1914.

Chubachi, M., and K. Taira. "Poverty in Modern Japan: Perceptions and Realities." In *Japanese Industrialization and Its Social Consequences,* ed. Hugh Patrick and L. Meissner, 391–437. Berkeley: University of California Press, 1976.

Civil Code of Japan. Translated by Ludwig Lönholm. Tokyo: Maruya & Company, 1898.

Clancey, Gregory. *Earthquake Nation: The Cultural Politics of Japanese Seismicity 1868–1930.* Berkeley: University of California Press, 2006.

Clark, Scott. *Japan, A View from the Bath.* Honolulu: University of Hawai'i Press, 1994.

Coman, Katharine. *The History of Contract Labor in the Hawaiian Islands.* New York: Macmillan Company, for American Economic Association, 1903; reprint, New York: Arno Press, 1978.

Conroy, Hilary. *The Japanese Frontier in Hawaii, 1868–1898.* Berkeley: University of California Press, 1953.

Crump, John. *The Origins of Socialist Thought in Japan.* New York: St. Martin's Press, 1983.

Dai jūichi kai Tokyo shi tōkei nenpyō: 1914 (Eleventh annual yearbook of Tokyo statistics: 1914). Tokyo Shiyakusho, 1914.

Dai ni kai Tokyo shi tōkei nenpyō: 1902 (Second annual yearbook of Tokyo statistics: 1902). Tokyo Shiyakusho, 1904.

Danly, Robert Lyons. *In the Shade of Spring Leaves: The Life of Higuchi Ichiyō With Nine of Her Best Short Stories.* New York: W. W. Norton and Company, 1984.

de Bary, Brett. "Sanya: Japan's Internal Colony." In *The Other Japan,* ed. E. Patricia Tsurumi, 112–118. Armonk, NY: M. E. Sharpe, Inc., 1988.

de Bary, Wm. Theodore, Carol Gluck, and Arthur E. Tiedemann, compilers. *Sources of Japanese Tradition,* 2, part 1 (1600–1868). 2nd edition. New York: Columbia University Press, 2006.

De Becker, J. E. *The Nightless City or the History of the Yoshiwara Yūkwaku.* Rutland, VT: Charles E. Tuttle Company, 1971.

De Vos, George, and Hiroshi Wagatsuma. *Japan's Invisible Race: Caste in Culture and Personality.* Rev. ed. Berkeley: University of California Press, 1966.

Dore, Ronald P. *Shinohata: A Portrait of a Japanese Village.* New York: Pantheon Books, 1978.

Dorrance, William H., and Francis S. Morgan. *Sugar Islands: The 165-Year Story of Sugar in Hawai'i.* Honolulu: Mutual Publishing, 2000.

Drixler, Fabian. *Mabiki: Infanticide and Population Growth in Eastern Japan, 1660–1950.* Berkeley: University of California Press, 2013.

Duensing, Dawn E., ed. *Pā'ia: Evolution of a Community.* Pā'ia, Maui, Hawai'i: Pā'ia Main Street Association, 1998.

Ehrenreich, Barbara. *Dancing in the Streets: A History of Collective Joy.* New York: Metropolitan Books, 2006.

Fairfax, Irwin. "Smallpox in Japan." *Public Health Reports (1896–1970)* 25, no. 35 (September 2, 1910): 1205–1208. http://www.jstor.org/stable/4565307.

Fowler, Edward. "The Buraku in Modern Japanese Literature: Texts and Contexts." *Journal of Japanese Studies* 26, no. 1 (Winter 2000): 1–39.

———. *San'ya Blues: Laboring Life in Contemporary Tokyo.* Ithaca, NY: Cornell University Press, 1996.

Freire, Paulo. *Pedagogy of the Oppressed.* Translated by Myra Bergman Ramos. New York: Continuum, 2007.

Frühstück, Sabine. *Colonizing Sex: Sexology and Social Control in Modern Japan.* Berkeley: University of California Press, 2003.

Fuess, Harald. *Divorce in Japan: Family, Gender, and the State, 1600–2000.* Stanford, CA: Stanford University Press, 2004.

———. "Informal Imperialism and the 1879 'Hesperia' Incident: Containing Cholera and Challenging Extraterritoriality in Japan." *Japan Review* 27 (2014): 103–140. http://www.jstor.org/stable/23849572.

Fujii Hidegorō. *Shin Hawai'i* (New Hawai'i). Tokyo: n.p., 1900.

Fujimoto, Taizo. *The Nightside of Japan.* London: T. Werner Laurie, 1915.

———. *The Story of the Geisha Girl.* London: Forgotten Books, 2012. Originally London: T. Werner Laurie, 1917.

Fujino Yutaka. *Wasurerareta chiiki shi o aruku: kingendai Nihon ni okeru sabetsu no shosō* (Walking the history of the forgotten regions: Various aspects of discrimination in modern Japan). Ōtsuki Shoten, 2006.

Fujita Hiroo and Urano Masaki, eds. *Toshi shakai to risuku: yutaka na seikatsu o motomete* (Urban society and risk: Seeking the abundant life). Tōshindō, 2005.

Fukutake, Tadashi. *Japanese Rural Society.* Translated by Ronald P. Dore. Ithaca, NY: Cornell University Press, 1967.

Fukuzawa Yukichi. *An Encouragement of Learning.* Translated by David A. Dilworth and Umeyo Hirano. Tokyo: Sophia University, 1969.

Garon, Sheldon. *Molding Japanese Minds: The State in Everyday Life.* Princeton, NJ: Princeton University Press, 1997.

———. *The State and Labor in Modern Japan.* Berkeley: University of California Press, 1987.

Gerteis, Christopher, ed. *Critical Readings on the History of Industrialization in Modern Japan.* Vol. 2. Leiden: E. J. Brill, 2013.

Gill, Tom. "Skid Row, Yokohama: Homelessness and Welfare in Japan." Nippon.com. November 27, 2014. http://www.nippon.com/en/column/g00232/.

———. *Yokohama Street Life: The Precarious Career of a Japanese Day Laborer.* Lanham, MD: Lexington Books, 2015.

Gordon, Andrew. *The Evolution of Labor Relations in Japan: Heavy Industry, 1853–1955.* Cambridge, MA: Council on East Asian Studies, Harvard University, 1985.

———. *Labor and Imperial Democracy in Prewar Japan.* Berkeley: University of California Press, 1991.

———. *A Modern History of Japan from Tokugawa Times to the Present.* New York: Oxford University Press, 2003.

———. "Social Protest in Imperial Japan: The Hibiya Riot of 1905." *Asia-Pacific Journal* 12, issue 29, no. 3 (July 20, 2014). http://apjjf.org/site/search/level/2/author/andrew%20gordon.

Gotō Ken'ichi. *Kindai Nihon to Tōnan Ajia* (Modern Japan and Southeast Asia). Iwanami Shoten, 1995.

Gray, Francis du Plessix. "Profiles: The Sugar-Coated Fortress." *New Yorker,* March 4, 1972, 41–79.

Griffis, William Elliot. *The Mikado's Empire.* 2 vols. New York: Harper and Brothers, 1906.

Gu Ayatoshi. "Tokyo fuka hinmin no jōkyō" (Conditions among the poor people in Tokyo's city districts). In *Meiji Tokyo kasō seikatsu shi* (Tokyo's poor in the Meiji era: A history of daily life), ed. Nakagawa Kiyoshi, 77–87. Iwanami Shoten, 1994. Originally in *Sutachisuchikku Zasshi,* January 20, 1891.

Gulick, Sidney L. *Hawaii's American-Japanese Problem: A Description of the Conditions, A Statement of the Problems and Suggestions for their Solution.* Honolulu: Honolulu Star-Bulletin, 1915.

Guyonnet, Emilie. "Young Temporary Workers Create Their Own Unions." *Asia-Pacific Journal: Japan Focus* 9, issue 16, no. 4 (April 18, 2011). http://apjjf.org/2011/9/16/Emilie-Guyonnet/3518/article.html.

Hackman, Money, and Peter Fetchko. *Japan Day by Day: An Exhibition Honoring Edward Sylvester Morse and Commemorating the Hundredth Anniversary of His Arrival in Japan in 1877.* Salem, MA: Peabody Museum of Salem, 1977.

Haga Eizō. *Meiji Taishō hikka shi* (History of Meiji-Taisho press infractions). Shikōsha Shobō, 1924.

Hagiwara, Yuki, and Isabel Reynolds. "In Japan, 1 in 6 Children Lives in Poverty, Putting Education, Future at Stake." *Japan Times,* September 10, 2015. http://www.japantimes.co.jp/news/2015/09/10/national/social-issues/one-six-japanese-children-live-poverty-threatening-education-future/#.V_-V26Nh2T8.

Hall, John Whitney, and Richard K. Beardsley. *Twelve Doors to Japan.* New York: McGraw-Hill, 1965.

Hane, Mikiso. *Peasants, Rebels, Women, & Outcastes: The Underside of Modern Japan.* Updated 2nd ed. Lanham, MD: Rowman & Littlefield, 2016.

———, ed. *Reflections on the Way to the Gallows: Voices of Japanese Rebel Women.* New York: Pantheon Books, 1988.

Hanes, Jeffrey E. *The City as Subject: Seki Hajime and the Reinvention of Modern Osaka.* Berkeley: University of California Press, 2002.

Hanley, Susan B. "Urban Sanitation in Preindustrial Japan." *Journal of Interdisciplinary History* 18, no. 1 (Summer 1987): 1–26.

Hara, Aaron I. "The Issei Experience." *Hawaii Herald* 11, no. 10 (May 18, 1990): 4–10.

Harada, Margaret N. *The Sun Shines on the Immigrant.* New York: Vantage Press, 1960.

Harada Tōfū. *Hinminkutsu* (The slums). Daigakukan, 1902.

Hastings, Sally Ann. *Neighborhood and Nation in Tokyo, 1905–1937.* Pittsburgh, PA: University of Pittsburgh Press, 1995.

Hawai'i Times, ed. *Hawai'i jijō* (Hawai'i facts). Honolulu: Hawai'i Times, 1964.

Hayashi Hideo. *Ryūmin* (Displaced people). *Kindai minshū no kiroku* (Records of modern commoners). Vol. 4. Shinjinbutsu Ōraisha, 1971.

Hazama, Dorothy Ochiai, and Jane Okamoto Komeiji. *Okage Sama De: The Japanese in Hawai'i: 1885–1985.* Honolulu: Bess Press, 1986.

Hearn, Lafcadio. *In Ghostly Japan.* Rutland, VT: Tuttle Publishing, 1971.

Henshall, Kenneth G. *Literary Life in Tōkyō, 1885–1915: Tayama Katai's Memoirs (Thirty Years in Tōkyō).* Leiden: E. J. Brill, 1987.

Hita Sei. "Hinminkutsu" (The slums). Illustrated by Morita Gekō. *Fūzoku Gahō* 176 (November 10, 1898): 9–11.

Hori, Joan. "Japanese Prostitution in Hawaii During the Immigration Period." *Hawaiian Journal of History* 15 (1981): 113–124.

Horikiri, Tatsuichi. *The Stories Clothes Tell: Voices of Working-Class Japan.* Translated by Reiko Wagoner. Lanham, MD: Rowman & Littlefield, 2016.

Horioka, Charles Yuji. "Consuming and Saving." In *Postwar Japan as History,* ed. Andrew Gordon, 259–292. Berkeley: University of California Press, 1993.

Hosoi Wakizō. *Kōjō aishi* (Sad history of the factory girls). Iwanami Shoten, 1982.

House, Edward H. *Japanese Episodes.* Boston: James R. Osgood and Company, 1881.

Howell, David L. "Fecal Matters: Prolegomenon to a History of Shit in Japan." In *Japan at Nature's Edge: The Environmental Context of a Global Power,* ed. Ian J. Miller, Julia Adney Thomas, and Brett L. Walker, 137–151. Honolulu: University of Hawai'i Press, 2013.

———. *Geographies of Identity in Nineteenth-Century Japan.* Berkeley: University of California Press, 2005.

Huffman, James L. *Creating a Public: People and Press in Meiji Japan.* Honolulu: University of Hawai'i Press, 1997.

Ikeda, James K. "A Brief History of Bubonic Plague in Hawaii." *Proceedings of the Hawaiian Entomological Society* 25 (March 1, 1985): 75–81.

Imai Konomi. "The Woman's Movement and the Settlement Movement in Early Twentieth-Century Japan: The Impact of Hull House and Jane Addams on Hiratsuka Raichō." *Kwansei Gakuin University Humanities Review* 17 (2012): 85–109. http://kgur.kwansei.ac.jp/dspace/bitstream/10236/10536/1/17-6.PDF.

Inoue, Yasushi. *Chronicle of My Mother.* Translated by Jean Oda Moy. Tokyo: Kodansha International, 1982.

——. *Shirobamba: A Childhood in Old Japan.* Translated by Jean Oda Moy. New York: Weatherhill, 1991.

Inouye, Jukichi. *Home Life in Tokyo.* London: KPI, 1985. Originally published 1910.

Inumaru Giichi, ed. *Shokkō jijō* (Factory workers' conditions). 3 vols. Iwanami Shoten, 1998 (originally published in 1903).

Irish, Ann B. *Hokkaido: A History of Ethnic Transition and Development on Japan's Northern Island.* Jefferson, NC: McFarland and Company, 2009.

Irokawa Daikichi. *The Culture of the Meiji Period.* Translation edited by Marius B. Jansen. Princeton, NJ: Princeton University Press, 1985.

——. *Shinpen Meiji seishin shi* (History of the spirit of Meiji). Rev. ed. Chūō Kōron, 1973.

Ishizuka Hiromichi. "The Slum Dwellings and the Urban Renewal Scheme in Tokyo, 1868–1923." *The Developing Economies* 19, no. 2 (June 1981): 169–193. doi/10.1111/j.1746–1049.1981.tb00431.x.

——. *Toshi kasō shakai to "saimin" jūkyo ron* (On urban lower class society and the living situations of paupers). Kokusai Rengō Daigaku, 1979.

Ishikawa, Takuboku. *Romaji Diary and Sad Toys.* Translated by Sanford Goldstein and Seishi Shinoda. Rutland, VT: Charles E. Tuttle Company, 1985.

Ito, Ken K. *Visions of Desire: Tanizaki's Fictional Worlds.* Stanford, CA: Stanford University Press, 1991.

Itō Takashi and George Akita. "The Yamagata-Tokutomi Correspondence: Press and Politics in Meiji-Taishō Japan." *Monumenta Nipponica* 36, no. 4 (Winter 1981): 391–423.

Iwata, Masami, and Akihiko Nishizawa. *Poverty and Social Welfare in Japan.* Melbourne: Trans Pacific Press, 2008.

Izumi Kyōka. *In Light of Shadows: More Gothic Tales.* Translated by Charles Shirō Inouye. Honolulu: University of Hawai'i Press, 2005.

Jansen, Marius B., ed. *The Cambridge History of Japan.* Vol. 5: *The Nineteenth Century.* Cambridge, UK: Cambridge University Press, 1989.

"Japan in 1909." *British Medical Journal* 1, no. 2681 (May 18, 1912): 1139–1140. http://www.jstor.org/stable/25297233.

Japan: Statistics of Cholera Epidemic: Typhoid Fever." *Public Health Reports (1896–1970)* 26, no. 2 (January 13, 1911): 31. http://www.jstor.org/stable/4565828.

Johansson, S. Ryan, and Carl Mosk. "Exposure, Resistance and Life Expectancy: Disease and Death during the Economic Development of Japan, 1900–1960." *Population Studies* 42, no. 2 (July 1987): 207–235. http://www.jstor.org/stable/2174175.

Johnston, William. *The Modern Epidemic: A History of Tuberculosis in Japan.* Cambridge, MA: Council of East Asian Studies, Harvard University, 1995.

Kaburagi Kiyokata. *Meiji no Tokyo.* Iwanami Shoten, 1989.

Kagawa Toyohiko. *Hinmin shinri no kenkyū* (Research on the mental state of the poor). Keiseisha Shoten, 1915.

Kamishima Jirō. *Kindai Nihon no seishin kōzō* (The spiritual structure of modern Japan). Iwanami Shoten, 1961.

Kaneko Fumiko. *The Prison Memoirs of a Japanese Woman.* Translated by Jean Inglis. Armonk, NY: East Gate Books, 1991.

Kanzawa Toshiko. *Mukashi mukashi obaachan wa* (Long, long ago . . . granny). Fukuinkan Shobō, 1985.

Kashiwabara, Sidney. "The Life of Hans Hankuro Kashiwabara." Bishop Museum, Ms. Group 210.1.

Katz, Michael B. *In the Shadow of the Poorhouse: A Social History of Welfare in America.* New York: Basic Books, 1986.

Kawabata, Yasunari. *The Scarlet Gang of Asakusa*. Translated by Alisa Freedman. Berkeley: University of California Press, 2005.

Kawakami, Kiyoshi K. *Asia at the Door: A Study of the Japanese Question in Continental United States, Hawaii and Canada*. New York: Fleming H. Revell Company, 1914.

Kawashima Yasuyoshi. *Fujin kateiran kotohajime* (Early women's and family columns). Yūgen Kaisha, 1996.

Keene, Donald. *Dawn to the West: Japanese Literature in the Modern Era—Fiction*. New York: Henry Holt and Company, 1984.

———. *Dawn to the West: Japanese Literature in the Modern Era—Poetry, Drama, Criticism*. New York: Henry Holt and Company, 1984.

Keisatsuchō tōkeisho: 1900 (Police department statistics: 1900). Tokyo Keisatsuchō, 1901. Also: 1907 volume (1908).

Kida Jun'ichirō. *Tokyo kasō shakai* (Tokyo's lower class society). Chikuma Shobō, 2000.

———. *Tokyo no kasō shakai: Meiji kara shūsen made* (Tokyo's lower class society: From Meiji to war's end). Shinchōsha, 1990.

Kimura, Yukiko. *Issei: Japanese Immigrants in Hawaii*. Honolulu: University of Hawai'i Press, 1988.

Kindai shomin seikatsu shi (Writings on the lives of commoners in recent times). *Byōki, eisei* (Illness and sanitation). Vol. 20. San'ichi Shobō, 1995.

Kingston, Jeff. *Japan in Transformation 1945–2010*. 2nd ed. New York: Pearson Education Limited, 2011.

Kinoshita, Naoe. *Pillar of Fire*. Translated by Kenneth Strong. London: George Allen & Unwin, 1972.

Kinzley, W. Dean. "Japan's Discovery of Poverty: Changing Views of Poverty and Social Welfare in the Nineteenth Century." *Journal of Asian History* 22, no. 1 (1988): 1–24.

Kodama-Nishimoto, Michi, Warren Nishimoto, and Cynthia Oshiro, eds. *Hanahana: An Oral History Anthology of Hawaii's Working People*. Honolulu: Center for Oral History (formerly Ethnic Studies Oral History Project), Social Science Research Institute, University of Hawai'i–Mānoa, 1984.

Kokumin Taimususha, ed. *Shashin gojūnen shi* (A fifty-year history: Photographs). Tokyo: Kokumin Taimususha, 1915.

Konishi Shirō and Oka Takeshi, eds. *Hyakunen mae no Nihon* (Japan a hundred years ago). Peabody Museum of Salem E. S. Morse Collection. Shogakukan, 1983.

———. *Mōsu no mita Nihon* (The Japan Morse saw). Peabody Museum of Salem E. S. Morse Collection. Shogakukan, 2005.

Kotani, Roland. "A Trouble at Paia." *Hawaii Herald* 11, no. 10 (May 18, 1990): 41–45.

Kubota, Gaylord C. "The Lynching of Katsu Goto." *Waimea Gazette*, February 1998, 12–16.

Kumazawa, Makoto. *Portraits of the Japanese Workplace*. Boulder, CO: Westview Press, 1996.

Ladenson, Alex. "The Japanese in Hawaii." PhD dissertation, University of Chicago, 1938.

Lensen, George Alexander. "The Attempt on the Life of Nicholas II in Japan." *Russian Review* 20, no. 3 (July 1961): 232–253. http://www.jstor.org/stable/126401.

Lewis, Michael. *A Life Adrift: Soeda Azembō, Popular Song, and Modern Mass Culture in Japan*. London: Routledge, 2009.

Linhart, Sepp, and Sabine Frühstück, eds. *The Culture of Japan as Seen Through Its Leisure*. Albany: State University of New York Press, 1998.

Lockwood, William W. *The Economic Development of Japan: Growth and Structural Change 1868–1938*. Princeton, NJ: Princeton University Press, 1954.

———, ed. *The State and Economic Enterprise in Japan*. Princeton, NJ: Princeton University Press, 1965.

Loftus, Ronald P. *Telling Lives: Women's Self-Writing in Modern Japan*. Honolulu: University of Hawai'i Press, 2004.

Lone, Stewart. *The Japanese Community in Brazil, 1908–1940*. Hampshire: Palgrave, 2001.

———. *Japan's First Modern War: Army and Society in the Conflict with China 1894–95*. London: St. Martin's Press, 1994.

———. "Remapping Japanese Militarism: Provincial Society at War 1904–1905." *Japanese Studies* 25, no. 1 (May 2005): 53–63.

Lublin, Elizabeth Dorn. *Reforming Japan: The Women's Christian Temperance Union in the Meiji Period*. Vancouver: University of British Columbia Press, 2010.

MacLennan, Carol. "A Kilauea Sugar Plantation in 1912: A Snapshot." *Hawaiian Journal of History* 41 (2007): 1–34.

Maeda Ai. *Text and the City: Essays on Japanese Modernity*. Edited by James A. Fujii. Winston-Salem, NC: Duke University Press, 2004.

Maeyama Takashi. *Hawai no shinbōnin: Meiji Fukushima imin no kojin shi* (One who persevered in Hawai'i: Personal history of a Meiji-era immigrant from Fukushima). Ochanomizu Shobō, 1986.

Mainichi Shinbunsha Tosho Henshūbu, ed. *Shashin Meiji Taishō 60 nen shi* (A 60-year history of the Meiji and Taishō eras: Photographs). Mainichi Shinbunsha, 1956.

Mani, Anandi, Sendhil Mullainathan, Eldar Shafir, and Jiaying Zhao. "Poverty Impedes Cognitive Function." *Science* 341 (August 30, 2013): 976–980.

Mansfield, Stephen. *Tokyo: A Cultural History*. Oxford: Oxford University Press, 2009.

Marcus, Marvin. *Reflections in a Glass Door: Memory and Melancholy in the Personal Writings of Natsume Sōseki*. Honolulu: University of Hawai'i Press, 2009.

Masuda, Sayo. *Autobiography of a Geisha*. Translated by G. G. Rowley. New York: Vintage, 2004.

Matsubara Iwagorō. *Saiankoku no Tokyo* (Darkest Tokyo). Min'yūsha, 1893; Iwanami Shoten, 1988; Kodansha Gakujutsu Bunkō, 2015.

———. *Sketches of Humble Life in the Capital of Japan*. Edited by F. Schroeder. Yokohama: The "Eastern World" Newspaper, Publishing and Printing Office, 1897.

Maus, Tanya. "Ishii Jūji, the Okayama Orphanage, and the Chausubaru Settlement: A Vision of Child Relief through Communal Labor and a Sustainable Local Economy, 1887–1926." PhD dissertation, University of Chicago, 2007.

Meiji nijūninen Yoshino-gun suisaishi (Records of the 1889 flood in Yoshino district). 11 vols. Totsukawa Rekishi Minzoku Shiryōkan.

Meiji no kurashi no kan (Meiji life volume). *Me de miru Edo Meiji hyakka* (Visual images of important Edo and Meiji-era happenings). Vol. 5. Koku sho Kankōkai, 1996.

Meiji Taishō Tokyo sanpo (Walking through Meiji and Taishō Tokyo). Jinbunsha, 2003.

Melendy, H. Brett. *Hawaii: America's Sugar Territory 1898–1959*. Lewiston, NY: Edwin Mellen Press, 1999.

Mensendiek, C. William. "Protestant Missionary Perceptions of Meiji Japan." *Kyōkai to Shingaku* (Church and theology). Tōhoku Daigaku, March 1986, 233–273.

Mihapoulos, Bill. "Women, Overseas Sex Work and Globalization in Meiji Japan." *Asia-Pacific Journal: Japan Focus* 10, issue 35, no. 1 (August 27, 2012). http://www.japanfocus.org/-Bill-Mihalopoulos/3814/article.html.

Milly, Deborah J. *Poverty, Equality, and Growth: The Politics of Economic Need in Postwar Japan*. Cambridge, MA: Harvard University Asia Center, 1999.

Minami Hiroshi and Asakura Kyōji, eds. *Hanzai* (Crime) 2. *Kindai shomin seikatsushi* (Records from the daily lives of modern commoners). Vol. 16. San'ichi Shobō, 1991.

Miyamoto Tsuneichi. *The Forgotten Japanese: Encounters with Rural Life and Folklore.* Translated by Jeffrey S. Irish. Berkeley, CA: Stonebridge Press, 2010.

———. *Wasurerareta Nihonjin* (Forgotten Japanese). Iwanami Shoten, 1984.

Moore, Dunlop. "Japan: Report from Yokohama." *Public Health Reports (1896–1970)* 17, no. 49 (December 5, 1902): 2770. http://www.jstor.org/stable/41471591.

Mori Kiichi. *Nihon no kindaika to rōdōsha kaikyū: kaikyūzō no rekishiteki tenkai* (Japanese modernization and the laboring class: The historical development of class structure). Nihon Hyōronsha, 1979.

Mori Ōgai. *Youth and Other Stories.* Edited by J. Thomas Rimer. Honolulu: University of Hawai'i Press, 1994.

Moriyama, Alan Takeo. *Imingaisha: Japanese Emigration Companies and Hawaii 1894–1908.* Honolulu: University of Hawai'i Press, 1985.

Moriyama Shōichi. *Shitamachi no hishi* (Secret history of the low city). Tokyo Shuppan Sentā, 1943.

Morse, Edward S. *Japan Day by Day.* 2 vols. New York: Houghton Mifflin Company, 1917.

Muramatsu Shōfū, ed. *Akiyama Teisuke wa kataru* (Akiyama Teisuke speaks). Dai Nihon Yūbenkai Kōdansha, 1938.

Naff, William E. *The Kiso Road: The Life and Times of Shimazaki Tōson.* Honolulu: University of Hawai'i Press, 2011.

Nagai, Kafū. *A Strange Tale from East of the River and Other Stories.* Translated by Edward G. Seidensticker. Rutland, VT: Tuttle Publishing, 1965.

Nagatsuka Takashi. *The Soil: A Portrait of Rural Life in Meiji Japan.* Translated by Ann Waswo. Berkeley: University of California Press, 1989.

Naikaku Tōkeikyoku. *Ichōbyō ni yoru shibō tōkei: 1899–1908* (Statistics on deaths from digestive illnesses, 1899–1908). Naikaku Tōkeikyoku, 1914.

———. *Eisei ni kansuru byōga enami tōkeihyō* (Illustrated statistical tables on health). Naikaku Tōkeikyoku, 1911.

Nakagami, Kenji. *The Cape and Other Stories from the Japanese Ghetto.* Translated by Eve Zimmerman. Berkeley, CA: Stone Bridge Press, 1999.

Nakagawa Kiyoshi. "Ambitions, 'Family-Centredness' and Expenditure Patterns in a Changing Urban Class Structure: Tokyo in the Early Twentieth Century." *Continuity and Change* 15, no. 1 (2000): 77–98.

———. *Gendai no seikatsu mondai* (Modern life issues). Rev. ed. Hōsō Daigaku Kyōiku Shinkōkai, 2011.

———, ed. *Meiji Tokyo kasō seikatsu shi* (Tokyo's poor in the Meiji era: Accounts of daily life). Iwanami Shoten, 1994.

———, ed. *Nihon no toshi kasō* (Japan's urban lower classes). Keisō Shobō, 1985.

———. "Senzen ni okeru toshi kasō no tenkai, jō" (Evolution of the urban lower classes in prewar Japan, part one). *Mita Gakkai Zasshi* 71, no. 3 (June 1978): 58–104. Also "Ge" (part two), 71, no. 4 (August 1978): 73–119.

———. *Senzen Tokyo toshi kasō* (Prewar Tokyo's urban lower classes). Kokuren Daigaku ningen to shakai no kaihatsu puroguramu kenkyū hōkoku gijutsu no iten hen'yō kaihatsu Nihon no keiken purojekuto. Vol. 8. Kokusai Rengō Daigaku, 1982.

Nakamura Masanori. *Rōdōsha to nōmin* (Laborers and farmers). *Nihon no rekishi* (The history of Japan). Vol. 29. Shōgakkan, 1976.

Nakayama, Patsy Y. "Plantation Days." *Hawaii Herald* 11, no. 10 (May 18, 1990): 16–19.

Nakayama Yasuaki, ed. *Shinbun shūsei Meiji hennen shi* (Chronological compilation of Meiji-era press articles). 15 vols. Honpō Shoseki, 1982.

Narita Ryūichi, ed. *Toshi to minshū* (Cities and their peoples). Yoshikawa Kōbunkan, 1993.

Natsume, Sōseki. *And Then*. Translated by Norma Moore Field. Ann Arbor: Center for Japanese Studies, University of Michigan, 1997.

———. *Botchan*. Translated by Umeji Sasaki. Rutland, VT: Charles Tuttle Company, 1968.

———. *Light and Darkness, an unfinished novel*. Translated by V. H. Viglielmo. Tokyo: Charles Tuttle Company, 1971.

———. *The Miner*. Translated by Jay Rubin. Tokyo: Charles Tuttle Company, 1988.

Nedan no Meiji Taishō Shōwa fūzoku shi (History of Meiji/Taishō/Shōwa customs: Prices). 4 vols. Asahi Shinbunsha, 1981.

Nihon Fūzoku Shi Gakkai, ed. *Nihon fūzoku shi jiten* (Encyclopedia of the history of Japanese cultural practices). Kōbundō, 1979.

Nihon Fūzoku Shi Shinbun Henson Iinkai, ed. *Nihon fūzoku shi shinbun* (History of Japanese customs: Newspapers). Nihon Bungeisha, 2000.

Nihon jitsugyōshi hakubutsukan junbishitsu kyōzō shiryō: shashin no bu (Old materials collected in preparation for the Japanese museum of practical business affairs: Photographs). 2 vols. Kokubungaku Kenkyū Shiryōkan, Tokyo.

Nimura Kazuo. *The Ashio Riot of 1907: A Social History of Mining in Japan*. Translated by Terry Boardman and Andrew Gordon. Durham, NC: Duke University Press, 1977.

Nishida Taketoshi, ed. *Toshi kasō shakai: Meiji zenki rōdō jijō* (Lower class urban society: Labor conditions in the early Meiji era). Seikatsusha, 1949.

Nitta, Jirō. *Death March on Mount Hakkōda*. Translated by James Westerhoven. Berkeley, CA: Stone Bridge Press, 1992.

North, Scott. "Limited Regular Employment and the Reform of Japan's Division of Labor." *Asia-Pacific Journal: Japan Focus* 7, issue 7, no. 3 (February 9, 2009). http://apjjf. org/2014/12/15/Scott-North/4106/article.html.

Odo, Franklin, and Kazuko Sinoto. *A Pictorial History of the Japanese in Hawai'i 1858–1924*. Honolulu: Bishop Museum Press, 1985.

Ogawa, Dennis M. *Kodomo no tame ni—For the sake of the children: The Japanese American Experience in Hawaii*. Honolulu: University of Hawai'i Press, 1978.

Ogi Shinzō. *Tokyo shomin seikatsu shi kenkyū* (Research on the history of Tokyo commoners' lives). Nihon Hōsō Shuppankai, 1979.

Oka, Yoshitake. *Five Political Leaders of Modern Japan*. University of Tokyo Press, 1986.

Okada Yasuo and Minami Hiroshi, eds. *Byōki eisei* (Sickness and hygiene). *Kindai shomin seikatsushi* (History of the lives of modern commoners). Vol. 20. San'ichi Shobō, 1991.

Okahata, James, ed. *A History of Japanese in Hawaii*. Honolulu: The United Japanese Society of Hawaii, 1971.

Okamoto, Shumpei. *The Japanese Oligarchy & the Russo-Japanese War*. New York: Columbia University Press, 1970.

Okano Takeo. *Meiji genron shi* (History of the Meiji press). Ōtori Shuppan, 1974.

Orwell, George. *Down and Out in Paris and London*. London: Harvest Book, Harcourt, Inc., 1933.

Ōtani Matsujirō. *Waga hito to narishi ashiato: hachijūnen no kaiko* (My journey: A memoir of eighty years). Honolulu: M. Otani Company, 1971.

Partner, Simon. "Peasants into Citizens? The Meiji Village in the Russo-Japanese War." *Monumenta Nipponica* 62, no. 2 (Summer 2007), 179–209.

———. *Toshié: A Story of Village Life in Twentieth-Century Japan*. Berkeley: University of California Press, 2004.

Pellegrini, Christopher. *The Shochu Handbook: An Introduction to Japan's Indigenous Distilled Drink.* Dublin, OH: Telemachu Press, 2014.

Platt, Brian. "Japanese Childhood, Modern Childhood: The Nation-State, the School, and 19th-Century Globalization." *Journal of Social History* 38, no. 4 (Summer 2005), 965–985.

Pyle, Kenneth. "The Emergence of Bureaucratic Conservatism in the Meiji Period." *Undercurrent* 1 (March 1983): 13–29.

Rubinger, Richard. "Who Can't Read and Write? Illiteracy in Meiji Japan." *Monumenta Nipponica* 55, no. 2 (Summer 2000): 163–198.

Saga, Junichi. *Confessions of a Yakuza: A Life in Japan's Underworld.* Translated by John Bester. Tokyo: Kodansha International, 1991.

——. *Memories of Silk and Straw: A Self-Portrait of Small-Town Japan.* Translated by Garry Evans. Tokyo: Kodansha International, 1987.

Sako, Teruhito, and Suzanne K. Steinmetz, eds. *Japanese Family and Society: Words from Tongo Takebe, a Meiji Era Sociologist.* New York: Haworth Press, 2007.

Sakurada Kurabu, ed. *Akiyama Teisuke den* (Biography of Akiyama Teisuke). Vol 1. Bunshōdō, 1977.

Sand, Jordan, and Steven Wills. "Governance, Arson, and Firefighting in Edo, 1600–1868." in *Flammable Cities: Urban Conflagration and the Making of the Modern World,* ed. Greg Bankoff, Uwe Lübken, and Jordan Sand. Madison: University of Wisconsin Press, 2012.

Sandai genronjin shū (The works of three generations of journalists). 8 vols. Jiji Tsūshinsha, 1962.

Sansom, George. *A History of Japan: 1334–1615.* Stanford, CA: Stanford University Press, 1961.

Sato, Hiroo. *Pahoa Yesterday.* Hilo: Hawai'i Japanese Center, 2002.

Scidmore, Eliza Ruhamah. *Jinrikisha Days in Japan.* New York: Harper and Brothers, 1891.

Scott, James C. *Domination and the Arts of Resistance: Hidden Transcripts.* New Haven, CT: Yale University Press, 1990.

Seidensticker, Edward. *Low City, High City: Tokyo from Edo to the Earthquake.* Rutland, VT: Charles E. Tuttle Company, 1983.

——(after Okamoto Kida). *The Snake That Bowed.* Tokyo: Printed Matter Press, 2006.

Seikatsu to fūzoku (Daily life and customs). *Nijūseiki fuoto dokyumento* (Twentieth-century photographic documents). Vol. 3. Gyosei, 1991.

Shibusawa, Keizō, ed. *Japanese Life and Culture in the Meiji Era.* Translated by Charles S. Terry. Tokyo: Ōbunsha, 1958.

——, ed. *Seikatsu* (Life). *Meiji bunka shi* (History of Meiji culture). Vol. 12. Hara Shobō, 1979.

Shibuya, Ryūichi. "The Emergence of Private Pawn Shops: Japanese Government Policy." *Japanese Experience of the United Nations University Human and Social Development Program Series* 59 (1983). http://d-arch.ide.go.jp/je_archive/society/wp_je_unu59.html.

Shiga, Naoya. *A Dark Night's Passing.* Translated by Edwin McClellan. Tokyo: Kodansha International, 1976.

——. *The Paper Door and Other Stories.* Translated by Lane Dunlop. Rutland, VT: Tuttle Publishing, 1992.

Shimazaki Tōson. *The Broken Commandment.* Translated by Kenneth Strong. University of Tokyo Press, 1974.

——. *Chikuma River Sketches.* Translated by William E. Naff. Honolulu: University of Hawai'i Press, 1991.

Shimonaka Kunihiko, ed. *Nihon zankoku monogatari* (Tales of Japanese inhumanity). 7 vols. Heibonsha, 1959–1960.

Shiomi Sen'ichirō, *Chōya Shinbun*, ed. *Edo no kasō shakai* (Edo's lower classes). Akashi Shoten, 1993.

Shokkō jijō (The conditons of factory workers). Nōshōmusho Shokōkyoku, 1903. Also see Inumaru Giichi.

Smethurst, Richard J. *Agricultural Development and Tenancy Disputes in Japan, 1870– 1940*. Princeton, NJ: Princeton University Press, 1986.

——. *A Social Basis for Prewar Japanese Militarism: The Army and the Rural Community.* Berkeley: University of California Press, 1974.

Smith, Henry D. "From Sketch to Print: Kiyochika's Ryōgoku Fire and Hakone-Shizuoka Prints." 1991. http://www.columbia.edu/~hds2/pdf/1991c_Kiyochika_sketchbooks.pdf.

Smith, Robert J., and Ella Lury Wiswell. *The Women of Suye Mura.* Chicago: University of Chicago Press, 1982.

Smith, Thomas C. *The Agrarian Origins of Modern Japan*. New York: Atheneum, 1966.

A Social History of Kona. 2 vols. Honolulu: Center for Oral History (formerly Ethnic Studies Oral History Project), Social Science Research Institute, University of Hawai'i–Mānoa, 1981.

Sōga Yasutarō. *Gojūnen no Hawai'i kaiko* (Memoir of fifty years in Hawai'i). Osaka: Osaka Kosoku Printing Company, 1953. "Sakkon no hinminkutsu: Shiba Shin'ami-chō no tansa" (The slums these days: An investigation of Shiba's Shin'ami-chō), *Hōchi Shinbun*, November 13–December 11, 1897. In *Meiji Tokyo kasō seikatsu shi* (Tokyo's poor in the Meiji era: A history of daily life), ed. Nakagawa Kiyoshi, 154–187. Iwanami Shoten, 1994.

Stanley, Amy. *Selling Women: Prostitution, Markets, and the Household in Early Modern Japan*. Berkeley: University of California Press, 2012.

Statistics Bureau, Ministry of Internal Affairs and Commerce. "Historical Statistics of Japan." http://www.stat.go.jp/english/data/chouki/28.htm.

Steele, M. William. "Mobility on the Move: Rickshaws in Asia." *Transfers* 4, no. 3 (Winter 2014): 88–107.

Sugihara Kaoru and Tamai Kingo, eds. *Taishō Osaka suramu: mō hitotsu Nihon kindai shi* (Osaka slums in the Taishō era: Another history of modern Japan). Shin Hyōron, 1996.

Sugimoto, Yoshio. *An Introduction to Japanese Society*. Cambridge: Cambridge University Press, 1997.

Sumii, Sué. *The River with No Bridge*. Translated by Susan Wilkinson. Tokyo: Tuttle Publishing, 1989.

Suzuki, Akihito, and Mika Suzuki. "Cholera, Consumer and Citizenship: Modernisations of Medicine in Japan." In *The Development of Modern Medicine in Non-Western Countries: Historical Perspectives*, ed. Ebrahimnejad Hormoz, 184–203. London: Routledge, 2009.

Suzuki Hiroyuki. *Toshi e* (Toward cities). *Nihon no kindai* (Japan's modern era). Vol. 10. Chūō Kōron Shinsha, 1999.

Suzuki, Jiro. "My Autobiography." Bishop Museum, Ms. Doc. 277. February 2, 1981.

Suzuki Kōichi. *Nyūsu de ou Meiji Nihon hakkutsu* (Uncovering Meiji Japan through the news). Vol. 7. Kawada Shobō Shinsha, 1995.

Tabata Shigekiyo, Mizuyama Takahisa, and Inoue Kimio. "Kōu ni yoru ten'nen damu no keisei to kekkai" (The creation and disintegration of the natural dam created by rainfall), in *Ten'nen damu to saigai* (Natural dam and disaster), 86–104. Kokon Shoin, 2002.

Tachibana Yūichi. *Hyōden Yokoyama Gennosuke* (Yokoyama Gennosuke: A critical biography). Sōjusha, 1977.

——. *Meiji kasō kiroku bungaku* (Literary recollections of the Meiji lower classes). Sōjunsha, 1981. Also Chikuma Gakugei Bunkō, 2002.

Taira, Koji. "Urban Poverty, Ragpickers, and the 'Ants Village' in Tokyo." *Economic Development and Change* 17, no. 2 (January 1969): 155–177.

Taishū bunka jiten (Dictionary of mass culture). Kōbundō, 1991.

Takei Nekketsu. *Hawai'i ichiran* (An overview of Hawai'i). Honolulu: Motoshige Shijundō, 1914.

Tamai, Kingo. "Images of the Poor in an Official Survey of Osaka, 1923–1926." *Continuity and Change* 15, no. 1 (2000): 99–116.

Tanikawa Ken'ichi, ed. *Shōfu* (Prostitution). *Kindai minshū no kiroku* (Records of modern commoners). Vol. 3. Shinjinbutsu Ōraisha, 1972.

Tanizaki, Jun'ichiro. *Childhood Years: A Memoir.* Translated by Paul McCarthy. Tokyo: Kodansha International, 1988.

———. *The Gourmet Club: A Sextet.* Translated by Anthony H. Chambers and Paul McCarthy. Tokyo: Kodansha International, 2001.

Tayama Katai. *Country Teacher.* Translated by Kenneth Henshall. Honolulu: University of Hawai'i Press, 1984.

Teranishi, Juro. *Evolution of the Economic System in Japan.* Cheltenham, UK: Edward Elgar, 2005.

Terry, T. Philip. *Terry's Japanese Empire: A Guidebook for Travelers.* Boston: Houghton Mifflin Company, 1914.

Tokyo fu tōkeisho (Statistics of the city of Tokyo). 11 vols. Tokyo Fu, 1901–1909.

"Tokyo no hinmin" (Tokyo's poor). *Jiji Shimpō,* October 11–November 29, 1896. In *Meiji Tokyo kasō seikatsu shi* (Tokyo's poor in the Meiji era: A history of daily life), ed. Nakagawa Kiyoshi, 90–153. Iwanami Shoten, 1994.

Tokyo shi tōkei zuhyō (Statistical charts for the city of Tokyo). Tokyo Shiyakusho, 1914.

Tokyo-to Yōikuin, ed. *Yōikuin hyakunenshi* (Centennial history of orphanages). City of Tokyo, 1944.

Torrance, Richard. "Literacy and Literature in Osaka, 1890–1940." *Journal of Japanese Studies* 31, no. 1 (Winter 2005): 27–60.

Toyama, Tetsuo. *Eighty Years in Hawaii.* Tokyo: Tosho Printing Company, 1964.

Tsuda Masumi. *Nihon no toshi kasō shakai* (Japan's urban lower classes). Minerva Shoten, 1972.

Tsurumi, E. Patricia. *Factory Girls: Women in the Thread Mills of Meiji Japan.* Princeton, NJ: Princeton University Press, 1990.

Tsurumi Shunsuke, ed. *Kyōkoku o mezashite* (Aiming to be a strong nation). *Nihon no hyakunen* (Japan's 100 years). Vol. 3. Chikuma Shobō, 1963.

Tsutsui, William M., ed. *A Companion to Japanese History.* Oxford, UK: Blackwell Publishing, 2007.

Tsuzuki, Chushichi. *The Pursuit of Power in Modern Japan: 1825–1995.* Oxford: Oxford University Press, 2000.

Turner, Victor. *The Ritual Process: Structure and Anti-Structure.* Ithaca, NY: Cornell University Press, 1969.

Ubukata Toshirō. "Kenpō happu to Nisshin Sensō" (Promulgation of the constitution and the Sino-Japanese War). In *Jānarizumu no shisō* (Philosophy of the press), ed., Tsurumi Shunsuke. In *Gendai Nihon shisō taikei* (Comprehensive outline of modern Japanese thought), ed. Matsumoto Sannosuke. Vol. 12, 80–112. Chikuma Shobō, 1965.

Uchikawa Yoshimi and Matsushima Eiichi, eds. *Meiji nyūsu jiten* (Encyclopedia of Meiji news). 9 vols. Mainichi Komiyunikēshiyon Shuppanbu, 1983–1986.

Uchimura, Kanzō. *The Complete Works of Kanzō Uchimura.* 8 vols. Tokyo: Kyobunkwan, 1973.

Uno Chiyo. *Confessions of Love.* Translated by Phyllis Birnbaum. Rutland, VT: Tuttle Publishing, 1989.

Uno, Kathleen. *Passages to Modernity: Motherhood, Childhood, and Social Reform in Early Twentieth Century Japan.* Honolulu: University of Hawai'i Press, 1999.

Waikīkī, 1900–1985: Oral Histories. 4 vols. Honolulu: Center for Oral History (formerly Ethnic Studies Oral History Project), Social Science Research Institute, University of Hawai'i–Mānoa, June 1985.

Waipi'o: Māno Wai: An Oral History Collection. 2 vols. Center for Oral History (formerly Ethnic Studies Oral History Project), Social Science Research Institute, University of Hawai'i–Mānoa, 1978.

Wakita Haruko, Anne Bouchy, and Ueno Chizuko, eds. *Gender and Japanese History.* 2 vols. Osaka: Osaka University Press, 1999.

Wakukawa, Ernest K. *A History of the Japanese People in Hawaii.* Honolulu: Toyo Shoin, 1938.

Waswo, Ann. *Modern Japanese Society, 1868–1994.* Oxford: Oxford University Press, 1996.

———. "The Transformation of Rural Society, 1900–1950." In *The Cambridge History of Japan: 6: The Twentieth Century,* ed. Peter Duus, 541–605. New York: Cambridge University Press, 1988.

Waswo, Ann, and Nishida Yoshiaki, eds. *Farmers and Village Life in Twentieth-Century Japan.* London: Routledge Curzon, 2003.

Watanabe, Sharlene K. *Japanese Immigration: Abstracts of Articles from Hawaiian Planters Records, 1884–1896.* University of Hawai'i Library, 1975.

Webb, Beatrice, Diary, 6 March 1911 to 8 December 1916. London School of Economics Digital Library. London School of Economics. http://digital.library.lse.ac.uk/objects/lse:six767gol/read#page/1/mode/2up.

Wilcox, Carol. *Sugar Water: Hawaii's Plantation Ditches.* Honolulu: University of Hawai'i Press, 1996.

Yamamoto Taketoshi. *Kindai Nihon no shinbun dokusha sō* (Structure of newspaper readership in modern Japan). Hōsei Daigaku Shuppankyoku, 1981.

———. "Meiji sanjūnen zenhan no shinbun dokusha sō" (The structure of newspaper readership at the turn of the century). *Shinbun Gaku Hyōron* 16 (March 1967): 93–123.

Yamanaka, William K. *Kipu-Huleia: The Social History of a Plantation Community, 1910–1950.* Seattle: n.p., 1996.

Yanagida, Kunio, ed. *Japanese Manners and Customs in the Meiji Era.* Translated by Charles S. Terry. Tokyo: Ōbunsha, 1957.

Yanagita Kunio. *Fūzoku hen* (Customs). *Meiji bunka shi* (History of Meiji culture). Vol. 13. Yōyōsha, 1954.

———. *Meiji Taishō shi sesō hen, shinsōban* (A history of the Meiji/Taishō era: Conditions of the world, new edition). Kōdansha Gakujutsu Bunko, 1993. Also 2nd ed.: *Meiji Taishō shi sesō henge.* Kōdansha, 1976.

Yano Toraji. *Ohchō hachijūgo nen: omoide tenten* (Eighty-five years of blessings: Bits of memory). Bishop Museum, Ms. Group 187. 1973.

Yasuoka Norihiko. *Kindai Tokyo no kasō shakai—shakai jigyō no tenkai* (Lower-class society in modern Tokyo: Development of social services). Akashi Shoten, 1999.

Yazaki, Takeo. *Social Change and the City in Japan: From Earliest Times Through the Industrial Revolution.* Translated by David L. Swain. San Francisco: Japan Publications, 1968.

Yokoyama Gennosuke. *Meiji fugō shi* (A history of Meiji millionaires). Chikuma Shobō (Chikuma Gakugei Bunkō), 2013.

———. *Naichi zakkyo go no Nihon* (Japan after the secluded era). Iwanami Shoten, 1954.

———. *Nihon no kasō shakai* (Japan's lower-class society). Iwanami Shoten, 1949. Originally published 1899.

———. *Yokoyama Gennosuke zenshū* (Complete works of Yokoyama Gennosuke). Edited by Tachibana Yūichi. Shakai Shisōsha, 2001 (vols. 1–4); Hōsei Daigaku, 2005 (vol. 5).

———. *Yokoyama Gennosuke zenshū* (Complete works of Yokoyama Gennosuke). Meiji Bunken, 1972.

Yumoto Kōichi. *Zusetsu Meiji jibutsu kigen jiten* (Illustrated dictionary of the origins of Meiji objects). Kishiwa Shobō, 1998.

Yutani, Eiji. "'Nihon no Kaso Shakai' of Gennosuke Yokoyama." PhD dissertation. University of California, Berkeley, 1985.

Page numbers in boldface type refer to illustrations.

About the Author

THE AUTHOR OF EIGHT BOOKS on Japanese history, James L. Huffman is a former journalist who spent his career teaching undergraduates at the University of Nebraska–Lincoln, Indiana Wesleyan University, Williams College, Dartmouth College, and, for thirty years, at Wittenberg University, where he is H. Orth Hirt Professor of History Emeritus. His works include *Creating a Public: People and Press in Meiji Japan, Japan in World History,* and *Japan and Imperialism.* Since retirement, Huffman has lived in Chicago, where he is a full-time writer and part-time theater enthusiast. In 2017, he received the Association for Asian Studies Award for Distinguished Contributions to Asian Studies.